D1120252

Z. A. "Zeke" Prust

FIFTH EDITION

GRAPHIC COMMUNICATIONS

The Printed Image

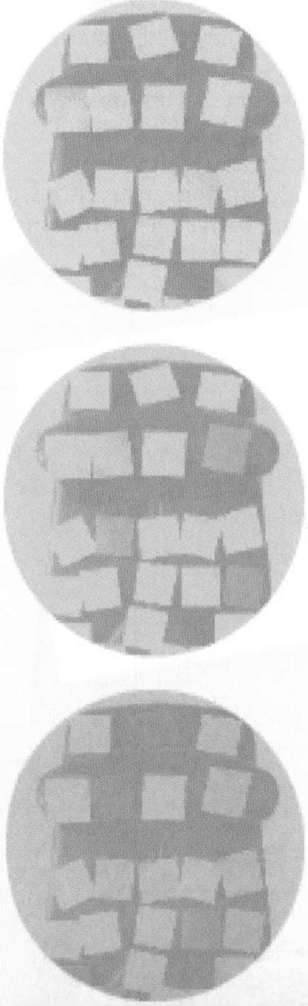

Publisher
The Goodheart-Willcox Company, Inc.
Tinley Park, Illinois
www.g-w.com

The Goodheart-Willcox Company, Inc. Brand Disclaimer: Brand names, company names, and illustrations for products and services included in this text are provided for educational purposes only and do not represent or imply endorsement or recommendation by the author or the publisher.

The Goodheart-Willcox Company, Inc. Safety Notice: The reader is expressly advised to carefully read, understand, and apply all safety precautions and warnings described in this book or that might also be indicated in undertaking the activities and exercises described herein to minimize risk of personal injury or injury to others. Common sense and good judgment should also be exercised and applied to help avoid all potential hazards. The reader should always refer to the appropriate manufacturer's technical information, directions, and recommendations; then proceed with care to follow specific equipment operating instructions. The reader should understand these notices and cautions are not exhaustive.

The publisher makes no warranty or representation whatsoever, either expressed or implied, including but not limited to equipment, procedures, and applications described or referred to herein, their quality, performance, merchantability, or fitness for a particular purpose. The publisher assumes no responsibility for any changes, errors, or omissions in this book. The publisher specifically disclaims any liability whatsoever, including any direct, indirect, incidental, consequential, special, or exemplary damages resulting, in whole or in part, from the reader's use or reliance upon the information, instructions, procedures, warnings, cautions, applications, or other matter contained in this book. The publisher assumes no responsibility for the activities of the reader.

Library of Congress Cataloging-in-Publication Data

Prust, Z. A., 1924–
    Graphic communications : the printed image / Z.A.
 "Zeke" Prust.
        p. cm.
    Includes index.
    ISBN 978-1-60525-061-8
    1. Printing--United States. 2. Electronics in printing--
 United States. 3. Digital printing--United States. I. Title.
    Z116.P78   2010
    686.20973--dc22

                                                      2008041008

INTRODUCTION

The graphic communications field (sometimes called graphic arts or simply *printing*) has undergone sweeping changes in recent years with the introduction of computers and digital technology in virtually every aspect of the industry. Digital image capture and manipulation, electronic prepress operations, computer-based systems for managing most aspects of a business, computer-to-plate technology, electronic control systems on presses and bindery equipment, and many other advances have changed the fundamental ways that most printing and related operations are performed. It is probably safe to say that the industry has seen more extensive changes in the 15 years than have taken place in the five centuries since Johannes Gutenberg began printing from movable type in the mid-1400s.

Graphic Communications reflects these changes in the industry, with chapters devoted to in-depth coverage of color science, electronic prepress and digital printing, digital image capture, color management, and flexography. Other chapters provide important information on design and layout, text composition, page composition, stripping and imposition, contacting, the business aspects of printing, and careers in graphic communications have been extensively revised. Strong emphasis has been placed on safety and workplace health matters and on environmental considerations.

Information on new methods and equipment has been incorporated throughout the book, while information on processes that have become obsolete has been condensed and treated in a historical context. The aim is to better prepare today's graphic communications student for a career in this rapidly evolving field.

Since "a picture is worth a thousand words," *Graphic Communications* is highly illustrated. To clarify the complex processes of the industry, literally hundreds of full-color illustrations are used. Color is also used to enhance the educational value of many of the line art illustrations and to stress safety rules given throughout the text.

Graphic Communications is a valuable source of information for anyone entering any area of the printing industry today. This text will help you become well-versed in most aspects of printing technology.

Z.A. Prust, Ed.D.

ABOUT THE AUTHOR

Z.A. Prust is retired after having taught 40 years. He has been honored with several awards throughout his career, including the Fred J. Hartman Award from the International Graphic Arts Education Association and the Award of Excellence from the Graphic Arts Technical Foundation. During his career, he taught printing at the junior high school, high school, and college levels. The majority of his teaching career was spent at Arizona State University, and he retired as the Associate Director of the Division of Technology and the Graphic Communications Program Coordinator. He was elected to the

Ben Franklin Honor Society of Printing Industries of America. He has served on many local, regional, and national committees and has been a member of several professional and social groups. In addition to **Graphic Communications**, Prust is the author of several articles in communications and printing magazines and journals. Two awards have been given in his name since 1987: the Z.A. "Zeke" Prust Award of Recognition at Arizona State University and the Z.A. Prust Industry Achievement Award, Printing Industries Association, Inc., of Arizona.

ACKNOWLEDGMENTS

The author and publisher wish to express their appreciation to the following individuals, companies, and organizations for their cooperation in furnishing photographs, line art, and technical information used in this book:

3M Company
A.B. Dick Company
Accel Graphic Systems
Accurate Steel Rule Die Mfg., Inc.
Advance Graphics Equipment
Agfa
American Color Corp.
American Roller Company
ATF
Autotype USA
Baker Perkins Limited
basysPrint Corporation
Bobst Group, Inc.
Bowling Green State University,
    Visual Communication
    Technology Program
Brookfield Engineering
    Laboratories, Inc.
Carpenter-Offutt Paper Co.
Center for Metric Education,
    Western Michigan University
Central Missouri State University
Compugraphic
Doboy Packaging Machinery
Domino Printing Sciences plc
Duplo USA
DuPont
Dynagram, Inc.
Earmark, Inc.
Eastman Kodak
Epson America, Inc.
Essex Products Group
Flexographic Technical
    Association, Inc.
Fuji Graphic Systems
Fuji Hunt Photographic Chemicals, Inc.
Fuji Photo Film U.S.A., Inc.
General Binding Corp.
Gerber Systems Corporation
GIT, Arizona State University

Graphic Arts Technical Foundation
GSMA
Hagan Systems, Inc.
Hantscho
Heidelberg Harris
Heidelberg, Inc.
ICG North America
imacon
Inter-City Paper Co.
Interlake Packaging Corp.
International Paper Co.
Interthor, Inc.
Iris Graphics, Inc.
Jack Klasey
John Walker
Justrite Manufacturing Company
King Press Corporation
Lab Safety Supply, Inc., Janesville, WI
Linotype-Hell
Mark Andy, Inc.
Martin Marietta Corp.
Matthias Bauerle GmbH
Max Daetwyler Corporation
McCain Manufacturing Corp.
Mead Publishing Paper Division
Mee Industries Inc.
MegaVision
Melbourne Museum of Printing
    (Australia)
MGI Digital Graphic Technology
Minolta Corporation
Multigraphics
NAPL
National Association of Quick
    Printers, Inc.
National Soy Ink Information Center
nuArc Company, Inc.
Océ Display Graphics Systems
Orbotech, Inc.
Pantone, Inc.

Paper Converting Machine
    Company
Polychrome Corporation
Presstek, Inc.
Printing Industries of America:
    Center for Technology and
    Research
Rollem
Safety-Kleen
Scitex America Corp.
Screaming Color–Chapter One
Screen Printing Association
    International
Screen-USA
Sonoco Products Co.
Southern Forest Products Assn.
Strachan Henshaw Machinery, Inc.
Supratech Systems, Inc.
Tensor Group, Inc.
Tetko, Inc.
The L.S. Starrett Co.
The Peerless Group of Graphic
    Services
The RAIDinc Z 2, courtesy of
    RAID, Inc.
The S. D. Warren Company
Thomas Detrie and C. Phillips
U.S. Bureau of Engraving and Printing
US Sublimation
USA Today
Van Son Holland Ink
Variquick
Western Litho
Westvaco Corporation
Xanté Corporation
Xerox Corporation
X-Rite, Incorporated
www.PrintingTips.com, owned by
    Austec Data Inc. dba Tecstra
    Systems

BRIEF CONTENTS

ⒸONTENTS

Chapter 3
Measurement   62

Chapter 4
Typography   78

Chapter 8
Digital Image Capture   158

Chapter 9
Color Science, Vision, and
Space   182

Chapter 10
Color Management 206

Chapter 11
Analog Film, Equipment, and Processing Information 232

Chapter 12
Imposition and Layout   252

Chapter 13
Digital Printing Technology   262

Chapter 14
Lithographic Platemaking   276

Chapter 15
Lithographic Press Systems 292

Chapter 16
Sheet-Fed Offset Press Operation and Troubleshooting 312

Chapter 17
Relief Printing 330

Chapter 18
Flexographic Printing   338

Chapter 19
Gravure Printing   352

Chapter 22
Ink   402

ACADEMIC LINKS

THINK GREEN

CAREER LINKS

FEATURES OF THE TEXTBOOK

Important Terms appear in green bold-italic type where they are defined. These terms are identified when they are introduced and are included in the glossary.

Figure References within the body of the text are printed in bold type. This makes them easy to locate and identify.

Running Glossary entries appear in green near their related terms. These entries can be used as a quick-reference guide to the definitions of the Important Terms in a chapter.

Learning Objectives appear at the beginning of each chapter. They are designed to make you aware of what you will be able to accomplish after studying the chapter.

Academic Links use questions and activities to relate chapter content to math, science, and history.

Safety Tips identify activities that can result in personal injury, if proper procedures or safety measures are not followed.

Digital Prepress

Learning Objectives

After studying this chapter, you will be able to:

- Identify different computer platforms.
- Explain the characteristics of different types of storage devices.
- Differentiate between various output devices.
- Explain the processes used in text and graphics preparation.
- Summarize the features of page composition programs.
- Identify the techniques used in creating digital design files.
- Explain the proofreading process.
- Explain the preflighting process.
- Compare types of production proofs.
- Explain digital prepress workflow.

Important Terms

bank
burnish
chase
composing stick
compositor
font
form
furniture
galley
job case
Linotype

Ludlow
matrix
Monotype
movable type
quoins
relief printing
scriber
slugs
spaceband
template

The term *composition* generally refers to the production and organization of all images to be printed. In graphic communications, however, composition can also mean setting type or words, not just line art or photographs. The *compositor*, or typesetter, is the person who sets the type.

Composition methods have changed throughout history as new technology has been introduced. Hand composition of wood or metal type was the primary composition method from the 1400s to the early 1900s. This method involved physically assembling separate letters into words, sentences, paragraphs, and pages. Many of the materials published using hand composition are works of art. The design and spacing of type is outstanding. Machine methods, which rapidly assembled molds and cast an entire line of type in metal, were introduced at the end of the late 1800s. This method remained an important technology for a half-century. In the late 1960s, equipment for photographic setting of type began to appear. While typesetting remained in widespread use into the early 1990s. The role of personal computers in composition has grown steadily since being introduced in 1984. Today, the computer is the primary method of composition for materials that will be presented in printed or electronic form. This chapter discusses these major composition methods.

RELIEF COMPOSITION

Printing from a raised surface is called *relief printing*. The name comes from the fact that the image area of the type is in relief to, or raised above, the nonimage area. The raised surface is covered with ink and pressed against paper or another substrate to produce an image, **Figure 6-1**.

compositor: A person who sets type; also referred to as a typesetter.

relief printing: The process of printing from a raised surface. Ink is applied to the raised image and transferred to the paper or other substrate.

movable type: Individual type characters, usually cast in metal, that can be assembled into words, disassembled, and later reassembled into different words.

Figure 6-1. First, the surface of the raised image is inked. After it makes contact with the substrate, an image remains on the surface of the substrate.

Relief printing dates back more than ten centuries, to the use of wooden relief type in China. The first relief printing was done using carved wooden blocks. This composition method was a long and tedious process, and was suitable only for pictures or a small number of words.

The modern process of printing traces to the development of movable type in the mid-1400s by Johannes Gutenberg in Mainz, Germany. Gutenberg made molds that could be used to cast individual metal blocks, each holding one raised letter. The blocks could be produced in quantity and assembled into words. Since the typeset letters could be taken apart and the letters reassembled into different words, the blocks were termed *movable type*. The first books printed using movable type by Gutenberg and his associates were copies of the Christian Bible, **Figure 6-2**.

The art of printing with movable type quickly spread to other cities across Europe. Two hundred years later, in 1639, the first press was established at Harvard Academy in Cambridge, Massachusetts. The first newspaper regularly published in North America was printed in Boston by John Campbell in 1704.

ACADEMIC LINK

Manual Copyfitting Calculations

Without the automated features of layout and design software programs, manual calculations would have to be performed to determine how much space is required for a given block of type.

A block of type with a total of 310 characters is to be set in a 10-point sans serif typeface, with a line width of 18 picas. For this particular typeface, 2.9 characters fill one pica of space. To determine the space required for the text:

1. Multiply the number of characters that fill one pica of space (2.9) by the line length (18) to find the number of characters possible per line:
   $2.9 \times 18 = 52.2$
   The result is rounded to the nearest whole number (52).

2. Find the number of typeset lines required for the text by dividing the total number of characters in the text (310) by the number of characters per line (52):
   $310 \div 52 = 5.96$
   Round the result of this equation up to the nearest whole number (6 lines).

3. Multiply the typeface point size (10) by the number of typeset lines (6) to find the depth of the text:
   $10 \times 6 = 60$

4. Convert the measurement from points to picas. One pica is equal to 12 points.
   $60 \div 12 = 5$ picas
   The text block measures 5 picas deep and 18 picas wide (line width).

Find the space required for a block of type with 275 characters set in a 12-point sans serif typeface, with a line width of 22 picas. 2.5 characters of this typeface fill one pica of space. Work the calculations on a separate piece of paper.

Whenever you are working with chemicals, take several precautions against harmful solvent

Do not attempt to identify a solvent by sniffing it.

Keep lids and covers on cans and drums.

Do not use large quantities of solvents in one area.

- Clean up spills immediately.
- Know the proper handling, cleanup, and disposal procedures for the chemical you are using.

Store oily rags in an approved safety can.

Specialists need to determine safe levels of solvents and determine safe...

Vapors should be exhausted away. Solvents and the area kept well ventilated. Some operator may require the operator to wear a respirator. The proper respirator for each situation must be selected...

wear a...
exceed...
produce...
allowed...
complete...
includes an individual training facility...
as well as other training facilities...

Solvents can also be harmful to...
Read the container label before using a chemical. Typically, it is determine what to do in case of contact. Typically, it is recommended that the affected area be flushed with water for at least 15 minutes and then treated by a doctor. Personal protective devices such as goggles, face shields, gloves, and aprons must be worn when handling chemical solvents.

The chemicals can irritate the skin or damage rubber or plastic gloves or aprons when working with platemaking chemicals. Never touch your face for pinholes before working. Never touch a or eyes with gloves that have been in contact with a chemical.

Contact lenses should *not* be worn when working with chemicals. If splashed in the eyes, the chemicals can seep under the lenses and cause severe burns. Face shields and splash goggles are the best form of eye and face protection.

Wearing an appropriate apron will keep chemicals from reaching clothing and soaking through to the skin. Food and beverages should never be allowed to come into contact with chemicals. Chemicals that are corrosive, flammable, or poisonous should be properly labeled and stored in a safety cabinet, **Figure 2-17**.

Many platemaking chemicals are concentrated. When diluting an acid, always pour the acid into the water. The opposite method would produce a dangerous splattering of the acid. Never add water to concentrated acid.

Ink Mists

Rapidly rotating press rollers throw tiny droplets of ink into the air, creating an ink mist. These droplets are tiny enough to be inhaled. Ink mists often contain pigments, polymers, plasticizers, resins, and solvents that can prove harmful. Face shields and respirators

Figure 2-16. In many cases, a...approved respirator is required...airborne mists of chemicals, inks, dust, paint, or other contaminants are present. (3M Company)

...programs used to produce graphics electronically, layout materials appear as object-oriented or bitmapped images. Using these programs, the designer can create very complex documents. These illustration packages will be discussed in greater detail in Chapter 13.

Think Green features touch on chapter-related topics and give an example of how the industry is working toward making products and processes safer for the environment.

Suggested Activities at the end of each chapter help you apply chapter concepts to real-life situations and develop skills related to the content.

Career Links highlight career opportunities in the graphic communications industry. Helpful quotes from industry experts are included in each link.

Summaries highlighting the chapter content are provided for each chapter. This feature provides a review of major concepts covered in the chapters.

Review Questions are included at the end of each chapter. The questions can be used to check your comprehension of the text material.

Related Web Links identify Web sites related to chapter content. These Web sites may expand on chapter concepts or introduce more environmentally focused information.

The **Appendices** include information on various typefaces, as well as several conversion tables and other useful reference information.

The **Index** is detailed and serves as a valuable reference tool.

The **Glossary** is comprised of the terminology in the textbook.

---

152 CAREER LINK

Preflight Technician

The preflight technician uses digital imaging technology to achieve the planned requested job. When using this technology, the preflight technician takes the electronic files that are given to him or her by the customer and checks them for all aspects of completeness. It is very similar to the checklist a pilot goes over before the plane takes off; the formalized preflight manual checklist makes sure everything is in order. Therefore, the preflight technician tasks are critical to the elimination of output problems of the electronic files. Preflighting software can speed up the process. Sometimes checklists and software are both used by the preflight technician.

Some of the responsibilities of the preflight technician include making sure submitted discs are not damaged; ensuring discs are readable; checking in-house font availability; checking for missing material on submitted discs; checking for correct size indications; checking for proper trapping and adequate bleeds; and checking for font problems, All these preflighting tasks ensure the digital job

...ability to work closely with the customer and other departments is an imperative attribute.

The preflight technician should have formal postsecondary graphic communications training in digital technology; an associate degree is often stated as a requirement in the job description. It is also beneficial to be familiar with the printing process and production workflow. Preflight technicians must have good communication and basic problem-solving skills, be comfortable with the pressure of deadlines, and be proficient with computer applications.

"Students entering the graphic communications discipline need to have a variety of skills for employment in our ever-changing industry. They need to be versed in the practical application of traditional web and offset printing, digital printing, prepress and prepress software, print management, and to have a firm understanding of the Internet and how it relates to the printing industry."

Tony Mancuso
Typography Unlimited, Inc. (TUI)

THINK GREEN

Paper Waste Overview

Paper is a large part of the graphic communications industry. However, there is growing concern about the various effects of paper waste today. The obtaining of virgin pulp is a cause of deforestation around the world. This, in turn, is leading to the extinction of inhabitants of the forest who rely on those trees for food and shelter. The disposal of large amounts of paper has increased the size of landfills. One easy way to reduce paper waste is to recycle paper and buy products that use recycled material. Several printers are working to be more...

Suggested Activities

1. Research Gutenberg's invention of metal type. Create a timeline of events... this invention.
2. Investigate the history of relief printing describe the earliest example you can... relief printing. Include the materials used... location the item was produced, and how... item was used.
3. Explain the history and purpose of the C... Job Case.

Related Web Links

Hamilton Wood Type Printing Museum
www.woodtype.org
Web site of the Hamilton Wood Type Printing Museum, which contains some historical information on the use of wooden relief type.

Briar Press
www.briarpress.org
Briar Press is a community of letterpress printers, book artists, and press enthusiasts dedicated to the preservation of letterpress-era equipment and the art of fine printing.

The Forest Stewardship Council
www.fscus.org
Standard-setting organization dedicated to preserving forests.

Summary

The information given in this chapter largely relates to analog processes. The means by which images are prepared for transfer to a substrate has changed dramatically over the years. Hand or mechanical methods of composing type was common for 500 years. The changes that have led to digital processes are explained in this chapter and should be viewed from a historical standpoint of the industry.

Review Questions

Please do not write in this text. Write your answers on a separate sheet of paper.

1. The person who sets type is called a(n) _____, or _____.
2. Letterpress is another name used for _____ printing.

template: A pierced or cut guide, usually plastic, used to create lettering and symbols, or to draw shapes by hand.
scriber: A tool for following a template; an attached pen deposits ink onto a sheet of paper.
burnish: To rub down a dry transfer image onto a substrate with a smooth wood, plastic, or metal tool.

---

472 Graphic Communications

APPENDIX A

Several typefaces are presented here, grouped by each of the five classifications. As you study the... designs, refer to the components identified below for features to compare.

Typeface

When discussing typefaces, using the correct terminology ensures effective communication.

---

510 Graphic Communications

INDEX

A

achromatic vision, 202–
adaptation, 201–202
A/D converter, 160–161
additive color formation
additives, 403
adhesive bonding, 373
adhesive-coated paper,
adjacency, 202–203
afterimages, 201
aging, 203
aliasing, 136–137
American National Standards Institute (ANSI), 453
analog charge, 160–161
analog format, 159
analog images, 159
anilox roll, 340–341, 348
antialiasing, 136–137
antihalation backing, 234–235
apprenticeship, 465
aqueous inks, 267
art preparation requirements, 25–26, 355
artwork, 25
ascenders, 83
assembly procedures, 256–258
    quality control devices, 258
automatic film processing, 248–249

brake mechanism, 258–259
brayer, 411, 413
brightness, 93, 190, 213, 397
brownlines, 226–227
brush system, 305
burned edges, 376–377
burnished, 124–125
business, 443–454
    basics, 444–451
    copyright laws, 454
    costs, 446–447
    job estimates, 447–448
    matching jobs to equipment, 450–451
    organizing work, 449–450
    planning, 443–444
    standards and specifications, 453–454
    trade customs, 451–453
business plan, 443–445
    developing, 443
    establishing organization, 443–444

banding machine, 438–439
bank, 121
barrier guards, 43
base material, 234–235
basic size, 68–69, 392–393
basis weight, 70–71, 393
batteries, 165
Bezier curve, 137
binding, 32–33, 431, 432–438
    edition, 436–437

calibration schedules, 216–217
calligraphy, 85
camera bed, 238–239
carbonless paper, 388
careers, 456–469
    creative positions, 459–460
    educators, 463
    engineers and scientists, 463
    entrepreneurship, 468–469
    finding jobs, 466

489

GLOSSARY

A

A/D converter: A device used to convert an analog charge into digital form. The result of this conversion is stored as pixel data. (8)

...ss to all colors; ability to see
...y, and black. (9)
...t eyes make in different
...s driers, lubricants, waxes,
...to ink to impart special
...rable properties, or
...ties. (22)
...ed on mixing red, green, and blue light in various combinations to create a color reproduction or image. (7)

additive color formation: Theory based on mixing red, green, and blue light in various combinations to create a color reproduction or image. (9, 10)

adjacency: A property of the eye that changes the perception of a color based on the adjacent or surrounding color. A color will appear brighter if surrounded by dark colors, or darker when surrounded by light colors. (9)

afterimage: An image that viewer continues to see after the actual object is no longer in sight. The image is created by the eye's attempt to restore equilibrium. (9)

aliasing: The process in which smooth curves and other lines become jagged because an image is enlarged or the resolution of the graphics device or file is reduced. (7)

analog charge: A series of electrical impulses created with the light received by the CCD. (8)

analog format: The principal feature of something in...

apprenticeship: A method of job training in which an employee in a union shop receives classroom training and on-the-job experience as a means of becoming an experienced journeyman. (25)

aqueous inks: Inks that are based on a mixture of water, glycol, and dyes or pigments. (13)

artwork: The graphic elements (line art and photographs) used in producing printed products. (1)

ascender: The part of a letter that extends above the body height. (4)

automatic film processing: A process that uses a mechanical device used to develop the latent image on photographic material. (11)

automatic trap: Trap set by building art with common colors. See also *trapping*. (7)

autotracing: A feature of some graphics programs; allows bitmapped images to be converted into object-oriented format. (7)

B

banding machine: Device that is used to wrap and bond a plastic or metal band around a bundle of booklets, books, boxes, or other products. This holds the products together for shipping. (23)

bank: A compositor's workstation; used to hold a job case when hand-setting foundry type. (4)

barrier guards: Machine guards that can be hinged or moved. (2)

base material: The layer of film that supports the emulsion. It is commonly made from plastic or a special grade of paper. Most of today's graphic films use a...

---

reduces the prominence of jaggies by surrounding them with intermediate shades of gray or color. (7)

antihalation backing: A biodegradable dye coating on the back of most films that absorbs light so it will not reflect back to the emulsion and produce a shadow or double image. (11)

control its shape. Named after French mathematician Pierre Bezier. (7)

binding: The process of joining together multiple pages of a printed product by various means including sewing, stapling, spiral wire, and adhesives. (1, 23)

bit: Binary digit. The basic unit of digital information. (7)

bit depth: The number of bits of color or grayscale...

CHAPTER 1

Overview of Graphic Communications

Learning Objectives

After studying this chapter, you will be able to:

- Explain the important role of graphic communications in our technological society.
- Identify the major processes commonly associated with the graphic communications industry.
- Summarize the four printing classifications.
- Recall the segments of the printing industry.

Important Terms

artwork	image carrier
binding	impactless printing
book printing	in-plant printing
commercial printing	line art
computer-to-plate (CTP)	newspaper printing
continuous tone copy	package printing
copy	page composition
editing	periodical printing
electrostatic printing	photoconversion
financial printing	printing
finishing	printing press
flexography	process camera
forms printing	process colors
graphic communications	quick printing
image assembly	substrate

The term *graphic* relates to the visual, or things we can see. The term *communication* refers to the exchange of information in any form. Therefore, *graphic communications* is the exchange of information in a visual form, such as words, drawings, photographs, or a combination of these.

Graphic arts used to be the common name for the study of the processes used in the printing industry. Graphic communications is now a more accurate term, because the printing industry creates products that visually convey messages. The term *graphic science* might also be used, since so many of the sciences—mechanics, physics, electronics, chemistry—are involved in various aspects of graphic communications.

This is an extremely challenging time for anyone involved in graphic communications. Advances in electronics and the application of these advances to graphic communications processes have made it vital to keep up-to-date with changes in equipment capabilities and operating procedures.

One fact is crystal clear: if you fail to keep up with new technology, you could fall behind and not be aware of more efficient types of equipment and processes. This could cause your company to lose any competitive edge. The result could be antiquated techniques and inferior products or higher costs. Either could cause you to lose customers and profits.

The purpose of this chapter is to briefly explain the role of graphic communications in a technological society and identify the basic processes in this fast-changing industry. It will help prepare you to more fully comprehend the many aspects of graphic communications that are presented in detail in later chapters.

ACADEMIC LINK
History of Print

The invention of printing is directly correlated to the development of a substrate on which an image could be printed. The earliest examples of recorded information are generally considered to be art forms, not printing.

The earliest form of a book was created by the Sumerians on clay tablets around 3300 B.C. A stylus was used to press characters into wet clay. Ancient Egyptian writings on papyrus have been discovered that date to approximately 2600 B.C. Papyrus was made from the stalks of papyrus plants, which were abundant along the Nile River. The papyrus stalks were cut into thin strips, layered, and pressed or pounded together to form a smooth sheet.

The beginning of paper as we know it today is attributed to Ts'ai Lun in China, about 105 A.D. He used bark, cotton, and fishnets to make pulp and strained the fibers using a large, framed screen. When the strained pulp dried, the sheets of paper that remained were thin, flexible, and smooth.

Over the next 1000 years, papermaking spread to India, the Middle East, Spain, Italy, and Europe. As each region implemented this method, small changes were made that affected the appearance, durability, and cost of the paper. For example, Arabians used linen fibers instead of wood in the pulp. Also, Italian paper-makers began using watermarks in the late 1200s as a way of identifying their products.

WHY IS COMMUNICATION IMPORTANT?

People are constantly communicating. We take part in the communication process when we talk, surf the Web, watch television, send text messages, blog, or obey a "One-way Street" sign.

graphic communications: The exchange of information in a visual form, such as words, drawings, photographs, or a combination of these.

The method or medium of communication used will vary based on the specific needs of the individuals involved. For example, speech, or verbal communication, is satisfactory in certain situations but has its limitations. With verbal communication, there is no record of the exchange of ideas or thoughts. People can misunderstand or even totally forget the message. This is one of many reasons graphic or visual images are and continue to be extremely important, **Figure 1-1.** The ability to exchange complex data in so many different ways sets humans apart from other living organisms. Without the ability to communicate, the human race would live in a far different world.

Graphic communications is the lifeblood of our technological society, influencing the population of the world wherever and whenever a product is printed. It affects education to a very high degree: how individuals think, see things, and draw conclusions, result to a great extent from what they have read and seen.

People often have a need for practical knowledge, such as directions on how to build a shed or repair a bicycle. For such knowledge, they often turn to manuals and textbooks. Textbooks are a form of organized knowledge that can be consulted for immediate use or stored for future reference. Without books and other printed materials, people seeking knowledge would be greatly deprived. Much of our heritage and knowledge would be lost.

Textbooks, magazines, and journals all advance the information needs of our society. Advertising is another form of information. The printed advertisement, whether in a local newspaper or a national magazine, is a widely used means of conveying selling messages to potential buyers. The variety of printed products seems to be endless. Books, newspapers, greeting cards, packages, stamps, fabrics, labels, order forms, advertisements, manuals, and maps are only a few examples.

PRODUCING VISUAL IMAGES

In the past, the term *printing* was used to cover all facets of the graphic communications industry. However, with present technology, printing is too limited a term to include the advanced technology found in a typical facility. Many electronic systems, such as digital printing, have been added to the production of graphic images. Today, traditional printing is just one part or aspect of the rapidly growing graphic communications industry.

Printing is now understood to imply using ink to place an image on a *substrate*. The many operations necessary to reach that point, as well as the steps completed to prepare a printed product for final use, are detailed in this book. See **Figure 1-2.**

Before any job can be printed, the product must be thought out from beginning to end. It must be properly designed. Specifications or measurements for all variables must be given, and a quote, or an estimate of costs, must be calculated.

Design ensures the printed image conveys the intended message. The graphic designer takes an idea and puts it in an appropriate visual presentation. The selection of the type style and pictorial material, which includes art forms and photographs, can make the final product either acceptable or unacceptable.

Specifications are guidelines used to determine the format and cost of the final product. The development of specifications varies considerably from one facility to another, but typically includes such items as paper weight or thickness, color use, type of binding, and finishing methods.

A quote or quotation lists the prices and quantities for production of printed goods and services. The cost estimate is based on the job specifications and represents the final cost to manufacture the printed product. If the quote is accepted, which means there is agreement between two parties, work can begin. See **Figure 1-3.**

Figure 1-1. Graphic communications involves the exchange of messages in a visual form. A visual message is less likely to be misunderstood or overlooked than a verbal message.

Figure 1-2. This web of printed images is leaving the press to start the binding process. This machine folds, perforates, and chops web sheet into signatures. (Hantscho)

Figure 1-3. The quote is given to the customer after evaluation of issues including the cost of materials, size of run, and use of color.

Figure 1-4. A printed product usually includes both copy and artwork.

Copy and Art Preparation

Most printed products have a combination of written material, called *copy*, and pictures, called *artwork*. Although one or the other may be more important in some situations, they are usually equally important in communicating information, **Figure 1-4.**

The amount of copy, also termed the *manuscript* or *text,* will vary with each type of job. For instance, a magazine article and an advertisement will differ significantly in length, style, content, and purpose.

Most writers today use a computer and word processing software to develop their manuscript. The use of the computer has become almost universal because it allows easy modification of copy and correction of spelling, sentence structure, and punctuation errors. The completed text can be output to a printer to provide a paper copy, and saved in electronic format for use in succeeding steps of the production process. See **Figure 1-5.**

Line art, also called line copy, is an object-oriented graphic drawn by a graphic artist. Traditionally, line art was produced manually, using technical ink pens to draw solid black lines on a white background. Most line art today is produced using computer software. Line art is also available in the form of electronic clip art. See **Figure 1-6.**

substrate: Any material with a surface that can be printed or coated.

copy: The text elements (words) used in producing printed products.

artwork: The graphic elements (line art and photographs) used in producing printed products.

line art: An illustrated image drawn by hand or using computer software.

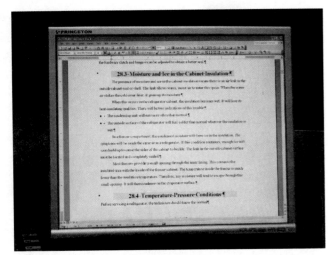

Figure 1-5. The computer has become an important part of every phase of graphic communications. Writers and editors commonly use a computer or word processor because it allows for easy revision and formatting of text.

Another form of artwork is the photograph, or *continuous tone copy.* Unlike line copy, which has only solid black and white tones, continuous tone copy has gradations of tones or shades from light to dark. Continuous tone copy must be converted to a

Figure 1-6. Electronic clip art is a readily available source of illustrations for printed materials. With suitable software, clip art images can be combined or altered to meet specific situations.

halftone image, or tiny dots, for printing. A scanner may be used for the screening process, which breaks up the continuous tone image into tiny dots. The press plate or *image carrier* needs distinct solid and nonsolid areas (provided by the dots and surrounding spaces) to place inked images on the substrate. **Figure 1-7** shows a greatly magnified view of the dots in a halftone image.

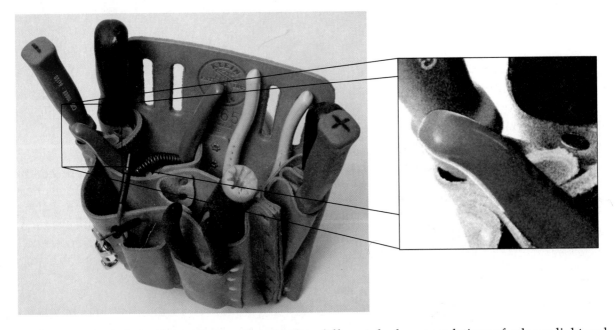

Figure 1-7. An original photo is a continuous tone that has different shades or gradations of color or light and darkness. A halftone, or screened photo, is made up of tiny dots that look like a continuous tone when printed. The screen can be seen easily in the enlarged section at right.

Editing

Editing is the final preparation of the author's or writer's manuscript for publication. It involves checking the text, line art, and photographs. The two classifications of editing are content editing and copy editing.

In content editing, an editor checks the material to make sure it is up-to-date, technically accurate, organized in a logical sequence, and covers all important ideas.

Copy editing is usually done after content editing. Copy editing is done to correct spelling and punctuation, to mark for style, and to ensure proper grammar. Consistency within the designated format or style is critical during copy editing.

As with writing, editing is usually done on a computer today. The writer's manuscript will typically be submitted in electronic form. The edited electronic file, in effect, becomes the typeset text. In many operations, the file will be imported to a page composition program and combined with graphic elements to create a finished page or other product, such as a brochure or multipage catalog. For operations still working with phototypesetting equipment and manual paste-up, the electronic text file becomes the input for the phototypesetter.

Page Composition

It is essential that printed material be attractive in design, hold attention, and transmit the desired message to the reader. To make this possible, text and graphic elements must be arranged on a page or pages. The process begins with design, progresses to layout, and is finally completed as *page composition*.

The initial design, or idea in basic form, is worked out by making a series of thumbnail sketches. Next, a rough layout is prepared. This is an actual-size visual of the page that accurately shows the space for type and position of different illustrations. Finally, a comprehensive layout is done. This detailed sketch clearly shows style, size, and format to be used in the final printed piece.

The assembly of all the necessary components or elements on the page (matching the layout) is typically done electronically. Electronic page composition has replaced mechanical paste-up in many printing operations. The text, line art, and photographs, which are all in digital form, can be arranged and manipulated to assemble the design. See **Figure 1-8.** The completed pages are then output to a printer or platemaker.

Figure 1-8. Electronic page composition has replaced manual paste-up in most operations. Page composition software allows the operator to position elements on the page and make all needed alterations.

Photoconversion

Photoconversion is a general term for processes that use light to place the original image onto a light-sensitive material. This broad category includes the use of process cameras to make negatives and screened or halftone images, digital cameras and scanners used for image capture, and exposure units for platemaking. This area of the printing plant is being eliminated in many facilities that no longer use negatives or positives.

Traditionally, a *process camera* has been used to make enlargements, reductions, and same-size reproductions of originals for use in page composition or stripping work. Depending on the purpose for which the reproduction is needed, the camera may be

continuous tone copy: An image with an infinite number of tone gradations between the lightest highlights and the darkest shadows.

image carrier: A press plate or other intermediate used to transfer identical images onto a substrate.

editing: The final preparation of the author's or writer's manuscript for publication, including checking the text, line art, and photographs.

page composition: Prepress process of setting type and image layout for a page.

photoconversion: The processes that use light to place the original image onto a light-sensitive material.

process camera: Device used to make enlargements, reductions, and same-size reproductions of originals for use in page composition or stripping work.

used to produce a film negative (opposite original), a film positive (film like original), or a print (photo like original). It is sometimes used to make a screened photo or halftone from a continuous-tone original.

Process cameras have either horizontal or vertical facing lenses, **Figure 1-9.** Some must be used in a darkroom, which is an area that can be made devoid of light for working with photographic material. Others are daylight cameras and can be used in normal room light.

As is the case in most graphic communications areas, computers have greatly changed the process of photoconversion. Scanned images are combined with text and electronically generated line art, using page composition software.

A widely used device today for many image-capture tasks is the electronic scanner. Both drum-type and flatbed scanners are used extensively in graphic communications work. Scanners convert the light, dark, and color values of the original to digital form, allowing the image to be stored as an electronic file. The image can then be altered or enhanced in a number of ways by using computer software. The image can be enlarged or reduced, color-corrected or modified, combined with other images, or processed in many other ways. Use of a scanner and computer is the most common method today for making color separations for printing.

Separations

When color photographs must be reproduced in a printed piece, separations are needed. Each separation is a halftone positive or negative representing one of the *process colors* used for printing: cyan, magenta, yellow, and black. Each separation is used to make the plate for that color. When run on the press,

Figure 1-9. This is a vertical process camera. This type of camera is commonly used to make Photostats, enlarge or reduce copies, screen halftones, and make film positives or negatives. (nuArc Company, Inc.)

each color is printed in register, or alignment, with the others to produce a full-color illustration. See **Figure 1-10.**

Image Assembly

The process of assembling line and halftone negatives or positives into pages has traditionally

Figure 1-10. To print a full-color image, color separations have to be made of a full-color photo. Each separation represents one of the three primary colors (cyan, magenta, and yellow). A fourth separation is made for black. Then, the four colors of ink are deposited on top of each other as the paper runs through the press. (Westvaco Corporation)

been called stripping. Today, the process of putting together pages is more often electronic and is referred to as *image assembly*.

In the stripping process, pieces of negative or positive film are physically taped in place on a carrier sheet or base. The film pieces, when assembled, make up a single page or several pages, called a flat. A number of pages may be assembled as a unit called a form. Location of the pages on the form is in a particular order, or imposition, so the pages will be in proper order when printed and folded.

Image assembly is done electronically, with all the page elements in the proper size and place. Electronic stripping and imposition software has allowed the computer to take over these tasks as well. The output of the imagesetter, when used with such software, is large sheets of film with multiple pages properly imposed for making the printing plate or plates.

Platemaking

The process of placing an image on a plate is called platemaking. The plates are the means by which many copies can be made as duplicates of the original through the printing process. Printing plates transfer identical images onto a substrate.

The method used to make a plate varies with each printing process. Plates can be produced mechanically, electronically, or photographically. The most commonly prepared type of plate is used for offset lithography, the most widely used printing process. The *computer-to-plate (CTP)*, or direct-to-plate system, uses an imagesetter to prepare the plate instead of using a negative. The plate is prepared directly from the electronic file, without any negatives involved.

PRINTING PROCESSES

Printing can be considered as a process involving the use of a *printing press* to transfer an image from an image carrier to a substrate, usually paper. Most often, printing involves making duplicates of the printed product in large quantities.

The two basic types of presses are sheet-fed and web-fed. The sheet-fed press prints on single or individual sheets of paper. A web-fed press uses a long, single sheet or ribbon of paper. Web-fed presses are used for longer runs than sheet-fed presses. A run is a press operation for complete job. See **Figure 1-11.**

The graphic communications industry generally recognizes four major printing processes: relief, planography, intaglio, and porous. A fifth category, impactless printing, has come into general use in recent years. See **Figure 1-12.**

Relief Printing

The relief process is the oldest method of printing, and requires a raised image. Ink is spread on the raised image areas, and transferred to paper by direct pressure. See **Figure 1-13.** Two types of relief printing are letterpress and flexography. The letterpress process prints from metal plates, and the process is seldom used today. Until recent years, however, it was the most widely used printing process. Examples of products once printed by letterpress are business cards, stationery, labels, business forms, tickets, cartons, magazines, reports, wrappings, newspapers, and books.

---

process colors: The four colors of ink used for color printing: cyan, magenta, yellow, and black (CMYK).

image assembly: The process of electronically assembling line and halftone negatives or positives into pages.

computer-to-plate (CTP): Imaging systems that take fully-paginated digital materials and expose this information to plates without creating film intermediates.

printing: A process involving the use of a specialized machine to transfer an image from an image carrier to a substrate.

printing press: A specialized machine used to transfer an image from an image carrier to a substrate, usually paper.

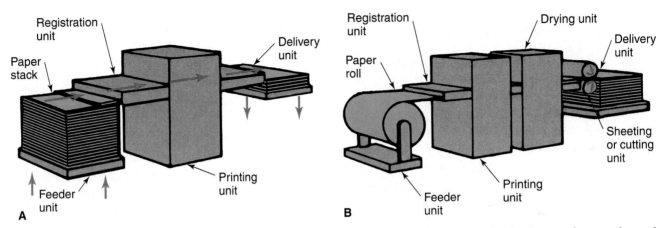

Figure 1-11. The two basic types of printing presses. A—The sheet-fed press moves single sheets of paper through impression system. B—The web-fed press prints on a long ribbon of paper. It is used for longer press runs.

Process	How It Works
Relief	Ink is spread on raised image areas and transferred to paper by direct pressure.
Planography	A flat printing plate accepts ink and repels water. The image is transferred from the plate to a cylinder, then onto the paper.
Intaglio	The image area is etched into the plate and then inked. The cylinders then transfer the images onto the paper.
Porous	A plate is attached to a screen and ink is forced through the screen mesh.
Impactless	Ink or toner is used to produce images from a computer.

Figure 1-12. The five major types of printing processes.

Although letterpress use has declined, another relief printing process has been growing in popularity. The process of *flexography* uses a flexible plastic or synthetic plate with a relief image to print on a substrate. Plastic bags, labels, and other packaging materials are commonly printed by this process. Some of today's newspapers and books are printed by flexography.

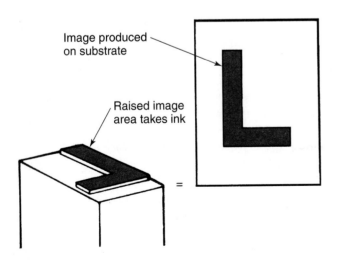

Figure 1-13. Letterpress printing transfers ink from a raised image area to a substrate.

Planography

Planography is the process of printing from a flat (nonraised) surface, and is based on the concept that water and oil do not readily mix. Water keeps ink from sticking, so nonimage areas are made to accept water. In this process, the image areas of the printing plate accept ink and repel water; nonimage areas accept water, which keeps ink from sticking. See **Figure 1-14.**

The most widely used form of planography is the printing process called offset lithography. In this form of printing, the inked image is first transferred, or offset, from the printing plate to a rubber cylinder or roller, then from the roller to a substrate. Both sheet-fed and web-fed presses are used in offset lithography. Lithography is widely used for all forms of commercial printing and publishing.

A form of offset lithography that is rapidly growing in popularity is waterless printing. It uses ink viscosity, rather than a dampening solution, to keep image and nonimage areas separate, and is increasingly used for both quality and environmental reasons.

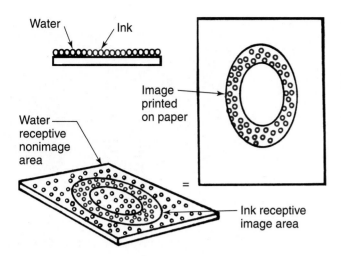

Figure 1-14. Planography has the image area and nonimage areas on a flat surface. The image area is receptive to ink, and the nonimage area is receptive to water.

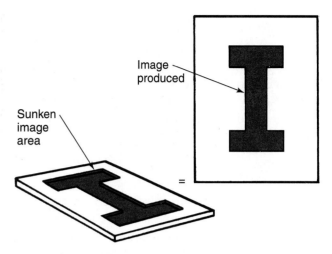

Figure 1-15. Gravure or intaglio printing has an image area that is sunken below the plate surface to hold ink.

Intaglio Process

In the intaglio process, the image area is sunken into the image carrier, as shown in **Figure 1-15.** Gravure printing is the most commonly used type of the intaglio process.

Two characteristics are common to the gravure process. First, both line work and photographs are screened. In effect, the total cylinder or gravure plate is a halftone. Once the images are etched in the plate, it is very difficult to alter them. Second, the gravure cylinder, which carries the image and nonimage area, is dipped in a tray of ink. The nonimage area must have the ink removed before the image is printed. The doctor blade is important because it removes the ink from the nonimage area. The blade is a steel strip that is fitted into a clip, and it is in contact with the cylinder. This leaves ink only in the sunken areas of the cylinder.

The gravure process is considered to be an excellent, high-speed, long-run means of producing a superior product. Some of the typical materials printed by this method are magazines, catalogs, newspaper supplements, package printing, metal surfaces, and vinyl surfaces.

Porous Printing

Porous printing is basically a stencil process, in which an image carrier is attached to a screen and ink is forced through the open mesh areas. Screen printing is the most used of the porous printing methods. See **Figure 1-16.**

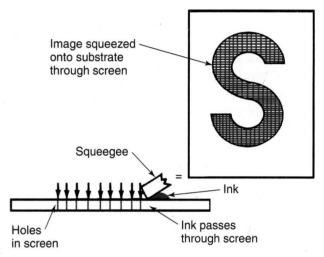

Figure 1-16. Screen printing is a form of porous printing. Small holes in the image permit ink to pass through and deposit on substrate.

Screen printing is a versatile method of printing on many types of surfaces. It is capable of doing line and halftone work. Some of the screen printing work in the electronics field is very precise and the equipment highly sophisticated. Special inks are required for screen printing.

The artwork is assembled much like that for lithographic work. Laying out to size, with all of the elements in position, will generally be acceptable. Overlays are necessary for additional color work. The techniques vary slightly when using photographic or hand-cut stencils. The presses for the screen process

flexography: A relief printing process that uses flexible printing plates.

can be manual or highly automated.

A wide variety of applications exists, including packaging, clothing and other fabric items, and printing on nonabsorbent surfaces such as glass. Many tiny electronic circuits are produced with a type of screen printing. Another unusual application is printing the conductive materials on automobile rear windows for defrosting circuits.

Impactless Printing

Impactless printing, also called pressureless printing, does not require direct contact between an image carrier and the substrate. Ink-jet printing is one of the examples of the impactless process. Ink droplets are formed and forced through very small nozzles onto the substrate. Most of the units use a computer to control the image generation. The computer controls where, and how much, ink is forced onto the substrate. See **Figure 1-17.**

Electrostatic printing systems and laser printers are also being used to produce high-quality images. The electrostatic method uses the forces of electric current and static electricity. It is commonly found in office copying machines. Machines capable of producing copies in multiple colors have become common in recent years, **Figure 1-18.**

Figure 1-18. This color digital production system enables customers to send electronic files directly to the digital full-color copier/printer. It provides an affordable way to produce short-run full-color prints of documents such as proposals, menus, reports, presentations, sales flyers, brochures, and other materials that are currently printed in black-and-white because of quality, turnaround, and cost considerations. (Xerox)

BINDING AND FINISHING

Once an image has been printed on a substrate, some form of binding and finishing is usually required. These are the final steps to completing the printing job.

Binding

Binding is the process of joining together multiple pages of a printed product by various means including sewing, stapling, spiral wire, and adhesives. Binding requires complex equipment, as shown in **Figure 1-19.**

The binding process for most printed products requires one or more of the following steps: folding, scoring, gathering, collating, stitching, and trimming.

- Scoring is the creasing of a heavier sheet of paper or paperboard to assist in the folding of the material.

- Folding is required when a large sheet contains two or more pages of a product. Sheets containing 8, 16, or 32 pages are common in production of books and periodicals. The folded groups of pages are called signatures.

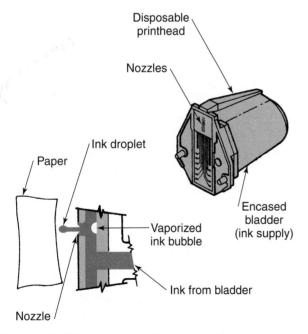

Figure 1-17. This diagram illustrates the basic principle of ink-jet printing. (A.B. Dick Co.)

Figure 1-19. A binding machine is used to hold multiple sheets together to form one product, such as a book.

- Gathering is the process of bringing several signatures together in the proper order.
- Collating is the process of placing pages (usually single sheets) in the correct sequence.
- Stitching is a stapling process by which pages of a signature are held together.
- Trimming is the cutting of material after printing to produce even edges. **Figure 1-20** shows an example of a semiautomatic operation for cutting stock.

Finishing

Finishing includes various processes that enhance the final printed product. Some of the more common finishing operations include embossing, die-cutting, stamping, punching, drilling, round cornering, and padding. Laminating and coating are also considered finishing processes.

- Embossing produces a raised design on paper or other material. This process uses pressure and heat to mold the paper fibers.
- Die-cutting uses rules or blades to cut paper or other sheet materials into designs.
- Perforating is a similar operation that cuts a series of holes or slits in the stock to allow part of it to be torn off easily. It is used extensively for tickets and coupons, often in conjunction with the process of numbering.
- Numbering is the process of printing numbers in sequence on each piece.

Figure 1-20. Trimming is done to make all sheets even on edges. This is a large computer-controlled cutter that automatically trims stock to size.

- Stamping refers to the application of a metal foil to almost any type of material, such as leather, paper, or cloth. A combination of embossing and foil stamping can also be done in one operation.
- Lamination is the process of bonding plastic film, by heat and pressure, to a sheet of paper to protect its surface and improve appearance. See **Figure 1-21.**

impactless printing: Term for several types of printing that do not require direct contact between an image carrier and the substrate.

electrostatic printing: A printing method that uses the forces of electric current and static electricity.

binding: The process of joining together multiple pages of a printed product by various means including sewing, stapling, spiral wire, and adhesives.

finishing: A general term that applies to the many operations carried out during or following printing.

Figure 1-21. Laminating is a finishing operation that puts protective coating over the image.

Figure 1-22. Products from each segment of the printing industry.

- Coating is done for the same purpose, and may be done as a finishing operation, or as part of the printing process, depending on the application. For example, a spot coating of gloss or dull varnish to part of a page is often applied during printing. The varnish is a design element to draw attention to the area of the page where it is applied.

SEGMENTS OF THE INDUSTRY

The graphic communications industry can be divided into segments or classifications, **Figure 1-22.** A few of the major segments are described briefly in the following paragraphs.

Commercial Printing

The *commercial printing* segment of the industry encompasses all sizes and types of printing operations. These range from small local shops with one or two employees to large companies with several plant locations and hundreds or thousands of employees. Products produced in the commercial printing segment are as varied as the company sizes, from simple one-color envelopes and letterheads to full-color product brochures and sales displays to complex and sophisticated annual reports for giant corporations. This segment of the graphic communications industry is dominated by the offset lithography printing process. See **Figure 1-23.**

Quick printing consists of shops specializing in rapidly completing short-run printing and photocopying work. Both independently owned and franchised quick printing operations are designed to serve the needs of business customers. Equipment in such shops may include both small offset duplicators and photocopiers with varying capabilities, including color.

Periodical Printing

The *periodical printing* segment of the industry consists of plants that are designed primarily to print magazines. Web-fed offset lithography is used extensively, but a shift to gravure appears to be taking place in periodical publication.

Newspaper Printing

Although *newspaper printing* was done for many years on web-fed presses using the letterpress process, most operations have switched to offset lithography. Because of the widespread use of computer technology and satellite transmission, national newspapers are published through a network of regional printing sites. This greatly simplifies distribution of the product. See **Figure 1-24.**

Figure 1-23. This is a large sheet-fed offset lithographic press, one of the types widely used in commercial printing. Paper sheets are picked up on right. They are then pulled to the left for printing.

Figure 1-24. These folded and gathered newspapers coming off a large web-fed offset lithographic press are being printed at a regional site for a national publication. Electronics technology has made possible printing of the same newspaper at multiple sites for easier distribution. (USA Today)

Book Printing

Book printing includes the production of trade books, such as general interest nonfiction and fiction, sold in bookstores and other retail locations and textbooks providing instruction on a great variety of subjects. At one time, many book publishers operated their own printing facilities. Today, however, most contract with large specialized printing operations.

commercial printing: A segment of the graphic communications industry that produces various products for customers, including forms, newspaper inserts, and catalogs.

quick printing: A subdivision of commercial printing, consisting of shops specializing in rapidly completing short-run printing and photocopying work for business customers.

periodical printing: That segment of the graphic communications industry consisting of plants that are designed primarily to print magazines.

newspaper printing: A segment of the graphic communications industry that involves publishing and printing daily or weekly newspapers.

book printing: Graphic communications industry segment that produces trade books and textbooks.

Web-fed offset lithography is the process usually used in book production.

In-Plant Printing

The *in-plant printing* segment of the industry covers printing facilities operated by companies whose business is not the production of printed materials. A typical use of in-plant printing is the production of owner's manuals, repair manuals, and parts lists for such products as power tools, material-handling equipment, or vehicles of various types.

Forms Printing

The *forms printing* segment of the industry designs and prints special paper forms used in many businesses. The types of forms vary from simple sales receipts or message pads to multipart carbonless order forms to continuous perforated forms for use in special impact printers. Label printing is also done by some forms printers, as well as by companies specializing in labels. Most label printing is done on papers with a pressure-sensitive adhesive backing, using specially designed small web-offset lithographic presses. Business forms printing is declining because the public is choosing to use digital equipment to print forms.

Financial Printing

Financial printing involves a variety of printed materials. Typical products include checks, bonds, currency, lottery tickets, legal documents, various certificates, registration material, and loan materials. This printing classification is highly specialized and generally controlled by the federal government. Maintaining security of many of these documents is imperative.

Package Printing

Package printing has become one of the large segments of the industry. Look at all the packages you see in the grocery store. Would you buy cereal if you did not see what it looked like? The images are printed on many different types of materials. Plastic, paper, cardboard, corrugated board, and foil are a sampling of the many types of materials used for packaging. It is a growing industry.

Summary

Graphic communications is an umbrella term to identify printing processes that place an image on a variety of surfaces we call substrates. It has a rich history that has preserved the art of communication. It is a dynamic challenging industry. Individuals working in the industry have skills that vary greatly. The creative person, the writer, the manager, the operator, the technician, and the engineer have typical skills needed by employees of a printing facility. These facilities use various processes to create a product that records and preserves thoughts and ideas of individuals. The products produced by various segments of the industry reflect the capabilities of each process.

Review Questions

Please do not write in this text. Write your answers on a separate sheet of paper.

1. Why are graphic images considered important compared to verbal communication?

2. Any material on which printing can be done is called a(n) _____.

3. A quote lists the _____ and _____ for production of printed goods and services.

4. Which of the following is the most common way of generating copy for printing?
   A. Computer.
   B. Hot type.
   C. Scanning.
   D. Photocomposing.

5. True *or* False? Line art is a type of drawing consisting of continuous tones.

6. Explain the term *halftone*.

7. Which of the following is *not* a process color used in printing a full-color photograph?
   A. Magenta.
   B. Yellow.
   C. Green.
   D. Cyan.

8. In your own words, describe the following types of printing: flexography, gravure, screen printing, impactless printing.

9. _____ is the printing process used most extensively in the commercial printing segment of the graphic communications industry.

10. What type of printing is ink-jet printing?
11. Name at least three steps that are considered part of the binding process.
12. What subdivision of commercial printing specializes in rapidly completing short-run printing and photocopying work?
13. What process is usually used in book production?

Suggested Activities

1. After getting permission to visit a printing plant, identify the variety of products the plant produces. What is the printing process used to produce these printed products?
2. Select an individual or a discovery that has contributed to the advancement of the industry. Verbally present your findings to the class.
3. Explain the basic differences among the following printing processes: relief printing, planography, intaglio process, porous printing, and impactless printing.

Related Web Links

Make Your Mark
www.makeyourmark.org
Online resource to create projects and learn about graphic communications careers.

Virtual Museum Printing Press
www.imultimedia.pt/museuvirtpress/index_i.html
History and information on printing press technology.

GAIN—Graphic Arts Information Network
www.gain.net/eweb/startpage.aspx
Resources include career and general printing information.

Graphic Arts Online
www.graphicartsonline.com
Current events in graphic communications.

Graphic Arts Education and Research Foundation
www.gaerf.org
Organization with resources about accreditation.

Graphic Communications Central
teched.vt.edu/GCC
Provides educational material in the graphic communications field for teachers and students.

International Graphic Arts Education Association, Inc.
www.igaea.org
Organization with resources for educators and professionals.

GreenPrint
www.printgreener.com
Information and resources on green printing.

in-plant printing: Term for printing facilities operated by companies whose business is not the production of printed materials.

forms printing: Industry that designs and prints special paper forms used in many businesses.

financial printing: A segment of the graphic communications industry consisting of plants that primarily print materials such as checks, currency, and legal documents.

package printing: Industry that uses images printed on many different types of materials, such as plastic, paper, cardboard, corrugated board, and foil.

CHAPTER 2

Safety and Health

Learning Objectives

After studying this chapter, you will be able to:

- Recall the purpose of a plant safety and health program.
- Explain the importance of machine guards and personal protection.
- Apply the safe handling of materials, tools, and equipment, as well as proper techniques for lifting.
- Identify the correct handling, storage, and disposal of chemicals and other materials.
- Explain plans for fire prevention within a plant.
- Explain roper noise control in a plant.
- Summarize an ergonomically correct computer workstation.
- Explain ways to reduce and eliminate waste for environmental compliance.

Important Terms

barrier guards
decibels (dBA)
ergonomics
lockout devices
machine guards
Material Safety Data Sheet
   (MSDS)
nip points
personal protective devices

spontaneous
   combustion
tagout device
toxic substance
volatile organic
   compounds (VOCs)
waste stream

Personnel in the graphic communications industry may be confronted with many hazards in the course of performing their duties. These include hazards of a mechanical, chemical, flammable, or electrical nature. While the industry has many safety and health problems common to other fields, this chapter will emphasize the recognition and control of those areas with the greatest potential for injury, illness, or environmental contamination. Later chapters will describe safety rules for specific processes performed in a graphic communications facility. Other sources of health and safety information available to you on the job are equipment manuals and machine labels.

It is vital for workers in a graphic communications plant to know basic safety practices. Because of the wide variety of processes performed, the potential for injury, illness, or death always exists. It is up to you to keep the work environment safe and healthy for your coworkers and for yourself. The checklist at the end of this chapter will be helpful in performing a safety inspection of a graphic communications facility.

SAFETY AND HEALTH PROGRAM

A safety and health program is an effective means of providing a safe working environment. The purpose of such a program is to recognize, evaluate, and control potential hazards in the workplace. See **Figure 2-1.**

Unguarded machinery, improper lifting methods, chemical contaminants, flammable and combustible materials, ungrounded wires, noise, and even poorly designed computer workstations are all potential health hazards.

An effective safety program begins with informed employees. The Occupational Safety and Health Administration (OSHA) has issued a Hazard Communication Standard known as the "Worker's Right to Know Law." It requires the employer to communicate information to workers about chemical hazards in the workplace. It generally requires employees to be afforded a safe and healthy work environment, be advised and trained concerning any hazardous materials to which they are routinely

Figure 2-1. A graphic communications facility can be a safe and enjoyable place to work. However, if safety rules are not followed, it can be very dangerous. (Variquick)

exposed, have access to information about chemicals used, and be advised of their rights and obligations under the act.

To ensure the success of the safety and health program, management leadership is essential. The person responsible for the safety and health program must have the authority to carry it out. Everyone in the establishment must be aware of the program. A safe operation largely depends on all plant personnel being properly informed of potential hazards.

Safe conditions depend on a constant vigilance for possible hazards. That is why periodic inspections are one of the most important aspects of a successful safety and health program. **Figure 2-2** provides

Safety Inspection Checklist	Satisfactory	Unsatisfactory	Not Applicable	Dangerous	Remarks
I. Housekeeping					
A. Clean and orderly work area					
B. Proper materials available for housekeeping					
C. Floor holes (drains) covered					
D. Materials available for cleaning					
E. Maintenance schedule used					
F. Properly marked aisles					
G. Proper storage facilities					
H. Proper disposal systems					
I. Warnings and cautions posted					
J. Containers labeled					
K. Open aisles and fire lanes					
L. Proper handling devices					
M. Vacuuming used where possible					
II. Personal Protective Equipment					
A. Eye protection					
B. Foot protection					
C. Head protection					
D. Protective clothing					
E. Ear protection					
F. Respiratory equipment					
III. Administration					
A. Safety program					
1. Education-safety personnel					
2. Incentives					
B. Procedures					
1. Recordkeeping					
2. Accident and injury handling					
3. Emergency evacuation plan					
4. Posting					
C. Job hazard analysis					
IV. Equipment/Machinery					
A. Fixed guarding					
B. Movable guarding					
C. Equipment placement					
D. Maintenance					
E. Mechanical controls					
F. Proper enclosure					

Figure 2-2. A safety inspection checklist that can be used for evaluating workplace safety conditions.

	Satisfactory	Unsatisfactory	Not Applicable	Dangerous	Remarks
V. Electrical					
A. Grounding					
B. Wiring					
C. Circuits identified					
D. Switch location					
E. Extension cords					
F. Portable electrical equipment					
VI. Chemicals					
A. Storage					
B. Ventilation					
C. Proper identification					
D. Handling devices					
E. Clean-up methods					
F. Disposal					
VII. Fire Protection					
A. Flammable materials					
1. Safe storage (cabinet)					
2. Proper labeling					
3. Proper containers					
4. Disposal of rags					
B. Fire equipment					
1. Fire extinguishers					
a. Right type for location					
b. Clearly visible					
2. Automatic sprinkler					
3. Blankets (same as fire extinguishers)					
4. Smoke detectors					
5. Flame and fume arrestors					
6. Proper waste disposal					
C. Fire drills					
1. Proper exits signs					
2. Availability of exits					
3. Dissemination of exit information					
4. Education of employees					
D. Periodic checking					
VIII. First Aid					
A. First aid facility provided					
B. Qualified first aid personnel					
1. Nurse provided					
2. First aid training available					

Figure 2-2. *(Continued)*

a safety checklist for identifying problems in a graphic communications facility so corrective action can be taken.

MECHANICAL HAZARDS

Many on-the-job physical injuries are the result of mechanical hazards that can be controlled if:

- Machines are properly guarded.
- Energy isolating devices are locked out and tagged out during maintenance.
- Workers properly use personal protective equipment.
- Workers are trained to handle materials, tools, and equipment safely.

Machine Guarding

Hazards are posed by the reciprocating, rotating, and shearing actions of various types of machinery in the industry. See **Figure 2-3.** Therefore, properly placed guards on mechanical equipment are very important for the operator's protection.

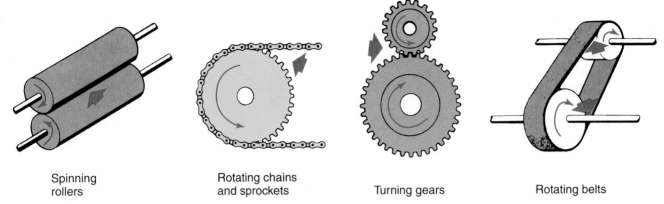

Spinning
rollers

Rotating chains
and sprockets

Turning gears

Rotating belts

Figure 2-3. These mechanisms found in a graphic communications facility can cause serious injury.

Rotating motions create hazards in two areas: at the point of operation and at the points where power or motion is being transmitted from one part to another. Any rotating or reciprocating part is dangerous. Contact with loose clothing, hair, and even skin can cause severe injury.

Typical rotating mechanisms are spindles, flywheels, horizontal or vertical shafts, cams, and collars, **Figure 2-4.** Whenever something projects from the rotating unit, the machine becomes even more dangerous. Extreme care must be taken when working in an area with rotating units, even though they are properly guarded.

Machine guards protect parts of the human body from being electrocuted, cut, squashed, or hit by flying fragments. Guards also protect the equipment from foreign objects. Metal and plastic are two materials commonly used as guards. Most machines in the graphic communications industry require some type of guard. See **Figure 2-5.** If a guard is in place, do not remove it to perform an operation. Likewise, do not use equipment when guards are missing, broken, or out of adjustment. The risk of severe injury to yourself or to others is too great.

Machine guards are necessary wherever hazardous machine parts are within reach of the operator. Make sure guards are in place over belts, chains, flywheels, cutters, pulleys, shafting, fasteners, punches, drills, clamps, gears, rollers, cylinders, shears, and all other points of operation.

Figure 2-5. Always keep guards and covers in position when you operate a press or other type of equipment. Guards primarily protect people from injury, but they also keep objects from entering and damaging the press. Covers perform the same general function. (Heidelberg Harris)

Figure 2-4. Rotating objects, especially those with projecting parts, pose a constant danger on presses and other equipment. They can cause serious cuts, wrap clothing around shafts, and pull the operator into the equipment.

Nip points exist where two cylinders meet or come close to one another. Cylinders can produce tremendous pulling and crushing force that can severely injure a person, sometimes causing permanent disability. Gears and rollers also have nip points. Many guards are pressure-sensitive and automatically stop the movement of the machine when an object becomes wedged between the guard and the cylinder. See **Figure 2-6.**

Barrier guards keep a person out of the operation area but can be hinged or moved. On newer equipment, when the guard is moved out of position, power is cut off, and the machine will not run.

Just because a machine or press looks small does not mean it is incapable of causing serious injury. Without a guard, the operator's clothing can easily be caught and pulled into the nip point. Long hair can also get drawn into nip points. Always tie back long hair and wear an industrial hair net, a cap, or headband when operating machinery. Do not wear jewelry of any kind, not even a watch, when operating equipment, **Figure 2-7.**

Some machines require specialized types of guarding. For instance, a typical safety device on a guillotine paper cutter prevents cutting until the pressure clamp is in position. A similar safety feature is one that will not permit machine operation if a light beam is blocked by some object, such as a hand. A common control device on a paper cutter requires both hands of the operator to be on the operating controls, **Figure 2-8.**

A paper cutter blade is very sharp; all precautions should be taken to avoid injury when cutting stock or handling the blade. When operating a cutter, make it

Figure 2-7. Always dress properly for work. The press operator is not wearing jewelry or a watch and is wearing an apron to keep clothing out of the press.

Safety buttons

Figure 2-8. Note the two control buttons on this cutter. Both safety buttons must be pressed simultaneously to operate the blade. The dual mechanism ensures the hands are out of the way when cutting.

machine guards: Metal or plastic enclosures that cover moving machine parts and protect the operator from being cut, squashed, or hit by flying fragments.

nip points: The point of contact where two cylinders, gears, or rollers meet or come close to one another.

barrier guards: Machine guards that can be hinged or moved.

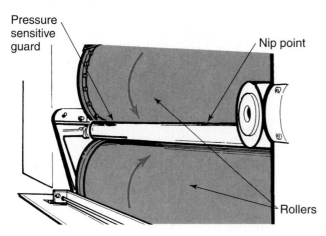

Figure 2-6. A nip point occurs where two rollers come together. This press has a pressure sensitive guard that shuts it off if anything is pulled into the nip point.

a habit to never reach for a jammed piece of paper. Follow safety procedures indicated on the machine labels or equipment manual.

Cleaning and maintaining equipment should be done when the machine is disconnected. Do not rely on a safety interlock when working on a piece of equipment. Make sure the power is *off* at the main switch!

Lockout Devices

When someone is working on a piece of equipment, the electrical power supply must be cut off. "Locking out" equipment is the only sure way to prevent injuries that could result from unexpected energizing or startup of the machine. *Lockout devices* utilize either a key or combination-type lock to hold an energy isolating device, such as a manually operated electrical circuit breaker, in the safe position to prevent the machine from energizing.

A *tagout device* is a prominent warning, such as a tag securely fastened to an energy isolating device. When you find a tagged power box, make no attempt to restore the power. The tag should be removed by the person who placed it. See **Figure 2-9.**

Many pieces of equipment have flip covers to prevent run/reverse or inch buttons from accidentally being pressed. The inch button on the press allows the operator to move the press a very short distance. The cover on the run/reverse button must be flipped

shut during plate gumming, blanket work, or any other operation that requires a press to be inched. The OSHA-approved "inch safe service" method must be utilized when washing rollers on the press and when washing blankets on the press and binding equipment.

Personal Protection

Besides making sure machines are properly guarded and locked out, you can take additional steps to protect yourself and others from injury.

As cautioned earlier, never wear watches, rings, ties, bracelets, scarves, or loose clothing while working with machinery. Remember that loose long hair is a hazard, as is a rag partially tucked in a pocket and hanging out.

Wear appropriate safety equipment, **Figure 2-10.** Eye protection should be worn when you are pouring/pumping hazardous chemicals, when you are operating a saw, a grinder, or any machine that can cause material to fly and strike you or other shop workers. Use earplugs or another type of hearing protection in noisy areas. Wear gloves to protect your hands when necessary. Choose gloves that suit the job while giving you the best possible protection and freedom of movement. Nitrile or butyl rubber gloves will protect your hands when handling inks,

Figure 2-9. Lockout devices and tags are used to prevent accidental operation of machinery.

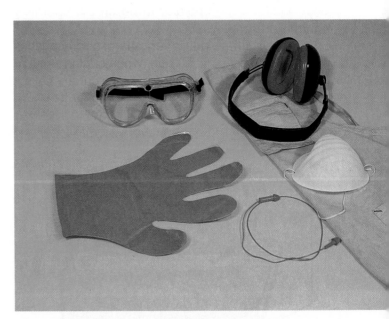

Figure 2-10. Wear personal protective equipment. Shown are approved eye protection, an apron to protect clothing, plastic gloves for handling oils and solvents, earplugs, and a dust mask. For some situations, a respirator must be worn, since it provides much greater protection than a dust mask.

oils, solvents, and other chemicals. Wear an apron to keep clothing from being pulled into machinery. A dust mask is suitable for some airborne particles, but an approved respirator must be worn when operations produce ink mists. Certain operations, such as press, bindery, and storage, may require foot protection.

Tools, Materials, and Equipment Handling

Keep the graphic communications facility organized. Return all tools, equipment, and supplies to their proper storage areas after use.

To prevent falls, keep floors dry and clear of tools and supplies. Clean up liquid spills immediately. Nonskid mats, adhesive strips, or coating materials may be applied to the floor around work areas, **Figure 2-11.**

Do not stand skid pads or pallets on edge. They are heavy enough to cause serious foot or leg injuries if they fall on someone. Always store them flat in a designated area.

Cuts from sharp materials are common injuries. Never carry sharp objects in your pockets. They can easily puncture the skin. Some materials are banded with metal strapping. When cut, the strapping can spring and cause severe lacerations. Use extreme care if you must cut strapping, and wear proper protective equipment, such as safety glasses with side panels, a full face shield, and leather gloves.

As described earlier, keep all guards, shields, and covers in place. They perform the important function of keeping your hands and other body parts out of the equipment.

Never use or adjust any equipment unless you have been properly trained to do so. Make sure you have seen a demonstration or have supervision before using any equipment. Only properly certified employees should operate a forklift, straddle lift, or motorized pallet jack. Riders are never permitted on material handling equipment.

Always work and act like a professional when in a graphic communications facility. Horseplay endangers the safety of individuals. A joke is an accident waiting to happen. If you are not sure about a safety rule or procedure, ask your supervisor.

When operating a press, keep these factors in mind:

- Never turn on a press unless you are sure all tools have been removed from it and all mechanisms have been set correctly.
- Make sure no one is near the press before starting the equipment.
- Check to make sure all press guards are in place.
- Keep your hands clear of the press when it is running.
- Do not try to grab paper, lubricate parts, or do anything that places your hands near the rollers and nip points while the press is running.
- Have an assistant present whenever you are cleaning or running a press. If you were to get caught in the machinery, the assistant could turn off the press.

Tips for Safe Lifting

Routine on-the-job lifting and materials handling can lead to injury. Too often, a person lifts a heavy load without seeking assistance from another person or from a mechanical device. See **Figure 2-12.** When lifting an object, keep your knees bent and your back straight. Leaning over while lifting is poor practice, **Figure 2-13.** These safety instructions will lessen the risk of serious injury to the worker who is using his or her body to lift or move materials:

- **Clear a pathway.** Before you move things from one place to another, be sure you have a clear pathway.

Figure 2-11. Nonskid mats help prevent slipping. (Courtesy of Lab Safety Supply, Inc., Janesville, WI)

lockout devices: A key or combination-type lock used to hold an energy isolating device in the safe position to prevent the machine from energizing.

tagout device: A prominent warning device securely fastened to an energy isolating device, to indicate that electrical power is off and must remain off until the tag is removed.

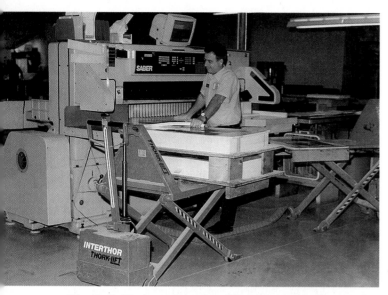

Figure 2-12. A combination lift table and pallet truck eliminates bending and lifting. (Interthor, Inc.)

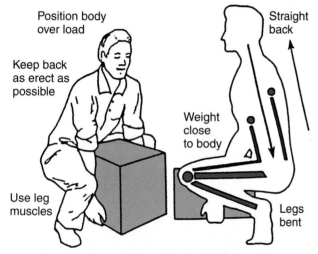

Position body over load

Keep back as erect as possible

Use leg muscles

Straight back

Weight close to body

Legs bent

Figure 2-13. Prevent painful back injuries by using the correct lifting technique. To help maintain a straight back, keep your head up and look straight ahead.

- **Check weight.** Check the object's weight to see if you will need help lifting it.
- **Request help.** Ask for help from another person if you need it, or use mechanical lifting equipment.
- **Keep your back straight.** Your back should be straight and vertical to the ground. Keeping your head up and looking straight ahead will help maintain this position.
- **Lift with your knees.** If you can, bend your knees when lifting; don't stoop over the object.

- **Keep objects close to your body.** Always bring the object as close to your body as possible. Never twist your body. Move your feet to turn and place a load next or behind your body.
- **Tighten your stomach.** Tighten your stomach muscles. This helps your back stay in balance.
- **Deliver carefully.** Use care when you put the object down. Follow the same guidelines as you would for lifting.

Compressed Air

Compressed air should *never* be used to clean off clothes or do general cleanup work. An air nozzle can force air through the skin and into the bloodstream, a condition that can cause death. Compressed air can also stir up paper dust, making breathing difficult and causing eye irritation.

When compressed air is used for an acceptable purpose, nozzle pressure should not exceed 30 psi (pounds per square inch) or 207 kPa (kilopascals). Always wear safety glasses when using an air nozzle.

CHEMICAL HAZARDS

Several chemicals are used in the printing industry. You may come in contact with substances such as solvents, platemaking chemicals, ink mists, and various fumes and gases. In order to work safely, you should know how to handle these chemicals and dispose of them properly.

Chemical Handling and Disposal

Depending on their chemical structure, certain substances are more harmful than others. A poisonous substance is termed a *toxic substance*. The amount of a toxic substance an individual is exposed to and the duration of that exposure affect the degree of harm the substance can cause. For example, oxygen is part of the air we breathe, and in normal amounts, it keeps us alive. However, a very high concentration of oxygen can be toxic.

The first line of defense against toxic substances is to know the types of chemicals you are using and the hazards involved. Chemicals should be handled with extreme care. Read the labels on chemical containers to learn specific handling procedures and potential health hazards. See **Figure 2-14.**

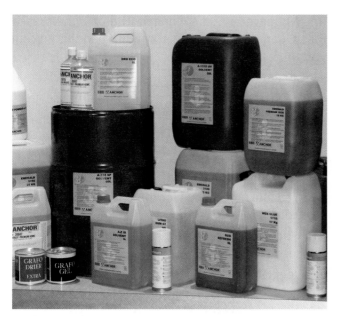

Figure 2-14. All chemical containers should be labeled. Read labels carefully before using chemicals, and note safety warning and actions to take in an emergency.

Be aware of the health risks posed by toxic substances in a graphic communications facility, and take measures to avoid harm. Chemicals can enter the body through the skin, by inhalation, or by ingestion. Wear *personal protective devices* appropriate to the level of hazard. Protective devices for working with chemicals include safety glasses, face shields, plastic or rubber gloves, respirators, boots, and full safety suits. See **Figure 2-15.** While exposure to some chemicals may have short-term effects, exposure to others may cause long-term health problems, even cancer.

When disposing of chemicals, do not pour them down a drain or sewer. They must be discarded in an environmentally safe manner. Some chemicals, such as photographic fixer, can be recycled to recover the silver that was dissolved from the film emulsion. Check the manufacturer's recommendations, as well as state and local environmental protection requirements, for proper disposal. Stiff fines are imposed for improper disposal of hazardous waste.

Types of Chemicals and Agents

The chemicals and chemical agents that pose hazards to workers in the graphic communications industry are commonly classified in four categories:

- Organic solvents.
- Platemaking chemicals.

Figure 2-15. A typical hazard identification chart with icons identifying personal protection required for various hazard categories.

- Ink mists.
- Gases, fumes, and dust.

Volatile Organic Solvents

Some of the most common organic solvents found in the industry are blanket and roller washes, fountain solutions, plate cleaners, glaze removers, degreasers, and film cleaners. Many blanket washes used to clean the press blankets contain *volatile organic compounds (VOCs)*, toxic substances that help the washes work well and evaporate quickly. However, the VOCs pass into the air in the pressroom, the workers' lungs, and the outside air.

Some solvents are more harmful than others, but the following should *not* be used: benzene, carbon tetrachloride, gasoline, chloroform, and carbon disulfide.

toxic substance: A poisonous substance.

personal protective devices: Clothing or equipment worn for protection from potential bodily injury associated with chemical use or machine operation.

volatile organic compounds (VOCs): Toxic substances contained in blanket and roller washes, fountain solutions, plate cleaners, glaze removers, degreasers, and film cleaners.

Breathing solvent vapors can be very harmful. Do not rely on your nose to warn you of vapors. Specialists need to be employed to measure airborne solvents and determine safe levels.

Vapors should be exhausted away from the operator and the area kept well ventilated. Some vapors may require the operator to wear a respirator. The proper respirator for each situation must be selected by an expert, **Figure 2-16.** Be sure to wear a respirator if the vapors in the surrounding air exceed the permissive exposure levels shown on the product's MSDS. For any industry that has an MSDS allowable levels statement, you must successfully complete extensive respirator protection training that includes an individual medical exam and fit testing, as well as other training factors.

Solvents can also be harmful to skin or eyes. Read the container label *before* using a chemical to determine what to do in case of contact. Typically, it is recommended that the affected area be flushed with water for at least 15 minutes and then treated by a doctor. Personal protective devices such as goggles, face shields, gloves, and aprons must be worn when handling chemical solvents.

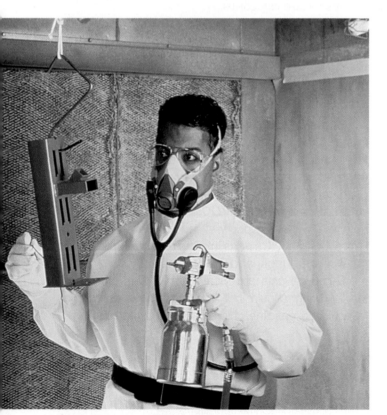

Figure 2-16. In many industrial occupations, an approved respirator is required whenever fine airborne mists of chemicals, inks, dust, paint, or other contaminants are present. (3M Company)

Whenever you are working with chemicals, take these general precautions against harmful solvent vapors:

- Do not attempt to identify a solvent by sniffing it.
- Keep lids and covers on cans and drums.
- Do not use large quantities of solvents in one area.
- Clean up spills immediately.
- Know the proper handling, cleanup, and disposal procedures for the chemical you are using.
- Place soiled rags in an approved safety can, keeping its lid closed.
- Ventilate the work area as needed.
- Wash your hands before eating.

Platemaking Chemicals

The chemicals used to prepare image carriers can irritate the skin and cause burns. Always wear rubber or plastic gloves or apply barrier creams when working with platemaking chemicals. Inspect gloves for pinholes before working. Never touch your face or eyes with gloves that have been in contact with a chemical.

Contact lenses should *not* be worn when working with chemicals. If splashed in the eyes, the chemicals can seep under the lenses and cause severe burns. Face shields and splash goggles are the best form of eye and face protection.

Wearing an appropriate apron will keep chemicals from reaching clothing and soaking through to the skin. Food and beverages should never be allowed to come into contact with chemicals. Chemicals that are corrosive, flammable, or poisonous should be properly labeled and stored in a safety cabinet, **Figure 2-17.**

Many platemaking chemicals are concentrated. When diluting an acid, always pour the acid into the water. The opposite method would produce a dangerous splattering of the acid. Never add water to concentrated acid.

Ink Mists

Rapidly rotating press rollers throw tiny droplets of ink into the air, creating an ink mist. These droplets are tiny enough to be inhaled. Ink mists often contain pigments, polymers, plasticizers, resins, and solvents that can prove harmful. Face shields and respirators

CAREER LINK

Safety Specialist

Employee health and safety is an important concern in businesses of all sizes. From the operation of equipment and work environment, to the resources available to employees, federal and state regulations help companies create and maintain a safe workplace. Many larger companies hire a safety and health specialist, or safety supervisor, to oversee the implementation and maintenance of appropriate health and safety guidelines.

The duties of this specialist are listed as examples and may vary with levels of job classification. Typical duties include establishing training needs for work areas; keeping records and reporting issues; conducting safety inspections; implementing changes that are found to lack compliance; reviewing accident, injury and illness reports; and explaining safety and health rules and standards to employees.

Some of the job qualifications require knowledge of basic OSHA and EPA rules and regulations; knowledge of safety techniques and applications; knowledge of safety practices in the industry; and the ability to coordinate, organize, and supervise work activities.

The safety specialist must have a basic knowledge of mathematics, physics, and chemistry. He or she must have good communication skills. This individual should also have a basic knowledge of accounting and budgeting. Some companies may specify that they be certified as safety professionals. Most safety professionals have graduated with a bachelor degree in safety management. The degree title may vary from one educational institution to another. Seminar courses may also be taken to prepare for certification. An exam must be taken and passed to be certified.

"The best companies emphasize the full implementation of a comprehensive written safety program that is clearly communicated to all employees through effective employee training, safety idea involvement, and disciplinary action for those who choose to break the safety rules."

John Holland
Assured Compliance Solutions

Figure 2-17. Chemicals, safety cans, and flammable containers should be stored in an approved safety cabinet. (Justrite Manufacturing Company)

should be worn for protection. Controls such as face shields and respirators are necessary where a relatively large amount of ink mist is produced, such as at newspaper facilities.

Gases, Fumes, and Dust

Gases, fumes, and dust are chemical agents commonly found in graphic communications facilities. Proper ventilation is imperative in areas where vapors and particulate matter are generated.

Ozone (O_3) is a great concern. It is a colorless, poisonous gas in the upper atmosphere, where it occurs naturally in what is known as the ozone layer, and it shields the earth from the sun's dangerous ultraviolet rays. However, at ground-level, it is a pollutant with highly toxic effects. Ozone damages human health, the environment, crops, and a wide range of natural and artificial materials. One source of ground-level ozone is the breakdown of VOCs found in solvents. Ozone gas is also created by carbon arcs, some antistatic devices, and ultraviolet ink-curing units used in printing plants.

Another hazard is carbon monoxide (CO), an odorless and colorless gas. CO is produced by the incomplete combustion of carbon-based fuels and natural and synthetic products. After being inhaled, CO molecules enter the bloodstream, where they inhibit the delivery of oxygen throughout the body. Low concentrations can cause dizziness, headaches, and fatigue; high concentrations can be fatal.

Fumes can be produced by molten materials. Acids or corrosives also give off fumes. Corrosive-resistant rubber or plastic gloves and aprons and eye protection must be worn when handling corrosives. Many fume-producing materials are very toxic and should be considered extremely hazardous. The work area must be well-ventilated and well-lit.

A common cause of dust in graphic communications facilities is paper. Microscopic particles of dust can be inhaled and lodge in lung tissue, causing respiratory disease and lung damage. Respirators with dust filters should be worn in areas where paper dust exists. Systems for controlling dust and scrubbing the air are available for use in large industrial settings, **Figure 2-18.**

Figure 2-18. Tiny fog droplets sprayed by an overhead humidification system scrub dust and chemicals from the air in this graphic communications facility. (Mee Industries Inc.)

Material Safety Data Sheets

OSHA requires employers to keep a list of all hazardous chemicals used on their premises, maintain a file of *Material Safety Data Sheets (MSDS)* on the chemicals, and train their employees to use the chemicals and respond properly should an accident occur. An MSDS gives the chemical name (common, synonyms, and formula); and the name, address, and/or telephone number of the manufacturer. See **Figure 2-19.**

The MSDS provides such information as:

- Flammability and reactivity data (vapor pressure and flash point information).
- Medical/health hazards.
- Overexposure limits/effects.
- Spill procedures.
- Personal protection information.

Sometimes you may need additional information about a chemical. The manufacturer or supplier should be able to supply specific information.

FIRE PREVENTION

Most graphic communications facilities use flammable and combustible materials. Therefore, fire prevention is a crucial part of a plant safety program.

Paper dust or antisetoff powders may explode if concentrated where a spark could ignite the mixture. Antisetoff powders are sprayed on printed sheets to eliminate the possibility of the fresh ink from transferring to the backside of the next printed sheet. Solvent vapors are another source of explosion danger. Avoid spillage. When pouring solvent, make sure the area is properly vented and no ignition source is present.

Ink- and solvent-soaked rags must be placed in an approved and covered metal waste can, **Figure 2-20.** The volatile vapors are then trapped inside the container. The contents of the waste can must be disposed of daily to minimize the possibility of *spontaneous combustion*. Do not store oily or ink-soaked towels in a container that does not meet safety regulations.

Fire prevention should be a priority on the shop floor. Practice these safety precautions to reduce the risk of fire:

- Pick up dust using a vacuum cleaner; do *not* blow dust with an air hose.
- Report leaking solvent containers.
- Wipe up solvent and oil spills.

Material Safety Data Sheet #309
For Printing Inks and related Materials
OSHA Hazard Communication Standard, 29 CFR 1910.1200

Date of preparation: 05/04/06
Revised: 05/14/07

I. PRODUCT IDENTIFICATION

Manufacturer: Gans Ink and Supply Co, Inc.
Address: 1441 Boyd Street
             Los Angeles, CA 90033

Emergency phone: (323) 264-2200

HMIS HAZARD IDENTIFICATION

Health
1
Flammability
2

Reactivity
0

Product Class: Blanket and Roller Wash
Trade Name: Aqua Wash

Manufacturer's code: S-1840

II. HAZARDOUS INGREDIENTS

Material	CAS #	%	Exposure Limits		Units
Aromatic Petroleum Distillates	64742-95-6	50.8	OSHA PEL		100 ppm
			ACGIH/TLV		100ppm
Petroleum Distillates	64741-65-7	43.0	Not established		

III. PHYSICAL DATA

Boiling Range: °F: 300-347	**Vapor Density (Air = 1):** > 1
	Vapor Pressure: 1.4 mm Hg @ 68 DEG. F.
Relative Density (H₂O = 1): 0.83	**Evaporation Rate:** Slower than Ether
Material Density Lbs./Gal: 6.93	**Solubility in Water:** Negligible
% Volatiles by Volume: 93.5	**% Solids by Weight:** 6.5
VOC Lbs/Gal: 6.48 g/L: 776.1	**Appearance/Odor:** Clear liquid with solvent odor

IV. FIRE AND EXPLOSION DATA

Flash Point °F: 104 TCC		**Auto-ignition Temperature** °F: Not established	
Flammable Limits in Air	**Lower Limit:** 0.01		**Upper Limit:** 7.0

Extinguishing Media: Alcohol foam, CO2, Dry Chemical, Water fog.
Special Fire Fighting Procedures: Combustible. Use self-contained breathing apparatus.
Water may be used to cool closed containers to prevent pressure build-up.
Unusual Fire & Explosion Hazard: Fire-exposed containers should be cooled with water to prevent pressure build-up, which could result in container rupture.

V. HEALTH HAZARD INFORMATION

Effects of Overexposure
Inhalation: Respiratory disorders may be aggravated.
Skin Contact: May cause irritation. Prolonged or repeated contact may result in dermatitis.
Eye Contact: May cause irritation.
Ingestion: Do not take internally. May be harmful if swallowed.
Emergency & First Aid Procedures
Inhalation: Remove to fresh air and provide oxygen if breathing is difficult.
Skin: Wash affected areas with soap and water. Remove contaminated clothing.
Eye Contact: Flush eyes immediately with large amounts of water for at least 15 minutes.
Ingestion: Do not induce vomiting. If vomiting occurs spontaneously, keep head below hips to prevent aspiration of liquid into the lungs. Seek attention immediately.
Acute Health Hazard: May cause irritation to nose, eyes and skin. May also cause CNS (central nervous system) depression, which may be evidenced by giddiness, headache, dizziness and nausea, in extreme cases unconsciousness and death, may occur.
Chronic Health Hazard: Prolonged or repeated contact may result in dermatitis and damage to central nervous system, liver and kidneys.

1

VI. REACTIVITY INFORMATION

Stability (Thermal, Light, etc.): Stable.	**Conditions to avoid:** Avoid heat, sparks and open flame.
Hazardous Polymerization: Will not occur.	**Incompatibility (materials to avoid):** Strong oxidizing agents.

Hazardous Decomposition or By-products: Thermal decomposition may yield carbon dioxide and / or carbon monoxide.

VII. ENVIRONMENTAL PRECAUTIONS

Steps to be taken in event of spill or release: Remove all sources of ignition and provide ventilation. Large spills may be pumped to salvage vessels. Small spills may be picked up with an absorbent material.
Waste Disposal Method: Place in tightly closed containers and dispose of in accordance with local, state and federal regulations.

VIII. SPECIAL PROTECTION INFORMATION

Ventilation Requirements: Use explosion proof ventilation as required to control concentrations.
Personal Protective Equipment
Respirator: Use self-contained breathing apparatus where vapor concentration may be above TLV limits. Where vapor does not exceed TLV limits, use NIOSH/MSHA approved respirator.
Skin: Wash hands thoroughly before eating or using the washroom.
Safety showers and eyewash stations should be provided.
Protective Gloves: Chemical resistant gloves.
Eye: Safety glasses, splash goggles or face shield. Contact lenses should not be worn.

IX. SPECIAL PRECAUTIONS

Handling and Storage: Keep away from heat, sparks, and open flames. Keep containers closed when not in use. Use with adequate ventilation.
Other Precautions: Ground equipment to prevent accumulation of static charge.
Do not cut, weld, drill or grind on or near containers.

X. SHIPPING DATA

Flammability Classification: Flammable Liquid, N.O.S. (Petroleum Distillates, Mineral Spirits), 3, UN 1993, PG III
OSHA: Combustible liquid - Class II.
DOT: Combustible liquid.

XI. ADDITIONAL NOTES

U.S. Federal Regulations
SARA(Superfund Amendments and Reauthorization Act of 1986) Title III:
SARA Section 313 Toxic Chemical List(TCL):
This material does not contain chemicals subject to the reporting requirements.
TSCA Section 8(b) Inventory Status:
All components of this product are either exempt or listed on the TSCA Inventory.

State and Local Regulations
California Proposition 65:
This product contains chemicals known to the State of California to cause cancer and birth defects or other reproductive harm.
Benzene (trace)
Toluene (trace)

The information herein is presented in good faith, based on the data available to us and is believed to be correct as of the date hereof. However, Gans Ink and Supply Co., Inc. make no warranty, expressed or implied regarding the accuracy of this data or the results to be obtained from the use thereof. Gans Ink and Supply Co., Inc. assume no responsibility for any damages of any nature directly or indirectly resulting from the use of or reliance upon the information contained herein. Users must make their own determination as to the suitability of the product for their purpose prior to use. In accordance with good practices of personal cleanliness and hygiene, handle with due care and avoid unnecessary contact with this product.

2

Figure 2-19. Part of a Material Safety Data Sheet for a hazardous solvent, providing information on ventilation and personal protective equipment. Always check the MSDS before working with any chemical.

Figure 2-20. An approved waste container should be used to dispose of flammable rags or towels. Empty the can regularly. (Justrite Manufacturing Company)

• Always use a spouted safety can when transferring small amounts of solvent, **Figure 2-21.** Make sure flame arrestors in safety cans are intact.

• In solvent-transfer operations, properly ground and bond equipment to prevent sparking, **Figure 2-22.**

• Properly label solvents and other flammable materials.

• Do not dump solvents into drains; store and dispose of them in compliance with state and local environmental protection standards.

Material Safety Data Sheets (MSDS): A document, produced by a chemical manufacturer, that summarizes the physical properties of a particular chemical and the health and safety hazards associated with its use.

spontaneous combustion: Ignition by rapid oxidation without an external heat source.

Flame
arrestor

Figure 2-21. Flame arrestors are an important feature of safety cans. Heat is dissipated and absorbed as it passes through the arrestor. (Justrite Manufacturing Company)

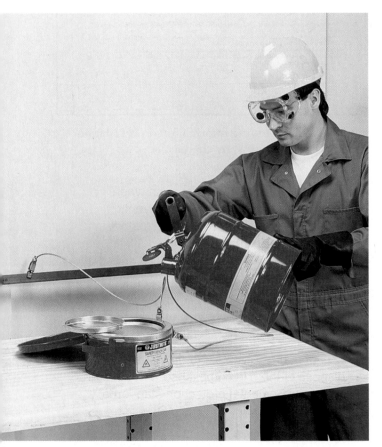

Figure 2-22. Flowing liquids can charge cans with static electricity. Static buildup can cause fires and explosions. Bonding and grounding wires prevent sparks from jumping by allowing the electric charge to balance safely. (Justrite Manufacturing Company)

- Watch for potential sources of fire, such as an overflowing safety container, dust buildup on equipment, and open chemical containers.
- No smoking! Inks, solutions, chemicals, paper, paper dust, and other substances all pose a serious fire hazard.

Know where fire extinguishers are located and how to use them. See **Figure 2-23.** Do not attempt to fight a fire if you are not trained or authorized by your employer, if more than a couple of ounces of chemicals are burning, or if you cannot fight the fire with your back to an exit for easy escape. Also know the fire evacuation routes. For higher visibility, many facilities outline aisles and walkways with yellow paint. Keep walkways, stairways, and exits free of obstructions. Being able to respond quickly and efficiently in a fire can mean the difference between a simple incident and a disaster.

Noise

Unwanted and excessively loud noise is found in many industrial facilities. Excessive noise can lead to permanent hearing loss. The best way to protect against ear damage is to control the noise. When those controls do not reduce the noise to an acceptable level, ear protection must be worn.

Noise levels are measured in units called *decibels (dBA)*. **Figure 2-24** illustrates allowable exposure time to various decibels. A reading of 90 dBA is the maximum allowable limit for an eight-hour day. If the amount is greater than 90 dBA, a specific time limit is established.

If noise exceeds permissible levels, unwanted sound must be engineered out of the operation, or personal hearing protection devices must be provided and worn. Hearing protection devices include earmuffs, earplugs, moldable inserts, and noise-reducing headsets, **Figure 2-25.** Folder and web press operators usually need to wear hearing protection as their equipment typically produces noises over 90 dBA.

decibels (dBA): A unit for expressing the intensity of sound.

Fire Extinguishers and Fire Classifications

Fires	Type	Use	Operation
Class A Fires Ordinary Combustibles (Materials such as wood, paper, textiles.) *Requires... cooling-quenching*	**Soda-acid** Bicarbonate of soda solution and sulfuric acid	Okay for use on **A** / Not for use on **B C D**	Direct stream at base of flame.
	Pressurized Water Water under pressure	Okay for use on **A** / Not for use on **B C D**	Direct stream at base of flame.
Class B Fires Flammable Liquids (Liquids such as grease, gasoline, oils, and paints.) *Requires...blanketing or smothering.*	**Carbon Dioxide (CO_2)** Carbon dioxide (CO_2) gas under pressure	Okay for use on **B C** / Not for use on **A D**	Direct discharge as close to fire as possible, first at edge of flames and gradually forward and upward.
Class C Fires Electrical Equipment (Motors, switches, and so forth.) *Requires... a nonconducting agent.*	**Foam** Solution of aluminum sulfate and bicarbonate of soda	Okay for use on **A B** / Not for use on **C D**	Direct stream into the burning material or liquid. Allow foam to fall lightly on fire.
	Dry Chemical	Multi-purpose type: Okay for **A B C**, Not okay for **D**. Ordinary BC type: Okay for **B C**, Not okay for **A D**	Direct stream at base of flames. Use rapid left-to-right motion toward flames.
Class D Fires Combustible Metals (Flammable metals such as magnesium and lithium.) *Requires...blanketing or smothering.*	**Dry Chemical** Granular type material	Okay for use on **D** / Not for use on **A B C**	Smother flames by scooping granular material from bucket onto burning metal.

Figure 2-23. Not every fire extinguisher will put out every kind of fire. Check the label on the extinguisher. Using the wrong extinguisher may electrocute you or produce toxic fumes.

ACADEMIC LINK
Measuring Sound

Sound is measured in decibels, which is a value that represents the pressure of a sound. OSHA mandates that sound measurements be taken when exposure reaches 85 decibels and above. When the sound level is greater than 90 dBA over an 8-hour workday, hearing protection is necessary.

For the purpose of standardized measurement, the threshold of human hearing is 0 dBA. Prolonged exposure to any sound over 85 dBA can cause permanent hearing damage. Pain caused by sound can occur around 120 dBA. The following are some examples of common sounds and the approximate decibel level of each:

Jet engine on takeoff	140 dBA
Front row of a rock concert	120 dBA
Chain saw or pneumatic drill	100 dBA
Lawn mower	95 dBA
Vacuum cleaner or hair dryer	70 dBA
Normal conversation	60 dBA
The hum of a refrigerator	40 dBA
Quiet library	30 dBA
Rustling leaves	10 dBA
Threshold of human hearing	0 dBA

Consider the sounds you are exposed to everyday. Do any of the sounds reach dangerous levels? Is ear protection available in areas of prolonged exposure to high levels of sound?

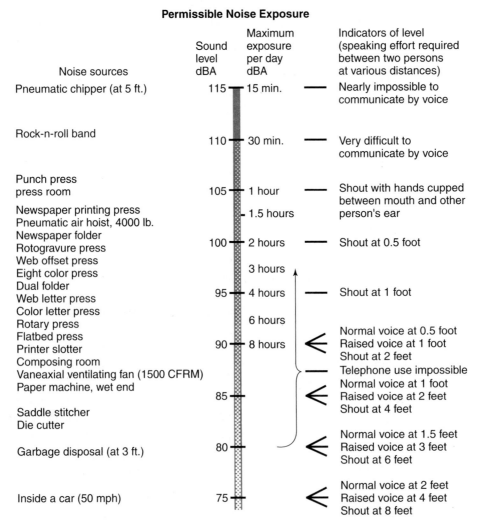

Permissible Noise Exposure

Noise sources	Sound level dBA	Maximum exposure per day dBA	Indicators of level (speaking effort required between two persons at various distances)
Pneumatic chipper (at 5 ft.)	115	15 min.	Nearly impossible to communicate by voice
Rock-n-roll band	110	30 min.	Very difficult to communicate by voice
Punch press press room	105	1 hour	Shout with hands cupped between mouth and other person's ear
Newspaper printing press Pneumatic air hoist, 4000 lb.		1.5 hours	
Newspaper folder Rotogravure press Web offset press	100	2 hours	Shout at 0.5 foot
Eight color press Dual folder		3 hours	
Web letter press	95	4 hours	Shout at 1 foot
Color letter press Rotary press		6 hours	
Flatbed press Printer slotter Composing room	90	8 hours	Normal voice at 0.5 foot Raised voice at 1 foot Shout at 2 feet
Vaneaxial ventilating fan (1500 CFRM) Paper machine, wet end			Telephone use impossible Normal voice at 1 foot
	85		Raised voice at 2 feet Shout at 4 feet
Saddle stitcher Die cutter			Normal voice at 1.5 feet
Garbage disposal (at 3 ft.)	80		Raised voice at 3 feet Shout at 6 feet
Inside a car (50 mph)	75		Normal voice at 2 feet Raised voice at 4 feet Shout at 8 feet

Figure 2-24. Some permissible noise exposures established by OSHA. When employees are subjected to sound exceeding the levels prescribed, administrative or engineering controls must be made. If such controls fail to reduce sound levels within the permissible levels, personal protective equipment must be provided.

Figure 2-25. Ear protection is often needed in the pressroom or the bindery where equipment noise is loud enough to damage your hearing. This radio headset reduces noise by 23 dBA while allowing for team communication. (Earmark, Inc.)

Figure 2-26. Wear approved eye protection if you are near harmful sources of light that produce ultraviolet or infrared rays. Do not look directly at bright light when working with platemakers and cameras. (NuArc)

LIGHT HAZARDS

Light sources common to graphic communications facilities can be hazardous. Ultraviolet (UV) light, for example, can damage unprotected skin and eyes. Potentially harmful sources of light include pulsed xenon and mercury vapor lamps, UV-ink curing units, and the ozone lights used on antisetoff devices. True UV rays cannot be seen but *are* harmful; avoid contact with them. See **Figure 2-26.**

Even though most new equipment is shielded, care must be taken to protect the eyes when working in areas with platemaking equipment and drying systems. Infrared (IR) light and laser beams are also potentially harmful. When working in areas where they are in use, take special precautions to protect your eyes.

ERGONOMIC HAZARDS

A mismatch between the physical requirements of the job and the physical capacity of the worker can cause painful conditions. *Ergonomics* is the science of fitting the job to the worker.

In recent years, the body of knowledge about ergonomics has expanded along with the use of computers in the workplace. In graphic communications, a task such as page layout and design, formerly performed by manually cutting and pasting text and images to boards, is now done electronically utilizing desktop publishing software. Therefore, consideration must be given to the effects of computer use on human health, **Figure 2-27.**

J. J. Keller and Associates, Inc., of Neenah, Wisconsin, prepared the following checklist as an evaluation tool to determine if computer workstations are appropriate for the worker.

- When seated, the operator should maintain proper posture. Are thighs horizontal?
- Are the lower legs vertical?

ergonomics: The science of fitting the job to the worker.

Figure 2-27. Workstations that are designed for health and comfort are important when you spend hours working at a computer.

- Are the feet flat on the floor or on a footrest?
- Are the wrists flat?
- Is the chair easy to adjust?
- Does the chair have a padded seat with a rounded front?
- Does the chair have an adjustable backrest?
- Does the chair provide lumbar support?
- Does the chair have casters?
- Is the keyboard detachable?
- Are the height and tilt of the work surface on which the keyboard is located adjustable?
- Do keying actions require minimal force?
- Is there an adjustable document holder?
- Are the document holder and the screen the same distance from the eyes?
- Are the document holder and the screen close together to avoid excessive head movement?
- Are armrests provided where needed?
- Are glare and reflections avoided?
- Does the monitor have brightness and contrast controls?
- Does the operator judge the distance between eyes and work to be satisfactory for viewing?
- Is the topmost line of display no higher than the operator's eyes?
- Is there sufficient space for knees and feet?
- Are adequate rest breaks provided for task demands?
- Have employees had training for posture at the workstation?
- Have employees been trained in proper work methods?

Ergonomic issues are presently not regulated by OSHA, but the "general duty" clause has been used to cite ergonomic hazards. California does have a state ergonomics standard and several other states are moving in that direction.

ENVIRONMENTAL COMPLIANCE

Most of the safety and health guidelines discussed in this chapter are mandated by OSHA for the protection of the individual worker. Another federal initiative, the Clean Air Act Amendments (CAAA), requires the Environmental Protection Agency (EPA) to periodically review and revise national air quality standards to ensure they fully protect human health.

The CAAA continue to significantly impact lithographic printers. An EPA standard changed the National Ambient Air Quality Standards for ozone and particulate matter from 0.12 parts per million (ppm) to 0.08 ppm measured over an eight-hour period. Printers must now fully comply with the new emission standard.

CAAA Background

The Clean Air Act Amendments are divided into eleven titles. Not all of the titles directly affect the printing industry, however.

Title I is concerned with reducing the use of VOCs, which significantly contribute to photochemical reactions in the atmosphere. VOCs are the prime ingredient in forming smog, which is ground-level ozone. For example, the cleaning solvents used in the printing industry emit VOCs and are, therefore, subject to government regulation. Plants face stiff fines for not following VOC emission regulations.

The Air Toxins Provisions of Title III have significantly affected the printing industry, as well. The Title lists 189 regulated toxic air pollutants, many of which are found in graphic communications plants. The EPA has published a list of industry groups targeted for regulation, including major sources in the printing and publishing industry. Sources were required to install the best available air pollution control devices or Maximum Achievable Control Technology (MACT) within three years; new facilities were required to comply upon startup.

Most hazardous air pollutants used by printers are also VOCs. To date, the use of materials that contain low amounts of VOCs has provided a popular, alternative method for printers to meet state and federal VOC emission requirements without the costs of additional control equipment.

Under Title V, each state is required to establish rules for issuing permits for all major sources of VOCs and air toxins. The title requires facilities to obtain air permits if their emissions exceed certain limits, based on where they operate.

Clean Water Act (CWA)

The Clean Water Act (CWA) governs water pollution control, regulating discharges of pollutants to U.S. waters. The commercial printing industry produces a number of pollutants potentially regulated by the CWA. Provisions and permit regulations are broad and administered by the United States EPA. Laundry effluent guidelines will most affect printers who send their shop rags to laundries. Hazardous oil spill regulations may apply to a printing facility if it works with oil and is located near a municipal storm sewer that discharges to or near a body of water.

Further information on these acts and amendments is available from the United States EPA or the appropriate state agency for environmental protection.

Reducing and Eliminating Waste

Typical wastes of the commercial printing industry include paper, photochemical solutions and films, inks and ink-contaminated solvents, equipment cleaning wastes (solvents, dirty rags, filters, and absorbents), and lubricating fluids from machinery.

Lithographic, gravure, flexographic, letterpress, and screen printing operations share four primary steps:

- Image processing.
- Production of the image carrier.
- Printing.
- Finishing.

Each step generates waste and contributes to the **waste stream**. See **Figure 2-28.** However, many opportunities exist for reducing or eliminating these wastes. Described below are the wastes generated by each step in the printing operation and some pollution prevention practices that can be employed.

Wastes Generated by Printing Operations

Waste Stream	Process	Composition
Solid waste	Image processing	Empty containers, used film packages, outdated material
	Platemaking	Damaged plates, developed film, dated materials
	Printing	Test production, bad printings, empty ink containers
	Finishing	Damaged products, scrap
Wastewater	Image processing	Photographic chemicals, silver
	Platemaking	Acids, alkali, solvents, plate coatings (may contain dyes, photopolymers, binders, resins, pigment, organic acids), developers (may contain isopropanol, gum arabic, lacquers, caustics), and rinse water
	Printing	Spent fountain solutions (may contain chromium)
Cleanup solvents and waste ink	Printing	Lubricating oils, waste ink, cleanup solvent (halogenated and nonhalogenated), rags
Air emissions	Makeready, printing	Solvent from heat-set inks, isopropyl alcohol fountain solution, and cleaning solvents

Illinois Environmental Protection Agency Office of Pollution Prevention

Figure 2-28. Wastes generated by printing processes.

waste stream: The solid, liquid, or contained gaseous material that is produced and disposed of, incinerated, or recycled by a facility.

Image Processing

Wastes from this step include used film and wastewater containing photographic chemicals and silver.

Sending used or spoiled film and paper to silver reclaimers is currently practiced by much of the printing industry. Systems are also available for on-site reclamation; the silver is then collected by a refiner for reuse, **Figure 2-29.** Silverless films are also available. Silverless films are processed in a weak alkaline solution that is neutralized prior to disposal, resulting in nonhazardous wastes. Substituting silverless films eliminates the need for sending waste film to a metal reclaimer. Electrostatic films are a type of silverless film that are also used frequently.

New technologies, such as computer-to-plate technology, have eliminated some of the film chemistry and the waste streams associated with films. A rapidly expanding segment of the commercial printing market is digital printing, which is suitable for short- to medium-run color jobs such as brochures, catalogs, direct mail pieces, fliers, and newsletters. See **Figure 2-30.**

Figure 2-30. Digital color press. Digital printing is an increasingly popular alternative to offset printing for short- to medium-run length jobs. One of its benefits is minimizing impact on the environment by eliminating prepress steps requiring chemicals.

Production of the Image Carrier

Lithographic platemaking generates wastewater that may contain acids, alkalies, solvents, plate coatings, and developers. Wastewater from letterpress and flexographic plates may contain high concentrations of heavy metals. Switching from chemical processing to water processing of lithographic plates and film may eliminate development wastewaters that currently require pretreatment before discharge.

Printing

Cleaning solvents and waste ink are the primary wastes associated with the printing process. Air emissions containing VOCs from petroleum-based inks and cleaning solvents are also part of the waste stream.

Typically, printers manually clean the printing equipment using a rag wetted with an organic solvent. These solvents normally contain alcohol and have low flash points that are usually less than 140°F (60°C). The rag often drips excess solvent onto the floor during cleaning. Furthermore, the solvent quickly evaporates, generating VOC emissions. Dirty rags containing solvents, waste ink, oil, dirt, and other contaminants are often sent to commercial laundries. Ink and "spent" solvents in the towels cause two major concerns for laundries and local sanitary sewer systems handling the laundry's effluent: volatility and flammability.

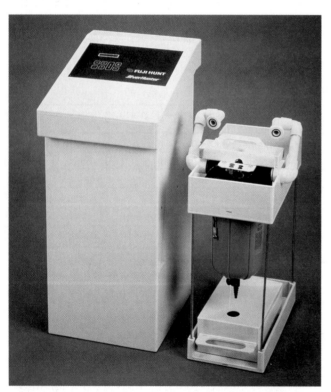

Figure 2-29. An electrolytic, recirculating silver recovery unit. The unit maintains low silver levels in the fixer tank, minimizing the amount of silver carried over into the wash tank. The complete system, including secondary metal ion exchange columns, will recover 99% or more of the available silver, meeting hazardous discharge requirements of 5.0 ppm or less. (Fuji Hunt Photographic Chemicals, Inc.)

Several manufacturers have developed low-VOC solvents with high flash points and low toxicity. Blanket washes made from vegetable oils and their fatty acid esters, terpenes (found in essential oils and plant resins), less volatile petroleum components, or a mixture of these substances have proven suitable substitutes. Compared to standard solvent-based washes that can contain up to 100% VOCs, the VOC content of vegetable ester washes is typically 12% to 30%. Vegetable and water mixtures drop to as low as 2%.

Some viable pollution prevention measures include using a less-volatile solvent, applying solvents conservatively using squeeze bottles or plunger cans, and wringing out excess solvent from rags using a centrifuge and reusing the recovered solvent.

Ink recovery machines make on-site reclaiming an option. Solvent recycling companies can also perform the task for printing operations that generate small quantities of ink and solvent wastes.

Substitute inks, such as UV-cured inks and water- or vegetable-based inks, are suitable for some printing applications. UV-cured inks contain no solvent and dry by exposure to ultraviolet light. They are nearly 100% solids and have a VOC content of 1% or less. UV-printed papers can be repulped and recycled as an added environmental benefit. Vegetable oils use fewer fountain additives than do mineral oils and accordingly reduce chemical use, **Figure 2-31.** Fountain additives are added to speed the drying of ink, as well as the flow characteristics and abrasion resistance.

Figure 2-31. Vegetable oils in inks are a sustainable resource and free of VOCs. While soybeans are the primary oil source for these inks, oils from linseed, rapeseed, and sunflower seeds are also used. (National Soy Ink Information Center)

Finishing

Most of the waste from finishing operations is scrap paper. Scrap paper from printing operations can be recycled into new paper. The market for recycled paper is good, shaped by depleted landfill space, tightening access to forest resources, changes in consumer awareness and preferences, and government restrictions. Technological improvements in recycled paper, such as stronger fiber and improved pulp, will continue to provide incentives for printers to send wastepaper to commercial paper recyclers and to buy recycled paper for printing.

Buying recycled paper is just the beginning. States are increasingly adopting totally chlorine-free paper purchasing policies. Chlorine, a chemical compound used to bleach paper products, has been linked with ozone depletion. Legislation for state purchase of chlorine-free paper is being modeled after laws mandating state purchase of recycled products.

Process Evaluation

An excellent way to uncover new methods for reducing and eliminating waste is to evaluate the steps in the printing process. The review can be incorporated into the plant's overall safety and health program. Follow these directions for conducting a review:

- Record each step in your printing process, from purchasing raw materials to shipping the finished product.

- Diagram the process, noting every point where materials are used and wastes are created. (Include steps that are indirectly part of the process, such as waste disposal and electricity use.)

- Where wastes are generated, estimate the cost of lost raw material, and costs resulting from collecting, tracking, and disposing of the wastes.

- Examine the diagram to pinpoint where the wastes are produced, and determine a plan for waste reduction. For example, you may be able to consolidate chemicals, replacing infrequently used ones with multiple-use chemicals.

Maintaining Tools, Equipment, and Machines

To operate safely and efficiently, the tools, equipment, and machines used in communication graphics must be regularly maintained according to the manufacturer's requirements and recommended procedures. Failing to perform required maintenance, or not following recommended procedures, can cause injury to workers, or damage to equipment and machines. It can also void the manufacturer's warranty and require costly repairs or replacement.

For many tools, equipment, and machines, maintenance procedures and requirements can be found in the owner's manual. More complex machines, such as printing presses, usually will have a separate maintenance manual.

Maintenance activities typically include:

- Cleaning, adjustment, and lubrication of specific areas or assemblies.

- Measuring to find whether tolerances are correct and making necessary adjustments to bring them "into spec."

- Checking alignment of parts and tightness of fasteners.

- Measuring wear on moving parts and adjusting or replacing parts as needed.

- Testing and calibrating electronic equipment to provide correct output.

To be sure maintenance is done at the recommended intervals, many companies keep a maintenance log. It lists the procedures to be done and the time when they should be performed. As each maintenance task is completed, the worker responsible signs and dates the log.

Summary

Accidents in the workplace are very costly to the person involved and the company. Efforts need to be made to inform all personnel in the facility of hazardous areas and conditions. Coexistence of people and machines requires the establishment of a safe working environment. Machines must be used in the manner they were intended. Proper use of protective devices is a safeguard against hazardous areas and materials. Production in the printing facility has an impact on the environment. It is imperative to handle resources responsibly.

Review Questions

Please do not write in this text. Write your answers on a separate sheet of paper.

1. What is the purpose of a workplace safety and health program?

2. Machine guarding protects the operator from hazards posed by what four types of machine action?

3. Which dangerous condition exists where two cylinders meet or come close to each other?
   A. Shear point.
   B. Rip point.
   C. Nip point.
   D. Cut point.

4. How should you dress when operating machinery in a graphic communications facility?

5. How can you help maintain a straight back when lifting a heavy object?

6. What are inks, blanket wash, fountain solutions, and plate cleaners examples of?
   A. Inorganic solutions.
   B. Organic solvents.
   C. Tetrachlorides.
   D. Benzenes.

7. How should you dispose of ink- and solvent-soaked rags?

8. A dBA reading of _____ is the maximum allowable limit for an eight-hour day without ear protection.

9. What is *ergonomics*?

10. Standard solvent-based washes can contain up to 100% VOCs, while vegetable ester washes contain _____% VOCs.

Suggested Activities

1. Using the checklist in this chapter, inspect the graphic communications laboratory.

2. Select a specific piece of equipment and make a safety checklist.

3. Check the location of fire extinguishers within the school building(s).

4. What is the maximum legal weight to be lifted by a person?

5. Demonstrate the proper way to lift an object.

6. Choose a liquid that is used in the laboratory, and find the Material Safety Data Sheet of the material on the Internet. Report on the hazards listed for your consideration.

Related Web Links

Occupational Safety and Health Administration (OSHA)

www.osha.gov
Online information on laws for safety in the workplace.

Environmental Protection Agency (EPA)

www.epa.gov
History and information on laws for protecting the environment.

Printers' National Environmental Assistance Center

www.pneac.org
Resources include information on law compliance in the printing industry.

Sustainable Green Printing Partnership

www.sgppartnership.org
Information on background of environmental issues with printing, as well as resources on becoming an environmentally compliant printer.

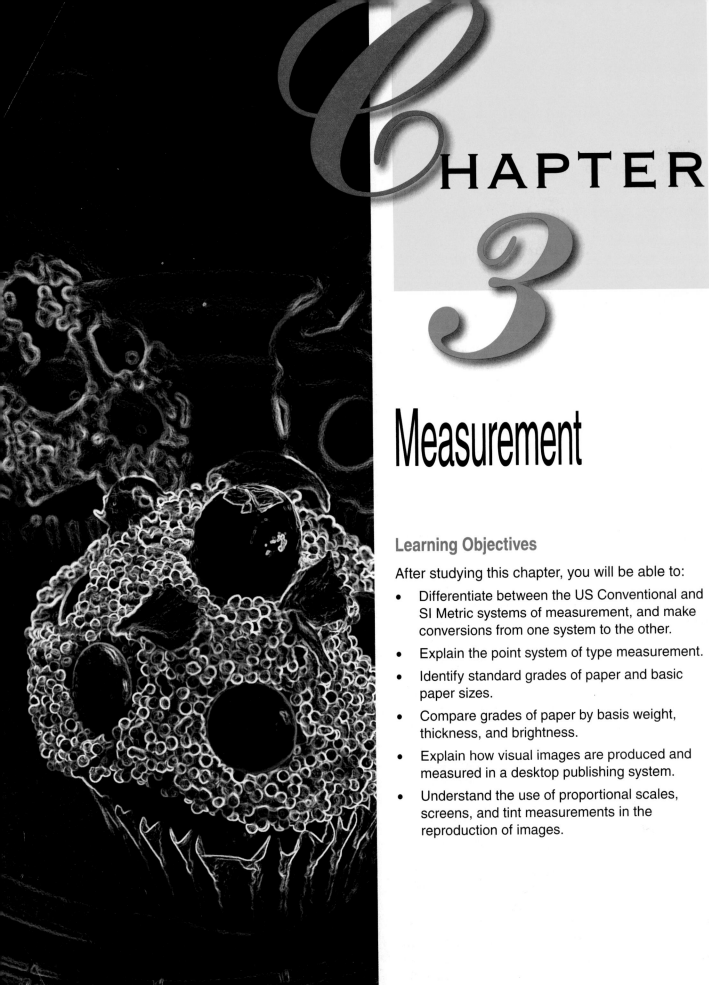

CHAPTER

3

Measurement

Learning Objectives

After studying this chapter, you will be able to:

- Differentiate between the US Conventional and SI Metric systems of measurement, and make conversions from one system to the other.

- Explain the point system of type measurement.

- Identify standard grades of paper and basic paper sizes.

- Compare grades of paper by basis weight, thickness, and brightness.

- Explain how visual images are produced and measured in a desktop publishing system.

- Understand the use of proportional scales, screens, and tint measurements in the reproduction of images.

Important Terms

basic size	nonpareils
basis weight	paper caliper
chromaticity	paper sizes
color separation	pica
densitometer	pixels
desktop publishing system	point
didot point system	point system
dots per inch (dpi)	proportional scale
E gauge	reams
grades	reflection densitometer
gram	resolution
grayscale	screen
illumination	screen angles
ISO series	screen tint
leading	SI Metric system
line gauge	spectrophotometer
liter	transmission
luminance	densitometer
meter	type sizes
metric conversion chart	US Conventional
metric prefixes	system
moiré pattern	

Measurement is used in almost every aspect of graphic reproduction. This chapter covers different systems and methods of measurement and demonstrates how vital they are to the graphic communications industry. The chapter begins with a discussion of the two most widely used systems of measurement: US Conventional and SI Metric. The point system of measurement, used throughout applications in graphics and design, is also discussed. The different standards used to measure paper sizes and weights are then covered. The chapter concludes with a discussion on developing technology in the production of images and the use of common measuring devices in the graphic communications industry. A thorough understanding of this chapter will prepare you for later chapters that apply different uses of measurement.

MEASUREMENT PRINCIPLES

Throughout history, systems of measurement have been necessary in all parts of society. Different forms of measure have not only served as a means to describe quantities or values, but have also provided the basic functions required for communication. Some of the first measuring terms used referred to parts of the human body. For instance, the distance

spanned by four fingers was known as four digits, while the hand was also a common measuring unit, representing about 4″. The length of a forearm was once called a cubit, and the length of a person's foot represented the distance of 1′.

More sophisticated measuring systems evolved as the growth of industry and trade created the need for standardization. Common agreement on units of measure developed as more accurate and consistent methods of measurement came into use.

The two most commonly used systems of measurement today are the *US Conventional system* and the *SI Metric system*. The US Conventional system was derived from the English system of weights and measures, which evolved from traditional standards and was established in many parts of the world by the 19th century. The metric system, by contrast, was designed specifically as a standard measuring system in response to the need for standardization. It originated in France in 1790 and became recognized as a worldwide coordinated system.

The U.S. Constitution empowered Congress to establish uniform standards for weights and measures. Today, the National Bureau of Standards ensures uniformity. The most common conventional and metric measurements are listed in **Figure 3-1.**

In 1866, the United States legalized the metric system as a standard for weights and measures. But the system has remained largely unused in U.S. industry despite the Metric Conversion Act, which established a national policy to coordinate conversion to metric standards.

METRIC SYSTEM

The metric system is the most commonly used system of weights and measures in the world. While the system is not typically used in the United States, it is recognized as the international standard.

The metric system is a decimal system based on values of 10. The system was originally developed with the *meter* as the standard unit of length, the *gram* as the standard unit of mass, and the *liter* as

US Conventional system: The standard system of weights and measures used in the United States.

SI Metric system: The modern version of the metric system, based on seven internationally recognized units of measure.

meter: The standard unit of length in the metric system.

gram: The standard unit of mass in the metric system.

liter: The standard unit of capacity in the metric system.

Approximate Equivalents			
Unit	US Conventional	SI Metric	Use
Length	inch (in) feet (ft) yard (yd) mile (mi)	millimeter (mm) meter (m) meter (m) kilometer (km)	Paper, wrapping material, plates, wire rolls, scales, press calibration Covers, tapes, binders
Pressure	pounds per square inch (psi)	kilopascal (kPa)	Web press ink pressure, air pressure, vacuum
Power	horsepower (hp)	kilowatt (kw)	Electric motor rating
Torque	pound-feet (lb-ft)	newton-meter (N•m)	Bolt tightening
Volume or Capacity	fluid ounces (oz) quart (qt) cubic inch (in^3)	milliliters (ml) liter (L) cubic centimeter (cc)	Ink, oil Plate chemicals Storage, shipping
Mass or weight	ounce (oz) pound (lb)	gram (g) kilograms (kg)	Postage, padding cement, chemicals, shipping, supplies
Speed	feet per second miles per hour (mph) revolutions per minute (rpm)	meters per second kilometers per hour (km/h) revolutions per minute (rpm)	Web press speed
Application rates	fluid ounce per square foot (fl-oz/ft^2) ounces per square feet (oz/ft^2)	milliliters per square meter (ml/m^2) grams per square meter (g/m^2)	Applying materials, ink coverage, estimating

Figure 3-1. Customary units of measure and metric equivalents. Common uses for each measurement are listed at right.

the standard unit of capacity. The SI Metric system (the *Systeme International d'Unites,* or International System of Units) is a modernized version of the metric system established by international agreement. The SI Metric system is built upon a foundation of seven base units of measure, as listed below:

- **Length** = *meter (m)*
- **Mass** = *kilogram (kg)*
- **Time** = *second (s)*
- **Electric current** = *ampere (A)*
- **Temperature** = *Kelvin (K)* or degree *Celsius (°C)*
- **Amount of substance** = *mole (mol)*
- **Luminous intensity** = *candela (cd)*

Metric Prefixes

The process of making different computations involving measure is simpler when using the metric system because metric units are structured in multiples of 10. *Metric prefixes* indicate multiples or divisions of these units. See **Figure 3-2.**

Rules of Metric Notation

Several rules are observed when expressing figures in metric notation. The following are standards used when abbreviating metric quantities:

- Unit symbols are not capitalized unless the unit is a proper name (mm).
- Unit symbols are not followed by periods (mm).
- Unit symbols are not pluralized in an abbreviation (10 g).
- A space separates the numeral from the unit symbols (2 mm).
- Spaces, not commas, are used to separate large numbers into groups of three digits (21 210 km).
- A zero precedes the decimal point if the numeral is less than one (0.11 g).

Metric Conversion

Since there is still widespread use of US Conventional measures in the graphic communications industry, it is sometimes necessary to convert to or from metric values. For instance, if a chemical

ACADEMIC LINK

Converting US Conventional Measurements to Metric

From time to time, it may be necessary to convert values from metric to US Conventional format, or vice versa. Simple multiplication skills are the only requirement to complete the conversions. A complete table of conversion factors is provided in Figure 3-3, but the following are some common conversion factors:

- There is 0.3048 meter in one foot, and 3.281 feet in one meter.
- There are 25.4 millimeters in one inch, and 0.03937 inch in one millimeter.
- There are 3.7854 liters in one gallon, and 0.2642 gallon in one liter.
- There is 0.04536 kilogram in one pound, and 2.2046 pounds in one kilogram.

For example, to calculate the number of meters in 12.5 feet, the equation is:

12.5 (number of feet) × 0.3048 (standard conversion factor) = 3.81 meters

Perform the following conversions on a separate piece of paper.

1. 6 liters to gallons.
2. 105 millimeters to inches.
3. 5 kilograms to pounds.

Common Metric Prefixes				
mega (M)	=	1 000 000	or	10^6
kilo (k)	=	1000	or	10^3
hecto (h)	=	100	or	10^2
centi (c)	=	0.01	or	10^{-2}
milli (m)	=	0.001	or	10^{-3}
micro (μ)	=	0.000 001	or	10^{-6}
Examples				
kilogram	=	1000	grams	
milligram	=	0.001	gram	
dekometer	=	10	meters	
centimeter	=	0.01	meter	
hectoliter	=	100	liters	
decimeter	=	0.1	meter	

Figure 3-2. Prefixes are used to identify units in the metric system.

quantity is given in liters and the equipment uses mixture ratios in quarts, one of the values has to be converted to the other system.

A *metric conversion chart* can be used to change a metric value to a conventional value or a conventional value to a metric value. See **Figure 3-3.** Values are converted from one system to another by multiplying known quantities by a specific number.

TYPE MEASUREMENT

Type sizes are used to distinguish different measures of printed type. The units of measure most commonly used for sizes of type in English-speaking countries are the point and pica, known as the *point system*, or the American point system. Type sizes are measured in points, while line lengths are given in picas and points.

The *point* measures approximately 0.01383″. The *pica* measures approximately 0.166″. Twelve points equal a pica, and six picas equal approximately one inch.

metric prefix: Word prefix that indicates multiples or divisions of measuring units in the metric system.

metric conversion chart: A table of equivalencies used to convert US Conventional and metric values from one system to another.

type size: Measurements that describe the size of printed type, commonly expressed in points.

point system: The system of print measurement used throughout the graphic communications industry in the United States.

point: One of the principal units of measure used in the graphic communications industry.

pica: One of the principal units of measure used in the graphic communications industry.

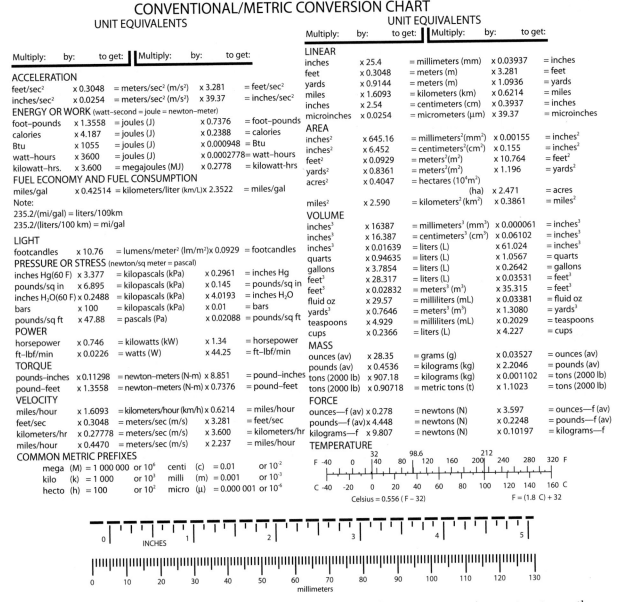

Figure 3-3. A metric conversion chart can be used to change values from one measuring system to another.

A *line gauge* is an instrument used to measure type sizes and line lengths in picas or inches. See **Figure 3-4.** Line gauges typically measure up to 72 picas (approximately 12″). One side of the gauge is marked in inches, and the other side is marked in picas and *nonpareils*.

Didot Point System

The American point system was adopted for use in the United States in 1886. It was based on the Fournier point system developed in 1737 by Pierre Simon Fournier, a French typographer. The Fournier point was later modified by a French printing family known as the Didots. The *didot point system*, based on the French inch, became the conventional printer's measure used in Europe and remains the standard today. The didot point is equal to 0.0148″. Twelve didot points equal the didot pica. A didot pica is equal to 0.1776″.

Metric Type Sizes

Metric units are also used to measure sizes of type. For example, millimeters can be used to give the equivalent sizes for either pica point (American point system) or didot point (European point system) sizes. One pica point equals 0.351 mm. One didot point equals 0.376 mm. Equivalent measures for the metric, pica, and didot point systems are shown in **Figure 3-5.**

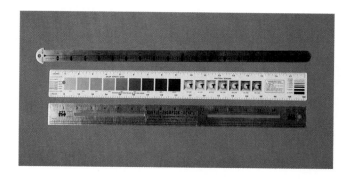

Figure 3-4. A set of line gauges with scales in both picas and inches, used to measure type sizes and line lengths.

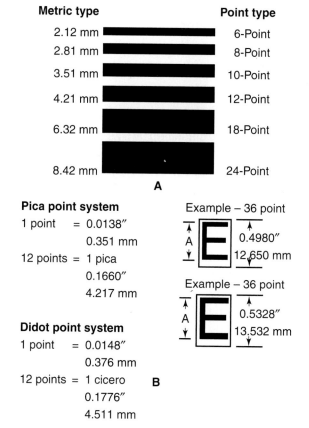

A

Pica point system

1 point   = 0.0138″
            0.351 mm
12 points = 1 pica
            0.1660″
            4.217 mm

Example – 36 point

A | E | 0.4980″
        12.650 mm

Didot point system

1 point   = 0.0148″
            0.376 mm
12 points = 1 cicero
            0.1776″
            4.511 mm

Example – 36 point

A | E | 0.5328″
        13.532 mm

B

Figure 3-5. Standard point and metric sizes type. A—Metric type is measured in millimeters, while type in the point system is measured in points. B—Different equivalents for type sizes in point, metric, and didot units.

Measuring Point Size

The point size or metric size of a letter is not a measurement from the top to the bottom of the letter itself. The point size also includes a small amount of white space above and below the letter for line spacing. Different styles of type have different amounts of white space above and below the letter

shape. Some typographers can identify a point size on sight. Others use an *E gauge* or similar measuring device, **Figure 3-6.**

The E gauge has a series of capital "E" letters with point sizes indicated for each letter. The correct point size can be determined by placing the gauge flat over a line of type and matching the letter "E" closest in size to the letters in the line.

A comparison of two different typefaces having the same point size but different letter heights is shown in **Figure 3-7.** The typefaces are both printed in 24-point type. However, the actual size of the letters is different. Identifying the correct point size is difficult without having typographical experience or without using an E gauge.

The amount of vertical space between lines of type is also measured in points and is called *leading*. An E gauge has a series of line spacing grids marked

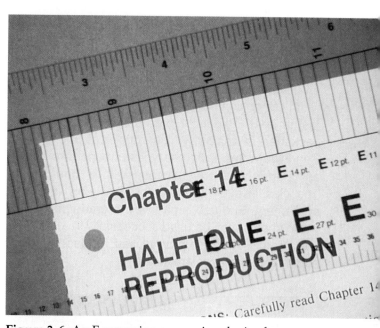

Figure 3-6. An E gauge is a measuring device for different point sizes of type and leading. The uppercase "E" in the chapter title is set in 24-point type.

line gauge: A device used to measure type sizes and line lengths in picas or inches.

nonpareil: Measuring unit on a line gauge that is equal to one-half pica.

didot point system: The standard system of print measurement used in Europe.

E gauge: A device used to measure point sizes and leading of printed type.

leading: The vertical distance separating each line of typeset copy, measured in points from one line to the next.

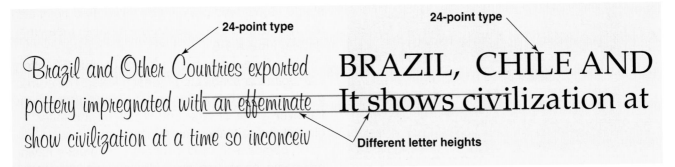

Figure 3-7. Two typefaces with the same point size but different letter heights. The point size of a letter includes the measurement of white space above and below the letter.

with point sizes that can be used to approximate leading. When the gauge is placed over several lines of type, the grid that most closely matches the spacing between the lines indicates the leading point size. Refer to Figure 3-6.

MEASURING PAPER SIZES

Paper sizes are designated in length and width dimensions and are given in either inches or metric units. Paper for business use is commonly packaged in *reams*, which consist of 500 sheets. See **Figure 3-8.** Different types of paper are known as *grades* and are classified with a *basic size*. The classification of paper grades lacks universal agreement. End use is one way to grade paper, but some sheets may be used successfully in more than one area. Some commonly used grades of paper and their basic sizes are listed:

- **Bond** = 17″ × 22″
- **Book** = 25″ × 38″
- **Offset** = 25″ × 38″
- **Cover** = 20″ × 26″
- **Text** = 25″ × 38″

Envelopes

Envelopes are classified by size and distinguished by styles that serve a special use. Business envelope sizes are usually designated by number. The most commonly used size is a Number 10, which measures 4 1/8″ × 9 1/2″. Window envelopes are available in the same size and are generally used for invoices or statements.

Envelopes used for wedding announcements and invitations or other formal occasions commonly measure 5″ × 6″. Open-end envelopes are larger types used for mailing reports, pamphlets, magazines, and other materials. Common sizes are 9″ × 12″ and 8 3/4″ × 11 1/4″.

Postal regulations should be reviewed in order to meet current mailing standards. Envelope sizes must comply with regulations so additional charges are not assessed for mail deliveries. See **Figure 3-9.**

ISO Sizes

Standard sizes for paper and envelopes have been established by the International Organization for Standardization (ISO). The sizes, known as the *ISO series*, are given in both SI Metric units (millimeters) and US Conventional units (inches). US Conventional units were discussed earlier. ISO sizes are commonly grouped into three series. A-series sizes are used for general printing requirements. B-series sizes are used for posters. C-series sizes are used for postcards, folders, and envelopes.

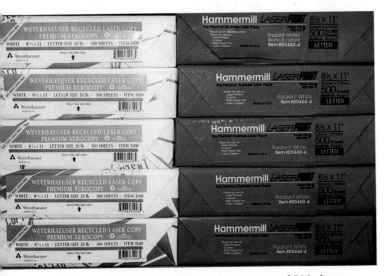

Figure 3-8. Paper packaged in reams of 500 sheets. Labels identify the paper size.

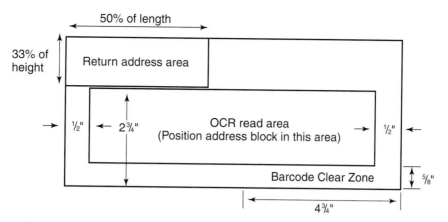

Figure 3-9. A dimensional standards template used to determine if letter size is acceptable for normal handling in mail delivery. A—Horizontal and vertical lines indicate minimum requirements for length and height. B—The upper-right corner of the letter must fall within the shaded area of the template to meet standards.

The A-series and B-series metric paper sizes are rectangular. Their sizes are based on the ratio of the two sides having the proportion of one to the square root of two (1:1.416).

The ISO-A size of paper is based on the area of one square meter, as shown in **Figure 3-10.** Each cut reduces the size of the sheet by 50% of the previous size; for example, the size of A2 is double that of A3. Each ISO-A measurement is listed in **Figure 3-11.**

ISO-A and ISO-B metric paper sizes are considered to be trimmed sizes. However, there are other series used to classify sizes for normal trims, bleed work, and extra trims. See **Figure 3-12.** Nearly all folded and gathered printed material needs to have a normal trim, but an image that runs off a printed page must have greater trim area. Control devices on the printed sheet require more space and extra trim.

ISO Sizes	Metric (mm)	Conventional (″)
A0	841 × 1189	33.11 × 46.81
A1	594 × 841	23.39 × 33.11
A2	420 × 594	16.54 × 23.39
A3	297 × 420	11.69 × 16.54
A4	210 × 297	8.27 × 11.69
A5	148 × 210	5.83 × 8.27
A6	105 × 148	4.13 × 5.83
A7	74 × 105	2.91 × 4.13
A8	52 × 74	2.05 × 2.91
A9	37 × 52	1.46 × 2.05
A10	26 × 37	1.02 × 1.46

Figure 3-11. ISO-A metric and conventional paper sizes.

ISO-B paper sizes are listed in **Figure 3-13.** The different sizes are based on the same ratio used in measuring ISO-A sizes (1:1.416). A comparison of ISO-A, ISO-B, and ISO-C paper sizes is shown in **Figure 3-14.**

The sizes for ISO-A sheets are compatible with the sizes for ISO-C envelopes. See **Figure 3-15.** One envelope size, designated DL, is not derived from ISO-A, ISO-B, or ISO-C sizes. DL are special envelope sizes and are not North American designations.

paper size: Measurements that describe the length and width dimensions of paper. Sizes are expressed in inches or metric units.

ream: Five hundred sheets of paper.

grade: Category or class of paper.

basic size: The standard length and width, in inches, of a grade of paper.

ISO series: The series of standard paper and envelope sizes established by the International Organizations for Standardization (ISO).

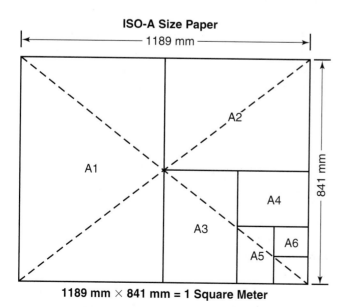

Figure 3-10. ISO-A metric size paper. The dimensions are based on the area of one square meter.

ISO Sizes for Normal Trims		
ISO Size	Metric (mm)	Conventional (″)
RA0	860 × 1220	33.66 × 48.03
RA1	610 × 860	24.02 × 33.86
RA2	430 × 610	16.93 × 24.02
ISO Sizes for Bleed Work or Extra Trims		
ISO Size	Metric (mm)	Conventional (″)
SRA0	900 × 1280	35.43 × 50.39
SRA1	640 × 900	25.20 × 35.43
SRA2	450 × 640	17.72 × 25.20

Figure 3-12. ISO trimmed paper sizes for normal trims, bleed work, and extra trims. (Center for Metric Education, Western Michigan University)

ISO Sizes	Metric (mm)	Conventional (″)
B0	1000 × 1414	39.37 × 55.67
B1	707 × 1000	27.83 × 39.37
B2	500 × 707	19.68 × 27.83
B3	353 × 500	13.90 × 19.68
B4	250 × 353	9.84 × 13.90
B5	176 × 250	6.93 × 9.84
B6	125 × 176	4.92 × 6.93
B7	88 × 125	3.46 × 4.92
B8	62 × 88	2.44 × 3.46
B9	44 × 62	1.73 × 2.44
B10	31 × 44	1.22 × 1.73

Figure 3-13. ISO-B metric and conventional paper sizes. (Center for Metric Education, Western Michigan University)

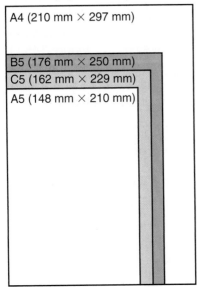

ISO-A, B, and C Paper Sizes

A4 (210 mm × 297 mm)
B5 (176 mm × 250 mm)
C5 (162 mm × 229 mm)
A5 (148 mm × 210 mm)

Figure 3-14. Common ISO-A, B, and C paper sizes.

THINK GREEN
ISO 14001

The International Organization for Standardization has also created standards based on the idea of reducing the impact organizations and industry have on the environment. The ISO 14001 standard deals with several aspects of environmental management. For example, this standard covers the general stages of controlling environmental impact by listing ways to set goals within an organization. While it doesn't specify how to reduce waste and VOC emissions, it does list guidelines for managing an organizational plan to reduce environmental impact. This standard is not required in the United States, although several companies are working toward certification. For more information on ISO standards, see www.iso.org.

PAPER WEIGHT

Most grades of paper are classified by their *basis weight*, which is a measure of the number of pounds in a ream of paper cut to its basic size. Each grade of paper is available in many different weights. See **Figure 3-16.**

The Technical Association of the Pulp and Paper Industry uses metric units to measure the weight of paper. The weight is expressed in grams per square meter (g/m^2). Factors for converting conventional weights of paper to metric units are listed in **Figure 3-17.** The conversion factors for changing from conventional weights of 500 sheets to grams per square meter are listed in column A. The conversion factors for changing weights from grams per square meter to conventional weights are listed in column B.

Using the conversion factors shown, a ream of coated book stock would be expressed as 100 g/m^2, or 67.5 lbs. (100 × 0.675). A ream of good writing paper would be listed as 85 g/m^2, or 22.61 lbs. (85 × 0.266).

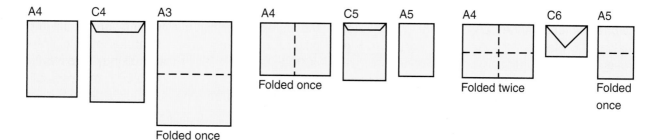

Figure 3-15. ISO-A Sheets of paper and ISO-C envelopes have compatible sizes.

Common Paper Weights (1000 sheets)		
Grade	Size (″)	Weight (pounds)
Bond	17 × 22	26, 32, 40, 48, 56
Book	25 × 38	60, 70, 80, 90, 100
Offset	25 × 38	50, 60, 70, 80, 100
Cover	20 × 26	100, 120, 130, 160, 180

Figure 3-16. Common grades of paper are available in a number of weights.

Conversion Factors for Ream Weights			
Grade of Paper	Conventional Size (″)	A Metric to Conventional	B Conventional to Metric
Writing	12 × 22	0.266	3.760
Cover	20 × 26	0.370	2.704
Cardboard	22 × 28	0.438	2.282
News	24 × 36	0.614	1.627
Book	25 × 38	0.675	1.480

Figure 3-17. Multiplying factors for converting paper weights from metric or conventional units.

Paper Thickness

Several types of caliper devices are available for measuring paper thickness. The ***paper caliper*** or micrometer is an accurate device used to measure the thickness of paper. It can also be used to determine the thickness of a printing plate. See **Figure 3-18.**

Paper Brightness

Paper is also classified by its brightness, based on the American Forest and Paper Association (AFPA) standards. Number 1 quality is the brightest, reflecting 85% to 87.9% of blue light; number 5 quality is classified as having the least brightness, as shown in **Figure 3-19.** Within each grade, papers are offered as virgin or recycled stock. Recycled stock may not be as bright as virgin stock.

Figure 3-18. A paper caliper is used to measure paper thickness. (Photo courtesy of The L.S. Starrett Co.)

Quality	Brightness
Number 1	85.0 to 87.9
Number 2	83.0 to 84.9
Number 3	79.0 to 82.9
Number 4	73.0 to 78.9
Number 5	72.9 and below

Figure 3-19. AFPA standard grade classifications for all finishes of paper. Brightness is measured by the percentage of blue light reflected from the paper's surface. (The S. D. Warren Company)

IMAGE MEASUREMENT

The rise of desktop publishing in the graphic communications industry has revolutionized the approach to the production of visual images. The use of computers has replaced many of the methods previously used in the design of printed materials.

basis weight: The weight, in pounds, of a ream of paper cut to its basic size.

paper caliper: A device used to measure paper thickness.

A *desktop publishing system*, consisting of a computer, printer, scanner, and publishing software, has taken the place of traditional methods used in operations such as typesetting and color separation. Most of the printed images found in publications and other media are now produced electronically. Equipment commonly used in desktop publishing is shown in **Figure 3-20.**

The growth of digital technology has led to improvements in image quality and higher levels of productivity. As technology continues to expand, desktop publishing will play an even greater role in graphic communications.

Monitor Viewing Conditions

Color monitors may be used to display and view digital images. The latest version of *ISO 3664—Viewing Conditions for Graphic Technology and Photography* establishes specifications for viewing of monitor independent of any form of hard copy. The specifications given in the ISO standard include guidelines for adjusting such controls as *chromaticity*, or color quality; *luminance*, or amount of light; *illumination*, or brightness of light; and environmental conditions, such as surrounding conditions and glare.

Resolution

Resolution describes the visual quality of an image and is a measure of elements that define the image. The resolution of an image is measured in *dots per inch (dpi)* or *pixels*. A pixel is a tiny rectangle that is only visible as a dot on a computer

Figure 3-20. The components of a desktop publishing system include a computer, scanner, and publishing software. Output is typically to a laser printer.

screen. The screen display of a computer monitor is measured in horizontal rows and vertical columns of pixels. A high-resolution computer monitor rated at 1600 × 1200 pixels is able to display a resolution of 1600 pixels horizontally and 1200 pixels vertically.

Laser printers and electronic scanners used in desktop publishing are identified by a measure of dpi for image resolution. A laser printer rated at 600 dpi can produce a resolution of 600 dots for each horizontal or vertical inch. A scanner that scans images at 1200 dpi can produce a file with an image resolution of 1200 dots per inch.

Scanning and File Sizes

The Warren Standard indicates that there is a simple way to govern how images should be scanned. Photographic material must be screened to break it down into tonal ranges. Various designated line screen figures are recommended for various types of stock. Doubling the line screen at which the image will be printed provides the number of dots per inch at which the image should be scanned. Scanning at different resolutions will change the file size and the amount of storage space needed; so will changing the type of file. A bitmap file contains the smallest amount of color information, while a CMYK color file contains the largest amount. See **Figure 3-21.**

PHOTOCONVERSION MEASUREMENT

Images are generally enlarged or reduced by certain percentages for use in photographic reproduction. Traditional methods used in halftone photography relied on measuring scales, screen tints, and process cameras. While desktop publishing has introduced new methods in the printing process, traditional procedures of producing images and other forms of measurement are still used in the graphic communications industry.

Proportional Scale

When images are to be enlarged or reduced, the correct percentage for reproduction can be determined by using a *proportional scale*. See **Figure 3-22.** The inside of the scale contains a rotating wheel that compares the size of the original to the reproduction size. The numbers along the inner scale represent the size of the original, and the numbers along the outer scale represent the size

File Sizes at Various Resolutions				
		Bitmap	Grayscale	RGB	CMYK
35mm	120 dpi	3 kb	19 kb	57 kb	76 kb
	170 dpi	6 kb	38 kb	114 kb	152 kb
	220 dpi	9 kb	64 kb	191 kb	254 kb
	300 dpi	15 kb	118 kb	353 kb	470 kb
	400 dpi	27 kb	210 kb	628 kb	838 kb
	600 dpi	60 kb	471 kb	1.38 Mb	1.84 Mb
4″ × 5″	120 dpi	36 kb	282 kb	844 kb	1.10 Mb
	170 dpi	72 kb	565 kb	1.65 Mb	2.21 Mb
	220 dpi	119 kb	946 kb	2.77 Mb	3.69 Mb
	300 dpi	220 kb	1.72 Mb	5.15 Mb	6.87 Mb
	400 dpi	391 kb	3.05 Mb	9.16 Mb	12.2 Mb
	600 dpi	879 kb	6.87 Mb	20.6 Mb	27.5 Mb
8″ × 10″	120 dpi	141 kb	1.10 Mb	3.30 Mb	4.39 Mb
	170 dpi	283 kb	2.21 Mb	6.62 Mb	8.82 Mb
	220 dpi	473 kb	3.69 Mb	11.1 Mb	14.8 Mb
	300 dpi	879 kb	6.87 Mb	20.6 Mb	27.5 Mb
	400 dpi	1.53 Mb	12.2 Mb	36.6 Mb	48.8 Mb
	600 dpi	3.43 Mb	27.5 Mb	82.4 Mb	109.9 Mb

Figure 3-21. File sizes that will result from scanning images of different sizes at various resolutions in the common formats: bitmap, grayscale, RGB color, and CMYK color. (The S. D. Warren Company)

Figure 3-22. A proportional scale is used to size images for enlargement or reduction.

for reproduction. When the two sizes are aligned, the percentage for enlargement or reduction is indicated by an arrow pointing to a windowed scale inside the wheel.

A proportional scale can be used to determine percentages for both the length and width of an image in either conventional or metric units. An image shot at 100% indicates that the image will be reproduced at the same size, while an image shot at 50% indicates that the image will be reduced by half its original size.

Screens

Halftone photography *screens* are used to change continuous tone photographs into dotted halftones for printing. Screens are measured in lines per inch in conventional units and lines per centimeter in metric units. In conventional units, screen sizes below 75 lines are considered to be coarse, while sizes above 133 lines are considered fine. The greater the number of lines, the finer the screen. See **Figure 3-23.**

desktop publishing system: A computerized system commonly used in the graphic communications industry to produce type and images.

chromaticity: The color quality of an image.

luminance: The amount of light in an image.

illumination: The brightness of light in an image.

resolution: An image's sharpness or clarity.

dots per inch (dpi): Measuring units for image resolution.

pixel: Acronym for *picture element*, the tiniest image component in a digital imaging or display system.

proportional scale: A measuring device used to determine the correct reproduction percentage for the enlargement or reduction of images.

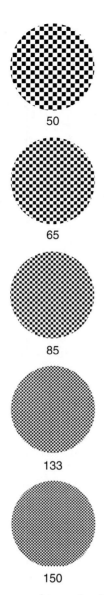

Figure 3-23. Screens used to make dotted halftones. The larger the screen number, the finer the screen.

Screen Rulings per Inch	Screen Rulings per Centimeter
50	20
65	26
75	30
100	40
120	48
133	54
150	60
175	70
200	80

Figure 3-24. Screen sizes compared in conventional and metric units.

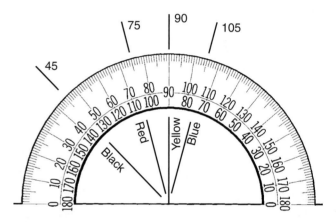

Figure 3-25. Standard screen angles used in making color separations.

Conventional screen sizes can be converted to metric units by dividing the number of lines per inch by 2.54. To convert metric screen sizes to lines per inch, multiply the number of lines per centimeter by 2.54. A comparison of conventional and metric screen sizes is shown in **Figure 3-24.**

In the digital world, the photos are scanned and the desired screen pattern and size are part of the program and are designated to the operator.

Screen Angle Measurement

Different **screen angles** are used when making **color separations** for each primary color for four-color printing. Screen angles are measured in degrees. A scale giving the screen angles for each color is shown in **Figure 3-25.**

To print properly, each separation must have the correct screen angle: a 45° screen angle is normally used for black, a 75° angle for magenta, a 90° angle for yellow, and a 105° angle for cyan. The line patterns on each screen have a specific angular relationship to prevent a **moiré pattern**. Screen angles are explained more thoroughly in Chapter 11.

Tint Percentages

A **screen tint** provides a hard dot screen that will produce evenly spaced dots that represent a tone percentage of a solid color. See **Figure 3-26.**

A 10% tint, for example, would result in 90% less ink deposited than an image printed without a screen tint. The resulting image would be very light. A 90% tint would print with 10% less ink and would produce a dark image.

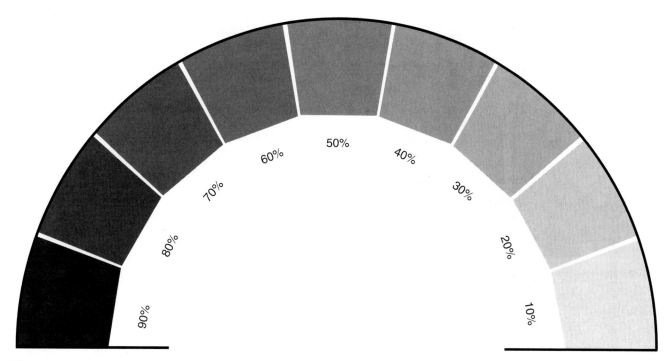

Figure 3-26. Common screen tint percentages. Larger percentages produce a darker screen, while smaller percentages result in a lighter screen.

Grayscale

A *grayscale* is a continuous tone strip with different shades of gray ranging from light to dark. It is used for visually gauging film exposure and development during chemical processing. Numerical values along the scale indicate the density of an image. See **Figure 3-27.**

Digital Control Strip

In industry, the digital control strip is called the target and is primarily used as a control device for pre-press proofs. It is also used to monitor and control production printing presses. The target must go through all of the steps required to create and print a product. See **Figure 3-28.**

Densitometer

A *densitometer* is a device used to measure the density of an image. See **Figure 3-29.** There are two types of densitometers commonly used in graphic

reproduction. One measures the reflection of light, while the other measures the transmission of light.

A *reflection densitometer* is used to give a reflected light measurement that indicates the tone values of printed materials or photographic prints. A *transmission densitometer* is used to measure light

screen: Used to change continuous tone photographs into dotted halftones for printing.

screen angles: Angular relationships of line screens used in making color separations for four-color printing.

color separation: Process of dividing the colors of a multicolored original into the printing primaries (CMY) and black (K).

moiré pattern: A visually undesirable dot-exaggerating effect that occurs when two different screen patterns are randomly positioned or superimposed.

screen tint: Reproduction screen used to provide a tint percentage of a solid color.

grayscale: A continuous tone strip used to visually gauge exposure of an image.

densitometer: An electronic instrument that uses a photocell to accurately measure the amount of light reflected from or through different one values.

reflection densitometer: Instrument used to accurately determine different tone values, such as the highlights and shadows of an original.

transmission densitometer: Color measurement device that measures the fraction of incident light conveyed through a negative or positive transparency without being absorbed or scattered.

Figure 3-27. A grayscale uses a series of tones to measure image density.

Figure 3-28. A digital control strip.

Figure 3-29. A densitometer measures reflected or transmitted light to read the density of an image.

passing through a material. Both devices measure the tone range, or contrast, of an image.

A densitometer can be used to determine the correct exposure for making a halftone screen from a photographic print. Measurements are taken to identify the lightest and darkest areas of the print or any other areas needed to calculate exposures.

Spectrophotometer

A *spectrophotometer* is a measuring device used to determine color values, such as chromatic value, (h*; hue) brightness (L*), and saturation (C*, chroma), with which color can be clearly classified quantitatively in accordance with the color perception of the human eye. It operates on the principle that any color can be described as an additive mixture of spectral colors.

Summary

Various positions within the graphic communications industry require the employee to have mathematical knowledge necessary to do a variety of calculations as well as being able to operate measuring devices. Becoming familiar with the different systems and methods of measurements are essential for competency in selected areas of the printing facility.

Review Questions

Please do not write in this text. Write your answers on a separate sheet of paper.

1. Name the two most commonly used systems of measurement.
2. What are the standard units for length and mass in the SI Metric system?
3. List five common metric prefixes.
4. Which of the following is an incorrect metric notation?
   A. 33 mm.
   B. 0.39 km.
   C. 34,000 km.
   D. 42 kPa.
5. Convert the following values:
   A. One inch = _____ millimeters
   B. 12 meters = _____ yards
   C. 10 quarts = _____ liters
   D. 12 milliliters = _____ fluid oz
   E. 400 pounds = _____ kilograms
   F. 25 meters/second = _____ feet/second
   G. 68°F = _____ °C
6. A point measures approximately _____ of an inch.
7. The pica is approximately _____ of an inch.
8. What are two devices commonly used to measure the point size of type?
9. The amount of vertical space between lines of type is called _____ .
10. A ream of paper consists of _____ sheets.
11. Name four common grades of paper.
12. List the three ISO series for paper and envelopes and the uses for each series.
13. What is the basis weight of paper?
14. List four components of a typical desktop publishing system.
15. Image resolution is measured in _____ or _____.

16. Screen sizes below 75 lines are considered _____, while sizes above 133 lines are considered _____.

17. A screen angle of _____ degrees is normally used for the color black when making color separations.

18. Why must each color separation screen angle be set differently?

19. A 10% screen tint would result in _____ ink deposited than a 20% tint.

20. A _____ is used to measure the density or darkness of an image.

Suggested Activities

1. Using an E gauge, measure the size by matching at 6 different sizes of the letter *E*.

2. Convert the following linear measurements to metric units: 10 inches, 3 feet, 12 yards, and 60 miles.

3. Look at labels found on paper cartons, cans, tubes and printing plates and list the US Conventional and metric measurement found on each unit.

4. List the applications of mathematics in the printing industry.

Related Web Links

Technical Association of the Pulp and Paper Industry (TAPPI)

www.tappi.org

Online resource dedicated to providing solutions in the industry of pulp, paper, packing, and converting.

International Organization for Standardization (ISO)

www.iso.org

Information on various standards within industry.

Conservatree

www.conservatree.com

Resources include information on recycled and environmental paper.

desktopPublishing

www.desktoppublishing.com

Free information and resources on desktop publishing.

spectrophotometer: Instrument capable of measuring light of different colors or wavelengths.

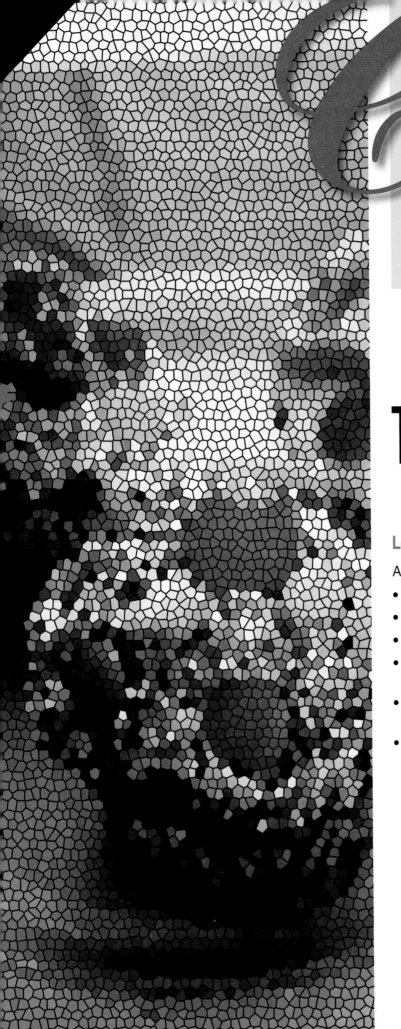

CHAPTER 4

Typography

Learning Objectives

After studying this chapter, you will be able to:

- Summarize the development of type styles.
- Identify the basic terms used to describe type.
- Summarize seven typeface classifications.
- Explain the difference between a family, a series, and a font of type.
- Identify the common type sizes and units used in typography.
- Explain the factors that contribute to the legibility of type.

Important Terms

ascender
black letter
body type
brightness
calligraphy
character compensation
characters
composition depth
condensed typefaces
cursive
definition
descender
display type
em quad
en quad
expanded faces
eye span
font
foundry type
heavy elements
ink darkness
italic type
justify
kerning
legibility
letterspacing
ligatures
light elements
line length
loose set
manuscript
Modern Roman typefaces
negative leading

Novelty typeface
oblique
Old English
Oldstyle Roman
    typeface
opacity
pi characters
point size
reverse type
Roman typeface
sans serif
script typeface
serif
set size
small caps
smoothness
Subiaco face
text
tight set
tracking
Transitional Roman
    typeface
typeface
typeface family
typeface series
type metal
typographer
typography
visibility
weight
widow
wordspacing
x-height

This chapter introduces the role that typefaces play in producing printed images. Typefaces are important, not only to the communication of thoughts, but to the overall appearance or aesthetic characteristics of the printed image. Careful study of this chapter will help you understand the information presented in later chapters.

TYPEFACES

Typefaces are distinctive visual symbols that are used to compose a printed page on paper or another substrate. *Characters* are the individual visual symbols in a particular typeface. An assortment of characters, such as letters, numerals, punctuation marks, and special symbols, is necessary to put words into print.

Just as every person has a name, every typeface has a name. It would be very difficult to identify specific typefaces without names, just as it would be difficult to identify individual human beings if there were no names. There are literally thousands of typefaces available to the producer of printed products. With the introduction of computerized typesetting, the number of new typefaces has increased dramatically and continues to grow steadily.

Typography

Typography is the art of expressing ideas in printed form through the selection of appropriate typefaces. The *typographer* must determine how the manuscript should be expressed in type, as well as other details of reproduction and physical format.

For example, if the typographer is selecting a typeface to use in an advertisement for a new electronic device, he or she would *not* select an old-fashioned-appearing type style with ornate, curly letters. A modern, clean-looking type would be more appropriate and representative.

Typeface Terminology

The alphabet used for English and most European languages consists of only 26 letters. However, since there are thousands of typefaces, the letters of that alphabet are represented in many different ways. To be able to differentiate among the various typefaces, you must understand the basic terms relating to type and know how typeface characteristics affect the printed image.

The fundamental terms relating to a typeface are shown in **Figure 4-1.** They include:

- **Uppercase.** The capital letters, usually abbreviated as *caps*.

- **Lowercase.** The body letters, abbreviated as *lc*.

- **Body height.** The distance from top to bottom of the lowercase letters, not including the ascenders and descenders. Also called *x-height*.

typeface: Distinctive designs of visual symbols used to compose a printed page.

characters: The individual visual symbols, such as letters, numerals, and punctuation marks, in a particular typeface.

typography: The art of expressing ideas in printed form through the selection of appropriate typefaces.

typographer: A print designer who determines how a manuscript should be expressed in type as well as other details of reproduction.

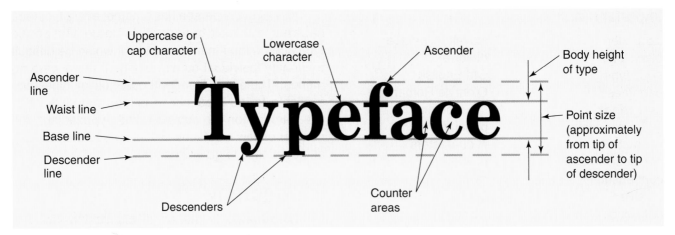

Figure 4-1. Basic terms relating to a typeface.

- **Ascender.** The part of a letter that extends above the body height.
- **Descender.** The part of a letter that extends below the body height.
- **Base line.** An imaginary line drawn along bottom of body height letters. Descenders go below it.
- **Waist line.** An imaginary line drawn along the top of body height letters.
- **Counter.** The nonprinting area surrounding a letter or inside the loop of a letter, such as d or p.
- **Point size.** A vertical measurement used to identify or specify the size of a typeface. Measurement is approximately from the top of the ascender space to the bottom of the descender space, with the em space taken into account. The measurement of the typeface varies with each type style.

Basic terms relating to specific characters, as shown in **Figure 4-2,** are:

- **Hairline.** A thin line or element of the character.
- **Stem.** The vertical part of the character.
- **Stroke.** The thickness of a line forming a character element.
- **Stress.** The slant or tilt of a character.
- **Serif.** The thickened tips or short finishing-off strokes at the top and bottom of a character.
- **Set width.** The distance across a character from side to side.

Later sections of this chapter, and other chapters, will discuss these terms in greater detail. You will learn how these typeface components and characteristics can be used to alter the form and function of words, sentences, and the general "look" of the printed image.

TYPE STYLE DEVELOPMENT

Throughout history, humans have striven to perfect the art of making written or printed images. The scribes of medieval Europe produced hundreds of beautiful and masterful letter forms as they hand-lettered book pages. The scribes developed very beautiful lettering, making each character into an art form. Across Europe, the style of the letters varied from country to country, or sometimes even from region to region within a country.

When the process of mechanical printing from individual pieces of type was introduced in Europe in the 15th Century, typographers modeled their letters on those drawn by scribes. Each letter was cut by

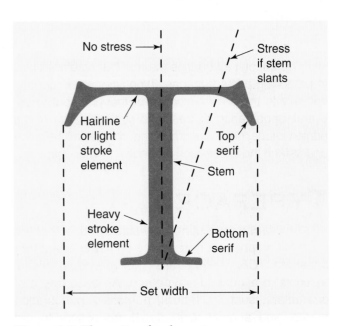

Figure 4-2. The parts of a character.

hand from hard metal to form a punch, which then was driven into softer metal to make a mold. The mold, in turn, was used to produce many copies of the letter. Molten *type metal* (an alloy of lead, tin, and antimony) was poured into the mold to form an individual piece of type that could be aligned with type containing other letters to form words and sentences. **Figure 4-3** shows a piece of *foundry type* produced by the modern version of this method. Although it is used only in a few specialized applications today, foundry type was the major form of type used for printing from the 1400s through the mid-1900s.

New printing methods introduced in the past 50 years have given rise to photographic and electronic methods of typesetting. These methods, which will be described later, also made it easier to design and produce new typefaces. Many of these new faces are radically different from those that have been widely used for many years.

Black Letter

The *manuscript* style of lettering used by the scribes of Germany, France, Holland, and other countries was similar to the type style known today as *Old English*, also called black letter or text, **Figure 4-4.** This letter style was the basis for development of the earliest metal type, since the typographer or printer typically imitated the manuscript style common to a locality or geographic area.

Figure 4-3. Foundry type, cast in metal, was the major form of type used by printers for more than 500 years. Ink was applied to the raised surface of the letter and transferred to paper to form an image.

𝕲𝖗𝖆𝖕𝖍𝖎𝖈 𝕬𝖗𝖙𝖘 𝕯𝖎𝖘𝖕𝖑𝖆𝖞 𝖔𝖋 𝕱𝖎𝖓𝖊 𝕻𝖗𝖎𝖓𝖙𝖎𝖓𝖌 𝕽𝖊𝖛𝖊𝖆𝖑𝖘 𝕾𝖐𝖎𝖑𝖋𝖚𝖑 𝕬𝖗𝖗𝖆𝖓𝖌𝖊𝖒𝖊𝖓𝖙 𝖔𝖋 𝕿𝖞𝖕𝖊

Figure 4-4. Black letter is a style of type based on hand lettering done by scribes in European countries. (ATF)

Development of the Roman Type Style

As the art of printing developed, changes in type styles also increased. This was especially true in Italy, where many of the German printers had migrated. The German black letter type styles gradually were replaced by a more delicate and lighter type style that became known as the Roman typeface. Several books were printed in an early version of the Roman face known as the *Subiaco face*.

A major figure in the development of the Roman type style was Nicolas Jenson. He was a master engraver for the French government who learned the new craft of printing in Mainz, Germany, and later moved to Italy.

Jenson is credited with designing and cutting the Roman letter forms that first appeared in printed pieces in 1469 and 1470. His designs, **Figure 4-5,** were based on the letters cut into stone monuments by the ancient Romans. Since the letters on the monuments were all capitals, Jenson developed Roman lowercase letters that would merge readily into word forms. This was significant, since we recognize words by their shape. The Jenson designs were the models used by type designers for hundreds of years. Nicolas Jenson is credited with printing about 150 books during his ten years in Italy.

Jenson followed the traditions of the manuscript scribe in his lowercase letters. When enlarged,

type metal: A low-melting-point alloy of lead, tin, and antimony used to cast foundry type.

foundry type: Individual pieces of metal type that could be aligned with type containing other letters to form words and sentences for printing on paper.

manuscript: A style of hand lettering used by the scribes of Germany, France, Holland, and other countries in the Middle Ages.

Old English: A text typeface often used for such applications as diplomas, certificates, and religious materials.

Subiaco face: An early version of the Roman typeface, used for several books and named for the town where the printing was done.

ABCDEFGHIJKLMNOPQR
STUVWXYZ
abcdefghijklmnopqrstuvwxyz

Figure 4-5. Nicolas Jenson modified Roman letters and developed a lowercase alphabet so that it would more readily form words. This is a modern version of his typeface.

these letters revealed the feeling of the pen-drawn letter on a parchment surface. Each letter could be considered independently, yet they merged into the identity of the word.

Many other designers produced type styles in Italy during the same period. The slanted *italic type*, modeled on a form of handwriting, was developed and first used by Aldus Manutius, a printer in Venice.

The black letter, Roman, and Italic type styles were used universally in Europe for two centuries. For a time, black letter was dominant in Germany and the Roman face was used primarily in Italy. Eventually however, Roman became the principal letter style used in all countries except Germany.

Modern Typefaces

As noted, the early type styles were adapted from hand-drawn or stone-carved letters. By the 1700s, however, the emphasis changed to producing typefaces by copying from those styles that already existed, rather than working from original sources. Aesthetics were no longer an important design factor. Types became thinner and lines became much sharper.

The decline in the quality of type design throughout Europe and England continued through much of the 1800s. The decline was reflected in the poorly printed books of the era.

In 1890, William Morris, an English architect, artist, and poet, set out to demonstrate that books could again be beautiful. His interest brought about the revival of many early typefaces, such as Jenson, Garamond, Janson, and Caslon. These faces are the basis for many of the typefaces used today in book publication. See **Figure 4-6.**

Claude Garamond, a French printer, was influenced by Nicholas Jenson's Roman typeface, but designed a more elegant and refined face that was typically French. Garamond's 1540 design was redesigned in 1919 in the United States. The redesign

BRAZIL, CHILE AND OTHER
A It shows civilization at the time so

AT BRAZIL AND OTHER
It shows civilization at a time so
B remote that it is doubtful whether

CHESS-KNIGHT
C After an apprentice

SOME KNIGHTS OF
D After an apprentice as

Figure 4-6. Roman typefaces revived for modern use are the basis of many faces employed today. A—Today's Garamond type is faithful to the original style. (ATF) B—The Caslon face is considered a classic. (ATF) C—Baskerville developed a type with letter forms designed specifically for printing. D—The extreme contrast of elements in Bodoni identifies it as a modern Roman typeface. (ATF)

resulted in a light-lined, more open design that would print more clearly.

The Janson typeface of today is a recutting of the face issued in about the year 1675 by Anton Janson. Janson modified the manuscript letter by lightening the lines for better printing on a rough-surfaced stock.

Also designed for printing on rough stock was the typeface issued by William Caslon in England in about the year 1722. Caslon's typeface was an immediate success. The design by Caslon continued the trend toward lighter lines and more open design for better printing.

The English printer John Baskerville developed a typeface that is considered the beginning of the transition from letters based on manuscript to letters designed solely for printing. This type style was suitable for printing on smooth paper. Baskerville established a paper mill, type foundry, and printing office in Birmingham, England, and conducted extensive experiments with type and paper from 1750 to 1758. Baskerville's principle of considering type, paper, ink, and presswork together was the basis of today's planning of a printed job.

Another widely used type style was designed by Giambattista Bodoni, an Italian printer active in the late 1700s and early 1800s. Bodoni's typeface had greater differences between the light and heavy elements than any other face at that time, and is considered to be a modern Roman typeface. Bodoni typefaces used today show extreme difference between light and heavy elements. The typeface known as *Bodoni Book* has less pronounced contrast between elements, and closer to Bodoni's earlier designs.

Contemporary Typefaces

Contemporary typefaces are primarily the contributions of the 20th century, and can be divided into three groups. First, there are the modern versions of the basic book faces of the early printers, as described in the preceding section. Second, there are the modifications of the basic book faces made for newspapers. Third, there are the many new display faces. The substantial increase in the number of typefaces paralleled the rapid growth of advertising and commercial printing during the first half of the 20th century.

Today, thousands of faces are in existence. While this number seems large, think of the carpenter or auto technician who keeps a large chest of tools so the right one will be available when needed. In the same way, a typographer needs many tools so he or she can choose the correct typeface for a specific job. For use in computerized typesetting, numerous typefaces are available on CD-ROM. Printed samples of the faces available on the disc allow the designer to easily select a specific font.

Sometimes, typefaces will look very much alike, yet have different names. Since typefaces cannot be copyrighted, it is possible for a designer to change a typeface slightly and gave the style a new name.

Roman Typeface Elements

Three elements contribute to the appearance of a character in a Roman typeface and help to differentiate between faces. They are the heavy elements, light elements, and serifs.

The *heavy elements* of the type character give it identity, while the *light elements* tie the heavy elements together. The contrast between heavy and light elements help give a typeface its distinctive character. See **Figure 4-7.**

The curves of the characters should vary to emphasize difference or unlikeness of the letters and to neutralize the vertical thrusts of the letters.

The *serifs* found on the *bottom* of letters imply the horizontal base line, helping tie the letters together to

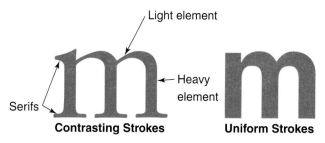

Figure 4-7. The contrast between heavy and light strokes makes differences in letter shape more pronounced. Serifs are finishing strokes at the tips of letters. Uniform strokes have the same thickness, so there is no contrast.

form words. The *top* serifs contribute to the unique appearance of the letter and help readability. The *ascenders* and *descenders* are also useful as identifiers and assist in the recognition of a word, **Figure 4-8.**

TYPEFACE CLASSIFICATIONS

The number of typeface classifications is not totally agreed on, since some experts will list more classifications than others. For the purposes of this book, seven classifications will be identified:

- Roman
- Sans serif
- Square serif
- Black letter
- Script or cursive
- Novelty or Decorative
- Italic (a variation of other classifications)

italic type: A slashed type, modeled on a form of handwriting.

heavy elements: The darker strokes of a type character that give it identity.

light elements: The hairlines or other less-dark strokes that tie together the heavy elements of a type character.

serif: The thickened tips or short finishing-off strokes at the top and bottom of a Roman typeface character.

ascender: The part of a letter that extends above the body height.

descender: The part of a letter that extends below the body or baseline.

Readability

Figure 4-8. Top serifs and ascenders are critical to readability. Cover the top half of word and try to read it. Then, cover the bottom half and read. Note how ascenders help you identify the word.

Roman

The **Roman typefaces**, or serif typefaces, are numerous in number and are the most widely used. The characteristics commonly associated with Roman types are the contrast between the heavy and light elements, and the use of the serifs.

Roman typefaces are further classified into three groups: Oldstyle, Transitional, and Modern. These are shown in **Figure 4-9.**

Oldstyle Typefaces

The **Oldstyle Roman typefaces** have a rugged appearance, with relatively little contrast between heavy and light elements. The fillets of the serifs, or where two fillets meet, are curved. Oldstyle letters look better as words; therefore, faces such as Caslon and Garamond were typically used for book text matter.

Transitional Typefaces

Transitional Roman typefaces are a remodeling of Oldstyle typefaces. Greater contrast is evident between the heavy and light elements. The characters were also wider than the equivalent Oldstyle characters. John Baskerville improved on the Caslon typeface and produced Baskerville, the first typeface used to print on smooth paper. The Oldstyle characters were designed to print *into* thick, rough paper, rather than on the surface of thinner and smoother stock.

Modern Typefaces

The most distinguishing feature of **Modern Roman typefaces**, first designed by Bodoni in 1789, is the increased contrast between the very thin, light elements and heavy elements. The Bodoni typeface has long ascenders and descenders and the serifs are straight lines without fillets.

Sans Serif

"Sans" in French means "without." Therefore, the classification *sans serif* is used for typefaces without serifs. See **Figure 4-10.** This typeface classification is second only to Roman in popularity today. Sans serif typefaces usually have a *monotone* appearance, meaning that the heavy and light elements are approximately the same thickness. While most are formed with strokes of uniform weight, a few sans serif faces have heavy and light elements.

Square Serif

Square serif typefaces are usually formed with strokes of equal weight, like sans serif types, but have finishing-off strokes added. The shape of the serif is square or block-like and the serif has the same weight as the main portion of the letter face, **Figure 4-11.**

Very seldom is a square serif typeface used for straight matter composition or text of a page, because it is not as easy to read as type with thinner serifs. These contemporary typefaces are most often used as display or headline types.

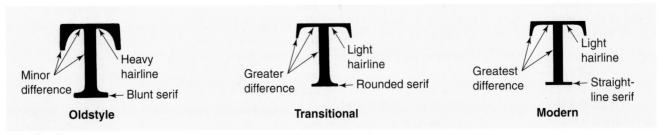

Figure 4-9. Roman typefaces are classified into groups of Oldstyle, Transitional, and Modern. The differences in stroke weights and serifs are shown.

Serif   Sans Serif

Figure 4-10. A sans serif typeface is normally formed with strokes of uniform thickness, and has no finishing strokes.

THE EARLY PRINTER
They instructed some of

Figure 4-11. On a square serif typeface, the serif strokes are often the same weight as the rest of the letter strokes. This sample is set in the typeface named Stymie.

Black Letter or Text

The *black letter*, or text typeface, resembles the *calligraphy* of German monks of the 1400s. Black letter is most often used for printed materials relating to special occasions. Certificates, wedding and graduation announcements, religious materials, diplomas, and official documents are typical examples.

A text face set in all capital letters is very difficult to read, **Figure 4-12.** For this reason, the use of both capital and lowercase letters is recommended when setting copy.

Script or Cursive

Both script and cursive typefaces are designed to simulate handwriting. The distinction between them is whether the individual letters in a word are joined or not. The letters in a *script typeface* are joined; letters in a *cursive* face are not. See **Figure 4-13.** The contrast of characters varies with the typeface design. Like text typefaces, script and cursive typefaces are used primarily for special effects. They are used for headlines, announcements, invitations, and letterheads. Since they are hard to read when copy length is more than a sentence or two, script and cursive types are seldom used for setting a full printed page or a large block of body copy.

UNIVERSITY

Figure 4-12. Black letter typefaces are very difficult to read when set in all capital letters.

Where to look for your rain-beau

for the one man in ten who

Orders regularly entered, verbal

A

Good neighbors to the North of us

Limited Time Only

Remember the sounds of San Francisco

B

Figure 4-13. Script typefaces have joined letters; cursive letters are separate. A—Examples of script typefaces. B—Examples of cursive styles.

Novelty or Decorative

The *Novelty typeface* classification is used for a wide variety of types whose primary intent is to command special attention, **Figure 4-14.** A Novelty

Roman typeface: A type style based on the capital letters cut into stone monuments by the ancient Romans.

Oldstyle Roman typeface: A group of typefaces that have a rugged appearance, with relatively little contrast between heavy and light elements.

Transitional Roman typefaces: Typefaces that are a remodeling of Oldstyle faces.

Modern Roman typefaces: Typefaces that have increased contrast between very thin, light elements and heavy elements.

sans serif: The classification for typefaces without serifs, or stroke endings.

black letter: A classification of type consisting of faces that resemble the hand-drawn lettering of German monks in the Middle Ages.

calligraphy: The art of hand-drawing letters, also known as *manuscript writing*.

script typeface: A typeface designed to simulate handwriting, in which the letters are joined.

cursive: A typeface designed to simulate handwriting, in which the letters are not joined.

Novelty typeface: A typeface designed primarily to command special attention, express a mood, or provide a specific appearance for a theme or an occasion.

Figure 4-14. Decorative typefaces are intended to draw your attention. They are normally used for headlines in advertisements and similar applications.

typeface, sometimes called occasional or decorative, must be carefully chosen to express a mood or provide a specific appearance for a theme or an occasion. Each style has individuality and is suited for a special situation. These faces are not intended to be used as body copy.

Italic

Italic type is a slanted version of the upright letter, and is often treated as a separate classification. Most Roman faces have a companion italic of related design, **Figure 4-15.** In electronic composition, the term *oblique* is sometimes used to describe a simulated italic character produced by electronically slanting an upright Roman character. Italic type is often used to indicate emphasis in body copy. It is also used for titles, for foreign words, for terms being defined, and for quotations. Poetry is often typeset in an italic face.

Reverse Type

Reverse type usually consists of white characters on a solid black or color background. This is done occasionally and can be done to stress the importance of the message or information in the copy. For example, a small newspaper advertisement might be reversed to make it stand out on the page and be noticed. Care must be used in choosing a typeface and type size for reversing. Many types are difficult to read when reversed, especially in small point sizes. See **Figure 4-16.**

Typeface Families, Series, and Fonts

In addition to the classifications discussed so far, typefaces can be grouped by specific style of type. The term associated with a given style is called family. The total range of sizes of one type style of a given font is called a type series. A font is the complete set of letters, figures, punctuation marks, special characters, and ligatures contained in a typeface.

Typeface Family

A *typeface family* consists of the variations of one style of type, **Figure 4-17.** The design elements

---

Characters in complete font

A B C D E F G H I J K L M N

O P Q R S T U V W Z Y Z &

$ 1 2 3 4 5 6 7 8 9 0

a b c d e f g h i j k l m n o p q

r s t u v w x y z . , - ' : ; ! ?)

fi ff fl ffi ffl &

Qu QU

Italic Typeface

Characters in complete font

A B C D E F G H I J K L M N

O P Q R S T U V W Z Y Z &

$ 1 2 3 4 5 6 7 8 9 0

a b c d e f g h i j k l m n o p q

r s t u v w x y z . , - : ; ! ? ')]

fi ff fl ffi ffl &

Qu QU

Companion Typeface

Figure 4-15. An italic is a slanted companion version of a Roman typeface.

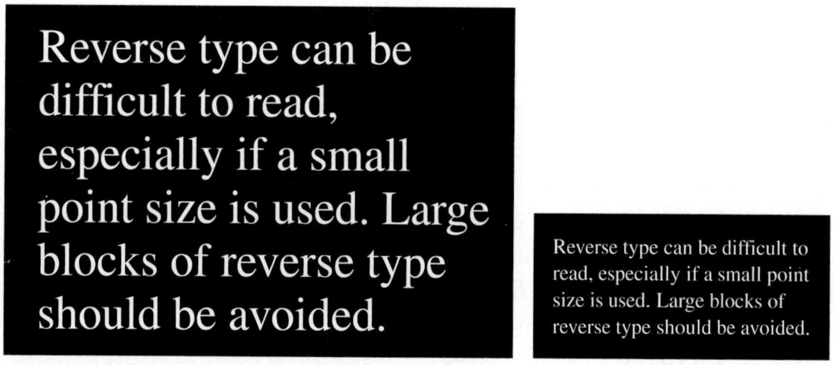

Reverse type can be difficult to read, especially if a small point size is used. Large blocks of reverse type should be avoided.
Reverse type can be difficult to read, especially if a small point size is used. Large blocks of reverse type should be avoided.

Figure 4-16. While reverse type can be effective as an attention-getting device, legibility suffers when the type is too small. Compare these examples on 18-point and 8-point type.

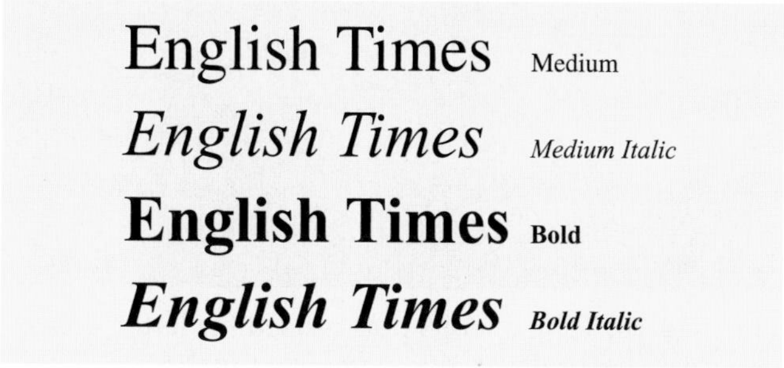

English Times Medium
English Times Medium Italic
English Times Bold
English Times Bold Italic

Figure 4-17. A type family is made up of all the variations within one style of type, such as different weights or stresses.

Typeface
Regular
Typeface
Expanded
Typeface
Condensed
Typeface
Extra condensed

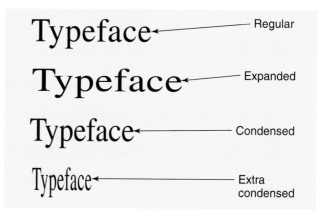

Figure 4-18. Width variations in a given typeface might include regular, expanded, condensed, and extra condensed type.

of the characters sets one family apart from another. Even though some typefaces are very similar in appearance, this does not make them part of the same family. As an example, Garamond is one family, and Caslon is another, even though their design is very similar. Refer to Figure 4-6.

Every variation of the designated typeface style becomes a part of that family. Knowledge of the variations in character widths and weights within a family is important to working effectively with type.

Width Variations

Some typefaces are designed to include width variations. These include the normal width types, as well as types with condensed, extra condensed, and expanded widths. Examples of such variations are found in **Figure 4-18.**

The ***condensed typefaces*** are intended to get more words in less space. They are used rather than going to a smaller typeface. ***Expanded faces***, also called *extended faces*, fill more space without going to a larger point size.

Weight Variations

The ***weight*** of a letter refers to the image area. The readable image might have a light, medium, bold, or extra-bold printing surface. Refer to Figure 4-17. With this range of weights, it is possible to vary the contrast for words or lines of type without changing the point size.

oblique: In electronic composition, the term used to describe a simulated italic character produced by slanting an upright Roman typeface.

reverse type: White characters on a solid black or color background.

typeface family: A grouping consisting of all the variations of one style of type.

condensed typefaces: Those intended to get more words in less space by narrowing the width of the characters.

expanded faces: Those intended to fill more space without going to a larger point size.

weight: The degree of boldness of the printing surface of a letter.

Typeface Series

A *typeface series* is the range of sizes of each typeface in a family, **Figure 4-19.** The common type sizes used in printing are 6, 8, 10, 12, 14, 18, 24, 36, 48, 60, and 72 point. In traditional relief printing, type in sizes 96 points and larger was made from wood, rather than metal, **Figure 4-20.**

The introduction of phototypesetters allowed the use of sizes, such as 7, 9, and 11 point, that were not common to the relief process. More recently, electronic (computer-based) composition has made it possible to generate typefaces in virtually any size needed, even in hundredths of a point increments. This can be a major advantage in design and copyfitting.

Type Font

A *font* consists of all the characters, such as letters, numerals, punctuation marks, and symbols that make up a specific typeface. Examples include 9-point Bodoni or 12-point Helvetica Bold.

When applied to foundry type, where each character is on a separate piece of metal, "font"

has a somewhat different meaning. As shown in **Figure 4-21,** a foundry type font consists of different quantities of each character in one size and style of type. This is necessary because the individual

Figure 4-20. Type over 96 points used for letterpress printing was traditionally made from wood.

8 Point Spartan Medium

10 Point Spartan Medium

12 Point Spartan Medium

18 Point Spartan Medium

24 Point Spartan Medium

36 Point Spartan Medium

48 Point Spartan Med

72 Point Spart

Figure 4-19. A typeface series is a full range of sizes of one typeface.

AAAAAABBBBBCCCCCDDDDEEEEE(G
EEEEFFFFFGGGHHHHIIIIIIIJJJKKKKLLLL.O
LLLMMMMMMMNNNNNNNNNOOOOOOO,–
OPPPPPQQRRRRRRRSSSSSSTTTTTTUZ
TTTUUUUVVVWWWWXXXXYYYYZZZ
&&&$$$$111?111222333444555666777
888999000((())).........,,,,,,,,,,,""""!!;;::""""——??
aaaaaaaaaaaaaaaaaaabbbbbbbbcccccc
cddddddddddddeeeeeeeeeeeeeeeeerr
eeeeffffffffffffgggggggggggghhhhhhhhhiiiiiiiiiiri
iiiiiiiijjjjjjjjjkkkkkkllllllllllllmmmmmmmmmnnnnss
nnnnnnnnnnnnnnoooooooooooooooos
oppppppppqqqqqrrrrrrrrrrrssssssssssssss
xsttttttttttttttuuuuuuuuuuuvvvvvvvwwwwwwff
● ● ● ● ● ● ● ●   ` ` ` ` `
wxxxxyyyyyyyyzzzz,,,,   ---""""::,;;!!??

Figure 4-21. A foundry type font consists of a full assortment of characters for one size typeface. The varying number of characters is based on frequency of use: more *e* characters are needed than *x* or *z* characters.

characters are physically assembled into words, **Figure 4-22.** Enough copies of each character must be available to make up a number of words.

The kinds and total number of characters differ from font to font. While most will include a full set of cap and lowercase letters, the numerals 0 to 9, and the usual punctuation marks, they often will differ in the symbols and special characters they include. For example, some fonts include *ligatures*, which are joined letter combinations such as *fi, ff, fl, ffi,* and *ffl*. Other fonts might include *small caps*, which are capital letters smaller than the normal caps of the font.

typeface series: The range of sizes of each typeface in a family.

font: In computer-based or phototypesetting composition methods, it consists of all the characters that make up a specific typeface.

ligatures: Joined letter combinations, such as *fi, ff, fl, ffi,* or *ffl*, found in some typefaces.

small caps: Capital letters smaller than the normal caps of the font.

Figure 4-22. Setting copy in foundry type involves selecting individual pieces of type and assembling the letters in a holder called a *stick*. This method was used by printers for hundreds of years.

In fonts for computer or phototypesetting, such symbols as stars, asterisks, arrows, percent signs, or checkmarks are known as *pi characters*, **Figure 4-23**. In foundry type, such special characters are called sorts or dingbats.

TYPE AND TYPESETTING MEASUREMENTS

While people in most occupations measure in units of inches, fractions of inches, centimeters, or millimeters, people working in graphic communications use special measuring units with names like points and picas.

Points and Picas

The two principal units of measure used in the graphic communications industry are the point and the pica. Points and picas were described in Chapter 3.

Points are used to measure the vertical height of a line of type, while picas are used to measure *line lengths* and *composition depth*. The *point size* of type is based on distance from the top of the ascenders to the bottom of the descenders, as shown in **Figure 4-24**. The point size of type should not be confused with the *x-height*, which is the height of the lowercase *x*.

The size of type is difficult to distinguish when in print, because two typefaces of the same point size may have x-heights that are quite different. The letters of one typeface may appear to be larger or smaller than the letters of the other, but lines set in the two faces would require the same amount of vertical space. See **Figure 4-25**.

Type sizes that range from 4-point through 12-point are usually referred to as *text* or *body type*. Sizes above 12-point are referred to as *display type*.

Figure 4-23. Symbols such as these are known as pi characters, sorts, or dingbats. They add to the interest of printed materials.

Figure 4-24. The point size of type is measured from the top of the ascenders to the bottom of the descenders.

Mm *Mm* Mm **Mm**

Figure 4-25. Typefaces of the same point size may vary greatly in body height, as shown by the lowercase letters here. These typefaces are all set in 36-point.

ACADEMIC LINK

Notation and Conversion of Picas and Points

Pierre Fournier le Jeune developed the first standardized system of typography measurement in the early 1700s. This system was further refined in the late 1770s by Françoise-Ambrose Didot with the addition of points as a unit of measure within picas. This measurement standard is still in use today.

- 1 point is 0.01383″, with 12 points in 1 pica.
- 1 pica is 0.166″, with 6 picas in approximately 1 inch.

Layout and design software programs note pica values as a whole number with a lowercase "p," which is followed by the points value. Using this notation style, a measurement of 4 picas and 5 points is presented as 4p5.

Convert each of the following notations to the equivalent measurement in inches on a separate piece of paper.

1. 3p6
2. 10p2
3. 2p3
4. 7p4
5. 11p1

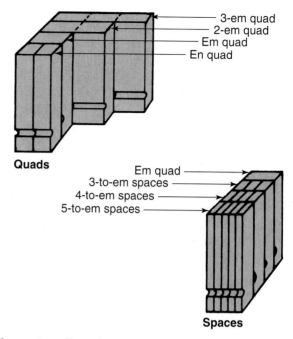

Figure 4-26. Foundry type used blocks called quads for spacing. Blocks narrower than the en quad were referred to as spaces.

has made it possible to change the set width of characters, and the words they make up.

When the character is electronically expanded or condensed, the height is not changed, **Figure 4-27.** For example, 12-point type with a 12-set would be

pi characters: In fonts for computer or phototypesetting, such symbols as stars, asterisks, arrows, percent signs, or check marks.

line length: The distance from the left to right sides of a line or body of copy, usually measured in picas.

composition depth: The space measuring from the beginning of a composition until the end of the composition.

point size: A vertical measurement used to identify or specify the size of a typeface.

x-height: The height of the lowercase "x." Also called *body height.*

text: Words, sentences, paragraphs. Also see *black letter* and *body type.*

body type: Type sizes that range from 4-point through 12-point that are used for setting straight matter.

display type: Type sizes above 12-point, used to emphasize the importance of a message and capture the reader's attention.

em quad: In foundry type, a nonprinting type block that is a square of the type size, typically used to indent the beginning of the paragraph.

en quad: In foundry type, a spacing element half an em quad in width, typically used to separate words.

Ems and Ens

The em is a unit of printer's measure equal to the height and width of the capital M in the given size of type. For example, in 12-point type, an em would measure 12 points wide and 12 points high; in 18-point type, an em would be 18 points wide and 18 points high. In foundry type, an *em quad* was used to indent the beginning of a paragraph. Sentences set in foundry type were separated by spaces that were half an em quad in width. That spacing element was called an *en quad*. See **Figure 4-26.**

Set Size

As you learned, point size refers to the height of the type character. *Set size*, or set width, refers to the width of a character. Electronic composition

THIS IS 12 POINT WITH 8 SET.

THIS IS 12 POINT WITH 12 SET.

THIS IS 12 POINT WITH 14 SET.

Figure 4-27. Set size is a modern term that refers to width of characters. Computerized typesetting allows letters to be condensed or expanded easily.

normal. If 12-point is programmed as "8-set," the type would be condensed. If 12-point is programmed for a "14-set," the type would be expanded. Although width of the character is changed, spacing between characters remains the same.

Letterspacing and Wordspacing

Letterspacing refers to a change of spacing between letters, while *wordspacing* involves varying the spacing between words, **Figure 4-28.** When carefully done, increasing or decreasing the space between letters and words can improve the legibility of type. It is also possible to increase or decrease the copy length to fit an allocated space by altering the letterspacing or the wordspacing.

If letterspacing other than normal is used, it is expressed as *loose set* or *tight set*. Spacing is expressed in units, with different composing systems varying in capability. Full units and half units are common. Loose set (plus units) and tight set (minus units) give the designer freedom to change the spacing to best fit the desired style or available space.

Character compensation is a method of tight-setting copy by electronically reducing very slightly the width of each character and space. This results in a reduction of white space between characters, allowing the copy to shrink and fit a smaller space.

	Tight:	Letterspace changes distance between characters.
	Normal:	Letterspace changes distance between characters.
A	**Loose:**	Letterspace changes distance between characters.
	Tight:	Wordspace changes distance or space between words.
	Normal:	Wordspace changes distance or space between words.
B	**Loose:**	Wordspace changes distance or space between words.

Figure 4-28. Letterspacing compared to wordspacing. A—Letterspacing alters amount of space between each character or letter. B—Wordspacing changes space between complete words.

Tracking

Tracking is a feature of computer typesetting programs that allows you to control the letter and word spacing together. The common choices for tracking are very tight, tight, normal, loose, and very loose. See **Figure 4-29.** Tracking makes it possible to delete and add more copy in a completed document.

Horizontal *scaling* of letters is often an option, as well. This is not a form of letter spacing, since the actual widths of the characters are changed, but the proportion of character to space is not.

Justifying Type

Letterspacing and wordspacing are used to *justify* lines of type so the lines are all equal in length. This results in blocks of copy with even left and right margins (like the paragraph you are reading right now). Justification can be done automatically with modern typesetting equipment.

Widow

A *widow* is a very short word, or part of a word, that forms the final line of a paragraph. The rest of the line is empty. There are various ways to avoid this undesirable amount of white space. The line can be lengthened, or the previous line can be shortened by adding or deleting words. Another way to fix widows is to change the letterspacing and wordspacing.

Kerning

Kerning is a typesetting technique that that involves closing up space between certain characters in the alphabet to improve the appearance and readability of the word. Kerning is normally done for letters that are top- or bottom-heavy.

For example, as shown in **Figure 4-30,** the capital letter "T" is top-heavy and the space between it and the next letter would appear to be too wide.

Letter Tracking Very Tight
Letter Tracking Tight
Letter Tracking Normal
Letter Tracking Loose
Letter Tracking Very Loose

Figure 4-29. Letter tracking allows letterspacing and wordspacing to be varied simultaneously.

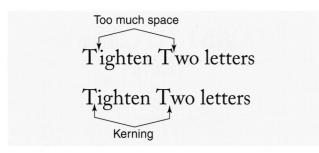

Figure 4-30. Kerning is similar to letterspacing, but changes only spaces between specific letters to improve appearance and readability.

Kerning moves the adjoining letter closer to the "T" for better appearance. **Figure 4-31** illustrates a number of letter combinations that can be improved in readability by using kerning.

LEGIBILITY FACTORS

Legibility, sometimes termed *readability*, is a measure of how difficult or easy it is to read printed matter. When selecting a typeface, legibility can be a very critical factor.

The major consideration when selecting a typeface is *purpose*. If the content of the copy is the main purpose, as in a textbook, legibility of the printed page should be the aim in selecting a typeface. When appearance is of major importance, as in designing an advertisement, then the aesthetic characteristics of the type must be given more attention.

The type you are now reading is what a printer calls *straight matter*. Straight matter is usually below

To	Wa	Va	PA	y.
To	Wa	Va	PA	y.
v.	p,	ay	VA	AT
v.	p,	ay	VA	AT
AW	LT	Yo	Fr	Fo
AW	LT	Yo	Fr	Fo

Figure 4-31. Examples of letter combinations before and after kerning. (Compugraphic)

14-point type. Display type is 14-point type or above and is used as headings and focal point material. Examples of products in which straight matter is used extensively are books, newspapers, magazines, and pamphlets.

Good legibility of the straight matter is the result of a proper combination of type, paper, and ink. It can make reading printed material less tiring to the eyes. Many printed pieces will have thousands of readers of varying ages and physical conditions. This makes good legibility a high priority.

Physical factors that contribute to legibility in the printed pages are: visibility, letter forms, definition, type size, line length, and leading.

Visibility

Visibility results from the contrast of the dark typeface against the light reflected by the paper. This is due to the paper's brightness, smoothness, and opacity, as well as the ink darkness and type style.

The term whiteness is *not* used because **brightness** is a property of both white and colored papers. The brightness of paper varies greatly.

set size: The width of a typeset character.

letterspacing: Changing the spacing between typeset letters, for better appearance or to fit copy in a given space.

wordspacing: Changing the spacing between typeset words, for better appearance or to fit copy in a given space.

loose set: Term describing wider than normal letterspacing.

tight set: Term describing narrower than normal letterspacing.

character compensation: A method of tight-setting copy by electronically reducing the width of each character and space very slightly.

tracking: A feature of computer typesetting programs that allows control of letter and word spacing together.

justify: To adjust letter-spacing and word-spacing so lines of type in a block are all equal in length, resulting in even left and right margins.

widow: A very short word, or part of a word, forming the final line of a paragraph.

kerning: A typesetting technique in which space between certain pairs of characters is tightened to improve appearance and readability.

legibility: A measure of how difficult or easy it is to read printed matter.

visibility: A legibility factor that results from the contrast of a dark typeface against the light reflected by the paper.

brightness: Often referred to as lightness luminosity, brightness can be defined as a value indicating how light or dark a color is.

The smoother the paper, the more light it reflects; therefore, paper *smoothness* also affects visibility of the images. A paper with high *opacity* does not allow print from the opposite side to show through.

The contrast of the printed material is affected by *ink darkness*. That term is used rather than *ink color* because both black and colored inks have degrees of darkness. Darkness depends on the ink's covering power; complete coverage hides the surface of the paper.

The type style is also a factor; the thicker the elements of the letter, the more ink will be deposited on the paper for contrast. As type size decreases, this factor gains in importance.

Definition

Definition refers to the sharpness or distinction of the printed image. Sharply defined letter forms are essential for easier reading. The relationship between the typeface and paper is very important. A small typeface requires a smoother paper for good definition. Top-quality pressmanship contributes to sharp images on the page.

Special consideration must be given when placing type over a screened background, because poor definition may result. See **Figure 4-32**. The same principle applies when the background for type is a halftone image, such as a photo of clouds or foliage.

Type Size

The legibility of copy, as it relates to type size, increases dramatically up to 10-point type. This increase flattens out with larger type sizes. Straight matter set in 10-point type is considered a norm for comfortable reading by young and middle-aged adults. **Figure 4-33** compares blocks of copy set in three different point sizes.

The x-height of the font also contributes to legibility. A large x-height would increase the size of the letters, and decrease the length of ascenders and descenders.

Line Length

Line length, also called *line width*, is the distance from the left to right sides of a line or body of copy. It is usually measured in picas.

Eye span is the width people can see with one fixation (sweep or adjustment) of the eye muscles. With body copy, the normal eye span is about one

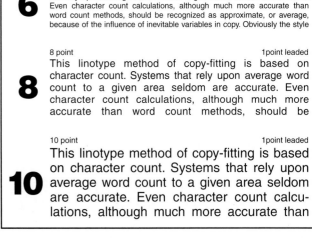

Figure 4-32. Selecting the proper typeface for placement on a screen pattern is very important to legibility.

---

6 6 point   1 point leaded
This linotype method of copy-fitting is based on character count. Systems that rely upon average word count to a given area seldom are accurate. Even character count calculations, although much more accurate than word count methods, should be recognized as approximate, or average, because of the influence of inevitable variables in copy. Obviously the style

8 8 point   1 point leaded
This linotype method of copy-fitting is based on character count. Systems that rely upon average word count to a given area seldom are accurate. Even character count calculations, although much more accurate than word count methods, should be

10 10 point   1 point leaded
This linotype method of copy-fitting is based on character count. Systems that rely upon average word count to a given area seldom are accurate. Even character count calculations, although much more accurate than

Figure 4-33. Smaller type sizes (those below 10-point) are difficult to read for the average person. The same copy is shown here in 6-point, 8-point, and 10-point type.

and one-half alphabets (about 40 characters). This width will vary with typeface classification and size, however.

When the width of the line corresponds to the eye span of the reader, the physical task of reading is made easier. Longer lengths require extra physical effort when reading (the more eye fixations per line, the more effort required). Horizontal travel of the eye is considered more tiring than moving vertically from one line to the next.

Line Spacing

Line spacing determines the distance separating each line of copy. It is measured in points from one line to the next. This spacing is also called leading (pronounced *ledding*), since lines of hand-set foundry type were separated by strips of lead-based type metal. See **Figure 4-34.**

When line spacing is equal to the size of the type, the type is said to be *set solid*. For example, if the typeface is 12-point and there is no extra line spacing, it would be set solid. On a specification, the size would be written 12/12 (in spoken form, "twelve on twelve").

When a customer or designer wants more space between lines of type, one or more points of leading would be added. For example, 10-point type might be used with 2 points of leading. The specifications would be written as 10/12 (ten on twelve). The typeface point size is normally written before the line spacing.

Many of today's typesetting systems have the capability of reducing spacing below the type size. This interline spacing is called **negative leading** or *minus leading*. The specifications might be written as 10/9 (ten on nine). This means the space between lines is to be reduced by one point.

Proper leading helps the reader's eye to readily separate one line from another. The white space gives the eye better access to the top portions of the lowercase letters. The tops of letters are the more unlike portions, and contribute most to word identity.

Leading also unites a line horizontally. Close word spacing will help to achieve unity in the line. Visibility is increased when extra leading is used on paper with low brightness. The extra leading lightens the tone of the page, and tends to make the type seem larger.

It is also possible to fit copy into a designated area by changing leading. By increasing leading, the copy will take up more space. Decreasing leading does just the opposite.

TYPEFACES FOR DISPLAY

Display type is intended to draw attention to a message. To emphasize the importance of the message and capture the reader's attention, display lines are larger in size. Generally, the smallest typeface size used in display is 14-point.

The position of the display line also gives it prominence. The words of that line supply the language and theme of the printed page or a block of copy. For this reason, it may be necessary to keep a complete thought in one line. This is shown in **Figure 4-35.**

Different weights of type can be used for emphasis by contrast. Different sizes show the relationship between principal and subordinate thoughts. Selection becomes very important to make sure that the typeface fits the intended use.

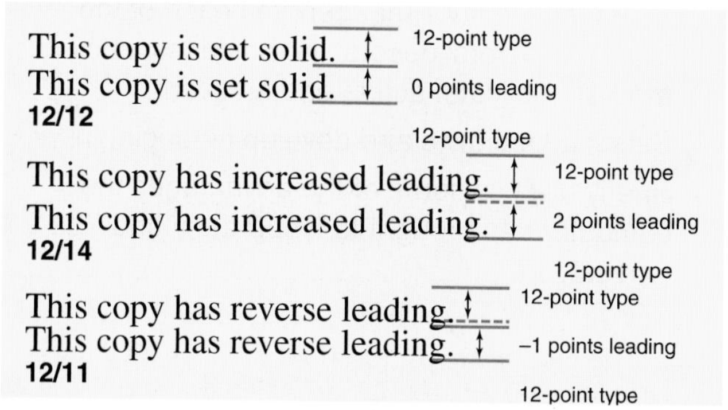

Figure 4-34. Linespacing, usually called leading, is the amount of vertical space separating one line of type from the next.

smoothness: Freedom from surface irregularities.

opacity: The quality of a paper that does not allow print from the opposite side to show through.

ink darkness: A factor that affects the contrast of printed materials.

definition: The sharpness or distinction of the printed image.

eye span: The width of body type a person can see with one fixation (sweep or adjustment) of the eye muscles.

negative leading: The practice of reducing spacing below the type size, resulting in lines that are set very close together vertically.

Towns getting together to fight against sprawl

By Marles Humphrey
Special to the Tribune

Residents of Crystal Lake and Lakewood long have been aware that urban sprawl threatens to blur the boundaries that preserve the two towns' distinctive characters.

Until recently, however, the two communites failed to engage in any cooperative efforts to address the issue.

That might change following a recent meeting between representatives of Crystal Lake and

Figure 4-35. Newspaper headlines are an example of display type in use. Note that the major thought, "Towns getting together," is on the first line. The subordinate or secondary thought is on the second line. This is commonly done in newspapers.

Summary

The style of the letter that makes up a word means very little to the person on the street, but the designer selects the type face design to match the thought within the message. Some letters are more massive while some give you the feeling of speed or direction. These letters have character and contribute to the pleasing design of the printed piece. Type style selection plays an important role in the design of a printed product

Review Questions

Please do not write in this text. Write your answers on a separate sheet of paper.

1. What are *characters*?
2. The art of expressing ideas through the selection of appropriate typefaces is called _____.
3. Define the term "body height."
4. An ascender extends _____ and a descender _____ the x-height letters.
5. What is the base line?
6. The finishing-off stroke at the top or bottom of a character is called a _____.
7. Who is credited with designing and cutting the first Roman typefaces?
8. Which designer first developed a typeface with letters designed solely for printing?
9. List and describe the seven basic typeface classifications.
10. Other than the use of serifs, what is the major difference between Roman and sans serif typefaces?
11. The _____ type style is based on the handwritten lettering of German scribes.
12. A typeface _____ consists of the variation of one style of type.
13. A type _____ consists of the letters, figures, and punctuation marks that are of one size and style.
14. *True or False?* The point size of a typeface is the same as its x-height.
15. Which is the larger unit of measure, the em or the en?
16. Changing the distance between words in a line of copy is called _____.
    A. letterspacing
    B. leading
    C. kerning
    D. wordspacing
17. _____ refers to changing the distance between some letters of a word to improve appearance of the type.
18. Name and describe at least three physical factors that affect legibility.
19. When the line spacing dimension is equal to the size of the typeface, the type is said to be _____.
    A. reverse leaded
    B. letter spaced
    C. set solid
    D. tight set
20. On a type specification, what does *10/12* mean?

Suggested Activities

1. Select a type style that denotes each of the following factors: decorative, boldness, ancient, modern, delicate, action and an event.
2. Select a type style and develop its origin.
3. Briefly discuss some of the advantages the computer has brought to typography and typesetting.

Related Web Links

I Love Typography

www.ilovetypography.com

Information and articles discussing different sorts of type.

A Brief History of Type

www.redsun.com/type/abriefhistoryoftype

Detailed information on the history of type.

Typotheque

www.typotheque.com

History and samples of fonts and typefaces.

CHAPTER 5

Design and Layout

Learning

After studying this chapter, you will be able to:

- Summarize the role of the graphic designer.
- Explain the elements of design.
- Explain the principles of design.
- Explain the elements of layout.
- Explain the factors that determine how a layout design is developed.
- Differentiate between the design methods used in layout.
- Recall the methods used in preparing illustrations for layout.

Important Terms

body type	lines
color	mass
color formation	primary colors
color wheel	principles of design
composition	proportion
comprehensive layout	refined layout
contrast	rhythm
copyfitting	rough layout
design	shapes
elements of design	specifications
elements of layout	texture
formal balance	thumbnail sketches
illustrations	unity
informal balance	white space
layout	

Figure 5-1. A graphic artist is commonly involved in several stages of production, from designing visual materials to performing layout tasks.

In graphic communications, *design* refers to the application of proper methods to create a product that is both artistic and functional. A successful design requires the skillful use of design elements and principles.

This chapter will cover the primary elements and principles of design and layout. Knowledge of common design techniques is critical in producing a layout and evaluating the visual quality of a product.

THE GRAPHIC DESIGNER

The role of the graphic designer varies greatly within the graphic communications industry. This is because of the overlapping duties that are performed throughout the process of design and layout. In some companies, the same artist who is responsible for producing artwork may also be required to perform certain layout tasks. See **Figure 5-1.** It is very important for the design person to work closely with the printer, since the planned design could cause problems when it arrives to be printed. Limitations relating to folding, press size, and paper capabilities could be potential problem areas.

Today's graphic designer might be an artist who prepares the artwork necessary for a portion of a product. Artwork could include freehand sketches, technical art, lettering, and calligraphy. In many cases, the graphic designer has little knowledge of the processes used in graphic reproduction. But the designer may also be responsible for pasting up camera-ready copy or producing a finished product with page layout software. This illustrates that the specific duties performed by design and layout personnel are very difficult to define clearly.

In the simplest of situations, a design artist would create the art images needed by the layout artist. Many companies, however, do not have the luxury of hiring people who only have specific design or layout skills. In many companies, the design artist translates ideas into art and is also involved in layout and production in various stages.

Once the layout design is approved by a client or outside source, the elements are usually gathered and assembled by the same person who created the design. The design artist must initially express a visual idea. The idea becomes the foundation of the layout and is then developed into the final product.

Planning and organizing the design process is essential to having an efficient operation. A small printing facility, from a financial standpoint, often cannot afford to employ one person to perform design tasks. Therefore, designing may be left to the plant personnel, who may have very little design knowledge but are required to devise and complete layouts for production.

A knowledge of the fundamentals of design is required for both the design artist and the layout artist. The elements and principles of design are an accumulation of many factors that help solve the problem of producing an image that is both attractive and practical.

design: The application of proper methods to produce a product that is both artistic and functional.

CAREER LINK

Graphic Designer

Designs of printed products are created by graphic designers. Graphic designers use visual elements to get a message across. Their designs may be used in several different areas, such as book layouts, brochures, posters, annual reports, packaging or Web sites.

A company or client will give the graphic designer an idea of the message that must be conveyed. Once the graphic designer has this information and understands the needs of the client, he or she works to develop the visual elements that will convey the message. Graphic designers begin to develop their designs by creating rough sketches of their ideas, either by hand or by using appropriate software. In some cases, graphic designers also help printers by choosing materials such as the proper substrate. Final design copy is approved by the client often working with the printer.

While many graphic designers are employed by agencies, publishers, or printers, some are self-employed. However, all graphic designers must have similar education and training to assist them in skill development. Graphic designers use a variety of computer design programs. They must also be familiar with applications of color, layout, type, photography, and printing processes. Graphic designers must have and associate or bachelor's degree to be competitive in the job market. In addition, graphic designers must be skilled at planning, organizing, analyzing, and learning to use the most up-to-date technology.

"Graphic communications remains a strong and viable field today and will continue far into the future."

Mike Chiricuzio
Arizona State University

ELEMENTS OF DESIGN

Design involves the selection and arrangement of visual images to make a pleasing presentation. The text and illustrations used in a design will have a tremendous impact on the viewer; therefore, it is essential to develop a strong layout of visual materials.

A successful graphic designer must apply the fundamental elements of design. The basic *elements of design* are lines, shapes, mass, texture, and color.

Lines

Lines are design elements that form the shapes of an image. Lines can be used to give the printed image a personality. Lines can be loose and free or they can be straight and sharp. See **Figure 5-2.** The repetition of lines creates patterns and adds emotional impact to the visual image.

Lines can also be used as a form of universal language in communication. In other words, lines can be designed to create a message. Arrows and other symbols are examples of lines used as a visual form. See **Figure 5-3.**

Lines are often used to enhance or change the visual quality of styles of type. They can appear very harsh or very delicate. Lines play a highly important role in designing a layout that communicates effectively.

Figure 5-2. Lines can be used to denote a specific meaning. Curved, loose lines imply a free spirit. Lines drawn straight imply a more straightforward or disciplined theme.

Each of the three basic shapes is associated with a psychological meaning, as shown in **Figure 5-5.** The visual attitude portrayed by the triangle is one of conflict or action. The square projects an attitude of honesty or equality, while the circle conveys a feeling of protection or infinity.

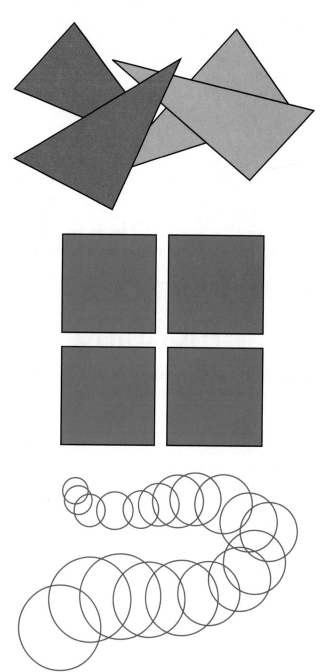

Figure 5-5. Different shapes are associated with psychological meanings. Squares show organization, while triangles display aggression and circles indicate motion.

elements of design: Lines, shapes, mass, texture, and color.

lines: Design elements that form the shapes of an image.

shapes: Elementary forms that define specific areas of space.

Figure 5-3. Lines can deliver a visual message when they are drawn as arrows or other symbols.

Shapes

Shapes are elementary forms that define specific areas of space. In many cases, a shape is defined by a line. The three basic shapes are the square, circle, and triangle. See **Figure 5-4.**

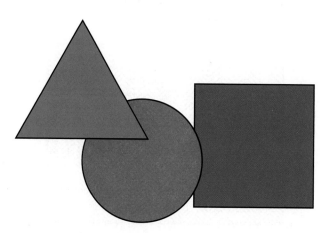

Figure 5-4. The three basic design shapes are the square, circle, and triangle.

Mass

Mass is a measure of volume that adds definition to shapes in a visual presentation. The mass or solid portion of the shape provides a visual relationship with the other elements. See **Figure 5-6.**

Different shapes of varying intensities, known as weights, can be used to emphasize or de-emphasize styles of type. See **Figure 5-7.** Unique shapes are made by combining the three basic shapes. See **Figure 5-8.**

Figure 5-8. A combination of shapes creates the physical form of an image.

Figure 5-6. Mass adds volume or weight to a shape by emphasizing part of an image.

Texture

The *texture* of a visual image is a projection of emphasized structure or weight. When gauging the texture of an object, the first inclination is to touch the surface. In graphic communications, texture is usually visual; there is no feeling gained through the sense of touch. See **Figure 5-9.**

Texture appears as a design element when the visual images reflect the meaning of lines, as shown in **Figure 5-10,** or when mass forms images that reflect a special technique. See **Figure 5-11.**

Texture varies and depends on the structure and weight of the individual letters, the amount of space between lines, and the amount of mass in a certain space. Actual texture for a printed image can be produced by embossing, which presses a shape or irregular surface into the substrate.

Color

Color is an important element to be considered when planning or designing a printed product. Color can draw attention and produce a strong emotional and psychological impact. Different colors have

Figure 5-7. Visual emphasis can be achieved by varying the weights or sizes of type or other images.

Figure 5-9. Lines can provide surface variation to give texture to an image.

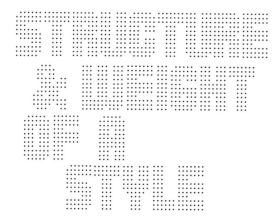

Figure 5-10. Texture of type can be a design element.

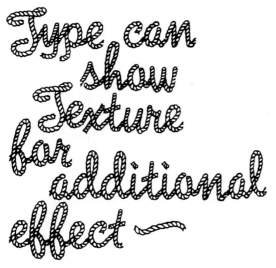

Figure 5-11. Lines added to type can provide texture. Here, they create a unique visual effect resembling rope.

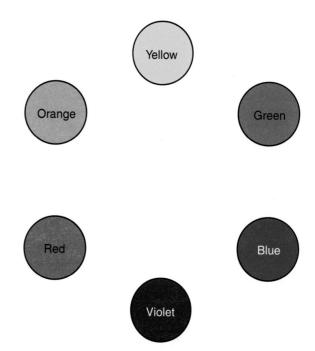

Figure 5-12. A color wheel is an arrangement of colors based on three primary colors: red, yellow, and blue.

The wheel is based on three *primary colors*, from which all other colors can be made. The primary colors are red, yellow, and blue. Mixing any two will produce a secondary color. The secondary colors are green, orange, and violet.

The additive and subtractive systems of *color formation* use different sets of primary colors to create secondary colors. The additive primaries are red, green, and blue. The subtractive primaries are cyan, magenta, and yellow. Color formation is covered in detail in Chapter 9.

The colors that are positioned across from each other on the color wheel are known as complementary colors. Red and green, orange and blue, and yellow and violet are complementary colors. See **Figure 5-13.**

Different shades and tints of a color, known as values, may be obtained by adding white or black to

traditional and symbolic meanings. A basic understanding of color is essential to creating a good design.

Color should be used to add interest and variety to a design. A small amount of color can heighten the visual quality of a page.

Color moods

Different colors project different moods. Yellow, orange, and red are warm colors and often denote aggression, excitement, and danger. Red is considered the most dramatic of these three. Blue, green, and violet are cool colors and are associated with nature and passiveness.

Color wheel

A *color wheel* is a visual tool that illustrates the basics of color. It is an arrangement of colors that provides a means of identifying colors in a consistent manner. See **Figure 5-12.**

mass: A measure of volume that adds definition to shapes in a visual presentation.

texture: A projection of emphasized structure or weight.

color: A visual sensation produced in the brain when the eye views various wavelengths of light.

color wheel: A visual tool that illustrates the basics of color.

primary colors: Colors that can be used to generate secondary colors.

color formation: Additive and subtractive systems that create secondary colors from primary colors.

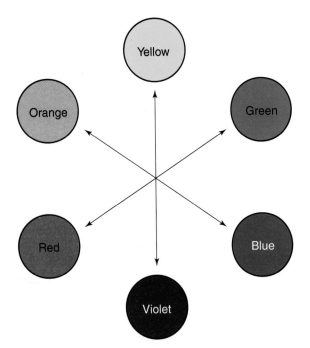

Figure 5-13. Complementary colors are the colors that are positioned across from each other on a color wheel.

a color. A color can also take on a different intensity when it is mixed with its complement. For example, when green is mixed with red, it will probably produce a brown. Striking color effects may be produced not only by mixing colors, but also by arranging colors in a layout so they have a direct effect on each other. Chapter 9 includes a detailed description of color theory and how it relates to graphic communications.

PRINCIPLES OF DESIGN

In the process of designing a printed product, many different ideas are generated through the use of design elements. To ensure the images have a pleasing relationship, design principles must be applied to sort out or select the right ideas.

The basic *principles of design* are balance, contrast, unity, rhythm, and proportion. These principles are used by the design artist to create an image that is both visually pleasing and functional.

Balance

Balance describes the even distribution of images to create a pleasing visual effect. Balance has one of the most important psychological influences on human perception. Consciously and unconsciously, people have a basic need for balance.

Balance must be maintained to ensure no one primary element dominates the layout. This principle can be used to draw attention and keep the reader's attention from jumping from one element to another.

This principle can be illustrated by the placement of letters on a scale, as shown in **Figure 5-14.** Visually, a judgment can be made by the value of each image. The type of balance in Figure 5-14A is symmetrical and is called formal. The type of balance in Figure 5-14B is asymmetrical and is called informal.

Formal balance is achieved when all of the elements on a page are of equal weight and are positioned symmetrically. *Informal balance* may be achieved by changing the value, size, or location of elements on a page. The use of various colors and color intensities can also create informal balance. For example, two squares of equal size but different color values, such as pink and dark red, will appear to be unequal in size when placed side by side.

Balance is a guiding principle of design. The layout should be considered as a whole when positioning the elements. See **Figure 5-15.**

Contrast

Contrast is the variation of elements in a printed product. When used, contrast gives meaning to a design. Lines drawn thick might have little meaning by themselves. Adding thin lines, however, can enhance the design and eliminate monotony. See **Figure 5-16.**

Styles of type can be contrasted to produce greater legibility and design variation. Some useful contrasts are round and straight, ornate and plain,

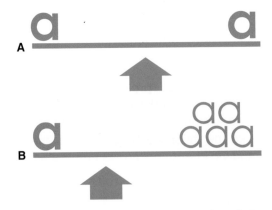

Figure 5-14. Balance in an image is produced through an equal positioning of elements. A—Letters placed symmetrically to achieve formal balance. B—Letters placed in uneven quantities to represent informal balance.

Figure 5-15. Balance in a design can vary depending on the desired visual effect. An unbalanced layout can be used to attract attention or imply leisure.

Figure 5-16. A variation of mass or other elements adds contrast and attracts attention to an area of an image.

and broad and narrow. An example of contrast is shown in **Figure 5-17**. A tall tree looks much taller if it is standing on a flat plane.

The relationship between an unprinted area and a printed area of an image can also be enhanced through the use of contrast. White space, when used effectively, creates contrast in an image. See **Figure 5-18**.

Figure 5-17. Using contrast emphasizes one element in relation to another. A tree appears taller when it is placed on a flat plane.

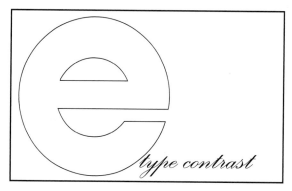

Figure 5-18. The use of white space creates contrast between the printed and unprinted areas of an image.

Care must be taken when combining contrasting elements so the uniform effect of the total design remains unaffected. A page of many contrasting designs might create confusion. See **Figure 5-19**.

Unity

Unity is the proper balance of all elements in an image so a pleasing whole results and the image is viewed as one piece. Every element must be

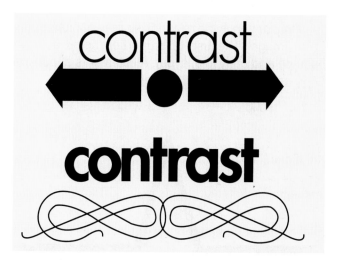

Figure 5-19. Too much contrast between elements can cause confusion.

principles of design: Balance, contrast, unity, rhythm, and proportion.

formal balance: A design principle that is achieved when the elements of a design are of equal weight and are positioned symmetrically.

informal balance: A design principle that is achieved by changing the value, size, or location of elements in a design.

contrast: The variation of elements in a printed product.

unity: The proper balance of all elements in an image so a pleasing whole results and the image is viewed as one piece.

in proper position to create a harmonious image. The characteristics of a design can be moved and manipulated to create an interesting and functional combination of elements.

Choosing type styles is also important to achieving unity. See **Figure 5-20.** A unified design is the result of viewing the layout as a whole and not as separate elements. This principle is also called harmony. See **Figure 5-21.**

Rhythm

The movement of a reader's eye is often determined by the shapes used in the image. The square reflects horizontal and vertical movement. The triangle reflects diagonal movement, and the circle reflects a curve.

Rhythm in a design results when the elements have been properly used to create visual movement and direction. See **Figure 5-22.** Rhythm can also be achieved through the use of a pattern or repetition. Patterns can be used in contrast with an element to create an effective design. See **Figure 5-23.**

Proportion

Proportion is the relationship between elements in an image. The use of proportion helps achieve balance and unity in a layout. All elements should be in proportion to each other. See **Figure 5-24.**

Figure 5-21. Unity results when all of the elements in an image are arranged as a whole.

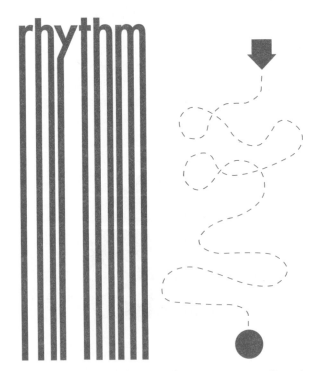

Figure 5-22. Images that imply movement or direction give rhythm to a design.

Figure 5-20. A type style that corresponds visually to the subject reflects unity in the design. Small dots forming the type represent stars in the sky.

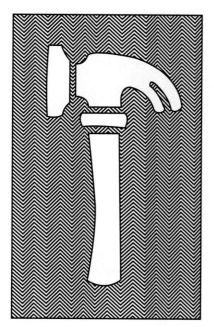

Figure 5-23. A balanced pattern of lines provides rhythm by contrasting with the rest of the image.

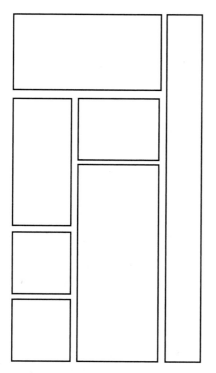

Figure 5-24. Elements arranged in proportion to each other produce a unified design.

When using different type styles, it is important that they are in proportion to the other elements on the page. See **Figure 5-25.** Using proportion is a means of developing an aesthetically pleasing relationship between each of the elements in the layout.

THINK **G**REEN
Reduction

Several companies in the printing industry are taking steps toward going green. Companies must determine how much waste they produce, as well as how much carbon dioxide is emitted due to the printing process. One of the first steps a company can take is to work toward reducing the amount of paper, water, and energy it uses in production. A company working to reduce waste is more vigilant, and the status of everything from energy use to VOC reduction will be accounted for. As a result, studies have shown reductions of this nature have had the greatest impact on the environment so far. For more information, go to www.epa.gov.

A basic knowledge of design elements and principles is key to understanding the guidelines used in layout. The finished layout must exhibit sound principles of design. The process of preparing a layout sheet is often performed by the same artist responsible for the design.

ELEMENTS OF LAYOUT

Layout is the arrangement of printing elements on a monitor screen or a layout sheet. The paste-up version of the base sheet, or mechanical, is made up of the elements ready for reproduction. Planning a layout involves choosing elements that best represent the design. The *elements of layout* are body type, display type, illustrations, and white space.

rhythm: The use of elements in an image to create visual movement and direction.

proportion: The relationship between elements in an image.

layout: The sketch or plan for the finished page followed by a paste-up artist when assembling a mechanical.

elements of layout: Body type, display type, illustrations, and white space.

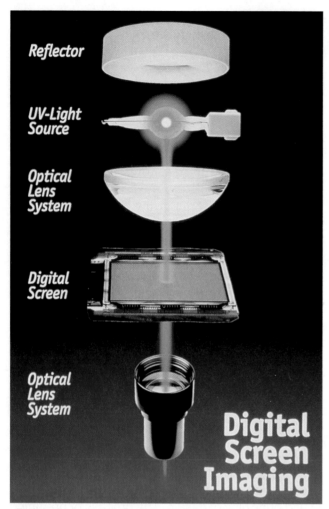

Figure 5-25. The size of type used in a design should be in proportion to the other elements.

The arrangement of elements in a layout must be pleasing to the eye and easy to read. The layout artist or designer is responsible for assembling the elements to make a *composition*. The layout artist plays a very important role in planning each job.

If the same elements were given to several artists, it is very probable that different layouts would be submitted. If each layout applies valid principles of design, it might be impossible to say one is better than another. Layouts may be judged differently by different people.

The major objective of the layout is that the printed material must be clearly seen and read. The layout artist must consider each element independently and determine how each one relates to the complete product.

Body Type

Body type is the printed type that makes up the text in a layout. Body type must be chosen to reflect the intent of the message. The text must be clearly

Figure 5-26. Selecting a proper typeface and type size for the layout is an important part of the design process.

legible and must relate to the topic. Typically, a topic aimed at a contemporary audience would use a modern typeface. See **Figure 5-26.** The placement of type requires proper spacing. White space can be just as important as the type itself.

Usually, the body type itself is not the focal point of the layout. The text will contain a message that expands on the other elements. All of the elements, including type, are positioned in a logical progression of importance to meet the layout objectives. Some layout elements will be primary, while others become secondary, according to the objectives of the layout.

Display Type

Display type is the type that conveys the main message of the layout. It is intended to draw attention. Newspaper and magazine headlines are typical examples of display type. See **Figure 5-27.** The display line is key to the success of a message. If the display type creates interest, the reader will proceed to the body.

The display type in an advertisement leads the reader to other information. After reading the display material, the person must be satisfied or directed to continue reading the text.

The style of display type is very important because it must correspond to the visual message. Some type styles can be very dramatic, as illustrated in **Figure 5-28.** In such cases, the topic and type style must be compatible.

Some type styles are directional and lead the eye of the reader. Sometimes, the layout designer

Figure 5-27. Headlines are a form of display type. They should draw attention and create interest in the image.

Figure 5-28. The style of display type used should reflect the message of the printed piece.

organizes the display line for an ad using hand-lettered display type.

The entire layout must be looked at when choosing a display typeface. The display line must

be distinctive and appropriate. To properly select a typeface, the job objective must be fully understood by the layout artist.

Illustrations

The *illustrations* in a layout include the ornamentation, photographs, and artwork, such as line art. Illustrations are common in most printed materials. For example, display ads typically include illustrations of the product.

The message provided by an illustration can be very revealing. See **Figure 5-29.** The old saying, "A picture is worth a thousand words," applies to many printed materials. Pictorial images are a very strong way of conveying a message. In some cases, an illustration may convey the message by itself. See **Figure 5-30.** Illustrations add another dimension to the layout; they can increase understanding of the product, as well as interest in the product.

White Space

White space includes areas of the layout that are void of printed images. Filling up the entire design space will not usually produce good results. The utilization of white space can add to the visual quality of a layout.

The distance between elements can be very valuable when white space is used according to sound design principles. It provides a brief period for absorbing the printed matter.

If used excessively, white space can be disorienting. When ideas are too greatly separated, flow and meaning can be lost. White space is very important and must be used properly to create flow, unity, and organization for the reader.

DEVELOPING A LAYOUT

There are a number of factors to consider in developing a layout. Five areas the layout artist

composition: The inputting or setting of type.

body type: Type sizes that range from 4-point though 12-point that are used for setting straight matter.

illustrations: The elements of layout that include the ornamentation, photographs, and artwork, such as line art.

white space: The areas of the layout that are void of printed images.

Specialties
of the house

Figure 5-29. A meaningful illustration can be used to convey a strong message.

Figure 5-30. Illustrations used in road signs can deliver a message with a minimum use of words.

must address are the objective of the project, the message the product will send, the style and format to be used, the layout requirements for production, and printing requirements. Each factor contributes to making decisions that will influence production of the final product.

Project Objective

The project objective is a statement that describes the intent or purpose of an identifiable end product. The objective outlines the goal of the layout artist. For example, an objective might state that the final printed piece should inform the reader, through text and illustrated material, how a piece of equipment will help in a specific production situation.

The objective describes what the information on the printed page is intended to do. Knowing the purpose helps the layout artist determine which text and illustrations will be best for the job.

Product Message

The message or visual effect delivered by a printed image helps determine how the layout will be planned. Identifying the audience gives direction to the layout artist. For example, one ad might be designed for young people, while another might be aimed at senior citizens. The design of each ad should be unique and must reflect the intent of the printed piece.

Design of the end product also determines the tone, or mood, of the message. If a lighthearted or humorous mood is intended, a dramatic photograph might not achieve the desired effect. All of the elements should reflect the message of the end product.

Style and Format

Style includes the text type, display type, and illustrations of the design. Some printed pieces will require a set style, while others do not. For instance, the style used in this textbook is quite different from the styles used in advertisements. The designer must choose the elements that will work best.

Deciding how to organize the format of the printed piece is of primary importance. The format is the style, size, spacing, group of pages, margins, and all printing requirements for a printed job. Will a single sheet carry the message, or will a booklet do a better job? The format will also be determined by its intended use. For example, if the printed piece is to be posted, it should not be printed on both sides.

Layout Requirements

The different methods of layout and the schedule to complete the job must be considered in planning a layout. A layout may need to be developed as a sketch, a rough, or a comprehensive. It may be necessary to perform all three.

A sketch is an idea in pictorial form with little detail. Sketches are often helpful because they provide a picture indicating possible placement of the elements. A rough layout is more illustrative of the final product; it provides the style of the type as well as the position of the elements. A comprehensive layout is the third and final method of layout. It is the presentation of what the finished product will indeed look like. See **Figure 5-31.** When planning a layout, the artist should decide which methods will be necessary to reach the final product in a timely manner.

An estimate of the time it will take to complete the job is essential from a planning standpoint. Most printed pieces are produced to meet a deadline and must be delivered by a specified date. The planner must decide whether the job can be completed in the time allowed.

Printing Requirements

The printing process that follows production has a strong influence on how a layout is developed. The size of the product, the quantity to be printed, paper requirements, color use, and operations following the printing must all be considered.

The finished dimension of a printed piece must be determined before beginning layout. The finished size will have a bearing on every production step. One important concern is the size of the press required to run the job. The finished size also determines the size of the paper to be used in printing.

The number of pages to be printed and the number of copies required are also factors to consider because they will help determine the printing requirements. Deciding the most economical way of printing the job is essential. The designer or editor must estimate the approximate number of pages to be printed so final plans for printing can be made.

Printing requirements include the kind of stock or paper to be used. The necessary stock must be available at the designated time for printing. A custom stock may need to be ordered and may require additional time. Other considerations in ordering stock are the size of the order, paper weight or thickness, and opacity.

Multicolor printing is another factor to consider when planning a layout. Different jobs require different uses of color. Printing a one-color or black-and-white job requires different layout methods from a two-color or four-color job. The layout artist must decide whether to use color when planning the layout.

Once the job is printed, further finishing operations might be required, such as trimming the job to the final size. Other finishing operations may include folding, scoring, creasing, varnishing, and binding. Knowing the operations that will be required after printing is important in planning the job.

LAYOUT METHODS

Choosing the right method to develop a layout can be very difficult and requires careful planning and thinking by the layout artist. The design methods used in layout are thumbnail sketches, the rough layout, and the comprehensive layout. Much of the decision depends on the factors that have already been discussed. The size of the job, the objective, and use of color are all important considerations. The layout artist must have a vision of how to arrive at the final product.

The layout can make or break the appearance of the final product. Many times, a number of layout ideas are discarded before one is chosen. Each method must be carefully analyzed to produce a strong, functional layout.

Thumbnail Sketches

Thumbnail sketches are simple, rapidly drawn designs for a layout. See **Figure 5-32.** Different approaches can be taken in drawing sketches. Sketching is a means of testing the visual appeal of a printed piece.

A   **B**   **C**

Figure 5-31. Different methods of layout. A—A sketch. B—A rough layout. C—A comprehensive layout.

thumbnail sketches: Simple, rapidly drawn designs of a layout.

Figure 5-32. Sketches showing the general relationship of elements provide a basis for the design.

The size of a thumbnail is not important. The sketch is generally smaller than the size of the printed product. The first sketch might not be the design selected, but each one will help the artist visualize the end product.

A soft pencil or felt-tip pen is typically used to draw thumbnail sketches. Even though the size is not important, the general proportion is required to indicate image relationships. The purpose of the sketch is to evaluate the weight of each element. The sketch shows the basic shape and tone of the total piece.

Rough Layout

A *rough layout* is a redrawn version of a thumbnail sketch, **Figure 5-33.** Once a specific thumbnail has been selected, refinement is necessary. The elements in a rough layout, or dummy, offer a truer visual meaning. In many cases, the rough layout must be checked and approved by the designer, client, and sometimes the printer.

The display lines and illustrations of a rough layout are very similar to the elements of the final product. The text material is located in a greeked, or illegible, block or whatever form it will take in the finished product. The rough layout has a closer resemblance to the intended printed piece than the thumbnail sketches.

Sometimes, a refined layout may be made, **Figure 5-34.** Since the *refined layout* is closer to the final layout, it can be used as the final layout when time is a major factor. Special notations for type size, type style, or color can be made on a tissue overlay or on the layout.

Comprehensive Layout

A *comprehensive layout* shows how the printed piece will look when finished. The layout artist is making a close version of the finished product; therefore, exact detail is essential. See **Figure 5-35.**

Figure 5-33. A rough layout is a sketched version of the final product.

Figure 5-34. A refined layout is sometimes made before doing a comprehensive layout.

Figure 5-35. A comprehensive layout is a detailed representation of the final layout.

The body type is usually ruled in and the display type is drawn as it will appear in the finished piece. Any art sketched previously now has a photograph or accurate line art in its place. Special effects become a part of the comprehensive layout, and colors can also be added.

Instructions, specifications, and notations are not placed directly on the comprehensive. A common practice is to attach an overlay sheet with tape at the top of the base sheet. The overlay sheet is usually translucent tissue paper so the comprehensive layout can be easily viewed along with any notations. The information is written on the tissue and serves as the specifications for the final preparation of art and copy.

The comprehensive layout should not be confused with the mechanical. The mechanical is pasted up and completed in the next step of production. The mechanical is the final stage of layout. It includes the body text and any other camera-ready images that are converted to film by a process camera or other means.

SPECIFICATIONS

Specifications, or specs, provide the information relating to type style, type size, line or column width, color use, page organization, and other facts pertaining to a printed product. Specifications are the overall guidelines used in layout.

Manuscripts are commonly marked with specifications identifying the typeface and type size to be used. The specifications are used to convert the original copy on the manuscript to the text in the final layout. See **Figure 5-36.**

Our teaching staff is creative and well qualified. Our focus is geared to the family and the role of the individual. Classes are offered for every age group.

Join our staff in discovering your many talents which can help your family better understand itself. Explore careers, interests, hobbies. Exercise in our gymnasium and attend the family seminars.

Daily hours are from 9:00 to 5:00 P.M. Evening sessions start at 7:00 P.M. and go until 10:00 P.M.

Big School
41 South Street
Haurent, MA
999-9000

A

Our teaching staff is creative and well qualified. Our focus is geared to the family and the role of the individual. Classes are offered for every age group.

Join our staff in discovering your many talents which can help your family better understand itself. Explore careers, interests, hobbies. Exercise in our gymnasium and attend the family seminars.

Daily hours are from 9:00 to 5:00 P.M. Evening sessions start at 7:00 P.M. and go until 10:00 P.M.

Big School
41 South Street
Haurent, MA
999-9000

B

Figure 5-36. Specifications identify the styles and sizes of type to be used in a design. A—The manuscript is marked to indicate type specs. B—Text in the final layout is arranged according to the specs.

rough layout: A redrawn version of a thumbnail sketch, closely resembling the final layout.

refined layout: Layout in which the positioning of the images represents the exact location of all images without having the composed material in place.

comprehensive layout: A detailed layout showing how the printed piece will look when finished.

specifications: The overall layout guidelines relating to such information as type style, type size, line width, color use, and page organization.

A spec sheet, sometimes called a style sheet, lists the specifications used in production. See **Figure 5-37.** The spec sheet is created before beginning a job. It contains information on type styles and sizes, art to be used, and color usage.

Specifications are also used in printing, binding, and finishing. A printing spec sheet may list information on the type of paper to be used, color specifications, and other requirements. See **Figure 5-38.**

COPYFITTING

Copyfitting is the process of fitting together copy and illustrations in a specific amount of space. It can be done by altering type size, leading, line length, or letterspacing. The layout planner or artist is heavily involved in copyfitting during various stages of production. If the amount of copy is greater than the space allocated, the total design is affected.

Copyfitting also involves estimating the amount of space needed for a certain amount of text. The amount of space needed must be known by the layout artist to design a comprehensive layout.

In desktop publishing, copyfitting is commonly completed for layout on a computer screen. See **Figure 5-39.** A desktop publishing system can be used to copyfit text and illustrations, move copy, draw line art, and finalize layout.

Specifications for *Graphic Communications*

Trim: 8-1/2 x 10-7/8
Gutter: 5p
Bottom Margin: 3p9
Thumb Margin: 4p
Top Margin: 3p to the base of the running head, 5p to the top of the first line of text
2 column format: 20p x 1p6 x 20p3

4-color process

Chapters are always to start a new left.

Typefaces used: Palm Springs, Helvetica (all in roman, bold, italic and/or bold italic).

Running Heads: Left hand pages, set folio flush left on left hand margin of left column. Folio sets in 9pt Helvetica medium. On 1p indent set Book Title. Book Title sets in 9pt Palatino. Right hand pages, set folio flush right on right hand margin of right column. Folio sets in 9pt Helvetica Medium. On 3p indent from right margin set Chapter Number and Title. Chapter number and title sets in 9pt Palatino, flush right on indent. Allow an em space between the number and title.

Chapters: Are to start a new left. The chapter opener takes a drop folio, 10pt Helvetica Bold, prints black, flush left on the outside margin, 2p below the normal text bed.

Chapter Opening Graphic: Photo falls in first column. Photo always runs vertically.

Chapter number: 240pt Commercial Script BT Regular, 100% Cyan. "C" in "Chapter" set as 240 point Commercial Script BT Regular, 100% Magenta, 100% Yellow. Rest of "Chapter" set as 60pt Copperplate Gothic BT Regular, all caps, 100% black.

Chapter title: 30pt Helvetica Narrow set flush left below chapter number.

Objectives: Heading sets Helvetica Bold Narrow, 14/16, p4 after.

Figure 5-37. A spec sheet lists type styles and sizes, along with information on art, the use of color, page margins, and other specific information needed to produce the printed piece.

PRINTING SPECIFICATIONS

Company _____   Contact _____
Address _____
Phone _____   Fax _____
Project Title _____
Description _____
_____

☐ Early budget   ☐ Late budget   ☐ Based on specs   ☐ Based on art

Date _____
Date prices required _____
Release date _____
Delivery date _____

Quantities _____
_____

Page count	☐ Plus cover, no. pages ___ ☐ Self cover	Proofs: ☐ Blueline ☐ Colorkey ☐ Matchprint ☐ Other ☐ Press check	No: ___

☐ Overs up to ____%
☐ Unders up to ____%
☐ No overs/unders

Flat size	Finished size

☐ New project
☐ Exact reprint
☐ Reprint w/changes

Paper

Form	# of Pages	Color	Basis Weight	Specify Cover or Book Weight	Name or Grade	Finish
Single Sheet						
Cover						
Fly						
Text 1						
Text 2						

Preparation

Electronic Prepress Output
Type of output _____
Software used and version no. _____
Fonts: _____

Disk Format   ☐ Single pages   ☐ Readers spreads   ☐ Printers spreads

Customer Furnish
☐ Complete camera ready art
☐ Windows on art for images
☐ Flapped for colors and screens
☐ Key lined for color break
☐ Masks furnished for outlines
☐ Composite negs. in ___ pg spreads

Maps charts   No. ___ Size ___   No. ___ Size ___   No. ___ Size ___

Line strip-ins   No. ___ Size ___   No. ___ Size ___   No. ___ Size ___

Half-tones   No. ___ Size ___ Outline ___   No. ___ Size ___ Outline ___   No. ___ Size ___ Outline ___

Duo-tones   No. ___ Size ___ Outline ___   No. ___ Size ___ Outline ___   No. ___ Size ___ Outline ___

Screens   No. ___ Size ___   No. ___ Size ___   No. ___ Size ___

Reverses   No. ___ Size ___   No. ___ Size ___   No. ___ Size ___

Color Seps.

No.	Original size	Finished size	Trans.	Refl	Scan	Cam.	Outline	Crossover	Scan to file	Lo/Hi res.
No. ___	___ x ___	To ___ x ___	☐	☐	☐	☐	☐	☐	☐	☐
No. ___	___ x ___	To ___ x ___	☐	☐	☐	☐	☐	☐	☐	☐
No. ___	___ x ___	To ___ x ___	☐	☐	☐	☐	☐	☐	☐	☐
No. ___	___ x ___	To ___ x ___	☐	☐	☐	☐	☐	☐	☐	☐
No. ___	___ x ___	To ___ x ___	☐	☐	☐	☐	☐	☐	☐	☐

Press

Cover _____ out _____ in _____ % Coverage _____	Fly _____ Side 1 _____ Side 2 _____ % Coverage _____	Text 1 _____ Side 1 _____ Side 2 _____ % Coverage _____	Text 1 _____ Side 1 _____ Side 2 _____ % Coverage _____
Varnish ☐dry ☐wet ☐spot ☐overall	Varnish ☐dry ☐wet ☐spot ☐overall	Varnish ☐dry ☐wet ☐spot ☐overall	Varnish ☐dry ☐wet ☐spot ☐overall
Solids ☐yes ☐no	Solids ☐yes ☐no	Solids ☐yes ☐no	Solids ☐yes ☐no
Bleeds ☐yes ☐no	Bleeds ☐yes ☐no	Bleeds ☐yes ☐no	Bleeds ☐yes ☐no
Coating ☐aqueous	Coating ☐aqueous	Coating ☐aqueous	Coating ☐aqueous
Coating ☐UV ☐spot ☐overall	Coating ☐UV ☐spot ☐overall	Coating ☐UV ☐spot ☐overall	Coating ☐UV ☐spot ☐overall

Bindery

☐ Soft fold   Fold to ___ x ___   No. of folds ___   ☐ Letter fold   ☐ Accordion   ☐ Round corner   ☐ Remoistenable gum
☐ Saddle stitch   ☐ Double saddle   ☐ Side stitch & tape   ☐ Perfect bind   ☐ Case bind   ☐ Spiral   ☐ Wire-O   ☐ GBC
☐ Perforate _____   ☐ Die Cut _____   ☐ Collate
☐ Drill _____   ☐ Emboss/size _____   ☐ Shrink wrap _____
☐ Score _____   ☐ Deboss/size _____   ☐ Mail   ☐ Label   ☐ Ink jet
☐ Glue pockets/size _____ No. _____   ☐ Foil stamp/size _____   ☐ Cust. supplies: _____
☐ Pockets no glue/size _____ No. _____   ☐ Trim only _____ x _____   ☐ Other

Shipping

Special packing _____
_____
(Bulk pack in cartons unless otherwise specified.)
No. of samples required _____   Delivery date _____
F.O.B. point _____   No. of local deliveries _____

Pricing

Vendor _____   Contact _____   Phone _____
Quantity   Estimated price
_____
_____

Figure 5-38. A printing spec sheet provides the guidelines used in printing a finished product.

copyfitting: The process of fitting together copy and illustrations in a specific amount of space.

Figure 5-39. Copyfitting for layout is commonly performed electronically using a desktop publishing system.

PROCESSING ILLUSTRATIONS

Photographs and pieces of line art used in layout are commonly edited or sized for reproduction by the layout artist by using computer applications. The principles used in design and layout must be followed when processing illustrations. The layout artist must make sure the illustrations are sized properly, and that they have the right contrast, unity, and proportion.

Today, most of these pictorial materials are shot using a digital camera and the images are stored in the computer. Changes or enhancements take place on the computer using available computer programs that are designed to assist in accomplishing the task of placing them in electronic form for the layout. Computer programs allow the operator to generate images of original artwork, while other programs offer clip art. The images can be transferred to the original document to finish the publication effort.

GRAPHICS PROGRAMS

In the programs used to produce graphics electronically, layout materials appear as object-oriented or bitmapped images. Using these programs, the designer can create very complex documents. These illustration packages will be discussed in greater detail in Chapter 13.

ACADEMIC LINK

Manual Copyfitting Calculations

Without the automated features of layout and design software programs, manual calculations would have to be performed to determine how much space is required for a given block of type.

A block of type with a total of 310 characters is to be set in a 10-point sans serif typeface, with a line width of 18 picas. For this particular typeface, 2.9 characters fill one pica of space. To determine the space required for the text:

1. Multiply the number of characters that fill one pica of space (2.9) by the line length (18) to find the number of characters possible per line:
    $2.9 \times 18 = 52.2$

The result is rounded to the nearest whole number (52).

2. Find the number of typeset lines required for the text by dividing the total number of characters in the text (310) by the number of characters per line (52):
    $310 \div 52 = 5.96$

Round the result of this equation up to the nearest whole number (6 lines).

3. Multiply the typeface point size (10) by the number of typeset lines (6) to find the depth of the text:
    $10 \times 6 = 60$

4. Convert the measurement from points to picas. One pica is equal to 12 points.
    $60 \div 12 = 5$ picas

The text block measures 5 picas deep and 18 picas wide (line width).

Find the space required for a block of type with 275 characters set in a 12-point sans serif typeface, with a line width of 22 picas. 2.5 characters of this typeface fill one pica of space. Work the calculations on a separate piece of paper.

Summary

When looking at a printed piece, you can see someone designed and laid out all of the elements that make up the visual product. Sometimes it requires extensive layout and design knowledge. The message is all-important. In many cases, the visual image must be artistic and functional. Techniques are critical in producing a printed product.

Review Questions

Please do not write in this text. Write your answers on a separate sheet of paper.

1. In graphic communications, design refers to the use of proper methods to produce a product that is both _____ and _____.
2. Explain the role of the graphic designer.
3. Which of the following is *not* an element of design?
   A. Shape.
   B. Texture.
   C. Mass.
   D. Beauty.
4. What are the three basic design shapes?
5. The _____ is a tool that illustrates the basics of color.
6. What are the three primary colors?
7. Name the five principles of design.
8. _____ is the proper balance of all elements in an image so a pleasing whole results and the image is viewed as one piece.
9. List the four elements of layout.
10. _____ is intended to draw attention to the printed piece.
11. What are five areas the layout artist must address when developing a layout?
12. A _____ is a rapidly drawn design of a layout.
13. A _____ layout shows how the printed piece will look when finished.
14. The guidelines that list information about the type style, type size, line width, color use, and page organization of a printed product are called _____.
15. How are photographs and pieces of line art commonly edited or sized for reproduction?

Suggested Activities

1. Select designs in a publication that stress the design elements of lines, shapes, mass, texture, and color.
2. Critic a magazine advertisement from the standpoint of balance, contrast, unity, rhythm, and proportion. What agreement exists between the evaluator?
3. Select an advertisement that appeals to you and explain the principles of design that make it desirable.

Related Web Links

Graphic Designers

www.bls.gov/oco/ocos090.htm
Government site with information on careers in graphic design.

Color Matters

www.colormatters.com
Resources and information on the human response to color in different environments.

Color Order Systems in Art and Science

www.colorsystem.com
History of the use of color in different applications.

Environmental Protection Agency

www.epa.gov
Information on reduction and recycling.

CHAPTER 6

Traditional Text Composition

Learning

After studying this chapter, you will be able to:

- Identify the techniques and materials associated with relief composition.
- Identify the techniques associated with cold type composition.

Important Terms

bank	Ludlow
burnish	matrix
chase	Monotype
composing stick	movable type
compositor	quoins
font	relief printing
form	scriber
furniture	slugs
galley	spaceband
job case	template
Linotype	

The term *composition* generally refers to the production and organization of all images to be printed. In graphic communications, however, composition can also mean setting type or words, not just line art or photographs. The ***compositor***, or typesetter, is the person who sets the type.

Composition methods have changed through history as new technology has been introduced. Hand composition of wood or metal type was the primary composition method from the 1400s to the early 1900s. This method involved physically assembling separate letters into words, sentences, paragraphs, and pages. Many of the materials published using hand composition are works of art. The design and spacing of letters and words is very time consuming, but the outcome is outstanding. Machine methods, which rapidly assembled molds and cast an entire line of type in metal, were introduced at the end of the late 1800s. This method remained an important technology for more than a half-century. In the late 1960s, equipment for photographic setting of type began to appear. Photographic typesetting remained in widespread use until the early 1990s. The role of personal computers in composition has grown steadily since being introduced in the 1980s. Today, the computer is the primary method of composition for materials that will be presented in either printed or electronic form. This chapter discusses each of these major composition methods.

RELIEF COMPOSITION

Printing from a raised surface is called ***relief printing***. The name comes from the fact that the image area of the type is in relief to, or raised above, the nonimage area. The raised surface is covered with ink and pressed against paper or another substrate to produce an image, **Figure 6-1.**

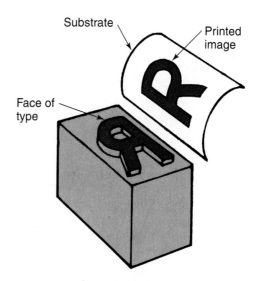

Figure 6-1. First, the surface of the raised image is inked. After it makes contact with the substrate, an image remains on the surface of the substrate.

Relief printing dates back more than ten centuries, to the use of wooden relief type in China. The first relief printing was done using carved wooden blocks. This composition method was a long and tedious process, and was suitable only for pictures or a small number of words.

The modern process of printing traces to the development of movable type in the mid-1400s by Johannes Gutenberg in Mainz, Germany. Gutenberg made molds that could be used to cast individual metal blocks, each holding one raised letter. The blocks could be produced in quantity and assembled into words. Since the typeset letters could be taken apart and the letters reassembled into different words, the blocks were termed ***movable type***. The first books printed using movable type by Gutenberg and his associates were copies of the Christian Bible, **Figure 6-2.**

The art of printing with movable type quickly spread to other cities across Europe. Two hundred years later, in 1639, the first press was established at Harvard Academy in Cambridge, Massachusetts. The first newspaper regularly published in North America was printed in Boston by John Campbell in 1704.

compositor: A person who sets type; also referred to as a *typesetter*.

relief printing: The process of printing from a raised surface. Ink is applied to the raised image and transferred to the paper or other substrate.

movable type: Individual type characters, usually cast in metal, that can be assembled into words, disassembled, and later reassembled into different words.

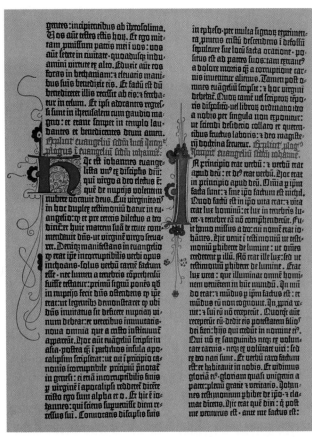

Figure 6-2. Johannes Gutenberg developed movable type and used it to print books, such as this Bible.

Figure 6-3. Individual pieces of foundry type were cast in molds. The type could be assembled in various combinations, sorted, and reused.

Materials Used for Relief Type

Relief type can be made from various materials, including wood, metal, rubber, or plastic. Some early printing in China was even produced using plates made of ceramic materials.

- Wood is well suited for large-point-size characters, since it is lighter than metal. Historically, it was used in relief printing for newspaper headlines and large posters. Wood type was relatively soft and could be easily damaged. For longer wear, the face of the type was placed on the polished end grain of the wood block.

- Metal was widely used to produce individual pieces of foundry type, which involved pouring molten metal into a *matrix* to form the characters, **Figure 6-3.** In machine composition for relief printing, hot metal was used with a series of molds to cast a full line of type at a time. The metal used to cast type is lead with some tin and antimony. Tin gives the type toughness and counteracts shrinkage. The antimony is added to give hardness to the type block and fluidity to the molten metal.

- Rubber can also be used to make images in relief. The most common application is the rubber stamp, which can be considered a form of relief printing.

- Plastic is the most modern material used in relief printing. A one-piece plastic plate with a raised image surface is used to print some newspapers and other long-run jobs quickly and efficiently, **Figure 6-4.**

First- and Second-Generation Image Carriers

An image carrier is the device on a printing press that transfers an inked image to an intermediate carrier, or directly to a substrate, such as paper. A first-generation image carrier is an original. Hot type that is formed by pouring molten metal into a mold is an example of a first-generation image carrier.

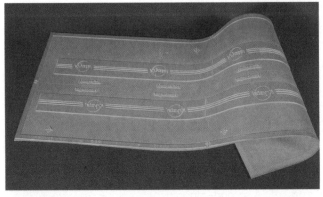

Figure 6-4. Rubber and plastic are common materials for plates used in flexography, the only relief printing process in commercial use today.

A second-generation image carrier is a copy produced by making a mold of an original, and then casting a metal plate, **Figure 6-5.** Such a plate might be produced for long press runs, since making many thousands of impressions can cause physical wear on the image carrier. If the second-generation plate becomes worn, the original image carrier can be used to make another plate to continue the press run.

Setting Metal Relief Type

Various methods are used to set type for the relief printing process. The oldest method of composition is hand-setting the individually cast characters, known as foundry type. Later, machine methods were developed for linecasting type and individual character composition.

Foundry Type

A compositor hand-setting foundry type selects the individual letters needed from a storage drawer called a *job case*. The job case is positioned on top of the compositor's workstation, known as a *bank*, as shown in **Figure 6-6.** Each job case holds a full font of type. A *font* of foundry type is the set of characters in one point size. It is made up of various numbers of each capital and lowercase letter, numerals, punctuation marks, and special symbols.

Each character is picked from the case and placed in a *composing stick*, **Figure 6-7.** The stick has a movable knee that can be set to the specified

Figure 6-6. A job case is placed on the compositor's workstation, called a bank.

line length. As each piece of type is positioned in the stick, the compositor's thumb places pressure on the characters to avoid spilling the type.

Type is set from left to right. The composed type appears upside down, so that the characters read correctly when printed on paper, **Figure 6-8.** When the stick is approximately two-thirds filled with type, the type is removed and placed in a *galley*. Additional type is set, as needed, and assembled in the galley. The type is then transferred to a metal frame called a *chase*. Wood or metal spacers, called *furniture*, are arranged around the block of type. See **Figure 6-9.** Arrangement of the furniture properly positions the block of type, called the *form*, for printing. *Quoins* are expanding metal locking devices used to wedge the form and furniture in place in the chase. The chase supports the type when positioned in the printing

matrix: A mold used with molten metal to produce individual pieces of foundry type.

job case: A storage drawer with individual compartments for the letters and spacing material used in hand-setting foundry type.

bank: A compositor's workstation; used to hold a job case when hand-setting foundry type.

font: A set of foundry type consisting of different quantities of each character in one size and style.

composing stick: A device used to hold foundry type when performing hand composition.

galley: A three-sided metal tray used to store type forms or slugs before they are assembled into page form.

chase: A metal frame that supports the type set into the galley for printing on a relief printing press.

furniture: Wood or metal spacers arranged around a block of type in a chase to position the type for printing.

form: The arrangement of a block of foundry type produced by a compositor.

quoins: Expanding metal locking devices used to wedge a type form and furniture in place in a chase.

Figure 6-5. A second-generation image carrier, such as this advertisement, is produced by casting a plate from a mold of the first-generation carrier. The plate is mounted on a wood base to bring it to standard type height (0.918″).

press. To print properly, metal relief characters must be of uniform height, aligned, assembled in a desired length and width, and locked up in a chase.

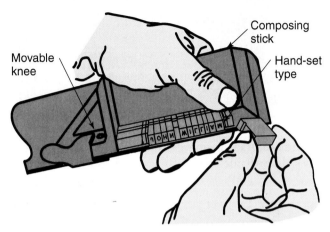

Figure 6-7. The composing stick is used to hold hand-set type. The stick is held in the left hand, with the thumb securing the last character set.

Figure 6-8. In relief type composition, composed type is read upside down and from left to right.

Figure 6-9. Type is positioned in a chase by using wood or metal furniture as spacers. (Melbourne Museum of Printing, Australia)

Linecasting Machines

In the 1880s, hot metal typesetting machines were introduced and provided a faster and more efficient composing method than hand-set type. Instead of individual pieces of type, these machines produced an entire line of type. The lines, called *slugs*, could be easily assembled into columns and pages for printing. Unlike the individual pieces of foundry type that had to be sorted and stored when the printing job was complete, the machine-produced slugs could simply be melted down and used to cast new lines of type.

The most common type of linecasting machine was the *Linotype*, **Figure 6-10.** It contained hundreds of brass matrices, or molds, stored in channels inside one or more magazines. Each matrix had one letter or symbol cut into it. Whenever the Linotype operator pressed a key on the keyboard, the corresponding matrix was released from the magazine and dropped down a guide to an assembly area.

Each word was assembled, letter-by-letter, with wedge-shaped *spacebands* between the words. Once the preset line length was reached, the line of matrices

Figure 6-10. The linecasting machine made relief composition more efficient. Matrices were formed into lines, cast in metal, and then distributed back into the magazines for reuse.

and spacebands was transferred to the casting position. Molten metal was forced into the die, creating a slug, **Figure 6-11.** The slug was automatically trimmed, forced out of the mold, and positioned in a galley.

The matrices and spacebands were then transferred to a distribution system that returned them to their proper places in the magazine, ready to be used again. The development of circulating matrices was a major breakthrough in machine metal composition, which allowed them to be used over and over to cast images as a single line of type.

The *Ludlow* is another type of linecasting machine that was used primarily to set larger point sizes, commonly used as display type. Although this machine produced a cast line of type, **Figure 6-12,** it was a variation of hand-setting. The large matrices were selected and arranged in order. After the display line was cast, the matrices had to be distributed into a storage case.

The *Monotype* is a more complicated composing machine that produced individual cast letters, rather than a line of type. This system was a two-part machine with a keyboard and a separate metal caster. The operator produced a punched paper tape by pressing keys on the keyboard unit. Holes in the paper tape were codes, which produced letters in the desired order once placed in the caster. However, the letters were not attached to each other.

COLD TYPE COMPOSITION

Cold type composition methods are so named to distinguish them from "hot metal" relief composition methods. Cold type composition ranges from hand

Figure 6-11. Slugs contain an entire line of type. They were much easier to assemble into columns and pages. (Melbourne Museum of Printing, Australia)

Figure 6-12. This is an example of a slug cast by the Ludlow machine.

and mechanical techniques to various forms of photographic typesetting and text generation on desktop computers. Because of the relative simplicity and low cost of computer-based text generation, traditional cold type methods are no longer used. Just as hot metal composition almost disappeared from commercial printing with the widespread adoption of phototypesetting methods, the phototypesetter has almost been entirely replaced by the computer.

Strike-On Composition

Before the introduction of phototypesetting systems, strike-on composition was used as a simple and rapid means of generating camera-ready text. The simplest piece of strike-on equipment was the standard typewriter. Later, special strike-on composers were introduced that could produce several different typefaces and point sizes. These composers also made it possible to vary wordspacing and produce justified columns with even left and right margins.

The IBM Selectric and the Varityper were two typical strike-on composers. They had a variety of type styles, but the operator had to type each line twice if the line was to be justified. First, the line is recorded in the machine. When the line is full enough to justify, a scale above the keyboard lines up with a color and a number. When this color and number are lined up on a dial, the machine automatically adds the right spacing as the line is reset.

slugs: An entire line of type produced by a hot metal typesetting machine.

Linotype: A type of mechanical linecasting machine allowing the compositor to use a keyboard to quickly assemble brass letter molds, then cast an entire line of type.

spaceband: Wedge-shaped devices used to justify a line of matrices in a hot-metal linecasting machine.

Ludlow: A type of linecasting machine that was used primarily to set larger point sizes, which were typically used as display type.

Monotype: A composing machine with a keyboard and a separate metal caster that produced individual cast letters.

Hand Composition Methods

Hand composition methods are utilized to a very limited extent today. Hand composition methods include using a pen, brush, template, or transfer letters to create type.

When using any type of hand composition, the tools and work area must be kept clean to produce quality work. The paper used also contributes to the quality of the finished image; a hard, smooth surface is preferable. The line quality is sharper when the proper paper surface is used.

Hand Lettering

Numerous letter forms are available today, but special designs can be difficult to find. It may be necessary for a graphic designer or artist to create images by hand, using pens and brushes. Special types of lettering and drawing pens are available to produce freehand lettering. The shape and tip size of the pens vary. The most common shapes are square, round, flat, and oval, **Figure 6-13.** Hand lettering is often created oversized, which allows for reduction during the photoconversion process. Reducing the images tends to sharpen them and helps hide minor errors.

Templates

Lettering also may be done using a *template*, which is a guide with a specific shape or letter cut into it. When the *scriber* (a tool for following the template) follows the template pattern, the attached pen deposits ink on the sheet of paper, **Figure 6-14.** Some templates allow for only one size and style of characters, while others accommodate a variety of character heights and permit changing the slant of the letter or shape.

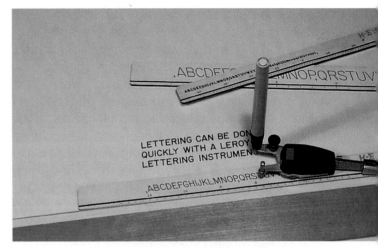

Figure 6-14. This template and scriber can be used to produce one size and style of type. A different template must be used to change size or style.

Dry Transfer Type

Dry transfer sheets are an inexpensive way of producing professional, camera- or plate-ready display type. Each sheet consists of a complete alphabet in a single type style, with varying numbers of each letter, **Figure 6-15.** The sheets include a greater number of the most commonly used letters (such as A, E, S, and T), and fewer of less-used letters (such as Q, X, Y, and Z). Many typestyles and sizes are available. Each letter is placed in position and *burnished* with a smooth wood, plastic, or metal tool. When properly burnished, the dry transfer image adheres to the sheet of paper.

Dry transfer is also used to create borders, decorative artwork, and shading. This is a very

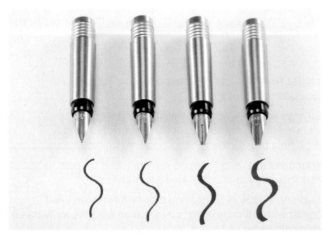

Figure 6-13. The special pens used in hand composition are available with tips in various sizes and shapes.

Figure 6-15. Dry transfer letters are first positioned, and then burnished to adhere the type to the paper. These letters are available in many styles and sizes.

THINK GREEN

Paper Waste Overview

Paper is a large part of the graphic communications industry. However, there is growing concern about the various effects of paper waste today. The obtaining of virgin pulp is a cause of deforestation around the world. This, in turn, is leading to the extinction of inhabitants of the forest who rely on those trees for food and shelter. The disposal of large amounts of paper has increased the size of landfills. One easy way to reduce paper waste is to recycle paper and buy products that use recycled material. Several printers are working to be more compliant with the environment. For example, printers are working toward meeting standards set by the Forest Stewardship Council in order to produce printed material coming either from recycled paper or from specific approved virgin pulp. For more information, see www.fscus.org.

inexpensive composition method to use when a limited number of camera- or plate-ready decorative images are needed.

Another form of transfer type is printed on a transparent carrier sheet with an adhesive backing. The desired letters are cut from the carrier and lifted off the base sheet. The letters are then positioned very carefully and burnished down onto a sheet of paper.

Summary

The information given in this chapter largely relates to analog processes. The means by which images are prepared for transfer to a substrate has changed dramatically over the years. Hand or mechanical methods of composing type was common for 500 years. The changes that have led to digital processes are explained in this chapter and should be viewed from a historical standpoint of the industry.

Review Questions

Please do not write in this text. Write your answers on a separate sheet of paper.

1. The person who sets type is called a(n) _____ or _____.
2. Letterpress is another name used for _____ printing.

3. A(n) _____ is the device on a printing press that transfers an inked image to the paper.
4. _____ type is an assortment of individually cast, metal characters used for relief printing.
5. Linecasting machines produce an entire line of type, called a(n) _____.
6. _____ methods of generating copy involve using a pen, brush, lettering template, clip art, or transfer letters.
7. When using dry transfer type, each letter is _____ onto the sheet of paper.

Suggested Activities

1. Research Gutenberg's invention of movable metal type. Create a timeline of events related to this invention.
2. Investigate the history of relief printing. Briefly describe the earliest example you can find of relief printing. Include the materials used, the location the item was produced, and how the item was used.
3. Explain the history and purpose of the California Job Case.

Related Web Links

Hamilton Wood Type Printing Museum
www.woodtype.org
Web site of the Hamilton Wood Type Printing Museum, which contains some historical information on the use of wooden relief type.

Briar Press
www.briarpress.org
Briar Press is a community of letterpress printers, book artists, and press enthusiasts dedicated to the preservation of letterpress-era equipment and the art of fine printing.

The Forest Stewardship Council
www.fscus.org
Standard-setting organization dedicated to preserving forests.

template: A pierced or cut guide, usually plastic, used to create lettering and symbols, or to draw shapes by hand.

scriber: A tool for following a template; an attached pen deposits ink onto a sheet of paper.

burnish: To rub down a dry transfer image onto a substrate with a smooth wood, plastic, or metal tool.

CHAPTER 7

Digital Prepress

Learning Objectives

After studying this chapter, you will be able to:

- Identify different computer platforms.
- Explain the characteristics of different types of storage devices.
- Differentiate between various output devices.
- Explain the processes used in text and graphics preparation.
- Summarize the features of page composition programs.
- Identify the techniques used in creating digital design files.
- Explain the proofreading process.
- Explain the preflighting process.
- Compare types of production proofs.
- Explain digital prepress workflow.

Important Terms

additive color
aliasing
antialiasing
autotracing
Bezier curve
bitmapped images
bits
byte
color management system (CMS)
comparison proofing
context-sensitive menu
cross-platform
design axes
dialog box
digital prepress system
dot pitch
drop-down menus
font set
gigabyte
graphical user interface (GUI)
hardware
ink-jet proofs
interpreter
Job Definition Format (JDF)
lossless compression algorithms
lossy compression algorithms
megabyte
modem
open press interface (OPI) system
output device
page description language (PDL)

page grid
palette
pasteboard
platform
PostScript
PostScript printer typeface file
PostScript Type 1 font
preflighting
print engine
proof
proofreading
proofreader's marks
RAID
random-access memory (RAM)
raster image processor (RIP)
selective compression
separation plates
smoothing
soft proofs
software
style sheet
subtractive color formation
suitcase file
template
text filter
toner
two-person proofing
vector fonts
vector images
WYSIWYG
WYSIWYP

Digital systems have penetrated every stage of the printing process: from formatting the author's manuscript, to platemaking and running the press. Maintaining a smooth workflow requires the consistency of digital data throughout the production process. Sustaining consistency, as well as compatibility, requires that everyone involved in the production process have an understanding of digital media.

In a perfect world, every piece of digital equipment, as well as every computer program and file produced, would be compatible. Unfortunately, this is not the case. For this reason, many organizations, such as the American National Standards Institute (ANSI), the International Standards Organization (ISO),

and the Joint Photographic Experts Group (JPEG), have created standards by which digital media and equipment must operate in order to be compatible. Due to the amount of information and the vast number of products available, this chapter covers general information that applies to digital prepress operations.

DIGITAL BASICS

The desktop computer has become the focal point of job creation and assembly of text and images into page layouts within the graphic communications industry. The computer and associated devices, in conjunction with the specialized graphics programs, are components in the *digital prepress system*, **Figure 7-1**.

A computer uses a binary system to process and store information in digital form. This means that the computer recognizes only two numbers or digits: 1 and 0. These digits represent two states, on (1) and off (0). The individual 1s and 0s are called *bits*, or binary digits, and can be combined into groups of eight digits to create a binary word, or *byte*. Since there are 256 possible combinations of 1s and 0s in an eight-digit byte (from 11111111 to 00000000), a special code was devised to assign a specific meaning to each combination.

Figure 7-1. Using word processors on a computer is the most common method of composing text for printed documents. A computer is also used for creating page layouts in page composition software.

digital prepress system: A computer-centered process that consists of preparing content, composing pages, and outputting the finished file.

bit: Binary digit. The basic unit of digital information.

byte: A binary word, or group of eight individual 1s and 0s.

The American Standard Code for Information Interchange (ASCII) provides a way to digitally store and process letters, numbers, punctuation marks, and symbols. When the letter C is pressed on a keyboard, for example, it is converted to a specific combination of 1s and 0s. Different combinations are assigned for the capital and lowercase forms of each letter. Once in digital form, the information can be processed by the computer's circuits and stored as digital or magnetic charges.

Regardless of size or complexity, a computer system has three major functions: input, processing, and output, **Figure 7-2.** Computer systems also have some means of storing information, either within the system, in a portable form, or both. There are a number of different methods and devices used for input, storage, and output. They are described in the following sections.

Computer Platforms

The *platform* of a digital prepress system is the computer system *hardware* used to operate various programs. Computer platforms include the elements necessary to create, assemble, and output data in the finished pages, **Figure 7-3.** Major computer platforms are PC (based on the Microsoft® *Windows*® operating system and the Intel® chip architecture), Apple® Macintosh®, and UNIX®. Once the platform is defined, software developers design and install corresponding software applications. **Software** is a computer program that initiates a specific function of the computer. Types of software include word processing, page composition, and graphics programs.

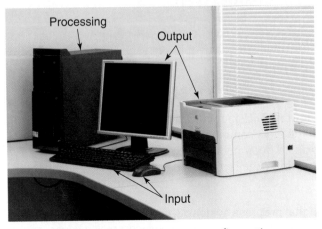

Figure 7-2. This computer system configuration illustrates the three main functions of input (keyboard and mouse), processing (CPU), and output (monitor and printer).

Figure 7-3. Desktop publishing allows graphic designers to create and edit both text and art.

Some file formats and devices are *cross-platform*, which means they can operate on or be used with different platforms. For example, a cross-platform word processing program allows users to create and modify documents using different operating systems, if necessary. Ideally, all computer systems involved in creating and producing a document or project would use the same operating platform. When this is not possible, using cross-platform applications and devices reduces errors due to file conversion and makes the entire process more efficient.

Macintosh®

The Macintosh® computer was introduced in 1984 and quickly became popular because of its ease of use and ability to generate high-quality graphic images. The Macintosh® system was designed around the concept of a *graphical user interface (GUI)*, which allowed for easy-to-understand, on-screen graphic representations of computing tasks. At that time, competing platforms were based on the more difficult method of typing commands to perform tasks. This platform was central to the development of Desktop Publishing (DTP) Systems and continues to play a major role.

Personal Computers (PCs)

The PC is the platform most often used in business environments. In the early 1990s, the original command-based operating system for PCs was replaced by Microsoft® *Windows*®, which was a GUI designed to give the PC the same ease of use as the Macintosh®. The introduction of versatile word processing programs, sophisticated illustration and graphics software, and powerful page composition software have made this platform a strong competitor to the Macintosh® for DTP applications.

UNIX®

UNIX® is a computer operating system that was developed in 1969 by a group of AT&T employees at Bell Labs. During the late 1970s and early 1980s, the influence of the UNIX® system within academic circles led to large-scale adoption of the operating system by commercial startups, the most notable of which is Sun Microsystems, Inc. The Macintosh® OS X operating system is a UNIX®-based operating system.

Today, UNIX®-like operating systems are commonly found, in addition to certified UNIX® systems. Linux® is a UNIX®-like computer operating system and one of the most common open-source operating systems. An open-source operating system is a computer system that has had part of the source code released so third parties can develop programs. Being a free, open-source system, the Linux® source code can be modified, used, and redistributed by anyone. It is used as an operating system for a wide variety of computer hardware, including desktop computers like the Macintosh® OS X, supercomputers, video game systems, and embedded devices, such as mobile phones and routers.

Memory Types

In addition to having a computer system capable of running programs, there must be some means of storing and transmitting data. Every computer system is equipped with a certain amount of physical memory, usually referred to as *random-access memory (RAM)*. RAM is the short-term memory the computer uses to store information in process. Systems can be updated and memory capabilities can be increased to enhance computing efficiency.

Because most page composition files are very large, there are many types of storage devices available that accommodate large files. Storage devices vary in terms of capacity, physical size, access capabilities, speed, reusability, and integrity. Storage capacity is measured in kilobytes (1024 bytes), megabytes (1024 kilobytes), and gigabytes (1024 megabytes).

A number of different types of devices have been developed to store and reuse digital files. Some of these devices use disks that contain magnetic tracks to hold the encoded data, while others laser write data onto specially coated discs. With the exception of the hard drive, storage devices make files portable, which allows a copy of the data to be loaded onto another computer.

Hard Drive

Both external and internal hard drives are common today, **Figure 7-4.** A hard drive contains one or more rigid, non-removable aluminum disks coated with a magnetic material. When the computer is operating, the drive motor spins the disk and a read/write head moves over the disk surface, which contains densely packed magnetic tracks. The head is used to write, or magnetize, information to portions of the tracks as they spin past the head. The head can also read, or play back, previously stored information.

The amount of information that can be stored on a hard drive has increased steadily from fewer than 10 *megabytes* to capacities measured in *gigabytes*. Almost unlimited storage capacity is available with a configuration known as a *RAID* (Redundant Array of Independent Disks), which connects a number of high-capacity hard drives together, **Figure 7-5.** The connected drives act like a single, huge hard drive, which is an advantage when managing extremely large files involving graphics and text. Virtually all digital prepress systems have an internal hard drive.

The single most critical occurrence for a hard drive is when it becomes inoperable, or crashes. The adage of "It isn't *if* your hard drive is going to crash, it's *when* your hard drive is going to crash" should be taken very seriously. Optimizing the drive for operational efficiency and regularly backing up the data should be part of standard operating procedures.

platform: The computer system that is used to operate software. The platform defines the standard around which a system can be developed.

hardware: A computer and its associated devices.

software: Computer programs that initiate and accomplish various computer-based tasks.

cross-platform: Describes applications, formats, or devices that work on multiple computer operating system platforms.

graphical user interface (GUI): A method of representing computer operations and programs on the screen with icons that can be selected with a mouse to perform activities.

random-access memory (RAM): Type of short-term computer memory that stores information in process.

megabyte: One million bytes; usually abbreviated MB.

gigabyte: One billion bytes, abbreviated GB.

RAID: Redundant Array of Independent Disks. A hard drive configuration that connects a number of high-capacity hard disk drives together.

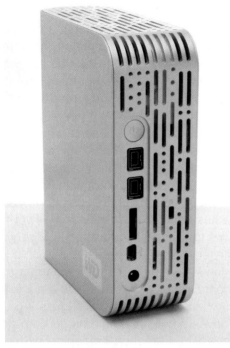

External Hard Drive   **Internal Hard Drive**

Figure 7-4. External hard drives are available in a range of storage capacities, from 500 gigabytes to 2 terabytes. Storage capacity is an important factor for internal hard drives as well, but access speed is an equally important consideration.

Figure 7-5. By connecting a number of high-capacity hard drives together, a RAID can provide an almost unlimited amount of data storage. (The RAIDinc Z 2, courtesy of RAID, Inc.)

CD and DVD Drives

The compact disc (CD) and digital video disc (DVD) drives have become standard features of desktop computers, with most equipped to write data onto the plastic disc. CD-R discs become "read-only" after data is written to them, and CD-RW discs are rewritable and can be recorded on many times. CDs range in capacity from 670 to more than 800 MB. The DVD was originally intended for use in the video industry, but has made its way into the graphic communications industry because of its very high storage capacity of 4.7 to 8.75 GB.

Flash Memory Cards

Flash memory cards are small, removable storage devices that have high storage capacity with fast access and retrieval speeds. Common examples of flash memory cards are CompactFlash® cards and USB flash drives, **Figure 7-6.** Applications for these devices include storing digital camera images, game system data, and audio files. Flash memory cards range in storage sizes from 8 megabytes to 32 gigabytes and have low voltage requirements. They are small in physical size, have fast write and erase speeds, and allow for easy file management.

Figure 7-6. The removable storage media commonly used for digital cameras, Personal Digital Assistants, and computer systems pack a great deal of capacity in a small space. Flash drives and memory cards are available in many different designs, all of which offer easy data transfer and portability. Storage capacity ranges from 1 to 64 GB.

Input Devices

There are a number of ways in which text or graphics information can be entered into the computer system. Methods range from manual entry, such as keyboarding, to electronic transmissions through a modem.

Keyboard

The computer keyboard is the most common way of entering text into a computer system. In addition to standard typing tasks, the keyboard may also be used to perform special functions through dedicated keys (such as the delete and insert keys). Special function keys carry out different tasks, depending on the program being used.

Mouse

Many computer systems rely extensively on input from the mouse. This navigation device is especially necessary for user interfaces and graphics. For example, a mouse is commonly used to cut content from one document and paste it into another.

Modem

A *modem* is an electronic device that converts digital signals into a form that can be transmitted over telephone lines, and from phone lines into the computer system. The technical name for this device is *modulator/demodulator*. Modems allow information to be sent from one computer to another, over distances great and small.

Scanner

Four types of scanners are used today to capture images: handheld, flatbed, film, and drum. Handheld scanners are small devices that are moved across the image area by hand. Flatbed scanners process images that are positioned on a flat glass surface or scan area that is stationary. The film scanner is intended to capture images of various types of film. The drum scanner scans images that are mounted on a rotating drum. Some types can quickly convert an entire page of type or printed material into digital form, **Figure 7-7.** Scanners are used extensively for image input. Scanners are discussed in more detail in Chapter 8.

Voice Recognition System

The premise of voice recognition technology is to use voice commands to control devices and to enter data simply by speaking into a microphone. Some of the major challenges in using this type of system include:

- Recognizing the voices of multiple users on the same system.
- Distinguishing homonyms, such as "there," "their," and "they're."

As the technology advances, the use of this system will extend into common applications within the industry. Presently, voice recognition is limited to common computer commands.

Output Devices

Most computer systems are connected to a variety of *output devices*, including monitors, printers, and external processing devices. Some output devices produce physical material, often referred to as *hard*

modem: A device used with computers to send and receive digital information through telephone lines.

output device: A piece of equipment used to display, produce, or transfer information processed by a computer, such as monitors and printers.

Figure 7-7. A flatbed scanner is commonly used to convert photographs, pages of type, or other printed materials into digital form. Optical Character Recognition (OCR) software is used for typed or printed originals.

copy. These include ink-jet and laser printers that produce copies on paper, and imagesetter and computer to plate equipment that outputs final film or printing plates.

Monitors

As content is entered using a keyboard or other input device, it is almost instantly processed by the computer and displayed on a monitor. The software used for word processing and page layout on computer systems provides a *WYSIWYG* (What You See Is What You Get) display on the monitor, **Figure 7-8.** Monitors used for page layout are usually large enough (17"–21" diagonal measure) to display an entire page, or even two page layouts.

In addition to display size, resolution and dot pitch are important characteristics to consider when choosing a monitor. The resolution is a monitor's ability to show fine detail and is stated in the number of pixels lined up across and down the screen. A typical high-resolution monitor has 1280 pixels horizontally across the screen and 1024 pixels vertically; this is expressed as 1280 × 1024. The resolution of monitors used in graphic communications range from 1024 × 768 to 1600 × 1280, or even higher. *Dot pitch* is a measurement of the vertical distance between rows of pixels on the monitor. The distance is expressed in fractions of a millimeter (stated in decimal form), with the image quality becoming crisper as the fraction becomes smaller.

A color monitor uses the *additive color formation*, based on the combination of red, green, and blue (RGB) to form white light. This

Figure 7-8. The WYSIWYG monitor display provides the user with a very close approximation of how material will appear when printed out. The screen in this figure is displaying an edited image. This image can later be exported to a page layout program, where it may be altered further, as needed.

creates a problem for the desktop publisher who is trying to achieve a WYSIWYG color environment. Since colors are displayed in RGB, it is difficult to match the printed results of a subtractive color environment. In the *subtractive color formation*, cyan, magenta, yellow, and black (CMYK) inks are combined to produce the printed image. This means that full-color representations of images on a monitor and on a printed sheet are achieved through different principles. To overcome this problem, a *color management system (CMS)* is installed to provide a monitor display that is closer to a CMYK representation of the final printed product. This software provides a *WYSIWYP* (What You See Is What You Print) display.

Printers

For proofing text, graphics, and page layouts, a printer is used to produce a hard copy on paper. The resolution of a printed image is measured in dots per inch (dpi) and ranges from 300 dpi (or less) to 1200 dpi (or higher), depending on the type and quality of printer. In some cases, final copy or page layouts can be output by a high-resolution laser or ink-jet printer to achieve quality sufficient for short-run reproduction by lithographic or xerographic methods.

Ink-jet printers

Ink-jet printers form images by using a print head that projects tiny droplets of ink onto the paper surface and provide a resolution of 300 dpi or more. Positioning the droplet is carefully controlled. Ink-jet printers are often used to make color proofs of graphics and page proofs to show a client, as a color-accurate representation of the final printed product, **Figure 7-9.**

Laser printers

Laser printers operate much like a photocopy machine. A photocopy machine uses reflected light to create an image on a drum, while a laser printer uses a laser beam to create an image on the drum, **Figure 7-10.** The laser printer has a *print engine* that translates the output of the computer into a bitmapped image for printing. A laser transfers the page image to a light-sensitive drum that has a positive electrical charge. As the laser light moves across the rotating drum, it emits the image drawn from printer memory. The polarity of the drum changes in the areas where the laser has transferred the image to be printed. *Toner* is a positively charged powder that is attracted only to the negatively-charged areas on a page to create an image. The paper with toner applied passes between heated rollers that fuse the powder onto the paper and produce a permanent image. Laser printers can produce images of 300 dpi and higher, and are typically available in both color and black-only models.

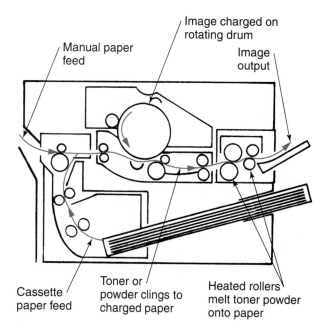

Figure 7-10. A laser printer produces an image by a scanning technique combined with electrostatic principles. Rollers feed paper through the printer at a constant speed. The paper source may be a cassette (tray) for multiple sheets, or a manual feed for single sheets.

Imagesetter and Computer-to-Plate Devices

When high-resolution images must be output for commercial printing, an imagesetter or computer-to-plate (CTP) device is used, **Figure 7-11.** A digital

Figure 7-9. An ink-jet printer can be used to produce a high-quality proof copy of graphics or page layouts. Output is relatively slow when compared to laser printers. (Epson America, Inc.)

WYSIWYG: A monitor display method used by word processing and page layout programs, in which the monitor displays a RGB representation of the printed output.

dot pitch: A measurement of the vertical distance between rows of pixels on a monitor, stated in decimal fractions of a millimeter.

additive color formation: Theory based on mixing red, green, and blue light in various combinations to create a color reproduction or image.

subtractive color formation: The combination of cyan, magenta, yellow, and black inks to produce a printed image.

color management system (CMS): An electronic prepress tool that provides a way to correlate the color-rendering capabilities of input devices, color monitors, and output devices to produce predictable, consistent color.

WYSIWYP: A monitor display method used by word processing and page layout programs that uses color management software to produce a CMYK representation of the printed output.

print engine: A small computer component inside a laser printer that translates the output of the computer into a bitmapped image for printing.

toner: Positively charged powder that is attracted to negatively charged image dots to make up the printed image on a page.

Figure 7-11. For highest quality output on photopaper or film, an imagesetter is used. This imagesetter offers six resolution settings ranging from 1000 dpi to 3000 dpi, and can output material up to 22″ (56 cm) in width. (Fuji Graphic Systems)

Figure 7-12. With the addition of an add-on device, many imagesetters are able to create plates as well as film. (FUJI Photo Film U.S.A., Inc.)

output station consists of two parts, the raster image processor and the digital output device. The digital output device can be used to output high-resolution text and graphic images onto paper, plates, or directly to a digital printing press.

The *raster image processor (RIP)* converts all elements of a page or image into a bitmapped image at the resolution of the selected output device. The RIP interprets the page composition information for the marking engine of the output device, such as an imagesetter, platesetter, digital printer, or large format devices, **Figure 7-12.** Output problems are most likely to occur during the ripping process. It is usually the responsibility of the operator to troubleshoot these problems. However, if the files have not been properly prepared, they may need to be returned to the point of origination for correction.

Page Description Languages (PDLs)

A *page description language (PDL)* serves as the interface between the page composition workstation and the RIP. PDLs are used in digital publishing to identify all the elements to be placed on the page, their respective positions on the page, and the page's position within the larger document, in a manner that the output device can understand. PDLs enable digital output devices developed by different

companies to interpret digital files from any number of personal computers and software programs. Common PDLs include Adobe® PostScript®, Adobe® PDF (Portable Document Format), and Hewlett-Packard PCL (Printer Control Language).

An *interpreter* is a computer program used with output devices that receive the PDL page descriptions and translates them into patterns of dots for a printer or pixels for monitor display. After receiving a page description, the interpreter constructs a representation of the page to suit the output device. For example, the interpreter can determine whether the output device is a black-only or color printer, an RGB video monitor, or a 2400 dpi platesetter. Once these parameters are defined, the interpreter modifies its instructions accordingly.

PREPARING CONTENT

Software used with digital imaging systems is classified by its role in the digital prepress process. This process essentially consists of preparing content, composing pages, and outputting the finished file to an imagesetter, a platesetter, or directly to a digital press. The software used in prepress work consists of word processors, draw and paint software, graphics editors, and page composition programs.

It is important to maintain the original text and image files when preparing content; make a copy of the original material and work from the copy. This ensures that the original material is available if data is lost or destroyed during prepress production, or if graphics must be drastically resized or modified.

Text Preparation

There are several options available when preparing text for the digital prepress process. The simplest method is to enter copy directly onto the page, while using page composition software. This is appropriate for materials that include only a small amount of text. When a large amount of text is included in a layout, it is better to compose the text using word processing software. Text may be scanned from a hard copy using an Optical Character Recognition (OCR) scanner, or imported electronically from a disc or through a modem connection. Once the text is electronically acquired, it is edited using a word processing program.

Word processing software is an efficient tool for creating and editing text. Originally designed for correspondence and similar tasks in the business environment, this software has allowed computers to replace phototypesetters in composing text for graphic communications applications. Many word processors have the capability of formatting both text and graphics. However, it is considered better to use the word processor strictly for text entry and editing, instead of trying to create an entire publication with it. This is particularly true if the publication requires extensive text formatting with numerous graphic elements.

Word processors typically include proofing tools that allow the operator to detect and correct errors in spelling, punctuation, and word division. These proofing tools go beyond mere spell-checking, as they are usually capable of detecting incorrect, extra, or missing punctuation, incorrect hyphenation; improper abbreviation; missing or incorrect capitalization at the beginning of a sentence; doubled words; and much more. This is a small sample of what proofing tools can do to increase typesetting efficiency.

To assist in formatting the text when it is placed in a page composition program, special codes may be incorporated to identify specific text attributes, such as headlines, subheads, or body text, **Figure 7-13.** Depending on the word processing program, the codes may be called styles, tags, or another similar term.

Figure 7-13. Formatting of special attributes, such as different sizes and forms of headlines or various types of lists, can be done by applying styles in a word processing program. In this screen example, the **Style** drop-down list is shown.

When the text is imported into the page composition program, the code is recognized and the specified text attributes are assigned to the copy. Such attributes may include type size, leading, alignment, and indents. This technique saves many hours of work once the text has been placed into the page composition.

Graphics Preparation

Graphic images can be created and saved in a variety of ways. Digital images can be created using paint programs, draw programs, digital photography, and electronic scanning. The electronic images created are saved in one of many file formats. The file format used for graphics is a very important consideration, because it determines how much an image may be manipulated and how well it will reproduce. Digital camera and digital scanner operation are covered in detail in Chapter 8.

Some graphics editing is possible with paint and drawing programs, but more extensive and precise

raster image processor (RIP): A device that interprets all of the page layout information for the marking engine of the output device.

page description language (PDL): A file format that describes a page's layout, contents, and position within the larger document in a manner the output device can understand.

interpreter: A computer program used with output devices that receive PDL page descriptions.

changes should be made with a full-featured image manipulation program, or image editor. Some of the most commonly used image manipulation programs include Adobe® Photoshop®, Macromedia® Freehand® MX, CorelDRAW®, and Adobe® Illustrator®.

Full-featured image editors allow almost any aspect of an image to be manipulated, including cropping, color and contrast, adding or removing visual information, and even combining images. See **Figure 7-14.** Experienced users of image manipulation programs can sharpen, blur, and smudge edges; mix, choose, and apply colors; paint, draw, work with multiple layers, clone, apply filters, create gradients and textures, adjust color, and print color separations, as well as composites. Many programs allow the user to restrict modifications to one area of a picture or to make picture-wide changes.

In digital prepress, graphics can be broadly divided into two groups, bitmapped images and vector images.

Bitmapped Images

Bitmapped images are graphics files that contain a map of pixels, each of which is assigned characteristics. See **Figure 7-15.** A continuous tone image (photograph) that has been digitized using a digital capture device is an example of a bitmapped image. In a simple black-and-white bitmap, one bit of information is assigned to each pixel: either it is on (black) or off (white). This information, in turn, determines where ink is placed on the paper when the image is printed. Graphics programs also store location information for each pixel, providing gray

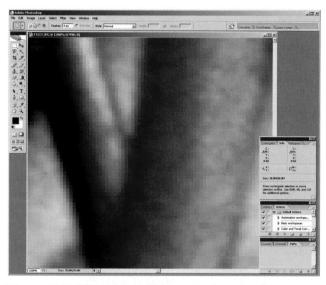

Figure 7-15. This piece of bitmapped art has been greatly enlarged to show the individual pixels.

scale and color data. Each pixel might require eight or even 32 bits of information to describe.

Working with bitmapped images

Artwork created by a paint program is a bitmapped image. When using a paint program, **Figure 7-16,** the rows and columns of squares that compose the image are visible by zooming in on any given area. Color may be added or deleted by filling in or emptying each square on the grid. When working with bitmap images, the individual pixels are edited, rather than whole objects or shapes. Through these actions, the image size, shape, or colors may be modified.

When bitmaps are enlarged or reduced, the edges can become ragged because they are composed of squares that do not create a smooth line. This process is referred to as aliasing. *Aliasing* is the process by which smooth curves and other lines become jagged due to the reduced resolution of the graphics device or file. *Antialiasing* is a software technique for diminishing jagged lines, or jaggies. These stairstep-like lines occur because the output device is not equipped with high enough resolution to represent a smooth line. Antialiasing reduces the prominence of jaggies by surrounding them with intermediate shades of gray or color, **Figure 7-17.** Shades of gray are used for gray-scaling devices, and color is used for color output devices. Although this reduces the jagged appearance of the lines, it also makes them fuzzier. Many programs provide an antialiasing option that is extremely useful when placing text in an image.

Another method to reduce jaggies is called *smoothing*. Some printers accomplish smoothing

Figure 7-14. When cropping an image in an image editing program, such as Adobe Photoshop, use the marquee tool to make a selection, and then trim the image.

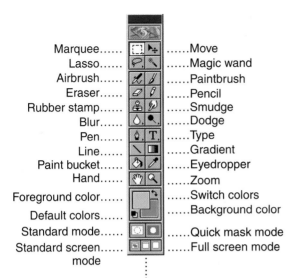

Marquee...... ......Move
Lasso...... ......Magic wand
Airbrush...... ......Paintbrush
Eraser...... ......Pencil
Rubber stamp...... ......Smudge
Blur...... ......Dodge
Pen...... ......Type
Line...... ......Gradient
Paint bucket...... ......Eyedropper
Hand...... ......Zoom
Foreground color...... ......Switch colors
Default colors...... ......Background color
Standard mode...... ......Quick mask mode
Standard screen...... ......Full screen mode
mode
Full screen mode with menu bar

Figure 7-16. Most paint programs are limited to the basic tools indicated above.

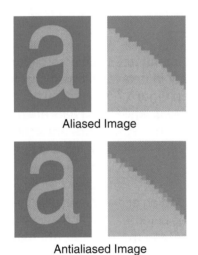

Aliased Image

Antialiased Image

Figure 7-17. The antialiasing technique helps smooth jaggies by filling in squares along the edge with color that varies slightly from that on the image.

by changing the size and horizontal alignment of dots to make curves smoother. Other printers reduce the size of those dots that make up a curved line to create a smoother appearance.

Some graphics programs incorporate an autotracing feature. *Autotracing* is a process for converting a bitmapped image into a vector image. Most autotracing packages read files in a variety of bitmapped formats (GIF and TIFF are very common) and produce a vector format file, such as an EPS. The conversion techniques used and the accuracy of the conversion process differs from one software package to another.

Vector Images

Vector images are represented as mathematical formulas that define all the shapes in the image, as well as their placement in a document. In computer graphics, a vector is a line that is defined by its start point and endpoint. A piece of line art generated by a drawing program is a vector graphic, **Figure 7-18.** A drawing program gives the designer control over shape, placement, line width, and object pattern, **Figure 7-19.**

A *Bezier curve* is a vector graphic named after French mathematician Pierre Bezier. It is defined mathematically by two endpoints and two or more other points that control its shape, **Figure 7-20.** Nearly all drawing programs support Bezier curves. The two endpoints of the curve are called anchor

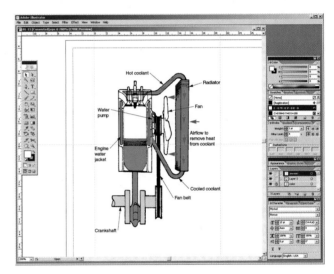

Figure 7-18. A drawing program generates vector images that can be easily scaled and modified because the object is defined geometrically.

bitmapped images: Graphics files that contain a map of pixels, each of which is assigned characteristics such as color and brightness, to make up the image.

aliasing: The process in which smooth curves and other lines become jagged because an image is enlarged or the resolution of the graphics device or file is reduced.

antialiasing: Software technique for diminishing the jagged edges of an image that should be smooth.

smoothing: A technique used by some printers to reduce jaggies.

autotracing: A feature of some graphics programs; allows bitmapped images to be converted into vector format.

vector images: Images that are defined in terms of mathematical parameters, which gives the artist or designer control over shape, placement, line width, and pattern.

Bezier curve: A vector graphic defined mathematically by two endpoints and two or more other points that control its shape.

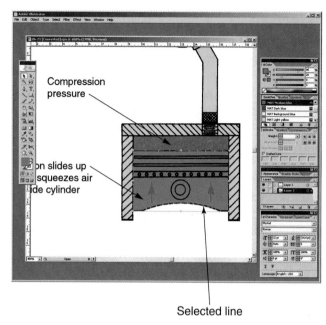

Figure 7-19. When a line is selected on a vector image, the nodes will be visible. The object can be modified by grabbing and dragging the line.

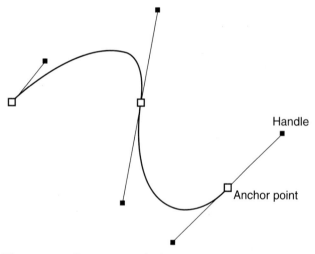

Figure 7-20. By moving the handles, or the control points, you can modify the shape of a Bezier curve.

points. The other points that define the shape of the curve are called handles, tangent points, or nodes. Attached to each handle are two control points. The shape of the curve can be modified by moving the handles or the control points.

There are several advantages to using vector images:

- Shapes can be resized without degradation because objects are defined geometrically.
- The images print the same, even when scaled to different sizes, and can be represented at any resolution, which makes them more flexible than bitmapped images.

- A computer can store vector images very efficiently, making them ideal for high-resolution output.

DIGITAL PAGE COMPOSITION

The assembly of text and graphic images into the final page is accomplished using a page composer. The most widely used page composition software packages today are Adobe® InDesign® and QuarkXPress®. Although the specific operations are somewhat different, an experienced operator can use either program to combine text and graphics and create a file in PostScript®. A PostScript® file can be output to a laser printer, platesetter, or even directly to a digital press.

Composition Software Features

The features offered by different page composition programs vary in details, but have many features in common. See **Figure 7-21.** A menu bar occupies the top of the screen, while scroll bars are on the bottom and one side. The scroll bars are used to shift the screen view up and down or left and right.

Pasteboard

A major portion of the screen display includes the page or pages being laid out and a work area, usually called the *pasteboard*. This area of the screen is used for temporary storage of layout elements (such as a piece of art or a section of typeset material) before moving them onto the layout page. The pasteboard can also be used to try out ideas for design elements, type treatments, and other composition changes.

Page Grid

The *page grid*, sometimes called a frame or baseline grid, is a nonprinted set of guidelines on each layout page. Guidelines for margins, columns, gutters, and other basic page elements are included in the grid. One important function of the grid is to align type horizontally when the page is arranged in two or more columns. The operator may choose to display or hide the grid lines.

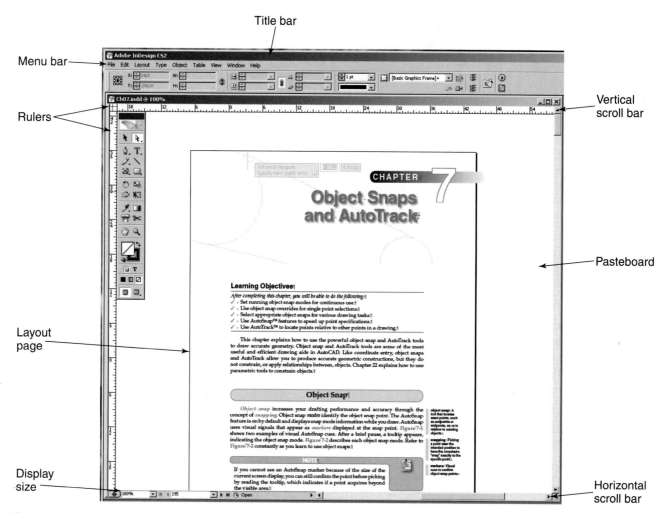

Figure 7-21. Screen layout of one popular page composition program with menu bar along the top and scroll bars down the right side and at bottom. The pasteboard is a work area, outside the page being composed, which is used for temporary storage and preliminary assembly of page elements.

Drop-Down Menus

By selecting one of the items on the menu bar, using the mouse or keyboard, a menu of choices extends down from the bar. These *drop-down menus* contain a number of choices that may be used to create or modify documents, **Figure 7-22.** The **Page** menu, for example, is used to insert, delete, or move pages within a document, and provides choices for quickly moving from page to page. Other common menu bar selections are **File**, **Edit**, **Style**, **Item**, **View**, **Utilities**, **Window**, and **Help**.

Some menus are *context-sensitive menus*— the menu that appears depends on the type of material being worked on. For example, the **Style** menu may display a list of choices that only apply to text when working with the text on a page. The list of available **Style** menu choices changes when working with an image on the page. Selecting some items in a drop-down menu prompts a submenu to display with additional choices, **Figure 7-23.**

pasteboard: An on-screen work area in page composition programs; used for temporary storage of layout elements before moving them onto the page.

page grid: A nonprinted set of guidelines on each composition page that includes guidelines for margins, columns, gutters, and other basic page elements.

drop-down menus: A selection list within software programs that extends downward from the menu bar on the computer display screen.

context-sensitive menu: The characteristic of a selection menu in page composition software in which the options that display are dependent on the type of material being worked on.

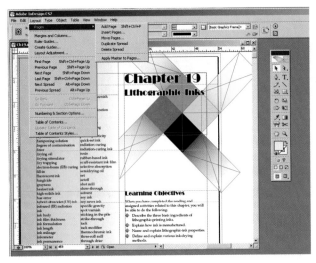

Figure 7-22. Selecting one of the items on the menu bar opens a drop-down menu with a number of choices.

Dialog Boxes

Selecting an item in a drop-down menu often opens a *dialog box*, which permits the operator to input additional information, **Figure 7-24.** This information may specify an action, input measurements, select colors, or apply a style. Some dialog boxes include drop-down lists, similar to submenus, which can be used to make a selection.

Palettes

A *palette* is a modified form of menu that can be resized and positioned on the screen to suit the operator's preferences. A palette can also be set to display or be hidden. When displayed, it always remains visible, overlaying any other images on the screen, **Figure 7-25.**

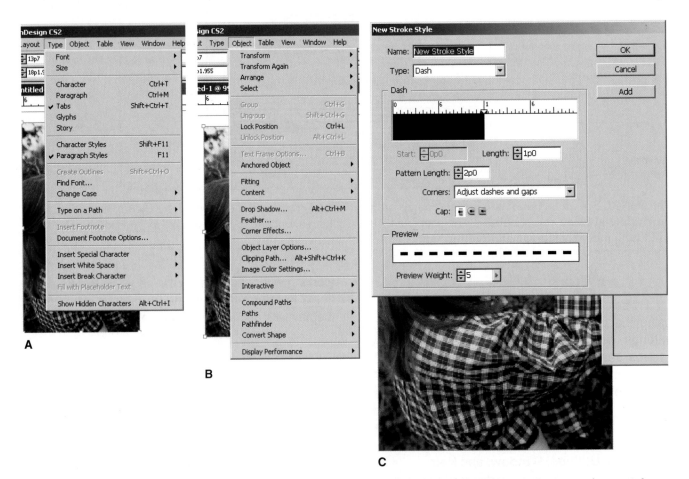

A

B

C

Figure 7-23. The options available within context-sensitive menus change, depending on the type of material being worked on. When **Style** is selected on the menu bar, one of these three menus will appear. A—The menu that appears when text is selected. B—The same menu for when images are selected. C—The menu for when lines or strokes are selected.

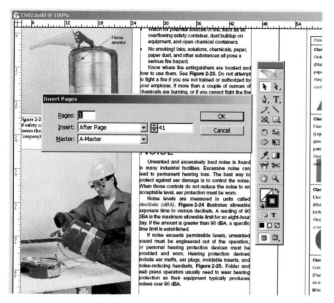

Figure 7-24. A dialog box permits the operator to input information. The dialog box in this figure appeared when the operator selected **Insert** from the **Page** menu. As shown, it allows entry of the number of pages to be inserted, and where they are to be placed. The **Master Page** drop-down list holds a list of master pages that were created for this document.

Figure 7-25. A palette is a list or menu that can be displayed or hidden, and can be positioned any place on the screen the operator chooses. This is the **Tool** palette, used for many layout functions.

Although there are more than six palettes available, the **Tool** palette is the most-often used because it allows the operator to perform many different layout functions. The **Tool** palette displays icons for the different tools available, including:

- **Item tool.** Select a box, line, or other item on the screen to be moved, resized, or reshaped.

- **Content tool.** Import and edit text and pictures. May also duplicate tasks performed by the **Item** tool.

- **Rotation tool.** Establish a point, and then rotate an item (box or line) around that point.

- **Zoom tool.** Enlarge or reduce the view of an item displayed on the screen.

- **Text Box tool.** Accurately position text on a layout. A submenu pops up to the side of the palette, which allows selection of different text box shapes.

- **Picture Box tools.** Available shapes, such as rectangular and rounded-corner, are displayed on the **Tool** palette. Selecting the rectangular **Picture Box** tool icon opens a pop-up menu with additional choices.

- **Line tool.** Draw a straight line at any angle. A pop-up menu allows selection of tools for drawing freehand line shapes.

- **Orthogonal Line tool.** Draw a line that is precisely horizontal or vertical on a page.

- **Line-Text Path tool.** Position straight lines of text at any angle. A pop-up menu provides other options, such as arranging text along a freehand-drawn line.

- **Linking tool.** Link text that is contained in two or more text boxes. This permits text to reflow freely from box to box or page to page, as dimensions or type sizes are changed.

Master Pages and Templates

The design of a document typically results in the repetition of certain attributes from page to page or section to section. Attributes such as column width, margins, page numbers, and headers and footers are often repeated. It is also common to have several

dialog box: A page composition software feature that permits the operator to input information, such as specifying an action, inputting a measurement, or selecting a color.

palette: A modified form of a program menu that can be resized and positioned on the screen to suit the operator's preferences.

different page formats within a document. The page geometry, typography, and other elements in each of these page formats can be set up as a master page, or template.

A *template* can be created that incorporates all the master pages and other formatting attributes. A new publication or page can easily be set up by opening the reusable template and customizing the page formats, as necessary. The main advantage of using a template is the increased productivity and less time spent recreating the same page information.

Importing Text

Although text may be directly input and edited in page composition programs, documents of more than a few paragraphs in length are usually created in a word processing program. The text file is then imported into the page composition program and placed in one or more text boxes.

The text formatting (boldface, italics, tabs, indents, line spacing, and similar parameters) that was applied in the original word processing document may be retained when the text is imported if a *text filter* is used. Text filters are available for major word processing programs. If no filter is available or the imported material is unformatted ASCII text, formatting must be applied through the page composition program.

Style sheets used in page composition programs (and in some word processing programs) are formatting tools that combine a number of attributes. A paragraph style sheet can include such information as alignment, indents, leading between lines, space before and after the paragraph, and such typeface information as font, point size, and kerning. Usually, different paragraph style sheets are created to format specific elements of a document, such as body text, main headings, subheadings, numbered lists, lists with bullets, or illustration captions.

A character style sheet is more specialized and is typically applied to single letters, words, or phrases. A character style sheet might be used to set off all illustration references in the text, for example, by specifying a type font and point size that is different from body text. A major advantage of using style sheets is the ability to accomplish changes quickly and thoroughly. For example, changing the attributes of a heading style from centered 18-point Helvetica Bold to flush left 16-point Cooper Black takes only seconds, and changing the style would alter every occurrence of that heading in the document.

Importing Graphics

Both bitmapped graphics created with paint programs and vector images created with drawing or illustration programs can be imported and placed in a picture box. Photographs are captured with a digital device, such as a camera or scanner, which converts them to a digital format. The digital file may then be imported to a picture box.

Once an image is in a picture box, it can be manipulated in various ways to suit the page layout. The image can be enlarged or reduced, cropped, moved around on the page, changed in color, or edited and altered in various ways. The amount of successful manipulation is affected by the format in which the graphic was imported. For example, bitmap images do not enlarge very well—as the image size increases, the pixels increase in size as well, which gives the image a jagged-edged look. When this occurs, the image is said to be "pixeled," **Figure 7-26.** Graphic file formats are covered in detail later in this chapter.

Drag-and-Drop Manipulation

Although keyboard commands are used for many functions of a page composition program, a mouse or other pointing device is commonly used for quickly and easily manipulating page elements. For example, a text box or picture box can be resized by clicking the mouse or pointer on a side or anchor point, and dragging the

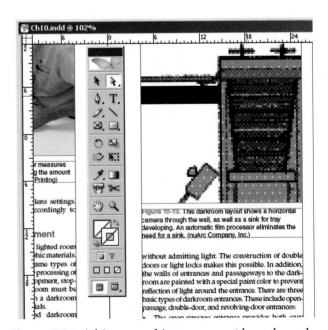

Figure 7-26. A bitmapped image cannot be enlarged by more than a small percentage, or the individual pixels will become visible. The image is said to be "pixeled," which is characterized by a blocky and ragged-edged appearance.

box to the desired size. In the same way, a section of text can be selected, dragged to a different place on the layout, and dropped into a new position. Material can be dragged off the page to the pasteboard for temporary storage or manipulation, or dragged off the pasteboard and dropped into the page.

Color Separations

Instead of the physical overlays used in conventional paste-up to prepare material for color printing, page composition software produces *separation plates* for each color on a page. For example, a page with black type and an illustration of a large red apple would be put out as two separation plates. If a platesetter is used for output, one separation plate is generated for the black images and a second separation plate is generated for the red images. If the page contained a full-color photograph, four separation plates would be created; one plate each for cyan, magenta, yellow, and black inks. These four process colors are used in combination to print all colors. Color science and its relation to printing processes are explored in detail in Chapter 9.

Font Formats and Management

Most applications that support text also provide a variety of fonts to choose from. The printer should use the same fonts as the original page composition, provided they can support them. The entire page composition can change if fonts are substituted. Font substitution can cause document reflow, bad word or line breaks, and loss of kerning and tracking. The fonts must be included in the project files if the production house or printer is expected to use them. Font utility software, such as Adobe® Type Manager® (ATM), Adobe® Type Reunion®, and Extensis® Suitcase™, can help manage and collect the fonts used in the original page composition.

Font Utility Software

Adobe® Type Manager® (ATM) creates bitmapped fonts in any size or style from PostScript® outline fonts. This provides WYSIWYG font representations on the screen. ATM also converts any missing font sizes and helps improve fonts printed on non-PostScript® output devices.

Adobe® Type Reunion® collects style variations in a pull-down menu and lists the style variations of a typeface together in a pop-up menu. Normally, the font menu displays active typefaces alphabetically by attribute, not alphabetically by name. Type Reunion® unifies a type family into a list that makes true typeface selection easier.

Font utility programs allow easier font activation or deactivation and enable the designation of *font sets*, or font lists. Font sets provide a quick list of the fonts used in a job, **Figure 7-27**. Font sets can be created for individual jobs and only the set needed may be activated.

Even though the page composition program may give a list of fonts contained in a document, they may not list the fonts used in imported EPS graphics. Therefore, you must record all fonts used in supporting files from the font sets because they are part of the page composition file. Fonts used within bitmapped graphics automatically convert into pixels and lose font information, so it is not necessary to record the fonts used within these files.

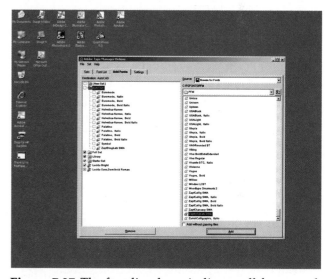

Figure 7-27. The font list above indicates all fonts used in a particular job.

template: In a page composition program, a reusable form that can be set up to include the page geometry, typography, and other elements of a page that recur in a document.

text filter: A page composition program feature that allows the original text formatting applied to be retained when the text is imported into the page composition program.

style sheet: A formatting tool that combines a number of attributes, such as type size, alignment, and other characteristics.

separation plates: Special outputs for each color on a page created by page composition software.

font set: The font list for a document. Font sets can be created for individual jobs and activate only the set needed.

Fonts represented with vector graphics are called *vector fonts*, also known as scalable fonts or outline fonts. The best example of a vector font system is *PostScript*. The PostScript font characters have no specific size and are described as mathematical definitions of the outline. PostScript output devices render the characters as designated.

As with vector images, vector fonts retain smooth contours when slanted, rotated, or scaled to any size. However, converting illustration fonts into vector graphics or object outlines can create problems for small type sizes and large text blocks. For example, outlining small type can create shapes that are too complex to print. Converting text to outline also makes editing more difficult, because the text is changed to a graphic instead of a font.

PostScript Type 1 Fonts

PostScript Type 1 is a format for vector fonts where each character in a typeface is stored as a PostScript language program. Because they are mathematical formulas, vector fonts take up less space in a printer's memory, and the quality of the characters is not affected when scaled to different sizes. PostScript Type 1 fonts can be rotated, outlined, or filled with patterns, and they produce smooth curves even at large sizes when used as display fonts.

PostScript Type 1 fonts are device-independent, which means that they can be used across a broad range of output devices. Any device that contains a PostScript interpreter can read PostScript Type 1 fonts. Although resolution varies among output devices, type generated from vector fonts is as sharp as the particular device can produce.

PostScript Type 1 fonts have two component files: a *suitcase file* for screen display and the *PostScript printer typeface file* for PostScript device output. These two components make a *PostScript Type 1 font*. Digital fonts require two files because the images on a computer screen are created differently from those reproduced onto paper. The screen font is a low-resolution pixel representation of the printer typeface, which does not allow for high-resolution output.

The suitcase file contains a set of screen font sizes and styles. Although the available sizes depend on the program, sizes usually range from 8 point to 72 point. Typical style choices include the primary font, italic, bold, and bold italic. Some font packages also include a variety of weights and widths. The printer typefaces are the actual PostScript files that define the shape of the letters through Bezier curve outlines. Every typeface requires a separate printer file to successfully output the composition.

TrueType Fonts

TrueType font technology was developed jointly by Microsoft® and Apple® as a cross-platform vector font. Although TrueType support is built into all *Windows*® and Macintosh® operating systems, they do not always translate well.

TrueType fonts have no specific sizes and work by combining the screen fonts and the printer typeface into one file (instead of the separate files used in PostScript). PostScript output devices must either convert TrueType fonts or substitute a PostScript font, which slows processing. If TrueType fonts can be imported successfully, they can provide many benefits in a cross-platform environment. Most prepress suppliers use PostScript Type 1 fonts as a standard, and may have limited TrueType fonts. To maintain a smoother workflow, it is best to avoid using both PostScript and TrueType fonts in the same document.

Multiple Master Fonts

Traditionally, standard type families had limited style variation. Adobe Systems Inc. developed multiple master fonts that allow variations to be created from a base design. Each multiple master font consists of the base font (the multiple master font itself) and one or more instances of the font, **Figure 7-28**. An instance is a rendition of the font that varies from other instances in one or more attributes, such as weight or width.

Multiple master fonts include one or more *design axes* for almost unlimited variations of typeface weight and width. A design axis is a variable typeface attribute (weight, width, style, optical size). The base font determines the range of variations available.

Font Organization

A filing system of fonts acquired should be developed on the computer's hard drive. Having an organized filing system makes it easier to collect and send the fonts associated with a document, or to reconstruct a document if problems occur. Such a filing system helps prevent mistakes caused by using the wrong font, mixing font types, or mixing typeface publishers.

Create a separate font folder inside the system fonts folder and file each job font by its name. Use separate folders to avoid mixing fonts from different publishers. For example, there may be a font named Adobe® Garamond and one named Agfa Garamond, **Figure 7-29.**

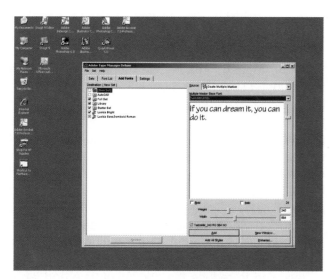

Figure 7-28. Settings for multiple master fonts can be modified within the program's type management utility.

Font Report

Most printers recommend that you create a report to verify document fonts. Customers often overlook fonts used in PostScript files. To make this task easier, most current software can compile a document report, **Figure 7-30.** For example, QuarkXPress® can create a report that indicates the fonts used and lists the embedded EPS files. Adobe® Illustrator® also indicates the fonts used. Adobe® InDesign® CS3 provides a font report that lists every open font on the computer and indicates the fonts used in the active file.

Figure 7-30. The layout and design of font reports varies from program to program, but they often include additional file information.

Preflighting Fonts

When *preflighting* files, all necessary font components should be copied to disc. By using one of the software utilities mentioned earlier, you can turn off all the fonts on a system and load the fonts directly to a printer-ready disc. If any fonts are missing, a prompt appears when the files are opened. Some programs

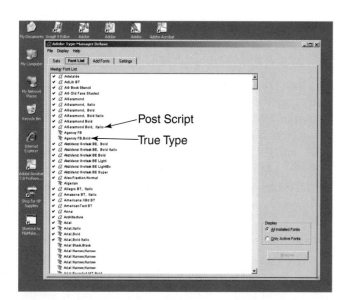

Figure 7-29. TrueType and PostScript fonts may be identified by the icons used within the type management utility.

vector fonts: Fonts represented with vector graphics, also known as scalable fonts or outline fonts.

PostScript: A programming language, commonly referred to as page description language.

suitcase file: One of two component files that make up a PostScript type family, used for the screen display of fonts.

PostScript printer typeface file: One of two component files that make up a PostScript type family, used for printing PostScript Type 1 fonts.

PostScript Type 1 font: Consists of all the variations of one style of type; includes the suitcase file and PostScript printer typeface file.

design axes: Variable typeface attribute.

preflighting: The process of checking documents for completeness to avoid unnecessary or unsuccessful processing.

substitute fonts or resort to the default font if fonts are missing from the file.

Problems also occur when fonts in a document have the same name as the printer's fonts, but are actually different fonts. Computers cannot distinguish between fonts that are named the same, but originate from different publishers. It may not always be possible to substitute one publisher for another. Avoid mixing publishers within the same typeface family because it complicates and slows the workflow.

Fonts are software and are subject to strict software licensing agreements. The user is responsible for maintaining licensed versions of the fonts used at their location.

CREATING DIGITAL IMAGE AND DESIGN FILES

There are several items to consider regarding the files themselves when creating digital design files. For example, the file format selected determines the type of modifications possible to the file and the type of file compression used affects the storage, portability, and resulting quality of the file. All of these decisions depend on the design environment and requirements of the printer.

File Formats

Many different image file formats exist; each varies in the way images are saved, how images can be modified, and how well images will reproduce. File formats contain a number of important aspects, including image placement, resolution, color, and background.

Tagged Image File Format (TIFF or TIF)

The tagged image file format (TIFF or TIF) is a raster graphic file used for exchanging bitmapped images between applications. Depending on the source application, a TIFF file can allow lossless or JPEG compression. Compression is discussed later in this chapter. The format supports bitmap, grayscale, RGB, CMYK, and indexed color models. TIFF files can also be exchanged among several platforms, including Mac® OS, DOS, PC, and UNIX®.

Tagged Image File Format for Image Technology (TIFF/IT-P1)

The tagged image file format for image technology (TIFF/IT-P1, also known as ISO 12639) is a device-dependent format used to describe four-color documents, including specifications for printing presses. TIFF/IT-P1 is a raster-based input format designed to be used with high-end color electronic prepress systems (CEPS). It is favored by the magazine industry for digital delivery of color advertising files. The P1, or "profile one," component was added when the format was accepted by the International Standards Organization (ISO) for consideration as an international standard. TIFF/IT-P1 is designed to reduce the additional time and labor required when CEPS cannot communicate easily.

Encapsulated PostScript (EPS)

The encapsulated PostScript (EPS) is one of the most stable file formats used in delivery to a digital output device. It is less convenient than a TIFF, but usually provides more stable output results. EPS provides a very reliable format for graphic images because it handles both vector and raster images.

The EPS format provides low-resolution previews for screen display and non-PostScript printing. The EPS format supports bitmap, grayscale, RGB, CMYK, spot color, and indexed color models.

EPS files can be used in the *open press interface (OPI) system*, which allows low-resolution images to be placed in a layout, but automatically replaces them with high-resolution image files for printing. If saved in ASCII data format, EPS pictures can be opened and read in a text editor.

Windows® Metafile (WMF) and PICT

The *Windows*® Metafile (WMF) is a graphics file format on Microsoft® *Windows*® systems. The PICT file format is a Mac® graphics file that is most commonly used with the Mac® OS QuickDraw software. Both WMF and PICT formats can hold bitmapped and vector images. Many non-*Windows*® platforms are able to utilize WMF files, but PICT files must be converted to be used on non-Mac® systems.

Desktop Color Separations (DCS 1.0 and DCS 2.0)

The desktop color separations 2.0 (DCS 2.0) file format is an EPS graphic saved as a single file that can include up to six plates (cyan, magenta, yellow, black, and two spot colors) and a master image. The desktop color separations 1.0 (DCS 1.0) format creates five separate files, one for each process color (CMYK), and a data or master file. The DCS format supports grayscale, RGB, spot color, and CMYK color models. DCS files print faster than standard EPS files and can contain both bitmap and vector graphics information.

Graphics Interchange Format (GIF)

The graphics interchange format (GIF) supports raster images and only handles up to 256 colors. GIF files offer lossless data compression, which makes them particularly effective for drawn images, animations, and images used on the Internet. Lossless data compression will be discussed later in this chapter.

Portable Document Format (PDF)

The Adobe® portable document format (PDF) has become a standard for electronic document distribution throughout the world. PDF is a universal file format that preserves all aspects of a native file, regardless of the application or platform used to create the PDF file. Anyone using Adobe® Reader® can view, navigate, and print the file exactly as the author intended.

Unlike the complex, continuous stream of data in PostScript files, PDF files are simple, compact, vector files. They process quickly and can be sent across the Internet or a network for remote proofing or printing. PDF files are also page-independent, so single pages can be replaced or altered without reprocessing the other pages. Page independence also allows printing pages in any order from a single file. The PDF file is also self-contained, meaning that the file has all the fonts and other resources needed to image it.

File Names

File naming conventions are often overlooked, or even ignored. However, carefully naming files helps keep work organized. Whether creating a standard in-house convention or following recommendations from a printer, the file format must be consistently applied.

Computer platforms and programs are subject to their own conventions. Even though some of the latest operating systems allow file names up to 255 characters, file names should be limited to fewer than 20 characters with a three-character extension.

Other general rules for file naming include:
- Use *only* alphanumeric characters; symbols should be avoided.
- File names should *not* begin with a space.
- Each file name should be unique.
- Use the appropriate file extension to identify file type, such as .tiff, .eps, or .pdf.

To avoid confusion, revised files should not be submitted with the same name as the original file. If you are using OPI software, however, it is important that the file names remain the same as the original. The file name serves as the link to the high-resolution image, and changing the file name requires that the link be reestablished, which causes delays.

File Compression

Before sending digital data to a printer, most publishers compress, or reduce, the size of the files. Some programs automatically compress the file when it is converted and decompress when it is viewed. Compressed files require less storage space, allow more efficient data management, and can be transmitted faster because redundancies and other unnecessary elements are eliminated from the original file.

Lossless Compression

A *lossless compression algorithm* refers to a data compression process in which no data is lost. The PKZIP compression technology is an example of lossless compression. The files are often referred to as ZIP files and typically have .zip as the file extension. PKZIP files with an .exe extension are self-extracting files, which can be unzipped simply by opening the file. Decompressing either of these types of files is called unzipping.

For most types of data, lossless compression techniques can reduce the file size by about 50%. Lossless algorithms used for image compression assume that the likely value of a pixel can be inferred

open press interface (OPI) system: A computer configuration and software that allows the designer to use low-resolution images when creating document layouts in page composition programs, and high-resolution images automatically replace the low-resolution images when the file is sent to an output device.

lossless compression algorithms: A mathematical formula for image compression that assumes that the likely value of a pixel can be inferred from the values of surrounding pixels.

from the values of surrounding pixels. Because lossless compression does not discard any of the data, the decompressed image is identical to the original.

Other common lossless compression methods are the Huffman method, Lempel-Ziv-Welch (LZW), and run-length encoding (RLE). Both the Huffman and LZW methods of compression are techniques where adjacent bits are replaced with codes of varying lengths. For example, this technique would encode the fact that zero occurs 20 times, rather than using 20 zeros. This information would use 4 bytes instead of 20. Run-length encoding (RLE) encodes digital data to reduce the amount of storage needed to hold the data without any loss of information. Each coded item consists of a data value and the number of adjacent pixels with the same data value. In other words, strings of the same character are encoded as a single number. This is a very efficient way of encoding large areas of flat color used in linework and text.

Lossy Compression

A **_lossy compression algorithm_** refers to data compression techniques in which some data is lost. Lossy compression methods attempt to eliminate redundant or unnecessary information. Most video compression technologies use a lossy compression. This improves the speed of data transfer, but causes slight degradation when the image is decompressed.

Lossy compression techniques include quantization, Delta Pulse Code Modification (DPCM), and JPEG. Quantization is a filtering process that determines the amount and selection of data to eliminate, so data can be encoded with fewer bits. DPCM measures one set of bits and then measures differences from that set. The differences are then encoded into fewer bits.

Lossless compression is preferred for printed images because each time a lossy compression is applied, more information is lost. The loss of data may not be noticeable on screen, but will be very noticeable in high-resolution printed output.

The JPEG file format was created by the Joint Photographic Experts Group, in collaboration with the International Standards Organization (ISO) and the Consultative Committee for International Telegraphy and Telephony (CCITT). The JPEG format was designed to establish an international data compression standard for continuous-tone, digital still images. JPEG compression is an open-system, cross-platform, cross-device standard that can reduce files to about 5% of their normal size.

JPEG is based on the discrete cosine transform (DCT) algorithm, which analyzes each pixel block, identifies color frequencies, and removes data redundancy. This algorithm requires the same amount of processing to either compress or decompress an image. JPEG compression can incorporate other algorithms, including quantization algorithms and one-dimensional, modified Huffman encoding.

JPEG is a popular standard for images used on the Internet due to its extreme compression capacity and ability to support 24-bit color. The JPEG file format allows the compression ratio and reproduction quality to be controlled at the point of compression, **Figure 7-31.** JPEG files contain bitmap information only and support grayscale, RGB, and CMYK color models.

A major goal of JPEG is to maintain the appearance of an image, rather than the actual data contained in the original. This works because we are visually less sensitive to high-frequency color. JPEG is a lossy compression, and therefore deletes some image information, but the decompressed image remains visually whole.

JPEG functions best for color and grayscale, continuous-tone images. Compressing images with high-contrast edges (such as line graphics or text) to significantly reduce the file size, adversely affects the portion containing the text. **_Selective compression_**

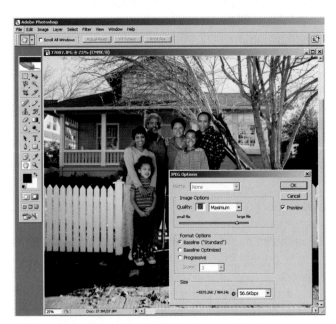

Figure 7-31. When saving a file using the JPEG compression option, there are several encoding options available.

enables users to specify different compression levels for the various elements within a single image. For example, EPS color image files embedded in a digital document result in a very large file. EPS-JPEG compression creates files for page composition software that are significantly smaller than standard EPS files. Images vary in the amount of data that can be compressed without affecting the visible quality. Experiment with quality settings to determine the maximum compression settings that do not perceptibly alter appearance. Since data is lost in each compression/decompression cycle, use JPEG compression at the maximum quality setting and only on final images, **Figure 7-32.**

PROOFREADING

A *proof* is any copy or art that is checked before going into print. In traditional typesetting, the proof is a galley pulled (printed) from the metal type or a printout on phototypesetting paper. In today's electronic production systems, a proof is typically a printout from a laser printer.

In traditional typesetting situations, manuscript was edited and marked for type size and style before being sent to the compositor. The compositor followed all editing instructions and set the copy exactly as it was written. After the copy was set, the *proofreading* process was carried out to detect and mark any typesetting errors. The marked proof would then be sent back to the compositor for correction, and a corrected proof would be produced and checked.

In digital composition methods, the author and editor create the final copy, which eliminates the separate typesetting step. This does not eliminate the need for proofreading, but changes the method and approach. The typeset copy is not compared to the original manuscript, since the typeset material *is* the manuscript. It must still be read carefully for errors and marked for corrections. After corrections are made, the copy must be checked again. In some operations, checking type corrections may be combined with proofing the laid-out pages.

Proofreading Skills

A proofreader has the very important job of making sure the final product meets the standards of expected quality and professionalism. In larger publishing and printing facilities, people are hired with expertise in proofreading. In smaller facilities, a variety of people may have this responsibility. Every printer, especially in a small plant, should be able to read proofs.

The proofreader must be a meticulous person and have the ability to accurately check individual letters in words, as well as look for combinations of letters. Proofreaders cannot scan a page, but must study each word separately. If proofreading is done poorly, the highest quality paper, best printing methods, excellent content, and other favorable aspects of the product will be ruined.

Proofreader's Responsibilities

The typical duties of a proofreader include:

- Check the spelling of all words.
- Ensure word divisions or hyphenations are correct.
- Verify that the style is consistent.
- Make certain that the size of type, line length, and spacing specifications are followed.
- Check that copy has not been omitted or repeated.

Proofreader's marks are widely used symbols that single out and explain copy changes or errors, **Figure 7-33.** The symbols are used to show when something should be taken out, added, or changed.

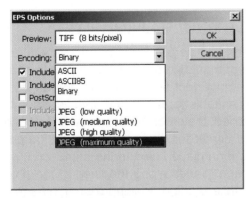

Figure 7-32. JPEG compression should be used at maximum quality to preserve the integrity of the data being compressed.

lossy compression algorithms: A mathematical formula for image compression in which data in an image that is least perceptible to the eye is removed.

selective compression: A compression option that allows the user to specify compression levels for different elements within a single file.

proof: Any copy or art that is checked before going into print.

proofreading: The process of checking for typesetting errors and marking them for correction.

proofreader's marks: Widely used symbols that single out and explain when something in typeset copy is to be taken out, added, or changed.

Punctuation			Spacing	
⊙	Period		#	Insert space
﹚	Comma		eq #	Equalize space
⊙	Colon		⌣	Close up
﹚	Semicolon		**Style of type**	
﹚	Apostrophe		wf	Wrong font
⸌⸍	Open quotes		lc	Lower case
⸜⸝	Close quotes		cap	Capitalize
=/	Hyphen		u lc	Initial cap, then lower case
⊦ ⊦ ⊦	Dash (show length)		sc	Small capitals
( )	Parentheses		c sc	Initial cap, then small caps
Delete and insert			rom	Set in roman
⸋	Delete		ital	Set in italics
⸋	Delete and close up		lf	Set in light face
out see copy	Insert omitted matter		bf	Set in bold face
stet	Let it stand		⸝3	Superior character
Paragraphing			⸜3	Inferior character
¶	Paragraph		**Miscellaneous**	
fl ¶	Flush paragraph		X	Broken type
① ②	Indent (show no. of ems)		⊙	Invert
run in	Run in		⊥	Push down
Position			sp	Spell out
⌐ ⌐	Move right or left		/	Shilling mark (slash)
⊓ ⊔	Raise, lower		⊙··	Ellipsis
ctr	Center		see l/o	See layout
fl L fl R	Flush left, right		? query	Query
=	Align horizontally			
‖	Align vertically			
↰ ⁓	Transpose			
tr #	Transpose space			

Figure 7-33. Some commonly used proofreader's symbols are presented in this chart. Although many of the symbols are considered standard, there may be some variation from company to company.

The appropriate proofreader's mark is placed in the margin of the page to indicate the type of correction to be made, **Figure 7-34.** This system is an efficient means of showing the compositor the location of the fault and the desired correction. Proofreading marks must be written clearly and should be exaggerated so they are not overlooked. When needed, the proofreader can write special notes pertaining to the marks in the border. Sometimes, an extra sheet of instructions may be attached to the copy or page layout.

Proofreading Methods

Comparison proofing, or one-person proofing, is done primarily to find such major problems as copy deletion, incorrect sequence, or copy duplication. It is most suitable for small jobs with little copy. Using this method, the proofreader scans through the proof once to check for obvious errors or changes. The proof is then placed next to the manuscript, and the proofreader traces along the lines of the proof with a pen while reading. Placing a straightedge across the copy and moving it slowly down the page is also helpful. To be consistent, the proofreader must always compare the proof with the copy, not vice versa.

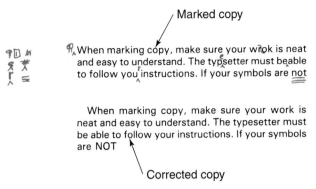

Figure 7-34. This is an example of how proofreader's marks are used to identify and correct copy problems. Note the caret placed at the point of error, and the correction symbol written in the margin.

Two-person proofing requires the reader to work with an assistant. This is the most common proofreading method when accuracy and speed are important. It is frequently used with larger jobs, such as a textbook. The two people are referred to as the reader and the copyholder. The reader follows the printed design proof (or computer screen display) to check closely for errors. The copyholder follows the original manuscript. Usually, the two take turns reading to each other. Each word must be carefully pronounced and the reading pace must not be too fast. The reader must have time to scan the letters of each word, check punctuation, style, and other items.

A special jargon or language often develops between the reader and copyholder. For instance, some readers pronounce each capital letter as "cap" and each period as "peer" to denote the beginning and end of a sentence.

Spell Check Programs

A spell check program, also called a spellchecker or proofing program, is incorporated into the majority of word processing software. Depending on the operator's preference, the program automatically checks the spelling of each word as it is typed, or all the words in a document when typesetting is complete.

A spell check program compares words in the document with those in the program dictionary. If a word is spelled incorrectly, a correction is suggested, **Figure 7-35.** The typesetter can accept the suggested spelling or may enter the proper spelling to be applied to the document. Spell check programs also permit unusual spellings or technical words to be added to the program dictionary.

Spell check programs can be very helpful to production speed and quality. When properly

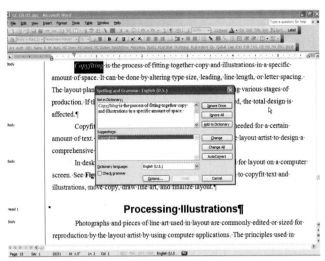

Figure 7-35. This spellchecker highlighted a word in the text and displayed it in a separate window. The most likely correct spelling is shown in the **Change To:** box, but one or more additional suggestions are often presented, as well.

used, they can greatly reduce typos and make the correction cycle much more efficient. A proofreader must still review the copy. However, with fewer typing errors, more attention can be given to checking style, illustration references, sequence, and other important content and typesetting aspects.

PREFLIGHTING

In addition to generating various types of proofs before sending files to a printer, the files should be preflighted. Preflighting is an orderly review of files to identify items that could cause problems at the output or prepress stage. To make sure preflighting goes smoothly, discuss file format and preparation with the printer while the project is still in the design stage. Knowing their requirements ahead of time will save both time and money.

According to the Printing Industries of America (PIA), some of the most common problems with the files customers provide are:

- Missing or incorrect fonts.
- Missing or incorrect trapping.
- File defined with incorrect color (RGB vs. CMYK).
- Scans supplied in wrong file format.
- Graphics not linked.
- Incorrectly defined or under defined bleeds.
- No laser proofs supplied.

Preflight Technician

The preflight technician uses digital imaging technology to achieve the planned requested job. When using this technology, the preflight technician takes the electronic files that are given to him or her by the customer and checks them for all aspects of completeness. It is very similar to the checklist a pilot goes over before the plane takes off; the formalized preflight manual checklist makes sure everything is in order. Therefore, the preflight technician tasks are critical to the elimination of output problems of the electronic files. Preflighting software can speed up the process. Sometimes checklists and software are both used by the preflight technician.

Some of the responsibilities of the preflight technician include making sure submitted discs are not damaged; ensuring discs are readable; checking in-house font availability; checking for missing material on submitted discs; checking for correct size indications; checking for proper trapping and adequate bleeds; and checking for font problems, All these preflighting tasks ensure the digital job is ready for the intended output device. The ability to work closely with the customer and other departments is an imperative attribute.

The preflight technician should have formal postsecondary graphic communications training in digital technology; an associate degree is often stated as a requirement in the job description. It is also beneficial to be familiar with the printing process and production workflow. Preflight technicians must have good communication and basic problem-solving skills, be comfortable with the pressure of deadlines, and be proficient with computer applications.

"Students entering the graphic communications discipline need to have a variety of skills for employment in our ever-changing industry. They need to be versed in the practical application of traditional web and offset printing, digital printing, prepress and prepress software, print management, and to have a firm understanding of the Internet and how it relates to the printing industry."

Tony Mancuso
Typography Unlimited, Inc. (TUI)

- Missing graphics.
- Resolution too high or too low in customer-supplied scans.

After the documents or pages have been created, proofed, and corrected, they are ready to send to the printer for output. At this point, the production department can begin preflighting. Preflighting begins with printing out color separations and composite hard copies. The printer can refer to these copies if problems are encountered with production, pagination, color, or even text flow.

Once the separations and composites are printed, all the graphics should be linked. All page composition programs allow the user to select link or reference options as the art is imported. In QuarkXPress®, for example, all the graphics in the document are linked to the Quark® file unless the art was created with the drawing tools in Quark®. There are many benefits to linking art files. If all the graphics are embedded in a document file and one piece of art is corrupted, the entire project can be lost. When the art files are linked instead of embedded, only the corrupt piece of art needs to be recreated.

When preflighting files, check to ensure every graphic used in the file is on the disc. If a graphic file is missing, the art will print as low-resolution images or bitmapped placeholders. Include the original art files in a separate directory for linked graphics that are in a non-editable format. Print a list of all files included on the disc(s), as well as how many discs are included for the project. Prepare a checklist to help verify that all graphic, font, and color components are present and correct.

After the basic preflighting is complete and proofs have been output, create a letter that outlines the software and fonts that were used to create the files, trapping requirements, print specifications, and any other pertinent information, **Figure 7-36.** Preflighting also requires checking fonts and the color palette. Font formats and management are covered in the previous section. For detailed information on color management, refer to Chapter 10.

File Submission Form

Book title/Part number _____

Order date _____ Blues date _____

Press date   Bill to P.O. number

Sales representative

CUSTOMER INFORMATION

Company name		Design house
Contact name		Design contact
Address		Address
City	State Zip	City	State Zip
Phone	Fax	Phone	Fax
Modem	Baud rate	Modem	Baud rate

FILE INFORMATION

Platform ❑ Macintosh ❑ IBM-PC (or compatible) ❑ UNIX (DEC) ❑ UNIX (Sun) ❑ VMS (VAX) ❑ Other ____

Operating system ❑ Macintosh version _____   ❑ MS-DOS version _____   ❑ Windows version _____

Media ❑ 3.5 inch disk ❑ 5.25 inch disk ❑ SyQuest (size___) ❑ 150 Mb DC (QIC tape) ❑ Bernoulli cartridge (size___)
❑ Zip cartridge ❑ Jaz cartridge ❑ Magneto-optical cartridge (size___)   ❑ CD-ROM

Fonts ❑ Type 1   ❑ TrueType   ❑ Complete font list, including manufacturer names, is attached on a
separate sheet   ❑ All printer and screen fonts are included on submission media

Files Files listed on other side are: ❑ Application files   ❑ PostScript files
Are files compressed? ❑ No   ❑ Yes (if yes, what compression software was used?_____version___)
Please complete the file list on the other side of this form.

Trapping ❑ Files do not need trapping ❑ Please trap the files for us
❑ Files need trapping, but we have taken the responsibility and done it ourselves

Proofs ❑ Single blueline ❑ Folded blueline   ❑ Blackprint   ❑ Matchprint   ❑ Iris

Artwork ❑ Digital scanning (to be placed in file) ❑ Conventional scanning (to be stripped into film)

Pagination ❑ Total page count _____   ❑ Page map included on separate sheets

Other Special instructions attached on separate sheet

A

B

File Name	Application/version	Trim size	Bleed amount	No. of pages	Halftone screen	Neg. or Pos.	RREU or RRED	Color separations
Chapter 01	QuarkXPress 3.31	8.5x11	1/8in.	16	133	Neg	RRED	CMYK/ PMS 367
								C M Y K/ PMS ____
								C M Y K/ PMS ____
								C M Y K/ PMS ____

Figure 7-36. If the printer does not provide a standard submission form, design a file submission form and file list that includes the basic information shown in this sample.

PRODUCTION PROOFS

Depending on the complexity of a project and previous arrangements with the printer, a number of proofs must be reviewed before the job goes to press. Proofs serve as samples for the customer and guidelines for the press operators. Proofs can be made directly from digital files, viewed online, or run off on a proof press. Cost variations often determine the type of proofs requested at different stages of prepress production. The most commonly used proofs today are soft proofs and digital proofs, **Figure 7-37.**

Soft Proofs

Soft proofs are electronic files that represent what the final printed page will look like. These proofs may be press-ready files created using the project composition files submitted to the printer. Soft proofs may be delivered via e-mail or accessed on the Internet, and are most often saved as PDF files. Soft proofing jobs has become a common industry practice, as it takes advantage of information technology to save the time and expense involved in producing printed proofs. Additionally, the client is able to review proofs in a significantly shorter time frame and may instantly approve pages or send comments through e-mail or a secure Web site.

Online soft proofs are posted and managed using Web-based applications specifically developed for electronically proofing documents. While each printer may not use the same interface, the functions and tools available to proof a job are similar from one application to the next. Some of the common Web-based proofing applications are Kodak InSite, eProof, inMotion, and proofHQ.

Digital Proofs

The two most common types of digital proofs used today are laser proofs and ink-jet proofs. Laser proofs are printed onto paper using electronic files. They are produced by an industrial laser printer and may be in black and white or use four colors. They are an inexpensive type of proof. However, the quality is said to be less than that of ink-jet proofs.

Ink-jet proofs are produced by a printing process that generates four-color proofs directly from the digital files. Ink-jet proofing is often used as a contract proof, replacing the press proof. The color simulates what will be produced on a press. However, there is often no halftone dot, so conventional screening problems such as moiré patterns cannot be predicted. Ink-jet proofs can be presented early in the proofing process because they are very inexpensive.

Matchprint™ Digital Halftone has become an industry-standard halftone contract proof. The actual digital file that will be used to create the printed pages is sent to a precalibrated ink-jet printer to produce

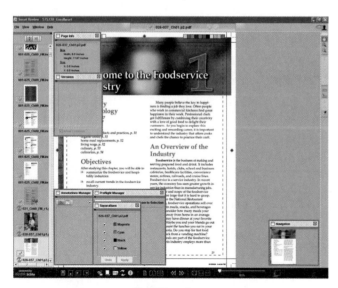

Soft Proofs

Digital Proofs

Figure 7-37. Different types of proofs. Printed color proofs commonly include colors bars, registration lines, and cut marks on the page. Soft proofs include the same information in color proofs, but the client may approve or reject each page individually.

THINK GREEN
Soft Proofs

With the growing use of technology in the graphic communications industry, as well as the increased concern for environmental issues, soft proofs are becoming more widely used than digital proofs. Soft proofs reduce the use of paper in multiple rounds of checking proofs. They eliminate the use of ink and the creation of any VOCs in the production of printing proofs. There is also no transportation involved since soft proofs are sent over the Internet. While some companies are concerned about the quality of soft proofs, others have found that with monitor calibrations, the on-screen page should match the printed page. Companies have found soft proofs to be a more efficient alternative to hard copy proofs because of the turnaround time and ease of use. For more information, see www.pneac.org.

a printed proof. This enables accurate evaluation of the file for trapping, moiré, and other conventional printing problems.

DIGITAL PREPRESS WORKFLOW

The changes resulting from the transition of conventional prepress methods to digital have brought about many workflow enhancements and radically changed the processes in the prepress department.

PDF Workflow

In a PDF workflow, the PDF file is used to create the film or plates needed by the print production facility. The PDF file contains all of the necessary information, such as the fonts, graphics, images, text, and document layout. No further prepress steps remain to be completed by the production department. Portable document software typically saves a document bitmap, the ASCII text, and the font data. Even with compression, most PDF files may be many times larger than the native file.

The PDF file format allows incorporation of an extended job ticket. An extended job ticket is an electronic document that contains all the instructions required for processing a job, **Figure 7-38.** It includes customer information, proofing directives, trapping, imposition and ripping parameters, and even finishing and shipping instructions. The job ticket specifications can be easily viewed and modified by everyone who has access to the file.

The PDF file is practically an ideal preflighting tool. If all the necessary elements are not present at the time of file creation, the user is warned. PDF files also provide a single file for viewing, distributing, archiving, editing, and printing small file sizes, and a built-in preview. PDF files can access many types of files including EPS, TIFF, PICT, QuarkXPress®, PageMaker®, and PostScript® from applications on both Macintosh® and PC platforms.

Job Definition Format (JDF)

The *Job Definition Format (JDF)* is a file format that automates the printing workflow, from design to production, and was developed through a partnership between Adobe®, Agfa, Heidelberg®, and Man Roland. This file format is based on Extensible Markup Language (XML) and provides a standard format that is compatible with any JDF-enabled equipment.

JDF files are similar to an embedded electronic job ticket, in that they can contain information on the document designer, fonts used, images contained, stock type and size, ink colors, bindery instructions, and other static data. In addition, the file may contain instructions for JDF-enabled devices used in the production process, including ink fountain settings on a press and the configuration of bindery equipment. Throughout the production process, the

comparison proofing: A proofreading method done primarily by one person to find such major problems as copy deletion, incorrect sequence, or copy duplication.

two-person proofing: A proofreading method that requires the reader to work with an assistant, called the copyholder.

soft proofs: Press-ready, electronic files that represent what the final printed page will look like and are most often PDF files that can be viewed on a computer monitor.

ink-jet proofs: A type of job proof that provides four-color proofs generated directly from the digital files.

Job Definition Format (JDF): A file format based on Extensible Markup Language (XML), which provides a standard format that is compatible with any JDF-enabled equipment.

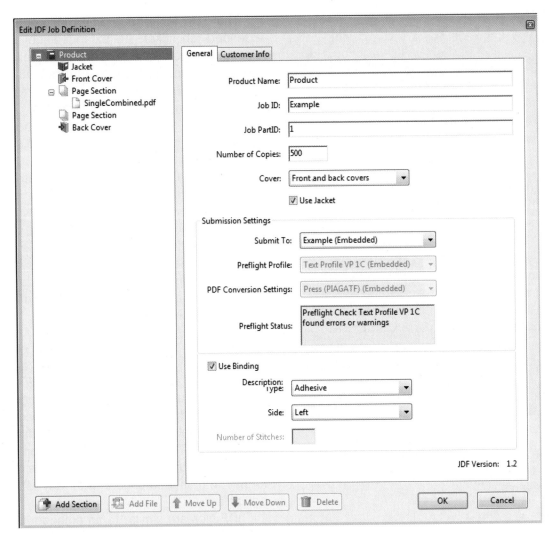

Figure 7-38. A job ticket contains several files, which allow the operator to access customer information, specific page data, processing details, and finishing specifications.

information and instructions contained in a JDF file may be manually amended to allow for adjustments or additions, such as completion dates, delivery schedules, and client contact information.

This technology expedites production, reduces errors that occur in the processes, and automates the workflow of print production. Other workflow solutions that are designed to optimize print manufacturing processes include Kodak Prinergy™, Agfa :Apogee Suite, Heidelberg® Prinect®, and EFI OneFlow®.

Summary

Today's prepress professional must be knowledgeable in both traditional graphic arts techniques (such as fonts, mechanical trapping, and color separations), and strong computer skills (including the ability to navigate intranet and Internet networks). Today, a single prepress professional is capable of performing the duties of several conventional prepress personnel from only a few years ago. These expanding skills and responsibilities will continue to grow as new technology and workflow techniques enhance prepress functions, and extend into all graphic communications processes, including press and bindery operations. In the near future, a single prepress operator may be able to control a print job, from creation to fulfillment, with commands from a single computer workstation. The possibility of this type of change emphasizes the importance of digital and workflow technology, and will further change the career opportunities and skill requirements in the graphic communications industry.

Review Questions

Please do not write in this book. Write your answers on a separate sheet of paper.

1. List the three major functions of a computer system.
2. A computer processes and stores information using the _____ system: a series of 1s and 0s.
3. Explain the function of computer *software*.
4. What is a *cross-platform* device?
5. List three different storage devices and describe the characteristics of each.
6. What do the letters WYSIWYG represent?
7. Explain the purpose of *color management software*.
8. What is the function of a *raster image processor*?
9. Define *page description language* and give examples of common PDLs.
10. Explain the difference between *vector images* and *bitmapped images*.
11. Two software techniques for diminishing jaggies are _____ and _____.
12. A(n) _____ is a vector graphic that is defined mathematically by two endpoints and two or more additional points that control its shape.
13. Which of the following is *not* a common feature of the computer screen display for a page composition program?
    A. Scroll bars.
    B. Pasteboard.
    C. Scanner port.
    D. Menu bar.
14. List five tool icons commonly found on the tool palette of page composition programs.
15. A reusable _____ contains all the master pages and other formatting attributes that make up a multipage document.
16. What is the purpose of a *style sheet*?
17. Explain the purpose of *font utility software*.
18. What are TrueType fonts? How do they differ from PostScript fonts?
19. Name three image file formats and describe the characteristics of each.
20. What are the general rules to follow when naming files?
21. What is the difference between *lossless compression* and *lossy compression*?
22. A(n) _____ is any copy or art that is checked before going to print.
23. What are *proofreader's marks*?
24. What is *preflighting*?
25. Identify the types of production proofs and explain how each is generated.
26. What are some advantages to using the PDF file format?

Suggested Activities

1. Prepare a workflow chart of a typical digital prepress department.
2. Select a product you want to print that includes line work and photographic images. Choose the computer platform to operate the software you will use to prepare the prepress project documents. Explain your equipment selection.
3. What ergonomic factors should be considered when setting up a computer workstation?
4. List the computer programs commonly used in your school and explain the unique features of each program.
5. Make an appointment to visit the prepress department of a printing plant. Describe the preflight plan used by the prepress personnel.
6. Research various printing facilities and make a list of the job titles found in the prepress department.

Related Web Links

The International Cooperation for the Integration of Processes in Prepress, Press, and Postpress Organization

www.cip4.org

CIP4 brings together vendors, consultants and end users in the print communications, graphic communications industry, and associated sectors to define future versions of Job Definition Format (JDF), to study user requirements, and to design a JDF Software Development Kit (SDK).

Merriam-Webster Online: Proofreaders' Marks

www.merriam-webster.com/mw/table/proofrea.htm

A table of commonly used proofreaders' marks and the meaning of each.

Printers' National Environmental Assistance Center

www.pneac.org

Resources include information on soft proofs in the printing industry.

CHAPTER

8

Digital Image Capture

Learning Objectives

After studying this chapter, you will be able to:

- Recall the difference between analog format and digital format.
- Identify the various types of light sensors used in imaging devices.
- Compare the characteristics of different CCD array configurations.
- Recall the different types of resolution.
- Identify different types of digital cameras.
- Summarize the function of each component on a digital camera.
- Understand the importance of proper lighting and its effect on the captured image.
- Recall the specific characteristics of each type of scanner.
- Explain how spatial resolution and tonal resolution affect the performance of digital imaging devices.
- Identify the use of common image manipulation program tools.

Important Terms

A/D converter	optical character
analog charge	recognition (OCR)
analog format	oil mounting
bit depth	paint effects
charge-coupled device	photomultiplier tube
(CCD)	(PMT)
CMOS APS	quantizing
digital format	resolution
drum scanner	retouching tools
dynamic range	scan area
film scanner	scanner
filter	screen ruling
flatbed scanner	spatial resolution
handheld scanner	sweet spot
histogram	tonal resolution
interpolation	unsharp masking
layers	(USM)
mask	well sites
mottling	XY scanning
Newton's rings	technology

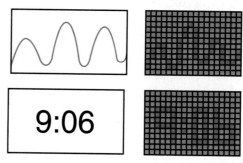

Figure 8-1. The curved line and time on the left represent analog format. The same curved line and time displayed on the right represent a digital format.

Since its introduction, digital imaging has had a steadily increasing impact on the printing industry. Computer software allows images to be quickly modified by changing or adding colors, removing unwanted components, or even combining multiple images. When paired with a computer modem, electronic images can be transmitted almost instantly around the world.

Some prepress operations may still depend on scanners for film and photo reproduction. However, digital cameras offer accurate RGB-to-CMYK conversion capabilities, which allows image files to bypass the scanning and color separation procedures and move directly into production flow.

ANALOG AND DIGITAL IMAGES

Photos taken with a film-based camera are in *analog format*. The principal feature of something in analog format is that it is continuous. Just as the volume control on a TV increases the sound in smooth increments from soft to loud, the image on a film negative has smooth gradations of tone from light to dark. In contrast, something in *digital format* consists of values measured at distinct points or positions, **Figure 8-1.** When an image in analog format is converted to digital format, each of

the distinct points represents variances in brightness and color of the image. These points are recorded as pixels (picture elements). Pixels are arranged in rows and columns to form a grid. An analog image is recorded into a digital format by assigning each pixel a set of numbers that designate position, brightness, and color.

When digitizing an image, using a large number of pixels, or dots per inch (dpi), produces more detail in the image, or better resolution. Additionally, setting a high *bit depth* results in smoother color gradations. The greater the bit depth, the more colors or grayscales are represented. For example, an 8-bit color image is comprised of 256 colors. But, a 24-bit color image can portray 16.7 million colors. A large color range is only useful if light sensors within the imaging device are capable of detecting a great number of distinct colors.

All digital imaging input devices function approximately in the same way: they expose the original with light and measure the amount of red, green, and blue light reflected back or transmitted through the object. These measurements are converted into digital data, which is then recorded onto an internal or external disk. The type of light-gathering sensors used by the imaging device determines both the dpi and bit depth. This is the key difference among various types of digital cameras, camera backs, and scanners.

analog format: The principal feature of something in analog format is that it is continuous. An image in analog format has smooth, continuous gradations of tone from light to dark.

digital format: Data stored with measured values and distinct points or positions. A digital image is stored with distinct points of varying brightness and color, which are recorded as pixels.

bit depth: The number of bits of color or grayscale information that can be recorded per pixel. The greater the bit depth, the more colors or grayscales can be represented.

LIGHT SENSORS

Both flatbed scanners and digital cameras use light-gathering sensors to gather information about an image. Just as film in a conventional camera records an image when light strikes it, these sensors use light to record an image electronically.

CCD Sensors

Charge-coupled devices (CCD) are solid-state chips composed of hundreds or even thousands of separate photosensitive elements known as *well sites*, or photosites. Each of the well sites in an array has a slightly different sensitivity from every other site.

The CCD converts light reflected from the subject matter into an *analog charge*, or series of electrical impulses. The charge is converted from analog to digital form through an *A/D converter*, and stored as pixels using binary code to represent the tonal values and detail of the subject. The A/D converter creates the digital image by converting the analog charge into a series of steps. This process is called *quantizing*.

Efficient CCD design is a trade-off between *resolution*, the sharpness and clarity of an image, and *dynamic range*, the gradations from light to dark. As individual well sites become smaller, the resolution of the CCD array increases. However, smaller well sites are less efficient at registering light intensity, so dynamic range suffers if they become too small. Most CCDs are designed to strike a balance between resolution and dynamic range.

The performance of a CCD is often measured by its output resolution, which is a function of the number of well sites on the CCD surface and shape of the pixels. A CCD for video technology has rectangular pixels, while sensors for computers are designed with square pixels.

Cameras are available with a variety of CCD configurations, including single-array/single-exposure, single-array/three- or four-exposure, single-array/one-, three-, or four-exposure, and trilinear-array/single-exposure. Scanners using CCD technology always use a trilinear array. The type of CCD configuration used by a camera, camera back, or scanner usually determines its cost, as well as the quality of the images it produces.

Because CCD sensors are inherently monochromatic, special filters are needed to separate the red, green, and blue (RGB) light reflected by an object. Designers have developed a number of ways to enable their digital imaging devices to capture color.

Single-Array/Single-Exposure

Cameras that use a single CCD array and a single exposure rely on RGB filtration decals to gather red, green, and blue color information, **Figure 8-2.** The filter decals may be arranged in rows to create a striped array, or a discontinuous pattern to create a mosaic array. With this method, three or four CCD well sites are used to gather RGB data for a single pixel. This results in a single-channel resolution that is one-third or one-fourth what it would otherwise be. Therefore, it is necessary to compensate for these low values by interpolating additional RGB data from neighboring pixels. A channel is one of the semi-transparent overlays that compose electronic images. For example, an image in RGB color is composed of red, green, and blue channels. In CMYK color, the image is composed of the four-color separations: cyan, magenta, yellow, and black.

Interpolation is a mathematical technique used to increase the apparent resolution of an image. Interpolation increases image resolution by adding data in intermediate shades of gray or color to surrounding areas. This may reduce the jagged appearance at the edges of the image, but it may also make them fuzzier. Interpolation generates varying degrees of image quality. Since interpolation yields higher resolution, it can smooth transition between gray or color gradation.

Single-Array/Three- or Four-Exposure

Single-array/three- or four-exposure CCDs use three or four exposures to create pure RGB data for

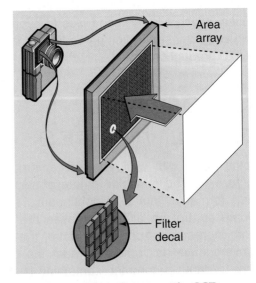

Figure 8-2. The resolution for a specific CCD corresponds to the total number of pixels and is determined by multiplying the horizontal by vertical pixel counts.

each pixel, **Figure 8-3.** The fourth exposure, when used, is a double pass to improve green rendition. The exposures are made through a rotating color-filter wheel positioned in front of the camera lens or CCD array. The advantage of individual exposures for RGB capture is more accurate color rendition because no interpolation is needed. The drawback is longer overall exposure times that do not tolerate movement during exposure.

Single-Array/One-, Three-, or Four-Exposure

This design uses a single mosaic CCD array with one or more exposures. When RGB data is captured using three or four exposures, the CCD array is repositioned between each of the exposures by piezoelectric motors, **Figure 8-4.** The CCD array changes position to align itself with the appropriately filtered light path that provides data for the respective pixels. This approach allows pure RGB data to be gathered for each pixel without resorting to interpolation.

Digital cameras that use this design often provide a single-exposure mode to stop motion and extend the camera's versatility. When operating in single-exposure mode, the mosaic CCD array gathers 25% of the total pixel resolution for the red and blue channels and 50% for the green channel. The remaining pixel resolution is interpolated to bring each channel up to 100%.

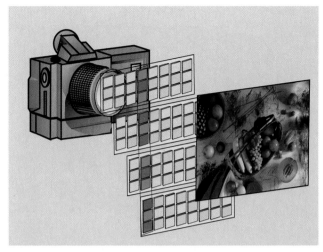

Figure 8-4. A single array/one-, three-, or four-exposure design uses a single mosaic CCD array with one or more exposures.

Trilinear-Array/Single-Exposure

In a trilinear-array/single-exposure configuration, three CCD chips are built into the camera, **Figure 8-5.** After light passes through the lens, it is split into three portions that travel to individual CCD arrays. The individual arrays are filtered to independently record red, green, and blue. This configuration achieves a non-interpolated RGB image capture without the need for multiple exposures. However, cameras with this design tend to be both bulky and costly. In order to keep the camera competitively priced, it is necessary to use moderate resolution CCD chips.

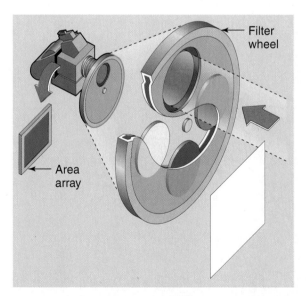

Figure 8-3. A three-exposure CCD area array captures tricolor image information through RGB filters positioned on a rotating wheel in front of the lens or the film plane.

charge-coupled device (CCD): A solid-state, light-sensitive chip receptor that converts light into an analog charge; commonly built into image capturing devices.

well sites: Hundreds or thousands of photosensitive elements on a CCD.

analog charge: A series of electrical impulses created with the light received by the CCD.

A/D converter: A device used to convert an analog charge into digital form. The result of this conversion is stored as pixel data.

quantizing: A filtering process that determines the amount and selection of data to eliminate, which makes it possible to encode data with fewer bits.

resolution: The sharpness and clarity of an image.

dynamic range: The gradations from light to dark that a digital imaging device can read or produce.

interpolation: A mathematical technique used to increase the apparent resolution of an image. Image resolution is increased by adding data in intermediate shades of gray or color to surrounding areas.

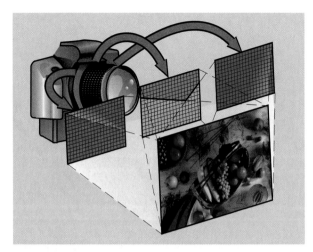

Figure 8-5. Three CCD arrays are built into a trilinear array/single-exposure camera.

CMOS APS Sensors

A complementary metal oxide semiconductor active pixel sensor, or **CMOS APS**, is a low-cost light sensor chip commonly used in low-end digital cameras. A basic point-and-shoot camera that uses a CMOS APS sensor can capture images at 1000 × 800 dpi. This is 2.6 times the resolution obtained by the common 640 × 480 dpi digital camera. CMOS APS chips have many advantages, including lower power consumption than CCDs, analog-to-digital conversion capabilities on the chip, and even integrating signal processing, such as image compression and color encoding.

DIGITAL CAMERAS AND CAMERA BACKS

Photojournalists require easy-to-handle cameras that can freeze motion in a single exposure. Product or still-life photography requires cameras with the ability to capture fine detail and tonal nuances. The specific needs of the photographer and desired results determine which digital camera or camera back design should be used.

Digital cameras and camera backs are available in a number of designs and range of capabilities. A digital camera back attaches to and replaces the back of a film-based camera. This back has an electronic sensor to capture the image. Rather than using film, the film-based camera is now a digital camera. Digital cameras and camera backs can be divided into three main categories: studio, field, and point-and-shoot.

Studio Cameras

Studio cameras include most of the high-end, digital camera backs designed for commercial use. These cameras are characterized by high- or ultra-high resolution and excellent, non-interpolated (pure RGB data) color rendition, **Figure 8-6.**

When digital cameras are used in a photography studio, images can be viewed on a computer monitor to evaluate progress. The ability to refine composition and lighting by viewing progressive changes eliminates the need for film, chemical processing, and, most importantly, the one-to-two hour wait for film verification.

Low-resolution, for-position-only (FPO) image files are available within minutes. FPO files can be dropped into the client's layout while work continues in the studio. The client is quickly provided with materials that allow visual assessment of the project. The client can take the FPO files, which are typically 72 dpi, and use them to complete the project's design. The final, color-separated CMYK images are often ready for placement in the master document within 24 hours.

Scanning Backs with Trilinear Arrays

Scanning camera backs usually use trilinear CCD arrays, **Figure 8-7.** In place of a square or rectangular chip, a trilinear array uses three rows of

Figure 8-6. Studio cameras are versatile and available in several sizes. (MegaVision)

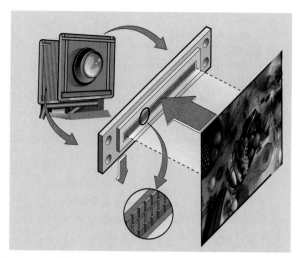

Figure 8-7. This trilinear array CCD camera back with three embedded color filters captures RGB data in a single pass.

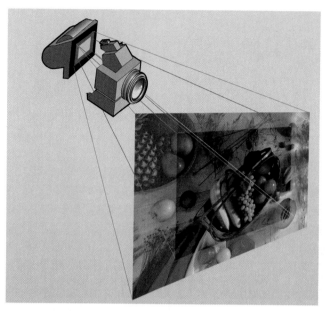

Figure 8-8. The CCD array of digital camera backs is often smaller than the film format.

CCD elements (one each for red, green, and blue) that run across the shortest side of the image capture area. When an exposure is made, the trilinear array moves slowly across the width of the film plane. As the array moves, it measures the light intensity of a predetermined number of pixel positions and writes image information as a stream of digital data. To scan at maximum resolution using this type of camera back, the image capture process may take as long as ten minutes.

Format Differences

With many digital camera backs, the CCD array is often smaller than the film format for which the camera was designed, **Figure 8-8.** The size difference between the CCD array and the format of the host camera creates two significant problems: the image seen in the viewfinder is larger than the live image area, and the narrow angle of view created by the CCD array increases the lens focal length.

When the image seen in the viewfinder is larger than the live image area, it must be cropped to accurately display the angle of view that corresponds to the CCD array. For instance, the live image area of a 35 mm film-based camera is 24 mm × 36 mm. However, the CCD array fitted to a 35 mm camera reduces the live image area to approximately 8 mm × 12 mm. A similar size discrepancy occurs with medium-format cameras. The potential live image area of a 6 cm × 6 cm square format design is reduced to about 3 cm × 3 cm, approximately 1/4 of the original area. With the viewing area cropped to 25% or less of its original size, arranging the compositional elements

becomes increasingly difficult. This is especially true when trying to distinguish subtle tonal differences or fine detail.

The CCD array creates a narrow angle of view of the live image area, which increases the lens focal length 2 to 2.6 times. For example, a 50 mm normal focal length lens placed on a 35 mm camera with an 8 mm × 12 mm CCD array becomes, in effect, a 130 mm medium-length telephoto. To compensate and approximate the normal angle of view, a 20 mm lens is required. For a medium-format camera using a 3 cm × 3 cm CCD array, a normal focal length lens of 80 mm is transformed into a 160 mm telephoto. A 40 mm lens is needed to provide a more accurate angle of view.

Most digital camera backs introduce a different format when used in place of the host camera's native film back, **Figure 8-9.** However, manufacturers have introduced camera backs with CCD arrays that measure the same size as their film counterparts. The capability of using a camera back with a full-format CCD array offers two advantages over other hybrid designs. First, the dimensions of the image seen in the viewfinder are close to, if not identical to, those of the image captured by the CCD array. Second, there is no change in lens focal length between film and digital formats.

CMOS APS: Complementary metal oxide semiconductor active pixel sensor. An active light sensor chip commonly used in low-end digital cameras.

Figure 8-9. This camera back is mounted on a high-quality, medium-format camera. (MegaVision)

Figure 8-10. Many types of digital point and shoot cameras are available in the marketplace today. Each has different capabilities and features.

Figure 8-11. Digital SLR cameras allow lenses to be interchanged to meet the needs of any shooting environment and subject matter.

Field Cameras

Field cameras are so named because of their portability. These cameras must be capable of stopping motion. This means the RGB data is usually gathered in a single exposure with a single CCD array. Although several manufacturers offer designs that use multiple arrays and gather pure RGB data, most field cameras use interpolation schemes to produce moderately high RGB resolution. As a result, their color fidelity is usually somewhat less than the studio camera's.

Point-and-Shoot Cameras

A point-and-shoot type of camera comes in a variety of sizes and features, **Figure 8-10.** Many digital cameras are designed to be used by causal or amateur photographers. A digital SLR (single lens reflex) camera is most often used by serious and professional photographers. Full digital SLR cameras allow lenses to be interchanged, **Figure 8-11.** For example, this allows a macro lens to be removed and replaced with a lens that has greater distance capabilities.

DIGITAL CAMERAS

When buying a digital camera, it is important to select a camera that fits your needs. The size and price of cameras varies greatly and model changes come with surprising frequency. Cameras have many features and options that differentiate various models. Carefully evaluate the characteristics of the cameras that fit your needs.

The pixel is a very small square dot that is used to make a picture. A high number of pixels means increased picture resolution, which determines the printing quality. **Figure 8-12** shows typical resolutions for some common applications.

Digital cameras use removable memory cards to record picture data. Some of the common types of memory cards are CompactFlash®, xD, and SD. See **Figure 8-13.** The available storage capacity of memory cards varies; 4 GB cards have less available storage capacity than 16 GB cards. However, the cost of a memory card increases as the storage capacity increases. Storage media can be formatted and used over and over again.

The images are stored as digital files in format design as JPEG, RAW, or TIFF files. JPEG files capture small and fast, but also have file compression that may introduce artifacts that degrade the image greatly. TIFF files are large and can slow down

Resolution	Application
640×480	E-mail and 3×5 prints
1200×1600	5×7 prints
2016×3040	9×12 prints

Figure 8-12. Typical resolutions for common applications.

Figure 8-13. Digital cameras have a port on the camera body that accommodates only the type of memory card cited in the camera's specs.

shooting, but have no compression artifacts. RAW files are smaller than TIFFs. Special software, which may not be found on all cameras, is required to read the RAW files.

Digital Camera Components and Features

Though the main components of a camera typically remain the same from model to model, the capabilities and features may differ greatly. Be aware of the different options available on various camera models.

Lens

Some lenses are permanently attached to the camera, while others can be detached and replaced with another lens. Lenses on digital cameras have two types of zoom options: optical and digital zoom. Optical zoom is a true function, which uses the camera's optics to change the closeness of the photographed object. This is an important feature to evaluate before purchasing a digital camera. Digital zoom is a software feature that does not rely on the abilities of the lens. When using digital zoom, some

of the detail in a picture is almost always lost. The lens aperture determines the speed of the lens. The lower the f-stop setting, the faster the lens (f-1.8 or f-2.8). A fast lens can capture low-light images by giving more exposure to the CCD.

Viewfinder and LCD

Optical viewfinders on digital cameras serve the same purpose as those on film camera, which is to frame the scene and shoot the picture. For photographers who wear glasses, an optical viewfinder equipped with an adapter allows the focus of the viewfinder to be adjusted.

Most digital cameras also have a liquid crystal display (LCD) screen on the back of the camera that displays the exact image being photographed. Look for a sharp LCD screen that shows an excellent image in both bright and dim light. The size of the LCD screen does not determine the size of the final image. The LCD screen also allows in-camera review and editing of images, which may be accomplished before downloading the photos to a computer.

Batteries

Digital cameras require a large amount of power because the image sensor, LCD screen, flash unit, and microprocessor are all powered at the same time. Three common types of batteries are alkaline, lithium-ion, or nickel-metal-hydride. Alkaline batteries are convenient because they are available at many local retail and convenience stores. While many of these batteries are rechargeable, alkaline batteries do not have a long life. The rechargeable lithium-ion or nickel-metal-hydride batteries are longer lasting and require a charging module. Most cameras also come with a built-in rechargeable battery.

Flash

Lighting conditions may often require additional illumination, **Figure 8-14.** A flash unit on the camera addresses that need. When shooting people or animals, it is recommended that the camera have a red-eye-reduction flash. Many cameras have a built-in flash, while others are equipped with a hot shoe (attachment point) for an external flash unit. The hot shoe allows the flash to be secured to the camera and electronically connects it to the camera.

Image Stabilization

Image stabilization is a camera feature that detects and counteracts camera movement. This feature is particularly useful when handheld shots

Figure 8-14. To compensate for various lighting conditions, various flash units may be attached to a camera or be added to the shooting environment.

are taken at slower shutter speeds or with long focal-length lenses. Knowledge of this feature is imperative to eliminate blurred images caused by camera shake.

Optical image stabilization is a mechanism that is found in handheld still cameras and video cameras. It is a feature built into the lens to assist in the stabilization of the recorded image by varying the optical path to the sensor. Digital image stabilization is used in some video cameras to counteract motion.

Exposure Modes

Digital cameras are programmed with a fully automatic mode, which allows the operator to point the camera and shoot an image. When reviewing a camera's exposure control, look for aperture and shutter priority modes. The full manual mode allows the operator total control of the camera's settings.

Even though digital point-and-shoot cameras do not completely rival their conventional counterparts, the introduction of affordable, higher-quality point-and-shoot cameras has increased their use by nonprofessionals. Many lower-end cameras now offer advanced features originally found only on professional equipment.

Image Capture Time

The amount of time required to write image-capture files to disc limits the performance of all digital cameras and digital camera backs. Write times tend to be longer for trilinear scanning backs, but field cameras and some point-and-shoot designs may face a similar problem. Even though image capture by an area array requires only a fraction of

a second, the size of the camera's internal buffer determines how many sequential exposures can be made before the camera must pause to write the files to an internal or external storage device.

The buffer is a temporary storage area that enables the manipulation of data before it is transferred for internal or external storage. With a small buffer or with high-resolution files, the camera may need to pause after every exposure. More sophisticated designs may permit up to a dozen sequential exposures before a pause is required to write to disc.

With lower-resolution single-array/single-exposure cameras, the write-to-disc time is often 1–3 seconds. Higher-resolution field cameras may need as long as 12 seconds. Digital cameras that depend on a rotating filter wheel to make individual RGB exposures on a single CCD usually require 5–30 seconds to write the image-capture files to disc. Because trilinear arrays use a wide range of resolution settings, the write-to-disc time may be as short as 30 seconds or as long as 10 minutes.

Lighting Considerations

When shooting with film-based cameras, lighting adjustments are usually made by changing the direction of light, its degree of diffusion, its color, or its intensity. The photographer can use lens filters, light deflectors, different types of lightbulbs, or different types of film to acquire the desired results. Although many of the same lighting methods are used when shooting with digital cameras, there are several special requirements.

The standard color temperature reference for digital cameras and daylight film emulsions is 5500 K, **Figure 8-15.** This reference corresponds to lighting conditions under a clear blue sky with unobstructed sunlight (roughly between 10:00 a.m. and 2:00 p.m.). These qualifications are necessary because daylight, being subject to the movement of sun, clouds, and weather fronts, is extremely variable. For instance, if the sun is obscured by clouds, color temperature rises because the proportion of warm, direct light is decreased.

The direction of daylight and how the light falls on the subject being photographed affects the color temperature. If the light is from the north sky with the sun obscured, the color temperature may rise to 10,000 K or higher. This results in very cool, bluish light. In early morning or late evening, when the sun is low on the horizon, the color temperature may fall to 2500 K to 3500 K.

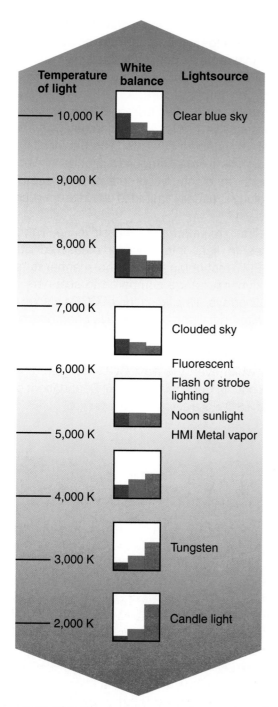

Figure 8-15. This illustration approximates the color temperature of some common light sources. (Agfa)

three to ten minutes. Scanning backs record pixel information three rows at a time as they step across the image-capture plane. Slight variations in light intensity can cause banding in certain regions of the image, instead of an even tone.

Normal surges in the electrical current cause fluctuations in light intensity. Due to the sensitivity of scanning CCD arrays, this fluctuation in lighting results in tonal irregularities in the image. To counteract this problem, several manufacturers offer flicker-free lighting solutions that smooth out current surges. Hydrargyrum medium-arc iodide (HMI) lighting provides another alternative to the problems presented by tungsten lighting. HMI lights are a high-intensity flicker-free source of illumination that is balanced for 5500 K output. The greater illumination intensity allows photographers to shoot at smaller lens apertures, which produces greater depth of field. A drawback of HMI lighting is the extreme heat output compared to tungsten sources. This makes it difficult to place filters and screens in front of the lamps or to photograph perishable food items.

The most commonly used lighting for commercial studio photography is an electronic flash or tungsten. Daylight is not usually used because of its variability and the additional lighting controls required to maintain consistent color temperature. In addition to freezing motion, an advantage of electronic flash is its consistent color temperature. It simulates the effect of shooting under constant daylight conditions, which lends a consistent visual appearance to ongoing projects, such as shooting for product catalogs.

When a digital camera uses multiple exposures to gather RGB data, it is important for the color temperature to be constant throughout the exposure cycle. Most manufacturers build their electronic flash equipment to deliver a color temperature of 5500 K regardless of flash duration or intensity. If the color temperature shifts during exposure, it affects the gray balance of the resulting image. When this occurs, color correction may be necessary using image-editing software. For this reason, it is not practical to shoot with three- or four-exposure RGB image-capture cameras under variable daylight conditions.

Handheld digital cameras designed for single-exposure use have much more flexibility in terms of their lighting requirements, **Figure 8-16.** Moderately expensive field cameras have built-in flash-synchronized connections that simplify use with a variety of electronic flash equipment. Focal plane shutters permit a range of flash-synchronized shutter speeds and make it possible to combine multiple light sources for a single exposure. Many of

Before the advent of electronic flash, 3200 K was the standard for tungsten lighting used by studio photographers and cinematographers. During the last few decades, the widespread use of electronic flash has decreased the use of tungsten lighting. However, certain digital camera designs have caused a resurgence in the use of tungsten lighting.

Cameras that use trilinear scanning arrays depend on constant and steady lighting conditions because RGB exposure times often extend from

Figure 8-16. Features of this camera include a built-in flash and a lens that can be rotated to shoot from almost any angle or be detached completely and used with a cable connection. (Photo courtesy of Minolta Corporation)

these cameras provide an electronic bias for often-used light sources such as electronic flash, daylight, tungsten, and fluorescent.

Less expensive point-and-shoot digital cameras include built-in electronic flash capability. This feature enables them to provide greater consistency under variable shooting conditions including daylight, tungsten light, and fluorescent light. Since the flash is designed to be the primary light source, off-color secondary lighting is less detrimental to good grayscale.

SCANNERS

A *scanner* is an electronic device that measures the color densities of an original image, stores those measurements as digital information, manipulates or alters the data, and uses the data to create four-color separations. Scanners use either a CCD array or photomultiplier tubes to capture the image as a raster or bitmapped graphic.

A scanner's imaging quality is affected by many variables, including dynamic range, resolution, quality of optics, the light source used, the number of bits per color, and aperture. Differences in any of these variables explains why the sharpness of an image of 4000 dpi resolution can vary from one scanner to another. *Unsharp masking (USM)* is the increase of tonal contrast where light and dark tones come together at the edges of an image. USM is accomplished electronically on a color scanner by comparing readings taken through two different-size

apertures, and adding the signal difference between the two readings to the signal from the larger aperture. This signal reduces density in the lighter areas of the original and increases density in the darker areas, creating a sharper picture.

A *photomultiplier tube (PMT)* is composed of highly sensitive photocells that transform variations in light into electric currents. The photocells create input signals to the computing circuits in electronic scanners. In electronic prepress production, PMT technology is usually limited to use in drum scanners, **Figure 8-17.**

PMTs are extremely sensitive to light, and changes in light intensity are measured at each pixel. PMT technology allows the scanner to "see" a wider dynamic range compared to scanners based on CCD arrays. This limitation of CCDs also explains why image data from CCD arrays often needs to be interpolated.

PMTs can detect optical densities (D) from 0.0 D to 4.0 D, while even the best CCD scanners can only detect optical densities up to 3.7 D, and most cannot exceed 2.8 D. For a scanner with a range of 0 D–3.0 D, the

Figure 8-17. Drum scanners use photomultiplier tubes (PMTs) as the light-sensing device instead of a CCD array. (Fuji Photo Film U.S.A., Inc.)

difference between the lightest and darkest detectable intensities is 1000:1. In a scanner with a range of 4.0 D, this difference is 10,000:1. This means that PMT scanners can distinguish ten times more shades or tones for each pixel than typical CCD scanners. This is especially important in the shadow areas of an image, where PMT scanners deliver much more shadow detail than CCD scanners.

Depending on the type of scanner, almost any type or size of original material can be scanned. This includes film negatives or positives (transparencies), photographic prints, printed media, drawings, graphs, and text. Text scanning requires the use of an *optical character recognition (OCR)* system. Scanners do not distinguish text from illustrations and represent all images as bitmaps. Therefore, you cannot directly edit text that has been scanned. To edit text read by an optical scanner, you must use an OCR system to translate the image into ASCII characters.

Many scanners allow the operator to specify whether RGB or CMYK color separations are to be made. There are four basic types of scanners in use: handheld, drum, flatbed, and film.

Handheld Scanner

Handheld scanners are small devices that you move across a piece of paper or image by hand. Handheld scanners are often called half-page scanners because they can only scan 2″–5″ at a time. Handheld scanners are adequate for small pictures and photos, but they are impractical for scanning large amounts of text or graphics, **Figure 8-18.**

Drum Scanner

The *drum scanner*, or rotary scanner, scans images mounted on a rotating drum, **Figure 8-19.** The drum spins quickly in front of a stationary reading head. As the drum rotates, the original material is illuminated by a halogen or pulsed xenon arc (PXA) lamp that pans slowly across the front of the drum. Light is transmitted through or reflected from the original, then passed through an aperture to the PMT light sensors where color measurements are made.

Most drum scanners use a set of three PMTs. Each of these sensors gathers information on one of the three additive primary colors (red, green, and blue). This allows all color information to be gathered

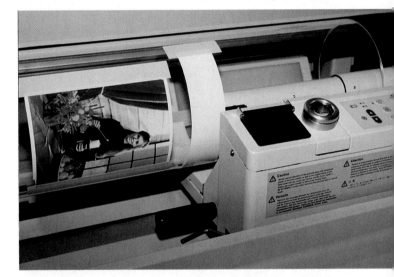

Figure 8-19. To capture images with a drum (rotary) scanner, the original material is mounted on a rotating drum.

scanner: An electronic imaging device that measures the color densities of an original, stores the measurements as digital information, manipulates or alters the data, and uses the data to create four color separations.

unsharp masking (USM): A function of some scanners that increases tonal contrast where light and dark tones come together at the edges of the images.

photomultiplier tube (PMT): A light-sensing device composed of highly sensitive photocells that transform variations in light into electric currents.

optical character recognition (OCR): A system used to translate the bitmap image of scanned text into ASCII characters.

handheld scanner: A small scanner is moved across a page or image by hand. Also referred to as *half-page scanners*.

drum scanner: A type of scanner that scans images mounted on a rotating drum.

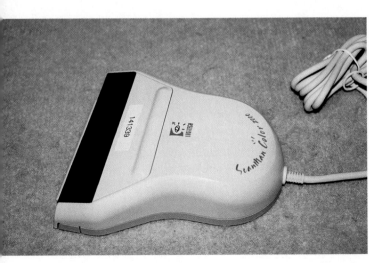

Figure 8-18. Hand-held scanners can scan small areas of text and photos.

in a single pass. Less-expensive drum scanners may have only one sensor, which requires three passes to gather the RGB information. Drum scanners may also use a fourth PMT sensor for unsharp masking.

Some drum scanners are capable of resolutions as high 12,000 dpi or 12,000 scanning samples per inch (spi). This is enough to enlarge an image by almost 50 times.

A scanner's versatility determines the kinds of jobs and volume of work that can be performed. Drum scanners can handle mixed media without any special masks, frames, or carriers. They can perform batch scans of mixed media, and permit the operator to mount artwork on removable drums while another drum is in use. *Oil mounting* can also be used with drum scanners. In this process, transparent originals are coated with a small amount of oil or gel to reduce scratches and imperfections, **Figure 8-20.**

In general, drum scanners have a larger scanning area than flatbed units. Many offer scanning drums of 20″ × 24″ or greater. Large drum sizes allow large originals to be scanned or batch scanning of a greater number of smaller originals. One important limitation of drum scanners is that originals must be thin (1.8″ or less) and flexible enough to be wrapped around a drum. Drum scanners are available as horizontal or vertical units, **Figure 8-21.** Vertical drum scanners take up less space; some of the drums have "pockets" to hold images in place. With some vertical scanners, the centrifugal force within the spinning drum holds images in place.

Flatbed Scanner

Flatbed scanners process images that are placed on a glass bed, or *scan area*, **Figure 8-22.** The scan area varies in size from machine to machine, and can be as small as 8.5″ × 11″ (216 mm × 280 mm) or

Figure 8-20. When using oil mounting, originals are coated with a small amount of liquid and held in place with a flexible insert. When the scanner rotates, the originals press against the interior wall of the drum, which forces the oil into a uniform layer. (ICG North America)

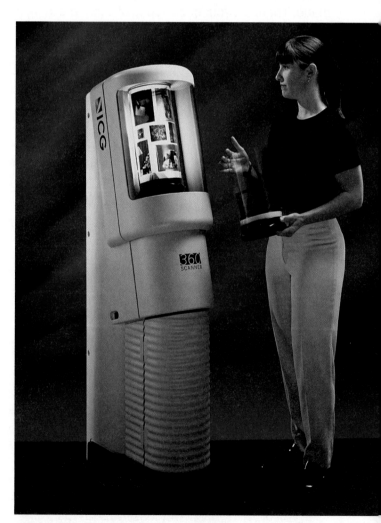

Figure 8-21. Vertical drum scanners require less floor space than horizontal models. (ICG North America)

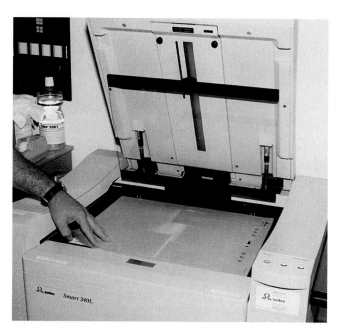

Figure 8-22. In this example, images are placed on the glass bed of the scanner and covered with a translucent sheet.

Figure 8-23. This desktop scanner uses a stationary bed, so the scanning head moves across the scan area.

larger than 13″ × 18″ (330 mm × 457 mm). Flatbed scanners are designed with either a stationary or moving bed. If the bed is stationary, the scanning head moves, **Figure 8-23.** If the bed moves, the scanning head is stationary.

Most flatbed scanners use trilinear CCD arrays and a single pass to capture images. After light passes through or is reflected from the image, it is split into three portions that travel to individual CCD arrays that are filtered to record red, green, and blue independently. Some flatbed scanners provide the user with a choice of resolution. A higher-resolution image commonly requires the interpolation of data.

The linear array in a scanner is arranged in a row on a single silicon chip. If the bed is stationary, the movement of the light source within the scanner (along with a mirror) directs consecutive lines of image data onto the CCD array via a second mirror and a lens unit. The full length of the image is read simultaneously as a line.

With the use of a magnetic image holder, some manufacturers have eliminated the glass between the image and the optics, **Figure 8-24.** This helps preserve sharpness, and reduce distortion and *Newton's rings*. These rings are undesirable color patterns caused by interference between the exposure light and its reflected beam from the closest adjacent surface. Newton's rings may reproduce as unwanted *mottling* of halftones or tint areas.

As with drum scanners, the versatility of a flatbed scanner determines the kinds of jobs and volume of work it can perform. Flatbed units can scan original materials that vary in thickness; many units can even scan three-dimensional objects. Flatbeds are adaptable to automation features, such as page feeders. Templates can be used to set up work with bar codes that specify size, location, and resolution requirements, **Figure 8-25.**

Although flatbed scanners are versatile and lower in cost than drum scanners, they do not match the output quality of drum scanners. For most ink-on-paper output, however, it is difficult to tell the difference between comparably priced flatbed and drum scanners.

One common complaint about flatbed scanners is the degradation of quality outside the 3″ area in the center of the bed called the *sweet spot*. Conventional flatbeds do not scan at full resolution across the

oil mounting: A method of mounting transparent original material onto a drum scanner. The originals are coated with a small amount of mounting oil or gel to reduce scratches and imperfections before being mounted on the drum.

flatbed scanner: A type of scanner that scans images placed on a glass bed, or scan area.

scan area: The section of a scanning device on which images are placed for scanning.

Newton's rings: An undesirable color pattern that results from interference between the exposure light and its reflected beam from the closest adjacent surface.

mottling: The blotchy or cloudy appearance of an image, instead of a smooth, continuous tone.

sweet spot: A 3″ or 4″ area in the center of a flatbed scanner at which the scanner scans material at full resolution.

Figure 8-24. On this scanner, images (reflective or transparent) are mounted in a magnetic holder and placed on the light table. The original is automatically flexed into the scanner and rolls past the image sensor. (imacon)

Figure 8-25. Many scanner manufacturers provide formatted and unformatted templates or holders for use with flatbed scanners. (Scitex America Corp.)

entirebed. Therefore, unless the original is small enough and centered directly in the sweet spot, resolution quality decreases toward the outer edges of the image. This also makes batch scanning more difficult.

XY scanning technology overcomes this problem by optimally positioning the scanning head along an XY axis. The scanner head slides both horizontally and vertically beneath the bed, **Figure 8-26.** In traditional flatbed scanners, the scanning head moves in one direction only. This dual motion allows images to be captured with uniformly high resolution and sharpness over the entire bed surface. For example, an 8″ × 10″ original scanned at 300 dpi using an XY scanner may be enlarged up to 2700% for top-quality poster production. If the same job were performed on a conventional flatbed, the uneven resolution would limit enlargement to about 400%. The practical limit of non-interpolated images from high-end flatbed scanners is about 5000 dpi.

Film Scanner

Film scanners are specially-designed CCD scanners that allow the user to capture images from various types of film. Some scanners are designed specifically for 35 mm film or slides, **Figure 8-27.** Film scanners are usually small enough to place on a desktop. As with flatbed CCD scanners, imaging speed and resolution capabilities depend on the quality of the CCDs.

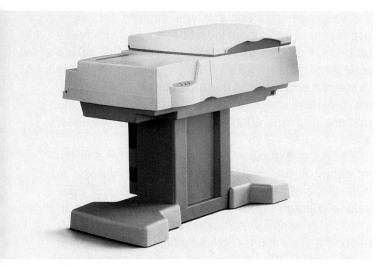

Figure 8-26. The scanning head on this multipurpose flatbed scanner can be positioned at any point beneath the platen, allowing XY scanning. (Fuji Photo Film U.S.A., Inc.)

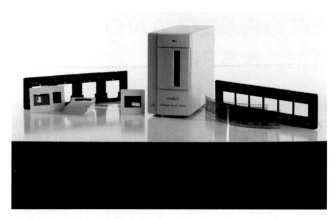

Figure 8-27. A film scanner can digitally capture images from film or slides.

Image Capture Time

Image capture time depends on the scanner's resolution capabilities and the type and number of images being scanned. The computer system's hard drive capabilities also affect a scanner's image capture time. Many scanners provide a preview image within 8–15 seconds and can complete a high-resolution scan within 60 seconds.

A scanner can be set up to send image files directly to the computer's hard drive or to an external storage device. When working with image files, or any large file, working off the hard drive is recommended due to speed of processing and stability.

Many scanners provide background processing, which allows the operator to view scans while the scanner continues working. When batch-scanning 25

originals, for example, the first two or three pre-scans can be opened as soon as they are complete. The operator can tighten crops, specify magnification, color-correct, and submit the scans to the scan queue. By the time all 25 pre-scans are complete, several high-resolution scans will also have been completed.

As the scanner continues working on the high-resolution scans, the operator can open and examine the first scans in an image editing program. If one of the high-resolution images is not acceptable, it can be disposed of and the pre-scan may be recalled and sent back to the scan queue. All initial cropping, sharpening, and other parameters are still valid, which means very little time is wasted.

Light Sources

Most flatbed and film scanners use a fluorescent light source. Some systems even use dual fluorescent lamps. Drum scanners use tungsten halogen, quartz halogen, or PXA lamps as a light source. Active cooling systems are required to keep the units from overheating and to keep CCD sensitivity at its highest levels.

IMAGE FILE SIZE AND RESOLUTION

The size of a digital image file in megabytes (MB) determines the reproduction size possible within a specific screen ruling. The *screen ruling* is the number of ruled lines per inch (lpi) on a halftone screen.

To calculate file size, multiply the number of horizontal pixels by the number of vertical pixels in the CCD array. The product is the file size for a single channel or black-and-white rendition. For RGB color, multiply the file size for one channel by three. For example, if the horizontal and vertical dimensions of a CCD array are 3060×2036 pixels, multiply these dimensions to find the file size for a single channel. In this case, the product is 6,230,160, or just over six megabytes. To get RGB color, multiply 6 MB $\times$ 3 to get a file size of 18 MB.

XY scanning technology: Scanning technology that optimally positions the scanning head along an XY axis.

film scanner: A specially designed CCD scanner that captures images from various types of film.

screen ruling: The number of ruled grid lines per inch (lpi) on a halftone screen.

The next step in this example is to determine if the pixel resolution is sufficient to output a 5″ × 7″ image at a 200 lpi screen ruling. High-quality reproduction requires two pixel samples for each line of resolution. So, a minimum image resolution of 400 dpi is necessary to use a screen ruling of 200 lpi. By multiplying the 5″ × 7″ image dimensions by 400 dpi, resolution is 2000 × 2800. The total minimum file size is 5.6 MB per channel. Therefore, in this example, the original file size of 6 MB per channel is slightly more than needed to maintain the desired quality. Typically, a high-resolution image should be about twice the line screen value.

Spatial and Tonal Resolution

Spatial resolution refers to the ability of a digital imaging device to address data in horizontal and vertical dimensions. See **Figure 8-28.** Digital imaging devices should also be evaluated in terms of tonal resolution. *Tonal resolution*, or bit depth, is the number of bits of color or grayscale information that can be recorded per pixel. An 8-bit digital image capture device can record 256 colors or levels of gray per channel. Increased tonal resolution in digital cameras allows the camera better exposure latitude. Exposure latitude is the amount of overexposure or underexposure of an image that is acceptable for final production. Better exposure latitude allows the photographer to shoot in difficult lighting situations with greater confidence.

When using an 8-bit digital camera, shooting a subject at the correct exposure is critical to obtain good highlight and shadow rendition. In many lighting situations, an 8-bit tonal scale is just long enough to provide good highlight and shadow detail, but only if the midtone is placed exactly in the correct position.

The exposure latitude is similar to what photographers experience when shooting fine grain transparency films. If it is not within 1/3 f-stop of the correct midtone position, the image will be either underexposed or overexposed. Overexposure results in the loss of highlight detail; underexposure results in the loss of shadow detail.

When using digital cameras and camera backs with 12 bits or more of tonal resolution per channel, the increase in exposure latitude means the photographer has a greater margin for error. Midtone placement may be off by as much as one full f-stop in some cases. The longer tonal range resulting from increased bit depth permits the camera to render good highlight and shadow detail, despite difficult lighting situations or exposure miscalculation.

To properly evaluate image capture files, it is necessary to open them in an image-editing software program that provides a *histogram* display of the pixel information, **Figure 8-29.** In graphic form, the histogram appears as a horizontal display of highlight, midtone, and shadow values that correspond to the number of pixels affected in each part of the tonal scale.

A good exposure is characterized by smooth tapering of the highlight and shadow values at opposite ends of the scale. If the display of pixel values appears cut off at either end, the highlight or shadow information has been lost due to incorrect exposure. To ensure correct highlight, midtone, and shadow detail, it is best to make a new image capture of the subject using the predetermined exposure adjustment.

IMAGE FILE STORAGE AND TRANSFER

Ongoing advances in digital technology have made it possible to design increasingly high-resolution cameras and scanners. The 2000 × 2000 CCD array used in many medium- and large-format cameras produces a file size of 4 MB per channel (12 MB for an RGB file). For handheld 35 mm cameras, resolutions as high as 2036 × 3060 pixels (18 MB RGB file) are available. Ultra-high resolution CCDs with pixel dimensions of 4000 × 4000 (48 MB), are commonly used by commercial photographers.

With higher resolution capabilities, the captured image files have steadily grown in size. Storage devices, such as flash drives, CDs, and internal/external hard drives, are used to store the larger image files. Because digital cameras are often used to capture images "on the fly," they require unique transfer speed and storage capabilities. For example, quick and adequate file storage is essential for digital cameras used in news gathering and sports coverage.

Internal and External Storage Devices

Many digital camera backs and most scanners rely on a computer workstation to store image files, and are connected to the workstation while in use. Some field cameras include internal hard drives with storage capacities ranging from 16 MB to 4 GB, or

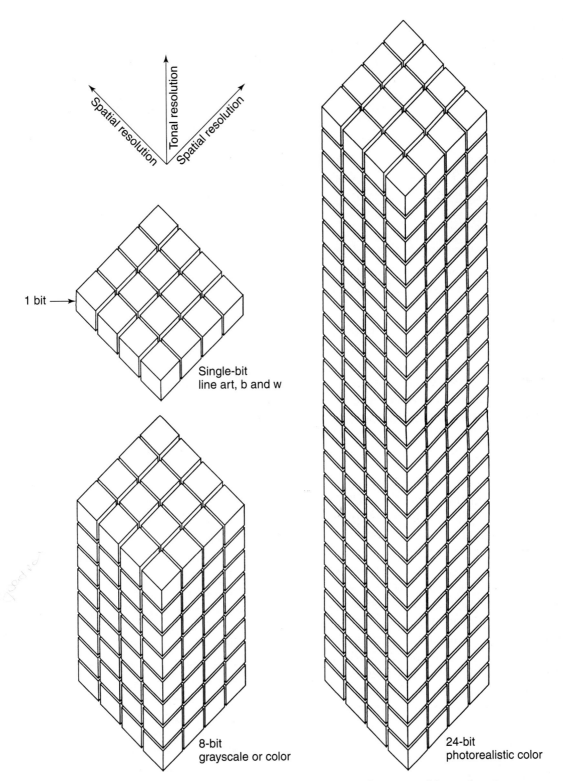

Figure 8-28. Spatial resolution refers to the ability of a digital imaging device to address data in two dimensions—horizontal and vertical.

spatial resolution: The ability of a digital imaging device to address data in horizontal and vertical dimensions.

tonal resolution: The number of bits of color or grayscale information that can be recorded per pixel. The greater the bit depth, the more colors or grayscales can be represented.

histogram: A graphic display of highlight, midtone, and shadow values that correspond to the number of pixels affected in each part of the tonal scale.

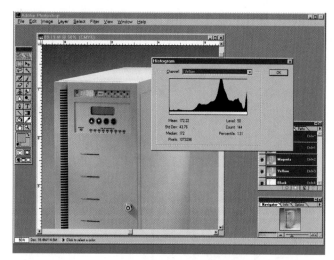

Figure 8-29. A histogram provides a graphic display of how the pixel values in an image are distributed.

more. While it is convenient to have digital images automatically write to a hard disk drive, files cannot be downloaded without temporarily removing the camera from an active shooting situation. To avoid this problem, photographers can use a removable storage device known as digital film or PCMCIA cards.

Data Transfer

Most serial and parallel ports have been replaced by the Universal Serial Bus (USB). The USB is designed to allow various peripherals to be connected to a standardized socket. The three most common types of USB plugs are Type A, Type B, and Type Mini-B, **Figure 8-30.** Type A plugs are found on various types of storage devices and peripherals, such as keyboards and computer mice. Type B plugs are commonly found on printer cables. Type Mini-B plugs can be found on various devices, such as digital cameras. The speed of USB cables depends on their specifications. For example, a USB 1.1 cable transfers data at a rate of 1.5 megabits per second, while a USB 2.0 transfers data at a rate of 480 megabits per second.

The FireWire device was designed as a high-speed serial bus to connect hard disks, audio, and video equipment. FireWire was designed for the higher performance required by audio and video applications, whereas USB is much simpler.

Figure 8-30. The most common types of USB plugs.

IMAGE MANIPULATION

Once an electronic image has been captured and transferred, editing can be done through an image manipulation program. For slides or film negative, it is best to use first generation images to ensure the sharpness and tone quality of the image. Some of the most commonly used manipulation programs are Adobe Photoshop™, Macromedia Freehand™, CorelDRAW!™, and Adobe Illustrator™. The type of program that can be used depends on the computer platform and image format.

With full-featured image editors, the user can manipulate any aspect of the image, including cropping, color and contrast, adding or removing visual information, and even combining images. Background clutter can be eliminated, and unwanted elements in the picture can be erased. See **Figure 8-31.** Most image editing programs offer similar tools and applications and allow changes to be made in a single area, multiple areas, or the entire image. Most programs also allow work to be done in layers, the application of filters and masks, paint effects, and retouching.

- *Layers* allow the user to create multiple levels of artwork that reside on separate, overlapping layers in the same document. Think of the layers as a stack of clear plastic sheets, with part of an illustration on each sheet. On the portions of the sheets with no illustration, the layer is transparent and you can see through to the layer below. By creating and working in layers, it is easier to modify objects without affecting all aspects of the artwork, **Figure 8-32.** Separate layers take up additional storage space, so they should be merged or flattened when editing is complete.

Figure 8-32. Displayed is the magenta channel of the CMYK color mode for this image. The small box in the right corner displays the image in full color or in one of the channels.

Figure 8-31. Image manipulation can be used to improve the content of a photo, in addition to aesthetic attributes. A—In the original photo, the neckline of the woman's jacket did not line up. B—The tools of an image manipulation program were used to align the top of the jacket. (The Peerless Group of Graphic Services)

- *Filters* are used to apply special effects to bitmap images, including textures and patterns, **Figure 8-33.** For example, a color halftone filter simulates the effect of using an enlarged halftone screen on each channel, or color separation, of the bitmap image. For each channel, the halftone filter divides the image into rectangles and replaces each rectangle with a circle, **Figure 8-34.** Applying filters to large bitmap images can be time-consuming. To save time, some filters allow you to preview the effect that they create.

Figure 8-33. When applying filters, you can preview the effect and make a variety of adjustments, including the direction of light.

- The *paint effects* feature in most image manipulation programs performs the same functions as a paint or draw program. Various tools allow the user to fill in and erase colors, create and add color, and assign and adjust color values and gradations.

layers: A feature of image editing programs that creates multiple, editable levels of a single piece of artwork.

filter: A feature of image manipulation programs used to apply special effects to images, such as textures and patterns.

paint effects: A feature of image manipulation programs that contains several tools that allow the user to create and color images.

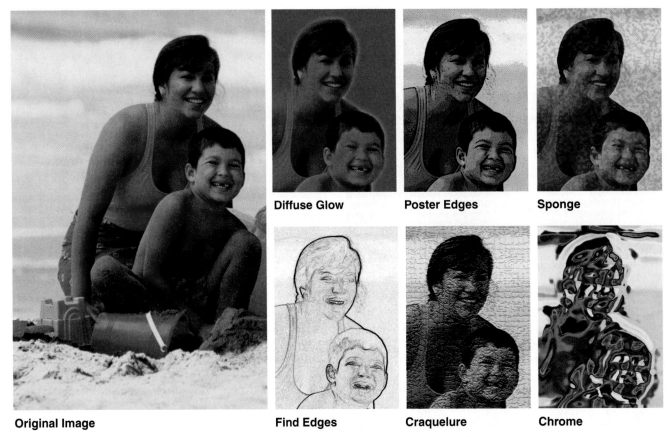

Original Image   **Diffuse Glow**   **Poster Edges**   **Sponge**

Find Edges   **Craquelure**   **Chrome**

Figure 8-34. The images above illustrate several of the filters that can be applied to a photo.

- *Retouching tools* perform similarly to methods used in darkroom photography. The user can "dodge" areas that are too dark and lack detail. Burn tools increase exposure to areas that are too light. Retouching tools also include features for adjusting color, contrast, hue, and saturation.

- *Masks* are used to isolate an area to protect it from the effects and changes applied to the rest of the image. When a part of an image is selected, the remaining area (not selected) is masked and protected from editing. Semitransparent masks allow an area of an image to be partially affected by changes. Masks can consist of a single path or a compound path, **Figure 8-35.**

Image Replacement

Automatic picture replacement (APR) and open prepress interface (OPI) systems allow low-resolution images to be used in the initial layout of material. When files are returned for imagesetting, the high-resolution images automatically replace the low-resolution FPO files. This saves time and prevents storage problems created when working with large, high-resolution image files. Using APR and OPI systems allow prepress professionals to work on color-correcting and editing the images while they are simultaneously being positioned in layouts, cropped, and proofed.

APR/OPI Limitations

Artwork must be properly sized and rotated before it is scanned. All art should be labeled with the percentage enlargement or reduction and the angle of rotation, **Figure 8-36.** When low-resolution scans are returned, they should be placed in the layout at 100% size and 0° rotation. Images may be cropped and (if absolutely necessary) resized. Resizing after scanning should be kept to a minimum to prevent loss in quality. If the image must be rotated or resized drastically, it should be rescanned.

APR/OPI files should not be renamed. The file name serves as the link to the high-resolution replacement image, and changing the name will cause delays while the link is reestablished. The FPO images should never be opened with image-editing software and resaved in a different format.

Figure 8-35. The mask applied in the image allows the user to modify its color and pattern without affecting the rest of the image.

Figure 8-36. The size and rotation (if any) of an original must be clearly marked when preparing material for scanning.

FUTURE TRENDS

Digital imaging devices have become a driving force in redefining the traditional boundaries that separate the disciplines of photography and printing. Personal computer technology and desktop publishing innovations have transformed prepress processes. Today, original artwork is likely to be a digital file produced in a paint or draw program, or captured with a scanner or digital camera.

With advances in digital imaging technology, the role of the photographer as a member of the creative team is evolving. When shooting film-based images, photographers have often been preoccupied with pushing the limits of the medium to achieve the best visual result for viewing on a light table. From the photographers' perspective, it is imperative to make maximum use of the film's tonal image range and color gamut.

Color separators long ago realized that the full tonal range of a photographic transparency could not be transferred to ink on paper. The transparency color gamut, using high-quality dye pigments, far exceeded what could be reproduced with a CMYK ink set on a lithographic press. Photographers were not necessarily concerned with these production complications until digital photography provided the ability to control how an RGB-to-CMYK conversion affects the appearance of their images.

Just a few years ago, the photographer's job was finished when the art director signed off on the transparency film. The transformation from film to digital image file was in the hands of the color separator. With a digital camera, the photographer is compelled to take on new responsibilities. In place of common transparent media, the end result is an RGB image-capture file.

Many photographers seek to gain a competitive advantage by taking the next step and delivering print-ready CMYK files that can be dropped into a document layout. In doing so, they have assumed what was formerly the job of a color separator. Along with this new responsibility is the opportunity to have the final say in how the image-capture file will print on press.

retouching tools: Tools used in image manipulation programs to modify images in ways similar to methods used in darkroom photography.

mask: A feature of image editing programs that protects a specified area of an image from changes, filters, and other effects applied to the rest of the image.

CAREER LINK

Traditional or Digital Camera Operator

The traditional camera operator creates an image that is recorded on silver halide film and is developed to make a permanent image. The digital camera operator records the image electronically. Each camera operator has a desired outcome when shooting an image. It may be to record an event, to tell a story, or to create a picture. This requires the operator to select the proper equipment to accomplish the desired goal. Achieving the proper effect, such as subject enhancement, is essential. Lighting is often a major consideration. Some of the common positions of camera operators are portrait photographers, commercial and industrial photographers, news photographers, studio camera operators.

The operator must be technically proficient. There is a great emphasis on creativity, imagination, and self-expression. When using the digital camera, the images are often stored on CDs. The operator now becomes involved with computer technology. This requires the operator to be familiar with editing software. The photographer can manipulate digital images to create the desired outcome. Once the desired effects are obtained, the images can be stored. Patience is highly desirable as well as accuracy. Attention to detail and communication skills are imperative.

The operator must have a technical understanding of photography and camera operation. The training for the necessary skills may be acquired at technical schools, colleges, universities, and specialty schools. On-the-job training is a possibility at some firms.

"Advancements in the prepress area have had a profound effect on graphic designers, illustrators, and photographers, all of whom now work on computer screens instead of drawing boards. From the creative stages to the print-ready file, our world is now digital."

Frank Romano
Rochester Institute of Technology

Summary

Digital imaging has changed the industry dramatically. In many printing firms, analog form no longer exists. Many devices are used in the industry to capture electronic images, including digital cameras, camera backs, and scanners. Digital cameras are used by many people, from casual users to professionals. Choosing a camera that fits the need of the operator is an important step that requires many considerations. No matter the type of equipment used, the finished product must meet the original specifications and intended application.

Review Questions

Please do not write in this book. Write your answers on a separate sheet of paper.

1. The colors and lines of an image in _____ format are continuous. The colors and lines of an image in _____ format consist of values measured at distinct points.
2. Explain how *CCD sensors* operate.
3. How does *interpolation* function to affect the appearance of an image?
4. Identify the four different CCD arrays and list the unique characteristics of each.
5. What are two problems created when there is a difference in size between a camera's film format and the CCD array of a camera back?
6. Why do cameras using trilinear arrays require constant lighting conditions?
7. Name the most commonly used types of lighting for commercial studio lighting.
8. What is *unsharp masking*?
9. When scanning text, you must use a(n) _____ system to translate the bitmapped image into ASCII characters.
10. Explain the process of *oil mounting*. What type of scanner must be used for oil mounting?
11. Describe how *XY scanning* technology has improved the capabilities of flatbed scanners.
12. What is *spatial resolution*?

13. Explain the use of a *histogram*.

14. List some typical storage devices used for images captured by common point and shoot cameras.

15. What purpose do *layers* serve in an image manipulation program?

16. _____ are used to apply special effects, such as patterns and textures, to bitmap images.

17. Which image manipulation tool would be used to protect an area of an image from changes and effects applied to the rest of the image?

Suggested Activities

1. Select two different digital cameras and make a comparison chart of the features and capabilities of each. Identify a typical user for each camera.

2. Visit a camera store and ask for a recommendation for the best storage card for a camera you own. Ask why one specific storage card is better than others available.

3. Take a picture of an image using 3 cameras with different megapixel ratings. Reproduce each image to 12″ × 18″. Make note of and describe any visible difference in resolution.

Related Web Links

DigitalcameraInfo.com

www.digitalcamerainfo.com

Offers information and reviews of available digital cameras, tips and guides, and updates on emerging technology.

Popular Photography Magazine

www.popphoto.com

Web site of Popular Photography magazine, with articles, tips, and equipment information.

CHAPTER 9

Color Science, Vision, and Space

Learning Objectives

After studying this chapter, you will be able to:

- Explain the basic principles of visible light.
- Recall various color space and organization methods.
- Summarize the characteristics of both additive color formation and subtractive color formation.
- Explain the basic principles of color separation.
- Recall various color measurement instruments and explain the use of each.
- Identify the parts of the human eye and recall the function of each.

Important Terms

achromatic vision
adaptation
additive color formation
adjacency
afterimage
brightness
chroma
chromatic adaptation
chromatic induction
chromaticity
chromaticity coordinates
color constancy
color gamut
color separation
color space
colorants
colorimeter
combination densitometer
complementary colors
cones
constructive interference
continuous spectrum
continuous tone
cornea
densitometer
destructive interference
detail printer
dichromatic vision
diffraction grating
direct screen photographic
   color separation
dye
electromagnetic spectrum
electronic color separation
fovea
gamut

hue
incident beam
indirect screen
   photographic color
   separation
iris
macula
monochromatic
   colorimeter
near-complementary
   colors
photopigments
pigment
process color printing
reflected beam
reflection densitometer
retina
rods
saturation
scanner
shade
spectrodensitometer
spectrophotometer
spectrum locus
subtractive color
   formation
successive contrast
tint
tone
transmission
   densitometer
trichromatic
   colorimeter
tristimulus values (X, Y, Z)
value
viewing booth

Color plays many important roles in our daily lives. Aside from the aesthetic benefits to our surroundings, the use of color on any medium can greatly enhance communication. Color can be used to grab attention, set a mood, or clarify images.

Colors should maintain consistency throughout the production process. This is especially true when so many products are recognized simply by the colors on their labels or logos. To accomplish this type of consistency, everyone from the graphic designer to the press operator should have a basic understanding of color.

COLOR SCIENCE

Without light, there is no color. Therefore, you must understand a few principles of light before understanding color science.

Principles of Light

The *electromagnetic spectrum* consists of bands of different wavelengths, ranging from radio waves to gamma rays, **Figure 9-1.** The wavelengths are usually measured in nanometers (nm). A nanometer is equal to one billionth of a meter. Another unit used to measure the wavelength of light is the Angstrom (Å). Ten Angstroms are equal to 1 nm.

Our eyes can detect only a very small part of the electromagnetic spectrum known as visible light, which includes wavelengths ranging from 400 nm–770 nm. Each wavelength is seen as a different color. Red light has the longest visible wavelength (630 nm–770 nm) and violet has the shortest (410 nm–440 nm).

Most light sources, including the sun, emit light that appears to be white. However, that light is actually a combination of roughly equal parts of all the visible wavelengths. Using a prism, **Figure 9-2,** white light can be broken down into six major colors: red, orange, yellow, green, blue, and violet. When sunlight is passed through a prism, a *continuous spectrum* is created that blends smoothly from one color to the next. Many other sources of light do not produce a continuous spectrum. A sodium vapor streetlight, for example, may produce bright yellow and blue, and also has dark regions in its spectrum. This difference in light sources greatly influences individual perception of colors.

Temperature of Light

The color of light is measured in degrees Kelvin (K). In terms of color temperature, blues and violets are the warmest colors and reds and oranges are the coolest, **Figure 9-3.** This range of colors can be demonstrated by heating a piece of metal called a black body. As the black body is heated, it emits light in a range of colors. Beginning with dull red, it moves

electromagnetic spectrum: The entire range of wavelengths of electromagnetic radiation, extending from gamma rays (very short) to radio waves (very long).

continuous spectrum: Spectrum of colors that is created when sunlight passes through a prism. The spectrum blends smoothly from one color to the next.

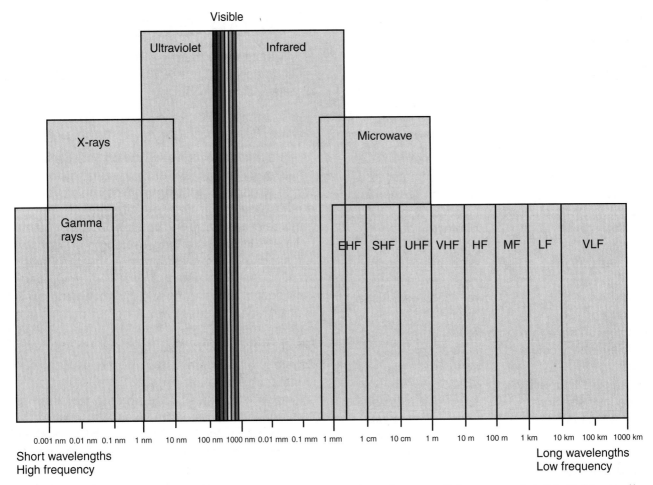

Figure 9-1. This illustration of the electromagnetic spectrum shows how small the range of visible light actually is. Each color has its own wavelength or frequency.

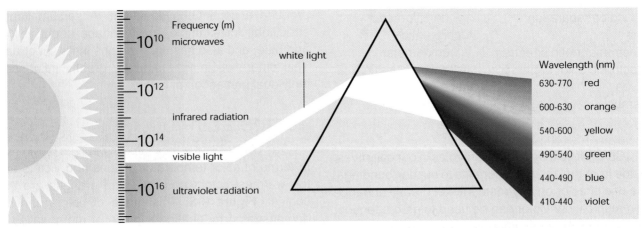

Figure 9-2. A prism disperses the light that passes through it, so our eyes can perceive individual wavelengths. The shorter waves are more dispersed than the longer waves. Because of this, the violet wavelength is always positioned at the bottom and the red wavelength is always at the top. (Thomas Detrie and C. Phillips)

Color Temperatures	
Blue skylight	10,000 K–18,000 K
Overcast sky	6250 K
Electronic photoflash	6000 K
Evening light	5000 K–6000 K
Morning light	5000 K–6000 K
Midday sunlight (direct)	4500 K–5500 K
Flashbulbs	4000 K
Professional photo lamps	3200 K–3400 K
Household bulb	2500 K–3000 K
Candlelight	1800 K–2000 K

Figure 9-3. Approximate color temperatures of some common light sources.

through orange, yellow, and white. If no chemical or physical change occurs, the metal eventually emits blue light. The color of light emitted from the black body can be described by its temperature.

Behavior of Light

When light travels through a continuous medium, it travels in a straight line. However, when light reaches a surface or boundary between two types of material, such as air or water, several things can happen. Some of the light may reflect from the surface, while some may pass through it. The light that passes through the second material may refract, or bend. In addition, some of the light may be scattered or absorbed.

Reflection

A beam of light coming toward a surface is called the *incident beam*. After the beam is reflected, it is called the *reflected beam*, **Figure 9-4.** Depending on the type of material causing light to reflect, the

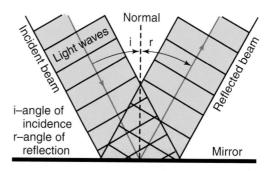

Figure 9-4. The angle of an incident beam (right angles to a surface), is equal to the angle of the reflected beam.

reflected beam may contain a different mixture of light waves than the incident beam. If the mixture is different, the new combination of wavelengths gives the material its color. For instance, a red book exposed to white light appears red because the surface absorbs all other wavelengths of color in the light. Only red wavelengths of the light spectrum are reflected off the red cover.

Refraction

When light passes through a surface at any angle other than a right angle, the speed of the light changes and its direction is altered, **Figure 9-5.** In other words, the light refracts. The type of material affects how much the light bends. Refraction can be demonstrated by placing a pencil in a glass of water. The pencil appears to be bent at the surface of the

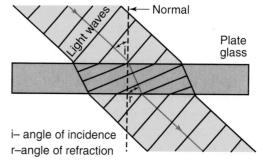

Figure 9-5. Refraction causes a beam of light to bend and slow down as it passes through a substance. The angle of refraction is less than the angle of incidence.

incident beam: The beam of light coming toward a surface.

reflected beam: A beam of light that has bounced off a surface.

water. Light from the top of the pencil comes directly to your eyes, while the light from the bottom passes through the glass and water.

Scattering

Scattering occurs when light waves strike the molecules of another substance. The molecules cause the waves to scatter. A clear sky appears blue because air molecules scatter a greater amount of shorter wavelengths (blue) than longer wavelengths in white sunlight.

Interference

When two light waves cross through the same spot, they interfere with each other. The interference between light waves occurs as constructive interference or as destructive interference. To illustrate interference, think of light as a wave with crests and troughs. *Constructive interference* occurs when the crests of multiple light waves pass through the same point at the same time. At this point, the light is brighter than any one wave can emit alone. *Destructive interference* occurs when the crest of one wave crosses the same point as the trough of another wave. The trough reduces the height of the crest, which leaves the spot very dim or even dark.

Diffraction

Light waves usually travel in straight lines. However, light waves diffract, or spread out, into curving waves when passing through an opening or slit, around a small object, or beyond an edge, such as the outline of a person or a building.

The diffraction of light is useful when studying colors in a light beam. For instance, scientists are able to separate the colors of light from a star using a *diffraction grating*. The grating uses thousands of thin slits to diffract light. Each color in the light diffracts by a slightly different amount, and the spread of colors can be large enough to make each color visible. Astronomers use this color information to determine the makeup of the star.

Diffraction can also be a hindrance. As the magnifying power of a high-quality microscope is increased, for example, the edges of the object being viewed begin to blur. The edges blur because the light diffracts when passing over the edge on its way to the eye.

COLOR SPACE

Both science and the graphic communications industry require precise color definition and classification. Words are imprecise in distinguishing and describing color. What one person identifies as yellow-green might be described by another as light green or "greenish." For this reason, various systems have been devised to establish universal terms for color classification.

The various color systems and color models describe colors through numerical or coordinate means. The numerical values or coordinates allow the colors to be defined within the system's parameters. These parameters define the system's *color space*. The term *space* is used because color data occur in three dimensions. The color space defines the limits by which the color model can be used. The full range of colors that can be defined by a color model is called a *color gamut*. To better define color space, many color models are triaxial. A triaxial system involves three axes (vertical, side-to-side, front-to-back). This section addresses the various color spaces in common use today.

Color organization begins with two small groups: pure chromatic colors and achromatic colors (white, grays, and black). All other colors exist within these two extremes.

The Color Wheel

A color wheel consists of a range of colors in the form of a circle and is useful for demonstrating the relationships among colors, **Figure 9-6**. The main colors on the wheel are primary colors (red, yellow, and blue). The secondary colors are orange, green, and violet. Other colors on the wheel are called tertiary, or intermediate, colors: yellow-green, blue-green, blue-violet, red-violet, red-orange, and yellow-orange.

Secondary colors are created by mixing equal amounts of two primary colors. For example, orange is made by mixing yellow and red. Green is made by mixing yellow and blue. Violet is made by mixing blue and red. The secondary colors are positioned between the primaries on the color wheel.

Tertiary colors are made by mixing a primary color with a secondary color. These colors are named after the two colors used to make them, with the primary color listed first. For example, yellow-orange is created by mixing the primary color yellow with the secondary color orange.

Color Triads

Any three colors that are an equal distance apart on the color wheel compose a color triad. The colors in a triad often go well together, so color triads are important design tools. The primary, secondary, and tertiary colors on the color wheel all form triads, **Figure 9-7**.

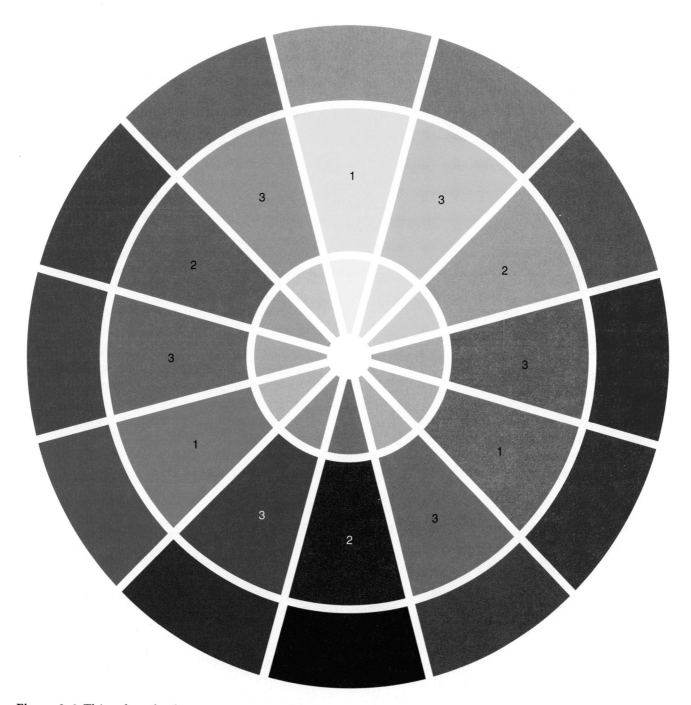

Figure 9-6. This color wheel presents the primary (1), secondary (2), and tertiary colors (3). The second ring represents normal values of the colors. The center ring shows tints of the normal values, and the outer ring shows shades of the normal values.

constructive interference: When two light waves cross a single point at the same time and combine to create brighter light than one wave can emit alone.

destructive interference: When two light waves cross at a single point at the same time and intersect to cause a dimmer light or a dark spot.

diffraction grating: An optical device used to study the colors in light.

color space: A three-dimensional area where three color attributes, such as hue, value, and chroma, can be depicted, calculated, and charted.

color gamut: Common expression for the entire (greatest possible) range of color that can be shown on a computer display or reproduced by another output device.

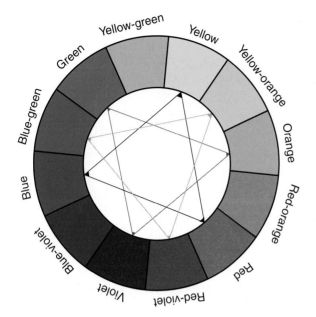

Figure 9-7. Triangles drawn in the center of the color wheel identify three different triads.

Complementary Colors

In color theory, two colors mixed in exact proportion to produce a neutral color (white, gray, or black) are *complementary colors*. On the HSV (hue, saturation, and value) color wheel, opposite colors are complementary. When properly mixed, they become a shade of gray. In the additive color model (RGB), they are paired in the following way: red and green, yellow and purple, and blue and orange. A color may also harmonize with colors that lie on either side of its complement, such as red with blue-green or with yellow-green. These colors are called *near-complementary colors* or split-complementary colors.

Shades, Tints, and Tones

Monochromatic color schemes are comprised of the shades, tints, and tones of a single color, **Figure 9-8.**

- *Shades* are created by adding black to a color. If black is added to red, the color maroon is created; maroon is a shade of red.
- *Tints* are created by adding white to a color. When white is added to red, the color pink results; pink is a tint of red.
- The *tone* of a color may be lowered or heightened by adding some of its complementary color. The tone of red can be dulled by adding a small amount of its complement, green.

The number of pure chromatic and achromatic colors is small compared to all color possibilities. The human eye can differentiate about 300 colors and about 150 shades of gray.

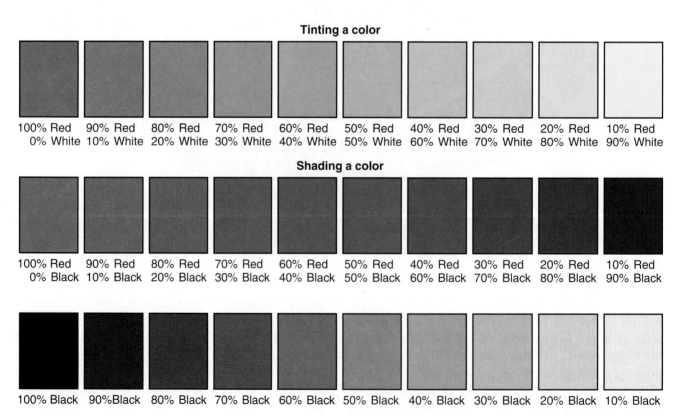

Figure 9-8. The top row shows various tints of red that are created by adding different percentages of white. The center row illustrates the shades of red created with different percentages of black. The bottom row is an array of values.

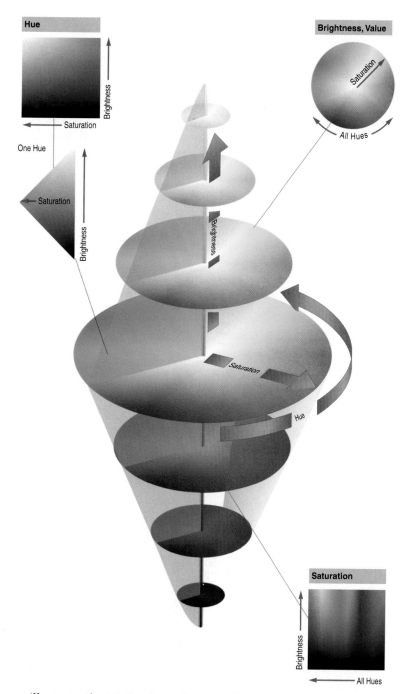

Figure 9-9. This diagram illustrates the tristimulus color space. Rotational movement around each circle varies the hue. Upward movement increases brightness. Radial movement from the center of each circle increases saturation. (Agfa)

Hue, Saturation, and Brightness (HSB)

It is impossible to definitively describe the appearance of a color. However, it is possible to describe a color's appearance in relationship to its environment. The eye differentiates colors according to the three basic criteria of every color: hue, saturation, and brightness (HSB). Together, these three characteristics define the relationship between colors in the HSB color model, **Figure 9-9.**

complementary colors: Any two colors that lie directly opposite each other on the color wheel.

near-complementary color: A color that harmonizes with colors that lie next to its complement on the color wheel.

shade: A color gradation created by adding black to a color.

tint: A color gradation created by adding white to a color.

tone: The degree of lightness or darkness of a color. The tone of a color may be lowered or heightened by adding some of its complementary color.

- *Hue* is the color of an object perceived by the eye, determined by the dominant light wavelengths that are reflected or transmitted.
- *Saturation* defines a color's degree of strength or difference from white. It can also be defined as the predominance of one or two of the three RGB primary colors.
- *Brightness* is often referred to as lightness or luminosity. The associated value indicates how light or dark a color is.

Hue, Value, and Chroma (HVC)

In the early 1900s, Albert H. Munsell developed a color organization and definition system based on human perception. The Munsell system identifies the three attributes of color as hue, value, and chroma (HVC). In Munsell's system, chroma indicates the intensity, or strength, of a color and its saturation, **Figure 9-10.**

- *Hue* is the color name and is indicated by the letter H, followed by a fraction. The top number

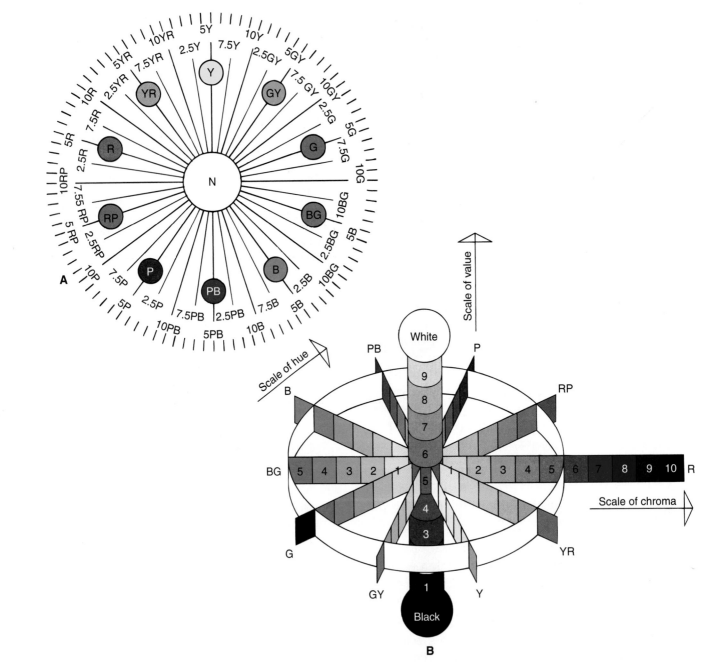

Figure 9-10. A—The Munsell color system includes hue notations of the five principal and five intermediate hue families. Each hue family is broken down into four parts: 2.5, 5, 7.5, and 10. The outer circle markings represent the 100 hues included. B—The system also includes a representation of the hue, value, and chroma relationships. The circular band represents hues in proper sequences. The center axis is the scale of value. Bands pointing outward from the center illustrate the steps of chroma, increasing in strength as indicated by the numbers.

of the fraction represents the value. The bottom number indicates the chroma.

- *Value* is the lightness or darkness of a color. It is shown on the central axis of the Munsell model as nine visible steps. The darkest value is at the bottom and the lightest value is at the top. The value of pure black is designated as 0/, pure white as 10/, and middle gray as 5/.

- *Chroma* is shown by the horizontal band extending outward from the value axis. The chroma value shows the amount that a given hue deviates from a neutral gray of the same value. The number of chroma steps varies because hues vary in saturation strength.

The popularity of Munsell's color system continues today because it separates the color-independent component, brightness (Munsell's value), from hue and saturation (Munsell's chroma). This enables two-dimensional color representation. In addition, it is perceptually uniform. Color distances on the model correspond to perceived differences between the colors. Every color has a specific location with this system.

The International Commission on Illumination (CIE)

To precisely match colors in the graphic communications industry, most ink and paper manufacturers have adopted the CIE system of color specification. CIE stands for Commission Internationale de l'Eclairage, or the International Commission on Illumination. In 1931, the CIE established a worldwide color measurement standard. The CIE system is a mathematical model of human color perception, **Figure 9-11.** Numerical values quantify the responses of the average human eye to different wavelengths of light.

The CIE defined several standard light sources, a standard observer, and standard viewing conditions. See **Figure 9-12.** The standard observer was chosen to have color vision representing that of the average person. Standard viewing conditions were determined using a dark background and only foveal vision. Foveal vision covers only about a 2° angle of vision. The CIE's angle vision is 10°. The wider angle provides a more accurate correlation with the visual perception for larger samples.

The CIE Uniform Color Space (CIE XYZ)

In order to determine accurate color measurements, information from three variables is required. The three variables are the light source, the color sample,

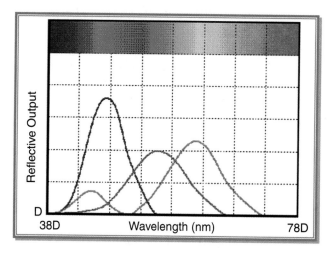

Figure 9-11. Responses of the average human eye to different light waves were used to establish the CIE color standard. As illustrated above, the human eye does not perceive color as equally spaced. Human perception of color is much greater in the center of the spectrum than on the ends.

Illuminant	Temperature
CIE source A, tungsten	2856 K
CIE source B, sunlight	4870 K
CIE source C, daylight	6770 K
CIE source D_{50}, daylight	5000 K
CIE source D_{55}, daylight	5500 K
CIE source D_{65}, daylight	6500 K

Figure 9-12. The CIE Standard Illuminants. D_{65} is the most widely used to represent average daylight conditions. D_{55} and D_{50} are other commonly used daylight sources.

hue: The color of an object perceived by the eye, and determined by the dominant light wavelengths reflected or transmitted.

saturation: An attribute of color that defines its degree of strength or difference from white. The extent to which one or two of the three RGB primaries is predominant in a color.

brightness: The lightness or luminosity of a color. An associated value indicates how light or dark a color is.

value: The lightness or darkness of a color; used in Munsell's color system.

chroma: A term used in the Munsell system to indicate the extent to which the color is diluted by white light.

and the receiver. After this information is gathered, a sample's *tristimulus values (X, Y, Z)* can be determined. The X, Y, and Z stand for red, green, and blue (RGB), respectively. Any color may be specified on the CIE XYZ color model by listing the amounts of the three primary colors required to match it. Certain methods are used to manipulate the data graphically or mathematically. Using measurement devices, computers, and computer software these values can be quickly determined.

The CIE XYZ color space is the parent system for nearly all color standards. Variations such as the CIE Yxy, CIELAB, and CIE Luminance Y models serve different scientific and technical purposes.

The CIE Chromaticity Diagram

The CIE chromaticity diagram (CIE Yxy color space) is a two-dimensional graph of hue and chroma, **Figure 9-13A.** *Chromaticity* refers to a quality of color that includes hue and saturation, but not brightness.

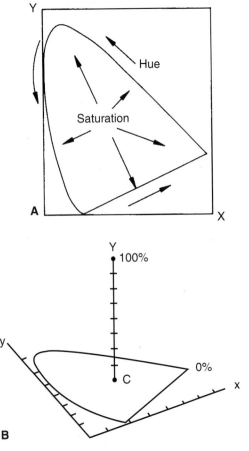

Figure 9-13. A—The CIE chromaticity diagram represents the hue and saturation of a specific color or the chromaticity coordinates of that color. B—The luminance value (Y) is seen as a vertical axis, rising up from a neutral position of the illuminant or light source.

As with Munsell's HVC color model, the CIE Yxy separates the achromatic component (Y) from the two chromatic components (xy). Two colors that are the same except for luminance would have the same chromatic definition, and therefore the same *chromaticity coordinates*. The chromaticity coordinates are represented by the x and y values. The color's brightness (Y) is specified by a number, not a location on the graph, **Figure 9-13B.**

The CIE chromaticity diagram has a horizontal x axis and a vertical y axis. When the chromaticity coordinates of visible light (380 nm–770 nm) are converted and plotted, the resulting points fall on a horseshoe-shaped curve known as the *spectrum locus,* **Figure 9-14A.** Since all visible colors are comprised of mixtures of light wavelengths, all visible colors must occur within the boundary formed by this curve. Connecting the spectrum locus curve endpoints forms a line called the purple line or the purple boundary. Colors on this line are mixtures of pure violet (380 nm) and red (770 nm) light, **Figure 9-14B.**

The colors plotted on the chromaticity diagram are relative to the light source used. The A, C, D$_{50}$, and D$_{65}$ labels in Figure 9-14A represent the location of the CIE standard light sources. The CIE values of dominant wavelength, purity, and luminosity are dependent on the color temperature of the light source used in making the measurements. In the CIE system, dominant wavelength relates to hue, and purity relates to chroma or saturation.

CIELAB

In 1976, the CIE revised the standards to create a more even distribution of colors. The result is the CIELAB model, **Figure 9-15.** The distance between colors corresponds to perceived color differences. The CIELAB model is the current standard for measuring the color of light and is very similar to Munsell's color model.

The CIELAB color space separates color and luminance into discrete color space dimensions. These dimensions are represented by the designations *L, A,* and *B.*

- **L.** The first dimension, which represents lightness. All colors of the same lightness lie in a plane. Lightness varies vertically.

- **A.** Indicates the red to green value. Positive a* values (+a*) appear reddish and negative a* values (−a*) appear greenish.

- **B.** Represents the yellow to blue value. Positive b* values (+b*) are yellowish and negative b* values (−b*) are bluish.

The a* and b* designations both represent a two-dimensional color subspace.

The human visual system is more sensitive to the L dimension, so digital systems allocate more data space to it than to the color components. This allows even more efficient coding of the color values.

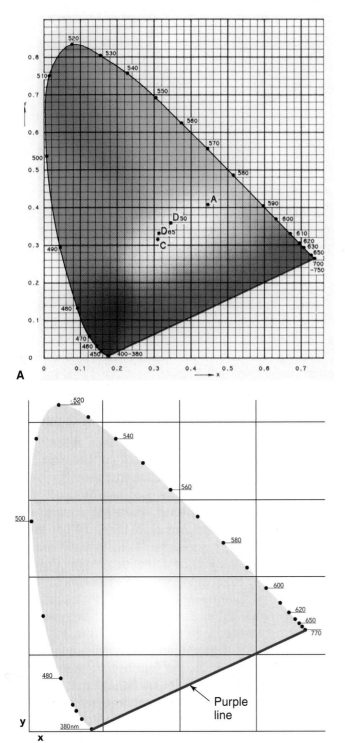

A

Figure 9-14. A—The CIE chromaticity chart. B—The bold line between 380 nm and 770 nm represents the purple boundary at the base of the spectrum locus. (Thomas Detrie)

The Pantone® System

The Pantone system of color specification is the most widely used system in the graphic communications industry. Unlike the HVC or HSB color models, the Pantone system is not based on equal visual differences in color. The colors used are based on ink colors common to the printing industry.

Manuals and swatchbooks provide Pantone color representations, names, and mixing formulas, **Figure 9-16.** The colors are usually presented on both coated and uncoated paper. Using the manuals or swatchbooks, designers, clients, and printers can effectively communicate color selections.

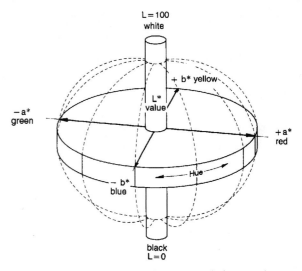

Figure 9-15. The CIELAB color space defines color based on our visual system's perception of color.

PRINTED COLOR

Creating colors can be accomplished using either additive color formation or subtractive color formation. *Additive color formation* is based on

tristimulus values (X, Y, Z): Three values that designate the amount of red, green, and blue light in an image.

chromaticity: A quality of color that includes hue and saturation, but not brightness.

chromaticity coordinates: The x and y values of the CIE Yxy color space; they represent the hue and saturation of a color.

spectrum locus: A horseshoe-shaped curve that results when the chromaticity coordinates of visible light are plotted on the CIE chromaticity diagram.

additive color formation: Creating colors by mixing red, green, and blue light in various combinations.

Figure 9-16. Pantone® offers printers, designers, and color professionals a variety of materials for choosing and using the Pantone colors. (Pantone, Inc.)

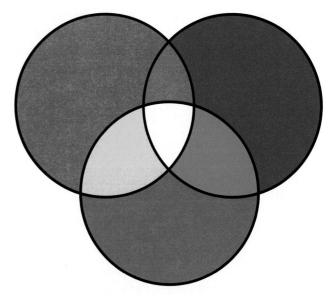

Figure 9-17. Additive color formation. Red, green, and blue additive primaries can be mixed in pairs to form magenta, yellow, and cyan. Mixing all three results in white light.

mixing primary colors of light; *subtractive color formation* is based on mixing colorants. *Colorants* are chemical substances that give color to such materials as ink, paint, crayons, and chalk. Colorants that dissolve in liquids are called *dyes*. Colorants that do not dissolve but spread as tiny solid particles through liquids or other substances, such as ink, are called *pigments*.

Additive and Subtractive Color Formation

In additive color formation, the primary colors of light (red, green, blue) combine to form other colors, **Figure 9-17.** Red, green, and blue are called the additive primary colors and are usually referred to as RGB. The human vision system, which is sensitive to red, green, and blue light, uses additive color mixing. Television sets and computer monitors create images in a full range of colors by combining dots of red, green, and blue light.

In subtractive color formation, color is seen by reflected light. Each of the subtractive primary colors—cyan, magenta, and yellow (CMY)—

absorbs (subtracts) other colors from the white light and reflects only its own, **Figure 9-18.** For example, a spot of cyan printed on a page absorbs red wavelengths of light, and reflects back only blue and green wavelengths that form the color cyan. A spot printed with black ink (or a black made by combining equal parts of cyan, magenta, and yellow) absorbs all the wavelengths and does not reflect any color. In the same way, a white paper surface reflects all the wavelengths, producing white light. Colorants of the subtractive primaries can be mixed together in equal proportions to form the additive primaries, **Figure 9-19.**

In *process color printing*, where only subtractive primary colors and black are used, the same principle applies. However, colors are mixed visually rather than physically. Varying combinations of tiny, closely spaced dots of cyan, magenta, and yellow ink absorb and reflect the different wavelengths of light to produce different colors. In the descriptions of color systems, black is designated with the letter *K*. Thus, the four process colors are described in abbreviated form as CMYK. Using black as the fourth color ensures a truer printed black and faster ink drying time. A black created by combining the other three colors would be muddy and require a heavier ink deposit on the paper and, therefore, increased drying time. Using black ink is also more cost-effective, since it is less expensive than color inks.

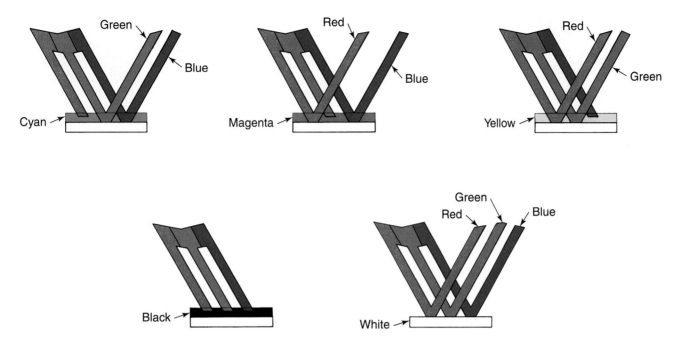

Figure 9-18. Subtractive color formation. Cyan, magenta, and yellow absorb wavelengths of some colors and reflect others back to the viewer. Black absorbs all the wavelengths, white reflects all of them.

Direct screen photographic color separation uses a process camera, a contact printing frame, or an enlarger to make color separation exposures. These exposures are made through a photographic mask and halftone screen onto high-contrast film. The color-corrected halftone separation negatives are produced in one step. The direct screen process can be used to make color separations from transparent and reflective copy.

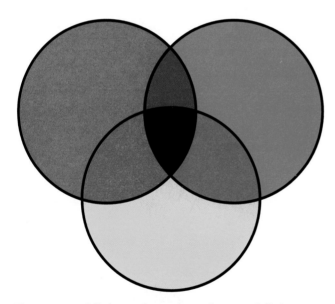

Figure 9-19. Mixing subtractive colorants. Mixing magenta, yellow, and cyan subtractive primaries in pairs forms red, green, and blue. Mixing all three produces black.

Color Separation

Color separation is the process of dividing the colors of a multicolored original into the subtractive, or printing, primaries (CMY) and black (K). The CMYK color separations are used to prepare printing plates, **Figure 9-20.** Common methods of making color separations are direct screen photographic, indirect screen photographic, and electronic.

subtractive color formation: Creating colors by combining cyan, magenta, yellow, and black colorants to produce a printed image.

colorant: A chemical substance that gives color to materials, such as ink, paint, crayons, and chalk.

dye: A type of colorant that dissolves in liquid.

pigment: A type of colorant comprised of fine, solid particles that do not dissolve, but spread through liquids or other substances.

process color printing: The method of printing full-color materials using the transparent cyan, magenta, yellow, and black inks.

color separation: The process of dividing the colors of a multicolored original into the printing primaries (CMY) and black (K). CMYK color separations are used to prepare printing plates.

direct screen photographic color separation: A method in which a process camera, contact printing frame, or enlarger is used to make color separation exposures through a photographic mask and a halftone screen onto high-contrast panchromatic film.

Figure 9-20. These four-color process printers were created with computer software. When printed, the combined images will create the four-color image.

The *indirect screen photographic color separation* method is a two-step process that produces *continuous tone* separations from full-color originals. Continuous tone implies an infinite number of tone gradations on the image. Halftone negatives or positives are made from the continuous-tone separation. Color values are separated in the first step and tone values are screened in the second step. The greatest advantage of the indirect method is that the negative can be retouched or enlarged. The opportunity to enlarge during the separation process allows the printer to produce large posters and display work. The indirect method can be used with transparent copy and reflective copy.

Electronic color separation is performed with a scanner. A *scanner* measures the color densities of an original, stores the measurements as digital information, manipulates or alters the data, and uses the manipulated data to create four film separations. Depending on the type of scanner, almost any type or size of original material can be scanned. This includes film negatives, transparencies, photos, printed media, drawings, graphs, and text copy. With so much of the work involved in the graphic communications industry being performed electronically, electronic color separation has replaced many of the older methods.

Color Separation Filters

The color separation process uses red, green, and blue filters to divide the original image into the CMYK process colors. Each color filter separates the necessary colors of light to produce its printer. To produce an image that represents each of the three subtractive primary inks (CMY), the complementary additive color filter is used, **Figure 9-21.**

A blue filter is used to produce the yellow printer. If an exposure is made with a blue filter, only the blue

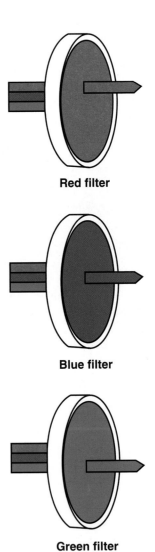

Red filter

Blue filter

Green filter

Figure 9-21. The principle of separating colors can be illustrated by reviewing the results of using red, green, and blue filters. A red filter transmits red and absorbs blue and green. A green filter transmits green and absorbs blue and red. A blue filter transmits blue and absorbs red and green.

elements of the copy pass through and expose the film. The black, or exposed, areas of the negative represent the blue areas of the original color copy. Unexposed, or clear, areas of the negative represent the colors absorbed by the filter. When the blue light image is printed in positive form with yellow ink (a blue light absorber), only red and green light waves are reflected, allowing the viewer to see the color yellow.

The green filter is used to produce the magenta printer. Only the green elements of the copy pass through the green filter and expose the film. The exposed areas of the negative represent the green areas of the original; the unexposed areas represent the blue and red light waves absorbed by the filter. When the image is printed in positive form with magenta ink (a green light absorber), only the blue and red light waves are reflected. The viewer sees the color magenta.

The red filter is used to produce the cyan printer. The red filter allows only the red elements of the copy to pass through and expose the film. The exposed areas of the negative represent the red areas of the original, and the unexposed areas of the negative represent the green and blue colors absorbed by the filter. When the image is printed in positive form with cyan ink (a red light absorber), only the green and blue light waves are reflected, so the viewer sees the color cyan.

The black printer, often referred to as the skeleton printer or *detail printer*, can also be created using different filters. The black printer is created with white light and is used to extend shadow details or density ranges. Printing a black ink over the three primaries improves and enhances shadow details of the reproduction. The black printer also helps compensate for CMY register problems.

Color Measurement

Precise standardized measurement is also part of color evaluation. Measuring instruments vary in both design and function. Some measure density, some measure color values, and others measure light waves. The most common color measuring instruments are spectrophotometers, densitometers, colorimeters, and spectrodensitometers.

Spectrophotometers

A photometer is used to measure light intensity. Adding the prefix *spectro* indicates that the instrument is capable of measuring light of different colors or wavelengths. When used for measurement in the graphic communications industry, a *spectrophotometer* converts this data to CIE color specifications. A spectrophotometer is the most accurate type of color measurement device.

The readout system of a spectrophotometer either plots spectrophotometric curves or provides the data from which the curves can be plotted. Spectrophotometric curves provide a contour or envelope that describes the reflection or transmission characteristics of a sample. The sample may be the image area on printed media, a color negative, or a positive color transparency.

Spectrophotometric curves describe the physical characteristics of viewing samples. They do *not* describe the colors as perceived by a person viewing the samples. For example, the curves for skin colors show that human skin has the lowest reflectance in the blue region and the highest in the red region of the spectrum. See **Figure 9-22.** Light skin has the highest reflectance at all wavelengths, but the curve is not very smooth. The reflectance for any specific wavelength is easily obtained from the curves. In the example at 700 nm, light skin has a reflectance of 70%, dark skin 45%, and very dark skin 15%.

Most spectrophotometers used in the graphic arts industry are limited to reading light waves in the visible spectrum. When reading light waves in the visible spectrum, the samples must be placed as close to the detector as possible to reduce the problem of light scattered by the system, **Figure 9-23.**

indirect screen photographic color separation: A two-step process in which continuous-tone separations are produced from full-color originals, and halftone negatives or positives are made from the continuous-tone separations.

continuous tone: An image with an infinite number of tone gradations between the lightest highlights and the darkest shadows.

electronic color separation: The process of separating process colors and black (CMYK) with an electronic (computer-assisted) imaging system.

scanner: An electronic imaging device that measures color densities of an original, stores those measurements as digital information, manipulates or alters the data, and uses the manipulated data to create four color separations.

detail printer: The black printer in a set of color separations.

spectrophotometer: A color measurement instrument that uses a prism or diffraction grating to spread light and isolates narrow wavelengths of light between 1 nm and 10 nm.

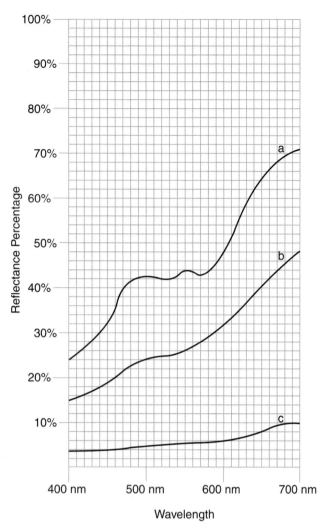

Figure 9-22. The spectrophotometric curves illustrate the reflectance of skin tones. Line "a" represents light skin, line "b" represents dark skin, and line "c" represents very dark skin.

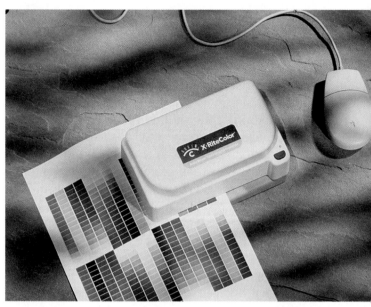

Figure 9-23. This strip-reading spectrophotometer can measure up to 800 color patches on A3 (11″ × 17″) media in eight minutes. It sends the resulting color measurement data (including colorimetric, densitometric, and spectral data), directly to computer software. (X-Rite, Incorporated)

Densitometers

Densitometers compute optical density; the light-stopping or light absorption ability of an image or surface material. The fundamental difference between a densitometer and a spectrophotometer is the bandwidth of light used. A densitometer uses red, green, and blue filters to isolate broad bands of light, the light being about 55 nm wide. A spectrophotometer uses a prism or diffraction grating to spread the light, and a slit to isolate narrow bands of light between 1 nm and 10 nm. The densitometer uses numbers, not curves, to express density. Depending on the type being used, densitometers can be used on negative or positive transparencies, photographs, or printed images.

- *Reflection densitometers* measure the amount of light that bounces off a photographic print or printed sheet at a 90° angle, **Figure 9-24.** It can be configured to make direct measurements of halftone values on printing plates.

- *Transmission densitometers* measure the fraction of incident light conveyed through a negative or positive transparency, without being absorbed or scattered.

- *Combination densitometers* measure both reflection and transmission densities.

Colorimeters

Colorimeters measure and compute XYZ color values in a way that models vision. The results are usually reported in a CIE color space. Colorimeters record all visible colors, but generally are not as precise as densitometers or spectrophotometers. Two types of colorimeters are the trichromatic colorimeter and the monochromatic colorimeter.

A *trichromatic colorimeter* allows the user to match a patch of light by combination of the three primary colors. Even though this instrument relies on the perception of the eye, it is a useful device for color measurement.

A *monochromatic colorimeter* does not measure types of color, but measures the intensity of a particular color. Unlike the trichromatic colorimeter, it does not depend on the perception of color by the eye.

CAREER LINK

Color Specialist

A high percentage of the jobs that are printed today have some color as a part of the finished product. The customers know what they want or like. When someone says the red is not red enough, the color specialist must work with that customer to meet the needs so the images are accepted. Customer approval of color images is a very critical step in the process of creating the finished printed product.

The color specialist must be an expert in understanding color theory. The end results of the specialist's work must ensure accurate color reproduction. Therefore, the color specialist must be competent in working with color calibrations, color separations, and color management. This expertise requires the application of color to types of media as well as to all printing processes. The ability to communicate clearly with customers and technicians is imperative. This person must be able to process, comprehend, and follow detailed written and verbal instructions.

A college education degree in graphic communications is recommended. Experience in the prepress area is imperative. Many of the high quality printers require that the color specialist be a G7 certified GRACoL expert. The G7 certification is a way of defining visual appearance. Belonging to this group classifies the specialist as an elite professional.

"Starting in 2000, the full-sized heatset web-fed presses were able to upgrade to closed loop color, presetting of inks and registration that really worked."

Pam Carritt
Courier Graphics Corporation

Spectrodensitometers

Spectrodensitometers serve all the functions of a spectrophotometer, densitometer, and colorimeter in a single instrument, **Figure 9-25.** In addition to

Figure 9-24. A reflection densitometer offers all the functions needed for prepress and print production in one single unit. The user can personalize the unit with only the functions required for their specific application. (Photo courtesy of GretagMacbeth, New Windsor, NY)

densitometer: An electronic instrument that uses a photocell to accurately measure the amount of light reflected from or through different tone values.

reflection densitometer: A color measurement device that accurately determines different tone values, such as the highlights and shadows of an original.

transmission densitometer: A color measurement device that measures the fraction of incident light conveyed through a negative or positive transparency without being absorbed or scattered.

combination densitometer: A color measurement device that computes both the reflection and transmission densities of an image or surface material.

colorimeter: A color measurement device that measures and compares the hue, purity, and brightness of colors in a manner that simulates how people perceive color.

trichromatic colorimeter: A color measurement device that relies on the perception of the eye to match a patch of light by combination of the three primary colors.

monochromatic colorimeter: A color measurement device that measures the intensity of a particular color and does not depend on the eye's perception of color.

spectrodensitometer: A color measuring instrument that serves all the functions of a spectrophotometer, densitometer, and colorimeter in one device.

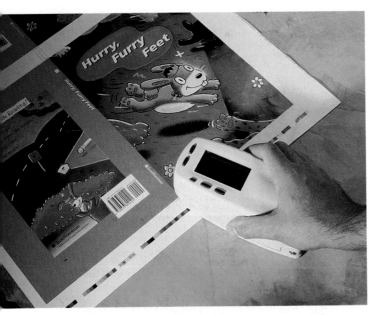

Figure 9-25. Spectrodensitometers are extremely valuable in color processing and quality control. The handheld device illustrated above provides both CIELAB and density data. (X-Rite, Incorporated)

measuring color value and optical density, many instruments can also be used to measure paper attributes and special colors.

THE HUMAN VISUAL SYSTEM

A photomechanical reaction that occurs in the eye when light stimulates retinal receptors allows us to see. The retinal receptors supply electrical impulse patterns to the brain. Images are formed in the mind and take on meaning for the viewer, **Figure 9-26.** Exactly how the brain makes us aware of colors is still much of a mystery.

Anatomy of the Eye and Vision

When light reaches the eye, it is focused onto the *retina*, a layer of light-sensitive cells at the back of the eye. See **Figure 9-27.** This occurs mainly by refraction at the front of the *cornea*, a transparent window at the front of the eye. A special lens behind the pupil and the eye's muscles control adjustments needed for focusing. The *iris* controls the amount of light entering the eye by altering the size of the pupil—from 0.08″ (2 mm) in bright sunlight to 0.3″ (8 mm) at night.

Our perception of light and color is determined by the light-sensitive nerve cells of the retina, known as *rods* and *cones*. There are about twelve million

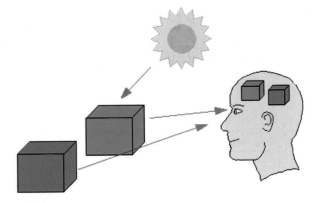

Figure 9-26. Color perception is dependent on the light-sensitive receptors of the eye. After information is collected by the eye, electrical impulses are sent to the brain where the images take on meaning for the viewer.

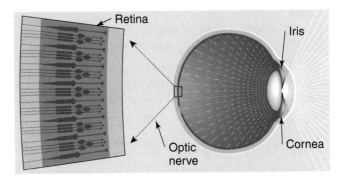

Figure 9-27. The rods and cones are located in the retina of the human eye.

rods and seven million cones in the human eye. The rods detect light intensity and are most sensitive to black, white, and shades of gray. Very little light is needed to stimulate the rods, so they are particularly important for night vision.

The retina has three types of cones that detect both intensity and wavelength (color). The cones contain light-sensitive chemicals called *photopigments* that respond to red, green, or blue. All colors are mixtures of signals from these three types of cone receptors. In other words, colors are perceived according to which cones are stimulated by wavelengths of light entering the eye. This color-mixing ability allows us to perceive a multitude of colors derived from the three primaries. For example, despite yellow's pure appearance, it is not a pure color. There is no retinal receptor sensitive to the yellow frequency. The color yellow is perceived through the combined activity of the red-sensitive and green-sensitive cones.

The *macula* is a small hollow in the middle of the retina. The cones are concentrated in the macula and diminish in concentration toward the edges of the retina. At the center of the macula is the *fovea*, the most sensitive part of the retina. The fovea is packed with cone cells and is the area of sharpest vision. Unlike rods, the cones need high levels of light. This is why colors often appear muted or absent at night.

Brightness and Intensity

The cones and rods of the retina are extremely sensitive light detectors. Even the smallest amount of radiant energy stimulates them. The intensity of light entering the eye causes the sensation of brightness.

Bright light bleaches the color-sensitive cones of the retina. This bleaching stimulates the nerves. After exposure to bright light, it takes time for the photochemical activity of the eye to return to normal. A good example of this effect is when a person is temporarily blinded by a camera flash. During the time a region of the retina is bleached, that region is less sensitive than surrounding regions. This can cause both positive and negative afterimages. *Afterimages* are created when the eye attempts to restore equilibrium. Gazing for some time at a green square and then closing your eyes causes a red square to appear as an afterimage. If the square is red, a green square will be the afterimage. This experiment may be repeated with any color and the afterimage is always the complementary color, **Figure 9-28.** The technical name for this color-vision effect is *successive contrast*.

Adaptation

The adjustment eyes make to lighting conditions is called *adaptation*. If the eyes experience low light for some time, the cones and rods grow more sensitive and light appears brighter. This is dark adaptation. Just as a photographer increases exposure time in a dim lighting situation, the dark adaptation of the eyes increases vision "exposure time" to raise sensitivity. Your eyes adapt to the color of light in much the same way. This is called *chromatic adaptation*. A good example of this effect is reading at night using a tungsten lamp that emits light with a yellow cast. The reader's eyes quickly adapt to the yellow color to the point that it is not even noticeable. If the reader steps outside and looks in the window, he or she would clearly see that the light has a yellow cast.

Adaptation makes it difficult to use your naked eye to determine such things as the amount of light needed in certain photographic situations. Adaptation is also part of the reason viewing booths are used when proofing printed materials. A *viewing booth* has color-balanced lighting (5000 K illumination), so anyone viewing the same printed materials sees

retina: A layer of light-sensitive cells at the back of the eye. When light reaches the eye, it is focused onto the retina.

cornea: A transparent window at the front of the eye that refracts light to the retina.

iris: An opaque diaphragm that contracts and expands to control the amount of light that enters the eye; the colored portion of the eye.

rods: Light-sensitive nerve cells of the retina that help us perceive light and intensity. There are about twelve million rods in the human eye.

cones: Light-sensitive nerve cells of the retina that help us perceive light and color (red, green, and blue). Cones detect both intensity and wavelength (color).

photopigments: Light-sensitive chemicals in the cones of the human eye. Photopigments respond to red, green, or blue light.

macula: A small hollow in the middle of the eye's retina where the cones are concentrated.

fovea: The most sensitive part of the eye's retina and the area of sharpest vision. It is located at the center of the macula and is packed with cone cells.

afterimage: An image that viewer continues to see after the actual object is no longer in sight. The image is created by the eye's attempt to restore equilibrium.

successive contrast: A color-vision effect that causes the viewer to see afterimages.

adaptation: Adjustment that eyes make in different lighting conditions.

chromatic adaptation: The adjustment our eyes make to color conditions.

viewing booth: A booth or defined area illuminated with color-balanced lighting (5000 K). Images are viewed at a 90° angle to reduce glare.

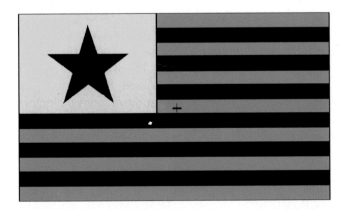

Figure 9-28. To see an afterimage, stare at the center of the flag for about 30 seconds. Then look at a white sheet of paper. You will see an image of the flag with its proper colors.

them under identical lighting conditions. The light temperature used in a viewing booth appears clear and color-balanced, and is ideal for making color comparisons, **Figure 9-29.**

Cones and rods in the eye adapt at different rates. Cone adaptation occurs in about seven minutes, while rod adaptation continues for an hour or more. Decreased light and increased visual sensitivity also reduces the ability to make out fine detail.

Adjacency

Adjacency is a change in color perception that is caused by colors adjacent to or surrounding a subject, **Figure 9-30.** If you place the same color against different background colors, the color appears different in each scenario. For example, a color looks brighter if the surroundings are dark, but the same color looks darker if surrounded by a lighter color. Additionally, a color looks more saturated if surrounded by a complementary color. This color-vision effect is called *chromatic induction* or simultaneous contrast.

Figure 9-30. When a color is viewed against a light background, it appears darker. When the same color is viewed against a dark background, it appears lighter.

Color Constancy

Color constancy is the tendency to perceive the color of an object to be the constant, even when environmental conditions (such as lighting) are changed. Skin tones are also commonly misperceived. When viewing the printed image of a person, for example, their skin color may appear correct due to the color maintained in the viewer's memory. The actual difference in color is apparent when the person is compared to the printed image.

Color Viewing Variables

Although the human vision system is both highly sensitive and accurate, it is also very subjective. Visual perception varies among individuals for many reasons and can even be affected by changes in emotional and physical states.

Color Blindness

The ability to see in color is not inherent to all animals. Although some birds, fish, reptiles, and insects have highly-developed color vision systems, it is almost certain that very few mammals below the primates possess color vision. Among humans, approximately 10% of males and about 1% of females, experience some degree of color blindness. Color blindness is the inability to tell colors apart.

A person with normal vision has cones that respond to all three of the additive primary colors (RGB). A color-blind person lacks one, two, or all three types of cones. Most color-blind people have *dichromatic vision* and can see only yellows and blues. They confuse reds with greens, and some reds or greens with some yellows. Very few people are truly blind to all colors. Those who are completely color-blind see only in shades of white, gray, and black, and are said to have *achromatic vision*.

Figure 9-29. Standardized viewing conditions are necessary to properly evaluate color reproduction. This viewing booth emits 5000 K illumination. (Photo courtesy of GretagMacbeth, New Windsor, NY)

Vision Fatigue

Random retinal impulses and involuntary rapid eye movements are essential to vision and keep the vision system perpetually active. Vision soon fades when an image becomes optically fixed on the retina. Movement of the eye sweeps the light pattern over receptors to continually signal the brain that the image is present. However, overuse fatigues the system and can impair color judgment. For example, viewing a saturated color for an extended period of time causes a second color to appear different because vision fatigue subtracts some of the first color from the image.

Aging

Even with the complete absence of light, random retinal impulses reach the brain. This continuous background of random activity creates a problem for the mind. The mind must decide whether the activity is "noise" or information. Internal visual noise increases with age and is partly responsible for the gradual loss of visual discrimination. Aging also impacts visual accuracy and adaptation.

Viewing Conditions

In addition to vision deficiencies and variations, external conditions also affect color judgment. External variables include diverse lighting types, different substrates, disparate viewing angles, unconventional illumination angles, and the size and shape of the color area, **Figure 9-31.** Because color vision requires sensory data, it is impossible to actually remember color; we can only compare color. However, accurate color comparison is almost impossible unless items are viewed under identical viewing conditions.

Summary

Color is an important and powerful factor in our everyday lives. When visiting a grocery store, notice the use of color in food packaging. If color was lacking on the package, the appeal of the product would also be lacking. This is because color often determines our selection or rejection of an item. Color selection is an important step in the printing process and understanding color is a critical quality in a printer. To ensure consistent use of color, standards and tools have been developed to assist both the designer and printer with color selection and application.

Review Questions

Please do not write in this book. Write your answers on a separate sheet of paper.

1. Our eyes are sensitive to only a small part of the electromagnetic spectrum. What is this range called?
2. A beam of light coming toward a surface is called the _____ beam.
3. How does light become refracted?
4. Explain the difference between the *constructive interference* of light and the *destructive interference* of light.
5. What is a *diffraction grating*?
6. What is a *color triad*?
7. How is a *shade* produced? a *tint*? a *tone*?
8. Identify and define the three criteria used in the HSB color model.
9. Explain the properties of Munsell's HVC color organization system.

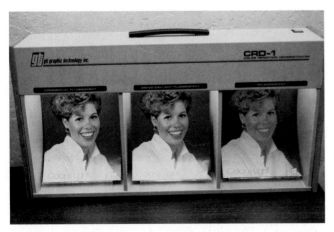

Figure 9-31. Differences in viewing conditions under 2500 K, 5000 K, and 6500 K illumination.

adjacency: A property of the eye that changes the perception of a color based on the adjacent or surrounding color.

chromatic induction: A change in perception where the eye causes a color to look different when surrounded by or adjacent to other colors.

color constancy: The tendency to perceive the color of an object to be constant, even when specific conditions (such as lighting) are changed.

dichromatic vision: A form of color blindness where only yellows and blues are visible.

achromatic vision: Blindness to all colors; ability to see only in shades of white, gray, and black.

10. Summarize how the CIE system standardized color specification.

11. What do the letters *LAB* represent in the CIELAB color model?

12. Which color specification system is based on ink colors common to the printing industry?

13. Describe the process of *additive color formation*.

14. Identify the *subtractive primary colors*.

15. Explain why black is used as the fourth process color.

16. Define *color separation* and give three examples of color separation methods.

17. Name four color measurement instruments and explain the use of each.

18. Which parts of the eye determine our perception of light and color?

19. Why is a viewing booth necessary to accurately compare colors?

20. Define *adjacency* and give an example of the effect.

21. What is the difference between *dichromatic vision* and *achromatic vision*?

Suggested Activities

1. Visit the physics lab of your school. Observe the visible light through a prism and identify the wavelengths.

2. Ink up the press with red ink, cut several different types of substrates, and run the substrates through the press. Once printed, notice the appearance of the red ink on the various types of substrates. Describe the differences in appearance.

3. Using a reflection densitometer, measure the density of several printed control strips. Explain your findings.

4. Select several color-printed pieces and view them under different types of light sources, including bright sunlight, fluorescent lighting, incandescent lighting, and natural indoor light. Describe the color variation in each situation.

Related Web Links

The Tech Museum of Innovation—Make a Splash with Color

www.thetech.org/exhibits/online/color

An online exhibit that explores characteristics of color, light, and the human eye.

The International Commission on Illumination

www.cie.co.at

Web site of the central bureau of the CIE. The site contains information on the various divisions of the organization, news bulletins, and resource links.

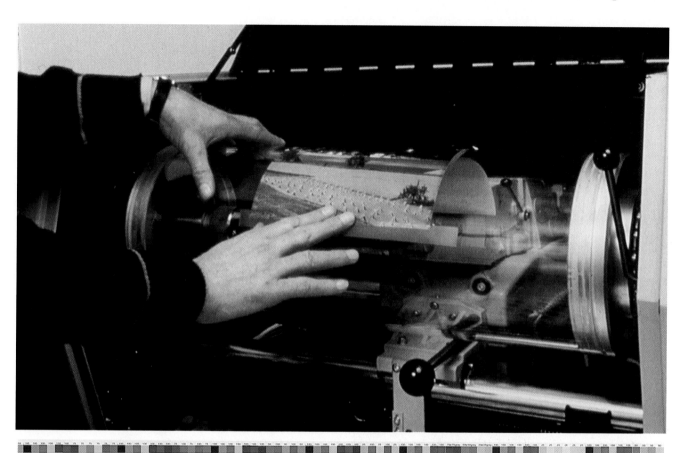

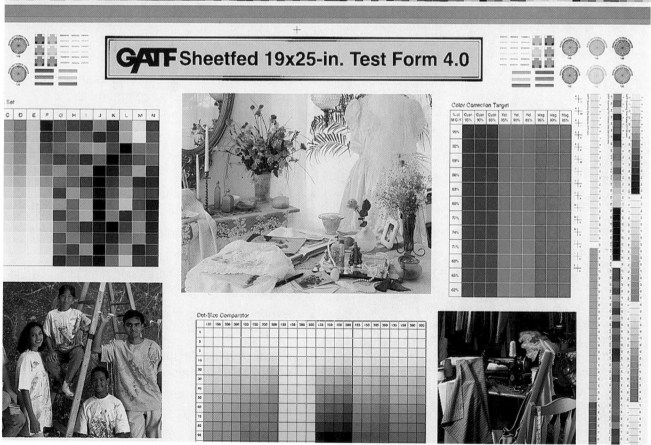

For optimum results in the final printed product, careful management of color must be maintained at all stages of the graphic communications process, from original image scanning to actual presswork. (Graphic Arts Technical Foundation)

CHAPTER 10

Color Management

Learning Objectives

After studying this chapter, you will be able to:

- Give several examples of color standards adopted by the graphic communications industry and explain how they are used.

- Explain how a color management system (CMS) regulates color conversion through the workflow.

- Explain several methods used for color separation and correction.

- Explain trapping and list conventional and electronic methods.

- Explain the various screening methods used in graphic arts.

- Explain how color may be affected in the preflighting stage.

- Recall proofing methods used in the graphic communications industry.

- Explain the importance of ensuring ink colors are used correctly.

Important Terms

additive color formation
automatic trap
blueline proofs
brightness
brownline proofs
calibration
characterization
choke trap
color control bar
color correction
color gamut
Color Key™ proofs
color management module (CMM)
color management system (CMS)
contrast
conversion
Cromalin™ proofs
digital blueline proofs
digital proofs
dot etching
dot gain
dot pitch
error-diffusion screening
gamma levels
gamut alarm
gamut compression
gamut reduction
gray component replacement (GCR)
grayscale
grayscaling
hinting
ICC color profile
International Color Consortium (ICC)
IT8 reflective target
knockout
lookup tables
Matchprint proofs
maximum resolution
overprinting
photographic masking
press proofs
refresh rate
screen flicker
soft proofing
spot screening
spread trap
stochastic screening
stroke
subtractive color formation
tone curve adjustment
trapping
undercolor addition (UCA)
undercolor removal (UCR)
video card
white point

Color management in graphic communications describes the systematic approach to color conversions from input to output devices. The conversions can involve output to monitors, to digital color printers or presses, or to film or plate material. The primary issue is getting the color transformation correct to ensure consistent and accurate color reproduction, regardless of the number or types of devices involved.

Computer monitors, digital proofing devices, and printing presses all render color differently. Documents viewed on-screen and output to different devices will have widely varying results. With an effective color management system, images can be scanned accurately, displayed on-screen correctly, and output as close to the original colors as possible.

STANDARDS, REGULATIONS, AND COLOR MODELS

Numerous means of regulating, testing, and reproducing color have been adopted by the graphic communications industry. Because ink and toner composition, printing presses, and substrate quality also affect the accuracy of color reproduction, their design and operation are also covered under many of the same standards.

The International Commission on Illumination (CIE)

Many computer, ink, and paper manufacturers have adopted the CIE system of color specification. As discussed in Chapter 9, CIE created the three-dimensional, device-independent CIELAB color model.

The CIELAB color model is an ideal color space for performing *color correction*. Instead of representing a color as a percentage of other colors, the CIELAB model puts the *grayscale* information in the L channel and uses the A and B channels for color information.

Grayscale is a means of showing the shades of gray that represent the image. When an image is converted to grayscale, all color information is discarded. The gray levels, or shades, of the converted pixels represent the luminosity of the original pixels. Because the grayscale channel is isolated in the CIELAB model, the user is able to apply sharpening and tonal settings without distorting the relationships of colors.

Grayscaling is the process of converting a continuous-tone image to an image in shades of gray. Continuous tone images, such as black-and-white photographs, use an almost unlimited number of shades of gray. Computers, however, can only represent a limited number of shades of gray (typically 16–256). Grayscaling requires large amounts of memory because each individual pixel

---

color correction: Adjusting images to optimize values for highlight and shadow, neutral tones, skin tones, and sharpness, to compensate for impurities in the printing ink and color separation.

gray scale: A continuous tone strip used to visually gauge exposure of an image.

grayscaling: The process of converting a continuous-tone image to an image in shades of gray.

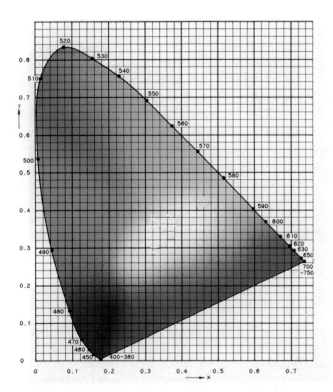

Figure 10-1. The horseshoe-shaped CIE chromaticity diagram contains the colors of the visible spectrum.

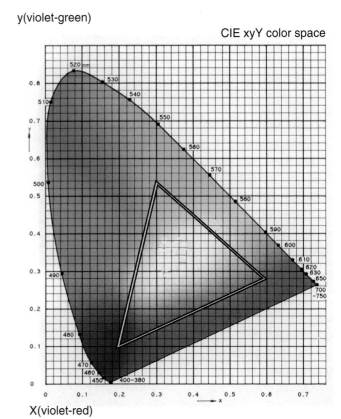

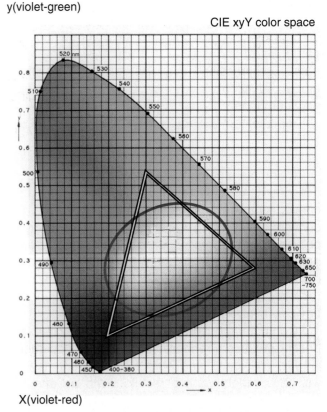

Figure 10-2. Gamut compression. A—The triangle represents the color space of a computer monitor. B—The oval represents the CMYK space of a printer.

can be a different shade of gray and is represented by 4–8 bits.

Although many image-editing programs allow the user to enhance the crispness of an RGB or CMYK image, halos and other distortions often occur when sharpening commands are applied. If possible, images should be captured and modified in the CIELAB color space and then converted to RGB or CMYK, depending on its final purpose. The CIELAB mode is also recommended for moving images between systems.

The color gamut of a device is usually displayed using the CIE chromaticity diagram, **Figure 10-1.** The CIE chromaticity diagram shows just two dimensions of the CIE Yxy color space: hue and chroma. Refer to Chapter 9 for a discussion of the Yxy color space. The achromatic component, or color's brightness, is represented by *Y* and is specified by a number, not a location on the graph.

The degree of inability of a device to display or print color is called its *gamut compression*. If the color plot of a computer monitor is superimposed on the CIE chromaticity diagram, it can be seen that the monitor can display only a fraction of the visible spectrum, **Figure 10-2A.** If the plot of printable colors is superimposed on the same chart, it is clearly visible that the gamut of most printing presses is even more limited, **Figure 10-2B.**

! No matter what type of color mode is used, some quality is lost each time an image is converted. To preserve image quality, use conversions sparingly and apply them once, only to the final image.

The International Color Consortium (ICC)

Until 1993, the formats used to describe the color behavior of particular devices varied by manufacturer. These multiple color standards were extremely impractical, because most graphic communications professionals use a combination of devices from different manufacturers.

In 1993, several leading manufacturers founded the *International Color Consortium (ICC)*. The ICC created a cross-platform standard for color management using *ICC color profiles*. These profiles are based on the CIELAB color space and function as standards for describing color characterizations of different devices. ICC color profiles contain information on the device's color space and the compensation required to bring the device to its ideal level of performance. Most graphic arts manufacturers have developed applications that support ICC color profiles.

Once a device profile has been created, the profile is then used by a color transformation engine, or *color management module (CMM)*. The CMM translates data from one device's color space to another.

Specifications for Web Offset Publications (SWOP)

In 1975, a review committee was formed to establish specifications to help eliminate variations in the materials being supplied to printers by prepress service bureaus. In 1976, the committee adopted its present name, Specifications for Web Offset Publications, or SWOP®. Although they are not mandated as such, the SWOP specifications are accepted as industry standards.

Initially, the specifications covered only the production of film and proofs for offset printing. However, as electronic technology has become more integrated in the production process, the specifications now concentrate on the use of electronic files and their impact on publication production. Electronic files are expected to meet the same high-quality standards

that have been expected of the graphic arts films and proofs supplied to the printer under SWOP.

SWOP has developed its specifications in accordance with many of the graphic communications standards established by such organizations as the American National Standards Institute (ANSI), the International Organization for Standardization (ISO), and the Committee for Graphic Arts Technologies Standards (CGATS).

Areas covered under the specifications include standard lighting for viewing proofs, electronic file formats, register marks, film requirements, ink measurement and control, and proofing, both on and off press. The specifications were also adopted for gravure publications.

YCC Color Space

Kodak's YCC color space is also important to the digital workflow. Developed for the Kodak Photo CD, this color space is device-independent and is suited for data compression and decompression. YCC is a variant of the RGB color space.

Color Rendition Charts

Color changes with time and environmental conditions. Many professionals use color test charts to make objective measurements. Charts such as the Macbeth ColorChecker™ are commonly used by photographers but can also be useful to the graphic communications professional, **Figure 10-3.**

The ColorChecker chart is composed of twenty-four 2″ (5 cm) square color patches made of matte paint applied to a smooth paper. The patches are selected Munsell colors that closely match real-object colors such as dark and light human skin, foliage, and blue flowers. The additive and subtractive primary colors and a six-step neutral scale are also included.

gamut compression: Technique used to compress colors to fit into a smaller color gamut to give the illusion that all color chroma, saturation, and value are present.

International Color Consortium (ICC): Organization established in 1993 by leading manufacturers to create a cross-platform standard for color management.

ICC color profiles: Profiles based on the CIELAB color space and used as standards for describing the color characterizations of different devices.

Color management module (CMM): Color transformation engine that translates data from one device's color space to another.

Figure 10-3. The ColorChecker chart has twenty-four 2" (5 cm) square color patches that closely match real-object colors such as dark and light human skin, foliage, and blue flowers. (Photo Courtesy of GretagMacbeth, New Windsor, NY)

Each patch can be identified by number; name; its CIE Yxy chromaticity coordinates; Munsell's hue, value, and chroma; an ISCC-NBS standard name (Inter-Society Color Council-National Bureau of Standards); and an assigned name, **Figure 10-4.** Subjective evaluations can be made by comparing the reproduction to the chart or by comparing the reproductions of different systems. Comparisons should be made under the proper viewing conditions.

The Pantone System

The Pantone® System of color specification is the most widely used system in the graphic communications industry. It is a universal color language that helps ensure color consistency throughout production. The Pantone System is based on ink colors common to the printing industry.

Designers, clients, and printers can communicate color selections using manuals or swatchbooks containing representations of the Pantone colors. The manuals and swatchbooks provide color simulations, names, and mixing formulas.

Pantone has developed software programs that allow the users of most computer systems to specify Pantone colors, **Figure 10-5.** The Pantone Matching Guide and the Pantone 4-Color Process Guide provide color control for solid color printing and process color printing.

The designer can select from one of the 1000 Pantone colors in the solid color range when using the

Pantone Color Formula Guide. With the Pantone 4-Color Process Guide, the user can specify any one of 3000 process tints. The colors are viewed with a fan guide displaying the colors in a spectrum, **Figure 10-6.**

Pantone has also developed chromaticity values for both Pantone Colors and monitor phosphors. These values allow monitors to display Pantone Colors that accurately represent the ink on paper. A color calibrator that compensates for monitor drift and phosphor decay is also available. The white balance can also be adjusted so the white screen on the monitor looks more like a press sheet illuminated in a printing plant.

Many printer manufacturers have been licensed to produce Pantone colors, but results vary with the resolution of the printer as well as the purity of the cyan, magenta, and yellow inks.

Using Spot and Process Colors

Defining spot and process colors correctly is essential for proper color separation. Most page composition programs provide editing features that allow the user to indicate the desired separation, **Figure 10-7.**

If spot colors are used in imported graphic files, the same colors must be defined in the page composition files. Illustration or image editing programs may name colors differently from page composition programs. Therefore, it is necessary to change the name in one file so that it matches the other exactly. If the names do not match, spot colors will separate as their CMYK equivalents. Some page composition programs automatically add the spot color to the color palette when importing graphics using that color, but do not automatically change the name.

When building process colors for output on a press, you should keep in mind that it is better to avoid too heavy an ink coverage. Maximum densities for the process colors vary for different types of presses and colors should be created with these values in mind.

Color Management Systems (CMS)

Color management for electronic imaging and reproduction involves more than the management of film color separations and ink composition. Electronic color reproduction requires a system of color management that will enable operators throughout

No.	Name	CIE (1931)			Munsell Notation		ISCC/NBS Name
		x	y	Y*	Hue	Value/Chroma	
1	Dark skin	.4002	.3504	10.05	3.05YR	3.69/3.20	Moderate brown
2	Light skin	.3773	.3446	35.82	2.2YR	6.47/4.10	Light reddish brown
3	Blue sky	.2470	.2514	19.33	4.3PB	4.95/5.55	Moderate blue
4	Foliage	.3372	.4220	13.29	6.65GY	4.19/4.15	Moderate olive green
5	Blue flower	.2651	.2400	24.27	9.65PB	5.47/6.70	Light violet
6	Bluish green	.2608	.3430	43.06	2.5BG	7/6	Light bluish green
7	Orange	.5060	.4070	30.05	5YR	6/11	Strong orange
8	Purplish blue	.2110	.1750	12.00	7.5PB	4/10.7	Strong purplish blue
9	Moderate red	.4533	.3058	19.77	2.5R	5/10	Moderate red
10	Purple	.2845	.2020	6.56	5P	3/7	Deep purple
11	Yellow green	.3800	.4887	44.29	5GY	7.08/9.1	Strong yellow green
12	Orange yellow	.4729	.4375	43.06	10YR	7/10.5	Strong orange yellow
13	Blue	.1866	.1285	6.11	7.5PB	2.90/12.75	Vivid purplish blue
14	Green	.3046	.4782	23.39	0.1G	5.38/9.65	Strong yellowish green
15	Red	.5385	.3129	12.00	5R	4/12	Strong red
16	Yellow	.4480	.4703	59.10	5Y	8/11.1	Vivid yellow
17	Magenta	.3635	.2325	19.77	2.5RP	5/12	Strong reddish purple
18	Cyan	.1958	.2519	19.77	5B	5/8	Strong greenish blue
19	White	.3101	.3163	90.01	N	9.5/	White
20	Neutral 8	.3101	.3163	59.10	N	8/	Light gray
21	Neutral 6.5	.3101	.3163	36.20	N	6.5/	Light-medium gray
22	Neutral 5	.3101	.3163	19.77	N	5/	Medium gray
23	Neutral 3.5	.3101	.3163	9.00	N	3.5	Dark gray
24	Black	.3101	.3163	3.13	N	2/	Black

Figure 10-4. This table provides the names and specification of color patches in the Macbeth ColorChecker Rendition Chart.

the production process to maintain and produce accurate color reproduction.

A *color management system (CMS)* uses software and hardware to ensure colors remain the same regardless of the device or medium used to display the colors. A CMS can correct for color shifts on a scanner; adjust color display on a monitor; and make proofing, printing, and viewing of color more accurate.

Correlating the color-rendering capabilities of input and output devices is a difficult task because different devices use different technologies and color models to produce colors. In addition, color is highly subjective.

Color management system (CMS): An electronic prepress tool that provides a way to correlate the color-rendering capabilities of input devices, color monitors, and output devices to produce predictable, consistent color.

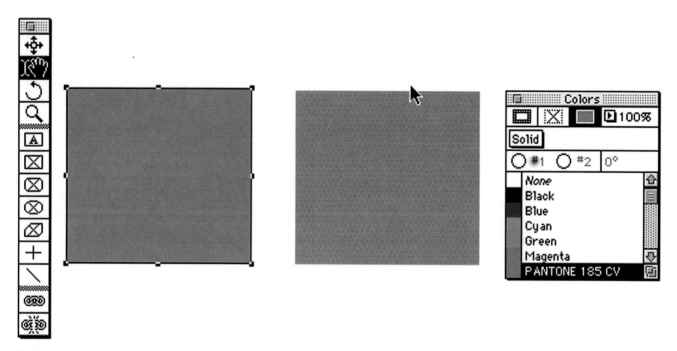

Figure 10-5. Many page composition and illustration programs allow the user to specify Pantone colors. Each program may render a color differently onscreen, as shown, even though the printed color would be as specified.

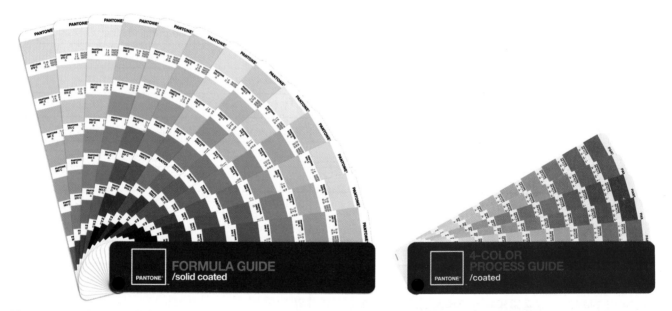

Figure 10-6. Pantone Color System. A—Pantone's Formula Guide allows the user to compare Pantone Colors to their closest CMYK version. B—Pantone's 4-Color Process Guide displays over 3000 CMYK color combinations. Colors are chromatically arranged and displayed with their CMYK percentages. (Pantone, Inc.)

There is quite a variety of color management systems available; the type you use will depend on your operating system as well as your output needs. As with most computer systems, similar applications operate in a similar manner and changing from one to another is a fairly simple process. Color management can be divided into three primary steps: characterization, calibration, and conversion.

Characterization

Characterization describes the color limitations, or profile, of a particular device. The profile defines how the device's specific color space relates to a device-independent color space. The profile can also be used to define the *color gamut* of a device.

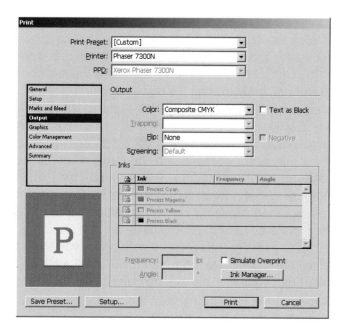

Figure 10-7. If you want a process color to separate to the proper CMYK plates, the process separation feature of the software should be turned on. When working with spot colors, you can have the color separate to its own plate by turning the separation feature off or simulate it in its corresponding 4-color equivalent by keeping it on.

A CMS depends on the device profiles that store the color characteristics of the devices being used. As a means of standardization, most device profiles are described with the device-independent CIELAB color space.

Some color management systems have a generic device profile describing the manufacturer's specifications for the product. However, if the device is not performing to those specifications, the profiles will not be accurate.

Calibration

One of the most important steps when setting up a CMS is calibrating the input device(s). The *calibration* process allows the user to understand the small color changes to an image that a particular device introduces each time the device is used. Regular calibration is necessary to bring the device in line with its intended specifications.

The calibration of any device requires the use of a standard. The device can then be calibrated by first determining its deviation from the standard. Once the deviation has been determined, the proper correction factors can be identified and applied. In graphic communications, it is necessary to calibrate everything from the scanner through the monitor, the

proofing device, and the actual press and paper on which the job will run.

Monitors

It is important to understand that the colors displayed on a computer monitor are different from those printable on a press. This is obvious when you look at the superimposed color gamut of a monitor on the CIE chromaticity diagram. Refer to Figure 10-2A. A monitor can be calibrated but it will never match the printed page perfectly because of the physics of color involved.

A CMS can be used to ensure your monitor provides as accurate color representation as possible. Before the CMS can begin characterization, four calibration elements must be set on the monitor to characterize it properly. These elements are the monitor's brightness, contrast, gamma levels, and white point.

Brightness is the attribute of light-source colors by which emitted light is ordered continuously from light to dark in correlation with its intensity. *Contrast* is the relationship between the lightest and the darkest areas of an image. Brightness and contrast levels are set manually with the controls on your monitor.

The *gamma levels* of a monitor are the degrees of contrast of the screen image. Gamma levels affect the distribution of tones between highlight and shadow areas of the original. The *white point* is the color that results when red, green, and blue channels are operating at full intensity. The white point defines the lightest area in an image. It is a movable reference

characterization: Describes the color limitations or color profile of a particular device.

color gamut: The range of colors that can be formed by all possible combinations of the colorants in a color reproduction system.

calibration: A process by which a scanner, monitor, or output device is adjusted to provide a more accurate display and reproduction of images.

brightness: Often referred to as lightness or luminosity, brightness can be defined as a value indicating how light or dark a color is.

contrast: The variation of elements in a printed product.

gamma levels: Degrees of contrast of a screen image of a monitor.

white point: A movable reference point that defines the lightest area in an image displayed on a cathode ray tube causing all other areas to be adjusted accordingly.

point that, when changed, causes all other areas to be adjusted accordingly.

White point temperature defines the coolness (bluish) or warmness (yellowish) of video white. In some monitors, the white point will tend toward blue; in others, toward a warmer color. The white point can be set to match the light under which proofs will be viewed to help standardize color at different stages of production.

The gamma levels and white point temperature of your monitor are set within the monitor's software and are typically adjustable from the control panel within the system software. Both the gamma level and white point of your monitor may vary according to the computer's age and operating temperature.

The next step involves the use of a colorimeter or spectrophotometer. When used for color measurement on a monitor, these devices use a rubber suction cup that affixes directly to the glass of the monitor, **Figure 10-8.**

Figure 10-8. Spectrophotometers are designed for use in many areas of graphic communications. A suction cup device is used for mounting the device on a computer monitor.

Once prompted, the CMS commands the monitor to broadcast different colors on the screen. The device measures the colors emitted and sends the data back to the CMS. The CMS creates a profile of the monitor's performance by relating the color values measured to ideal colors. If the monitor tends slightly toward blue, the CMS will know that it will need to subtract that percentage of blue from every color it processes.

It is not necessary to perform a complete measurement procedure every time the white point or gamma level setting is altered. Some color management systems can automatically adapt to a new white point and gamma level.

Along with regular monitor calibration, you should eliminate light glare from windows, skylights, and overhead lighting. This can be done by constructing a glare hood for your monitor and placing egg-crate diffusers on overhead lighting.

🛈 **Do not display the same pattern on your monitor for an extended time. If the same pattern is left onscreen for too long, the brightness of that area will be decreased due to the degradation of phosphors, or increased because the electrode surface will be activated more than in other areas.**

Monitor Limitations

It is not easy to accurately reproduce color on a computer monitor and it is practically impossible to display the exact colors of a printed image on a monitor. This problem exists because monitors and printing devices produce color through two entirely different processes. Monitors use additive color formation and printed images are formed by subtractive color formation.

In *additive color formation*, the primary colors of light (red, green, blue) combine to form other colors. Monitors using cathode ray tubes (CRTs) produce color by exciting red, green, and blue phosphors with a sweeping beam of electrons. The screen starts out as black, and images are created when the electrons hitting the phosphors generate combinations of red, green, and blue light. The screen becomes white when all the red, green, and blue phosphors are illuminated at the same time. The liquid crystal display (LCD) screens and light-emitting diode (LED) screens do not have cathode ray tubes. Since each of the monitors has millions of pixels, each of these pixels has a liquid crystal or an LED. The pixels become tiny lightbulbs capable of lighting up as colors.

Monitors are analog devices and must translate an image's binary data before being able to display it. Computers use a *video card* to translate and generate the corresponding electrical voltage levels needed to produce the colors on the monitor. For a monitor to display at its optimum resolution, the video card must be able to operate at the proper level. For example, at least 4 MB of video RAM (VRAM) is required when doing color work with a 24-bit display (16.7 million colors).

The video card uses color *lookup tables* and a digital-to-analog converter to coordinate the digital and analog color information. Lookup tables store the dot sizes needed to produce given colors. The type of video card used and the accuracy of the lookup tables will determine the quality of the conversion process.

In *subtractive color formation*, color is seen by reflected light. Each of the subtractive primary colors (cyan, magenta, and yellow) absorbs other colors from the white light and reflects only its own. In process color printing, colors are mixed visually, rather than physically. Tiny, closely spaced dots of cyan, magenta, and yellow ink absorb and reflect the different wavelengths of light to produce different colors. Refer to Chapter 9 for a review of RGB and CMY color formation.

Monitors vary by size and resolution quality. They should be chosen based on the tasks they are to perform. The overall size of the monitor should be considered first. For example, a 15″ screen may be the most cost-effective for RIP stations, but a 17″ screen would be more suitable for a scanning station. Designers working on page composition need monitors with screens measuring at least 21″, **Figure 10-9.**

Other criteria to consider are dot pitch, maximum resolution, and refresh rate. *Dot pitch* is the size of the pixels that make up the screen matrix. *Maximum resolution* is the maximum number of pixels that the screen can represent in both horizontal and vertical dimensions. Higher resolution provides a clearer image and allows the user to have more windows open on the screen at the same time.

The *refresh rate* is the speed with which the screen is redrawn. The refresh rate controls the amount of detectable *screen flicker*. Screen flicker can also be affected by lighting and the persistence of the screen phosphors.

Scanners

Most digital imaging equipment provides a means of performing characterization and calibration. For example, to assist in determining the characterization

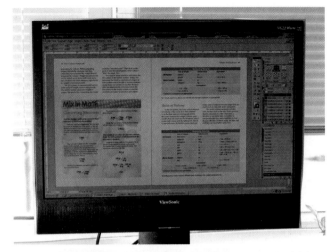

Figure 10-9. Designers working with page composition software should use as large a screen as possible. Larger screens are able to display the layout for a full two-page spread or an entire book cover image.

of a scanner, manufacturers will include a reference image and a set of reference values for that image. The reference image contains well-defined color patches and will typically be the IT8 reflective target or pattern, **Figure 10-10.**

IT8 Reflective Target

The *IT8 reflective target* is a standard color reference tool used to calibrate input and output devices. It is also known as a color target. Samples from the CIELAB color space are used to create the IT8 reference targets.

additive color formation: Theory based on mixing red, green, and blue light in various combinations to create a color reproduction or image.

video card: Board that plugs into a computer to give it display capabilities.

lookup tables: Chart stored in computer memory that lists the dot sizes needed to produce given colors.

subtractive color formation: The combining of inks in the colors cyan, magenta, yellow, and black to produce the printed image.

dot pitch: A measurement of the vertical distance between rows of pixels on a monitor, stated in decimal fractions of a millimeter.

maximum resolution: Maximum number of pixels that a computer screen can represent in both horizontal and vertical dimensions.

refresh rate: The speed with which the screen is redrawn.

screen flicker: Rapid changes in light intensity produced by a monitor screen.

IT8 reflective target: Standard color reference tool used to calibrate input and output devices.

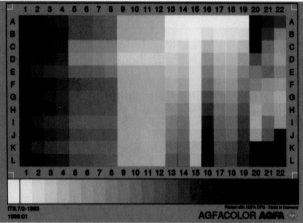

Figure 10-10. IT8 targets are available for various uses and from many different manufacturers. A—Kodak target. (Eastman Kodak Company) B—Agfa target. (Agfa)

Two targets currently used in the graphic communications industry are the IT8.7/1-1993 and the IT8.7/2-1993. The IT8.7/1 chart is used for scanner calibration. The target is used to measure the values of transmissive color being read by the input device. The IT8.7/2 is also used for input scanner calibration, but it is used to measure reflective color. Transmissive color is light conveyed through a negative or positive transparency without being absorbed or scattered. Reflective color is color that is seen by reflected light. The reference image is scanned and the measured results are related to the ideal values measured in the manufacturer's lab.

An ideal scanner would allow the user to scan images directly into an independent color space such as CIELAB. However, most scanners are limited to the RGB and CMYK color spaces. All scanners start with an RGB signal and many allow conversions to CMYK as the scan is being made. If the CIELAB color space is not available, RGB should be used because it provides greater flexibility for the scanned image.

Some scanners convert from the RGB scan signal to CMYK on-the-fly, automatically creating a color-separated file from the original image. This is a less desirable approach to scanning in RGB because it makes the file device-dependent and limits the potential uses of the image. CMYK files are locked into the color gamut of the output process for which they are separated. This makes the conversion to other spaces difficult or impossible, and causes the conversion back to RGB to result in a less-than-optimum image for RGB purposes. A CMS is usually capable of making CMYK to RGB conversions, but the color quality is reduced because the original scan was made to a reduced gamut CMYK space. Therefore, scans should be saved in the original CIELAB or RGB format to preserve the maximum amount of color, and to ensure the image can be used for a number of different purposes.

Color correction and modification are easier to perform in the CIELAB or RGB mode than in CMYK. An RGB or CIELAB image file is also about 25% smaller than the same image saved in CMYK. Some imaging programs allow the user to preview an image in CMYK and still keep the file in RGB or CIELAB color.

Calibration Schedules

Most circumstances do not warrant daily equipment calibration. However, some situations warrant device calibration on at least a monthly (if not weekly) basis. An example would be a printer that deals with large amounts of work. Operators can also develop a regimen for scanner characterization and calibration.

Determining a scanner's characteristics is a methodical process. Situations and equipment will vary, but by performing the following steps you will be able to determine the characteristics of a scanner.

- Gather an assortment of media and scan them at the scanner's default settings. Media will vary according to your scanner's capabilities, but when applicable, should include both transparent and reflective originals.

- Output the scans to your printer or imagesetter. Composite color proofs should be made from the film if you are using an imagesetter.

- Compare the color proofs to the originals under correct lighting.

- If a color measurement device is available, use it to obtain accurate readings.

Characteristics of the scanner can be identified at this point. You can determine whether the scans have a common color cast, if they are flat, or if they are all too heavy. Most scanning software provides controls in the form of highlight and shadow selection or tone curve adjustment to correct most common problems.

Tone curve adjustment involves the use of curves to make tonal adjustments. You can use curves to make precise adjustments to one area of the tonal range while maintaining the effect on other areas. For example, curves can be used to add or decrease the contrast of an image without changing the colors.

A lookup table listing the standard settings for all the scans should be created. This table should compensate for the scanner's characteristics. This lookup table will provide a good starting point for all your scans.

Save the original media, file, films, and proofs from one or two images that have been scanned with the new standard settings. The files should be output to film and a new composite color proof should be made at least once a month. The new color proof can be compared with the original to verify consistency. If the proofs are not close, you should check the output device calibration and processor status (chemical strength of the solutions used, temperature, speed), among other variables.

It is important to set all the controls of the scanner to neutral points before performing characterization. The neutral settings allow the user to return to the same starting point to continuously make successful scans.

Printers

Characterization and calibration of printing devices is also important to the accurate reproduction of color. The first step is to output a target file that is appropriate for the final printing process. After the target file is printed, it should be measured with a color spectrophotometer, **Figure 10-11.**

After the target is evaluated, profiling software can be used to create the printer's color profile. This profile is used by the CMS to adjust color inaccuracies in the printer as files are output.

The time needed to establish color management standards depends on the complexity of the operation. The calibration of monitors takes just a few minutes, while the calibration of scanners can require two hours. However, the procedure does not need to be repeated often because most scanners are stable performers. Printing presses and proof printers require more time because the number of color spot readings needed to build a profile is high. However,

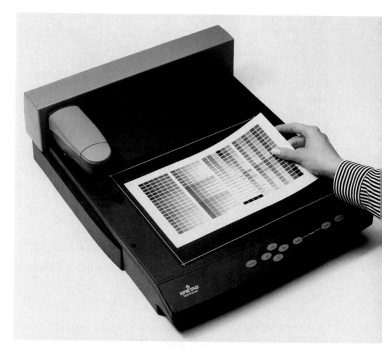

Figure 10-11. This spectrophotometer is mounted on an x/y table for automatic color measurement. (Photo courtesy of GretagMacbeth, New Windsor, NY)

for larger operations, automated color measurement instruments are available and are capable of making hundreds of readings in just a few minutes.

Color Conversion

The *conversion* step performs color correction between imaging devices. Color management systems are used to compensate for and select from the possible range of colors available on each device. In most imaging programs, images can be converted to, displayed in, and edited in eight image modes. These eight modes are bitmap, duotone, indexed color, grayscale, multichannel, RGB, CMYK, and CIELAB, **Figure 10-12.**

Your system and output needs determine which image mode best suits your work. For instance, if a publication is to be printed in black and white, the grayscale mode can be used to convert color images into high-quality black-and-white images.

When converting images from one mode to another, the conversion creates a permanent change to the color values in the image. For example, the four-channel CMYK space contains far fewer colors,

tone curve adjustment: The use of curves to make tonal adjustments to an image.

conversion: Step of color management systems that performs color correction between imaging devices.

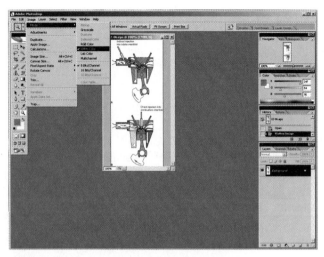

Figure 10-12. The user can easily choose image modes from a pull-down menu.

a narrower dynamic range, and a much smaller color gamut than the three-channel RGB space. Therefore, colors must be compressed to fit into the smaller color gamut. The gamut compression gives the illusion that all color chroma, saturation, and value are present, but there is always a loss of color.

> **!** Each conversion changes data so you should always save a backup copy of the original file.

One of the most effective ways of performing color conversions is to begin with the CIELAB color space. Because it is device-independent, based on numerical values, and has a large color gamut, the CIELAB color space allows the CMS to make calculations and conversions without damaging color values.

COLOR SEPARATION AND COLOR CORRECTION

Color separation is the process of dividing the colors of a multicolored original into the subtractive primaries cyan (C), magenta (M), yellow (Y), and black (K). The CMYK color separations can be made into films used to prepare printing plates or made directly into plates. Although there are several methods for making color separations, almost all color separation is now performed with an electronic scanner.

One of the biggest challenges in graphic communications is getting color to reproduce the way it should or even to predict what the printed colors will

look like. Color correction is complex because color functions are interconnected. For example, in an RGB system (such as a computer monitor or television set), a change in value changes chroma. For a brighter, more saturated red, the percentages of red, green, and blue must be adjusted. The percentage of red cannot simply be increased because that would increase lightness as well. To achieve a brighter red in a CMYK system, the cyan and black would need to be reduced and the yellow and magenta would need to be increased.

What used to be the job of prepress technicians is now often the responsibility of the designer. Before the advent of computers in prepress production, methods such as photographic masking and dot etching were used for color correction and manipulation.

Photographic Masking

Photographic masking is accomplished by creating film images from the original using filters. Photographic masks are measured by their percentage of light-stopping ability. For example, a 100% positive mask would block out all illumination when placed on a light table if it was in register and overlapping a negative image.

Dot Etching

Dot etching is used for modifying isolated areas of an image. Wet etching involves the use of chemicals to erode or build up the silver deposits on the film that form the different dot sizes. Dry etching refers to contacting techniques used to spread or choke the dot structure.

Color correction is now performed almost exclusively in electronic format. Most color management systems provide both automatic and manual means for color correction. Imaging programs provide tools and filters for setting highlights and shadows, adjusting midtones and color balance, modifying hue and saturation values, image sharpening, and changing both brightness and contrast. Although most imaging programs allow the user to perform these types of adjustments, the need for and the amount of color correction is still best determined by the results in the pressroom.

Shadow Clarity

In theory, by combining equal parts of cyan, magenta, and yellow, you can produce black. However, due to impurities present in all printing inks, a mix of these colors actually yields a muddy brown. To compensate, some cyan, magenta, and yellow is removed from areas where the three colors overlap, and black is added. Printing black ink over the three primaries improves and enhances shadow details of the reproduction.

The effect of having full colors with the primaries can be achieved in a number of ways, but prepress operators typically use undercolor removal, gray component replacement, and undercolor addition.

Undercolor Removal (UCR)

Undercolor removal (UCR) is a process of color correction typically associated with high-speed web printing. UCR can be accomplished with an electronic scanner, an image editing program, or photographic masking techniques, **Figure 10-13.**

The shadow details of a four-color separation will typically be represented as the three process colors overprinted with black. When printing with high-speed presses, it is not desirable to overlap layers of ink that are too heavy. Drying problems and ink trapping problems can occur with saturated ink layers.

The theory of UCR is to reduce the amount of magenta, yellow, and cyan in shadows and neutral areas of an image, and replace them with an appropriate amount of black. This is accomplished by reducing the shadow dot structure in the overlapping areas of the yellow, magenta, and cyan inks. UCR produces good shadow densities by using the black printer to its fullest capacity.

Gray Component Replacement (GCR)

Gray component replacement (GCR) is an electronic technique used to substitute black ink for calculated amounts of cyan, magenta, and yellow inks, **Figure 10-14.** Substitutions occur mainly in the neutral tones and in gray components of desaturated colors. When applying GCR, the black printer is used to replace a proportionate amount of cyan, magenta, and yellow anywhere the three colors overlap.

GCR separations tend to reproduce dark, saturated colors better than UCR operations. GCR separations also maintain better gray balance on press. Other advantages include better detail and contrast within the reproduction, reduced ink costs, reduction of ink setoff (unwanted ink transferring to adjoining sheet of paper), and reduced drying time.

Many scanner and electronic prepress equipment manufacturers have developed specific software packages for GCR. The type of separation you should use will depend on the substrate and requirements of the printer.

Figure 10-13. The image on the left is a full-range color separation. The image on the right illustrates the same image with a 30% undercolor removal, providing better shadow details.

photographic masking: Method of color manipulation that is accomplished by creating film images from an original using filters.

dot etching: Manual alteration of the dot structure to correct color. Also a contacting technique used to spread or choke the dot structure.

undercolor removal (UCR): Technique used to reduce the yellow, magenta, and cyan dot percentages in neutral tones by replacing them with increased amounts of black ink.

gray component replacement (GCR): The removal of equal amounts of cyan, magenta, and yellow areas of a four-color halftone and replacement of these colors with a higher proportion of black.

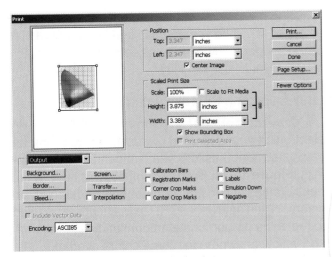

Figure 10-14. The separation setup box in most page composition programs allows the user to specify separation types and ink limits.

Undercolor Addition (UCA)

Undercolor addition (UCA) is the inverse function of undercolor removal. UCA is used to add cyan, magenta, and yellow after removing some of the black in the shadow areas. Undercolor addition is applied with gray component replacement because 100% GCR does not produce a good saturated black in print.

UCA helps produce rich, dark shadows in areas that might appear flat if they are printed with only black ink. The color added to the shadow or black areas will determine the warmth or coldness of the black.

The amount of undercolor addition is set with the same control used for GCR. Increasing the UCA amount increases the amount of cyan, magenta, or yellow added to the shadow areas. Check with your service bureau or printer for the appropriate values.

TRAPPING

When colors printed from separate plates border one another, the slightest amount of misregistration can cause gaps between printed objects (graphics and type). Printers use a method called **trapping** to create a small area of overlap between colors to compensate for potential gaps. Trapping can be defined as how well one color overlaps another without leaving a white space between the two or generating a third color.

Because responsibilities for color separation have shifted from trade shops to electronic page-production artists, trapping is typically performed during electronic page and image composition, **Figure 10-15.** Trapping must be considered any time

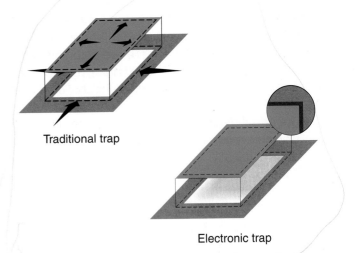

Figure 10-15. No matter which method is used, traditional or electronic, trapping still performs the same function.

two colors meet. Methods used to set traps include spread, choke, and automatic.

A **spread trap** is created by spreading the foreground over the background color, **Figure 10-16.** Spread traps are used when a lighter object knocks out of a darker background. Illustration programs that are limited to one type of trapping usually use spread traps.

Choke traps are performed by spreading the background under the foreground object. The object may appear to be squeezed or reduced in size.

Automatic traps are set by building art with common colors. As long as a **knockout** is not

Figure 10-16. Spread trap. A—If no allowance is made for misregistration (i.e. trapping), the paper will show through as white lines around the image. B—When trapping with uncommon colors, the stroke should be the same color as the object being trapped. Half the width will fall outside the edge and blend with the other color.

specified, and common colors are used, the shared component compensates for the space between the objects. For example, if two overlapping objects contain cyan as part of their CMYK values, any gap between them is covered by the cyan content of the object underneath. In **Figure 10-17,** no background shows through because both the letter and the background contain the same percentage of magenta.

Some illustration programs allow the user to perform trapping automatically by applying a trap filter. This type of trapping is intended for simple objects where parts can be selected and trapped individually. It does not work with gradients or patterns, however. Fortunately, most illustration programs provide an alternative trapping method that allows more complex work to be performed.

It is best to scale graphics to their final size before adding a trap, otherwise the amount of trapping will increase or decrease if you scale the object. For example, if you create a graphic that has a 0.5-point trap and scale it four times its original size, the result will be a 2.0-point trap for the enlarged graphic. Trapped files should also be imported into the page composition program at the same size. If they are scaled after they are imported, the traps will also be scaled and will need to be recreated.

Trapping Type

There are a variety of factors that must be considered when setting traps. They include everything from the kind of paper to pressroom conditions. These variables are extremely important when applying traps to type because spreading or choking may cause character distortion.

Applying process colors to type at small point sizes should be avoided because any amount of misregistration can make the text difficult to read. Trapping type at small point sizes can also result in hard-to-read copy. However, if it is necessary to trap type, always remember that smaller type requires a smaller trap to prevent distortion, **Figure 10-18.**

Text can also be trapped by first converting it to outlines and then placing a copy behind the original. A trap could then be created as with any other graphic object. However, when type is converted to outlines, *hinting* is lost. Hinting optimizes how type prints at small point sizes on printers with a resolution of 600 dpi or lower. Text can no longer be edited when converted to outlines because it becomes a graphic instead of type. You should contact your printer for recommendations.

Special Considerations

Trapping tools and capabilities vary with each illustration program, so you should refer to the user's guide for detailed instructions. However, there are several points that should be considered when creating traps, regardless of the program being used.

- In general, the lighter color is spread into the darker color. If there is no obvious lighter or darker color, then content is considered when determining the trap. For example, if text is one of the elements, it probably would not be spread over the background. However, it is okay to spread type over the background if the type is a very light color against a dark background. The dark background will hold the character shapes.

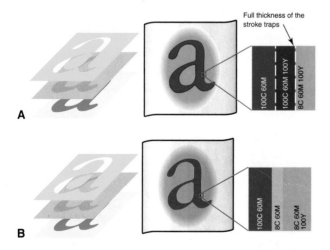

A **B**

Figure 10-17. Trapping with common colors. A— Although it is not always necessary to set a trap with objects using common colors, the trap tends to blend the object colors better. B—If a trap is not used, the common color may or may not show through as a third color surrounding the object.

undercolor addition (UCA): Undercolor addition is used with *gray component replacement* to produce better shadow quality.

trapping: Method used to create a small area of overlap between colors to compensate for potential gaps.

spread trap: Trap created by spreading the foreground over the background color.

choke trap: Trap performed by spreading the background under the foreground object.

automatic trap: Trap set by building art with common colors.

knockout: Clean break between design elements.

hinting: Application that optimizes how type prints at small point sizes on printers with a resolution of 600 dpi or lower.

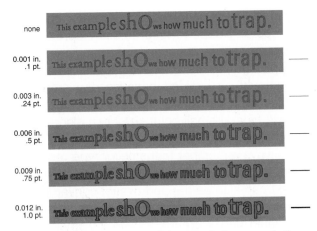

Figure 10-18. As the size of the trap is increased, the letter elements thicken and the serifs lose their delicacy.

- When trapping two light-colored objects, the trap line may show through the darker of the two colors, resulting in an unsightly dark border. For example, if you trap a light blue object into a light yellow object, a bright green border is visible where the trap is created. You can specify a tint of the trapping color (in this case, yellow) to downplay the trap line. Your printer can recommend the correct percentage of tint.

- When using an illustration program, artwork can be trapped by applying a colored *stroke* or outline to the elements requiring a trap. Half the width of a stroke will fall inside and half will fall outside the element it outlines. When a stroke is specified to overprint, the adjoining color will be trapped beneath the outside half. See **Figure 10-19.**

- Color gradations are difficult to trap because the best trap would be a gradation of colors. When trapping a gradation to a solid color, a common

color between the background and gradation should be selected. After a common color has been selected, a trap can be created.

- To trap lines electronically into a background of a different color, create two lines, one directly on top of the other, **Figure 10-20A.** The first line should be wide enough to create a trap.

- The need for trapping is eliminated if *overprinting* of colors is specified, **Figure 10-20B** and **C.**

- Trapping is intended to correct misalignment of solid tints in CMYK images and should not be created for continuous-tone images. Excessive trapping may generate a keyline effect or even crosshair lines in C, M, and Y plates. These problems may not be visible in the on-screen composite image and might show up only when output to film or plates.

- When using black to trap a black object that is a mixture of process colors, you should apply a 100% black stroke knocking out of the object to be trapped, **Figure 10-21.** This prevents misregistration from revealing the colors in the mixed black.

- EPS art should be trapped in the image creation program because page composition programs cannot trap EPS artwork.

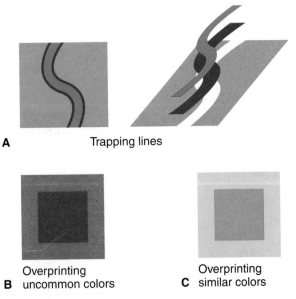

A   Trapping lines

B Overprinting uncommon colors

C Overprinting similar colors

Figure 10-20. A—The trap line must be wider than the original line in order to overprint it. B—The overprinted image adds its color completely to the background. C—The background color contains 30% cyan, and the image has 8% cyan. The largest percentage of color is used for the overprint, so the overprinting area contains 30% cyan instead of 38%.

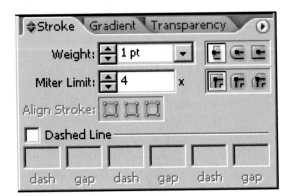

Figure 10-19. The most common method of trapping within an illustration program is to add a stroke on each element, and set the stroke to overprint. The width of the stroke should be twice the width of the desired trap.

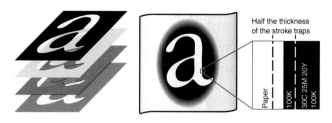

Figure 10-21. If 100% black is used for the stroke, none of the other process colors will show through.

- If photos are to be printed on a color background, they should always be choked by the surrounding background color.

  Trapping can be an extremely complex process. Although most page composition programs can be used to set traps, they are not always sophisticated enough to handle complex situations. Besides layout considerations, factors such as the type of paper, printing process, pressroom conditions, and expected *dot gain* must be considered. In most cases, your printer will determine if any trapping is needed and will tell you what parameters or values you will need to apply.

SCREENING

Proper screening is vital to producing a halftone of high quality for reproduction. This gives the full tonal range of pictorial material. Before computers took over most prepress functions, a variety of screening patterns were applied with a process camera. A screening pattern is the strategic placement of dots to create the illusion of a continuous-tone image. Conventional printing uses variable-sized dots in fixed spacing to reproduce photos, **Figure 10-22.** Digital printing uses smaller, fixed-size dots to create photorealistic images.

Currently, most imaging programs, raster image processors, and imagesetters provide the user with a variety of screening options. Screening options allow the user to do such things as eliminate moiré patterns while holding rosettes across the page, and apply higher screen frequencies at lower resolutions. Features often include the ability to shift angles to accommodate gravure, screen printing and flexography, and to render dots in a variety of shapes.

Spot Screening

Spot screening is a screening method in which dots are laid in a grid pattern based on the color tone. The spacing between the dot centers is held constant,

Figure 10-22. This is an enlargement of a halftone separation dot structure within a four-color reproduction.

but the dot size is varied to produce different shades or tones. Because the grids for different colors are offset at angles, a distinctive rosette pattern is created in the image. Stochastic screening attempts to overcome the rosette pattern that frequently mars images created with spot screening.

Stochastic Screening

Stochastic screening is a halftoning method that creates the illusion of tones by varying the number of micro-sized dots in a small area. Unlike conventional halftoning, the spots are not positioned in a grid-like pattern. The placement of each spot is determined as a result of a complex algorithm that evaluates and distributes spots under a fixed set of parameters. In stochastic screening, the spacing of dots varies, **Figure 10-23.** Stochastic screening is also referred to as frequency modulation (FM) dots or FM screening.

---

stroke: The thickness of a line forming a character element.

overprinting: When image elements are specified to be printed over or on top of other colors.

dot gain: Optical increase in the size of a halftone dot during prepress operations or the mechanical increase in halftone dot size that occurs as the image is transferred from plate-to-blanket-to-paper in lithography.

spot screening: Screening method in which dots are laid in a grid pattern based on the color tone. The spacing between the dot centers is held constant, but the dot size is varied to produce different shades or tones.

stochastic screening: Halftone method that creates the illusion of tones by varying the number of micro-sized dots in a small area.

Figure 10-23. Dot variation in placement and shapes is evident in this enlargement of a printed image.

Stochastic screens provide greater definition and detail in irregular shapes and expand the range of tones that can be reproduced through increased ink densities and improved color saturation. The disadvantage of stochastic screens is that tints or solid-color areas can sometimes appear grainy because the tiny dots are not really replaced in a random pattern.

To correct this problem and maintain the image's photographic attributes, most raster image processors (RIPs) provide additional screening options. Multiple screening options allow the user to select the best screening method for the type of image used. For best results, photos, line art, and vector graphics may each require different screening methods.

Error-diffusion screening

Error-diffusion screening places dots more randomly than stochastic screening. It uses data from surrounding cells to determine dot placement. The difference between the color tone requested and that printed for a cell is fed through a filter and carried to other cells as they are processed, diffusing the error across surrounding cells. Although this reduces graininess in solid areas, it can also cause the loss of image sharpness. However, error diffusion can create smoother transitions of colors or tones for certain types of images and result in better printed output. The type of screening method used will depend on the output device and the intended use of the image.

When RIPs were first introduced, they were designed for use with 200-dpi electrostatic printers. Variations of stochastic and error-diffusion screening between different manufacturers had an obvious impact on the visual appearance of printed images. RIP software developers have since developed screening patterns to the point that it is almost impossible to detect the difference.

Screening patterns can affect file-processing speed. If one pattern adds more dots for image sharpness, the file size will be larger and take longer to process. On the other hand, to process blends more quickly, the screening pattern on some RIPs will eliminate the top 5% and bottom 5% of the data.

PREFLIGHTING

During the design process, many colors may be defined, tested, and rejected. Rejected colors may remain in the files and should be removed from the color palette to speed printing and to ensure they are not accidentally used.

Ideally, the color palette in a page composition program would display *only* the colors used in the job. Unfortunately, this is not usually the case and unused colors will often be left in a layout. If an unused color is present, a *gamut alarm* will appear when preflighting the files and you will need to find and delete the color, **Figure 10-24.** If you cannot delete a color, it is probably an extra spot color from an imported graphic file. You will have to go back to the imaging program to delete the stray color. If stray color is not deleted, it will increase the chance that an incorrect color will be applied to the text or to a graphic.

Some composition programs include the additive primary colors red, green, and blue in the default color palette. These colors should be removed from your files because they are made of components of red, green, and blue light, not the CMYK colors.

Special colors, such as metallics or fluorescents, are not always available in an application's color palette. When using a special color, it should be defined as a spot color and given a unique name. You should contact your printer for detailed instructions.

PROOFING

Depending on the complexity of a project and the arrangement you have with the service bureau or printer, you will review a number of proofs before the job goes to press. Proofs are generated for performing corrections (text, layout, and color), and to provide a means for confirming a contract. Besides confirming that layout, fonts, and other design elements were not lost or deformed before reaching the output stage, proofs should be generated for checking color accuracy and resolution, **Figure 10-25.**

Figure 10-24. If there is an unused color present in the layout, a gamut alarm or warning will appear when preflighting files.

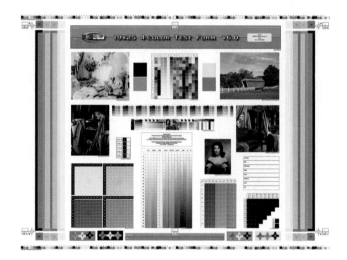

Figure 10-25. Test forms are available to check the capabilities of presses. (Printing Industries of America: Center for Technology and Research)

Proofs can be generated directly from film, run off on a proof press, or made directly from digital files. Cost variations will often determine what type of proofs you will request at different stages of prepress production. *Soft proofing* is the proofing of images on-screen.

Press proofs may still be one of the best verification proofs, but the digital proof is fast becoming the standard. *Digital proofs* are generated by outputting files on a high-resolution, high-quality printer, **Figure 10-26.** Initially, professionals in the industry could not place much faith in digital proofs. However, technological advancements have allowed many types of digital output devices to meet industry color standards for prepress proofing. Because of

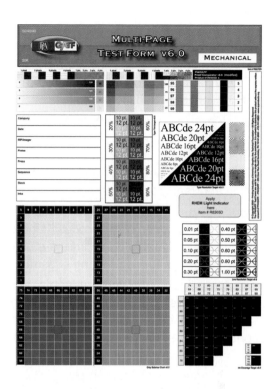

Figure 10-26. Digital test forms contain the same information as a conventional press form. (Printing Industries of America: Center for Technology and Research)

the accuracy and cost savings, digital proofs are replacing the conventional film-generated contract proofs that have been used for decades.

Film-Generated Proofs

Photomechanical proofing systems are categorized into single-sheet, or laminate color, proofing systems and overlay color proofing systems. The advantage of single sheet or laminate proofing is that the viewing light is reflected from a single surface and light refraction is limited. Film-generated proofs include Matchprint™, blueline, Cromalin™, brownline, and Color Key™.

error-diffusion screening: Screening method that places dots randomly.

gamut alarm: Warning used by many imaging or page composition programs to indicate the presence of colors that are out of the printing range.

soft proof: A proof of an image or page layout on a computer monitor.

press proofs: Proof generated with a proof press. One of the best verification proofs; also very slow and expensive.

digital proofs: Proofs generated by outputting files on a high-resolution, high-quality printer.

- *Matchprint proofs* are four-color proofs produced from the film that will be used to create the printed pages. They enable accurate evaluation of the film for trapping, moiré, and other conventional printing problems.

- *Blueline proofs*, or diazo proofs, are produced from positive imageset film. Blueline proofs can be imaged on both sides, folded and trimmed, and are extremely valuable for showing the position and registration of the printed material.

- *Cromalin™ proofs* are four-color proofs created from halftones using process toners and special film. Heat and pressure are used to transfer the image to the proofing substrate.

- *Brownline proofs*, or silverprint proofs, are created by exposing brownline paper through the negative flat on a platemaker. This method is commonly used to proof single-color flats.

- *Color Key™ proofs* are transparent sheets that are imaged from film, then physically fastened together in register. Proofs can be made from process-color separations, or from mechanically-separated art to show spot color.

Digital Proofing

As more of the industry moves to a CTP workflow, digital proofing has become extremely important. For digital proofs to replace film-generated proofs, they must accurately represent all the features of the traditional proof, including color fidelity, traps and overprints, representative screening, and quality in fine line details, **Figure 10-27.**

Color management systems can be used to compensate for all factors affecting the printing process. A quality CMS will compensate for such factors as ink hues, color contamination, press gains and losses, plate gains and losses, and the paper's color and absorptivity.

Depending on the system's capabilities, digital proofs can simulate results from any type of printing press. Most dye-sublimation printers and ink-jet printers are able to simulate both process inks and spot colors. These machines produce dotless color images that closely simulate the press sheet, at a much lower cost than conventional methods.

Many digital proofing systems can also simulate dot patterns and the dot gain expected on final output. This is especially useful because most customers insist on seeing the halftone dots or screen pattern before accepting the proof as a true indication of color and quality. Many digital output devices can be

Figure 10-27. Color proofing systems vary in size and capabilities. This system can produce proofs ranging in sizes from 11″ × 17″ to 25″ × 38″ at about one-third the cost of traditional methods. (Western Litho)

connected to the same RIP that runs the imagesetter and output halftone patterns that are identical to those that will appear on the final sheet.

Some electrostatic printers and high-quality printer/copiers can also simulate the printing inks of a press. They are commonly used for proof production, as well as short-run impressions of finished color printing. The same process used to calibrate printers is used for calibrating proofing devices.

Digital Blueline Proofs

Computer-to-plate workflows originally lacked a proof for checking final imposition before output to the platesetter. Several manufacturers have designed and produced two-sided signature proofs that are referred to as *digital blueline proofs*.

The digital blueline can be defined as a two-sided digital position proof for eight-page impositions (sixteen-page signatures). These proofs are usually printed on wide format ink jet proofers, **Figure 10-28.** In some proofers, after imaging on one side of the ink-jet media, the paper is flipped and repositioned. Other systems print both sides at once. Most systems allow proofs to be output in full color or in a single color to check basic layout and imposition. It is unlikely that this type of digital proof will eliminate the need for contract color digital proofs.

Automatic Proofreading Systems

Automatic systems can be used for proofreading plates, film, carton stock, stuffer sheets, label stock, textbooks, and a variety of other printed material. Some systems are capable of detecting details as fine as missing or partially missing periods in 3-point type, **Figure 10-29.** Sensors are mounted at various press stations to identify and warn the operator of defects such as streaking, stains, and under- or over-inking.

A database of pixels that make up the text and graphics of each sheet is generated by the system. During the inspection process, charge-coupled

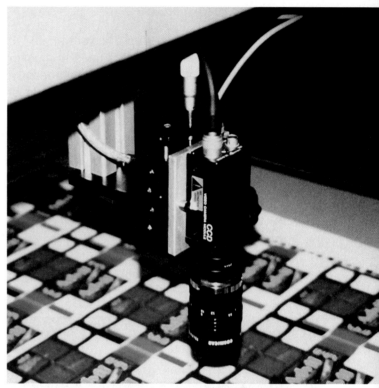

Figure 10-29. Automatic proofreading systems are able to complete their proofreading process in as little as three percent of the time required for traditional proofreading. (GSMA)

Matchprint proofs: Industry-standard contract proof produced from the actual film that will create the printing pages.

blueline proof: A photographic procedure in which light-sensitive compounds are applied to a substrate. The substrate is then exposed to intense blue light and developed with ammonia vapors or an alkaline solution to form an image.

Cromalin™ proofs: A type of single-sheet color proof.

brownlines: Single-color printing proofs that are used to evaluate the placement of page elements.

Color Key™ proofs: A color proofing system that generates a set of process-color transparent film positives from separation negatives so that registration and screen-tint combinations can be checked before actual press proofs are produced.

digital blueline proofs: Two-sided digital position proof for eight-page impositions.

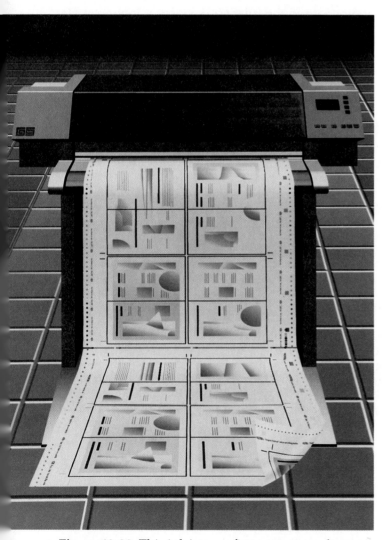

Figure 10-28. This ink jet proofing system produces two-sided digital imposition proofs. (DuPont)

devices (CCDs) are used to inspect printed sheets by searching for missing or unwanted pixels. Therefore, any combination of different languages, symbols, and graphics can be accurately proofread at the same speed as simple text. The operator can call up the file of inspected images that is made during proofreading and magnify any highlighted discrepancies.

Color Control Bars

A color control bar is a strip of colors printed in the trim area of a press sheet. It is used to monitor printing variables such as trapping, ink density, dot gain, and print contrast. It usually consists of overprints of two- and three-color solids and tints; solid and tint blocks of cyan, magenta, yellow, and black; and additional aids such as resolution targets and dot gain scales, **Figure 10-30.** Color control bars may also be referred to as color bars, color control strips, or proofing bars.

Color control bars should be output on any type of color proof. SWOP includes a list of characteristics that should be included on a color control bar as well as its position on the proof. Color control bars created for computer-to-plate (CTP) systems may require additional features than color bars generated for film.

Calibration and Characterization

Just as the calibration of scanners and monitors is vital to accurate color reproduction, proper characterization and calibration of proofing devices is vital to the production of accurate digital proofs. Before outputting a job to any type of digital output device, an output profile should be created. The output profile can be used to correct color inaccuracies in the printer, or it can be combined with a printing press profile to simulate the effect of the press on the proof printer.

The first step is to create a target file that is appropriate to the printing process. A four-color file

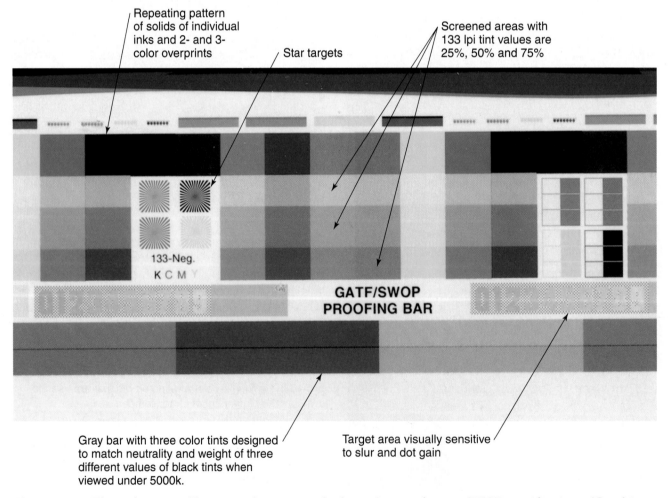

Repeating pattern of solids of individual inks and 2- and 3-color overprints

Star targets

Screened areas with 133 lpi tint values are 25%, 50% and 75%

133-Neg.
K C M Y

GATF/SWOP PROOFING BAR

Gray bar with three color tints designed to match neutrality and weight of three different values of black tints when viewed under 5000k.

Target area visually sensitive to slur and dot gain

Figure 10-30. This color control bar is used to assess whether color proofs meet SWOP specifications. (Graphic Arts Technical Foundation)

is made for a printing press. The target file is printed and then measured with a color spectrophotometer.

After the target is printed and evaluated, the profiling software creates a profile that describes the color capabilities of the device. This profile then becomes the output profile, which adjusts the color of the file as it is output. Using this output file, the proofing system can output proofs that will accurately depict what the job will look like when printed on the printing press. This can be done before film or plates are made.

Viewing Variables

As discussed in Chapter 9, there are many variables to consider when viewing or judging color. In addition to inherent human variables (color blindness, vision fatigue, aging), viewing conditions must also be considered.

Accurate color comparison is almost impossible unless items are viewed under exactly the same viewing conditions. For this reason, the graphic communications industry has established an illumination standard. Viewing booths have been designed with a neutral color environment and 5000 K illumination. This light temperature is color-balanced and is ideal for making color comparisons. Viewing booths are usually available in printers. Unfortunately, many customers do not have standardized viewing areas and cannot view proofs under the same lighting conditions as printers.

INK COLORS

Color reproduction systems should be engineered from the pressroom back to the point of creation. One of the first steps in the engineering of a color reproduction system is the analysis of process inks.

Process inks differ from one ink manufacturer to another. To evaluate the set of inks used in a specific printing facility, a set of color bars is printed under normal printing conditions. Most printers will furnish test patterns for comparison purposes.

Ink film density is read with a reflection densitometer. The densities recorded can be used to determine the working characteristics of a set of process inks. The four factors that best describe the working characteristics or impurities of the inks are strength, hue error, grayness, and efficiency.

Ink strength is important because it will identify the range and depth of colors that can be produced from a set of inks. This factor can be determined by visually comparing the density readings, and selecting the highest reading for the yellow, magenta, and cyan inks.

Ink hue error determines the percentage of the reflection of colored light from a specific color of ink. A hue is determined by the eye in terms of cone stimulation to colors of light. For example, the color or hue of magenta ink should absorb and prevent green light from reflecting off the paper surface, and allow all of the blue and red light to reflect. The ink impurities in the magenta ink pigmentation that distort this normal reflection ratio can be measured as a percentage of hue error.

The grayness factor for a set of process inks identifies the purity for the process colors. A color is considered grayed when it reflects less light of its predominant color than the white sheet of paper on which it is printed. For example, cyan should reflect 100% blue and green light, but is considered grayed in percentage because it reflects less blue than the white paper.

Ink efficiency is similar to hue error, but instead of measuring the percentage of error in the reflection of light, a positive percentage is expressed. The ability of the ink's color to filter out its complementary additive color and reflect the other two-thirds of the spectrum is the measurement of its efficiency. The higher the percentage of an ink's efficiency, the greater the gamut of possible colors, and the less color correction will be required. For additional information on inks and their formulation, see Chapter 22.

Summary

Modern graphic communications workflow relies on ICC profiles to control color reproduction throughout the process. Through the process of characterization, calibration, and conversion of one color space to another, modern color management has made the process of reproducing color more accurate and predictable. This cannot occur without a great deal of attention being given to the process or workflow of creating, adjusting, proofing, and reproducing the color. The challenge of color management lies in determining what the intended color is for the factors in the digital color workflow, in the face of occasional conflicting color requirements and capabilities.

Review Questions

Please do not write in this book. Write your answers on a separate sheet of paper.

1. What is the primary purpose of color management in the graphic communications industry?

2. Why is the CIELAB color space ideal for performing color correction?

3. What is *grayscaling*?

4. Why shouldn't color conversions be applied more than once to an image?

5. What areas of graphic communications are covered under SWOP?

6. What are the three primary steps of color management?

7. How is a color management system used to calibrate a computer monitor?

8. The _____ is a standard color reference tool used to calibrate scanners and printers.

9. Why does scanning an image into a CMYK color space limit its potential uses?

10. _____ replaces measured amounts of magenta, yellow, and cyan in shadows and neutral areas of an image with black.
    A. GCR
    B. UCR
    C. UCA
    D. RGB

11. When must *trapping* be considered?

12. Graphics should be scaled _____ (after/before) adding a trap.

13. What is the disadvantage of the stochastic screening method?

14. What makes a gamut alarm appear during the preflighting process?

15. What is a *digital blueline*?

16. Color control bars are used to monitor _____.
    A. dot gain
    B. print contrast
    C. trapping
    D. All of the above.

17. What four factors describe working characteristics or impurities of inks?

Suggested Activities

1. Request printed samples of various screening techniques from printers in the area. Examine the copies and write your observations of variations existing between the screening techniques.

2. Visit a printing plant, and identify the color management system used by the plant.

3. Look for printed products that required the use of spreads and chokes. Were the printed results of high quality?

Related Web Links

Color Matters—The Amazing World of Color Science

www.colormatters.com
Resources on science of color in graphic design as well as in other areas.

Munsell Palette

www.triplecode.com/munsell
Information and links to resources on using the Munsell system.

ColorManagement.com

www.colormanagement.com
Contains news and information about color management within the graphic communications industry.

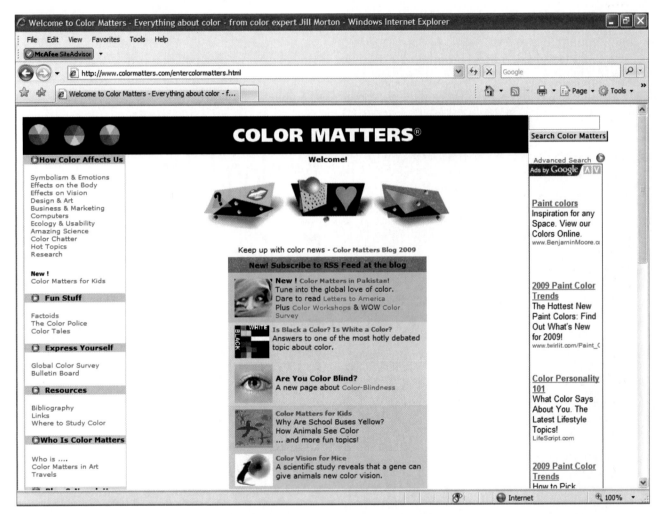

Web sites relating to color may include resources on graphic design, as well as information on the effects individual colors have on our senses.

CHAPTER 11

Analog Film, Equipment, and Processing Information

Learning Objectives

After studying this chapter, you will be able to:

- Explain the structure of film.
- Recall the various light sources and how to adjust them.
- Identify the major parts of a process camera.
- Explain the principles of continuous tone originals and halftone reproduction.
- Explain the processes involved in color separation and special effects.
- Recall the equipment needed to process film.
- Recall various contact printing applications.

Important Terms

antihalation backing
automatic film processing
base material
camera bed
color sensitivity
color separation
color temperature
contact printing
continuous tone
control strips
copyboard
copyboard controls
D log E chart
densitometer
density
density capacity
drawdown
duotone
electromagnetic spectrum
emulsion
emulsion sensitivity
film
film back
floor horizontal camera
focal plane
gamma
ground glass
halftone grade film
halftone screen process
high-key photograph
highlight

horizontal camera
lensboard
lensboard controls
low-key photograph
mercury vapor lamps
metal halide lamps
midtones
moiré pattern
overhead horizontal
  camera
photo-density range
posterization
process camera
protective overcoating
pulsed xenon lamps
quartz-iodine lamps
reflection copy
reflection densitometer
reflection density
  guide
sensitometry
shadow
tone-line process
transmission copy
transmission
  densitometer
tristimulus
tungsten-filament
  lamps
vertical camera
visible spectrum

This chapter discusses the film, equipment, and processing procedures necessary to convert original line art, continuous tone photographs, and special effects material to film negatives or positives. Films were used to produce printing plates and a final printed product. These procedures are becoming obsolete and are not commonly found in printing plants. A strong desire exists to improve ecology by eliminating wet chemistry. This is a contributing factor in the development of new processing systems. Some of these materials and procedures are still used today. However, since this is a dying part of the industry, detailed procedures will not be explained.

FILM STRUCTURE

Film is a material that is chemically altered after it is exposed to light. This allows it to capture an image that can be made permanent by chemical development. It is made up of the emulsion, base material, antihalation backing, and protective overcoating. See **Figure 11-1A.**

Emulsion

The *emulsion* is made up of chemical compounds that form a light-sensitive coating on the base material. The emulsion is usually made up of silver halides suspended in a gelatin. Although silverless light-sensitive materials are available, the silver halides are still the most common. Silver halides are compounds of silver and chlorine, bromine, or iodine. The three compounds formed are silver chloride ($AgCl$), silver bromide ($AgBr$), and silver iodide (AgI).

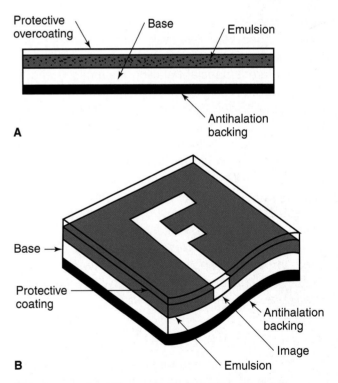

Figure 11-1. A—Film, or light-sensitive material, consists of four layers. B—When light strikes the film, it generates latent image on the film. Processing or developing will make the image visible.

film: A material that is chemically altered after it is exposed to light.

emulsion: Chemical compounds that form a light-sensitive coating on the base material.

The lighting used by graphic arts photography exposes the particles of silver halides in the emulsion. This produces a latent image. The parts of the emulsion that are exposed to light will change to black metallic silver during processing. This makes the latent image visible. See **Figure 11-1B.**

Conventional emulsions are generally thought of as being negative-forming, but it is possible to produce positives by special treatment of the film. Image reversal is the making of a positive from conventional emulsions. This can be done by a pretreating process from the manufacturer. Posttreatment might also produce a positive image. This means the processing steps change. Use the manufacturer's guide to produce the desired results.

Base Material

The *base material* of a film is the support for the emulsion. The two most common base materials are made of plastic or a special grade of paper. Most of today's graphic films use a polyester base. The polyester base is a very stable material and its size changes very little with relative humidity and temperature. This base has a long storage life. The manufacturer's special handling instructions should be followed.

Acetate-based films are not as stable as the polyester-based materials. Humidity will affect the base, causing it to change size. Polystyrene-based films are not affected by humidity, but temperature control is important. Photographic bases using special paper often have stability problems. They are subject to curl. The cost of these types of film is much less than the polyester bases.

Another base is glass. Glass-based films are used for special applications, such as those that require extreme dimensional stability. Glass is a very costly type of support material for film.

Antihalation Backing

The *antihalation backing* is a biodegradable dye coating on the back of most films. It absorbs light so light rays will not reflect back to the emulsion and produce a shadow or double image.

Protective Overcoating

The emulsion is quite fragile. The *protective overcoating* is a material that helps keep the emulsion from being scratched and marred while film is handled.

FILM DENSITY

The amount of darkness in the negative or positive is referred to as its density. *Density* is the light-stopping ability of a material: the ability to hold back or block light. Film also has a density capacity. *Density capacity* is the theoretical maximum density allowed by a film. Up to a certain point of exposure, the film will continue to have greater density. Once that point has been reached, density no longer increases and the film has reached its capacity.

Characteristic Curves

The *D log E chart* is a graphic representation, or characteristic curve of the relationship between exposure and density. It indicates how a given film reacts to light and development. On the chart, the vertical scale is typically the density (D) scale, and the horizontal scale is the logarithm (log) of exposure. See **Figure 11-2.** The three segments of the D log E chart are the toe, the straight line, and the shoulder. The toe represents the initial response to exposure. The straight line portion represents the exposure range that identifies the density development for each exposure. The shoulder is that portion in which more exposure would not increase the density.

The film used for line and halftone work is considered to be high-contrast film. As shown in Figure 11-2, the D log E chart for this film would be steeper than a low-contrast film. The slope of the chart is given as *gamma* (γ). Gamma is affected by development time. The longer an exposed piece of film is developed, the higher the gamma. Films do have latitude, which means that minor errors can take place without wasting materials. However, high-contrast films have less latitude than low-contrast films.

Color Sensitivity

Color sensitivity is a measure of how receptive a material is to the colors of light. Silver halide emulsions are normally sensitive to ultraviolet, blue-violet, and blue regions of the spectrum.

LIGHT

If you are using film, light is required for line photography for graphic reproduction. The light source is an important aspect affecting the operation of a process camera. It can greatly affect the quality

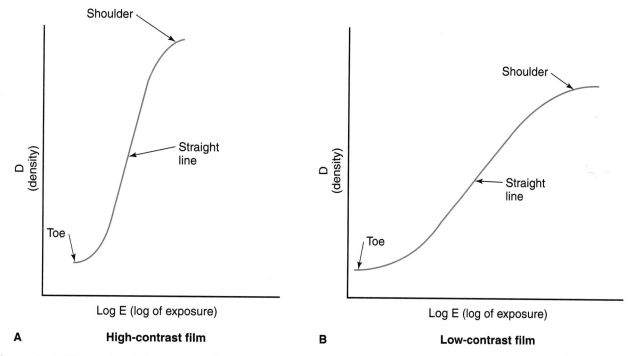

Figure 11-2. The typical D log E chart for film has a toe, straight line, and shoulder. The curve for high-contrast film is steeper than the curve for low-contrast film.

of the finished product. As the light strikes the original copy, some of that light is reflected into the camera lens. The lens directs the reflected light onto the film, exposing it to form a latent image. See **Figure 11-3.**

Light Sources

Sunlight is an excellent source of light because it contains all colors of the visible spectrum. The *visible spectrum* is the part of electromagnetic spectrum visible to the human eye. The *electromagnetic spectrum* is the entire range of wavelengths of electromagnetic radiation.

It is not practical to use sunlight as a light source for process camerawork. Other light sources used to expose film include tungsten-filament lights, quartz-iodine lamps, pulsed xenon lamps, mercury vapor lamps, and metal halide lamps.

Never look directly into a light source. The rays may be harmful to your eyes.

Pulsed xenon lamps are the primary light source for many process cameras found in graphic communications facilities. They are an excellent light source with spectral output close to daylight. See **Figure 11-4.**

Mercury vapor lamps produce radiation by passing an electrical current through gaseous

base material: The layer of film that supports the emulsion, commonly made from plastic or a special grade of paper.

antihalation backing: A biodegradable dye coating on the back of most films that absorbs light so it will not reflect back to the emulsion and produce a shadow or double image.

protective overcoating: A material that helps keep a film emulsion from being scratched and marred while being handled.

density: The light-stopping ability of a material. The ability to hold back or block light.

density capacity: The theoretical maximum density allowed by a given film.

D log E chart: A graphic representation of the relationship between exposure and density. It indicates how a given film reacts to light and development.

gamma: A measure of film contrast resulting from length of development.

color sensitivity: A measure of how receptive a material is to the colors of light.

visible spectrum: The electromagnetic wavelengths visible to the human eye.

electromagnetic spectrum: The entire range of wavelengths of electromagnetic radiation, extending from gamma rays to radio waves.

pulsed xenon lamps: The primary light source found in graphic communication facilities. These lamps are an excellent light source with spectral output close to daylight.

mercury vapor lamps: Light source that produces radiation by passing an electrical current through gaseous mercury.

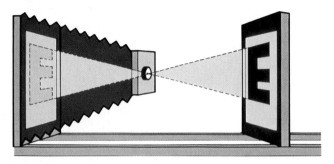

Figure 11-3. Light strikes the image and reflects into the camera lens. A lens directs the image onto light-sensitive material or film. This exposes image on film for reproduction.

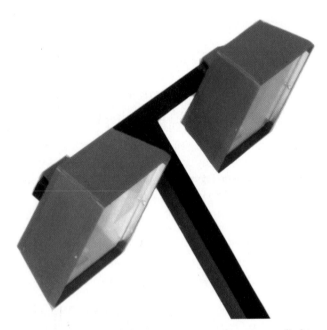

Figure 11-4. One of the many types of exposure lights used on process cameras.

mercury. At one time, these lamps were the primary means of exposing sensitive printing plates, but this is no longer true.

These lamps are high in ultraviolet radiation and provide a good light source for platemaking. Mercury lamps are a good means of exposing materials that require long periods of light exposure.

Metal halide lamps are mercury lamps that have metal halide additives. They are high in blue-violet radiation. Metal halide lamps are three to four times stronger than other light sources.

Tungsten-filament lamps are incandescent lamps with a tungsten filament surrounded by gases. The filament and gases are enclosed in a glass bulb. Tungsten-filament lights are deficient in the blue and ultraviolet rays and are excessive in the red rays.

Quartz-iodine lamps are incandescent lamps with a tungsten filament surrounded by iodine and inert gases. The tungsten filament, iodine, and inert gases are enclosed in a quartz bulb. The quartz bulb is smaller and can withstand higher temperatures than the glass bulb. The color temperature of this light source is greater than the tungsten-filament lights.

Cleaning the quartz-iodine bulb with a soft cloth is essential. The bulb should never be touched by your hands. This will greatly reduce the usable life of the bulb. Surface heat becomes greater in the touched area because of oils from your skin. This can cause rapid failure of the lightbulb.

Adjusting and Controlling the Light Source

Proper illumination is a critical consideration. The light source should be adjusted to the correct distance and angle. If adjustments are done improperly, then reflections, overexposure, underexposure, or other problems can occur. For most exposures, the typical light source angle is 45°. See **Figure 11-5.** However, you should refer to the operating manual for details of specific equipment.

Visible Spectrum

As previously mentioned, the electromagnetic spectrum is the entire range of wavelengths of electromagnetic radiation, which extends from very short gamma rays to very long radio waves. All forms of electromagnetic radiation travel in waves. The type of radiation is determined by measuring wavelengths. Wavelength is the distance from the crest of one wave to the crest of the next wave. See **Figure 11-6.**

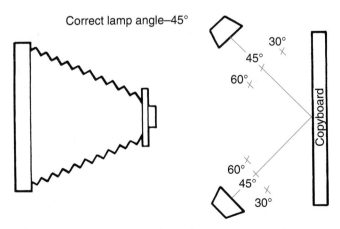

Figure 11-5. This is a typical lamp angle adjustment for most exposures. Refer to the camera operating instructions for details.

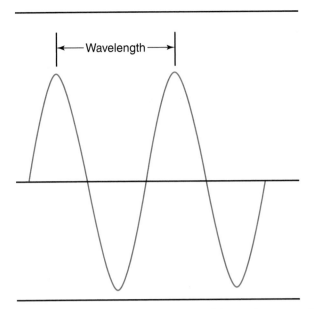

Figure 11-6. Wavelength is measured from the crest of one wave to the crest of the next.

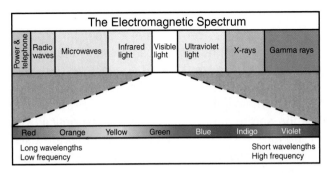

Figure 11-7. The visible spectrum is made up of various wavelengths, which correspond to the different colors.

Wavelengths are measured in nanometers. One nanometer is equal to one billionth of a meter. Another unit of measure used for measurement of wavelengths is the angstrom. Ten angstroms are equal to 1 nanometer.

The visible spectrum is a very small part of the electromagnetic spectrum, falling between gamma rays and radio waves. The visible spectrum is made up of various wavelengths. These wavelengths correspond to the different colors of the visible spectrum. The approximate positioning for each color in the visible spectrum, and its relationship to the electromagnetic spectrum, is shown in **Figure 11-7.** Color is discussed in detail in Chapter 10.

Color Temperature

Color temperature is the degree to which black must be heated to produce a certain color radiation. It is the method of rating the quality of a light source for color reproduction. Color temperature refers to the visual aspect of the light and does not necessarily apply to the photographic effect it will have on film. For example, mercury vapor and metal halide light sources may have the same visual aspects, but because they have slightly different spectral emissions, they might produce significantly different results on film.

Color temperature is measured using the Kelvin (K) temperature scale. On the Kelvin scale, 1 K is equal to –272.15°C. Absolute zero (0 K) equals –273.15°C. Color temperature must be considered whenever color separations are to be prepared for full-color work. Actual sunlight is rated at 5400 K, but for practical purposes daylight is considered 5000 K. Most full-color work is viewed at 5000 K. This temperature is the standard used for viewing and judging proofs and prints for consistencies.

The color temperature is a very important factor to be considered whenever viewing color work. A color viewing booth provides the correct color temperature for accurate color evaluation. Remember, printed pieces will not look the same under different light sources. Viewing in room light may *not* give a true representation of color.

GRAPHIC ARTS CAMERAS

The *process camera* is used to produce graphic images on photosensitive materials. Process cameras are designed to produce single-plane images, but some computerized cameras can also photograph three-dimensional objects. The process camera must be capable of producing single-plane images from line work, continuous tone work, and full-color work.

metal halide lamps: Mercury lamp that has metal halide additives.

tungsten-filament lamps: An incandescent lamp with a filament of tungsten metal surrounded by gases, all enclosed in a glass bulb.

quartz-iodine lamps: An incandescent lamp with a tungsten filament surrounded by iodine and inert gases, all enclosed in a quartz bulb.

color temperature: The degree to which black must be heated to produce a certain color radiation.

process camera: Device used to make enlargements, reductions, and same-size reproductions of originals for use in page composition or stripping work.

Process cameras are available in a variety of styles and sizes. The two major types of process cameras are the horizontal camera and the vertical camera. See **Figure 11-8.** The principles used for both cameras are the same, but their capabilities vary. The major parts of the two types of cameras also are the same, but the orientation of the optical axis of the lens is different. Electronic controls are used to control focusing, enlarging, reducing, illumination, and exposure.

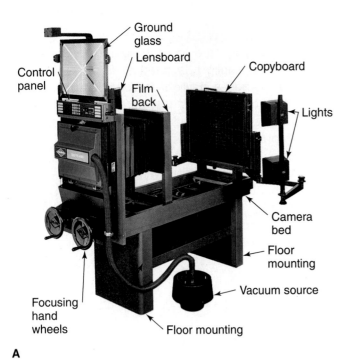

A

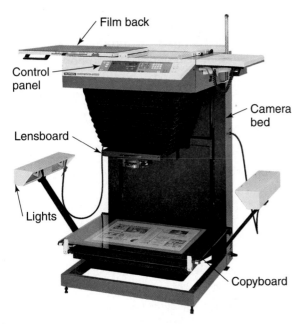

B

Figure 11-8. There are two types of process cameras. The major parts are the same for both. A—Horizontal camera. B—Vertical camera.

Camera Parts

Although the major parts of the horizontal and vertical process cameras are the same, many subparts are required and may vary from camera to camera. The major parts for both types of cameras are the camera bed, lighting system, copyboard, lensboard, film back, copyboard and lensboard controls, and ground glass.

The *camera bed* is the main support for the other camera parts. It determines the sturdiness of the camera. A well-constructed bed is essential for eliminating the possibility of poor alignment. The copyboard, lensboard, and film back must be in perfect alignment to ensure quality reproduction.

The lighting system varies from one manufacturer to another, but the manner in which lights are adjusted is of great importance. The lights must be capable of giving off even light and be sturdy enough to take the abuse of handling. They must also be designed for easy positioning and adjusting.

The *copyboard* is a glass-covered frame that holds the original image while it is being shot. The glass must be of high quality to eliminate the possibility of light distortion, which is a cause of reproduction problems. To ensure contact between the copy and the glass, the copyboard is either spring-loaded or uses a sponge material under the glass. The copy must have even contact with the glass. Some copyboards have a vacuum back that holds the copy in place.

> **All copyboards using glass must be handled with extreme care. If register pins are used, make sure they are of proper height. A pin that is too high or misaligned could break the copyboard glass. Handle the copyboard with care.**

The *lensboard* is the support that holds the lens in alignment with the optical axis of the camera. This part must be well constructed because it holds the lens of the camera. The lens must be held in constant alignment.

Process cameras have a hinged *film back* that supports the film in the *focal plane*. Some film backs have channels to hold various sizes of film, while others are perforated and use vacuum to support the film evenly over its surface.

Copyboard controls are used to position the copyboard in relation to other parts of the camera. *Lensboard controls* are for positioning the lensboard and making other adjustments to the lens. These controls are essential for same size reproduction, enlarging, or reducing. **Figure 11-9** shows how moving the copyboard and lensboard changes reproduction size. Controls may vary with make and model of camera. Always refer to the operating manual for specifics about a camera.

On most cameras, these controls are computerized and are manipulated using a control panel. Once the camera operator has the original image in place, the reproduction requirements (size and exposure) are entered using the control panel.

The *ground glass* is used to check for proper focus on the original copy before exposing a latent image on film. See **Figure 11-10**. The glass has a grained, matte, or frosted surface, and is mounted onto the back of the camera with hinges or on rails. It can be swung or slid into the focal plane in place of the film.

Vertical Camera

The *vertical camera* has a vertical optical axis. The copyboard and filmholder are perpendicular to the optical axis. Refer to Figure 11-8B. The vertical camera is a space-saving camera. It must usually be housed in a darkroom or an adjacent lighttight room.

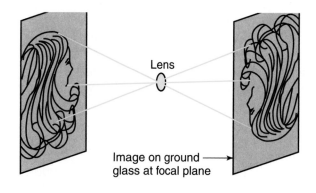

Figure 11-10. The image that will appear can be viewed on ground glass. Focus, sizing, and location of image on focal plane can be checked. (Screaming Color–Chapter One)

Horizontal Camera

The *horizontal camera* has a horizontal viewing plane. It is referred to as the darkroom camera because the film is loaded in the darkroom while the rest of the camera is outside the darkroom. This allows for an efficient operation. The two variations of horizontal cameras are the floor and overhead types.

The *floor horizontal camera* has a large bed that mounts on the floor of the facility. Refer to Figure 11-8A. The copyboard and lensboard slide on this bed.

camera bed: The main support for the other camera parts. It determines the sturdiness of the camera.

copyboard: A glass-covered frame at one end of a process camera that holds the original image while it is being shot.

lensboard: The support that holds the lens in alignment with the optical axis of the camera.

film back: The hinged assembly on the process camera used to hold a sheet of film flat in the focal plane.

focal plane: The plane on a camera where the images transmitted by the lens are brought to sharpest focus.

copyboard controls: Controls used for positioning the copyboard in relation to others parts of the process camera.

lensboard controls: Controls used for positioning the lensboard and making other adjustments to the lens on process cameras.

ground glass: A piece of grained, matte, or frosted glass mounted onto the back of the process camera with hinges or on rails.

vertical camera: A process camera that has a vertical optical axis.

horizontal camera: A process camera that has a horizontal optical axis.

floor horizontal camera: A horizontal process camera with a large bed that mounts on the floor of the facility.

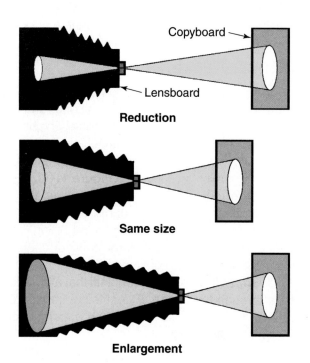

Figure 11-9. The process camera can be used to enlarge or reduce the size of the image by adjusting the lensboard and/or the copyboard. (Screaming Color–Chapter One)

The *overhead horizontal camera* has the camera bed and copyboard attached to the overhead framework of the camera. See **Figure 11-11.** It allows for easy access around the copyboard and lensboard, and tends to eliminate potential vibration problems.

Camera Operating Procedures

For efficiency, it is imperative to understand the basic procedures for operating a process camera. Each facility might have a suggested procedure, but following a basic plan can help eliminate the possibility of mistakes. Consistent procedures lead to a more profitable operation. The following basic steps are used for operating a process camera:

1.   Mounting the copy.
2.   Setting the light source.
3.   Making exposure adjustments.
4.   Focusing.
5.   Mounting the film.
6.   Setting exposure time.
7.   Exposing film.

CONTINUOUS TONE AND HALFTONE REPRODUCTION

Today, most continuous tone reproduction is done electronically. This is a brief explanation of how continuous tone photographs are prepared photomechanically using the halftone process. The halftone process is the procedure of converting a continuous tone original into a pattern of dots.

The term *halftone* comes from an old hand-engraving process that involved breaking the image up. A halftone reproduction gives the viewer an illusion of a continuous tone image when it is actually a tone pattern composed of dots that vary in size, but not density. See **Figure 11-12.**

Unlike line art, a photograph consists of many different shades or densities. Since a printing press only uses one shade or density of ink, the photo must be altered into a halftone containing a dot pattern corresponding to the many shades in the photo. Then the printing press can deposit ink on paper so the image will resemble a continuous tone photograph.

The printing press reproduces the image on the plate with only one color and density of ink. The reproduction of high-contrast copy or line copy conforms to this limitation. If the press operator is printing from a plate that has type matter and simple line art, then the press sheet will have the same image printed in one uniform color and density of ink. Refer to Figure 11-12. Halftone reproduction is the process of printing a continuous tone image, such as a photograph or painting, using the same one-color-per-plate printing process. Full-color images like Figure 11-12 require four plates to print the process colors of cyan, magenta, yellow, and black.

Continuous Tone

Continuous tone is a term used for an original that has not been screened to make a halftone, and has infinite tone gradations between the lightest highlights and the deepest shadows. Continuous tone can be broken down into the two subcategories of reflection copy and transmission copy. See **Figure 11-13.**

Reflection copy is an original image that is opaque. It reflects different amounts of light from the different tone values. Examples of reflection copy include photographs, oil paintings, chalk or charcoal renderings, and watercolor work.

Transmission copy is an original that allows light to pass through the image. Examples of transparent copy include 35 mm black-and-white or color slides and larger transparencies.

Both reflection and transmission forms of continuous tone copy require the use of a *halftone grade film*. This type of film is considered to be more sensitive and dimensionally stable than line negative film. This grade of film is used to make a negative of

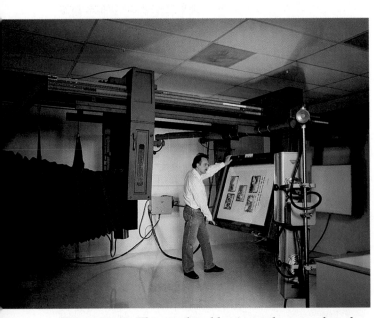

Figure 11-11. The overhead horizontal camera has the camera bed and copyboard attached to the overhead framework. It can be used for very large originals.

Figure 11-12. Look closely to see the small dot pattern in this reproduced photo. (Jack Klasey)

text or line copy and not continuous tone copy. The reproduction of continuous tone copy also requires the use of a halftone contact screen to record the dot pattern that is needed for the printing press.

Figure 11-13. Continuous tone images can be reflection copy, like the photo at right, or they can be transmission copy, as in the 35 mm slide or the large color transparency.

Continuous tone copy may consist of black-and-white or color images. The hues or colors in a color photograph can reproduce differently on black-and-white film. For example, depending on the nature of the film emulsion used, the red lipstick on the color portrait of a woman may turn out black or gray when printed as a black-and-white halftone. It takes practice and experience in the evaluation of color originals to make quality black-and-white halftones.

overhead horizontal camera: A horizontal process camera that has the camera bed and copyboard attached to the overhead framework.

continuous tone: An image with an infinite number of tone gradations between the lightest highlights and the darkest shadows.

reflection copy: An original that will reflect different amounts of light from the different tone values of the original.

transmission copy: An original that allows light to pass through.

halftone grade film: Film used to create halftones.

Halftone Screen Process

The *halftone screen process* is the procedure of converting a continuous tone original into a pattern of dots. This conversion is made with a halftone contact screen placed over the film. A fresh sheet of film is placed in the path of the imaging or main exposure.

Stochastic screening is a halftone reproduction method that creates the illusion of tones by varying the number of dots in a small area. This is different from the conventional halftone screens where spaced rows of dots of varying sizes give the illusion of various tones. Stochastic screening requires software because it is done electronically. See Chapter 10 for more information.

CONTINUOUS TONE EVALUATION

The continuous tone original to be used as camera copy for halftone reproduction will contain a wide range of tones. These tones range from the whitest value, referred to as the *highlight*, through gray values referred to as the *midtones*, to the darkest black called the *shadow*. See **Figure 11-14.**

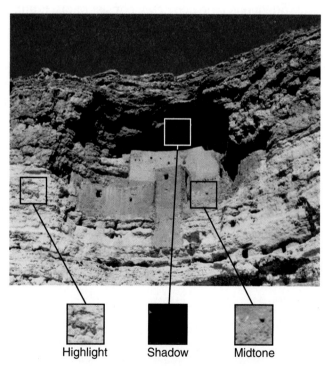

Figure 11-14. This grayscale shows the areas of highlights, midtones, and shadows. (Eastman Kodak)

Density

Density refers to the degree of blackness and is a measurement system used in photography. For example, a high-density image would be solid or almost solid black, and a low-density image would have an absence of black.

Density is expressed as a numerical value. Refer to Figure 11-14. For transmitted light, 0.00 would be clear film and 3.00 would be black. For reflected light, 2.00 would be the black and 0.00 would be white. Near the middle of these two densities would be gray, with a density value ranging from around 0.30–0.60. As you can see, as the density value becomes larger, the image becomes darker and vice versa.

There are a number of methods used to measure density. Density can be measured with a reflection density guide or a reflection or transmission densitometer.

Reflection Density Guide

A *reflection density guide* is used to compare a sample density to the image density. It has precalibrated density steps that are assigned numerical values, which represent the photo-density range. The *photo-density range* is the density difference between the highlight value and shadow value. Using this method, you have to visually compare the example density to the image density. This method is limited to visual accuracy.

Densitometer

A *densitometer* is an electronic instrument that uses a photocell to accurately measure the amount of light reflected from or passing through different tone values. See **Figure 11-15.** Densitometers provide an accurate way of assigning density values or determining if the values have been attained. There are several types of densitometers, including those that read reflected light, those that read transmitted light, and those that read either reflection or transmission copy. The significant differences in the types of densitometers is the amount of detailed information they give and the type of materials that can be measured.

High-Key and Low-Key Illustrations

Another set of terms used to evaluate continuous tone originals are high-key illustrations and low-key illustrations. A *high-key photograph* contains the most important details in the highlights, or lighter

Figure 11-15. Densitometers measure light passing through different tone values. (X-Rite, Inc.)

tones. A *low-key photograph* is primarily shadows, or darker tones. The important details fall between the midtones and shadows.

Paper Absorption

Another factor controlling tone reproduction and location is the type of paper surface used. An absorbent paper will cause the dot sizes to increase as the ink is absorbed into the paper and spreads.

Tone Range Limitations

When accepting original copy for halftone reproduction, the limitations of tone range should be explained. Most photographs will have a reflection density range of about 1.70. This is the difference between the highlight density value and the shadow density value in the photograph. Some professionally produced glossy prints can have a density range in excess of 2.00.

When using a coated stock with only one pass through the press, the printed press sheet has a density range capability of only about 1.60. This concern is magnified with the use of transparent originals that have a density range capability of about 3.00. The longer density ranges of the original will be compressed due to the nature of the printing process. Facsimile tone reproduction is the ultimate concern in halftone photography, but due to the total printing process limitations, some loss of detail and tonal separation will be experienced.

HALFTONE EVALUATION

When producing a halftone, several values must be identified in order to ensure the exact relationship between the halftone and a continuous tone photograph. Solutions can be stable at any level, but the proportions must be exactly calculated to properly develop the film or other material. The density must be calibrated, the exposure time must be calculated, and the chemical levels used in development must be stable.

Density

To produce a halftone of an original continuous tone photograph, the camera operator must first evaluate the photo density range. The highlight or whitest white of the photograph must be identified with either the use of a precalibrated reflection density guide or a reflection densitometer.

In halftone photography, a *reflection densitometer* is used to accurately determine different tone values such as the highlight and shadows of a reflection original. A *transmission densitometer* can be used to determine the opacity or amount of light-stopping capability for different areas of an original transparency or of the processed film negative.

halftone screen process: The procedure of converting a continuous tone original into a dot structure.

highlight: Tones with the lightest value. In halftone, the area with the smallest dots.

midtones: Tones with gray values.

shadow: Darkest parts of an image or photograph, represented as the largest dots in a halftone.

reflection density guide: Measuring instrument used to visually compare the example density to the image density.

photo-density range: The density difference between the highlight value and shadow value.

densitometer: An electronic instrument that uses a photocell to accurately measure the amount of light reflected from or through different tone values.

high-key photograph: Photo that contains the most important details in the highlights, or lighter tones.

low-key photograph: Contains primarily shadows, or darker tones.

reflection densitometer: Instrument used to accurately determine different tone values, such as the highlights and shadows of an original.

transmission densitometer: Color measurement device that measures the fraction of incident light conveyed through a negative or positive transparency without being absorbed or scattered.

When using either reflection or transmission densitometers, certain considerations should be observed. For black-and-white halftone applications, the densitometer should be set for a tristimulus reading. *Tristimulus* means that the densitometer is reading through all three color separation filters and not one specific part of the light spectrum.

Sensitometry is the study and measurement of the sensitivity of photographic materials, in relationship to exposure and development. *Emulsion sensitivity* is described by a standard numerical system known as the International Standards Organization (ISO) rating. The higher the number rating assigned to a film emulsion, the faster the film will react to a light exposure. For example, ISO 200 film is half as fast, or as sensitive to light, as ISO 400 film.

Exposure Time

To determine the exposure times for the halftone, select one of the exposure determining devices and follow the manufacturer's directions. To use the exposure determining devices, calibrate the exposure dials with the basic main exposure and basic flash exposure. In some cases, calibrate according to the main exposure with a predetermined percentage of bump exposure.

After calibration and the identification of the effective screen range, you must input the photo density information. This information is used to calculate the desired exposures.

Processing Halftones

Processing the halftone can be completed either in an automatic film processor or in processing trays using manual techniques. If a film processor is used, be sure to use the appropriate control strips to determine if the chemistry level is stabilized. *Control strips* are continuous wedges of film with graduated densities that are pre-exposed under exacting conditions and are used to test development solution in automatic processors.

COLOR SEPARATIONS

Color separation is the process of using red, green, and blue filters to divide the many colors of an original image into the three process colors (yellow, magenta, and cyan) and black. This process requires four halftone film negatives. Each halftone is exposed at

different screen angles on pan film so each represents a different printing ink. See **Figure 11-16.** Pan film is sensitive to all wavelengths of light. It is commonly used to make color separations. The four halftones are used to prepare the three process color and black printing plates. These plates also are referred to as printers.

The exposures creating the four different halftones are each altered through the use of color separation filters. The red filter is used to reproduce the cyan printer. Cyan ink is a red light absorber. It will represent the image of the red light absorbed by the original when printed in positive form. When the eye sees the cyan ink, it only identifies green and blue light reflection because the red light from the paper is absorbed by the ink layer.

The green filter is used in the reproduction of the magenta printer. Magenta ink is a green light absorber. It will represent the image of the green light absorbed by the original when printed in positive form. For the eye to see magenta, the green light must be absorbed by the ink, and only the red and blue are reflected.

The blue filter is used to reproduce the yellow printer because it represents only a blue light image on the negative. Yellow ink is a blue light absorber. When the blue light image is printed in positive form on the paper with yellow ink, only the red and green light rays will stimulate the eye and allow the brain to identify the color yellow.

The black printer is produced by partial exposure of the film through each of the previously used filters (blue, green, and red). A single exposure technique using a yellow or orange filter may also be used.

Figure 11-16. This is an enlargement of a halftone separation dot structure within a four-color separation. Each separation is used to print one color. When two or more colors overlap, a new color is created.

Screen Angles for Color Reproduction

Color reproduction uses four halftone negatives, each representing a different screen angle. The rotation of screen angles is designed to eliminate or minimize the undesirable *moiré pattern*. Each of the four screen angles is assigned to one of the separation colors. See **Figure 11-17.**

Yellow is assigned to the 90° angle for two reasons. The first reason is that the 90° screen angle is only 15° away from the 75° and 105° angles that represent a moiré. The slight moiré is not noticeable when a light yellow pigment is used. The second reason is that the human eye aligns images either on a horizontal or vertical format, and the light yellow dot structure is not as visible. The normal screen angle assignments are illustrated in **Figure 11-18.**

When printing separations containing considerable amounts of flesh tones and brown, it is suggested that the magenta and black angles be exchanged. The 45° angle of the magenta when imposed with the yellow at 90° provides a very pleasing 45° pattern. Since there is often a minimal amount of black in the flesh tones, its conversion to a 75° angle is less objectionable.

Black Printer

In pure color reproduction theory, the three process color inks each subtract one color of the visible spectrum and reflect the other two. The difficulty with this theory lies in ink impurities. The

Figure 11-17. A moiré pattern will result if the screen angles are not correct.

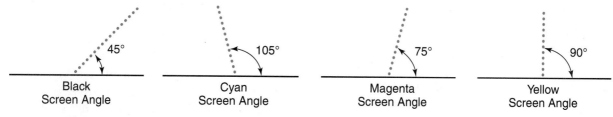

Figure 11-18. These are the normal screen angle assignments for color separations.

tristimulus: A densitometer reading through all 3 color separation filters.

sensitometry: The study and measurement of the sensitivity of photographic materials, in relationship to exposure and development.

emulsion sensitivity: A measure of how light-sensitive material reacts to light exposure.

control strips: Continuous wedges of film with graduated densities that are pre-exposed under exacting conditions.

color separation: Process of dividing the colors of a multicolored original into the printing primaries (CMY) and black (K).

moiré pattern: A visually undesirable dot-exaggerating effect that occurs when two different screen patterns are randomly positioned or superimposed.

inks used in the pressroom do not entirely absorb one part of the spectrum, and only reflect a percentage of the other two parts. For this reason, when the three subtractive primary pigments are overlapped, they produce a dark brown color instead of black.

The process black printer serves a dual purpose. First, the black printer is used to extend the shadow details or density ranges. Printing a black ink density over the three primary colors will improve and enhance the shadow details of the reproduction. Second, the black ink provides fine detail outlines and simplifies register problems of the three primary color overprints.

SPECIAL EFFECTS

Though many special effects can be created using computer software, they can also be created electronically by either a modification or conversion using standard techniques. These modifications and special effects are a designer's effort to capture an audience's attention.

Some original artwork lends itself to the desired effect better than other artwork. For this purpose, the designer and reproduction people must understand the limitations of the effects.

Duotone Techniques

The *duotone* is a special effect that consists of making a two-color halftone reproduction from a single color image. Each halftone has a different screen angle and tone range of the continuous tone original. There are four different classifications of duotones:

- Two-impression black duotone
- One color plus black duotone
- Color on a second color duotone
- Fake duotone

The designer can use duotones to create a mood or simulate process color separations. Duotone colors can add warm tones to a normal black-and-white illustration. See **Figure 11-19.**

The difficulties in producing a desired effect or a successful duotone come from the camera operator's abilities in evaluating tone values. Another factor contributing to the success of a duotone is the choice of colors.

For example, blues and greens will combine well with black for seascapes. But the designer must remember that a seashore in California is often sunny, depicting the color blue. The seascape in

Figure 11-19. This is an example of a one-color plus black duotone.

New England may be cloudy and better represented with green hues. Warm hues, such as yellows and reds, are often appropriate for sunsets or sunrises.

Posterization

Posterization is the technique of changing a black-and-white, continuous tone image into a multicolor or multitone reproduction. In this process, the continuous tone original must be converted into selected tone values. These selected tone values should enhance the details of the original continuous tone. The abstract reproduction should attract the attention of an individual by virtue of color or contrast.

The success of the posterization technique will greatly depend on the proper selection of the original continuous tone photograph. An ideal black-and-white photograph should have good contrast, with fine line detail. Photo texture or grain can also be useful for posterization.

There are four classifications of posterization. They are classified by the selected number of tone values or colors of ink. The number of tone values or colors can include the paper substrate for the

Figure 11-20. This two-tone posterization is a line reproduction of a continuous tone original.

Figure 11-21. This is an example of a three-tone posterization.

posterization. For the purposes of this description, the paper surface or color will be considered a tone or color value.

- **Two-tone posterization.** A line reproduction of a continuous tone original that is printed on a white or colored sheet of paper. See **Figure 11-20.**

- **Three-tone or three-color posterization.** Consists of two reproductions of the original, each having a different density, that will overprint the paper value. See **Figure 11-21.**

- **Four-tone or four-color posterization.** A reproduction of the original using different densities.

- **Multiple-tone posterization.** Posterization with more than four tones or colors. These are created using techniques similar to three-tone and four-tone posterizations.

Tone-Line Process

The *tone-line process* is used to convert continuous-tone originals into line reproductions that resemble pen-and-ink sketches or other fine-line drawings. In other words, it is used to create a detailed outline reproduction of a continuous tone original. This effect will remove the gray tone values. See **Figure 11-22.**

FILM PROCESSING

No matter how the latent image is produced on the film, it must be processed to make the image permanent. Processing film can be done manually or automatically. The manual processing method will not be explained since it is not a common practice in the printing industry. The manual method of tray processing is seldom found in printing plants today. Automatic processing units have become the state of the art for the development process of most light-sensitive materials. Darkrooms are a thing of the past in up-to-date plants.

duotone: A two color halftone reproduction from a black-and-white photograph.

posterization: The technique of changing a black-and-white, continuous tone picture into a multicolor or multitone reproduction.

tone-line process: The process used to convert continuous-tone originals into line reproductions that resemble pen-and-ink sketches or other fine-line drawings.

Figure 11-22. A tone-line reproduction only shows an outline of the original image.

Automatic Film Processing

Automatic film processing uses a machine to send the photosensitive material through the development steps. Some automatic film processors are used to process latent images created by a process camera or contact printer. See **Figure 11-23.** The exposed film enters the processor dry and travels through a developer, a stop bath, a fixer, a wash, and a dryer. Other machines process electronically-created latent images in a similar manner, but the output may be film, paper, or plates.

Other automatic processors are used to develop electronically-created latent images being output by an imagesetter. The processing procedure is similar to that of the other automatic processors, except these may produce film, paper, or press plates. Many development systems have been developed to be very environmentally friendly.

Automatic processors are able to produce a large quantity of high-quality film. Correct machine settings are essential for ensuring quality. Procedures for operating and maintaining automatic processors vary from model to model.

Each processor is equipped with a system to control time at each step. Usually, the speed of film travel determines the time in each step. The temperature and agitation is also automatically controlled and must be properly set. The total time the film is in the machine varies from one machine to another.

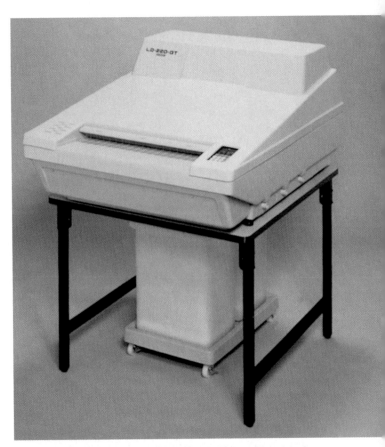

Figure 11-23. This automatic film processor is used to develop line film, contact film, and paper. It has an automatic chemical replenisher, which prevents developer fatigue and oxidation. (Screen–USA)

To keep the developing solution and other chemicals in proper balance, many of these processors are equipped with an automatic chemical replenisher. The replenisher adds chemicals to the solutions as needed, preventing chemical fatigue and oxidation. Some automatic processors require large quantities of chemicals. This can be very costly when the volume is not sufficient to keep the processor in constant operation.

Process control strips are essential to establish the machine settings and quality control. See **Figure 11-24.** Once the specific control is attained, however, consistency will be ensured. This means that every piece of photosensitive material is meeting quality standards. Anytime the development of the control strip is above or below the recommended step, the automatic processor must be readjusted.

Study the film processor manual carefully and follow the recommended processing procedures.

Store chemicals and photosensitive materials separately. Storage of both in the same area might affect film emulsions.

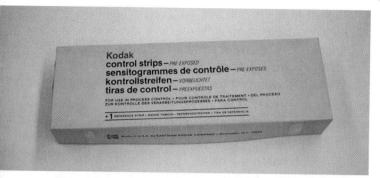

Figure 11-24. Control strips are vital in establishing proper machine operation and control of processing chemicals, temperature, speed, and other variables. Read the directions provided with the specific control strips

Processing Chemicals

Chemicals are necessary to process light-sensitive materials. Properly mixing and diluting processing chemicals, such as developer, stop bath, and fixing solution, is critical. Each manufacturer has a recommended procedure. Exact measurement is important to assure consistency. All chemical containers must be clearly labeled.

The containers for mixing and holding chemicals must be clean. Contamination can be a problem if someone is careless. If the same container and stirring rods are used for each chemical, make sure they are thoroughly cleaned before mixing each chemical.

(!) **Whenever mixing chemicals and water, always add the chemicals to the water. Extreme care must be taken not to splash the liquid. Developer and other chemicals often tend to irritate the skin. If possible, use tongs or wear gloves that are compatible with the solutions.**

(!) **Always wear eye protection when working with chemicals. If a chemical is accidentally splashed in your face, it may cause painful eye or skin burns. Go to the nearest eyewash station immediately.**

Ventilation

Proper ventilation is required to prevent a buildup of chemical fumes in the processing area. The amount of air exchange is set by federal, state, and local regulations. These regulations must be followed

THINK GREEN
Wet Chemistry

The progress of technology in the area of photography has begun to reduce much of the wet chemistry used throughout the process of film development and image reproduction. The use of digital photography is not only time-saving, it also removes the use of chemicals during the steps of processing film. One cause of concern when using the wet chemistry to develop film is the disposal of the chemicals so the ground and water supply do not become contaminated. There are environmental regulations in place for disposal of chemicals with which development businesses must comply; however, proper disposal is not checked for noncommercial film developers. Different types of chemicals may be poured down the drain, polluting the water. Digital photography eliminates the need for film development, leaving photographers without the need to use traditional film processing. For more information, see digital-photography.suite101.com.

to be in compliance with the law. Some ventilation systems remove dust particles and chemical fumes from the air. Dust removal is important for quality assurance and safety.

(!) **Do not work with chemicals in an unventilated area. Chemical fumes can be harmful if they are inhaled. Refer to Chapter 2 for more safety information.**

CONTACT PRINTING

Electronic imaging has replaced most manual applications. However, contact printing is still performed for such things as duplicating and proofing, and is needed as an application in some of the printing processes.

automatic film processing: A process that uses a mechanical device used to develop the latent image on photographic material.

Once a negative or positive is produced, a need may exist to develop new films from those originals. These new films can be made by contacting the original to another light-sensitive material. *Contact printing* is a process that produces a photographic print by exposing a light-sensitive material held against a negative or positive in a contact printing frame. The positive or negative is actually in physical contact with the film or photo paper during the exposure. The result is a contact print, often referred to as a contact, which is a same-size negative or positive reproduction. An accurate 1:1 size reproduction is ensured because of the nature of the contact printing process. In older plants, this area is usually in the darkroom. However, many printing plants have eliminated analog applications, so a specific area is no longer found in the facility.

Analog contact printing may be used to make negatives from positives; to make positives from negatives; to change contrast and tonal values; or to make proofs and plates.

Contact Printing Considerations

There are a number of considerations that should be kept in mind when contact printing. These considerations should become part of your working routine.

- If using a glass top or acetate overlay contact printing frame, make sure the glass or acetate is free of dust, fingerprints, tape residue, or opaquing solution.
- Avoid scratching the frame's surface with razor blades when removing tape residue.
- Use an approved backing sheet, and place the film in the frame with the desired side facing up.
- Always include a target control aid appropriate to the work being conducted.
- Be careful not to place fingerprints on the photosensitive material.
- Make sure the exposed film is dust-free.
- Position the exposed film so you do not scratch the film emulsion.
- Apply the vacuum slowly and visually inspect for good contact or *drawdown*, if possible.
- Make certain the vacuum gauge reads properly.

- Before exposing the film, wait until all air is exhausted between films and overlays. For less critical work, delay at least 30 seconds after the vacuum gauge has reached maximum reading. Wait up to two minutes for the more demanding jobs. This delay is very important.
- Make sure the frame is evenly lighted over the entire surface.
- Set the timer to the established values for the type of work and film being used.
- Process exposed film according to an established format for the type of film and application intended. Both manual and automatic processing are suitable for films used for contacting.

Summary

The four layers in film are the emulsion, the base material, the antihalation backing, and the protective overcoating. Although sunlight contains all the colors of the visible spectrum, it is not practical to use it for process camerawork. Process cameras must be able to produce single-plane images from different types of photographical work. Continuous photographs have not been screened and contain highlights and shadows. Halftone reproductions are composed of dots, giving an illusion of a continuous tone photograph. Automatic film processors are widely used today. Contact printing may be used for duplicating and proofing.

Review Questions

Do not write in this book. Write your answers on a separate sheet of paper.

1. Name the four layers of film.
2. What is *density capacity*?
3. The _____ is the entire range of wavelengths of electromagnetic radiation.
4. What are the basic parts of a process camera?
5. How does a halftone reproduction give the illusion of a continuous tone image?
6. What is a *densitometer*?
7. How do you prevent a moiré pattern?
8. What is *posterization*?
9. Explain the development process used in an automatic film processor.
10. List four applications for contact printing.

Suggested Activities

1. While visiting a facility, check the technique used to process materials automatically.

2. Identify five light-sensitive materials, and identify the techniques normally used to process these materials.

3. Select a printed full-color job after it is printed, and read the various densities on the control strip of the printed sheet. What do these readings represent?

Related Web Links

Kodak

www.kodak.com
Information on different sorts of analog and digital film, as well as projects and tips.

How Photographic Film Works

science.howstuffworks.com/film8.htm
Online resource detailing film construction and development.

Unblinking Eye

www.unblinkingeye.com
Articles on history of film and darkroom processing.

Digital Photography @ Suite 101

digital-photography.suite101.com
Resource providing several articles on the use of digital photography, including on the advantages over manual film processing.

contact printing: Process that produces a photographic print by exposing a light-sensitive material held against a negative or positive in a contact printing frame.

drawdown: The amount of time required to remove all air from a vacuum frame to allow the original and the film to achieve uniform contact before exposure.

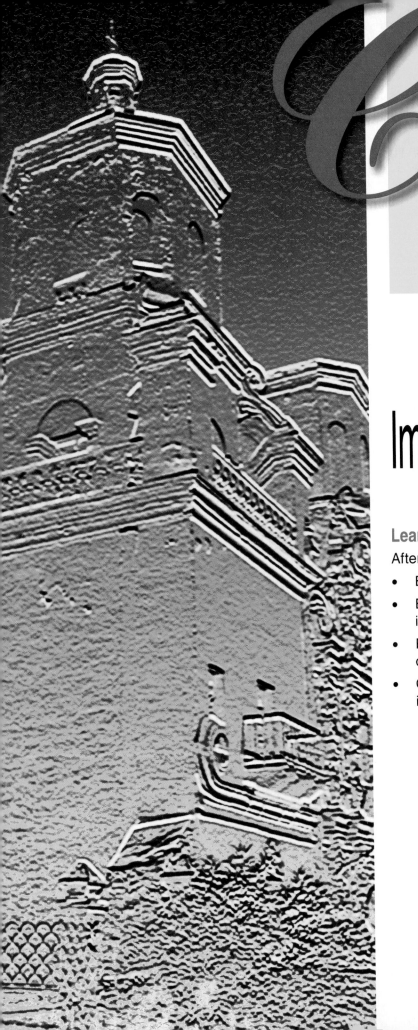

CHAPTER 12

Imposition and Layout

Learning Objectives

After studying this chapter, you will be able to:

- Explain the mechanics of a layout.
- Explain the three basic imposition layouts used in the industry.
- Recall assembly procedures and quality control devices.
- Compare manual imposition and electronic imposition.

Important Terms

control lines	portable document format (pdf)
creep	prepress
dummy	rasterized
flat	sheetwise imposition
form	signatures
front-end platforms	star target
gripper allowance	stripping
gripper edge	tick mark
imposition	work-and-tumble imposition
job ticket	work-and-turn imposition
plate bend allowance	

Imposition is the layout of various sizes and shapes of copy on a page in preparation for the production process. This department has been eliminated in most of the up-to-date printing plants. Software has been developed to accomplish these tasks. Most of the analog applications will be addressed from the historical standpoint to give the background for electronic development. This chapter will examine both the analog and electronic methods of image assembly with an eye to current and future technology.

Analog layout is done on a *flat*, a large base sheet that consists of assembled images, **Figure 12-1.** The flat is used to make the printing plate. *Stripping* is the physical assembly of those images on the flat. Image assembly requires the positioning and attaching of images to the base sheeting. The person doing the image assembly is called a stripper.

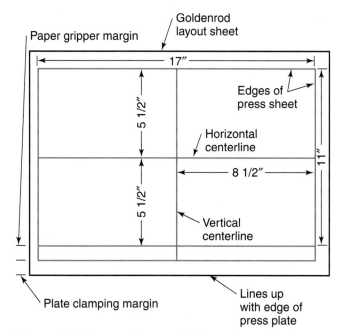

Figure 12-1. Layout lines on the base sheet of a flat help ensure accuracy during stripping and when feeding the sheets onto the press.

Making the flat is a critical part of the prepress process, since an error at this stage will show up in the final printed product. *Prepress* refers to the production steps carried out prior to printing.

MECHANICS OF LAYOUT

Page position, sequence, and folding patterns are issues that arise daily in prepress operations. To assist with imposition, a dummy is made. Most press sheets today have several pages imposed on the single sheet, and when folded together, they make a group of pages. This single sheet with multiple pages is called a signature.

Dummy

A *dummy* is a folded representation of the finished job. Right angle and parallel are the two most common types of folding, **Figure 12-2.** In the right-angle fold, each succeeding fold is made at a right angle to the preceding one. In the parallel fold, all folds are parallel with each other. The first fold is made from the center, out.

The final page size and fold is important. To make a dummy, use a blank sheet of paper that is the same size as the paper to be used for the print job. For an eight-page dummy, fold the sheet in half, then in half again. Number each page, and cut a notch through the tops of the folds, **Figure 12-3.** When the dummy is unfolded, the pages appear in proper sequence for layout, and the notches indicate the head of each page.

Signatures

To form a book or other multiple-page document, printed sheets are folded into sections that contain 4, 8, 16, or 32 pages. The folded sheets are called *signatures*.

imposition: The layout of various sizes and shapes of copy on a page in preparation for the photographic process.

flat: A large base sheet to which images have been attached for exposure onto a printing plate.

stripping: The physical assembly of film negatives and positives on a flat for platemaking.

prepress: The production steps that are carried out prior to printing.

dummy: A representative layout of a printed piece showing the folds, page numbers, and positions of text and illustrations.

signatures: Folded sheets that form multiple-page sections of a book. Each signature contains four, eight, 16, or 32 pages.

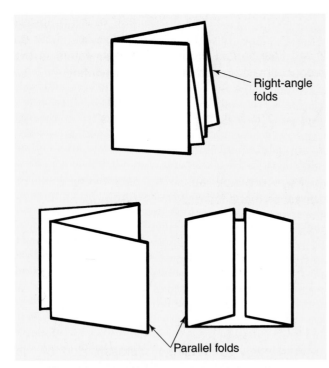

Figure 12-2. In a right-angle fold, each fold is at a right angle to the proceeding fold. In a parallel fold, all folds are parallel with each other.

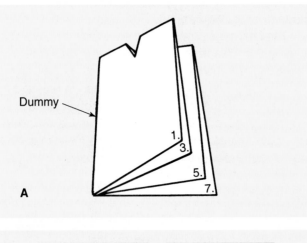

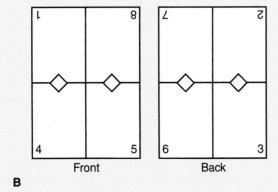

Figure 12-3. The dummy. A—The dummy is a folded and numbered representation of the printed sheet. B—When opened, the dummy pages will be in the correct position.

Each signature begins as a large sheet of paper printed front and back, called a press sheet. The group of pages on each side of the sheet is called a *form*. The pages on each form are laid out so when the signature is folded, trimmed, and bound, they end up in the proper sequence and position for reading.

An eight-page signature, for example, would have four pages printed on one side of the press sheet and four pages printed on the other side. After printing, the sheet is folded and ready for trimming and binding.

Workers in both the stripping and bindery departments must be familiar with the parts of a signature, **Figure 12-4:**

- The *head* is the top portion or top edge of the signature.
- The *thumb edge* is the edge where you would spread the signature to turn the pages.
- The *saddle edge* is the outside edge, opposite the thumb edge. It forms the backbone of the finished book. It may also be called the bind edge or spine edge.
- *Gutter* refers to the inside of the bind edge or saddle edge.
- The *open edge* is a side that is not folded, so the pages can be opened without cutting or trimming.
- The *closed edge* is a side that is folded and must be cut or trimmed to open the pages.
- *Foot* refers to the bottom of the signature.
- The *signature number* or *mark* is printed on the saddle edge to designate the sequence of the signatures. It ensures the signatures are in the correct order for binding.
- The *folio* is the page number of the signature.
- The *front folio* is the lowest page number in the signature.

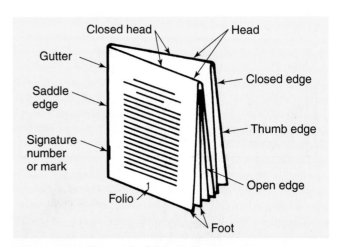

Figure 12-4. Parts of a folded signature.

TYPES OF IMPOSITION

Three types of imposition are commonly used in the industry: sheetwise, work-and-turn, and work-and-tumble. The type of imposition used depends on the press, the format size, and the number of pages. Before discussing imposition types, several terms should be defined.

An impression made on only one side of the final printed sheet is called a one-up impression.

Step-and-repeat means to expose the same image on a plate a number of times. Sometimes, a small form, such as a business card, will be stepped and repeated to fill the image area of the plate. Images are also stepped and repeated when a long run is required. Repeating the images reduces press time. See **Figure 12-5.**

A combination layout also utilizes the full area of a plate. While step-and-repeat imposition exposes the same form, a combination layout is made up of various size forms on the same printed sheet.

Sheetwise

Sheetwise imposition is generally used when two sides of the sheet are to be printed with separate flats. The front side of the sheet has one image, and the back side has another image. Since the images are different, two separate printing plates and two runs are required.

The *gripper edge*, the side of the flat that enters the press first, is the same for both. However, the guide edge changes. The first image uses the left guide; the backup image uses the right guide because the sheet has been turned over. In this case, pages 1, 4, 5, and 8 are printed on one side, while 2, 3, 6, and 7 are printed on the other side, **Figure 12-6.**

Work-and-Turn

Work-and-turn imposition requires a sheet twice as large as that needed for running the job sheetwise, **Figure 12-7.** The gripper edge is the same for both sides, but the guide edge is changed. When the sheet is turned over end-for-end, all the images printed on the first side will be repeated on the second side. The pages on the second side will properly back up the pages on the first side so the press sheet can be cut into two identical eight-page signatures.

Work-and-turn saves half the time of sheetwise imposition and uses only one plate. Work-and-turn imposition requires a larger press size, however.

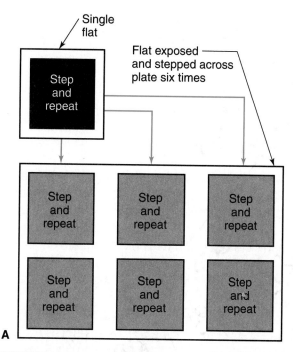

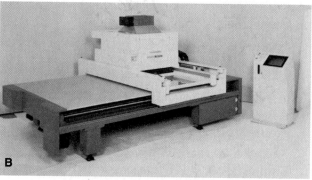

Figure 12-5. Step-and-repeat. A—Step-and-repeat produces the same image more than once on the same plate. B—A platemaker used for automated step-and-repeat exposures. (Screen-USA)

form: A guide for determining how images on a signature will be laid out to meet folding, trimming, and bindery requirements.

sheetwise imposition: A printing layout that uses separate flats and plates to print the front and back of a single press sheet. Different pages appear on each side of the sheet.

gripper edge: The side of the flat that enters the press and is held by the mechanical fingers of the press gripper.

work-and-turn imposition: A printing method in which one plate surface is used for printing both sides of a sheet without changing the gripper edge.

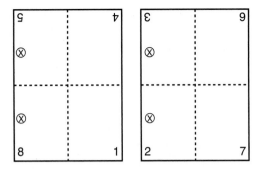

Figure 12-6. The sheetwise layout uses the same gripper edge (indicated by *x*'s) but different press guides.

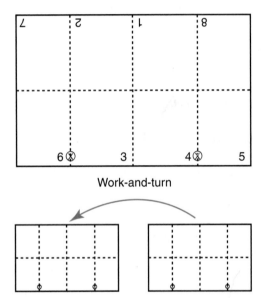

Work-and-turn

Figure 12-7. With work-and-turn, all of the images printed on one side of the sheet are also printed on the other side.

Work-and-Tumble

Work-and-tumble imposition also requires the sheet to be twice as large as for sheetwise imposition. Work-and-tumble imposition requires different gripper edges. The top becomes one gripper edge; then, the sheet is tumbled (or flopped), and the bottom becomes the gripper edge. The two gripper positions require the sheets to be trimmed and squared on all four sides. Only one guide edge is used.

Work-and-tumble imposition uses only one plate and requires only one press makeready. See **Figure 12-8.**

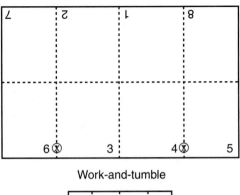

Work-and-tumble

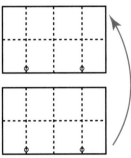

Figure 12-8. With work-and-tumble imposition, the top and bottom of the sheet become the gripper edges.

TYPICAL ASSEMBLY PROCEDURES

A stripper assembles negatives of images and attaches them in prescribed locations to a base sheet to create a flat. The negatives held in place on the base sheet are used to make an image proof or image carrier (such as a printing plate). This is a brief explanation of how to correctly position the film on the base sheet and prepare them for producing an image carrier.

1. Square the sheet. The goldenrod sheet must be squared and fastened to the light table with masking tape.
2. Locate the gripper edge or margin.
3. Locate the plate edge. Every press requires a portion of the leading edge of the plate to be inserted into a plate holding device. The inserted portion of the plate is called the *plate bend allowance* and varies with each press, **Figure 12-9.**
4. Keep the *gripper allowance* in mind, **Figure 12-10.** This allowance must be made on the flat and a visual indication given that no printed image can occur in this area. Allowance area will vary from press to press.

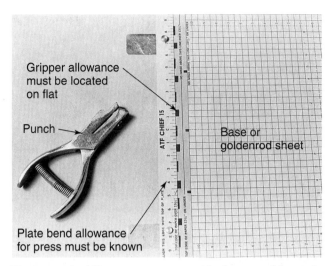

Figure 12-9. Allowances are provided on a goldenrod sheet for press grippers and plate.

5. Know the maximum sheet size the press will run. The press manual is the best source for information. If necessary, draw margins on the masking sheet.

6. Locate the control lines. *Control lines* are essential to accurately position the negatives, **Figure 12-11.** Control lines also assist in registering the flat on the

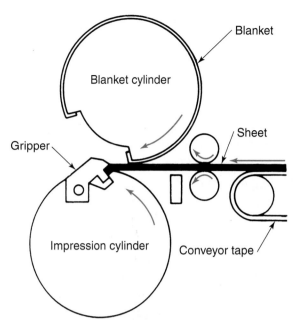

Figure 12-10. Grippers hold the sheet as it goes through the press. The stripper must allow for gripper room on the flat.

plate. Trim and registration marks are sometimes printed on the press sheet. These marks are also important to the bindery operation.

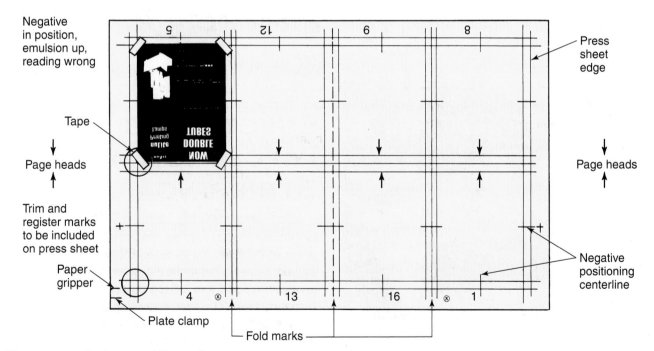

Figure 12-11. Basic control lines of concern.

work-and-tumble imposition: A printing method in which one flat is prepared, but the sheet is tumbled so the gripper edge changes when the second side is printed. Needs only one plate and press makeready.

plate bend allowance: A portion of the leading edge of the plate that is inserted into a plate-holding device.

gripper allowance: The unprinted space allowed at the edge of a printing sheet.

control lines: Markings on originals and along the margins of negative film flats to aid in color registration and correct alignment.

7. Cut a V-shaped notch in the lead edge of the flat. The notch is called a *tick mark* and identifies the gripper edge.

8. Trim the negatives. Allow at least 1/2″ of film to remain around the image area. The extra edge is necessary for taping the negative to the goldenrod sheet, **Figure 12-12.** Negatives should not overlap on the flat, so less than 1/2″ edge may sometimes be necessary.

9. Strip the first negative, either emulsion-side up or emulsion-side down.

Quality Control Devices

The quality of images and the accuracy of registration are best determined by the use of quality control devices. Developed by the Graphics Arts Technical Foundation, these devices are stripped onto the nonimage areas of the flat. Directions for use are given with each control device.

A common quality control device is a *star target*, **Figure 12-13.** The star target is a circular pattern of wedges used to detect smearing of ink. Other devices are a sensitivity guide, which is a grayscale used to gauge film or plate exposure; a dot gain scale used to gauge the dot areas on halftones; a slur gauge; and a color gauge to maintain accuracy of color reproduction, **Figure 12-14.**

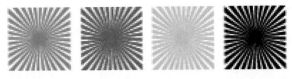

Figure 12-13. A star target is a quality control device used to detect ink slurring. (Graphic Arts Technical Foundation)

Figure 12-14. A color gauge is a quality control device.

Figure 12-12. Negatives should be trimmed with enough margin left for taping them to the goldenrod sheet.

ELECTRONIC IMPOSITION AND STRIPPING

Electronic stripping using a computer, display screen, and mask-cutting machine to automatically generate flats was considered state-of-the-art only a few years ago. In this technology, a mouse and a menu keypad are used to produce different shapes on the display screen. The resulting electronic data is used to run a mask-cutting machine or other output device such as an imagesetter, **Figure 12-15.** The output film is a single sheet with all the images in the proper location. In many cases, the film is ready to be used to produce a plate for the press. Less sophisticated systems use a machine to cut conventional mask overlays for the flat. More advanced systems go directly from electronically scanned data to the printing plate.

Figure 12-15. Electronic stripping methods allow an imagesetter to output film with all images properly positioned and ready for exposing a printing plate. (Orbotech, Inc.)

Imposition Software

One revolution in prepress operations has been the introduction of imposition software. Traditional imposition with stripping done by hand is time consuming, labor intensive, and costly. Imposition software significantly reduces all three expenditures by automating the prepress process for electronically published documents, **Figure 12-16.**

Software programs enable users to impose, preview, edit, proof, color separate, and print in a single application. Plates can be quickly created and saved as templates of unlimited size. Strippers can override templates and create a library of custom layouts.

A

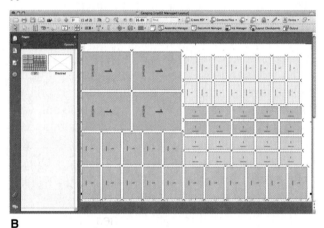

B

Figure 12-16. Imposition software. A—This wizard can create different standard impositions for folded or flat work. Results can be viewed and printed to a compatible printer or platesetter. B—Using this software, information such as the press, sheet size used, size of each product, and print quantity desired can be generated automatically. (Dynagram, Inc.)

Settings can be defined for gutter widths, paper-stock thickness, binding methods, bleed amount, and trim-page sizes. Layouts may be combined, blank pages inserted, and the forms precisely positioned onto a sheet of final film. Compensation for *creep* is done automatically.

tick mark: A V-shaped notch in the lead edge of the flat that identifies the gripper edge.

star target: A quality control device used to detect slurring of ink.

creep: A pushing out or extension of pages on the outer edge of a saddle-stitched book, caused by the greater thickness at the spine.

Portable Document Format

Computer-to-plate and computer-to-press technologies are advances in the printing industry requiring a totally digitized workflow, from creation of a document to its publication. Desktop publishing, using a combination of desktop computer hardware, peripherals, and sophisticated software, allows users to create, manipulate, and store text, graphic images, and entire documents prior to printing. New applications of these *front-end platforms* continue to revolutionize the printing industry.

Portable document format (PDF) files are quickly becoming the industry standard for delivering digital documents. PDF files are compressed and their small size makes them ideal for electronic distribution. As described in Chapter 8, PDF files are platform and media independent. They preserve the document's original layout, fonts, and graphics as one unit for electronic transfer and viewing. Compatible software reads and prints the file. Publishers frequently use a digital master file to distribute documents over electronic mail, the World Wide Web, CD-ROM, or other media. Recycling content into other media is easier and faster with PDF than with PostScript™, the workflow system that has dominated print production since 1985.

The *job ticket* is as important to the electronic prepress process as it is to the manual process. Attached to every PDF file, the job ticket travels with the file wherever it goes, allowing operators along the way to record, store, and manage information. The job ticket specifications can be easily viewed and modified by everyone who has access to the file.

When the file is *rasterized*, the raster image processor (RIP) will take the job ticket instructions and carry out the imposition order, color separations, and other image assembly procedures conventionally done by hand.

PDF publishing also eliminates the film-proofing stage. A viewing tool allows the designer to zoom in on the pixels and edit them before output to the imagesetter or proofer.

Summary

Extreme care is essential to properly place images in the correct location in the document. Mistakes are very costly. The three types of imposition are sheetwise, work-and-turn, and work-and-tumble.

Check the work during the performance of various tasks. Quality control can be ensured by use of various devices, such as a star target or dot gain scale. The programs available for positioning copy can be very simple or highly sophisticated. Knowing the capabilities of various programs is essential to ensure desired outcome.

Review Questions

Please do not write in this book. Write your answers on a separate sheet of paper.

1. Define *imposition*.
2. What is the purpose of a flat?
3. _____ refers to the production steps taken before printing.
4. True *or* False? Signatures are printed sheets folded into sections.
5. Describe the three types of press layout commonly used in the industry.
6. The side of a flat that enters the press first is the _____ edge.
   A. spine
   B. open
   C. gripper
   D. thumb
7. List three types of quality control devices.
8. _____ enable users to impose, preview, edit, proof, color separate, and print in a single computer application.
9. What is the name of the computer file format that has become the industry standard for delivering digital documents?
10. What is the purpose of a job ticket?

Suggested Activities

1. Inspect the binding of this book. How many signatures are bound together?
2. Visit a plant, and identify what type of control devices are located on the printing press sheet.
3. When visiting a plant, inquire about the digital workflow plan.

Related Web Links

Designer Info

http://designer-info.com/Home/homex.htm
Provides information needed to choose the right design tools and use them properly.

International Paper Knowledge Center

http://glossary.ippaper.com/default.
asp?req=knowledge/article/3
Learn about a variety of printing processes.

front-end platforms: The combination of desktop computer hardware, peripherals, and software that allow users to create, manipulate, and store documents prior to printing.

portable document format (PDF): A file format for representing documents in a manner that is independent of the original application software, hardware, and operating system used to create those documents.

job ticket: A work order that gives the imposition for a particular job and provides a checklist of general information for use by the stripper or others in the prepress department.

rasterized: To convert image data into a pattern of dots for the production of film.

CHAPTER 13

Digital Printing Technology

Learning Objectives

After studying this chapter, you will be able to:

- Explain how digital processes have affected the graphic communications industry.

- Compare digital printing technologies.

- Explain the practical uses of variable data printing and distributed printing.

- Recall the purpose of digital asset management systems.

- Summarize the advantages and disadvantages of digital printing.

Important Terms

aqueous inks
continuous ink-jet printer
digital asset management
  (DAM)
digital printing technology
direct imaging (DI)
distributed printing
dye sublimation
electrophotography
electrostatic printing
ionography
ink-jet printing

magnetography
makeready
piezoelectric ink-jet
  printer
software-as-a-service
  (SaaS)
solvent inks
thermal ink-jet printer
thermal transfer
UV-curable inks
variable data printing

DIGITAL PRINTING OVERVIEW

Digital printing technology is any reproduction technology that receives electronic files and uses dots for replication. An ink, toner, or any other dye- or pigment-based transfer system may be used. This type of printing eliminates the time-consuming and costly preparation of film, plates, and inks. Though not without limitations, digital printing provides customers with options that bring professional printing closer to the desktop with quick turnaround, flexibility, and cost-effective color short run printing.

Prior to digital technology, the production of printed materials did not lend itself to complete integration. However, the application of digital technology to all aspects of the workflow has reduced the number of steps and made the process simple and more productive, **Figure 13-1.**

Digital technology is now used to create text, capture or create images, create printing plates, and even apply ink or toner directly to the page. Computer applications and digital presses have made possible many printing options that were once unimaginable. See **Figure 13-2.** Jobs of four or more colors can be produced within hours. Print runs can range from just a few to a few thousand.

The major digital printing technologies include electrostatic and ink-jet printing technology. Both technologies have been available for many years, but recent advances in their speed and print quality have made them more competitive with conventional printing technology. There is a wide variety of applications for digital printing technology, including business cards, calendars, coupons, greeting cards, postcards, short run printing, and variable data printing. See **Figure 13-3.**

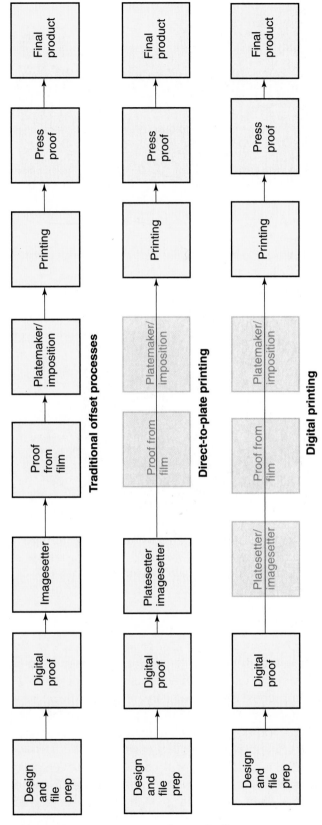

Figure 13-1. Comparing traditional offset processes with digital printing technology.

digital printing technology: Any reproduction technology that receives electronic files and uses dots for replication.

Figure 13-2. This four-color digital printer can print over 3,000 sheets per hour. (MGI Digital Graphic Technology)

Figure 13-4. This direct imaging press prints four colors in a single pass. Note the console on the right. (Heidelberg, Inc.)

Figure 13-3. Digital printing technology can be used to print several different products, including business cards, postcards, flyers, and personalized material.

Process of Direct Imaging

Digital printing, or *direct imaging (DI)*, is the process of sending a digital file directly to a press without the use of traditional offset or computer-to-plate processes or chemistry. It is also known as a computer-to-press system. DI presses eliminate the production steps and variables normally associated with offset platemaking processes.

Today's DI presses combine the versatility of offset with the convenience and ease of use of digital while delivering a high degree of speed, quality, and automation to the four-color printing market. DI presses provide good image quality and a significantly reduced environmental footprint because of the chemistry-free plates.

The DI press, **Figure 13-4,** reduces makeready time and improves productivity. The *makeready* is

the process of preparing a press for printing a job. The prepared digital files are sent via a high-speed network directly to the press, where plates are automatically advanced and mounted on the press plate cylinder and imaged simultaneously and in register, **Figure 13-5.**

Digital Workflow

The printing workflow consists of the various steps to create, prepare, and print materials. As discussed in Chapter 7, many changes have been made in the process of prepress workflow. Manual tasks are now done using various types of software. The preparation of text, graphics, and layout is completed on a computer. The general steps of a digital workflow, **Figure 13-6,** can be summarized as the following:

1. The creation of text and images.
2. Importing text and images to create page layouts.
3. Imposition and sheet assembly of laid-out pages.
4. Platemaking and printing based on the sheets on a DI press.

PDF workflows are commonly used in industry. PDF files allow users to include necessary pieces of a job in one file. With all the document information, such as fonts, text, and graphics, PDF files may be quite large. However, job ticket information, including everything from customer information to shipping information, can be incorporated into a PDF file, making it a versatile tool of the printing industry.

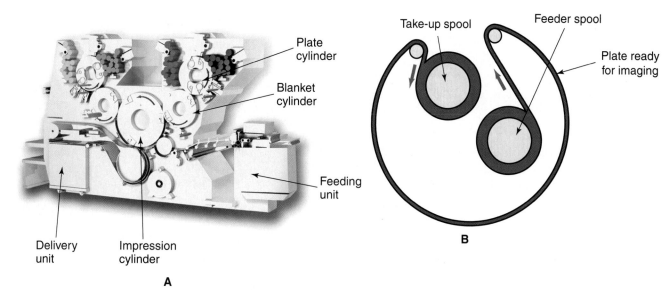

Figure 13-5. The workings of a direct image press. A—A cross section reveals a common impression cylinder. B—One method of automatic plate loading is to place both the feeder and take-up spools within the plate cylinder. (Presstek, Inc.)

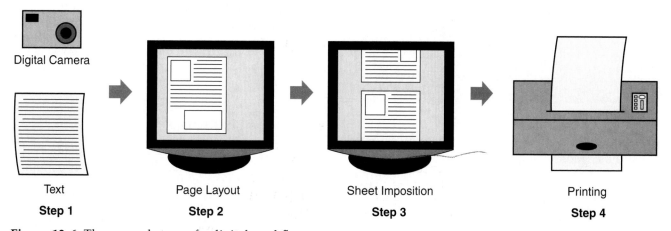

Figure 13-6. The general steps of a digital workflow.

DIGITAL PRINTING METHODS

Digital printing is done using various methods. The most common of these is ink-jet printing. Some techniques, such as electrophotography, are types of electrostatic printing. *Electrostatic printing* uses electrical charges to cause toner to fuse onto a page. Other common types of digital printing are iconography, magnetography, dye sublimation, and thermal transfer.

Ink-Jet Printing

Ink-jet printing is a direct-to-paper technology with no intermediate image carrier. It uses digital data to control streams of very fine droplets of ink

direct imaging (DI): The process of sending a digital file directly to a press without the use of traditional offset or computer-to-plate processes or chemistry.

makeready: The process of preparing a press for printing a job.

electrostatic printing: Type of printing that uses electrical charges to cause toner to fuse onto a page.

ink-jet printing: A direct-to-paper technology that uses digital data to control streams of very fine droplets of ink or dye to produce images directly on paper or other substrates.

THINK GREEN
Electronic Media Waste

Although digital technology is helping reduce the damage from existing threats to the environment, its continuing use and constant growth comes at a price. When computers and other types of electronics are replaced, the older machines that are thrown out become e-waste. E-waste is the fastest growing cause of toxic waste in the United States. The toxic chemicals found in e-waste can consist of lead and mercury. While these toxins can damage the environment, they are also harmful for your health. Exposure to lead can cause neurological damage and cancer. Mercury poisoning can cause damage to the nervous and endocrine systems. Recent policies regarding the disposal and recycling of e-waste have been adopted in several countries. Several electronics manufacturers have initiated recycling programs for their products. For more information, see www.ewaste.com.

Figure 13-7. Ink-jet printers can be used for variable data printing in various sizes.

Figure 13-8. Large format ink-jet printers may be used for posters, banners, and signs. (Océ Display Graphics Systems)

or dye to produce images directly on paper or other substrates. Most ink-jet printing is variable data printing of single or spot colors, such as direct mail advertising or large format posters, banners, or signage for limited distribution, **Figure 13-7.** Variable data printing is discussed later in this chapter.

Ink-jet printers are classified as either desktop, large format, or grand format based on the size of the reproduced image. Desktop printers are typically those that can produce images up to 13″ × 19″. Large format printers are those that typically produce images from paper rolls larger than 13″ in width and technically limited in length only by the length of the roll of substrate material, often 100′ or more. However, there are some large format specialized printers that print on sheets, especially in the world of art reproduction, often referred to as Giclée (pronounced *zhee-clay*). Large format ink-jet printers, **Figure 13-8,** are used extensively within the graphic communications industry for critical proofing applications. Ink-jet printers beyond the classification of large format are called grand format printers. They are commonly used to create outdoor signage using solvent inks.

Types of Ink-Jet Printers

The three main technologies used with ink-jet printers are thermal, piezoelectric, and continuous. The way the ink is dispersed onto the substrate is what makes the technologies different.

In a *thermal ink-jet printer*, the ink cartridges have an ink chamber with a heater and a nozzle. Electrical current is sent to the heater for a few microseconds to generate heat. This heat is transferred to the ink, which is superheated to form a bubble. The bubble expands through the firing chamber, and the ink is forced out of the nozzle, **Figure 13-9.** The ink then refills in the chamber. Thermal ink-jet printers use aqueous inks, which are discussed later in this chapter.

In a *piezoelectric ink-jet printer*, the piezocrystal is charged by an electric pulse. The electric pulse causes pressure, which forces droplets of ink from the nozzle, **Figure 13-10.** Piezoelectric ink-jet printers may use a wide variety of inks.

The *continuous ink-jet printer* is used commercially for marking and coding of products and packages, **Figure 13-11.** A continuously circulating flow of ink through the printhead is maintained while

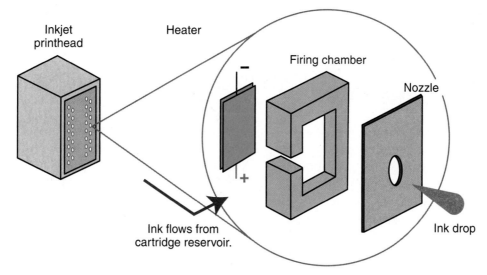

Figure 13-9. Exploded diagram of a typical thermal ink-jet printer.

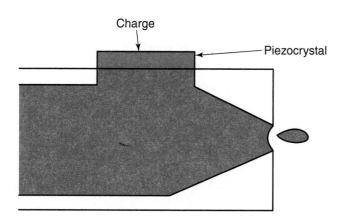

Figure 13-10. Process of a piezoelectric ink-jet printer.

Figure 13-11. Continuous ink-jet printers are used to mark and code products. (Domino Printing Sciences plc)

the power is on. In all other respects, it behaves like a thermal ink-jet printer. The printhead and the ink storage reservoir are separate components, and the ink storage reservoir also contains an area to store waste ink.

Types of Ink-Jet Inks

Several special inks are needed to create an image on a substrate using the ink-jet method of printing. The most commonly used inks are aqueous, solvent, and UV-curable.

Many of the desktop ink-jet printers use *aqueous inks*, based on a mixture of water, glycol, and dyes or pigments. Aqueous inks are able to withstand high temperatures that are needed to form a bubble without affecting the chemical makeup of the ink.

In *solvent inks*, the main ingredient used as the carrier of the dyes or pigments is considered to be high in volatile organic compounds (VOCs). Environmental concerns must be taken into consideration to meet

thermal ink-jet printer: Printer in which the ink is superheated to form a bubble, which expands through the firing chamber, forcing ink out of the nozzle.

piezoelectric ink-jet printer: Printer in which a piezocrystal is charged to cause pressure, which forces droplets of ink from the nozzle.

continuous ink-jet printer: Printer in which a continuously circulating flow of ink through the printhead is maintained while the power is on.

aqueous inks: Inks that are based on a mixture of water, glycol, and dyes or pigments.

ACADEMIC LINK

Volatile Organic Compounds

Volatile organic compounds (VOCs) are chemical compounds that emit vapors at normal room temperatures. These compounds are found in many common items, such as paints, varnishes, adhesives, aerosol sprays, household cleaning products, and air fresheners. Some common VOCs include,

- Formaldehyde: Found in liquid adhesives.
- Butyl acetate: Found in adhesive caulk, dry erase markers, and nail polish.
- Methylene chloride: Found in aerosol spray paint and paint stripping agents.
- Perchloroethylene: A chemical used in dry cleaning.

Short term exposure to VOCs can cause irritation of the eyes, nose, and throat, headaches, dizziness, or nausea. Long term exposure to some VOCs may cause damage to the liver, kidney, and central nervous system or may cause cancer.

It is recommended that products containing VOCs be avoided. If it is necessary to use products containing VOCs, follow all the safety instructions on the product label and use the product outside or in very well-ventilated areas.

Research common VOCs and evaluate your daily environment. What are the sources of VOCs around you every day? What steps can you take to reduce your exposure to VOCs?

government standards. When this ink is placed on the paper, the solvent evaporates very rapidly, sending the VOCs into the atmosphere while the colorant remains on the substrate.

There is a lack of VOCs in *UV-curable inks*. After the ultraviolet (UV) ink droplet is forced onto the substrate, it is subjected to UV light. The ink is polymerized. The result of the curing process is the instant hardening of the ink. The image produced by UV-curable inks is very sharp in appearance.

Types of Ink-Jet Printheads

The two main inkjet printhead designs are fixed-head and disposable head. The fixed-head ink-jet printer design has a built-in printhead that is expected

to last the life of the printer. When the ink runs out, the printhead can be refilled with ink. In the disposable head ink-jet printer, the cartridge is replaced when the ink runs out.

Electrophotography

Electrophotography is a widely used printing technique that is seen most often in photocopiers. In the electrophotographic process, an original image is reflected onto a drum coated with chargeable photoconductors that discharge in the nonimage areas after exposure to light. See **Figure 13-12**. The image receives dry or liquid toners in the charged area, and it transfers either to an impression blanket or directly to a substrate. The substrate is charged by the corona assembly, and the image is fused by heat, solvent vapor, or other fixing method. Most electrophotographic systems accommodate a wide range of paper finishes, weights, and sizes, **Figure 13-13**.

A common type of printer that uses an electrophotographic process is a laser printer. Laser printers use one system that contains a scanning bed and an imaging system. Software to connect the printer to the computer and the step of using a raster imaging processor (RIP) are added to the process. Multiple mirrors and a laser beam are used to expose the image on the drum, **Figure 13-14**.

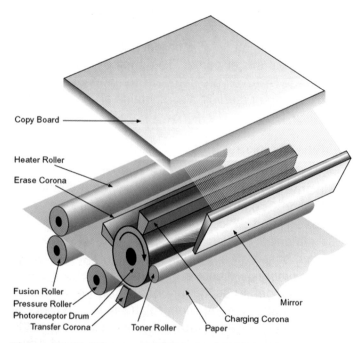

Copy Board
Heater Roller
Erase Corona
Fusion Roller
Pressure Roller
Photoreceptor Drum
Transfer Corona
Toner Roller
Paper
Charging Corona
Mirror

Figure 13-12. Diagram of an electrophotographic printer. (www.PrintingTips.com, owned by Austec Data Inc. dba Tecstra Systems)

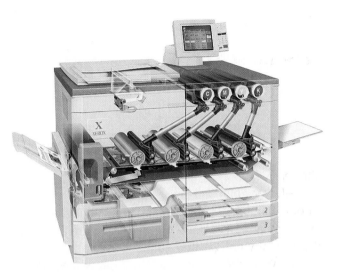

Figure 13-13. The electrophotographic printing system illustrated above includes a flatbed scanner and a previewing screen. This system also allows the addition of a sorter and automatic document feeder. (Courtesy of Xerox Corporation)

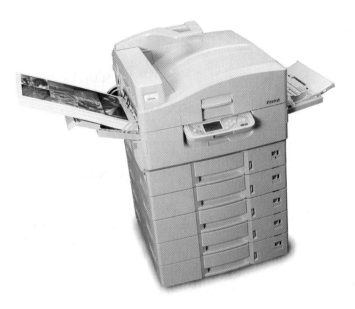

Figure 13-15. This electrophotographic printer is capable of printing high-quality, four-color printing jobs. (Xanté Corporation)

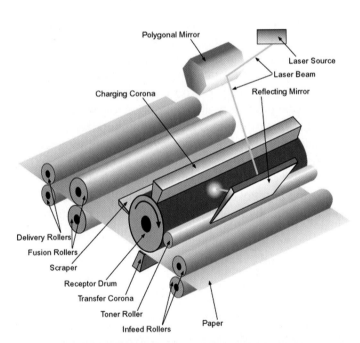

Figure 13-14. Diagram of a laser printing system. (www.PrintingTips.com, owned by Austec Data Inc. dba Tecstra Systems)

Electrophotographic printing has become more systemized by connecting the device to a network and viewing the output device as part of a system consisting of a page layout workstation, a scanner, a RIP, and a printer. In some instances, electrophotographic printing systems are being used to produce content and contract proofing, including final output copies. See **Figure 13-15.**

Ionography

Ionography is similar to electrophotography. However, instead of using mirrors to expose the image onto the drum, ionography uses an electron cartridge, or ion generator. A negative charge is dispersed from the electron cartridge. The charge is then transferred onto a heated nonconductive surface covered with a magnetic toner. The image is then fused onto the substrate. See **Figure 13-16.**

Misregistration may occur because of the pressure of the image transfer. Therefore, ionography is used mainly for single- or spot-color printing. Ionography systems are used for high-volume and variable data printing. Variable data printing is discussed later in this chapter.

solvent inks: Inks that have a main ingredient of a solvent that evaporates and produces VOCs.

UV-curable inks: Inks that are forced onto the substrate, then subjected to UV light to be polymerized.

electrophotography: Printing process that uses a drum coated with chargeable photoconductors, dry or liquid toners, and a corona assembly to produce an image on a substrate.

ionography: Printing process that uses an electron cartridge, a nonconductive surface, and a magnetic toner to produce an image on a substrate.

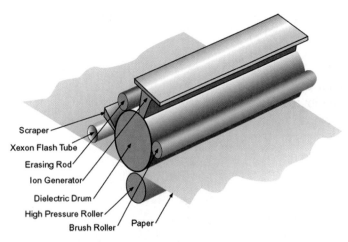

Figure 13-16. Diagram of an ionographic printer. (www.PrintingTips.com, owned by Austec Data Inc. dba Tecstra Systems)

Magnetography

In *magnetography*, the image is converted to a magnetic charge on a drum that then attracts magnetized toner. Similar to ionography, magnetography exposes an image onto a drum and then uses high pressure to fuse the toner onto the substrate.

As with ionography, magnetography is commonly used for single- or spot-color printing. The iron oxide contained in the core of the magnetic toner causes the toner to be darker on paper. One advantage magnetographic systems have over other digital printing systems is that they are faster than other types of systems. Magnetographic systems are commonly used for printing barcodes and other types of variable data printing. Variable data printing is discussed later in this chapter.

Dye Sublimation

Dye sublimation is a type of thermography. Dye sublimation is the process of using heat and pressure to change solid dye particles to a gas, which vaporizes as it permeates the surface of the substrate. See **Figure 13-17.** In dye sublimation printers, a ribbon is made up of cyan, magenta, and yellow panels of solid pigment. The ink panels pass over a thermal head, and as the panels are heated, the solid pigment becomes a gas, which transfers to the paper below the panels. The thermal head changes temperature to vary the amount of ink dispensed on the substrate. This makes dye sublimation a type of continuous tone printing process. After the three colored panels have been printed on the substrate, a lamination is applied to prevent smudging from warmth, **Figure 13-18.**

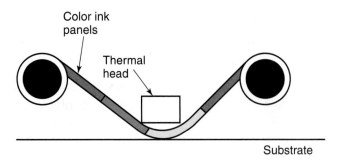

Figure 13-17. Diagram of a dye sublimation printer.

An advantage of dye sublimation is that the ink is dry as soon as it is done printing. A disadvantage is that once a panel has been used, it cannot be reused, resulting in higher costs of ink than other methods of printing. Dye sublimation is commonly used to print digital photographs and plastic cards, and it is also used to print on polyester.

Thermal Transfer

Thermal transfer is a type of thermography. The process of thermal transfer printing is very similar to dye sublimation. However, the ink panels are different in a thermal transfer printer. Rather than a ribbon of panels of colored solid pigment, thermal transfer printers use a different ribbon for each color. Thermal transfer printers have been used mainly for one-color printing, but newer systems with multiple ribbons of different colors are also used. The type of ink used for thermal transfer makes it difficult to control the amount of ink transferred to the substrate. This technique is commonly used for color proofing.

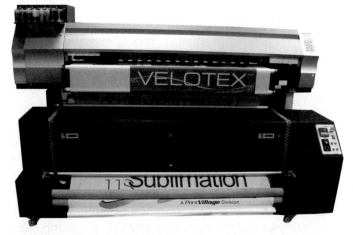

Figure 13-18. An example of a dye sublimation textile system with on-board curing. (US Sublimation)

DIGITAL PRINTING APPLICATIONS

Digital printing allows for more flexibility in the printing process. This flexibility and electronic workflow permit materials to be easily shared and customized. Many of the items people receive in the mail are the products of digital printing processes.

Variable Data Printing

Variable data printing is a printing process that is unique to digital printing systems. It enables quick and easy content changes at several points within a print run. The "on the fly" imaging device in all true digital printing presses allows customized and personalized materials to be produced. Customized printed materials typically target a specific audience or group, but not a particular individual. Personalized printed materials are unique and intended for a specific person.

Printing variable data items begins with the designer's work: a basic template of the printed material. Within the design, certain sections are designated as changeable fields. The data for these fields is held in a database or separate file and are applied during the digital printing process. The results of variable data printing include direct marketing mailers, area-specific sales flyers, and product mailings that include customer-specific messages.

Distributed Printing

Distributed printing is a system of digital printing in which the electronic files for a job may be sent anywhere in the world through a wide area network (WAN) and printed near the point of distribution. For example, a brochure can be sent electronically to a digital printing operation near a trade show location prior to the event. The brochure can be printed and delivered to the convention center or hotel, saving time and shipping costs. Also, national newspapers and magazines use distributed printing technology to print regional editions of the publications. A central or home office sends an electronic file to all its regional offices for the addition of local merchant ads and articles of local interest. The regional offices may then send the completed file to a local digital printing facility for production and distribution.

Distributed printing has limitations. Using color management systems at both ends of the process helps ensure color consistency, but it may still be necessary to send hard copies to clients if color fidelity is critical. Many companies prefer to proof the printed documents prior to a press run, either for their own proofing/approval purposes or to get final approval from a customer. Businesses using distributed printing on a regular basis may be able to provide local representatives for onsite approval.

Digital Asset Management

Digital asset management (DAM) consists of the protocol and resources established to handle all digital files and data. Common management tasks include downloading, processing, organizing, storing, and transmitting data. The types of data typically involved in digital printing processes includes design files, templates, images, font files, and databases. An effective data asset management system streamlines the business processes that involve handling digital data.

There are a number of applications where digital asset management systems are essential in managing a large amount of necessary digital information. For example, data libraries use asset management systems to manage the storage and retrieval of large amounts of infrequently changing media assets, such as archival documents, photos, and videos. Digital supply chain services that push digital content (music, videos, and games) out to digital retailers is another example of a business where digital asset management systems are essential.

Effective large-scale digital asset management solutions involve scalable, reliable, configurable

magnetography: Printing process that uses a drum, magnetic toner, and high pressure to produce an image on a substrate.

dye sublimation: A type of thermography that uses heat and pressure to change solid dye particles on a ribbon into a gas to produce an image on a substrate.

thermal transfer: A type of thermography that uses heat and pressure to change solid dye particles on multiple ribbons into a gas to produce an image on a substrate.

variable data printing. A digital printing process that enables quick and easy content changes at several points within a print run. The "on the fly" imaging resident allows customized and personalized printed materials to be produced.

distributed printing. A system of digital printing in which the electronic files for a job can be sent anywhere in the world, through a wide area network (WAN), for output. Commonly used for localized editions of newspapers and magazines.

digital asset management (DAM). The protocol and resources established to handle all digital files and data.

CAREER LINK

Digital Press Operator

Digital press operators are found in small printing shops, as well as larger printing plants. The operator works with digital printing presses and computerized systems to produce printed material, and is generally required to troubleshoot and maintain the press. Also, press output must be monitored for optimum image quality.

The requirements of a digital press operator include knowledge of various merge applications, multitasking and prioritizing skills, and possess mechanical and technical skills that apply to the operation of computerized systems. Following safety rules and practicing safe work habits are essential characteristics for an operator, as well. Necessary skills to be a digital press operator may be acquired at technical schools, colleges, and universities. On-the-job training may also be offered by some printing establishments.

"At a time when methods of communicating are becoming increasingly digital, printing on paper and countless other substrates has consistently proven to be the most reliable medium to convey ideas and images."

Michael Makin
Printing Industries of America

hardware and software products that can handle a great number of files, as well as many simultaneous users, workflows, or multiple applications operating on the system. Some management systems are offered as installed software with Web-based access, called *software-as-a-service (SaaS)*. SaaS systems manage and maintain data externally, and provide clients with system-specific software to facilitate data access through an internet connection. Industry-focused systems, such as AGFA's Apogee or Kodak's InSite, combine automated publishing workflows with digital asset management in a Web-enabled environment that supports multiple-user collaboration. For small-scale applications or individual use, some image viewer applications offer management capabilities, including backing up, organizing, and reading/writing metadata and keywords.

ADVANTAGES AND DISADVANTAGES OF DIGITAL PRINTING

There are certain areas in which digital and conventional printing each have distinct production and economic advantages. There are also many areas where they overlap, as emerging and conventional technologies adapt to meet the short-run market demands.

Conventional color printing requires long runs to absorb the high make-ready costs. However, computer-to-plate technology has eliminated many of the time-consuming and expensive steps involved in traditional printing. Digital printing has not yet surpassed the quality of traditional printing, but is considered comparable to the average viewer, **Figure 13-19.**

The term "on-demand printing" is often used solely to describe digital-to-paper printing. This is a misnomer, because all printers print on demand. If a

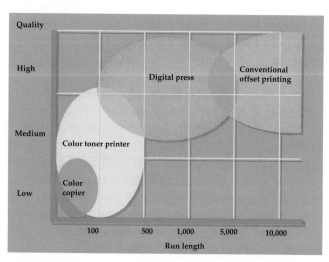

Figure 13-19. Color printing technology is available with various levels of quality and all types of run lengths.

customer "demands" an order, the printer will print it. On-demand printing is better described as short-run, distributed, just-in-time printing, no matter how it is produced.

Digital presses offer quick turnaround times, a great deal of flexibility, and cost-effective, printing for short color runs. Depending on finishing requirements, an experienced print shop using a digital press can typically turn around digital printing runs in 24–48 hours. With the proper full-color digital printers, digital printing can also provide a means to produce quick, cost-effective, high-quality proofs for gravure and offset printing.

The flexibility of digital printing exists because there are no plates or drums; digital presses are imaged on-the-fly. Last-minute changes can be made with little or no extra cost. Digital printing allows individual pages to be customized during print runs and enables electronic files to be transmitted almost anywhere in the world for printing. Digital printing provides a cost-effective means for printing out-of-print titles and short runs of manuals, books, and textbooks, **Figure 13-20.**

By eliminating much of the traditional press preparation, digital presses make the overall cost of short color runs affordable. Short-run, process-color printing includes very short printing runs that can range from one to several thousand copies. The unit cost may be higher with digital printing, but the overall cost is less expensive than on a traditional press. A short run on a traditional press would be prohibitively expensive due to the setup costs involved.

Although digital printing has many advantages, it also has its limitations. To the eye of experts, most digital presses do not produce the quality achievable by today's traditional offset presses. Digital presses are not intended to be replacements for conventional printing presses, but are meant for the types of jobs that aren't practical or possible on traditional presses.

As the quality of digital graphic arts technology continues to improve, the advantages it promises are certain to grow. These include lower costs, greater flexibility, and faster production time. New technology will also require the mastery of new skills for every step of the production process.

The trend toward all-digital design, storage, production, and reproduction is very exciting. However, this trend also involves the expansion of complex input and output options and application of consistent standards for product creation, transmission, and reproduction. As with all technology, you must continually update your knowledge and equipment to remain competitive.

Figure 13-20. This DocuColor™ system can produce color printed materials at a rate of about 80 pages per minute. This system also offers a variety of finishing options, including binding, punching, and booklet making. (Courtesy of Xerox Corporation)

software-as-a-service (SaaS). A type of data management system in which the data is managed and maintained externally. Clients access the data on demand using system-specific software and an internet connection.

Summary

While the demand for high-quality color printing is growing, run lengths and production cycle times are shrinking. Printers must keep pace with customers who work in this fast-paced digital world. The most common types of digital printing are ink-jet, electrophotography, ionography, magnetography, dye sublimation, and thermal transfer. Digital printing allows for variable data printing. Digital asset management systems are used to manage digital files and data.

Review Questions

Please do not write in this book. Write your answers on a separate sheet of paper.

1. _____ is any reproduction technology that receives electronic files and uses dots for replication.
2. Describe how a DI press works.
3. Which of the following is *not* a step of a digital workflow?
   A. Imposition and sheet assembly of laid-out pages.
   B. Creation of text and images.
   C. Paste-up to produce a mechanical.
   D. Importing text and images to create page layouts.
4. List three main technologies used with ink-jet printers.
5. What type of commonly used ink contains a great amount of VOCs?
6. _____ is the type of printing technology used by laser printers.
7. Name two common types of thermography.
8. Explain how materials are customized using variable data printing.
9. How does distributed printing save time and money?
10. How do SaaS systems provide digital asset management capabilities to clients?
11. List some advantages of digital printing compared to offset printing.

Suggested Activities

1. Visit a printing plant and determine what digital applications are being used in the facility.
2. Compare color digital printed images with conventional printed images for detail, color, dot structure, sharpness of image, and other selected factors.
3. What types of applications are appropriate for variable data printing?

Related Web Links

DyeSub

www.dyesub.org
Information about dye sublimation and thermal transfer.

eWaste

www.ewaste.com
Online information source for recycling electronic equipment.

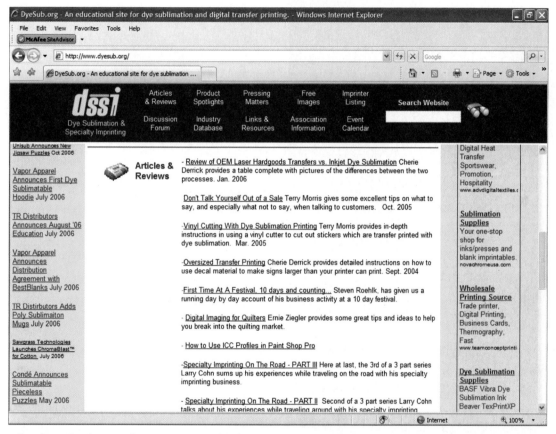

Because technology is always changing, some Web sites may provide up-to-date material pertaining to specific types of digital printing technology.

CHAPTER 14

Lithographic Platemaking

Learning Objectives

After studying this chapter, you will be able to:

- Understand the use of lithography as a printing method and explain how lithographic plates are used on an offset press.

- Summarize the types of equipment used in platemaking.

- Identify the main parts of a lithographic plate and explain how plates are classified.

- Explain how plates are exposed and developed on a platemaker.

- Identify the methods and equipment used in different platemaking systems.

- Recall the types of platesetters used in computer-to-plate applications.

- Understand computer-to-plate classifications.

- Recall common problems associated with the platemaking process.

Important Terms

blanket
computer-to-plate (CTP)
electrostatic plates
flat
laser plates
lithography
offset printing
photo direct plates
photopolymer plates
plate

plate coatings
plate coverings
plate grain
soft image
surface plates
thermal plates
vacuum frame
vignette
waterless plates

This chapter covers the different methods used in making and processing plates and the various types of plates used in offset lithographic printing. A *plate* is an imaged sheet designed for printing multiple copies on a press. This chapter will illustrate how different types of plates are made and introduce the various forms of equipment used in platemaking.

LITHOGRAPHY

Lithography is a method of printing directly from a flat surface, or plate, containing an image formed in ink. The lithographic process is also known as planography, which means printing from a flat surface. Basically, lithographic printing is based on the principle that oil and water do not readily mix.

The plate has a nonimage area that receives water and repels oil- or grease-based ink. The image area accepts ink and refuses water. **Figure 14-1** illustrates how ink and water act in lithographic printing. Even though this system is the most common, today some plates have been developed that have coatings that do not accept ink in the nonimage areas.

Lithography was developed as a method of printing from a flat stone surface, by Alois Senefelder, a German playwright, in 1796. Using a smooth piece of limestone, he drew an image with a grease-based material. When the stone was moistened, water would only be absorbed by the nonimage area of the stone; it would not adhere to the image formed in grease. When the stone was inked, only the grease-based image would accept the ink. Paper was placed on the stone, and pressure was applied to transfer the image. Images for stone lithography were drawn in reverse, since the image would mirror the printing surface, **Figure 14-2**. Prints were made by repeating the process of applying water and then ink to the stone.

As printing methods improved, metal replaced stone as the standard material for making lithographic plates. The development of *offset printing* led to the use of metal plates with printing presses.

The operation of an offset lithographic press involves the transfer of images from one surface to another. The image is offset from the plate to

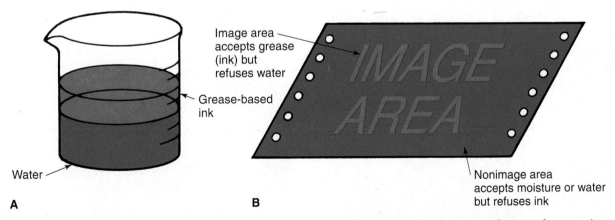

Figure 14-1. Lithography is a printing method based on the principle that oil or grease and water do not mix readily. A—If grease-based ink is poured into a container of water, the ink will normally separate and rise to the surface. B—Lithographic plates use the principle of ink and water repulsion for printing. The image area accepts ink but rejects water, while the nonimage area accepts water but rejects ink.

plate: An image carrier used for printing multiple copies on a press.

lithography: A method of printing directly from a flat surface or plate containing an image formed in ink.

offset printing: A printing method in which inked images are offset or transferred from one surface to another.

blanket: A resilient material that is attached to a cylinder and used as an image transfer material from the plate cylinder to the substrate.

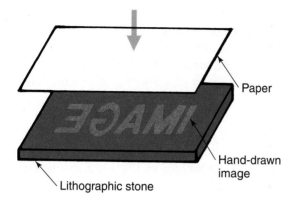

Figure 14-2. In stone lithography, images were drawn in reverse on a smooth stone surface to make prints.

a *blanket* and is then transferred to the paper, **Figure 14-3.** After the blanket receives the image in reverse form from the plate, the image transfers back to its original form on the substrate.

Printing methods continue to evolve as electronic platemaking and desktop publishing systems gain more use in the graphic communications industry. Traditionally, platemaking has involved the use of a plate coated with a light-sensitive material to capture images from a positive source. In this method, film is placed over the plate and the plate is exposed and then processed. Electronic platemaking does not use film and images are transferred from the original sources directly to the plates. Automatic plate processors, which combine image transfer with plate processing, are commonly used to make plates. While electronic methods of platemaking have become widely adopted, traditional platemaking techniques and equipment continue to be used in commercial applications of printing.

PLATEMAKING EQUIPMENT

Platemaking requires the use of a platemaker and processing materials or an automatic plate processor. A platemaker uses a light source to expose the plate from a piece of film or camera-ready copy. The plate is placed in contact with the original image inside a glass frame called a *vacuum frame*. After the plate is exposed, it may be processed by hand using chemicals in a developing sink, or processed by an automatic plate processor.

A self-contained platemaking unit is equipped with a light source, a light control or timer, a vacuum frame, a vacuum pump, and a motor. A flip-top platemaker is one example of a self-contained unit, **Figure 14-4.**

The vacuum frame holds the plate and stripped *flat* in close contact under the glass during exposure. The plate and flat are aligned and placed inside the frame on a rubber blanket, which is connected to a vacuum pump. The pump removes air between the blanket and the glass, sealing the plate and flat together. After the plate and flat have made close contact, the light source is turned on and the exposure is made. See **Figure 14-5.**

Figure 14-4. A flip-top platemaker used to expose plates. Exposure time is controlled electronically. (nuArc company, inc.)

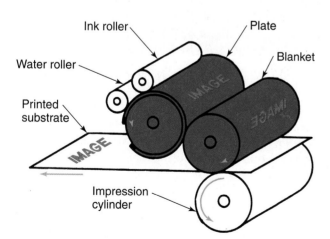

Figure 14-3. Components of an offset lithographic press. After the image is offset from the plate to the blanket, it is offset again to the substrate.

A source high in ultraviolet light is commonly used to expose plates. The light source must provide an even illumination across the plate area; a computerized control panel on the front of the platemaker houses the controls for vacuum and exposure time. After the plate is exposed, it is developed.

Automatic Plate Processors

Automatic plate processors are used to automatically prepare plates for the press. They are found in small and large printing plants, **Figure 14-6.** Processing chemicals are automatically applied and

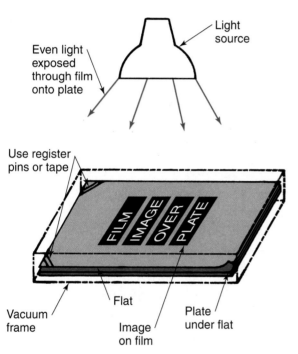

Figure 14-5. A plate is exposed once the film has been registered over the plate and a close contact has been made. The light source shines through the image on film and exposes the light-sensitive surface of the plate.

Figure 14-6. Plate processing is increasingly being done with automatic plate processors. (3M Company)

replenished when needed. Process monitoring is conducted to ensure the chemicals are at the proper strength for consistent development.

Automatic processing eliminates the task of processing plates by hand and assures consistent plate quality. The internal parts of a typical processor are shown in **Figure 14-7.** During automatic processing, the plate is transported through the unit at a predetermined rate of speed. It is fully developed and ready for the press when it leaves the processor, **Figure 14-8.**

LITHOGRAPHIC PLATES

The image and nonimage areas of a plate are kept separate chemically. This separation is necessary because the image and nonimage areas are essentially on the same plane.

Waterless printing plates are designed with a principle different from that used for the conventional lithographic plate. A waterless plate has a light-sensitive, ink-receptive photopolymer attached to its surface. The nonimage area is coated with an ink-repellent substance other than water. Since waterless printing does not use a dampening solution, possible chemical hazards are eliminated. Therefore, waterless printing is less harmful to the environment.

Plates are made of paper coated with plastic, cellulose-based paper, polyester, acetate, steel coated with plastic, chromium, aluminum, or stainless steel coated with copper. Aluminum is widely used because it is more receptive to water than grease. It is also flexible, lightweight, and can be easily grained.

Generally speaking, lithographic plates have three parts: the base or plate grain, the plate covering, and the plate coating. Plate materials and surfaces vary according to the use of the plate.

vacuum frame: A glass frame used to hold the film and plate in tight contact for exposure on a platemaker.

flat: Film mounted on a masking sheet.

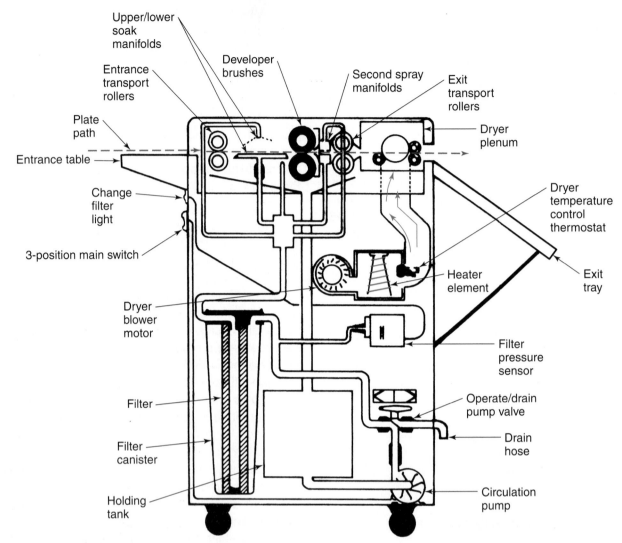

Figure 14-7. Components of an automatic plate processor. Rollers feed the plate through the processor as it is developed and dried.

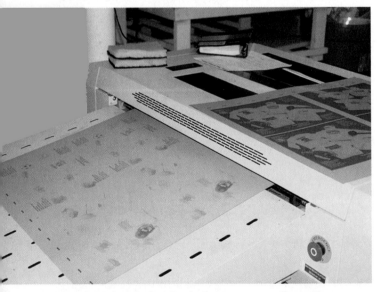

Figure 14-8. A finished plate emerges from the automatic plate processor, ready for printing.

Plate Grains

The *plate grain* of lithographic plate is the surface texture of the plate base. It can appear very smooth or quite rough when magnified. Several types of grains can be used. Each appears as a texture on the surface of the plate.

Mechanical grains include blasted and brushed grains. Blasted grain is formed by an abrasive applied by air pressure. Brushed grain is applied to the plate with abrasives and a brush. Chemical grains are formed by chemicals that etch into the plate. **Figure 14-9** shows several grain classifications for plates.

Paper and plastic plates are considered to be grainless plates. The surfaces of grainless plates are manufactured to hold moisture. The plate surface is chemically treated. The image areas, receptive to

THINK GREEN
Recycled Plates

Lithographic plates can be coated with a variety of metals. Some of the most commonly used are plastic, stainless steel, and copper. One that is becoming used more and more is aluminum. There are many advantages to using aluminum, but it is important to note that aluminum plates can be recycled. Several lithographic printing plants are going green, and a common attribute among them is that they use recyclable aluminum plates so the waste doesn't go to landfills. Recycling programs for aluminum plates are offered by multiple platemaking companies. Most of these services also provide tracking for printers so they can verify that their plates have been properly handled and recycled. For more information, see imagingnetworkonline.com/pages/scrap.html.

ink, are created by the light action. The nonimage area becomes receptive to water.

Plate Coverings

Plate coverings are layers of material bonded to the base of a plate. The covering assists in holding the image area on the plate surface.

Plate Coatings

Plate coatings are the surface layers of light-sensitive material that harden when exposed to light. Plates manufactured with a light-sensitive material to capture images are presensitized. The surface of presensitized plates are sensitive to light, and they must be handled according to manufacturers' specifications. Different types of coatings are used for various platemaking applications.

Diazo coating is one of the most commonly used. When a plate is exposed, active light strikes the diazo coating and the image area becomes inactive. The nonimage areas remain active and can be removed during plate processing. The inactive image area remains as a part of the plate for printing the image.

Photopolymers are plastic coatings put on plates designed to produce long-lasting images without requiring added protection. When light strikes the coating, the coating hardens and forms a strong image area.

Silver halide coatings contain silver salts and are used with diffusion transfer plates, which are exposed from a negative. The image areas are converted to metallic silver when light strikes the plate surface and when the plate is developed.

Electrostatic plates have carbon powders or liquids applied to the surface. The coating is fixed on the plate electrostatically. Although the surface of the plate is not coated with a light-sensitive material, light is used during the platemaking process to neutralize an electrical charge in nonimage areas.

Plate Classifications

Presensitized plates coated with light-sensitive material are called *surface plates* because of the

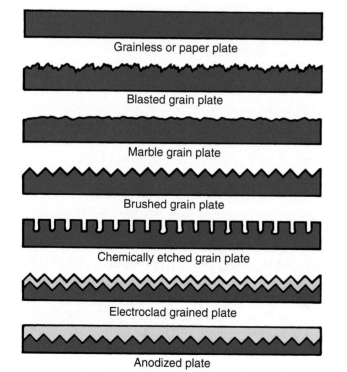

Figure 14-9. Different types of grain used to form a surface texture on a plate.

plate grain: The surface texture of a plate base.

plate coverings: Layers of material bonded to the plate base material, used to help hold the image area in place.

plate coatings: Layers of light-sensitive material on the surface of plates that form or harden when exposed to light.

surface plates: Presensitized plates coated with light-sensitive material.

coating on the surface of the plate. Surface plates are classified as either negative-acting, positive-acting, additive, or subtractive plates.

Negative-acting plates have image areas that harden when exposed to light. Negative film stripped on a flat is used to expose the image onto the plate.

Positive-acting plates are those in which the area exposed by light becomes the nonimage area. Positive film is contacted to the positive-acting plate to transfer the image. After exposure, the exposed nonimage area is removed in processing.

Additive plates have a developing solution added to the image during processing. Although additive plates are presensitized, developer is used to make the image more receptive to ink and more durable.

Subtractive plates are presensitized plates that are processed after exposure by removing the plate coating from the nonimage area.

Handling Plates

Lithographic plates must be handled carefully when they are processed and mounted on a printing press. Corners are sharp. Always handle plates with clean hands and use clean equipment to prevent fingerprints and dirty roller marks from appearing on the plate.

Lithographic plates attach to the plate cylinder of a printing press. Plates are classified by the way they are secured to the press cylinder. Classifications include straight bar plates, pin bar plates, or serrated plates, **Figure 14-10.** All three types of plates are commonly used with duplicator presses, but larger presses normally use straight bar plates.

A straight bar is a clamping device that is used to hold a plate over the entire length of the press cylinder. Pin bar and serrated plates have punched holes that are positioned with fittings on the leading and trailing edges of the press cylinder. If too much tension is put on the plate, the holes or slots tend to elongate.

PLATEMAKING SYSTEMS

Numerous advances have been made in the production of lithographic plates for offset printing in recent years. Automatic processing machines and electronic platemaking systems have replaced many of the manual techniques previously used to make plates. Newer systems involve the production of presensitized plates and vary depending on the type

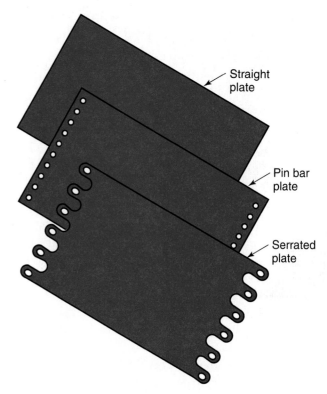

Figure 14-10. Plates use different methods for attachment to a press.

of plate used. This section of the chapter will present several of the most commonly used surface plates and different platemaking systems.

Photo Direct Plates

Photo direct plates are carriers that are imaged directly from a flat or camera-ready copy. The images on photo direct plates are commonly projected through a lens to the light-sensitive surface. Photo-direct platemaking systems are typically fully automatic, computerized systems. See **Figure 14-11.**

In this system, the camera-ready copy is placed faceup on a copyboard, **Figure 14-12.** An automatic registration control allows the operator to position the copy accurately and easily. Photo direct systems are often equipped with automatic centering, which positions copy for enlarging or reducing. The operator inputs the information on the control panel located in front of the system.

The photo direct plate system eliminates the use of a film intermediate. After the plate is exposed, it is automatically processed and is then ready to be mounted on the press. See **Figure 14-13.**

Figure 14-11. A photo direct platemaking system images the plate and processes it automatically. (3M Company)

Thermal Plates

Thermal plates are carriers that can be imaged optically or digitally through the use of heat. Heat, not light, is used to expose thermal plates. The

Figure 14-12. The original image or mechanical is placed on the copyboard for exposure in a photo direct platemaking system. (3M Company)

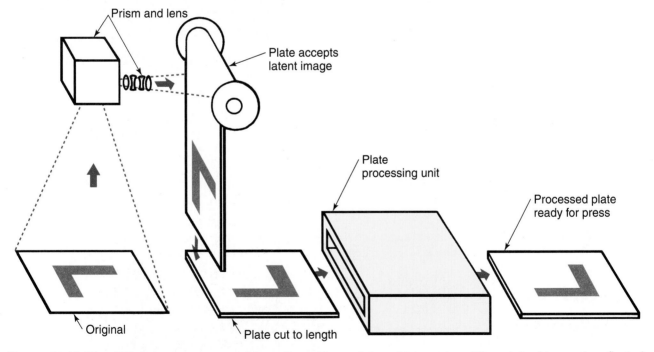

Figure 14-13. The different processes used in a photo direct platemaking system. The original image is reflected through the prism and lens onto the light-sensitive plate. The plate is then cut to length and fed through the processing unit. It emerges ready for use on the press.

photo direct plates: Image carriers that are imaged directly from camera-ready copy or a paste-up.

thermal plates: Image carriers that can be exposed optically or digitally through the use of heat.

base of the plate is metal and is similar to that of a conventional lithographic plate.

The coating of a thermal plate is a heat-sensitive polymer. A thermal plate can be processed automatically through aqueous processing, a method using water-based chemicals.

Another thermal platemaking system, using a red-laser diode as the imaging device, uses paper or film-based plates. See **Figure 14-14.** The plate material is supplied in rolls and automatically cut to length after exposure. Developing is performed by an in-line processor. The system is temperature-controlled and the developing chemicals are automatically replenished.

Laser Plates

Laser plates are imaged digitally by a laser platemaking system. Images from the flat or pasted-up material are scanned, and the digitized information is imaged directly to the polyester plate. Each line is exposed to the plate by the laser. Once all of the images of a page are on the plate, the plate is automatically processed. Due to static electricity, some toner is scattered over the plate by the printer. The plate must be cleaned and buffed before it is used on a press.

Photopolymer Plates

The plate material on a *photopolymer plate* is UV photosensitive. Ultraviolet light is used to expose the plate. When exposed, the UV light cross-links the polymers and hardens the image. The unexposed

areas are washed away by either alcohol or water. The plate is post cured in the exposure unit, dried, and then allowed to cool down.

Computer-to-Plate (CTP)

Computer-to-plate (CTP) technology uses a platesetter to accept digital files directly from a computer and then image light-sensitive or heat-sensitive plates. The system is an electronic network that eliminates the use of film as an intermediate, producing plates with high resolution, **Figure 14-15.** A typical CTP system can produce imaged plates with resolutions up to 4000 dots per inch (dpi).

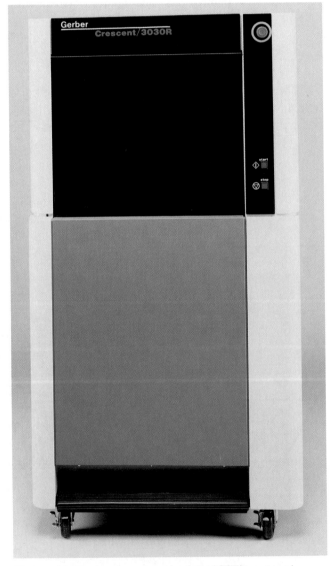

Figure 14-15. A computer-to-plate (CTP) system is used to image high-resolution plates. (Gerber Systems Corporation)

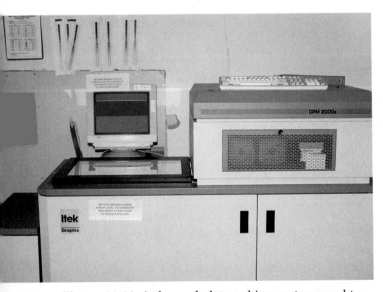

Figure 14-14. A thermal platemaking system used to image plates digitally.

Types of Platesetters

Several different types of platesetters are used in CTP applications. The final image quality is one of the factors to be considered when selecting any of the CTP plate systems. The three basic designs are flatbed, internal drum, and external drum.

Flatbed

On a flatbed unit, the plates are placed on a flat surface and imaged. This system makes it very easy to handle the plates. Usually a single imaging beam is deflected on the surface of the plate by using a rotating mirror. Sometime the bed of the platesetter moves and the line is written on the plate. The mirror remains centered over the plate. Another system requires a stationary flatbed and the imaging beam moves while each line is written to the surface of the plate. Because the mirror pivots, the length of the laser beam changes causing the distance to the plate to vary. To compensate for this, the laser is directed through a special lens, **Figure 14-16.**

Internal drum

The internal drum unit is a partial cylinder, **Figure 14-17.** The plate is placed on the inside of the C-shaped drum. It is held in place with a vacuum drawdown. A rapidly spinning mirror is in the center of the cylinder. As the mirror travels the length of the imaging area, the laser beam is deflected at a 90º angle and the image is written to the plate.

External drum

The external drum system uses a full drum with the plate mounted on the outside of the drum, **Figure 14-18.** The rotation speed of the drum speed depends on the system being used. Parallel to the drum is a multiple-beam laser head. While the drum is rotating, the laser head is moving the distance of the image area. This system does not require the use of a mirror.

CTP Plate Classifications

CTP plates are classified or described based on one of several characteristics: base substrate, emulsion type, exposure effect, exposure spectrum, exposure power, and/or emulsion debris.

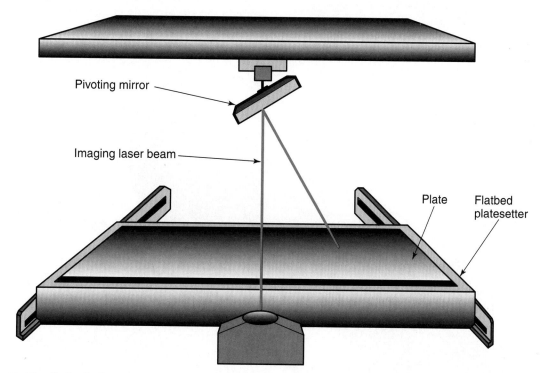

Figure 14-16. The flatbed platesetting system allows for easy plate handling, but the imaging technique limits the width of the imaged area.

laser plates: Carriers that are imaged digitally by a laser platemaking system.

photopolymer plates: Plastic relief plates commonly used in flexographic printing. The surface of a photopolymer plate contains a light-sensitive polymer coating that hardens after exposure.

computer-to-plate (CTP): Imaging systems that expose fully-paginated digital materials to plates in platesetters or imagesetters without creating film intermediates.

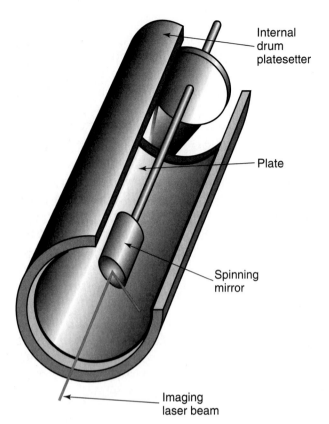

Figure 14-17. An internal drum platesetter uses a spinning mirror to deflect the laser onto the plate.

Base substrate

Base substrate is the material used to make the plate. Metal, polyester, and paper are common types. The most common metal CTP plate is made of aluminum. As in the analog offset plate, it is grained. The ink-receptive areas of the plate are the imaged areas. The metal plates are used for long-run jobs, which can range from hundreds of thousands to millions of copies.

Polyester or plastic plates are often used for runs up 25,000 copies. They are not grained but chemically treated to hold moisture. The plates come in a variety of thicknesses. The thicker plates are commonly used for longer runs.

Paper plates are made using a cellulose material. The plate thickness also varies and the plate is not grained. These plates are chosen for short runs using smaller equipment.

Emulsion types

Plate emulsions are the coatings that are placed on the base substrate. Several emulsions are used to coat the plates. The plate is imaged using a CTP laser with varying wavelengths of emitted light. The application determines what type of laser is used to produce the image.

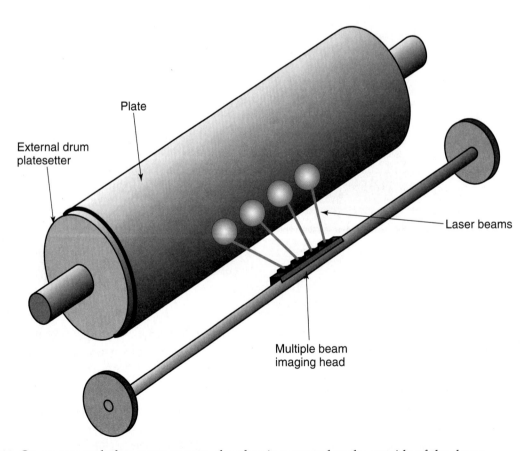

Figure 14-18. On an external platesetter system, the plate is mounted to the outside of the drum.

A silver/silver diffusion coating is made of photosensitive compounds. These are long-run plates. The material removed during processing is treated as hazardous waste. Proper handling of this waste is required by OSHA regulations.

A photopolymer coating made of light-sensitive plastic is used on some plates. This type of coating does not contain silver. These plates are developed in an aqueous solution. This eliminates the problem of hazardous materials. For extended runs, the plates are baked.

Hybrid coating consists of two coatings on a metal plate. The undercoat is a photopolymer and the top coat is photosensitive and made of silver halides. Two exposures are required. The top coat is exposed optically or digitally and the unexposed portion is removed. The remaining area acts as a mask during the next exposure, which requires ultraviolet light. The masked portion is removed during processing and that area becomes the image to be printed. Two hazardous wastes are created during this procedure: silver and photopolymer. Because of this, hybrid coating is not often used.

Thermal plates are coated with special polymers. An infrared laser beam creates heat to cause the necessary reaction to image the plate.

Exposure effect

CTP plates are available as negative- or positive-acting. When using the negative-acting plate, the exposed area of the plate, when processed, attracts ink while the nonimage area attracts moisture. The opposite is true of positive-acting plates.

Exposure spectrum

Portions of the electromagnetic spectrum are used to expose CTP plates. Thermal plates require infrared light for imaging while light-sensitive plates require visible light for imaging. UV-sensitive plates require an ultraviolet source for imaging. Different light wavelengths are needed to properly image the plate.

Exposure power

Various laser light sources have been identified and now the power required to image each type of emulsion is very important. Two types of emulsion are used on the plates. One is fast emulsion and the other is slow emulsion. The slow emulsion requires much more energy than the fast emulsion. The time factor may be very important in the production environment.

Emulsion Debris

With some types of plates, after imaging, the coating on the plate must be removed. This coating left on the plate is referred to as debris. Some types of CTP plates do not have debris left on the surface of the plate after imaging. The debris or no-debris forming plates are classified in three ways: ablation plates, controlled ablation plates, and nonablation plates.

After imaging, an ablation plate will contain debris from the areas that were removed. Before printing from an ablation plate, the debris must be washed away.

A controlled ablation plate also contains debris from the imaging process on the plate. However, with this process, a fountain solution helps dissolve the debris and ink rollers remove it from the plate. The material is deposited on the paper during the first revolutions of the printing process.

Nonablation plates, when imaged, do not leave debris on the plate, eliminating some environmental concerns.

Processless CTP Plates

As the name implies, processless CTP plates do not require chemical processing. The process is environmentally friendly and saves money even though the processless CTP plates are more expensive. The purchase of chemical processing equipment is no longer required. The balancing of the fountain solution requires some press adjustments. Since these plates are relatively new, further development is taking place.

Ink-Jet Plates

This type of plate does not require any form of exposure. The ink jets spray a special ink on the plate to form the image. The information from a digital file determines proper imaging transfer. These plates can be used immediately after imaging. The ink-jet platesetter is less expensive than the laser or thermal systems.

Waterless Plates

Waterless plates are presensitized plates that use an ink-repellent substance instead of water to separate the nonimage area from the image area. Waterless plates are manufactured as both

waterless plates: Presensitized plates that use an ink-repellent substance other than water to separate the nonimage area from the image area.

negative-acting and positive-acting plates. They are designed to be used on a lithographic press without a dampening solution.

The nonimage area of the plate is covered with an ink-repellent silicone rubber layer, while the image area is slightly recessed and coated with an ink-receptive polymer. The plate is designed differently from a conventional lithographic plate, **Figure 14-19.**

Plate exposure is done using conventional vacuum frames and light sources. After the plate is exposed, it is ready for processing. Silicone rubber repels ink so fountain solution is not necessary to keep the nonimage area clean. Special chemicals are used to process the plate. Although the surface is resistant to oxidation, the plate should be cleaned and stored with a protective sheet to prevent scratching.

Waterless printing requires the use of special inks which are thicker than conventional lithographic inks. While on the press, the ink is cooled to maintain an optimal viscosity level. Waterless plates are recyclable and are treated the same as conventional aluminum plates for recycling.

An aqueous plate is exposed to a light source and is then developed in a water-based solution, rather than with a solvent-based solution. Many water-based solutions are safe to dispose of in the sewer system. However, approval is necessary when disposing of any substance into the sewage system from the facility.

Processed-on-Press

One of the newest types of surface plates is processed-on-press. The plate is exposed and then mounted on the press. When the plate comes in contact with the fountain solution, the plate is developed. After several revolutions, the dampening solution reacts with the coating on the nonimage

areas of the plate. The plate is now developed and the printing process begins.

Electrostatic Plates

Electrostatic plates are light-sensitive plates that are imaged by a charge of electrostatic energy. When the plate is exposed and light strikes the nonimage area, the positive charge is eliminated from that area. The image area remains positively charged and receptive to ink. A negatively charged resin powder is then applied to the image area and fused. Electrostatic platemakers are designed to process electrostatic plates automatically.

COMPUTER-TO-PRESS SYSTEMS

First, the use of film was eliminated, and now the plate is being eliminated to create an image on a substrate. The image is placed directly on the cylinder. One system allows the cylinder to be removed when the product is printed. The image is then removed and the cylinder is used again for another printing job. Cylinders can be reimaged many times.

A typical computer-to-press network includes a digital color-proofing system and an electronic color correction system. A color proof is a prepress version of the final printed product. After a proof of the design is produced and evaluated, electronic color correction can be used to adjust the computer file before the file is sent to the imagesetter and the image carrier is made.

The use of computer-to-press technology is becoming commonplace in the graphic communications industry. By eliminating the use of film negatives and

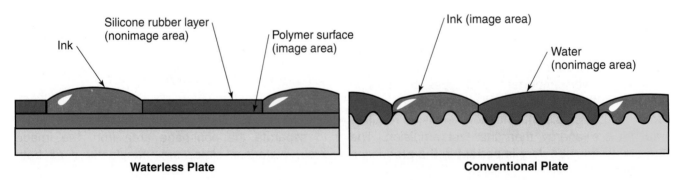

Figure 14-19. A comparison between a waterless plate and a conventional lithographic plate. Waterless plates are designed with an ink-repellent substance other than water to form the nonimage area. The image area is slightly below the nonimage area and is receptive to ink. (Polychrome Corporation)

ACADEMIC LINK
Coulomb's Law

In the field of electrostatics, Coulomb's Law is one of the principle foundations. French physicist Charles Augustin de Coulomb published some of his research and experiments in 1785, which included electrostatic forces. The force between positively and negatively charged items will either repel (two positives or two negatives) or attract (one positive and one negative) and is affected by the distance between the charged items.

The electrical force between two objects can be measured using the following equation:

$$F = k\ \frac{(q1 \times q2)}{r^2}$$

To find the electrical force (F), multiply the charge of the first object (q1) with the charge of the second object (q2), divide the product by the distance between the objects squared (r^2), and multiply the result with the constant value (k).

Coulomb's Law also has applications outside the field of electrostatics. Because protons have a positive charge and electrons have a negative charge, Coulomb's Law explains how atoms bind together to form molecules. Coulomb's Law also applies when studying crystal structures. Crystals are composed of charged particles called ions, which arrange themselves in such a way that the charges are balanced.

flats and by outputting plates directly from a computer, computer-to-press presents several advantages over traditional platemaking, including higher productivity and better image quality.

PLATEMAKING VARIABLES

The materials and equipment used in traditional platemaking systems must be properly applied to ensure the quality of a plate. Electronic platemaking and CTP systems have eliminated many of the variables commonly encountered in manual platemaking, but traditional methods continue to be used and have a critical effect on image quality.

Using Equipment

Selecting the correct equipment is one of the most important steps in the platemaking process. The components of a platemaker must be used properly when imaging plates.

A good vacuum frame is essential for proper drawdown. This creates firm, even contact between the plate and the flat. The vacuum frame must also be located at the right distance from the light source to ensure proper exposure. If the frame is too close to the light source, the plate may be overexposed. When the distance between the frame and the light source is too great, underexposure may occur.

Contact is an important variable to be considered in using the vacuum frame. When exposing the plate, it is essential that the flat be in firm, even contact with the plate. A soft, pliable vacuum blanket assists in ensuring good contact. If good contact is not made, the image will be larger than the original because light will escape under the edges and expose the plate. Film that is improperly stripped on the flat or that has an excessive amount of tape may also cause poor contact, **Figure 14-20.**

Soft Image

One of the most frequent problems affecting the quality of a plate is a *soft image*. This occurs when the outside edges of an image contain less density or tone quality than the inside portion of the image. A soft image is a common problem when working with halftones. In a soft image, the dots making up the image appear to be vignetted. A *vignette* is a photograph in which the background color gradually decreases in strength toward the edge.

To process a good lithographic plate, the flat must be of high quality. It is imperative that the film intermediate closely represent the original copy.

The softness of an image can be checked with darkfield illumination. This technique involves viewing the intermediate image with a black background and a light source. If the intermediate image has a dense center and there is less density around the edges, a soft image will commonly result.

electrostatic plates: Light-sensitive plates that are imaged by a charge of electrostatic energy.

soft image: A loss of image that occurs when the outside edges of an image contain less density or tone quality than that of the inside portion of the image.

vignette: Pictorial material (photograph) in which the background color gradually decreases in strength toward the edge until it appears as the stock.

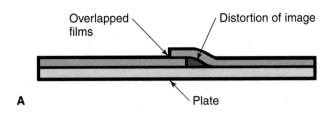

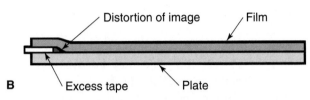

Figure 14-20. An improperly stripped flat can result in poor contact with the plates. A—Overlapped film causes a distorted image to result. B—An excess of tape prevents complete contact between the film and the plate.

Summary

The making and the processing of the plates has changed dramatically in recent years. EPA regulations have compelled manufacturers to make the total process more environmentally friendly. The material used for the base of lithographic plates has not changed much. Many printing plants now use computer-to-plate technology.

Review Questions

Please do not write in this text. Write your answers on a separate sheet of paper.

1. Explain the process of lithographic printing.
2. A _____ is used to provide contact between the plate and the original image for exposure on a platemaker.
3. True or False? Automatic plate processing eliminates the need to process plates by hand.
4. What are the three parts of a lithographic plate?
5. Name two types of mechanical grain applied to plates.
6. Name two types of plate coatings.
7. Plates that are manufactured with a light-sensitive material to capture images are _____.
8. When a positive-acting plate is exposed, the area struck by light becomes the _____ area.
9. Name three methods for attaching plates to a cylinder.
10. Thermal plates can be imaged _____ or _____ through the use of heat.

11. Which type of platemaking system scans images as digital data and transfers them directly to the plate?
12. List the types of platesetters used in CTP systems.
13. Name three types of base substrates.
14. Which plate has a coating of resin powder applied to its surface?
    a. Waterless.
    b. Silver halide.
    c. Diazo.
    d. Electrostatic.
15. A(n) _____ is a condition in which the outside edges of an image contain less density than that of the inside portion of the image.

Suggested Activities

1. Choose one of the many types of printing plates, and write a paper describing, in detail, the method used to create images on a carrier.
2. If you do not have a CTP system in your school, go with your class to a plant that has a system. Ask about changes that had to be made from the standpoint of production and personnel knowledge.
3. Make a flowchart of the workflow commonly used in one of the platemaking systems.
4. Trace the changes from the first known planographic carrier to present day systems.

Related Web Links

Fine Print Knowledge Center
www.fineprintschool.com/articles/offset-lithography
An online guide to print and design

The Imaging Network
imagingnetworkonline.com/pages/scrap.html
Online source for information about aluminum recycling.

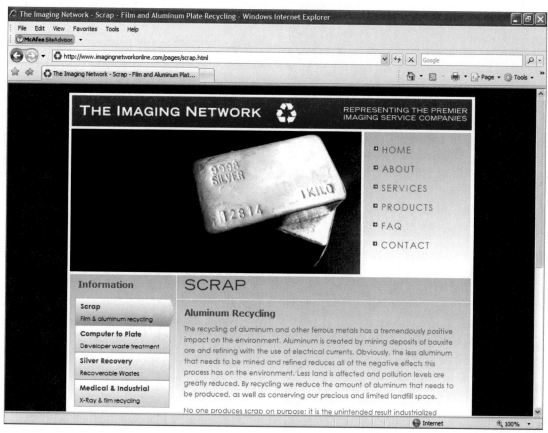

All facets of the graphic communications industry are working to become more environmentally friendly. Web sites contain information about companies who are dedicated to finding new ways to achieve this goal.

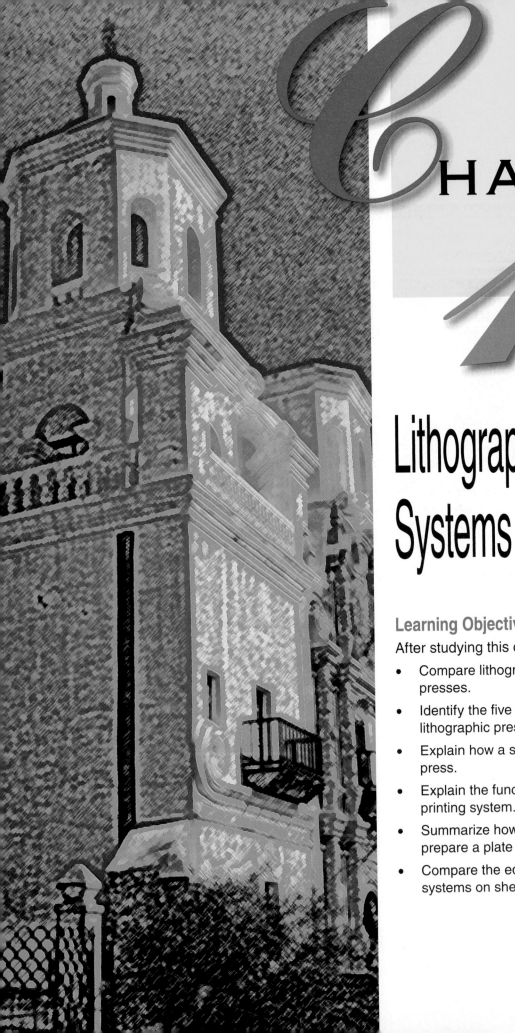

CHAPTER 15

Lithographic Press Systems

Learning Objectives

After studying this chapter, you will be able to:

- Compare lithographic sheet-fed and web-fed presses.

- Identify the five fundamental systems used in a lithographic press.

- Explain how a substrate travels through the press.

- Explain the function of each press cylinder in a printing system.

- Summarize how dampening and inking systems prepare a plate for printing.

- Compare the equipment used by delivery systems on sheet-fed and web-fed presses.

Important Terms

blanket cylinder	perfecting press
brake mechanism	pH scale
brush system	pH value
common impression	plate cylinder
cylinder	printing system
dampening system	register unit
delivery pile	sheet separators
delivery system	sheet-fed press
double-sheet detector	sucker feet
feeding system	two-cylinder printing
flying splicer	system
former board	undercut
impression cylinder	waterless press
inking and dampening	web splicer
system	web-break detector
inking system	web-fed press
molleton cover	zero-speed splicer

This chapter covers the different types of presses and press operations used in printing operations. It will introduce the five fundamental systems of a press and explain how each system functions. The next chapter covers the operation of offset presses.

LITHOGRAPHIC PRESSES

Lithography is a process of printing or transferring images from one surface to another. The lithographic system of printing from plates on a press is commonly referred to as an offset or indirect method. In the operation of a lithographic press, the image on a plate is offset from one cylinder to another, **Figure 15-1.**

During the traditional printing process, the plate is dampened and then inked. The plate has an image area that accepts ink and repels water and a nonimage area that accepts water and repels ink. This design is based on the principle that ink, a grease-based substance, does not mix readily with water; ink adheres to the image area only. When the plate is placed on a press, the image in ink is transferred from the plate cylinder to a blanket, which in turn transfers the image to the substrate, **Figure 15-2.** Waterless lithographic plate printing will be covered at end of the chapter.

Because the image is printed directly, or mirrored, from the plate to the blanket, it appears in reverse form on the blanket. When the image is offset again from the blanket to the substrate, it returns to its original form as it appears on the plate.

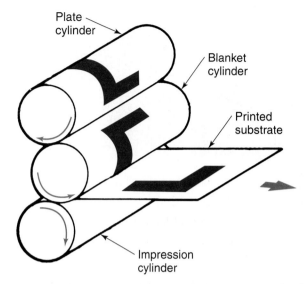

Figure 15-1. Offset lithographic printing is a method of transferring an image from one press cylinder to another.

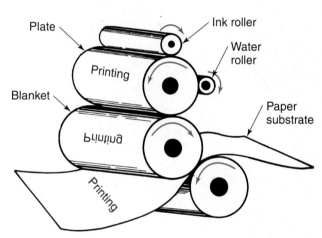

Figure 15-2. In offset lithography, the plate is dampened with water and then inked. The inked image is offset from the plate to the blanket, which then transfers the image to the paper substrate. (A.B. Dick Company)

Lithographic presses are classified as either sheet-fed presses or web-fed presses, based on how paper is fed through the system, **Figure 15-3.**

A *sheet-fed press* prints on individual sheets of paper as they are drawn through the system. Sheets are removed from a stack, one at a time, and fed through the press, **Figure 15-4.**

A *web-fed press* prints on one long, continuous web of paper that is drawn into the press from a roll. As the roll unwinds, images are printed on the web and the entire length of paper winds through the press, **Figure 15-5.**

sheet-fed press: A lithographic press that prints paper one sheet at a time as it is fed through the system.

web-fed press: A lithographic press that prints with one long, continuous web of paper that is fed from a roll.

Paper
stack

Registration unit

Delivery
unit

Feeding
unit

Printing
unit

Sheet-fed press

Paper roll (web)

Registration
unit

Drying
unit

Delivery
unit

Feeding
unit

Printing
unit

Sheeting
unit

Web-fed Press

Figure 15-3. A comparison of sheet-fed and web-fed press designs.

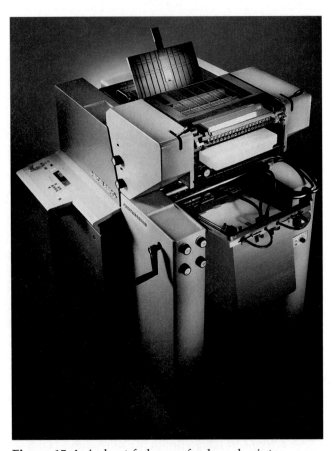

Figure 15-4. A sheet-fed press feeds and prints paper one sheet at a time. (Heidelberg USA)

Figure 15-5. A web-fed press prints on a continuous roll of paper, called a web, that feeds through the entire system. (Heidelberg USA)

The components making up each press system vary, depending on the design of the press. Each system must be working properly for the press to accurately print images on the substrate.

The feeding system is the mechanism that sends the substrate into the press. The printing system consists of the equipment used to offset the image from the plate to the substrate. The dampening system feeds water or fountain solution to the plate. The inking system feeds ink to the plate. The delivery system removes the paper from the press and stacks it for finishing operations.

Each system in the operation will be explored during the remainder of this chapter.

LITHOGRAPHIC PRESS SYSTEMS

The operation of a lithographic press is divided into five systems, each of which performs a basic function. The five basic press systems are the feeding system, printing system, dampening system, inking system, and delivery system, **Figure 15-6.**

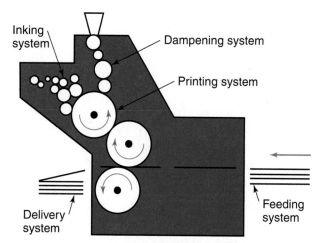

Figure 15-6. Five basic systems are used in the operation of a lithographic press.

FEEDING SYSTEMS

Paper is fed, printed, and delivered differently depending on the type of press used. *Feeding systems*, discussed next, are classified as sheet-feeding systems or web-feeding systems.

Sheet-Feeding Systems

On a sheet-fed press, sheets of paper are typically stacked on a feeding platform and removed one at a time by the press. Printing duplicators and presses are now equipped with automatic feeders to operate at high production speeds. The feeding system is divided into three operations. A stack of paper is placed by hand on the feeding platform, which serves as a guide for feeding each sheet into the press separately. Air-producing sheet separators positioned along the upper edges of the paper stack are used to separate the top sheet from the rest of the pile. Each sheet is then transported to the register unit, which positions, or registers, the paper for insertion to the press. This process is known as successive sheet-feeding. No two sheets overlap when they are fed, as shown in **Figure 15-7A.**

Some presses allow sheets to partially overlap when paper enters the press. This method, known as stream feeding, is typically used with high-speed presses, **Figure 15-7B.**

Some sheet-feeding systems are classified as continuous-feeding. A press equipped with a continuous-feeding system remains running while the platform is reloaded with paper. This system increases production since the press does not need to be stopped for reloading.

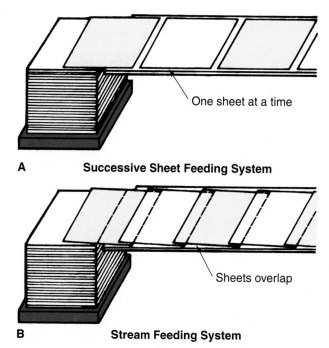

A   **Successive Sheet Feeding System**

B   **Stream Feeding System**

Figure 15-7. Sheet-fed presses can use a successive sheet feeding system or a stream feeding system. A—In successive feeding, one sheet at a time is fed through the press. B—Stream feeding allows sheets to partially overlap when they are fed, resulting in faster press speeds.

In general, if the paper is positioned properly on the platform and aligned with the feeding system, the sheets will be fed correctly, without causing a jam or misfeed. Any variation in the system could force the operator to stop the press. Most manufacturers of stock provide instruction for stacking different grades of paper.

When the press is running, the paper stack must remain at a certain height on the platform for best operation. Operating height can be monitored manually or with a control device. Some feeding systems contain gauges that provide readings on operating heights.

Sheet Separation

Sheets are separated on the platform using air nozzles called *sheet separators*. The air from the nozzles is directed toward the edges of the paper to separate the sheets. This system ensures the top sheet of the stack is picked up and transferred to the next press operation, **Figure 15-8.**

feeding system: A press system that transfers individual sheets of paper to the press and places them in register.

sheet separators: Air-producing devices that separate the top sheet from the rest of the pile in a feeding system.

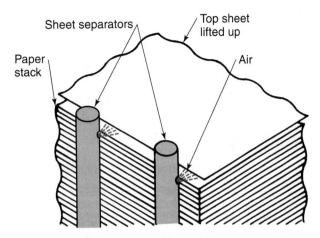

Figure 15-8. Sheet separators provide a flow of air to help guide one sheet at a time into the press.

The location of sheet separators depends on the design of the press. Sheet separators are most often located near the lead edges of the stack or on the sides. Sheet separation may also be aided by the use of thin brass or spring-steel devices known as fingers, **Figure 15-9.**

Paper is aligned on the platform by sheet guides. These are located on the sides and rear edges of the stack. Rear guides are usually weighted to assist in guiding only one sheet at a time.

Sheet Transfer

Sheets are commonly transferred from the stack and fed to the press by *sucker feet*. Sucker feet create a vacuum that removes sheets and positions them for access to the press-feeding pullout rollers. On smaller presses, the sucker feet are positioned at the leading edge of the sheet, **Figure 15-10.** Sucker feet may also be located at the rear edges of a sheet. The rear feet draw the paper forward to the pullout rollers, **Figure 15-11.**

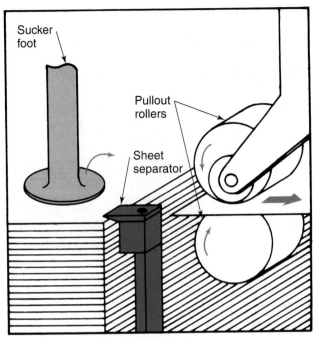

Figure 15-10. Sucker feet are used to lift and guide sheets of paper to the pullout rollers in a feeding system.

The amount of vacuum provided by sucker feet must be adjusted for each type of stock. A typical sheet-fed press equipped with sucker feet is shown in **Figure 15-12.**

Once a sheet is directed to the pullout rollers by the sucker feet, it is guided to the register unit for entry to the press. To ensure only one sheet passes through, all presses are equipped with a control device called a *double-sheet detector*. Double-sheet detectors sense paper thickness. When the sensor detects excess thickness, indicating multiple sheets, it activates a solenoid. The solenoid opens a deflector plate for removal of the sheets, **Figure 15-13.**

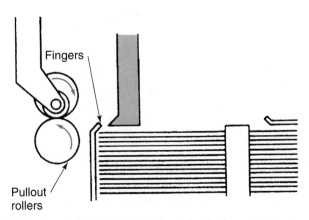

Figure 15-9. Fingers are devices that help separate sheets for feeding.

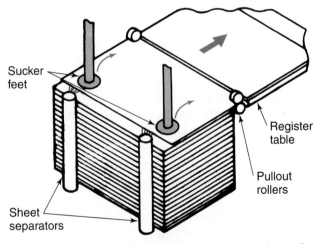

Figure 15-11. Sucker feet located at the rear edges of the paper draw sheets forward from the stack.

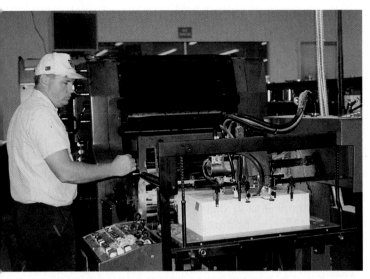

Figure 15-12. A typical sheet-fed press equipped with sucker feet to feed paper for printing.

Register Unit

A *register unit* is a mechanism that aligns the sheet for printing. Proper registration of the paper is critical to the operation of the press. Register units vary in design, but they must provide a means to feed the paper and align it in the same position for printing each time. Joggers are used to move the stock to the side guides. The most common register units have side guides for positioning, **Figure 15-14.**

The register unit consists of a register table that carries each sheet to the register stop, where paper is aligned with the printing system of the press. The register table uses conveyor tapes to carry sheets of paper to the register stop for entry to the press.

When a sheet of paper is fed through the register unit, it comes into contact with the register stop. The paper is then aligned square with the printing system, ready to be captured by the grippers on the impression cylinder, **Figure 15-15.**

Web-Feeding Systems

The feeding system on a web-fed press is designed differently from the system used on a sheet-fed press. Printing on a web-fed press is done on a continuous roll of paper that winds through a series of rollers, **Figure 15-16.**

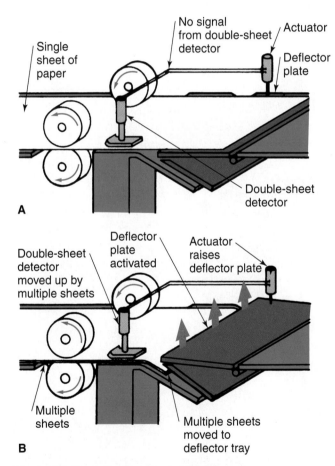

Figure 15-13. A double-sheet detector senses paper thickness as sheets are fed through the system. A—When a single sheet is fed, the detector remains inactive. B—When it senses excess thickness, the detector activates the deflector plate for removal of the paper.

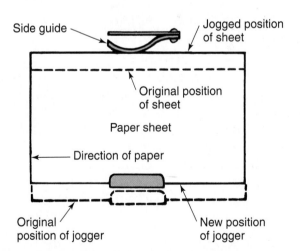

Figure 15-14. Joggers move paper into position against the side guides when it is fed to the register unit.

sucker feet: Devices that provide a vacuum to remove sheets from a stack and position them for access to the press.

double-sheet detector: A control device that prevents more than one sheet of paper from entering the press.

register unit: A feeding system mechanism that places paper in register for printing on a press.

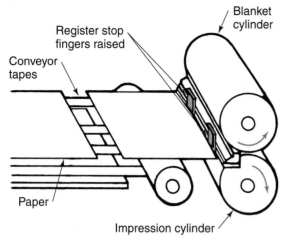

Figure 15-15. The register stop places paper in register, ready to pass through the printing system.

Figure 15-16. Paper travels through a web-fed press as one continuous web. The web winds through a series of rollers as it is printed. (Tensor Group, Inc.)

The movement of paper through a web-fed press is controlled by a paper tension device. Since a continuous web of paper is fed through the press, its tension must be closely regulated. Improper web tension can alter the registration of paper and affect print quality. In some cases, improper tension can cause the web to break, forcing shutdown of the press.

A **brake mechanism** is one of the most commonly used tension control devices on a web-fed press, **Figure 15-17.** The brake mechanism is attached to the paper roll and is designed to produce a slight amount of friction, or drag, on the web.

Web Splicer

When a new roll of paper replaces an existing roll while the press is running, a **web splicer** splices, or bonds, the end of the existing roll to the start of the new roll. Splicing allows the web to remain intact while it is being printed. Webs must be spliced accurately;

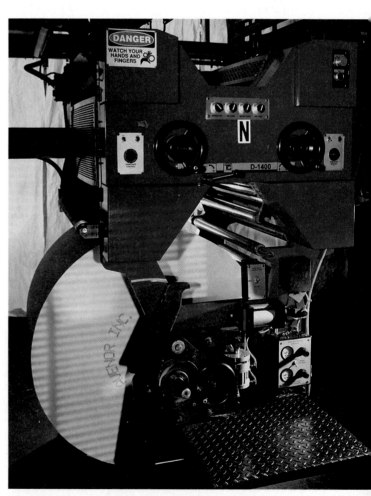

Figure 15-17. A brake mechanism provides the correct tension as the web is fed from the roll on a web-fed press unit like this one. (Tensor Group, Inc.)

an improper paper splice could cause a web break. Two types of web splicers commonly used are the zero-speed splicer and the flying splicer.

A *zero-speed splicer* uses a set of rollers called a festoon to draw out slack from the web before a splice is made. The festoon unit allows the new roll to be spliced to the old one while the press uses up the slack, **Figure 15-18.** When a splice is made, the two paper rolls are stopped, but the press continues to run from the web stored on the festoon.

The festoon rollers move up and down during the press run. As the web is fed through the press, the festoon unit draws out slack and moves up. When the web roll runs out of paper, the web rollers are stopped, and the festoon unit moves down to feed the press. The end of the new roll can then be taped to the end of the old roll. After the splice is made, the new roll is rotated up to speed before the paper from the festoon rollers is used up, keeping the press in operation.

A *flying splicer* is a device that bonds a new roll of paper to the existing web without stopping any operations

on the press. Neither web roll is stopped while the splice is made. The process is illustrated in **Figure 15-19.** An adhesive, such as double-sided tape, is applied to the end of the new web to make the splice.

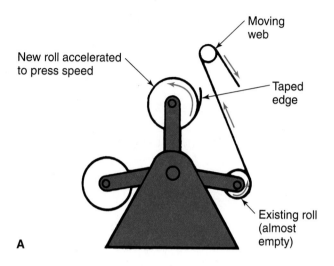

A

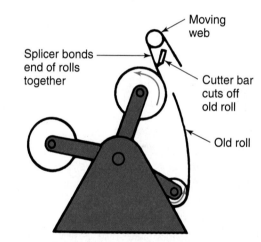

B

Figure 15-19. A flying splicer allows the press to remain in operation when a new roll is spliced to the moving web. A—When the existing roll of paper is nearly used up, the new roll is accelerated to the speed of the press. Double-sided tape is applied to the end of the new roll to make the splice. B—The splicer rotates the new roll to meet the moving web and cuts away the old roll. The new roll is then moved into operating position.

brake mechanism: A tension control device designed to produce a slight amount of drag on the web as it travels through a web-fed press.

web splicer: A device used to bond a new roll to the end of an existing web on a web-fed press.

zero-speed splicer: A splicer unit on a web-fed system that uses a set of festoon rollers to draw out slack from the web and feed the press while a splice is being made.

flying splicer: A splicer unit that bonds a new web to the existing web without stopping any operations on a web-fed press.

Figure 15-18. This web-fed press is equipped with a zero-speed splicer unit. The unit contains festoon rollers that allow web slack to build up for use on the press when a new web is attached and a splice is made.

When the existing web roll is nearly empty, the splicing unit rotates the new roll toward the existing roll and accelerates it to match the speed of the moving web. When the new web meets the moving web, the two ends are spliced together and the old web is cut. The new web becomes the moving web and is rotated into the running position previously occupied by the old web.

Web-Break Detector

A **web-break detector** is a device that automatically shuts down the press if the web snaps or tears. Modern web-fed presses operate at tremendous speeds. A web break can be disastrous, causing the incoming ribbon of paper to jam and wrap around the printing rollers, severely damaging the press.

A web-break detector uses a sensor to detect a break in the web. If a break occurs, the detector will kill power to the press instantly. It will also activate a mechanism that cuts off the incoming web before it reaches the printing system, preventing any incoming paper from entering the press.

PRINTING SYSTEMS

The **printing system** of a lithographic press consists of a group of cylinders that transfer images from the printing plate to the substrate. The components of a printing system are the plate cylinder, the blanket cylinder, and the impression cylinder, **Figure 15-20.**

The printing system accepts paper from the feeding system and uses the dampening and inking systems to print images from the plate. On an offset press, images are offset from the plate cylinder to the blanket cylinder, and then offset again as paper contacts the impression cylinder.

Three-Cylinder Printing System

The three-cylinder printing system has a plate cylinder, a blanket cylinder, and an impression cylinder. Each cylinder has a specific task. The purpose of each cylinder is discussed next.

Plate Cylinder

The **plate cylinder** holds the printing plate on the press. The components of a plate cylinder include the body, bearers, bearings, and a gear that drives the cylinder, **Figure 15-21.**

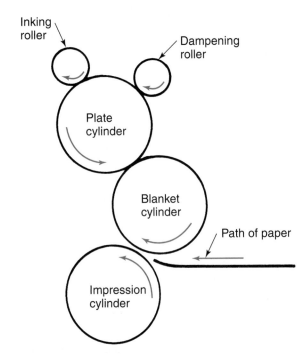

Figure 15-20. The three components that make up a printing system are the plate cylinder, the blanket cylinder, and the impression cylinder.

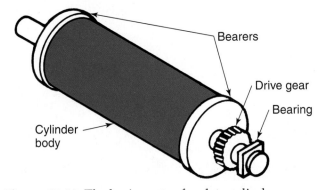

Figure 15-21. The basic parts of a plate cylinder.

A plate cylinder has a series of clamps that hold the plate in place. As discussed in Chapter 14, plates are classified as serrated, straight, or pin bar, **Figure 15-22.** The cylinder clamps are used to tighten or loosen the plates. Proper tension must exist between the plate and the plate cylinder. Excessive tension can place too much stress on the plate and cause it to crack or tear. Insufficient tension can affect registration and print quality.

The vertical space that lies between the surface of the plate cylinder bearers and the cylinder body is known as the **undercut**, **Figure 15-23.** The undercut allows for the thickness of the plate and packing. The size of the undercut can be determined by measuring the difference between the diameter of the cylinder bearers and the diameter of the cylinder

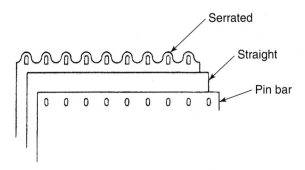

Figure 15-22. Different attaching methods for plates.

Serrated

Straight

Pin bar

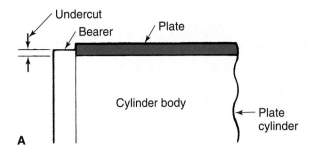

A

Undercut

Bearer

Plate

Cylinder body

Plate cylinder

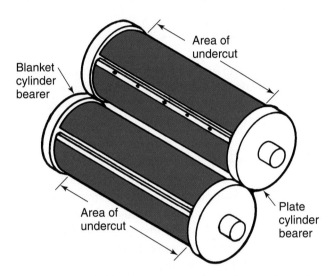

Blanket cylinder bearer

Area of undercut

Area of undercut

Plate cylinder bearer

Figure 15-23. Cylinder surfaces are undercut from the bearers to allow for plate and blanket thickness and packing.

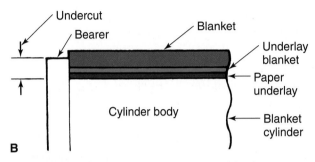

B

Undercut

Bearer

Blanket

Underlay blanket

Paper underlay

Cylinder body

Blanket cylinder

Figure 15-24. The undercut of a plate or blanket cylinder is equal to the difference between the diameter of the bearers and the diameter of the cylinder body. A—The plate cylinder body is undercut to allow for the thickness of the plate and packing. B—The blanket cylinder is undercut to allow for blanket thicknesses and packing.

body, **Figure 15-24.** Undercut can also be measured with a cylinder packing gauge, **Figure 15-25.**

Since the bearers of the cylinders ride on each other, the plate and blanket cylinders are commonly packed to achieve proper image transfer. The size of the undercut is usually stamped on the cylinder body.

Blanket Cylinder

The *blanket cylinder* holds the image-receptive blanket on the press and acts as an intermediate between the plate cylinder and the impression cylinder. During printing, the blanket receives the image in reverse from the plate and then offsets the image to the substrate in its original orientation.

The blanket cylinder consists of the same components as the plate cylinder. The blanket cylinder body holds the blanket in place with a set of clamps. Blankets are elastic and are designed to stretch around the cylinder. Blanket surfaces are commonly made of rubber and supported by a woven cloth base, **Figure 15-26.**

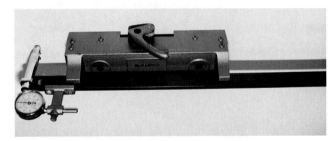

Figure 15-25. A cylinder packing gauge can be used to measure the amount of undercut on a press cylinder.

web-break detector: A device that automatically shuts down the press if the web snaps or tears.

printing system: A group of cylinders used to transfer images from the printing plate to the substrate. In a lithographic press, the printing system consists of a plate cylinder, a blanket cylinder, and an impression cylinder.

plate cylinder: A printing system component that holds the plate on the press.

undercut: The vertical distance between the surface of the cylinder bearers and the cylinder body. The undercut allows for the thickness of the plate or blanket and packing.

blanket cylinder: A printing system component that holds the image-receptive blanket on the press and receives the image from the plate cylinder.

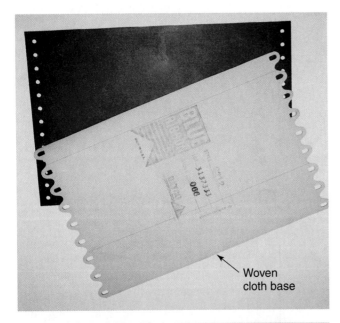

Woven
cloth base

Rubber
surface

Figure 15-26. Press blankets stretch to fit the blanket cylinder. The resilient surface of the blanket accepts the inked image from the plate.

Blanket sizes vary, depending on the size of the press. Like the plate cylinder, the blanket cylinder is also undercut. The undercut allows for blanket thickness and packing between the cylinders.

Impression Cylinder

The *impression cylinder* brings the stock to be printed into contact with the blanket cylinder. As paper travels between the impression cylinder and the blanket cylinder, the image is transferred from the blanket to the paper. The impression cylinder carries the substrate from the feeding system to the delivery system, **Figure 15-27.**

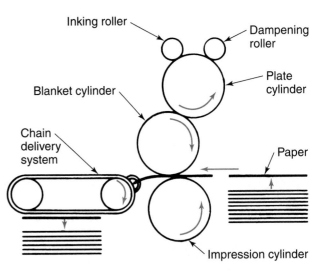

Figure 15-27. The impression cylinder brings the paper into contact with the blanket cylinder and provides the pressure needed to offset the image. (A.B. Dick Company)

The impression cylinder serves as the base component of a three-cylinder system. It applies the pressure needed to transfer the image from the blanket cylinder to the substrate. As paper passes between the cylinders, the impression cylinder must provide the correct amount of gap between the paper and the blanket to make the impression.

Two-Cylinder Printing System

Most presses operate with a three-cylinder printing system, but other systems are also used. A *two-cylinder printing system* is a press design that combines the printing operations of the plate cylinder and impression cylinder into one cylinder, **Figure 15-28.**

A combination cylinder serves as the main cylinder. It is twice the circumference of the blanket cylinder. When each impression is made, the blanket cylinder revolves twice, while the combination cylinder revolves once. The combination cylinder performs two operations as it revolves. In the first half of the turn, the image is offset from the plate segment of the cylinder to the blanket cylinder. In the second half of the turn, paper contacts the impression segment of the cylinder and the blanket cylinder and accepts the image.

Perfecting Press

A *perfecting press* is a printing system that prints both sides of the substrate simultaneously. As shown in **Figure 15-29,** the perfecting press consists of two

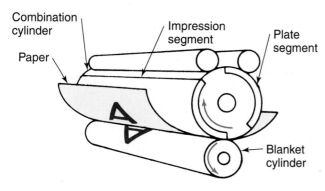

Figure 15-28. A two-cylinder printing system combines the plate and impression segments of the press into one cylinder. (A.B. Dick Company)

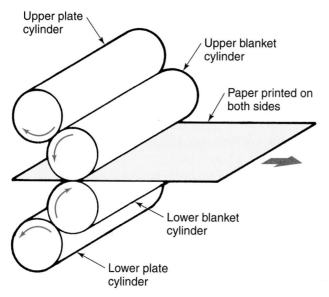

Figure 15-29. A perfecting press is equipped with two plate cylinders and two blanket cylinders to print both sides of the substrate simultaneously.

plate cylinders and two blanket cylinders. The pairs of cylinders are arranged above and below the path of the substrate. As the substrate comes into contact with both blanket cylinders, the upper cylinder prints one side of the substrate, while the lower cylinder prints the other side.

Common Impression Cylinder

A *common impression cylinder* is a press design commonly used for multicolor printing on web-fed presses. One large impression cylinder is central to the printing system, **Figure 15-30.** The cylinder is surrounded by a group of printing units. Each unit consists of a plate cylinder, a blanket cylinder, and inking and dampening systems. Each printing unit prints a separate color on the web as

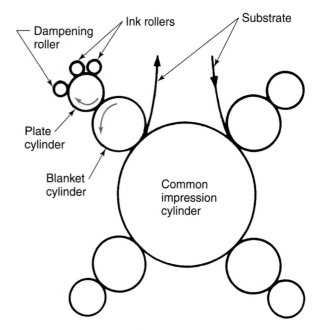

Figure 15-30. A common impression cylinder joined with a group of printing units is typically used for multicolor printing on a web-fed press.

it travels between the blanket cylinders and the common impression cylinder.

DAMPENING SYSTEMS

A *dampening system* is a group of rollers designed to apply moisture to the nonimage area of the plate. Before the plate is inked, the nonimage area is coated with fountain solution to separate it from the image area. When the plate is inked, only the image area is receptive to ink; the nonimage area repels ink.

The two most common types of dampening systems used on a press are the conventional dampening system and the continuous dampening system.

impression cylinder: A printing system component that brings the paper to be printed in contact with the blanket cylinder.

two-cylinder printing system: A press system that combines the printing operations of the plate cylinder and impression cylinder into one.

perfecting press: printing system that prints both sides of the substrate at once.

common impression cylinder: A web-fed press design in which one cylinder is surrounded by a group of printing units.

dampening system: A group of rollers designed to apply moisture to the nonimage area of the printing plate.

Conventional Dampening System

A conventional dampening system uses a series of rollers to distribute fountain solution from the fountain to the plate when the plate is positioned on the press. The basic components of a conventional dampening system are a dampening fountain, a fountain roller, a ductor roller, a distributor roller, and a form roller, **Figure 15-31.**

During the printing process, fountain solution is supplied to the dampening fountain by a bottle or similar reservoir. To keep the solution at the same level, many presses use a bottle that works by gravity feed to refill the fountain.

The fountain roller revolves in the fountain to draw out the solution. It transfers the fountain solution to the ductor roller, which moves back and forth, making intermittent contact with the fountain roller. The movement of the ductor roller controls the amount of fountain solution that is transferred to the rest of the system. Refer again to Figure 15-31.

The ductor roller is often covered with a *molleton cover*, a cloth tube that fits over the body of the roller. See **Figure 15-32.** Because water is not easily absorbed by the surface of a roller, the molleton cover keeps the ductor roller coated with fountain solution. Molleton covers help absorb and transfer the solution.

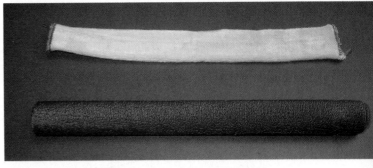

Figure 15-32. Molleton covers are used with dampening rollers to absorb and retain fountain solution as it is transferred to the plate.

As the ductor roller rotates, it carries the fountain solution to the distributor roller. The distributor roller is used to spread the solution evenly across the rollers and prepare the solution for placement on the plate. The number of distributor rollers used in a dampening system varies. Distributor rollers are classified as rotating rollers and oscillating rollers. Rotating rollers turn steadily in one direction to distribute the solution. Oscillating rollers move from side to side while rotating to achieve a more even distribution of the fountain solution.

The distributor roller transfers the solution to the form roller, which applies the solution to the plate. Different systems may use one or more form rollers and typically use a molleton cover to retain moisture.

Dampening system rollers should be regularly cleaned and adjusted to ensure the correct levels of pressure exist between each roller. Excessive pressure between the rollers can cause the rollers and plate surfaces to wear prematurely. Molleton covers must also be cleaned and rinsed thoroughly on a regular basis to remain effective.

Continuous Dampening System

A continuous dampening system is a system of rollers that distributes a continuous flow of fountain solution to the plate. This system eliminates the ductor roller, **Figure 15-33.** A transfer roller used in place of the ductor roller makes direct contact with the fountain roller to distribute the solution.

A metering roller is commonly used in a continuous dampening system. It serves the same purpose as the fountain roller but can be adjusted to control the flow of solution when it makes contact with the transfer roller. This presents an advantage over other dampening systems by allowing the

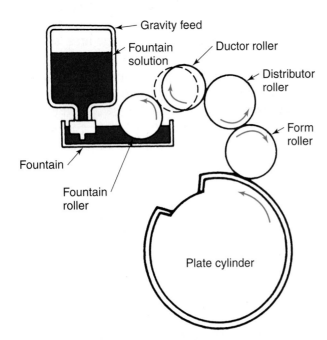

Figure 15-31. In a conventional dampening system, rollers are used to carry fountain solution from a fountain to the plate.

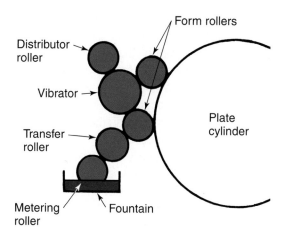

Figure 15-33. A continuous dampening system applies moisture to the plate with a continuous alignment of rollers. A transfer roller carries fountain solution from a metering roller to the rest of the system.

system to respond quickly to changes in fountain settings. When the press is in operation, the operator can adjust the flow of solution if there is not enough reaching the plate.

A *brush system* is a continuous dampening system that uses a brush roller to transfer solution from the fountain roller to the rest of the system. The brush roller is used in place of a transfer roller to control the flow of solution, **Figure 15-34.** The brush roller draws solution from the fountain roller and spreads it accurately to a distributor roller, which transfers the solution to the form roller.

Fountain Solution

The fountain solution used in a dampening system must be properly mixed to provide a consistent dampening material for the plate surface. The fountain solution is normally a combination of water, some type of acidic substance, and gum arabic. Water serves as the main ingredient of the solution. It is applied to the nonimage area of the plate and is used to repel ink.

Because ink is applied repeatedly to the plate, the fountain solution is also responsible for separating the nonimage area from the image area and ensuring the nonimage area remains receptive to water. A concentration of acid and gum arabic in the solution helps prevent the nonimage area of the plate from receiving ink. The solution is designed to desensitize the nonimage area, or keep it from becoming image receptive.

Fountain solutions are commonly identified by their *pH value*, a measurement that indicates the acidity or alkalinity of the solution. A *pH scale* provides numeric pH values ranging from 0 to 14, with 7 designated as neutral, **Figure 15-35.** A pH value less than 7 is an acidic solution, with a value of 0 representing the highest acidity. A pH value above 7 is an alkaline solution, with a value of 14 representing the highest alkalinity. Each successive pH value is 10 times the previous value. For example, a solution with a pH reading of 3.0 is 10 times more acidic than a solution with a pH reading of 4.0.

Plates have a recommended pH value that is used when mixing the fountain solution. Most plates are designed to use solutions with a pH reading between 4.0 and 5.5. Some presses are equipped with devices that automatically monitor the pH value of the fountain solution.

Solutions with a controlled pH level result in higher printing quality and reduce wear on the plate. A solution with a low pH reading can cause emulsification, or ink loss, and plate damage. A solution with a high pH reading reduces the ability of the plate to repel ink and can cause scumming, or excess ink in the nonimage area.

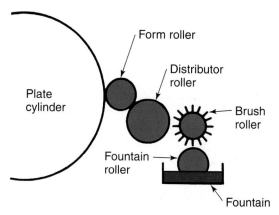

Figure 15-34. In a brush system, a brush roller spreads the fountain solution and is part of a continuous series of rollers.

molleton cover: A cloth tube that fits over the body of a dampening roller and helps it retain fountain solution.

brush system: A continuous dampening system that uses a brush roller to transfer fountain solution from the fountain roller to the rest of the system.

pH value: A measurement that indicates the acidity or alkalinity of a solution, as measured on the pH scale.

pH scale: A measuring scale used to determine the acidity or alkalinity of a solution. The pH scale is numbered from 0–14, with 7 designated as neutral. A pH value below 7 indicates an acidic solution; a value above 7 indicates an alkaline solution.

ACADEMIC LINK
Acidity/Alkalinity

The fountain solution used on printing presses keeps ink off areas on the plate that do not contain an image. To ensure that the solution performs optimally, it is important to regularly measure the pH of the solution. Maintaining the proper pH level impacts the quality of the printed material, as well as the wear on the printing plate.

The pH scale contains measurement values from 0 (acid) to 14 (alkaline), with 7 being neutral. Typically, the fountain solution pH reading for sheet-fed work is around 4.0. It is best to follow the manufacturer's directions when adjusting a solution's pH.

A change in pH by one unit of measure is actually a difference of 10 in the pH of the solution. For example, a change in pH from 7 to 8 is an increase of one unit of measure, but represents a 10 point jump in pH. This solution has gone from neutral (7) to alkaline (8). A practical example is lemon juice with a pH around 2 and stomach acid with a pH of about 1. The change in one pH unit represents a much greater difference in the actual acidity of the two liquids.

If each incremental pH value is a change of 10, what is the pH value change from 4.5 to 5?

waterless plates, which are designed differently from conventional plates. The surface of a waterless plate is a layer of silicone rubber that repels ink and keeps the nonimage area separate from the image area. The image area is recessed. It lies just below the plate surface and has an ink-receptive photopolymer coating. The silicone plate surface serves the same function as the fountain solution in a dampening system.

The inking system used by a waterless press is temperature controlled. As ink is applied to the plate, the surface is designed to repel a certain thickness of ink. The system must regulate the temperature of the ink to maintain the correct thickness. Several rollers in the system contain hollow tubes that are filled with water to remove excess heat. Water circulates through the rollers and cools the ink as it is transferred to the plate.

The use of waterless lithography is becoming more common in the graphic communications industry. Waterless presses have several advantages over conventional presses that use dampening systems. Waterless plates provide greater image quality by producing a higher density of ink when they are offset. The procedures involved in formulating fountain solutions and maintaining a dampening system are also eliminated, saving setup time. Waterless printing changes the image transfer system from a chemical/physical process to a mechanical process. The waterless system allows printers to create an environmental management system (EMS) that complies with the International Organization for Standardization (ISO) 14001 recommendations. These recommendations are intended to help industries create more environmentally sensitive work practices. This effort is voluntary.

Waterless Presses

A *waterless press* is an offset lithographic press system that does not use a dampening system during the printing process. A waterless press prints with

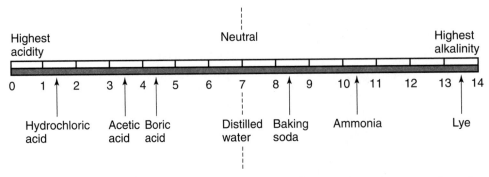

Figure 15-35. A pH scale measures the acidity or alkalinity of a solution. The scale ranges from 0 to 14, with 7 indicating a neutral solution. A value above 7 indicates an alkaline solution; a value below 7 represents an acidic solution. (A.B. Dick Company)

INKING SYSTEMS

An *inking system* consists of a set of rollers that carries a thin film of ink to the image area of a plate, **Figure 15-36**. The inking system, also known as an ink train, is responsible for maintaining a consistent flow of ink to the plate surface. A typical system includes an ink fountain, a fountain roller, a ductor roller, and a combination of distribution rollers and form rollers.

Ink is supplied to the system by an ink fountain. On larger presses, an ink agitator may be used to help maintain a consistent ink flow. An agitator is a revolving device that moves along the fountain and stirs the ink to keep it at the same flow level.

The fountain roller transfers ink from the fountain to the ductor roller. The ductor roller makes intermittent contact with the fountain roller and the distributor roller. The ink is then distributed by one or more distributor rollers to the intermediate rollers or directly to the form rollers. The form rollers place the final film of ink on the plate.

The number of distributor, intermediate, and form rollers used in an inking system varies according to the press. The number of rollers in the design provides an indication of the quality of the system. The greater the number of rollers, the more uniform the distribution of ink to the plate.

Inking systems are joined with dampening systems on some duplicators to form a combined *inking and dampening system*, **Figure 15-37**. The two systems are linked to apply both ink and fountain solution to the plate. In an integrated system, the entire set of inking and dampening rollers is first inked. Fountain solution is then added to the dampening fountain and fed to the system. Because ink is first distributed to the entire system, fountain solution

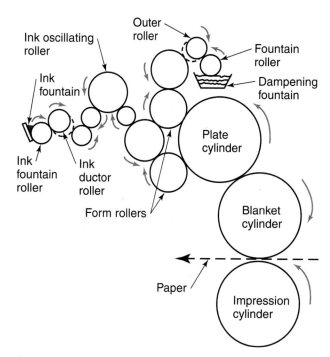

Figure 15-37. An inking and dampening system is a combined design that carries both ink and fountain solution to the plate. (A.B. Dick Company)

rides on the top of each roller after it is added. The form rollers connect the two systems and carry the ink and fountain solution directly to the plate.

DELIVERY SYSTEMS

A *delivery system* removes the printed substrate from the printing system of the press and prepares it for finishing operations. Delivery systems on sheet-fed presses are designed differently from those used on web-fed presses. On a sheet-fed press, the delivery system removes sheets of paper and places them into a stack called the delivery pile. On a web-fed press, the delivery system conducts a number of additional operations.

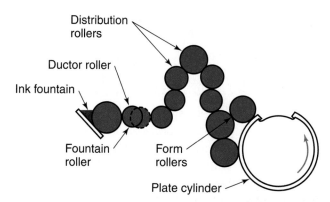

Figure 15-36. Ink is applied to the plate by a series of rollers that make up the inking system.

waterless press: An offset lithographic press system that eliminates the use of a dampening system during the printing process.

inking system: A group of rollers designed to carry ink to the image area of the printing plate.

inking and dampening system: A combined system of rollers that applies both ink and fountain solution to the plate during operation of the press.

delivery system: A press system that removes the printed substrate from the printing system and prepares it for finishing operations.

Sheet-Fed Delivery Systems

A sheet-fed delivery system removes sheets after they are printed and stacks them onto an outfeed table or tray. Sheet-fed delivery systems vary in design and use.

The most common delivery system used on a sheet-fed press is a chain delivery system, **Figure 15-38.** As a sheet of paper leaves the printing system, it is directed to the *delivery pile* by a pair of chains that serve as conveyor belts. Two delivery bars extending between the chains contain grippers that grasp the sheet and guide it through the system. The gripper bars are positioned along the length of the chains so one set of grippers pulls a sheet from the printing unit at the same time the other set of grippers delivers a sheet to the delivery pile. The pile is stacked on top of the outfeed table.

When a sheet is released by the gripper bars, it is aligned in the delivery pile by guides positioned along the sides of the pile, **Figure 15-39.** Proper alignment of the sheets is critical. The delivery pile must be uniformly arranged so the paper can be trimmed or folded after it is stacked. Two stationary guides and two jogging guides place each sheet in position and straighten the stack. The stationary guides are on two sides of the paper. The jogging guides are adjustable and move or jog the paper into place as it is fed to the pile, **Figure 15-40.** As the sheets build up, the outfeed table slowly drops under the weight of the pile.

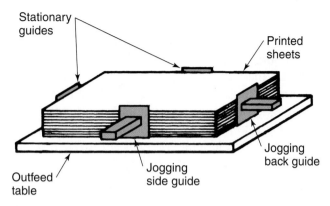

Figure 15-39. Guides are positioned to align delivered paper on the outfeed table.

Figure 15-40. Jogging guides can be adjusted to align the edges of the stack as paper is delivered.

Some delivery systems use a tray to hold the paper after it is printed. Duplicators are commonly equipped with an ejector system that uses rollers to feed the paper from the printing system to the delivery tray. Paper guides align the edges of the paper when it reaches the tray.

Web-Fed Delivery Systems

A web-fed delivery system is designed to provide a series of finishing operations in addition to the actual delivery of paper. The feeding and delivery systems used with web-fed presses are designed much differently from those used with sheet-fed presses. After the paper is printed, it is transferred to a group of units that make up the delivery system.

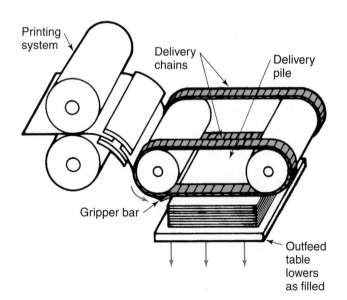

Figure 15-38. A chain delivery system driven by a pair of chain conveyor belts directs printed stock to a delivery pile.

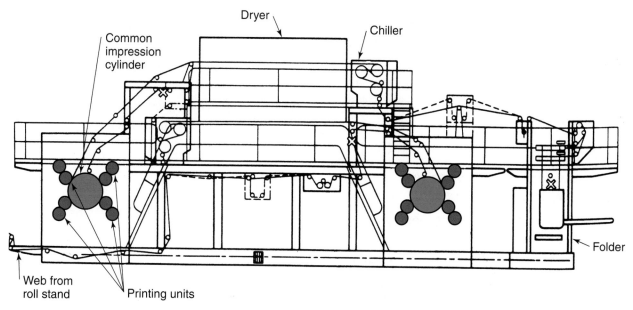

Figure 15-41. The delivery system of a web-fed press is commonly equipped with separate dryer, chiller, and folder units. (Baker Perkins Limited)

Different delivery systems are used on various web-fed presses. A typical system includes a dryer, chiller, and folder, **Figure 15-41.**

The dryer unit dries the ink printed on the web. The dryer operates at high temperatures and removes much of the moisture from the ink through evaporation. The web is then cooled by the chiller unit, which lowers the temperature on the web surface and hardens the ink. The system may also include a moisturizing unit to restore web moisture that is lost in the drying and chilling processes.

Once the web passes through the dryer and chiller units, it is transferred to the folder, where it is trimmed and folded into signatures. A signature is a folded sheet that is commonly printed on both sides and trimmed. A typical folder folds sheets using a *former board*, a curved or triangular plane that serves as the folding surface, **Figure 15-42.**

Other folder units are equipped with a series of rollers that produce folded signatures. A jaw folder uses a blade to feed the web through the system. As the web travels through the rollers, it is automatically folded and cut into signatures. The finished signatures are then delivered by a conveyor system to a delivery table.

Summary

The traditional lithographic printing process is often referred to as an offset method. The image on the plate is offset to another surface called a blanket and the image from the blanket is transferred to

Figure 15-42. A former board is used to make the first fold in the paper web. The folder unit cuts the paper web and makes additional folds to form the signature. (King Press Corporation)

delivery pile: A uniform stack of paper that accepts sheets from the delivery system of a sheet-fed press.

former board: A curved or triangular plane that serves as the folding surface on a web-fed press.

the substrate. Basically, the presses are classified as sheet-fed or web-fed presses. Five basic press systems make up the printing press. They are the feeding system, printing system, dampening system, inking system, and delivery system. To print an acceptable finished product, all of the systems must be properly adjusted.

Review Questions

Please do not write in this text. Write your answers on a separate sheet of paper.

1. A _____ press prints on one continuous roll of paper, pulled from a roll.

2. What are the five basic systems of a lithographic press?

3. Name two devices that are used in the feeding system to separate paper and feed sheets one at a time to a sheet-fed press.

4. A(n) _____ is a control device that prevents more than one sheet of paper from entering the press.

5. True or False? A register unit is a mechanism that aligns paper for printing.

6. Name two types of splicer units typically used on a web-fed press.

7. How does a web-break detector work?

8. What are the three cylinders that make up the printing system of a typical lithographic press?

9. The vertical space that lies between the surface of the plate cylinder bearers and the cylinder body is called the _____.

10. True or False? The impression cylinder applies the pressure needed to transfer the image from the blanket cylinder to the substrate.

11. Which of the following is a true statement about a common-impression cyclinder?
    A. One large impression cylinder is central to the printing system.
    B. The cylinder is surrounded by a group of printing units.
    C. Each printing unit prints a separate color on the web as it travels between the blanket cylinders and the common impression cylinder.
    D. All of the above.

12. Name the two most common types of dampening systems used on a press.

13. A _____ is a cloth tube that fits over the body of a dampening roller to help it retain fountain solution.

14. Which of the following would be an acceptable pH value for a fountain solution?
    A. 9
    B. 1
    C. 4.5
    D. 3.5

15. What are three finishing units commonly used by the delivery system of a web-fed press?

Suggested Activities

1. Visit a sheet-fed printing plant, and list the various types of systems found on the presses.

2. Visit a web-fed printing plant and describe how ink is dried on the printed roll stock. Is it a heat-set or a nonheat-set unit?

3. Print a two-color close register letterhead using register marks.

4. Write a few paragraphs describing safety devices found on a sheet-fed press and on a web-fed press.

5. Outline some of the factors to consider when choosing which type of press to use for a selected job.

Related Web Link

The Fine Print Knowledge Center
www.fineprintschool.com
An online learning resource for those interested in printing, publishing, and graphic design.

Some Web sites contain a great deal of resources for current and upcoming methods of printing, as well as older printing forms. Research these sites for background and historical information.

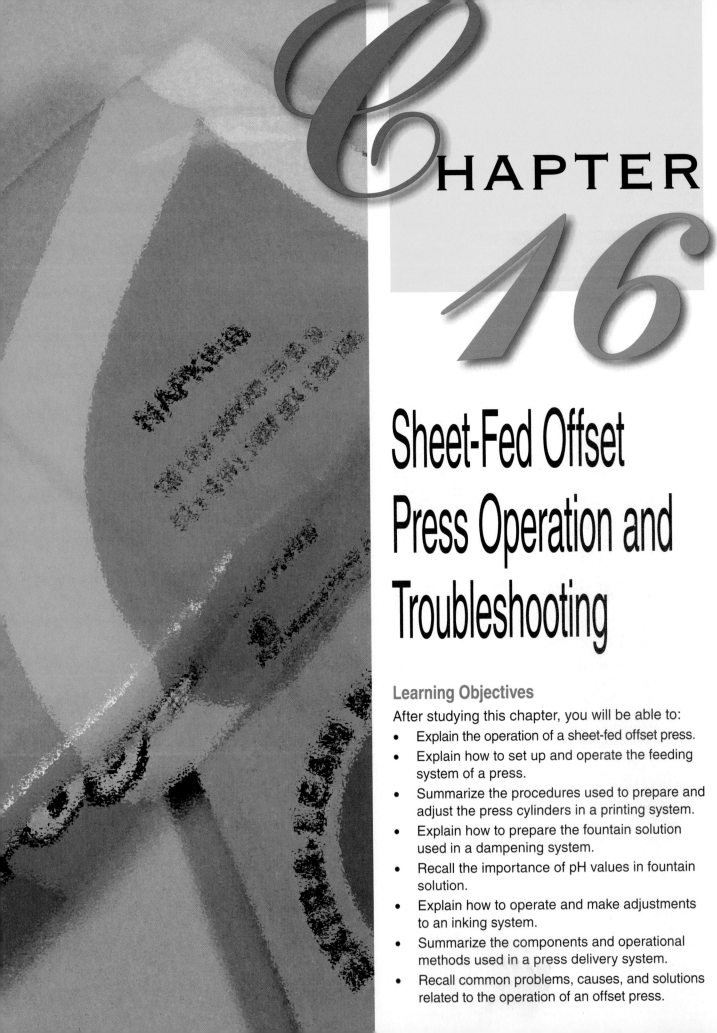

CHAPTER 16

Sheet-Fed Offset Press Operation and Troubleshooting

Learning Objectives

After studying this chapter, you will be able to:

- Explain the operation of a sheet-fed offset press.
- Explain how to set up and operate the feeding system of a press.
- Summarize the procedures used to prepare and adjust the press cylinders in a printing system.
- Explain how to prepare the fountain solution used in a dampening system.
- Recall the importance of pH values in fountain solution.
- Explain how to operate and make adjustments to an inking system.
- Summarize the components and operational methods used in a press delivery system.
- Recall common problems, causes, and solutions related to the operation of an offset press.

Important Terms

duplicator
ink agitator
ink keys
ink tack
setoff

Press designs vary, with different operational methods required for each type of press. Many systems, however, follow the same basic design principles as those used on a sheet-fed press. A press operator familiar with the design of a sheet-fed press, therefore, can use many of the same guidelines and techniques when operating other presses. For example, a *duplicator*, often found in small commercial print shops and in-plant printing operations, is a small sheet-fed press. It is used for short printing runs and can produce more than 10,000 impressions per hour (iph), **Figure 16-1**. Many of the same control devices used on large sheet-fed presses are common to duplicators. Knowledge gained from operating a duplicator can be used to run larger presses, such as those used for multicolor printing. These presses are much larger than duplicators, **Figure 16-2**. They usually contain several printing units, each of which prints a separate color.

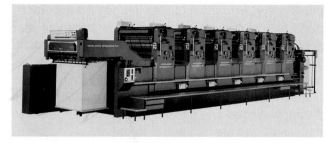

Figure 16-2. Large sheet-fed presses used in multicolor printing are equipped with several printing units, each of which prints a separate color. The knowledge gained from using a small sheet-fed press can be used to operate larger presses like this one. (Heidelberg USA)

The five fundamental operating systems of both sheet-fed and web-fed offset presses were introduced in Chapter 15. Recall that sheet-fed presses print on individual sheets of paper as they are fed through the press. Web-fed presses print on an entire web that travels continuously through the press. This chapter will focus on the operation of sheet-fed presses only. This is because web-fed presses are typically designed to operate automatically. Sheet-fed presses, however, require more manual setup for each press system.

The first section of this chapter will cover the different methods of preparing and operating each press system. Waterless press systems, increasingly used by commercial printers, will also be covered. The second part of the chapter will present common troubleshooting techniques used to maintain an offset press.

OFFSET PRESS OPERATION

In the operation of an offset press, the five different systems must be set up and adjusted to prepare it for printing. Each system performs a different function as paper is fed through the press and printed.

Recall that paper is drawn to the press from the feeding system. Parts of this system include a feeding platform, a group of devices that help separate and transfer sheets of paper, and a register unit that aligns the paper for printing. The feeding system is controlled by a series of guiding and registration devices that are adjusted when the system is set up. Paper is transferred from the feeding system to the

Figure 16-1. A duplicator is a small sheet-fed press commonly used for in-house printing applications.

duplicator: A small sheet-fed press typically used for short printing runs.

printing system, which offsets images from an inked plate to the printing substrate. In a three-cylinder printing system, images are offset from the plate to a blanket, then offset again to the substrate as paper travels between the impression cylinder and blanket cylinder, **Figure 16-3.** Each cylinder must be properly aligned and packed to provide the pressure necessary to transfer images to paper.

With the plate positioned on the press, water or fountain solution is applied to the plate surface by the dampening system, and ink is applied by the inking system. The nonimage area accepts fountain solution and repels ink, and the image area accepts ink and repels fountain solution. The separation of the image area from the nonimage area means only the inked image will be offset during printing. The rollers in the dampening and inking systems must be set up to provide the correct proportion of fountain solution and ink to the plate. On some presses, the two systems are combined into a single unit. When the press is operating, adjustments are sometimes necessary to maintain a consistent flow of fountain solution and ink.

After the image is printed, paper is transferred from the printing system and stacked for postpress operations by the delivery system. A typical delivery system uses chain conveyor belts and gripper bars to pull sheets of paper to an outfeed table or delivery pile. Pile guides are set to align the paper on the delivery pile, where sheets are stacked for such operations as folding, trimming, and binding.

Each system in an offset press must be set up and maintained for proper operation by the press operator. Presses are commonly equipped with a computerized control unit that allows the operator to set up the press by entering and reading data on a display, **Figure 16-4.** The computer collects, controls, and analyzes information about the various functions of the press.

Many types of presses must be adjusted manually. Before such a press is used, each system must be checked and set up according to specifications of the press.

! The press operator must have a thorough understanding of all press operations before setting up and running a press. Any adjustments to the press must be made when the press is not in operation. The operator must practice correct safety procedures when using the press. Damage to the press or injury can result if recommended procedures are not followed.

FEEDING SYSTEM OPERATION

The location and types of control devices in a feeding system vary, depending on the press design. The typical components of a feeding system are a feeding platform, paper guides, sheet separators, sucker feet, pullout rollers, a double-sheet detector, and a register unit, **Figure 16-5.**

When paper is placed on the platform, it is aligned into a uniform stack by the paper guides. The platform is usually lowered by hand. When the stack is at the right height, the top sheet should be in position to enter the registration unit. Sheet separators positioned along the edges of the paper are used to separate the top sheet from the rest of the stack by producing streams of air. Each sheet is then directed to the pullout rollers by the sucker

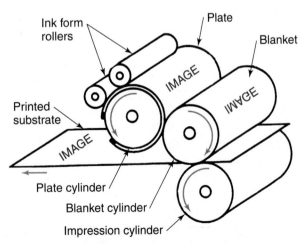

Figure 16-3. In offset lithographic printing, images are first offset from a plate to a blanket and then offset again to paper.

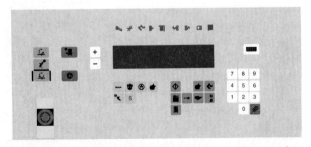

Figure 16-4. A computerized control panel is used to make automatic adjustments to the press. (Heidelberg USA)

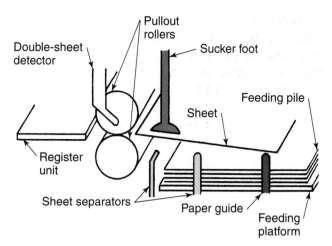

Figure 16-5. Typical components of a sheet-fed press feeding system.

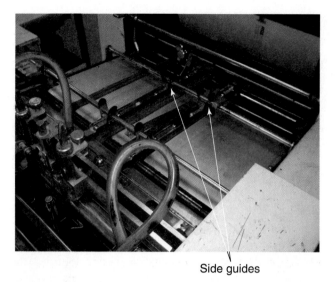

Side guides

Figure 16-7. Paper is placed in register with the press by side guides once it reaches the register stop.

feet, a set of vacuum devices that remove paper from the stack, **Figure 16-6.** When the rear edge of one sheet leaves the pile, the sucker feet pick up the next sheet.

As the paper passes through the pullout rollers, it comes into contact with the double-sheet detector. If more than one sheet is fed through the pullout rollers, the double-sheet detector activates and opens a deflector plate to remove the excess paper.

The register table uses a set of conveyor tapes to carry the paper to the register stop; when the paper reaches the stop, it is registered with the printing system by the side guides, **Figure 16-7.** The paper is then ready for printing.

Feeding System Setup

Proper setup of the feeding system is a critical part of operating the press. Paper must be registered correctly when it leaves the feeding system in order to receive a consistent transfer of images from the printing system. Proper setup is also essential in eliminating misfeeds. The following is a typical procedure for setting up and operating a feeding system on an offset press.

1. Lower the feeding platform to the operating height by turning the elevator handle. Adjust the paper guides to match the sheet size of the paper. Fan the paper and stack it on the platform, jogging it into place to meet the guides. Next, adjust the pile height and align the paper just below the sucker feet. During operation of the press, the pile must remain at the same height so sheets can be drawn off for printing, **Figure 16-8.** The elevator control knob is used to set the pile height. Turning the knob clockwise lowers the pile height, while turning it counterclockwise raises the pile height. Once the pile height is set, the platform will rise automatically to maintain the height of the pile when the press is in operation.

2. Adjust the sheet separators to control the flow of air separating the top sheet from the rest of the pile. The sheet separators are usually located at the front and rear edges of the stack. They can be moved up, down, forward, or backward. Adjust the airflow for the size and weight of the paper.

Sucker feet

Figure 16-6. Sucker feet draw sheets of paper from the feeding pile to the register unit.

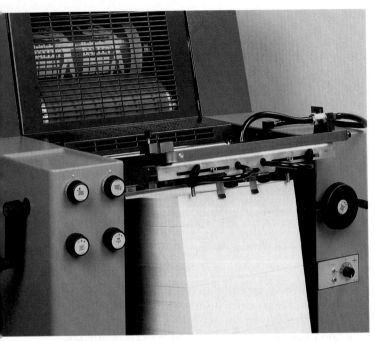

Figure 16-8. The feeding pile is set to remain at the same height during operation of the press. (Heidelberg USA)

3. Position the sucker feet so they are parallel to the bar controlling the operating height of the feeding platform. The sucker feet are typically arranged in a single row on a bar located above the paper, **Figure 16-9.** The sucker feet must be close enough to remove individual sheets of paper. Too much suction will draw more than one sheet of paper from the stack. Any sucker feet that extend beyond the edges of the sheet must be turned off. Like the airflow of the sheet separator, the amount of vacuum provided by the sucker feet can also be adjusted for the stock being used.

4. Adjust the pullout rollers and the double-sheet detector. The pressure between the rollers must be sufficient to draw each sheet of paper to the register table. Check the pressure by pulling a thin strip of paper through each set of rollers. As the strips are pulled through, there should be a slight amount of resistance. The pressure felt between the rollers must be equal. Adjust the pressure by tightening or loosening the control knobs on the side of each roller. After paper is fed through the pullout rollers, its thickness is determined by the double-sheet detector, **Figure 16-10.** If more than one sheet of paper is detected, a deflector plate opens to remove the paper.

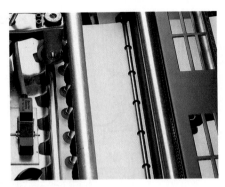

Figure 16-9. The sucker feet must be set parallel to the feeding pile height control bar. (Heidelberg USA)

5. Set up the register unit by positioning the side guides. Paper is transferred from the pullout rollers to the register unit by a set of conveyor tapes that run along the register table. When a sheet of paper reaches the register stop, the side guides bring the paper into register with the printing system. Refer to Figure 16-7. The register stop is a group of fingers that stop the paper before it is guided into position. After the paper is registered, the fingers rise or drop to allow the paper to pass to the printing system. The side guides are located on either side of the paper on the register table. One guide is designated as an active guide, while the other is designated as the stationary guide. The active guide jogs the paper into register when it reaches the register stop. To set the active guide, use the handwheel to manually advance the press until the guide reaches its most inward position on the register table, **Figure 16-11.** Reposition the guide by loosening the screw attached to the assembly. Then move the guide along the measuring scale to match the width of the paper. The stationary guide remains in a

Figure 16-10. The double-sheet detector is set to monitor paper thickness as sheets pass through the system. (Heidelberg USA)

Figure 16-11. A handwheel is used to manually advance the press when setting up the register unit. (Heidelberg USA)

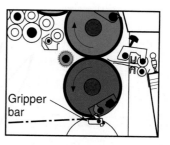

Figure 16-12. A gripper bar grasps the edges of the paper as it makes contact with the impression cylinder. (Heidelberg USA)

fixed position and meets the edge of the paper opposite the active guide. When a sheet of paper reaches the register stop, it is guided into position to accept the image.

PRINTING SYSTEM OPERATION

The printing system is the main unit of the press. It draws paper from the feeding system and then prints images from a printing plate. Recall that a three-cylinder system contains a plate cylinder, a blanket cylinder, and an impression cylinder. The cylinder bearers ride on each other as images are transferred from one cylinder to another. The plate cylinder holds the plate. The blanket cylinder holds the blanket. The impression cylinder provides the pressure needed to transfer the image from the blanket to the substrate as it revolves against the blanket cylinder. The impression cylinder also grasps paper from the feeding system after the paper is registered. Grippers located along a bar on the impression cylinder are used to draw the paper when it reaches the register stop, **Figure 16-12.**

The printing system operates in connection with the dampening and inking systems of the press. An even distribution of fountain solution and ink must reach the plate surface during a press run.

The printing system cylinders must be set up properly before operating the press. Position the plate correctly on the plate cylinder and mount the blanket properly on the blanket cylinder. Plates are commonly punched at the ends and attached to pin bar fittings on the plate cylinder. The plate cylinder has two pin bars, one to hold the lead edge of the plate and one to hold the tail end. A set of clamps lock the plate in place. Blankets are typically designed with the same punched fittings used by plates and are attached to lead and tail pin bars on the blanket cylinder.

The operation of the printing system has a direct effect on the appearance of the printed image. The cylinders must provide enough pressure to offset images and the plate and blanket must be mounted correctly. The following procedure is typical for setting up each cylinder in a three-cylinder printing system.

Plate Cylinder Setup

1. Clean the plate cylinder of any foreign particles or moisture, before mounting the plate. Using the handwheel on the operating side of the press, turn the press until the lead clamp of the cylinder is in position to receive the lead edge of the plate, **Figure 16-13.** With the clamp bar open, mount the plate on the lead pin bar and then tighten the lead clamp. Holding the tail end of the plate securely, use the handwheel to rotate the press until the tail clamp is in position to receive the tail end of the plate. Release the tail clamp and position the plate fittings over the tail pin bar. When the pins are inserted, tighten the tail clamp to lock in the plate.

2. Rotate the plate cylinder to adjust the printed appearance of the image. Some presses are equipped with a control device that can adjust the plate cylinder and raise or lower the image when it is printed. If the image is too high or too low on the plate, it may not offset to the correct position on the paper. To adjust the position of the image, loosen the plate cylinder locknut and turn the handwheel to rotate the cylinder. A scale is used to indicate the location of the image. The direction of the turn determines whether the image is raised or lowered, **Figure 16-14.** After adjusting the offset position of the image, retighten the cylinder. Some plate systems automatically load the plate to the plate cylinder eliminating the manual operation.

Figure 16-13. A mounted plate is held in place by lead and tail clamps on the plate cylinder. (Heidelberg USA)

Blanket Cylinder Setup

1. Measure the thickness of the blanket and determine the amount of packing needed to pack the cylinder. A micrometer is often used to measure blanket thickness. Determine the amount of undercut of the blanket cylinder. This is typically indicated on the cylinder body or listed in the press operating manual. When positioned on the press, the blanket commonly extends above the bearers to meet the plate on the plate cylinder. The distance that the blanket should extend above the blanket cylinder bearers is generally recommended by the press manufacturer. To calculate the amount of packing needed, subtract the blanket thickness from the undercut. This figure is the distance from the blanket surface to the bearers. Add this figure to the recommended distance past the bearers for the total thickness for blanket packing.

   Blanket and plate packing thickness can also be determined by using a cylinder packing gauge. The gauge can be used to measure the amount of pressure or squeeze that exists between the cylinders when the plate and blanket are both mounted on the press. To provide the pressure necessary to transfer images, the total thickness of the plate, blanket, and packing should exceed the combined undercut of the plate and blanket cylinders. The amount of squeeze typically ranges from 0.002″ to 0.004″ (0.051 mm to 0.102 mm).

2. Clean the surface of the blanket cylinder and mount the blanket. Inspect the cylinder for any loose particles or moisture. Then mount the blanket. Blankets commonly have a rubber surface and are punched with the same fittings used to mount plates on the press. Using the press handwheel, rotate the blanket cylinder far enough so that the lead edge of the blanket can

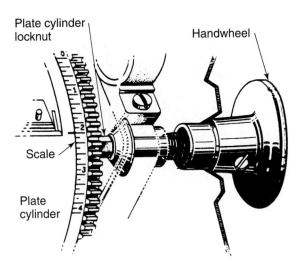

Figure 16-14. A printed image can be raised or lowered when it is offset from the plate by adjusting the position of the plate cylinder. (Multigraphics)

be positioned in the lead cylinder clamp. Attach the blanket and tighten the clamp. If any packing sheets are to be used, place them under the blanket. The sheets should fit entirely under the blanket without extending past the edges. Holding the blanket in place, turn the handwheel and rotate the cylinder until the tail end of the blanket can be positioned with the tail cylinder clamp. Attach the blanket and tighten the clamp, **Figure 16-15.**

3. Clean the blanket after operating the press to rid the surface of ink, foreign materials, or moisture from previous use. Wash the blanket with an ink solvent recommended by the manufacturer. After the wash is applied, wipe the blanket clean. Some presses are equipped with an automatic washing system to clean the blanket, **Figure 16-16.** The system uses a set of rollers to feed washing solution to the blanket. When the system is operated, a dampening roller transfers

Figure 16-15. A blanket is held in place on the cylinder by clamps. (Heidelberg USA)

Figure 16-16. This automatic washing system can be used to clean the blanket after a press run. (Heidelberg USA)

washing solution from a filled container to a metering roller. The metering roller carries the solution to an oscillating roller, which moves back and forth to apply solution to the blanket. After the blanket is cleaned, it should be wiped dry and placed in storage until needed for further use.

Impression Cylinder Setup

1. The impression cylinder must be free of any substances or residue that will affect the pressure needed to transfer the image from the blanket cylinder to the paper. A cloth dampened with ink solvent can be used to clean the cylinder surface. After cleaning the cylinder, wipe it dry.

2. Test the impression provided by the cylinder and adjust the cylinder pressure as needed. After running a number of sheets through the press, the system may require an adjustment to improve the quality of the impression. On some presses, the impression cylinder is spring-loaded and designed to adjust to the pressure of the system. Other presses are equipped with a manual control device that can be used to adjust the impression. The adjustment varies the amount of pressure between the blanket and the impression cylinder. To adjust the impression cylinder pressure, turn off the press and loosen the cylinder locking screw by hand. Next, turn the adjusting screw to adjust the impression. Turning the adjusting screw clockwise will increase the pressure, while turning it counterclockwise will decrease the pressure. After making the adjustment, tighten the cylinder locking screw and resume operation of the press.

3. New technology allows the register to be automatically adjusted using the control console.

CONVENTIONAL DAMPENING SYSTEM OPERATION

The dampening system must be set up to provide a steady flow of fountain solution to the plate. Although system designs vary, a typical system includes a dampening fountain, a fountain roller, a ductor roller, a distributor roller, and a form roller, **Figure 16-17.** Different dampening systems may be equipped with different combinations of rollers. For example, some presses are equipped with a combined inking and dampening unit. In this unit, ink and fountain solution are fed together across the rollers to the plate. A continuous dampening system does not use a ductor roller. Instead, each successive roller makes contact and the fountain solution is spread continuously through the system.

Fountain Solution

A typical fountain solution consists of water, gum arabic, and an acidic concentrate. Water repels ink when the fountain solution is applied to the nonimage area of the plate. A mix of gum arabic and acid

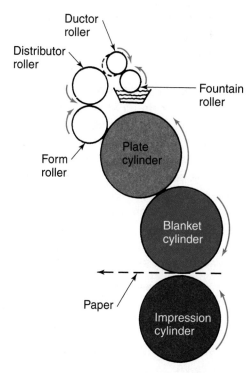

Figure 16-17. A group of rollers is used to carry fountain solution to the plate in a dampening system. (A.B. Dick Company)

keeps the nonimage area desensitized. Because the plate surface is repeatedly coated with ink, the nonimage area must remain desensitized. The chemicals making up the fountain solution must be in correct proportion with the water. The solution must contain enough water to repel ink and enough acid to desensitize the nonimage area. Different fountain solutions are recommended for use with plates by different plate manufacturers. In many cases, the acidic concentrate is supplied by a manufacturer and is mixed with distilled water to produce the solution. Whether the fountain solution is purchased or mixed by the press operator, it must be prepared based on the type of plate used.

Recall that fountain solutions are identified by their pH value and the pH scale ranges from 0 to 14. The midpoint, 7, indicates a neutral solution. Values below 7 are acidic solutions, and pH values above 7 are alkaline solutions. Each successive pH value is 10 times the previous value. A small difference in pH values can have a significant impact on the strength of the fountain solution.

Some presses automatically monitor pH values of fountain solutions. For those that do not, two common measuring devices are litmus paper and an electronic pH meter.

Litmus paper is dipped into the fountain solution and changes color or darkness depending upon the level of acidity in the solution. The paper is then removed from the solution and compared to a standardized scale that contains varying shades of color. Each color tone is marked with a pH value. The scale darkness that most closely matches the darkness of the litmus paper equals the pH value.

An electronic pH meter is a more accurate way to measure pH values. The meter is calibrated before use by measuring the pH value of distilled water. It should produce a reading of 7, or neutral. After the meter is calibrated, it can be used to measure the fountain solution pH. Submerge the probe, attached to the meter, into the fountain solution to get a digital readout of the pH value.

Check the fountain solution regularly and reformulate when necessary. Solution pH can change after a press run. The type of paper and ink used can also have an effect on the pH value of the solution. The fountain solution must keep the nonimage area of the plate water-receptive and desensitized. A fountain solution that is too acidic can make the nonimage area image-sensitive, which allows it to be ink receptive. A solution with a high acidity can also damage the plate.

Dampening System Setup

1. Formulate the fountain solution and measure the solution pH. Prepare the solution for the type of plate being used. Use the chemical blend recommended by the plate manufacturer. After the solution is mixed properly, fill the bottle that feeds the dampening fountain.

2. Adjust the flow of fountain solution to the press by setting the metering roller. On some dampening systems, the speed of the fountain roller can be adjusted to control the flow of the solution.

3. Check the level of pressure between the rollers. To ensure that an even flow of fountain solution is transferred from the fountain to the plate, the level of pressure between the rollers might require adjustment. The pressure between each set of rollers can be checked by positioning two thin strips of paper on either side of the rollers and pulling the strips through. The resistance on each strip should feel equal. If the pressure is not even, adjust one of the rollers to increase or decrease the pressure. The devices used to adjust roller pressure vary, depending on the type of press. Many presses have a locknut on the side of the roller that is loosened and an adjustable screw is turned to change the roller pressure. When adjusting roller pressure, check each roller.

4. Clean the dampening system after operating the press. Most combined inking and dampening systems have an automatic washing system. On other dampening systems, the rollers must be removed and cleaned manually. Remove molleton covers from the rollers and clean after each press run. Use solvent to remove any ink on the covers or roller surfaces.

WATERLESS LITHOGRAPHIC PRINTING OPERATION

The waterless lithographic printing system uses a waterless offset plate, which means the plate prints without using any water or dampening system. The nonimage area of the waterless plate is covered with ink-repellent silicone rubber. A special ink is required. The ink must remain within a certain temperature range to transfer the ink to the substrate. The ink rollers are cooled to the proper temperature. This process is more environmentally friendly than a conventional system because the chemicals in fountain solutions of a conventional system are eliminated.

INKING SYSTEM OPERATION

A number of control devices are used to operate an inking system. The ink fountain is equipped with an adjustable blade that regulates the flow of ink from the fountain to the rollers. A line of thumbscrews along the length of the blade, called *ink keys*, are used to adjust the position of the blade, **Figure 16-18.** The blade controls the thickness of the ink as it is drawn by the fountain roller. A small gap separates the blade from the roller surface; when the ink keys are loosened, the gap widens and the blade allows more ink to pass from the fountain. When the keys are tightened, the gap closes and the blade permits less ink to be drawn.

Ink distribution can also be controlled by adjusting the speed of the fountain roller. Higher speeds release more ink to the system and lower speeds release less ink. As the fountain roller rotates in the fountain, it stirs the ink to keep it flowing at a consistent level. Large presses are often quipped with an *ink agitator*. The agitator maintains a consistent flow of ink to the rollers.

When ink is drawn from the fountain, the pressure between the rollers must be sufficient to split the ink into a thin, even film. The pressure between the ink rollers can be checked by using the same technique employed to check dampening roller pressure.

There is a more accurate technique, however, to check the level of pressure between the ink form rollers and the plate. Turn on the inking system and coat the rollers with an even layer of ink. Mount and position the plate on the plate cylinder so it is in line with the form rollers. Lower the form rollers to make contact with the plate and examine the resulting ink stripes formed by the rollers. The stripes should be evenly spaced and measure approximately 1/8″ to 3/16″ (3.17 mm to 4.76 mm) in width along their entire length. Incorrect pressure will result in a poor image. Review the results of incorrect pressure shown in **Figure 16-19.**

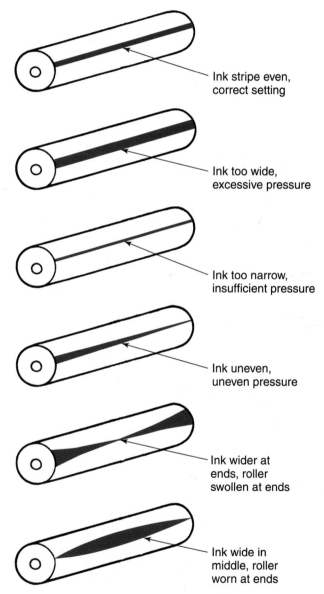

Figure 16-19. Different inking problems caused by excessive or insufficient roller pressure.

Figure 16-18. Ink keys are used to control ink thickness by adjusting the amount of gap that exists between the fountain blade and the ink roller surface. (Heidelberg USA)

ink keys: Adjustable devices used to control the flow of ink from the ink fountain to the printing plate.

ink agitator: A revolving device that is used to maintain a consistent flow of ink from the ink fountain.

Inking System Setup

1. Inspect the rollers and make sure they are clean and free of any dried ink, lint, or dust. Use solvent to remove ink from the rollers and to wash the fountain and fountain roller.

2. Once the system is clean, fill the fountain with ink. Use ink that is compatible with the fountain solution, the press, and the stock being printed. Use an ink knife to remove the ink from the can and to remove and discard any dried ink from the top of the can. Then fill the fountain.

3. Adjust the ink keys to produce an even flow of ink to the rollers. To decrease the flow of ink, turn the keys clockwise. To increase the flow of ink, turn the keys counterclockwise. Ink thickness can also be adjusted along the width of the fountain as the ink is transferred, **Figure 16-20.** If one side of the plate requires more ink than another portion of the plate, the keys controlling the corresponding area of the fountain can be adjusted to apply a greater amount of ink. A plate that contains a large halftone image, for example, may require more ink for the halftone portion than another portion containing type.

4. Adjust the speed of the fountain roller and ink the entire set of rollers. The fountain roller speed is typically controlled by an adjustable knob. While setting the speed, observe the movement of ink across the rollers and readjust the ink

keys to provide an even flow. On some presses, the ductor roller can also be set to make the necessary amount of contact with the fountain roller.

5. Check the pressure between the form rollers and the plate. After inking the rollers, bring the form rollers into contact with the plate and observe the ink stripes that form on the plate surface. The stripes should run parallel and appear even in width. If the stripes appear to be uneven, adjust the pressure by tightening or loosening the rollers.

6. Clean the ink fountain and system rollers after the press run. To clean the fountain, remove excess ink with a knife and use a cloth dampened with solvent to wash off any dried ink deposits. Ink rollers are cleaned with blanket or roller wash. Any leftover ink must be removed before it dries. Because ink tends to spread to the ends of the system, the roller ends must be carefully examined for ink buildup.

As was mentioned earlier, some presses are equipped with automatic washing systems. Move the rollers into cleanup position. Solvent is automatically carried by the distributor rollers and applied to the entire set of inking and dampening rollers.

DELIVERY SYSTEM OPERATION

A delivery system transfers printed sheets from the press and stacks them for finishing operations. Most sheet-fed presses use a chain delivery system to accomplish these tasks. The chain delivery system consists of a pair of chain conveyor belts that drive two or more gripper bars. The gripper bars grasp and move the paper from the impressions cylinder to the delivery pile. Stationary and jogging guides then align the paper on the stack. As the pile grows, the outfeed table drops.

When sheets of paper are stacked, the printed side of one sheet meets the unprinted backside of the next sheet and smudging or *setoff* can occur. Two types of drying devices are commonly used with delivery systems to prevent setoff. In one design, printed sheets are sprayed with an antisetoff powder or liquid that dries the ink and prevents it from being transferred. The powder or liquid is sprayed between the delivery of each sheet. Another system uses heat to dry the ink as sheets of paper are moved to the delivery pile.

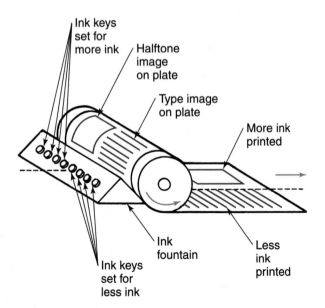

Figure 16-20. The ink keys can be adjusted to provide a greater flow of ink from different parts of the fountain to the plate.

Lithographic Press Operator

Lithographic press operators run many different types and sizes of printing presses found within the industry. On any type or size press, the operator must produce a product that matches the job specifications, is of high quality, and is completed on time to meet the customer needs. In addition to press operation, the operator must perform regular maintenance on the press and other printing equipment. Keeping equipment in excellent condition helps to ensure optimum output.

Other responsibilities of a lithographic press operator include preparing stock for printing, maintaining a clean and organized production area, monitoring product quality during production, observing all shop and equipment safety guidelines, and working closely with other team members to assure customer satisfaction. Operators are expected to have adequate knowledge of substrates and production processes. Mechanical knowledge of machines and tools is also considered beneficial.

Most of the lithographic press operator positions require a minimum of a high school diploma. Many operations require technical school or certification program training. Equipment-specific training is typically provided on the job or through manufacturer-sponsored training sessions. Knowledge in basic mathematics, chemistry, computers, and electronics is highly desirable.

"Whether your interests are technical in nature, or based in the areas of marketing or any aspect of communicating thoughts, ideas, or philosophies, I strongly encourage you to consider graphic communications for your future."

Mike Chiricuzio
Arizona State University

As paper is delivered and stacked, a buildup of static electricity can occur. To eliminate this buildup, some presses use an antistatic bar or strands of tinsel. This process helps keep each sheet separate and aids in the alignment of the stack.

As paper is drawn to the delivery pile from the press, it must be transferred correctly through each part of the delivery system. Each sheet must be guided into the same position when it leaves the press to prevent damage to the paper. When paper reaches the delivery pile, it must be arranged in a uniform stack for such finishing operations as folding, trimming, and packaging. The delivery system represents the final operating stage of the press.

Delivery System Setup

1. Adjust the chain delivery grippers to accommodate the type of stock being printed and the speed of the press. The opening of the grippers is controlled by a cam mounted on a shaft extending between the chains. As the gripper bars revolve along the chains, the grippers are forced open when they come into contact with the cam. To adjust the opening position of the grippers for releasing paper, set the cam dial. A high setting allows the grippers to hold each sheet longer before releasing it. A high setting with light stock will provide better stacking. A high setting should also be used for lower press speeds. When using heavy stock, the cam should be adjusted to a low setting to provide an earlier release point for the paper. A low setting will keep each sheet separate as paper is released and can also be used when operating the press at higher speeds.

2. Adjust the stationary and jogging guides to match the sheet size. To set the guides, feed a sheet of paper through the press and stop it just before it is released to the delivery pile. Adjust each guide to meet the edges of the paper. The jogging guides are usually adjusted by loosening a thumbscrew and moving the guide

setoff: A condition that results when wet ink on the press sheets transfers to the back of other sheets in a stack.

into place. Once the guides are in position, retighten the thumbscrews.

3. Presses are designed to run hundreds or thousands of sheets, so adjustments are often necessary to ensure the feeding and delivery systems are operating consistently. While running the press, observe both systems and determine whether each is functioning properly. Align the feeding system with the delivery system by turning the press handwheel and manually advancing the press to bring the systems into alignment. Adjustments may also be needed to reset other components in the delivery system, depending on the source of the problem.

4. Set the receding table control. The outfeed table can be set to lower at various rates, depending on such factors as the speed of the press and the type of stock used. A control knob or handle adjusts the receding table speed. The receding table should lower at the same rate that the feeding platform rises.

OFFSET PRESS TROUBLESHOOTING

Offset press operation involves many procedures and variables that determine the quality of the printed product. Printing problems encountered by press operators are often the result of working with a high volume of materials. Troubleshooting and maintenance play a critical part in operating a press, **Figure 16-21.** Regular press maintenance helps increase production and printing quality.

The setup procedures discussed in this chapter directly affect image quality. Each press component must be functioning properly to achieve consistent production. Because the components are interdependent, each press function affects the entire operation. The operator must be able to recognize a problem when it occurs, understand how it is caused, and determine how to solve it. For example, poorly printed materials may result from failure of the plate to keep the nonimage and image areas separate, improper packing of the plate or blanket, an incorrect combination of ink and fountain solution, or insufficient roller pressure. Numerous control devices and settings used on the press can make it difficult to identify the exact cause of the problem. When analyzing a problem, the operator must consider all the variables associated with the problem, and then decide which steps to take to fix

Figure 16-21. Making the right adjustments to the press can play a key role in troubleshooting printing problems.

the problem. Thorough analysis is key when looking for the source or cause of the problem.

Printing problems can usually be classified as either ink problems or press problems. Ink problems are caused by a variety of issues. One common problem results from the stickiness of the ink, or *ink tack*. This is cohesion between the ink film and the substrate. When the ink is transferred from one roller to another, the ink must split. A portion stays on the first roller, but another portion must transfer to the next roller. If ink has too much tack, or does not split, it cannot transfer properly from one roller to another, to the plate and blanket, or from the roller to a surface of the substrate, **Figure 16-22.** The properties of ink will be discussed in more detail in Chapter 22.

Press problems usually require adjustments to specific parts of the system. Newer presses are equipped with automatic control devices that allow operators greater control over image quality. However, manual adjustments are often necessary to correct a printing problem.

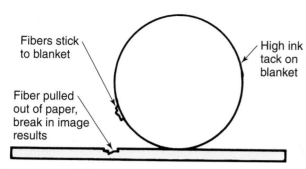

Figure 16-22. When ink tack is not matched to stock, the high tack can pull fibers off the paper.

Troubleshooting charts are commonly used by operators to analyze and solve printing problems. The troubleshooting chart in **Figure 16-23** lists several common ink and press problems, along with typical causes and corrections.

Summary

The principle of all lithographic presses is the same. However, the sheet-fed press prints on a precut sheet, while the web-fed press prints from a continuous roll of stock, which is then cut into sheets. Press designs vary, but the fundamental systems are found on the presses. The substrate must travel through the various systems to have an image placed on the stock. Knowledge of each system is imperative, and knowing how to diagnose press system problems is important for the operating role.

Review Questions

Please do not write in this text. Write your answers on a separate sheet of paper.

1. A _____ is a small sheet-fed press used in short printing runs.
2. List the five operating systems found in both sheet-fed and web-fed offset presses.
3. On the feeding system, the paper on the feeding platform is sent to the pullout rollers by the _____.
4. What are the two functions of the impression cylinder in a printing system?
5. True *or* False? Plates and blankets mounted on a press are held in place by a set of clamps.
6. The undercut surface of a press cylinder allows for _____ to adjust for different plate and blanket thicknesses.
7. Which roller makes intermittent contact with the fountain roller and distributor roller to transfer fountain solution in a dampening system?

Troubleshooting Guide: Ink Problems	
Chalking: Dried ink easily rubs off or is missing from the sheet.	
Cause 1. Insufficient amount of ink drier. 2. Ink absorbed by paper before setting properly. 3. Job printed with improper ink for stock used.	**Correction** 1. Add drier as suggested by manufacturer. 2. Add gum or binding agent to control absorption. 3. Overprint paper with varnish.
Hickeys: Ink spots surrounded by a white background.	
Cause 1. Particles of dried ink. 2. Dust specks or other contaminants. 3. Slitter or paper dust.	**Correction** 1. Remove dried ink when skimming ink from can. Clean press and remove all dried ink from fountain and rollers. 2. Improve cleanliness in pressroom. 3. Check feeding pile for loose edges.
Misting: A fine spray of misplaced ink.	
Cause 1. Ink film too soft. 2. Press speed too high. 3. Excess flow of ink. 4. Ink rollers damaged or out of round. 5. Poor lateral distribution of ink on rollers.	**Correction** 1. Stiffen ink with body gum or varnish. 2. Reduce press speed. 3. Adjust ink flow from fountain. 4. Inspect rollers and replace if necessary. 5. Adjust roller pressure or oscillating motion of vibrator roller.

Figure 16-23. There are many problems and solutions encountered during the printing problem. Review this chart to become familiar with some of the more common problems.

ink tack: A measurement of cohesion between the ink film and the substrate.

Piling: A buildup of ink on the ink rollers, plate, or blanket.

Cause	Correction
1. Ink too stiff or tacky.	1. Reduce tack by adding a reducing compound.
2. Emulsified ink.	2. Clean up press and use proper balance of ink and fountain solution.
3. Improperly ground ink.	3. Reformulate ink.
4. Blanket packed improperly.	4. Repack blanket.

Poor ink distribution: An uneven dispersion of ink, resulting in an excess of ink film in one area of the ink rollers.

Cause	Correction
1. Ink rollers glazed.	1. Deglaze or replace rollers.
2. Ink rollers "out of round."	2. Regrind or replace rollers.
3. Ink too stiff or tacky.	3. Add an ink-reducing compound to the ink supply.
4. Uneven ink fountain distribution.	4. Adjust ink keys.

Poor ink trapping: The misregistration of color images in multicolor printing. Occurs when the second color ink has a higher tack than the first color ink.

Cause	Correction
1. Excess tack in overprinted ink.	1. Reduce tack of ink that fails to trap. Reformulate each color of ink.
2. Insufficient drier used on first color printed.	2. Change drier.
3. Ink and fountain solution out of balance.	3. Reduce ink feed in problem areas, then minimize use of fountain solution.
4. Too much time taken after printing first color.	4. Perform additional color runs as soon as possible.

Slow drying: Condition that occurs when ink fails to cure quickly enough after printing, delaying multicolor printing runs.

Cause	Correction
1. Fountain solution too acidic.	1. Check pH and adjust value to between 4.0 and 5.5.
2. Insufficient amount of ink drier.	2. Add drier to ink.
3. Wrong ink used with paper.	3. Use proper ink for grade of stock.
4. Low temperature in pressroom.	4. Raise temperature to improve drying ability.

Press Problems

Blinding: The image area of the plate will not accept ink.

Cause	Correction
1. Excess gum in fountain solution.	1. Check solution and reformulate using procedure recommeded by manufacturer.
2. Fountain solution too acidic.	2. Check pH and adjust value to between 4.0 and 5.5.
3. Excess plate-to-blanket pressure.	3. Check roller pressure with cylinder packing gauge and repack blanket.
4. Glazed rollers.	4. Deglaze or replace rollers.
5. Improper ink tack.	5. Reformulate ink to match stock.
6. Contamination of plate during platemaking.	6. Thoroughly clean and rinse plate and regum surface.

Ghosting: Condition that occurs when a solid image prints unevenly or a faint, second image appears next to the original.

Cause	Correction
1. Glazed or hardened ink rollers.	1. Clean or replace rollers.
2. Excess fountain solution.	2. Adjust balance of ink and fountain solution.
3. Embossed or engraved blanket.	3. Replace blanket.
4. In multicolor printing, ink loss due to varying solids.	4. Minimize fountain solution or use opaque inks.

Image loss: An area of missing lines or halftone dots that make up the image.

Cause	Correction
1. Blanket wearing thin under pressure.	1. Repack blanket.
2. Glazed blanket surface.	2. Clean or replace blanket.
3. Swollen blanket.	3. Remove packing or replace blanket.
4. Smashed blanket.	4. Fill in smashed area or replace blanket.

Figure 16-23. (*Continued*)

Ink roller stripping: Failure of ink rollers to absorb ink.

Cause	Correction
1. Fountain solution pH too acidic.	1. Adjust pH to between 4.0 and 5.5.
2. Excess use of fountain solution.	2. Adjust fountain solution setting.
3. Ink rollers are desensitized.	3. Clean and etch rollers.
4. Glazed ink rollers.	4. Deglaze rollers.

Misregistration: Two overprinted images or color elements do not align when printed.

Cause	Correction
1. Excess ink tack.	1. Reduce tack.
2. Curled or wrinkled paper stock.	2. Reduce humidity of pressroom.
3. Printing pressures stretch paper stock.	3. Adjust impression (cylinder pressure).
4. Image improperly positioned on plate.	4. Remake plate with image in register.
5. Plate mounted improperly.	5. Reposition plate on plate cylinder.
6. Loose blanket.	6. Reattach blanket.

Mottling: Uneven amounts of ink in the solid portion of the image, causing printed sheet to appear cloudy.

Cause	Correction
1. Failure of ink to be absorbed uniformly by paper.	1. Formulate ink to grade of stock.
2. Excess fountain solution.	2. Adjust balance of ink and fountain solution.
3. Ink not resistant to water.	3. Add varnish to increase tack.

Picking: The lifting of paper fibers by the ink during printing.

Cause	Correction
1. Excess ink tack.	1. Reduce tack with a reducing compound.
2. Excess blanket-to-impression cylinder pressure.	2. Repack blanket or reduce cylinder pressure.
3. Poor quality of paper.	3. Use a better grade of stock.
4. Tacky blanket surface.	4. Clean or replace blanket.

Plate wear: Gradual disappearance of the image area from the plate surface.

Cause	Correction
1. Excess form roller pressure.	1. Check pressure by inking plate and observing ink stripes.
2. Excess pressure between plate and blanket.	2. Check roller pressure with cylinder packing gauge and repack blanket.
3. Fountain solution too acidic.	3. Check pH and adjust value to between 4.0 and 5.5.
4. Insufficient amount of ink.	4. Adjust ink keys.
5. Dried gum on plate.	5. Clean plate with water and solvent and regum surface.
6. Abrasive residue or debris from blanket or stock.	6. Clean blanket or check paper.

Scumming: Buildup of ink film on nonimage area of plate.

Cause	Correction
1. Ink too soft.	1. Add varnish to increase tack.
2. Excess use of ink.	2. Adjust balance of ink and fountain solution.
3. Sensitized nonimage area of plate.	3. Remake plate.
4. Incorrect fountain solution pH.	4. Check pH and adjust value to between 4.0 and 5.5.
5. Glazed blanket.	5. Clean or replace blanket.
6. Excessive printing pressure.	5. Reduce plate-to-blanket and blanket-to-impression cylinder pressures.
7. Glazed or dirty ink rollers.	6. Clean or replace rollers.
8. Dirty dampening rollers.	7. Clean or replace rollers.

Setoff: The transfer of ink from one sheet to the back of another on a delivery pile.

Cause	Correction
1. Too much ink carried to paper.	1. Readjust ink keys.
2. Excess acid in fountain solution.	2. Change pH value of solution to recommended level.
3. Insufficient amount of ink drier.	3. Add drier to ink.
4. Improper ink for stock.	4. Change ink to match stock.
5. Sheets clinging from static electricity.	5. Use static eliminators with delivery system.
6. Delivery pile too high.	6. Reduce pile height.

Figure 16-23. (*Continued*)

Slurring: An unwanted accumulation of halftone dots that result in a smeared image.	
Cause 1. Slippage in the impression phase. 2. Excessive pressure between plate and blanket. 3. Excess ink on coated stocks. 4. Piling of ink on paper. 5. Loose-fitting plate on cylinder. 6. Excessive tack; paper sticks to blanket at trail edge.	**Correction** 1. Reduce impression cylinder pressure. 2. Adjust pressure. 3. Adjust ink keys to reduce ink feed. 4. Change paper or use a moisture-resistant stock. 5. Reattach plate. 6. Add reducing varnish to ink or use ink with lower tack.
Tinting: Unwanted color tint in background of image, commonly caused by emulsification of ink in the fountain solution.	
Cause 1. Ink fails to repel water. 2. Improper fountain solution pH. 3. Ink and fountain solution out of balance. 4. Plate not properly desensitized.	**Correction** 1. Add varnish to soft ink to increase tack. 2. Adjust pH value to between 4.0 and 5.5. 3. Clean press and adjust mix of ink and fountain solution. 4. Prepare new plate.

Figure 16-23. *(Continued)*

8. Name two devices used to measure the pH value of a fountain solution.

9. What are ink keys?

10. Describe a common technique used to check the pressure between the ink form rollers and the plate.

11. A chain delivery system uses this device to draw paper from the press and release it to the delivery pile.
    A. Sucker feet.
    B. Grippers.
    C. Stationary guides.
    D. Jogging guides.

12. Explain the term *setoff*.

13. True *or* False? Most printing problems can be classified as either ink problems or press problems.

14. The measurement of cohesion between ink film and a substrate is called _____.

15. Using the chart in Figure 16-23, list three possible causes and corrections for each of the following printing problems: chalking, misting, picking, and scumming.

Suggested Activities

1. Answer the following questions after printing a job.
   A. What were some common problems encountered during the printing run?
   B. List the steps taken to complete the entire printing job.
   C. What calculations were made during the printing job?

2. What scientific principles can you identify that are needed in press design?

Related Web Links

Paper, Film & Foil Converter (PFFC) Online Magazine
pffc-online.com/mag/paper_role_tack_printing
Online magazine for the packaging industry.

Society for Imaging Science and Technology
www.imaging.org/resources/web_tutorials/printing_press/printing_press.cfm
Web tutorials about imaging technology.

Specialized offset presses have been developed to meet specific needs of printers and their customers. This web-fed offset press is designed specifically for the printing operations geared to rapid production of short-run, single-color books. It permits quickly and easily changing web width for different print jobs. (Strachan Henshaw Machinery, Inc.)

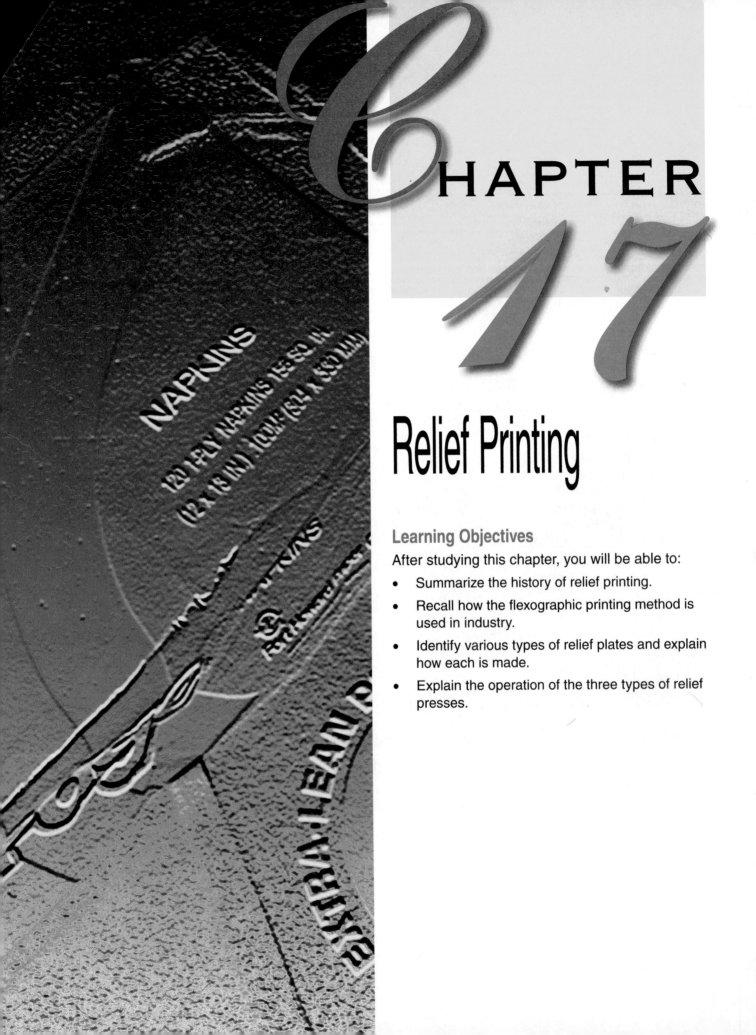

CHAPTER 17

Relief Printing

Learning Objectives

After studying this chapter, you will be able to:

- Summarize the history of relief printing.
- Recall how the flexographic printing method is used in industry.
- Identify various types of relief plates and explain how each is made.
- Explain the operation of the three types of relief presses.

Important Terms

drawsheet
electrotype
flexography
photoengraving
photopolymer plate
platen press
relief printing
rubber plates
stereotype

Relief printing, also known as letterpress, is a traditional printing method in which images are printed from a raised surface. Elements making up the image are raised (in relief) above the surface. The nonimage area is recessed and lies below the surface, **Figure 17-1.** After the image carrier or plate is inked, the raised surface is pressed against paper to print the image.

Relief printing has essentially been replaced by offset lithography as the standard commercial printing process. As we learned in Chapter 14, both the image and nonimage areas are on the same plane in lithographic printing. Relief printing applications, however, are still used in some areas of the graphic communications industry. A basic understanding of relief printing is still valuable to students interested in graphic communications. This chapter will explore those relief printing techniques that continue to be used today.

HISTORY OF RELIEF PRINTING

Chapter 6 explained the history of relief printing and the process of relief printing composition. In that chapter, we learned that relief printing was the first printing method developed and was the dominant form of printing in the world from the 1400s until the middle of the 20th century. The earliest uses of relief printing can be traced back to 8th century Chinese wood block images. Modern relief printing methods originated in the mid-1400s in Germany when Johannes Gutenberg invented movable type.

Prior to the invention of movable type, books were created one at a time using hand-lettering or carved wooden plates. With movable type, multiple copies of books could be printed, making them available to more people. The Gutenberg Bible remains one of the most famous books ever published. Its printing helped lay the groundwork for modern printing practices.

RELIEF PRINTING APPLICATIONS

Traditional relief printing methods have limited use today in commercial operations. They are used to some extent in printing packaging materials, **Figure 17-2,** and in finishing operations such as embossing, ticket numbering, perforating, and die

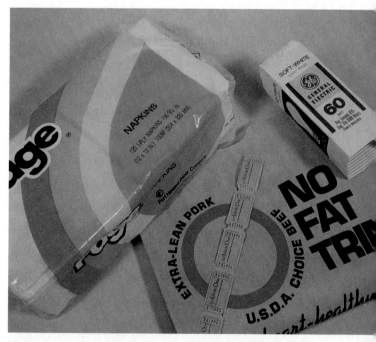

Figure 17-2. Packaging materials and numbered tickets are examples of products that are created using relief printing processes.

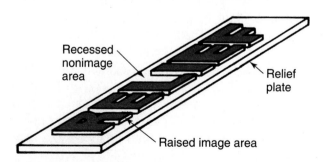

Figure 17-1. The relief process prints images from a raised surface that accepts ink. The nonimage area is recessed and lies below the raised image.

relief printing: The process of printing from a raised surface. Ink is applied to the raised image, then transferred to the paper or other substrate.

flexography: A relief printing process that uses flexible printing plates for printing long run jobs.

cutting. After paper is printed, it can be die-cut into a special design using letterpress equipment. The printed material is trimmed to a final shape by pressing it against a die mounted on a press, **Figure 17-3.**

Flexography, a type of relief process, is the only relief process still in use in the graphic communications industry. Flexography uses a curved or flexible plate made from rubber or plastic. When mounted on the press, the plate is wrapped around a plate cylinder. The plate is then mounted on a press, inked, and pressed against a printing substrate to produce an image.

Flexography is commonly used to print packaging materials, such as grocery bags, labels, and folding cartons. It is sometimes used to print paperback books, and newspapers.

Flexography offers several advantages over other printing methods. Because flexographic plates are made from rubber, they are very durable and can be used to print a large number of materials. Another advantage of flexographic plates is their use of fast-drying, water-based inks. Water-based inks are less harmful to the environment than solvent-based inks, which produce fumes as they dry.

Flexographic printing is covered in more detail in Chapter 18. The next section of this chapter will discuss the different types of plates used in relief printing.

Figure 17-3. Die cutting is a process that cuts printed materials into special designs.

RELIEF PLATES

In traditional relief printing, the original type form contained the characters used for printing. There was only one image carrier. This hand-set composition of individual pieces of movable type was a time-consuming process that often took weeks to accomplish. As the method evolved, duplicate plates were introduced to reduce wear on the form and to allow printers to produce more than one copy of a form at a time. In many cases, the original form served as a master plate and was then used to make duplicates. As a result, plates used in traditional relief printing are designated as either original or duplicate plates. Original plates can be used for direct printing or to make a duplicate plate. Duplicate plates are used for long press runs when one plate is expected to wear out before the printing is completed. Duplicates made from a master can also be sent to different locations for printing. Two of the most common types of duplicate plates used in relief printing are stereotypes and electrotypes.

Stereotypes

A *stereotype* is cast by pouring molten metal (an alloy of lead, tin, and antimony) into a mold or mat made from the original type form. The mat is produced by placing a blank rubber or paper sheet over the form and applying pressure to form an intaglio image (one that appears in reverse from the original). To produce plates for use on high-speed newspaper presses, the mats were curved to the same diameter as the press cylinders. The resulting curved plates could be locked in place on the cylinders for web-fed printing.

Electrotypes

An *electrotype* is produced from a mold through an electrochemical process. After a mold is made from the original type form, the intaglio image is sprayed with silver. The silver coating is a conductive material that forms a thin layer on the surface of the mold. The surface is then electroplated with a layer of copper or nickel to form a shell. When the shell that forms the relief image is removed from the mold, it is backed with a layer of lead or plastic to provide support. The electrotype is then attached to a base and ready to be printed, **Figure 17-4.**

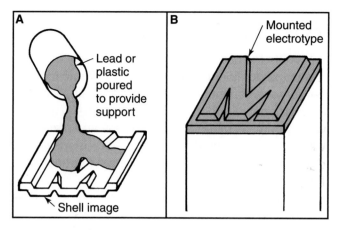

Figure 17-4. Electrotypes are duplicate plates that are formed through an electrochemical process. A—The shell containing the image is produced from a mold of the original form and is backed with a layer of lead or plastic. B—The newly formed plate is mounted on a base for printing.

Photoengraving

For many years, line art images had to be first carved by hand when they were printed along with type forms. This process changed in the 1800s when photochemical processes such as photoengraving were introduced. *Photoengraving* is a platemaking method that produces relief images by exposing a light-sensitive plate coating through a negative. The negative is a film version of the original image. After exposure, the nonimage portion of the plate is etched away with acid to produce the relief image. This process allows picture images to be reproduced by converting the two-dimensional image of a negative into a three-dimensional relief image.

Photoengraved plates consist of line or halftone images, or a combination of both. To expose the image, the negative containing the original image is placed facedown in contact with the plate. The plate receives a wrong-reading version of the image, which, when printed on the press, is transferred to the printing substrate in its original form.

The image area of the plate is formed when the light-sensitive coating is exposed. When the plate is developed, the unexposed coating of the nonimage area is washed away. The raised relief surface is produced when the nonimage area is etched to a designated depth with an acid.

While the basic principles of relief printing changed little after the invention of movable type, newer platemaking procedures continued to emerge. Different materials and procedures have been tried when making photoengraved plates. The most common materials currently used to make relief plates are rubber and plastic.

Rubber Plates

Rubber plates are flexible relief plates commonly used in flexographic printing. They have a raised image area that is formed from a mold or matrix. As discussed earlier, rubber plates are designed to wrap around the plate cylinder of a press.

To create a rubber plate, a matrix is first produced from the original image. The original is placed on top of the matrix material inside a hydraulic press, and the two are forced together through heat and pressure to form the matrix. Then a sheet of rubber is placed over the matrix on the press, and heat and pressure are applied to vulcanize the rubber and form a duplicate plate.

Rubber plates have several advantages over other plates used in relief printing. Rubber plates have a softer surface than metal plates and are compressible. They provide a smooth transfer of ink to materials with a rough surface, such as folding cartons and grocery bags.

Plastic plates are growing in popularity and have replaced rubber plates as the most commonly used flexographic plates. A type of plastic plate, the photopolymer plate, does not require a mold to be made from the original copy.

Photopolymer Plates

Photopolymer plates are light-sensitive plastic image carriers that are widely used in flexographic printing. The plate surface contains a hard, sensitized plastic coating or polymer that is bonded to a backing or base, **Figure 17-5.** Photopolymer plates are flexible and designed for long use. They are often used to print packaging materials.

---

stereotype: A duplicate relief plate that is cast by pouring molten metal into a mold or mat made from the original type form of composed characters.

electrotype: A duplicate relief plate that is produced from a mold through an electrochemical process.

photoengraving: A platemaking method that produces relief images by exposing a light-sensitive plate coating through a negative.

rubber plates: Flexible relief plates commonly used in flexographic printing.

photopolymer plates: Plastic relief plates commonly used in flexographic printing. The surface of a photopolymer plate contains a light-sensitive polymer coating that hardens after exposure.

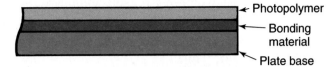

Figure 17-5. Photopolymer plates have a sensitized plastic surface layer that hardens after exposure to ultraviolet light.

A photopolymer plate is exposed through a negative by ultraviolet light. The polymer coating hardens to form a raised image area. The nonimage area remains soft and is washed out through processing with a water-based solution. After exposure and development, the plate undergoes a drying process. The plate is then re-exposed to ultraviolet light to further harden the relief image. This process strengthens the plate for extended use on the press. The basic steps used in exposing and processing a photopolymer plate are shown in **Figure 17-6.**

Photopolymer plates can also be imaged directly by lasers using computer-to-plate (CTP) technology. This process eliminates the need for film as an intermediary when the plate is made. An image is scanned and transferred directly to the plate by the computer and then the plate is automatically processed by washing out the nonimage area.

RELIEF PRESSES

While the use of letterpress has sharply declined, it was the dominant form of printing well into the 20th century and continues to be used in a few applications. In traditional letterpress, a chase containing the type form or plate is mounted on the press and positioned for printing. The surface of the plate is inked and pressed against the printing substrate to transfer the image.

Three types of relief presses are commonly used in the relief printing process: a platen press, a flatbed cylinder press, or a rotary press, **Figure 17-7.** The different equipment and operating procedures used with each type of press are discussed next.

Platen Press

A *platen press* produces printed materials by pressing a locked-up form or plate containing the image against a platen, the printing surface that holds the paper. Originally, hand-operated platen presses were used extensively by print shops. During press operation, sheets of paper were fed by hand and printed individually. Power-operated presses were developed later to feed, print, and deliver sheets automatically, **Figure 17-8.** Platen press designs vary, but components used include a feedboard, a bed, a platen, bails, grippers, and a delivery board.

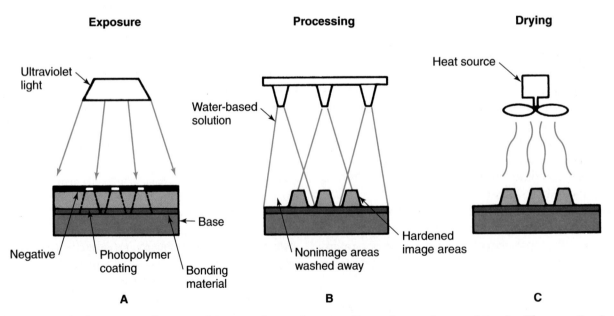

Figure 17-6. The basic procedures used in exposing and processing a photopolymer plate. A—The negative is placed over the plate and the exposure is made using an ultraviolet light source. B—During processing, a water-based solution is applied to wash out the nonimage area. The image area has hardened and is raised from the surface. C—A drying process is used to remove moisture from the plate before it is exposed again to strengthen the image.

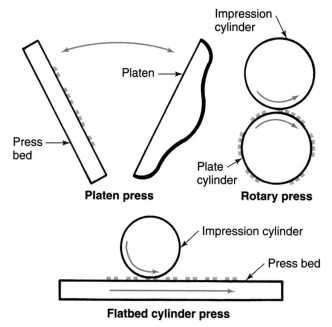

Figure 17-7. The three types of presses most commonly used in relief printing are the platen press, the flatbed cylinder press, and the rotary press.

Figure 17-8. A traditional power-operated platen press.

The type form is locked up in a chase, is placed in the bed of the press, and is locked in position. During the printing process, paper is stacked onto the feedboard and transferred to the platen. The type form is inked by a set of form rollers. The ink used on the rollers is supplied by an ink disk. The form and platen are pressed together to make the impression. After the sheet is printed, it is removed from the platen and placed on the delivery board.

To prepare the press for printing, the platen must be dressed with packing sheets. These sheets include tympan paper, hanger sheets, and a pressboard. Each sheet is attached to the platen and held in place by the bails. The bails are a pair of locking arms that clamp the sheets in place. The packing provides enough pressure between the surface of the platen and the form to transfer the image.

To pack the platen, hanger sheets are attached first and clamped down by the lower bail. A sheet of tympan paper, also called a *drawsheet*, is then placed on top of the hanger sheets and clamped under the lower bail. The drawsheet serves as the holding surface for the paper and can be used to make a test impression. With the drawsheet and hanger sheets in place, the pressboard (a heavy piece of stock) is positioned under the rest of the packing, but is not locked by either bail. The drawsheet is then clamped under the top bail.

As each sheet is transferred from the feedboard to the platen, it is aligned in the correct position to receive the image when it is printed. Sheets are aligned on the drawsheet by two bars of grippers, mechanical devices that close around the edges of the paper when it reaches the platen. The grippers must be placed so they guide each sheet into position without touching the type form. If the grippers make contact with the type form, the type will be smashed.

Hand-fed platen presses use gauge pins to align the paper on the drawsheet. The location of the gauge pins is determined by printing a test impression on the drawsheet and placing a sheet of paper over the image. The pins are inserted to fit the dimensions of the paper; typically at the top and left sides. When paper is placed on the platen, the gauge pins are used to hold each sheet in the desired position for printing. After the gauge pins are set, the test impression can be removed from the drawsheet with solvent.

Flatbed Cylinder Press

A flatbed cylinder press prints by producing contact between a flat surface or bed supporting the plate and a revolving impression cylinder that carries sheets of paper. The chase holding the plate or type form is mounted on the bed. The paper on

platen press: A relief press that prints by pressing a type form or plate against a platen, the surface that holds the paper to be printed.

drawsheet: A sheet of tympan paper that provides the holding surface for paper to be printed on a platen press.

the cylinder then rolls over the bed and receives the image from the inked form. The impression cylinder uses a set of grippers to grasp and deliver paper as it travels through the press. The pressure between the cylinder and the type is used to transfer the image.

Many of the same devices and techniques that are associated with platen presses are used to operate flatbed cylinder presses. Many sheet-fed flatbed cylinder presses are equipped with devices that draw and feed paper through the system automatically. Some cylinder presses are designed to print from flexographic plates and are used in multicolor printing.

Rotary Press

A rotary press prints the substrate as it travels between an impression cylinder and a plate cylinder, **Figure 17-9.** The impression cylinder draws paper into the printing unit and releases it after it is printed. The image carrier used by a rotary press is a curved plate that is mounted on the plate cylinder. Rotary presses typically use duplicate plates for long press runs and operate at high speeds. They are designed as both sheet-fed systems and web-fed systems and are commonly used in magazine and newspaper publishing, where longer runs are required.

Rotary presses used in multicolor printing are equipped with several printing units. Each unit contains a separate plate cylinder that prints a single color. In this design, a common impression cylinder is surrounded by several printing units. The common cylinder provides the pressure needed to transfer images from each plate to the paper as it is fed through the system.

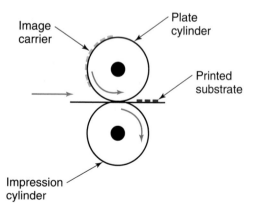

Figure 17-9. A rotary press is designed to print paper as it passes between a plate cylinder and an impression cylinder.

Labels in figure:
Image carrier
Plate cylinder
Printed substrate
Impression cylinder

ACADEMIC LINK
Printer's Math

Basic math skills are essential in performing daily tasks in a print shop. Calculating the amount of paper needed for a job, the correct proportions for ink and solution mixtures, and the per item cost of supplies are necessary for the efficient and successful operation of a printing business. The following are examples of how math is regularly applied in the print production process. Use your knowledge of basic math operations to solve each of these problems.

1. The finished pages of a printed book are 7.5″ wide. There is a 1/2″ margin around the type on both the left and the right side of each page. Additionally, the customer wants the pages to be perforated 1/4″ from the left edge. What is the total margin on the left side of the page? How much room is left on the page for printed material?
2. 100 sheets of cover stock measures 1.25″. How many sheets of cover stock are in a stack that is 34.75″ high?
3. A skid of 100 lb. coated stock contains 7,750 sheets of paper and costs $2,400. What is the per sheet cost of the paper?
4. 115 lbs. of black ink is needed to stock the supply shelves of the shop. The ink is available in 5 lb. cans. How many cans need to be ordered?
5. How many full-sized sheets of 23″ × 35″ paper must be ordered to print a job that involves 1200 pieces of 8.5″ × 11″?

Like other web-fed presses, web-fed rotary presses are designed to print high volumes of materials on a continuous roll of paper. The web winds through each system during operation of the press, **Figure 17-10.** Rotary presses used in flexographic printing are equipped with individual feeding, printing, drying, and delivery systems.

Figure 17-10. This web-fed rotary press prints on a continuous web (roll) of paper and is designed to operate at high speeds.

Summary

For hundreds of years, relief printing was the only method of placing an image on a substrate. That is no longer the case. There are many more printing methods available today. However, a small amount of printing is still done using the relief printing process, largely by specialty companies in the packaging industry. In these instances, relief printing provides quality printed items.

Review Questions

Please do not write in this text. Write your answers on a separate sheet of paper.

1. Relief printing creates images from a(n) _____ surface.
2. Using _____ type, multiple copies of a book can be printed.
3. List three finishing applications of traditional relief printing equipment.
4. True *or* False? Flexography is one of many relief processes used in the graphic communications industry.
5. What is the purpose of a duplicate plate?
6. Define the term *photoengraving*.
7. Which of the following plates provides a smooth transfer of ink to rough-surfaced materials?
   A. Photopolymer.
   B. Stereotype.
   C. Rubber.
   D. Electrotype.
8. Describe the process used to make a photopolymer plate.
9. List the three types of presses traditionally used in relief printing.
10. What two cylinders make up the printing unit of a rotary press?

Suggested Activities

1. Printing museums are found throughout the world. Research the location of printing museums and make this list available to everyone at your school. Request that students or staff visit these museums if they are traveling or vacationing in their vicinity.
2. Think about the invention of movable metal type. Write a short paper explaining the importance of this invention to present-day society.

Related Web Links

Printers' National Environmental Assistance Center

www.pneac.org/printprocesses
Provides descriptions of various print processes.

Experimental Arts

www.experimentalarts.com/lessons/relief_printing.htm
Online visual arts gallery that supplies instruction in various printing methods.

CHAPTER 18

Flexographic Printing

Learning Objectives

After studying this chapter, you will be able to:

- Describe the flexographic process.
- Recall various types of presses used in flexography.
- Identify the types of substrates, inks, and plates used in flexography.

Important Terms

anilox roll	photopolymer plates
doctor blade	plate elongation
FIRST	repeat length
flexography	viscosity
inline	volatile organic compounds
matrix	Zahn cup

OVERVIEW OF FLEXOGRAPHY

Flexography is a method of direct rotary printing that uses flexible relief image plates made of rubber or photopolymer material. The plates are attached to cylinders of various repeat lengths and inked by a cell-structured ink metering roll. This fast-drying, fluid ink is carried to plates that print on nearly any substrate.

Flexography was originally known as aniline printing because of the aniline dyes used to color the ink. However, aniline dyes and their harsh solvents left an odor on the product and came to be considered toxic. Eventually, the Food and Drug Administration banned their use on food packaging. Chemists began developing new inks and alcohol solvents as replacements. The term *aniline printing* remained in use until the late 1950s, when the process became known as flexography. Later, passage of the United States Clean Air Act spurred development of water-based inks using low-solvent or no-solvent inks. Today, flexography is often chosen because of the ability to print with clean, water-based, or no-solvent ultraviolet inks. The process is also less expensive than other printing methods.

Flexography satisfies the demand for high-quality graphics on packaging products. Corrugated boxes are the largest market for flexography. It is also used to print candy wrappers, shopping bags, milk cartons, cereal boxes, gift wrap, wallpaper, and many other goods.

PRESS DEVELOPMENTS

Prior to World War II, Europe was the leader in printing press engineering and innovation. After the war, the United States became much more competitive in the printing arena. Currently, flexographic press engineering and innovation comes from all areas of the globe.

Flexographic presses often house the equipment needed to perform the entire manufacturing process, **Figure 18-1.** These presses contain the machinery needed to slit, laminate, number, perforate, die-cut, emboss, and sheet (cut to size) a job. Presses range in web width from 2″–110″ (5 cm–279 cm). Unlike offset lithography, in flexographic printing just one roller applies ink to the printing plates. Lithographic printing uses several rollers to split and work the

Figure 18-1. Flexographic presses are widely used for printing packaging and labels. This is a seven-station, narrow-web label press. (Mark Andy, Inc.)

flexography: A relief printing process that uses flexible printing plates.

paste ink into a thin film. This is not necessary with flexographic inks. In addition, paste inks dry very slowly compared to flexographic inks which evaporate in fractions of a second. This makes flexographic inks ideal for printing on polyethylene, the material used for plastic grocery bags and similar products.

An ink fountain holds the ink. The fountain roller is made of soft or hard rubber and transfers the ink to the next roller in the chain, the *anilox roll*, **Figure 18-2.** The anilox roll surface is engraved with cells that carry ink up to the plate cylinder. The fountain roller moves at a slower speed than the anilox roll, creating a skidding action between the two rollers. This helps remove some of the excess ink from the anilox roll. The act of removing excess ink is called doctoring. Many presses slow the fountain roller to increase the doctoring action between the two.

Doctoring was done using a two-roll system for many years, until the doctor blade was introduced. The *doctor blade* is angled in order to clear excess ink from noncell areas. The doctor blade produces excellent, even inking of the cells in the anilox roll.

The image carrying plate is mounted on the plate cylinder and is made of rubber or photopolymer, **Figure 18-3.** The anilox roll inks the relief image plate with a continuous, metered supply of ink. The substrate is fed, under controlled tension, against the impression cylinder. The fast-drying ink prints on the absorbent or nonabsorbent substrate and dries instantly.

A recent improvement in the flexographic inking system is an enclosed, or chambered, dual-doctor-blade system, **Figure 18-4.** The chamber contains ink and it is applied directly to the anilox roll. Two doctor blades are placed at either end of the chamber and make contact with the anilox roll. The upper blade doctors the anilox roll. The lower blade, which acts as an ink-catch basin, is called the trailing or

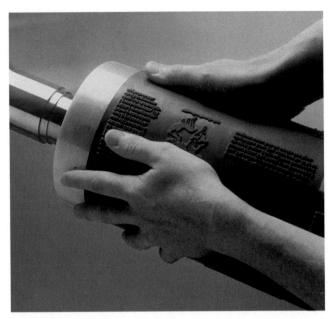

Figure 18-3. Rubber or polymer are used for the raised flexographic plate. (Strachan Henshaw Machinery, Inc.)

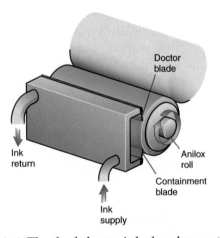

Figure 18-4. The dual-doctor ink chamber system is becoming common on presses. (Agfa)

containment blade. The ends of the enclosed unit have special wipers that prevent ink from coming out of the enclosed system. The dual-doctor ink-chamber eliminates the need for a fountain roller and pan. Most new presses are built with the chambered system, while many existing presses are being retrofitted for it.

FLEXOGRAPHIC PRESS TYPES

Flexographic presses are rotary printing machines. The cylinders print on every revolution to a moving web of substrate material. This very

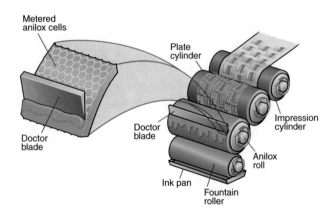

Figure 18-2. The flexographic ink delivery system uses an anilox roll engraved with tiny cells. (Agfa)

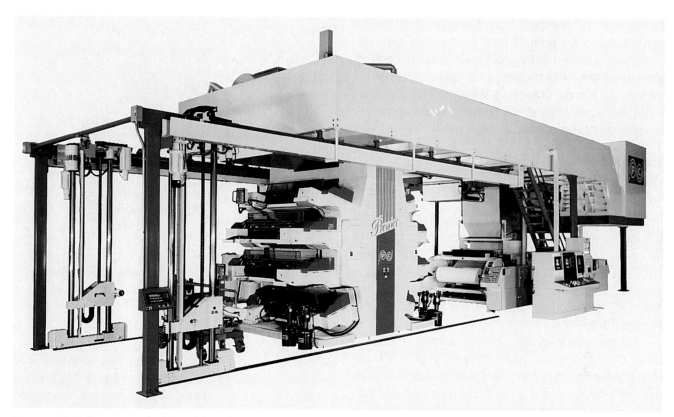

Figure 18-5. Every revolution of the plate cylinder creates the same image on a substrate. (Paper Converting Machine Company)

action makes for high press speeds, **Figure 18-5.** It is not uncommon for wide-web presses printing polyethylene to run at speeds of 750 feet per minute (fpm) or 228.6 meters per minute (mpm). Label presses can print up to 500 fpm (152 mpm). Press speed is relative to the type of work being done. Some jobs require lower speeds to print properly.

The design of the flexographic printing unit allows press manufacturers to build presses in any one of three configurations: the stack press, the central impression cylinder press, and the *inline* press.

Stack Press

The stack press was the first type of flexographic press developed and was used with aniline inks. In a stack press, printing stations are positioned one above another, or vertically. A two- to three-foot distance between the stations gives the web time to dry before the next color is printed. A typical stack-type press prints three colors down and three colors up on the web, **Figure 18-6.** Since the moving web is unsupported between the printing stations, pliable materials, such as polyethylene plastic, can stretch between stations and cause register problems. Unstretchable substrates, such as thick paper or

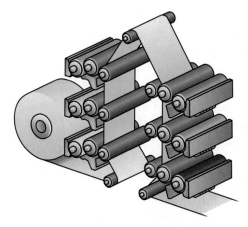

Figure 18-6. The stack press was the first type developed for flexographic printing. (Agfa)

anilox roll: A metal or ceramic roll engraved with cells that carry ink to the plate cylinder.

doctor blade: A thin metal blade that clears excess ink from the noncell areas of the anilox roll.

inline: Done as a continuous process on a single piece of equipment.

heavier gauge plastics, can hold register from station to station and are better suited for this configuration.

Stack presses with good web tension controls are used for work that does not require tight register. Fewer stack type presses are being manufactured today because other press types have proven more reliable for flexographic printing.

Central Impression Cylinder Presses

In the central impression cylinder (CIC) press, the web travels from one print station to the next around a central drum, **Figure 18-7**. The moving web is supported between stations, so the press is ideal for stretchable films needing a close register. The CIC drum does not allow the web to stretch, **Figure 18-8**.

CIC presses originally had four stations around the drum. Current presses, have drums up to 96″ (244 cm) in diameter, allowing for six to eight stations. The central cylinder has a gear that times and controls the turning of all print stations and keeps them in register.

CIC presses print on one side only. Because of their accuracy, CIC presses are ideal for printing on stretchable plastic film packaging.

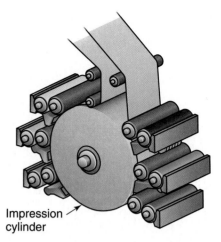

Impression cylinder

Figure 18-7. The central impression cylinder type of flexographic press supports the substrate by direct contact with the cylinder. (Agfa)

Inline Press

The inline flexographic press has separate print stations placed in a straight line, **Figure 18-9**. Each section has its own dryer. The stations are connected to one another by a long central shaft that keeps the stations in register. A single print station is similar to a gravure press print station, **Figure 18-10**.

Two sides can be printed in one pass with the aid of a turnover bar. Printing stations can be added to an inline press at any time to increase the number

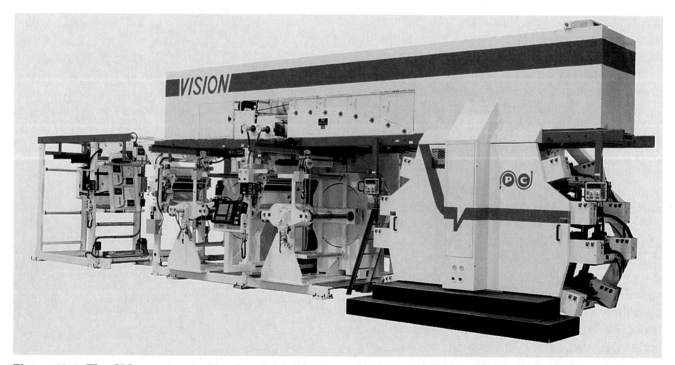

Figure 18-8. The CIC press is capable of producing high quality, close register work. Note: Guards have been removed from this press to show details. (Paper Converting Machine Company)

Figure 18-9. This inline web label press has six print stations. (Mark Andy, Inc.)

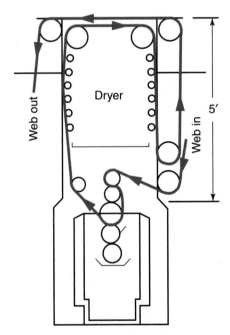

Figure 18-10. A single print station of an inline press, showing the path of the web.

Figure 18-11. A corrugated press is a type of inline press used for printing large sheets of linerboard for paper box manufacture. (Agfa)

six to eight color stations. They also are capable of die cutting, slitting, sheeting, numbering, and embossing. Most flexographic label shops use these smaller presses to print pressure-sensitive labels.

The advent of fully automated, computerized presses is not far away. Press controls are becoming more sophisticated, and numerous improvements have made flexographic printing comparable in quality to offset and gravure.

FLEXOGRAPHIC PLATES

Flexographic presses use flexible plates that conform to uneven surfaces. These plates have raised images, much like letterpress plates. In fact, letterpress photoengravings are used to vulcanize rubber into the relief-type plates. Flexographic plates can be made of molded rubber or photopolymer materials, and through laser imaging.

of colors it can print. Because of the distance the web must travel from one station to the next, inline register problems can occur. Sensitive tension-control devices are used to keep the web in tight register. Some inline presses are extremely wide-web machines, feeding webs up to 110″ (279 cm), with varying repeat lengths. These presses are used to print linerboard for corrugated boxes before corrugation takes place. See **Figure 18-11.**

Inline presses are also suited for printing narrow-web labels and forms that are 6″–18″ (15 cm–46 cm) wide, **Figure 18-12.** Narrow-web inline presses have

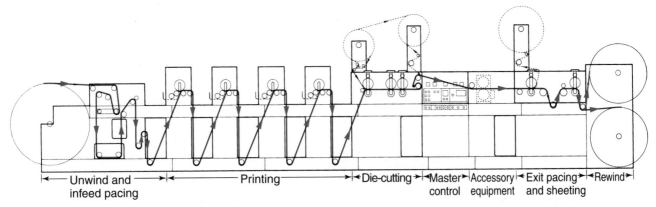

Unwind and infeed pacing ⟶ Printing ⟶ Die-cutting ⟶ Master control ⟶ Accessory equipment ⟶ Exit pacing and sheeting ⟶ Rewind

Figure 18-12. A narrow-web inline press with four color stations. (Flexographic Technical Association, Inc.)

Molded Rubber Plates

Molded rubber plates are created in a multistep process. An original photoengraving is etched from magnesium or made from a UV-sensitive polymer. The phenolic resin *matrix*, or mat, captures the details of the original plate, **Figure 18-13.** A hydraulic press generates the heat and pressure needed to mold the matrix board and plates. Because the mat can be used to make many rubber plates, this procedure is known as a duplicate platemaking process.

The original photoengraving is placed on top of the matrix board. Steel bearers on each side of the mold stop the press at the proper distance to produce the desired plate thickness. Upper and lower platens are heated to 307°F (153°C) and a pressure of 300 psi–1000 psi (2070 kPa–6900 kPa) is applied. The matrix board melts slightly and forms the mold. After 15 minutes, the press is opened, and the original plate is removed. All details of the original plate are impressed into the matrix.

When the matrix cools, a sheet of unvulcanized rubber is placed over the matrix, **Figure 18-14.** Cloth coated with silicone is placed on top of the matrix and rubber to prevent the rubber from sticking to the upper ram of the molding press. The press is closed, applying heat and pressure that cause polymerization

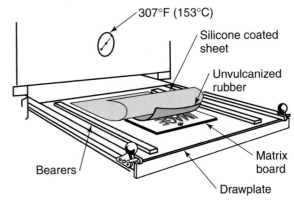

Figure 18-14. A molding press forces unvulcanized rubber into the recessed areas of the matrix, where it is cured by heat and pressure.

to occur and the rubber to vulcanize, **Figure 18-15.** The press is opened, and the plate is removed from the matrix. When the plate is mounted onto a cylinder, it prints onto the substrate as a readable image.

Rubber plate molding is a continuous process in flexography plants. Many jobs on wide-web cylinders require numerous plates made from the same mold. This process has its limitations. Small details and fine type styles may not reproduce well. The quality of process halftones is limited, as well. Even though rubber plates provide excellent ink transfer, their use has decreased as photopolymer plates have improved.

Photopolymer Plates

During the 1970s, chemists developed formulations of polymers (flexible plastic materials) that reacted to ultraviolet light and then solidify. Several companies produced sheet material with a nonstretchable base which, after UV exposure, can be washed out, leaving

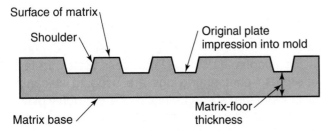

Figure 18-13. Matrix (mold) material is etched or formed to create a reverse image.

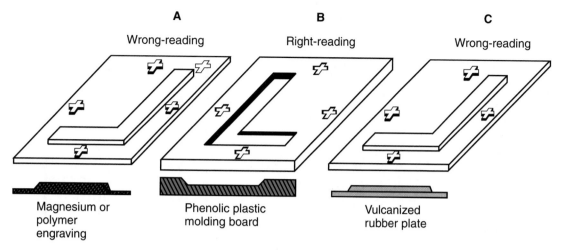

A Wrong-reading   **B** Right-reading   **C** Wrong-reading

Magnesium or polymer engraving   Phenolic plastic molding board   Vulcanized rubber plate

Figure 18-15. The sequence for making a duplicate rubber plate. A—The original is wrong-reading (reversed). B—The mold is right-reading. C—The plate is wrong-reading so it will print correctly on the substrate.

a sharp relief image on its surface. Photopolymer plates became a standard in flexography.

Photopolymer plates have advantages over molded rubber plates. Photoengravings and molding boards are not required, so a hydraulic molding press is unnecessary. The entire platemaking operation can be done in-house, rather than having to be sent out to a subcontractor, **Figure 18-16.**

The platemaking process begins with a laterally reversed negative on matte-based film. Matte-based film allows air to flow across the smooth polymer surface. The image area of the plate is exposed by UV light through the film negative. The UV light causes a reaction with a photo initiator in the plate material and sets off a cross-linking within the polymer that causes it to harden.

After UV exposure, the unexposed polymer material is washed out with water or another chemically reactive liquid. Once dry, the plate is exposed to intense UV light, which finishes the cross-linking phase. The finished relief plate feels like a rubber plate because the polymer contains a large amount of gum rubber, **Figure 18-17.**

Polymer material holds very fine screen size dots; excellent printing results are obtained with 200-line process screens. Photopolymer plate costs generally are higher than rubber plate costs, but the fine detail held by the polymer plates usually offsets the difference. Polymer plates also have a longer life than rubber plates.

Shore A Gauge is an instrument that is used to measure plate hardness. Measuring plate hardness is done in large solid areas of plate image. The purpose of measuring plate hardness is to serve as a guide to ensure proper plate processing and resulting image print quality.

Polymers dominate the flexographic platemaking industry. Costs are being reduced by printing from thinner plates that use less polymer. Less polymer needs to be etched away; therefore, less time is needed to produce the plates. Thin plates stretch less when placed on cylinders. Thin plates also print sharper images because they compress less on impression.

Laser Plates

Computer-to-plate processing transfers images directly from the computer to the plate, thus eliminating film. Some photopolymer plates can be

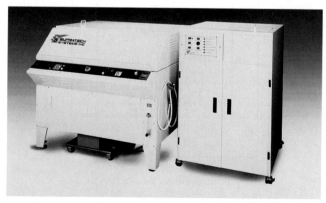

Figure 18-16. A platemaking system for processing photopolymer plates. The plates are washed out with water. (Supratech Systems, Inc.)

matrix: A mold used with molten metal to produce individual pieces of foundry type.

photopolymer plates: Plastic relief plates commonly used in flexographic printing that contains a light-sensitive polymer coating that hardens after exposure.

Figure 18-17. The rubber-like photopolymer plate has a nonstretchable plastic base that keeps it stable. (Supratech Systems, Inc.)

directly imaged by lasers. In recent years, laser-engraved rubber cylinders have been used to print wallpaper and other continuous pattern jobs.

PLATE ELONGATION

Because flexographic plates are made with soft material, they tend to stretch when mounted on the plate cylinder and may distort images and text. A circle, for example, may stretch to look like an oval, **Figure 18-18.** Allowance must be made for *plate elongation*.

The amount a plate stretches depends on the thickness of the plate and the diameter of the cylinder. Stretch can easily be calculated using the formula

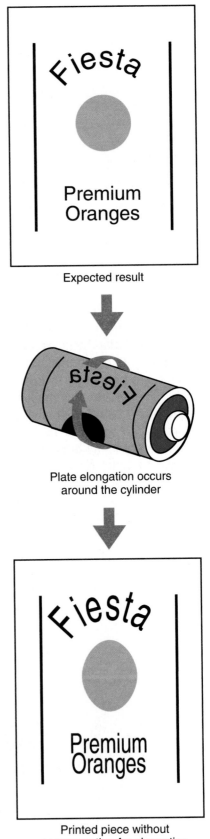

Expected result

Plate elongation occurs around the cylinder

Printed piece without compensation for elongation

Figure 18-18. If compensation is not applied by distorting the original art, the round image will print as an oval.

ACADEMIC LINK

Pi

The equation to calculate plate stretch includes the pi (π) value. But, what is pi?

Pi was first calculated and identified by Greek mathematician named Archimedes of Syracuse (287-212 BC). Pi is a value that represents the ratio of a circle's circumference to its diameter. This ratio remains the same, regardless of the size of a circle.

Pi (π) = 3.14159

Actually, pi is an infinite decimal, which means that the numbers after the decimal point go on forever. For practical use, either 3.14 or 3.14159 is used in common equations. A unique characteristic of pi is that the numbers to the right of the decimal point do not ever repeat in a recognizable pattern.

Pi is commonly used in equations to find area, volume, and other measurements that involve circles and cylinders.

Now, try to solve a plate stretch equation $(\pi \times 2T \div RL)$ where the plate thickness is .029″ and the cylinder repeat length is 13″.

software programs that allow for distortion are available for computer-generated art. In computer-to-plate imaging, compensation is not needed if the imaging is applied directly to a curved plate.

PLATE MOUNTING

Flexographic plates must be accurately mounted on press cylinders to provide proper registration to other plates on other cylinders. A mounting machine is used to mount plates.

The flexographic pin-register system has holes punched into the plate. These holes are fitted to pins on the mounting machine. Each cylinder is mounted with the same pin locations, to ensure perfect registration. Some narrow-web mounts use microscopes and small targets on two sides of the plates. The plates are carefully aligned with the dots, providing excellent register.

The latest type of mount is the television-monitored microscope camera/plate machine. Two TV monitors show enlarged dot areas on both ends of the cylinder. The microdots on the plate are then projected by the camera to the TV monitors, achieving dot-for-dot registration.

When both sets of dots are lined up, the plate is adhered using sticky-back mounting tape, a two-sided adhesive with a cloth center. One side sticks to the metal cylinder; the other holds the plate in place, **Figure 18-19.** Sticky-back tape comes in several thicknesses. The diameter of the cylinder determines the thickness of the tape. Most printers use 0.015″

$\pi \times 2T \div RL$, where T is the plate thickness and RL is the repeat length of the cylinder.

Compensation is applied by distorting (shortening) the original image in the curve direction. Flexographic

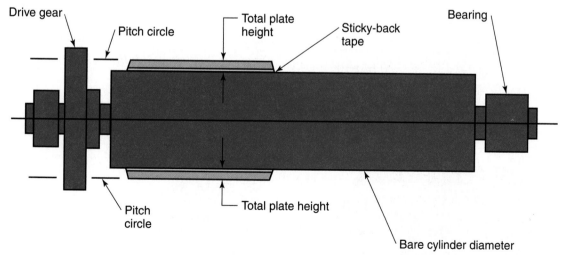

Figure 18-19. Sticky-back mounting tape is used to adhere the plate to the cylinder.

plate elongation: The physical stretching of an image carrier when mounted on the plate cylinder, which may distort images and text.

or 0.020″ (0.038 cm or 0.05 cm) thickness. The total plate height should be 0.002″ (0.005 cm) larger than the pitch circle diameter of the press drive gear.

ANILOX ROLLS

Plate inking is an important part of the flexographic printing process. The anilox roll must apply ink evenly and consistently to the relief image on the plate. The amount of ink applied to the plate surface directly affects the quality and sharpness of the image produced.

The surface of the anilox roll is engraved with cells, **Figure 18-20.** The ink capacity of each cell is calculated in billions of cubic microns. The larger the cells, the greater the volume of ink carried to the plates. Typically, the cells on the anilox are engraved at 45° angles. Laser-engraved cells have 30° or 60° angles. The number of cells per square inch (cpi) varies.

Proper screen ruling is crucial for image quality and must be correlated with anilox cell count. Anilox cells come in screen ruling sizes from 65 to 1200 lines. The higher the screen ruling, the higher the resolution, because there are more dots per square inch. The surface of an anilox roll with a 500-line screen engraving has 250,000 (500 × 500) cpi. A 1200-line screen has 1,440,000 cpi engraved into its surface.

Why must anilox rolls use certain screen sizes? For anilox rolls to ink fine process dots on a plate, several cells must contact each dot surface. The four-time rule of thumb applies. If you are printing a 150-line screen plate, use four times the screen size, or a 600-cell anilox roll. If you want to gain finer inking, a 700- or 800-cell anilox roll can be used to control print density. See **Figure 18-21.**

In flexography, the amount of ink delivered to the plate is regulated by varying the screen size and the anilox roll capacity. To increase ink volume, an anilox with a lower screen size is positioned on the press. The cells are larger and hold more ink as the cells per square inch decrease in number.

The emergence of the laser has changed the manner in which anilox rolls can be engraved. The versatile laser process cleanly engraves ceramic-coated steel rollers with screen sizes up to 1200 cpi. The plasma-coated ceramics are hard and long-wearing.

PRINT CYLINDERS

Flexographic cylinders have some distinct advantages. Printing cylinders are completely round, permitting them to print continuous patterns, such as wallpaper and gift wrapping. Cylinders are also removable. Because each press is adjustable, a wide range of repeat-length cylinders can be used. *Repeat length* equals one revolution of a press cylinder. Therefore, flexographic presses can print the exact repeat length of a job with minimum waste.

Each flexographic press is made to fit a certain pitch size. Pitch refers to the drive gears on the cylinders. For example, a 1/4″ (0.63 cm) circular pitch press has a range of repeat lengths of 7″–28″ (17.8 cm–71 cm). Each cylinder size increases by 1/4″ (0.63 cm) increments. For example, increases would move from 7 1/2″ (19 cm) to 7 3/4″ (19.7 cm) and from 8″ (20.3 cm), and 8 1/4″ (21 cm).

Three plate systems are used in flexographic printing. They are integral, demountable, and sleeve plate systems. The integral system is a one-piece cylinder and shaft with a circumference matched to the plate cylinder. Each revolution is a repeat length

Cells engraved into entire roll face

Bearing and drive gear journal

Bearing journal

Figure 18-20. Engraved cells cover the entire surface of the anilox roll. The cells carry the ink.

  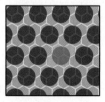

Cells are engraved on an anilox roll at one of three angles: 30, 45, or 60.

Ideally, the anilox should contain a minimum of 4 cells for every halftone dot.

Figure 18-21. Anilox cell angles should be 30°, 45°, or 60°. (Agfa)

of the image. This cylinder is very expensive but very accurate.

The demountable cylinder has a sleeve made of steel or aluminum. The circumference depends on the repeat length of the image. This system requires the gears and bearings to correspond to the cylinder diameter. They are installed to match the cylinder during mounting.

The sleeve system is lightweight and can accommodate a variety of repeat images. A single mandrel can be used to accommodate or support a single sleeve in a range of repeat image lengths. The plate cylinder mandrels are hollow and fitted for compressed air. To place the sleeve on the mandrel, air is forced into the sleeve to slightly expand it so it can be positioned on the mandrel. Once on the mandrel, the air pressure is released and the cylinder contracts to create a tight fit. To remove the sleeve, the reverse takes place.

Flexography printing plants store an array of cylinders, although few have all the cylinder sizes their presses will run. Typically, plants store repeat sizes that fit the general sizes of the types of work they do.

The bare cylinder diameter of all flexographic cylinders is made smaller in diameter to accommodate the thicknesses of the plate and the sticky-back tape. Refer again to Figure 18-19.

Cylinders must run true to their centers by standard tolerances. A cylinder should not wobble by more than 0.001″ (0.0025 cm) for general-type printing. A closer tolerance of 0.0005″ (0.0013 cm) is needed for process-type printing.

PRESS MAKEREADY

After plates are mounted onto cylinders, the cylinders are brought to the press and placed in the proper stations. Required aniloxes are installed. Each station is fed ink. Press adjustments are made, and the job begins to print. Registration is achieved by moving cylinders into a timed position. After final approval of a press web sample, the job is run.

Each type and size of press has its own makeready procedures. Generally, the larger the press, the longer the time needed to set up and change jobs. New systems have been developed that allow anilox rolls to be changed in minutes.

Because of their smaller cylinders and anilox rolls, narrow-web label presses require less changeover time than wide-web presses. Some presses have a slide-out print station that can be changed over in seconds.

Flexographic newspaper presses are engineered for short run times. Plate register systems allow quick plate-changing and register control. Many times the second turn of the press produces salable copy.

FLEXOGRAPHIC INKS

Flexographic printing uses inks that are more fluid than the inks used in lithography. Flexographic ink is free-flowing, it pumps easily into print stations and dries in fractions of a second.

The press operator is responsible for controlling ink's *viscosity*, or its resistance to flow. Viscosity is measured using a gravitational flow device, called a viscometer. A *Zahn cup* is one type of viscometer. The Zahn cup resembles a test tube and comes in different sizes that are designated with a number. Viscosity is determined by the number of seconds it takes for the volume of the cup to be emptied. Cup sizes range from 1 to 5.

To better understand viscosity, look at the relative viscosity of two common liquids. Water empties out of a #2 Zahn cup in 15.2 seconds. In the same size Zahn cup, heavy cream empties in 20 seconds. The higher the viscosity, the longer it takes a fluid to flow out of the Zahn cup. Always report measurements in the seconds it takes for the cup to empty, as well as the type of cup used.

Flexographic ink viscosities are between 19 and 55 seconds and can be measured by a #2 Zahn cup. The press operator thins the ink with solvent to acquire the proper viscosity. Most polyethylene films are printed with 21 second ink measured by a #2 Zahn cup.

The higher the ink viscosity, the thicker the film left on the substrate. High-viscosity inks print fewer impressions and dry slowly. The press must be slowed to allow time for drying between stations.

Proper ink viscosity is an important consideration for producing sharp, clean images. In large flexographic printing plants where precise measurement and control of viscosity, pH, and temperature are critical for controlling ink costs, a viscosity control system may be utilized, **Figure 18-22.**

---

repeat length: Distance equal to one revolution of a press cylinder.

viscosity: The internal resistance of an ink to flow. It is the opposite of fluidity.

Zahn cup: A gravitational flow device used to measure the viscosity of ink.

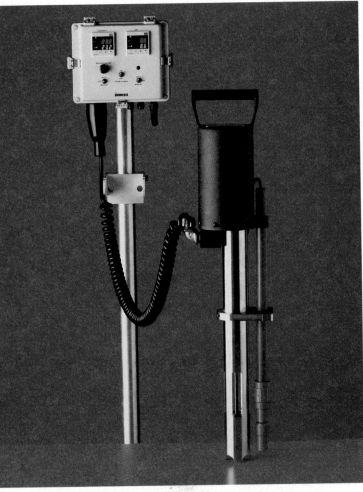

Figure 18-22. A viscometer system that features centralized monitoring and control of viscosity and pH. (Brookfield Engineering Laboratories, Inc.)

Types of Inks

Three types of flexographic inks are widely used in the graphic communications industry: alcohol-based-inks, polyamide inks, and water-based inks.

Alcohol-based inks come in a full range of dyes. Pigmented inks are also available. Polyamide inks are solvent-type inks requiring alcohol and acetates to dissolve their resins. Polyamide inks are widely used for general-purpose printing. These inks print successfully on nearly any substrate, including absorbent or nonabsorbent plastics. However, both alcohol-based and polyamide inks emit *volatile organic compounds (VOCs)*. Printers that continue to use solvent-type inks must install complex pollution control devices to catch and neutralize all VOC emissions from their plants.

Although water-based inks have been used in flexography for over 60 years, they are gaining wider use in the wake of new environmental laws. Water-based inks must maintain a critical pH. Viscosity of water-based ink ranges from 20 to 40 seconds, #2 Zahn cup. Water-based inks may or may not adhere to some substrates as well as solvent inks do. However, research continues to produce water-based inks with improved ability to print on nonabsorbent materials.

Inks cured by ultraviolet light are extensively used in flexographic printing. These high-viscosity inks have been adapted from the letterpress UV paste inks. Many printers are using UV-cured coatings for all types of printing.

FIRST

The intention of the *Flexographic Image Reproduction Specification and Tolerances (FIRST)* is to provide a common set of guidelines and data to be used as communication and production tools in the flexographic reproduction process. FIRST is a common set of specifications and communication protocols for the industry. FIRST is not a set of standards.

The FIRST specifications are meant to produce predictable, consistent results. The implementations of these specifications are the responsibility of the producer and intended to improve print quality, develop better raw materials, and grow the overall flexographic industry.

FIRST was developed and validated by flexographic industry professionals. Topics addressed by the FIRST documentation include color management, process inks, digital platemaking, expanded gamut ink sets, and plate-sleeve technology, to name a few. Included in the specifications are actual print samples on paperboard, corrugated board, film, envelope, and newspaper, along with litho printed paperboard for comparison purposes. The mission of the work is to understand customer graphic requirements for reproduction and translate their requirements into specifications for each area of the flexographic printing process.

Summary

Flexography has emerged and continues to grow as a major printing process. But like all printing processes, flexography has strengths and weaknesses. It can be done on large or small presses. Flexographic presses can do many inline operations, such as laminating, die-cutting, gluing, and folding. Flexographic printing can be done on a wide variety of absorbent and nonabsorbent substrates, including stretchable plastics. Many plate sizes allow for a wide range of printing image sizes. In addition, the process works well with water-based inks. Conversely, imaging of very small type can be a problem. Short runs are not economical. Generally, printing standards have not been established.

Review Questions

Please do not write in this book. Write your answers on a separate sheet of paper.

1. Why was flexography originally known as aniline printing?
2. What is the largest market for flexography?
   A. Milk cartons.
   B. Wallpaper.
   C. Plastic grocery bags.
   D. Corrugated boxes.
3. True *or* False? Unlike offset lithography, flexographic printing uses just one roller to apply ink to the printing plates.
4. The _____ surface is engraved with cells that carry ink up to the plate cylinder.
5. What device scrapes the ink off the anilox roll?
6. The cylinders on a flexographic press print on every _____ to the moving substrate.
7. Name three main types of flexographic press configurations.
8. Flexographic image carriers are commonly made from what two materials?
9. Explain how to compensate for plate elongation.
10. True *or* False? Sticky-back tape is one-sided.
11. Which of the following statements about anilox rolls is *not* true?
    A. The surface of the anilox roll is engraved with cells.
    B. The ink capacity of each cell is calculated in billions of cubic microns.
    C. The larger the cells, the greater the volume of ink carried to the plates.
    D. The number of cells per square inch (cpi) does not vary.
12. Repeat length equals _____ revolution of a press cylinder.
13. Name the types of plate systems used in flexographic printing.
14. What is meant by the term *press makeready*?
15. Identify three types of ink used in flexographic printing.

Suggested Activities

1. Collect plastic bags that have been printed by the flexographic process color method and check the color register. Write what you observe about the color register, ink coverage, and quality results.
2. Visit a grocery store and list some of the packages and containers that were printed by the flexographic printing process.
3. How can you tell the difference between products printed by the flexographic and gravure methods? Bring samples to class and explain the difference to the class. Do all students use the same criteria when showing the difference?

Related Web Links

FlexoExchange
www.flexoexchange.com/articles/articles.html
Informative articles from industry professionals regarding a variety of flexographic topics.

Printers' National Environmental Assistance Center
www.pneac.org
Supplies expert and reliable information on environmental issues related to the printing, publishing, and packaging industry.

volatile organic compounds (VOCs): Toxic substances that evaporate into the atmosphere, contributing to smog and causing health concerns.

Flexographic Image Reproduction Specification and Tolerances (FIRST): A set of guidelines and data to be used as communication and production tools in the flexographic reproduction process.

CHAPTER 19

Gravure Printing

Learning Objectives

After studying this chapter, you will be able to:

- Recall the four basic steps in gravure printing.
- Compare the advantages and disadvantages of gravure.
- Recall the reproduction requirements essential for printing a finished product with gravure.
- Summarize the methods of cylinder imaging.
- Explain the electrostatic assist process.
- Explain the properties of gravure inks.

Important Terms

color correction
electroplating
electrostatic assist
gravure
halftone gravure

intaglio
reflection copy
ribbons
stylus

DEVELOPMENT OF GRAVURE

For hundreds of years, artists have used sharp, pointed tools to cut images in metal plates. Before printing, the plates are covered with ink, and the ink fills in the etched images. Excess ink is removed, paper is pressed against the plates, and the etched images are transferred to the paper.

Sinking words, pictures, or designs into a printing plate or cylinder is a process called *intaglio*. Because the plates are hand engraved, the intaglio process is useful with line illustrations or type. Paper money, postage stamps, and stock certificates are some of the products printed by this process today, **Figure 19-1.**

Figure 19-1. This intaglio plate is used to print postage stamps. (U.S. Bureau of Engraving and Printing)

ACADEMIC LINK

U.S. Currency

In addition to using intaglio or gravure printing processes, the U.S. Bureau of Engraving and Printing makes use of several high tech processes to thwart that activity of currency counterfeiters. Intaglio and gravure printing add unique patterns and texture to paper currency, but additional identifiers have been added to the redesigned currency in circulation.

- **Watermarks:** Faint images that are part of the paper and are visible from both sides of the paper. Common watermarks on U.S. currency include portraits of historical figures and the numeric value of the currency.
- **Security threads:** A plastic strip embedded in the paper that displays the value of the bill. Depending on the denomination, security threads glow orange, green, or yellow when held under ultraviolet light.
- **Microprinting:** Tiny characters, words, or phrases printed on the bills that are usually not visible to the naked eye. The microprinted words are difficult, if not impossible, to be reproduced by counterfeiters.
- **Color-shifting ink:** Images or numbers printed on the bills change from copper to green when viewed at different angles. This effect is created by adding metallic flakes to the ink.

THE GRAVURE PROCESS

Intaglio was the forerunner to modern *gravure* printing. Like intaglio, gravure creates prints from images that are etched below the surface of the image carrier. In the past, acid was used to etch the

intaglio: A printing process in which words, pictures, or designs are engraved into a printing plate or cylinder.

gravure: A method of printing from cells or depressions that are engraved below the nonimage area of the printing cylinder.

images into the image carrier. Today, this process is rarely used in commercial applications in the United States. Instead, most images are etched on the printing plate or cylinder with electronically controlled cutting devices or with laser imaging technology.

Karl Klietsch (pronounced "Klic") is considered the inventor of modern gravure printing. With the advent of his grain screen photogravure etching process in 1878, printing continuous tone illustrations became possible. Klietsch further refined the process using a crossline screen and a sheet of light-sensitive (carbon) tissue. By 1890, the first rotary cylinder gravure press was built.

The dominant gravure process used today uses a metal cylinder as the image carrier. The engraved image area is recessed below the nonimage surface. The press rotates and prints continuously, at high speed, on both web-fed and sheet-fed stock.

The gravure process has four basic steps, as shown in **Figure 19-2.**

1. Ink is deposited on the surface of the image carrier and collects in microscopic ink cells below the surface.

2. Excess ink is removed from the nonimage area.

3. The substrate is pressed against the image.

4. The substrate absorbs or attracts the ink to produce a printed image.

The paper, usually fed by a web traveling about 30 mph (48 km/h), acts like a blotter, absorbing the ink from the microscopic ink cells. The cylinder can have as many as 22,500 ink cells per square inch. The amount of ink absorbed into the surface of the substrate depends on the size and depth of the ink cells, **Figure 19-3.**

Gravure Industry

Gravure printing is responsible for 15% to 18% of the printing done in the United States. The gravure printing industry employs tens of thousands of people. The U.S. Department of Commerce has identified gravure printing as an industry itself, with its own North American Industry Classification System (NAICS) code number: NAICS 323111, Commercial Gravure Printing.

The gravure industry is divided into three major markets: publication/advertising, packaging, and specialty products. Products typical of the publication/

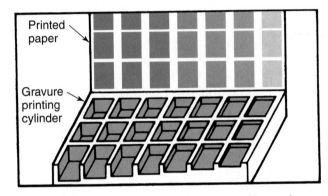

Figure 19-3. Magnified ink cells. Deep cells produce darker, denser image areas. Shallow cells produce lighter, less dense image areas.

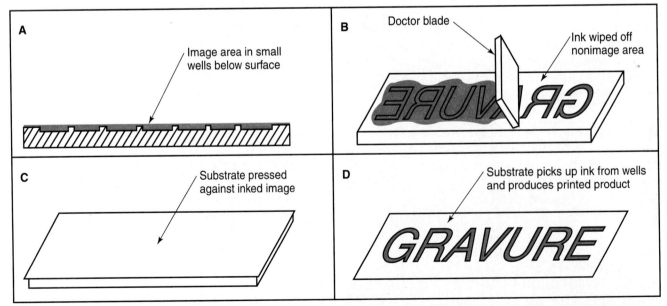

Figure 19-2. Basic steps for printing with gravure. A—Side view of an image carrier shows ink collected in tiny ink wells recessed below the nonimage surface. B—A doctor blade is slid across the image carrier to remove excess ink. C—The substrate is pressed against the inked image. D—The substrate absorbs the ink for a printed image.

advertising market are newspaper supplements, magazines, catalogs, advertising and promotional material, coupons, and stamps. Examples of packaging products are folding cartons; wrapping paper; flexible packaging, such as nylon, cellophane, and foil; and labels. Specialty printing products include wall and floor coverings, automobile windshield and glass tints, plastic containers, decorative laminates (furniture and countertops), and sanitary tissues.

Advantages and Disadvantages of Gravure

The main advantage of gravure printing is its simplicity. Gravure is a direct printing process that does not have to contend with ink and water balance, as does offset lithography. Eliminating the production variables typical of other printing processes, gravure presses can run at higher speeds.

Like letterpress, gravure image transfer requires pressure but, unlike letterpress, gravure also utilizes the natural tendency of paper to absorb ink from the tiny ink cells in the cylinder.

Gravure is capable of consistent, high-quality reproduction at a low per-unit cost on extremely long press runs. The microscopic cell structure of the image carrier results in the appearance of nearly continuous tone on the press sheet. Furthermore, the long life of the gravure cylinder sustains high-quality reproduction. The inks used in gravure printing dry rapidly, allowing for faster press speeds.

The main disadvantage of gravure is inherent in the printing cylinder. If an engraved gravure cylinder is damaged during shipping or production, the entire cylinder or set of cylinders may have to be re-engraved. Previously, the time involved in the preparation of the gravure cylinder made prepress operations more costly than for other printing processes. Newer technology has eliminated the photographic processes used to create an image on a plate. The older methods required many steps to complete. In this way, direct digital engraving has lowered platemaking costs and drastically reduced lead time, from weeks to hours.

GRAVURE PREPRESS CONSIDERATIONS

Several factors must be considered at the prepress stage. These include art preparation, page makeup, color reproduction, film preparation, and image carrier configuration. While most artwork is produced digitally, about 10% is still done on boards.

Art Preparation Requirements

Both line work and continuous tone images are reproduced with a screen pattern. Because the screen pattern disrupts fine lines, medium- or bold-faced styles are recommended for 8-point or smaller type. Small sans serif type styles reproduce better than small type in styles containing a hairline serif structure.

Reproduction films used in gravure, like those in offset lithography, will not reproduce light blue guidelines. Type matter should be proofed for consistent density and image structure. If possible, typesetting should be output directly to film. The film should equal the quality or density level required of the engraver.

Continuous Tone and Color Requirements

Continuous tone photographs or copy selected for reproduction should have average contrast and good tonal separation. To avoid a loss in quality, do not enlarge photographs more than 500% or reduce less than 20% of original size.

Reproductions for four-color gravure can be in the form of transparency copy (negative or positive film) or reflection copy. Transparencies produce the sharpest image. Common transparency sizes are 1.38″ (35 mm), 2.25″ × 2.25″ (57 mm × 57 mm), 4″ × 5″ (102 mm × 127 mm), and 8″ × 10″ (203 mm × 254 mm). Transparencies with balanced tones reproduce better than light ones. A photograph that has been produced using slow-speed film will have a smaller grain pattern than one produced with high-speed film.

Reflection copy includes such items as color photographs, watercolor or oil paintings, or any other opaque copy. In reproduction, white light is reflected from the copy and passed through filters before striking unexposed film. When reflection is a problem because images are not on the same plane, as with oil paintings, a color transparency can be made for reproduction.

---

reflection copy: An original that will reflect different amounts of light from the different tone values of the original.

Digital cameras are capable of producing high-quality photographic images. Many photographic images are produced utilizing digital technology. The same requirements regarding photograph quality apply to both conventional photography and digital images. For excellent results, the original must have high-quality features.

Color correction should be done before reproduction to compensate for impurities in the printing ink. Today, most separation and color-correction work is done electronically, but dot etching is still used in some cases. Dot etching is a manual correction technique that can be done on either the film separations or the plates.

Color evaluation and viewing of both originals and reproductions should be performed under uniform lighting conditions. The gravure industry uses the ANSI standard of 5000 K for viewing.

Image Carrier Configurations

The three basic gravure image carrier configurations are flat, split cylinder, and cylinder, **Figure 19-4.**

The flat image carrier is used on sheet-fed presses. It is used for limited runs requiring high-quality results, such as printing stock certificates and limited editions of fine art originals.

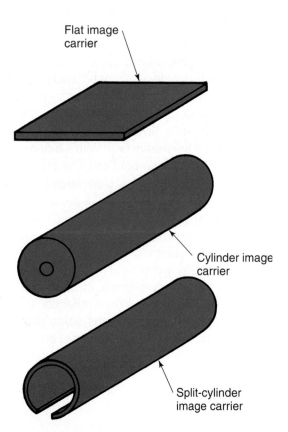

Figure 19-4. Basic image carrier configurations. The cylinder is able to produce a continuous image.

A split cylinder, or wraparound plate, is thicker than an offset plate. However, like the offset plate, it is flexible and designed to bend around a cylinder. In the U.S., sheet-fed gravure is used primarily for limited runs. In Europe and Asia, there is much greater use of this method. Some wraparound presses have as many as six printing units. They cannot produce an edgeless or continuous design because they use a clamping gap to hold the plate on the cylinder.

The cylinder is the most popular image carrier for gravure because it can print a continuous pattern. It is used for printing packaging, publications, and such products as laminates for furniture and floor coverings. A cylinder can be constructed either integral with or mounted on a shaft, **Figure 19-5.** Because of its popularity, the cylinder image carrier is the configuration that will be examined in this chapter.

GRAVURE CYLINDER ENGRAVING

Traditionally, cylinders have been produced using continuous tone films, carbon tissue, and chemical etching. Currently, cylinder imaging is done almost exclusively by direct digital input to electronic and laser cylinder production devices. The image is engraved by a cutting mechanism or a laser beam.

The engraving of gravure printing cylinders has undergone dramatic changes in the past few years. The quality of gravure cylinders has increased drastically.

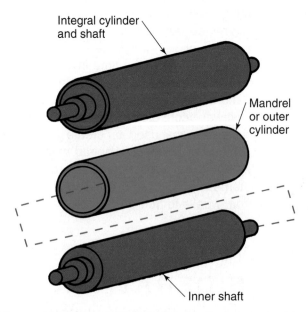

Figure 19-5. A gravure cylinder can be integral with the shaft. More commonly, however, a mandrel or outer cylinder is mounted on an inner shaft.

The newest manufacturing process produces lightweight polymer-based gravure cylinders. These lightweight cylinders can be stored easily, **Figure 19-6.** Steel cylinders were very heavy and required a great deal of room for storage.

Gravure Base Cylinder

The quality of the final image depends on the construction and preparation of the cylinder. Base cylinder refers to the gravure cylinder before it is imaged. The base is made of steel or aluminum and is ground and polished to a tolerance of 0.001″ (0.025 mm).

The base is copper-plated to an additional thickness of 0.006″ to 0.030″ (0.15 mm to 0.76 mm). The copper plating is applied by an electrical-chemical process known as *electroplating*, **Figure 19-7.**

The copper plating is oversized approximately 0.006″ (0.15 mm) in thickness, then ground down to its final diameter. A 1000-grit abrasive is used to polish the copper-coated cylinder smooth. The copper plating is tested for hardness, tensile strength, grain structure, and percent of elongation, **Figure 19-8.**

There has been experimentation with a variety of plate materials, including plastics, photopolymers, and ceramics. The results of these tests have not warranted changing to newer materials. Laser imaging has had success using zinc as an image carrier material.

Cylinder Imaging Methods

Transferring the image to the cylinder is accomplished using the electromechanical engraving

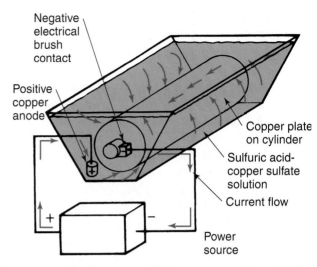

Figure 19-7. In the copper-plating process, the cylinder is submerged in an acid and copper sulfate solution. An electrical current is fed through the solution and the cylinder, causing the copper to electroplate onto the surface of the cylinder.

and chemical engraving processes. In recent years, laser engraving has experienced some success.

Electromechanical Engraving Method

Direct digital electromechanical engraving produces the most reliable cylinder for the press.

Figure 19-8. A copper-plated gravure cylinder. (Max Daetwyler Corporation)

color correction: Adjusting images to optimize values for highlight and shadow, neutral tones, skin tones, and sharpness. Compensates for impurities in the printing ink and color separation.

electroplating: An electrical-chemical process of applying copper plating to a gravure cylinder.

Figure 19-6. This machine can easily and quickly insert, remove, and store gravure cylinders.

Electromechanical engraving essentially replaced chemical engraving during the 1980s. Today, this engraving method accounts for 95% of all cylinder-making in the United States.

In direct digital engraving, the gravure cylinder is prepared using scanned data to drive an engraving machine, **Figure 19-9.** The scanner and the engraver are electronically linked. The scanner reads the original copy and converts it to electronic data or pulses.

Electronic circuits feed the digital information, stored in the computer file, to the engraving unit. A computer-controlled engraver receives the electronic pulses that are generated by the computer file, prompting a diamond *stylus* cutting tool or a laser device to form tiny ink wells on the image carrier surface. The diamond stylus vibrates at approximately 4500 oscillations per second, **Figure 19-10.**

The strength and duration of the impulses picked up from the scanning drum control the depth and size of the ink cell structure. The precision oscillating or cutting frequency is controlled by a quartz crystal, the type used in wristwatches.

Most of these machines have multiple engraving heads that work simultaneously. It takes about 40 minutes to engrave four *ribbons* of pages. Multiple-

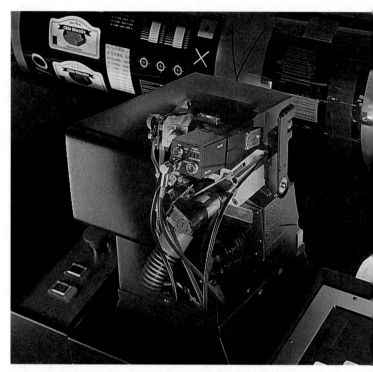

Figure 19-10. This high-frequency engraving head is cutting an image into a copper-plated gravure cylinder. The diamond stylus moves in and out to cut ink cells to the correct size and depth. (Max Daetwyler Corporation)

Figure 19-9. The image processing workstation is the heart of this fully automated direct digital engraving system. (Max Daetwyler Corporation)

THINK GREEN
Carbon Footprint

A carbon footprint is a measurement of how much the everyday behaviors of an individual, company, or nation can impact the environment. It includes the average amount of carbon dioxide put into the air by energy and gas used at home and in travel, as well as other more detailed aspects. The graphic communications industry as a whole has a large carbon footprint. The processes used in printing plants, such as in producing inks and paper, greatly impact the environment. The electricity that goes into producing these products causes the emission of great quantities of carbon dioxide. Recently, companies have begun to determine carbon footprint. Simply learning the details of a carbon footprint has become motivation enough for a company to work toward reducing it. However, not all companies have taken this first step. It is up to each company to do what it can to help reduce carbon dioxide emissions. For more information, see www.carbonfootprint.com.

Copper did not prove to be a suitable metal for use with the laser. Later research has shown that zinc is a more suitable metal base for laser engraving.

Max Daetwyler Corporation (MDC) manufactures high-speed electromechanical engravers and direct laser engravers. One type of engraver direct laser engraves images into a zinc material that is chrome-plated using traditional chrome tanks and polishers. This technology is being adopted in both publication and packaging gravure markets. The advantages of the direct laser method are quicker imaging, repeatability, significant ink savings, and greater stability (no mechanical tools). There is one engraving head from MDC that gives an intaglio look.

Publication engravers usually use multiple heads for engraving page formats or ribbons. Packaging or product engravers usually use a single head so that multiple images will match up. Very small gravure cells do not release ink well.

Cylinder Evaluation and Finishing

Once the gravure cylinder is etched or engraved, it must be closely inspected. Under 12× or greater magnification, the ink cell structure is checked for flaws. Cylinder correction can be accomplished by spot plating, burnishing with charcoal, lacquering, or other methods.

Once any necessary corrections are completed, the cylinder is plated in chrome to increase the life of the image carrier. Plating is typically 0.0003″ (0.008 mm) thick. Chromium is harder than copper and can better withstand the friction of the doctor blade.

Proofing of completed cylinders is an expensive process, but is done if the customer requires it. Less on-press proofing is done today because the cylinder engraving process has become more accurate and turnaround times have become shorter. On-press proofing is accomplished by using a proofing press. The set-up time adds to the turnaround time, and this is a cost factor. The on-press proof must still be evaluated, **Figure 19-11.**

Halftone Gravure Technology

Halftone gravure, sometimes called offset gravure, uses halftone color separations to produce films for the gravure process. It was introduced as a

head machines are used for publication printing. For packaging and product printing, single-head machines are the norm.

Chemical Engraving Method

Chemical engraving accounts for a small percentage of the gravure cylinder market in the U.S. and worldwide. The market share has dropped because of the continued growth of direct digital engraving.

The use of carbon tissue and chemical engraving is essentially nonexistent in the U.S. today, because of the environmental issues involved. Only 2% of the engraving is done by direct engraving.

Laser-Beam Engraving Method

Since being introduced in the late 1970s, the use of lasers for engraving has been limited. The cylinder was originally coated with plastic, and the laser functioned as a cutting tool. The laser vaporized the plastic to form the cells. An epoxy coating was used because the highly polished copper reflected 95% of the laser output, leaving only 5% for engraving.

stylus: A diamond cutting tool used to form the tiny ink cells on the metal surface of a gravure cylinder.

brought about the reality of filmless engraving. It is now possible to bring images directly from a prepress system into a computer for electronic engraving.

GRAVURE PRINTING PRESS

After the flexographic press, the gravure press has one of the simplest reproduction methods. Unlike offset, the gravure press does not require a dampening system. Cheaper grades of paper can be run at higher press speeds without the threat of web tear. If the web tears, the press stops, and the web must be threaded through the press system again before the press can be restarted.

Press Configuration

Gravure printing typically uses a web-fed or rotary press, **Figure 19-12**. Press speeds are given in feet per minutes (fpm) or kilometers per hour (km/h). Publication presses are rated at speeds of up to 3500 fpm (64 km/h). Packaging presses are rated at speeds up to 2500 fpm (46 km/h). Realistic operating ranges are from 2800 fpm–3300 fpm (51 km/h–60 km/h) in publication presses and from 600 fpm–1500 fpm (11 km/h–27 km/h) in packaging. A press running at 2000 to 2500 fpm has a web that is traveling around 30 miles per hour.

Figure 19-11. A quality control technician examines a digital proof to make sure the final product will meet the customer's specifications. (Max Daetwyler Corporation)

way to use films prepared for the offset process in gravure, instead of having to produce an additional set of continuous tone separations.

The gravure industry developed the technology in order to use generic halftone film for both offset work and gravure work. However, the use of halftone gravure has diminished as digital technology has

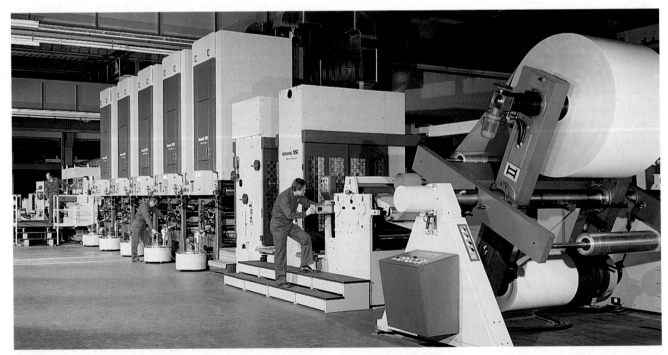

Figure 19-12. This multicolor gravure press prints from a web. (Bobst Group, Inc.)

Printing Units

The gravure press is made up of a number of printing units, each containing a printing cylinder. The web is fed through each unit, **Figure 19-13.** The combination of printing units can range from 4 to 16 or more. The number of units depends on the number of pages being printed and the amount of color work being produced.

Cylinder Action

At each unit, the cylinder is immersed in the ink fountain. As the cylinder turns, its tiny ink cells fill with ink. Modern gravure printing presses can have cylinders over 12′ (3.6 m) wide.

Doctor Blade

Doctor blade thickness is typically 0.006″ (0.15 mm), with a set angle of 20°. The blade can be stainless steel or plastic, but is usually made of blue-spring steel. Both thickness and set angle can vary.

Impression Roller

An impression roller usually applies pressure at 100 lb.–200 lb. per linear inch at the printing nip point. Impression rollers are made of rubber, neoprene, and other synthetic products.

Impression rollers should be tested for the degree of hardness as determined by the printing substrate. Resilience and solvent resistance are important to the continued quality of printing.

Substrates

Gravure printing is done on a wide variety of substrates, including inexpensive paper stocks. Paper should be evaluated by strength and ink absorption. Packaging and specialty products typically use such substrates as film, cellophane, cloth, plastic, and corrugated board. The gravure press runs about a 32-lb. newsprint stock and a 35- to 40-lb. coated stock for publication work.

Electrostatic Assist

Many gravure printing presses use a process known as *electrostatic assist* to improve ink transfer to the substrate, especially when the surface is hard or has poor ink receptivity. If ink transfer is incomplete or inconsistent, highlights or light tone values will have a speckled appearance, or color reproduction may shift in hue. In electrostatic assist, electrical charges between the impression roller (negative) and the printing cylinder (positive) create a force that achieves a nearly complete release of ink from the etched cells, **Figure 19-14.**

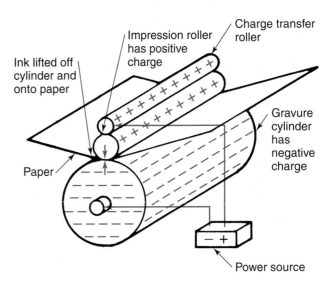

Figure 19-14. In electrostatic assist, a power source feeds a positive charge to the transfer roller which, in turn, transfers the charge to the impression roller and the paper. The gravure cylinder receives a simultaneous negative charge. A magnetic force is created, helping to pull ink out of the wells onto the substrate.

ribbons: Rows of pages engraved on a cylinder.

halftone gravure: A gravure method that uses halftone separations rather than continuous tone separations for image reproduction.

electrostatic assist: A process in which a power source feeds electrical charges between the impression roller and the printing cylinder, creating a force that helps release ink from the etched cells.

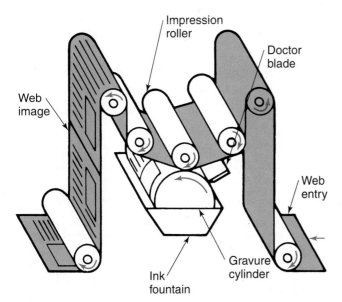

Figure 19-13. Movement of the web through a gravure printing unit.

Fires can occur on the gravure press when electrical charges are exposed to volatile solvent-based inks. Take all necessary precautions to prevent this from happening.

Gravure Process Inks

The process color inks used in gravure printing differ in both hue and composition from the average offset lithography and letterpress inks.

Classification of Gravure Inks

Figure 19-15 shows a general guide only. It cannot cover all technologies and technical variants used to address the needs and demands of an ever-changing gravure market. It is important to use technical information and proper handling information furnished by the manufacturer.

Ink Standards

Standards were adopted in 1984 for halftone gravure. The original objective was to establish a universal film, which could be used for both gravure and offset printing. For this to work, the gravure and offset ink colors had to be similar, and the decision

was made to modify the gravure coated paper Type B inks to be more similar to the offset SWOP colors.

The gravure yellow was made greener and cleaner, the red became bluer (more like a magenta), and the gravure blue, greener (more like cyan). The resulting ink, formulated for coated paper, was designated as Type B/SWOP.

The gravure Type A inks are designed for use on newsprint and supercalendered papers used mainly for supplement, insert, or tabloid work. SWOP standards do not exist for uncoated paper.

All publication gravure today is essentially using SWOP standards. The SWOP standards are not very applicable in packaging and product gravure, however.

Ink Properties

Common properties of gravure ink are opacity, drying speed, gloss, and fineness of pigment grind. Gravure inks are thinner than those used in other printing processes. The ink viscosity (weight) is much lower than most inks. They are usually diluted with 50% or more solvent.

Solvent-based gravure inks are highly volatile. The gravure pressroom should be isolated from unnecessary traffic. Ventilation must be excellent and fumes should be filtered through beds of charcoal to absorb both odors and vapors. Petroleum shortages, rising costs, and regulation by the U.S. Environmental Protection Agency has increasingly

Type	Function
Type A	This type of ink is mostly used for newspaper supplements, catalogs, advertising inserts, and similar publication work.
Type B	This ink is formulated mainly for publication printing on coated stock.
Type C	These inks are principally used for package printing on foil, paperboard, coated and uncoated paper, metallic paper, and some types of fabrics.
Type D	These inks work well when printing on plastic film.
Type E	These inks are often used on paper and paperboard, shellac or nitrocellulose-primed foil, and many coated papers and boards.
Type M	These inks are made from polystyrene resins that are used to produce low-cost top lacquers.
Type T	High gloss type of ink, but the health and safety hazards associated with chlorinated rubber has almost eliminated its use.
Type V	These inks are used to print on vinyl. Decorative products, which include labels, cartons, shrink sleeves, and wall coverings are typical examples.
Type W	These are water-based inks that are primarily used in package printing and product gravure.
Type X	Inks not associated any of the listed types are classified as Type X, Miscellaneous.

Figure 19-15. General classifications of inks.

forced the printing industry to substitute water-based inks for solvent-based inks.

Inks should never run too low in the press fountain, or air entrapment and foaming may occur. Like any other process inks, gravure inks contain impurities. Pressroom results determine the color correction requirements used in color separation. Inks are discussed in detail in Chapter 22.

Low-VOC Technology

In order to control pollution, inks are formulated to produce as few VOCs as possible. In many cases, water-based inks have replaced solvent-based inks. The industry is spending large amounts of money to comply with regulations.

Summary

The gravure process was stemmed from the intaglio process. Sharp instruments were used to cut images in metal plates. The ink covered the plate and the excess ink was removed from the plate leaving ink in the engraved areas. Today, the image is placed on the image carrier electronically. The gravure imaging system has changed from chemical processing to electronic imaging. The process is much more environmentally friendly. Solvent inks are being replaced with water-based inks, making the system compliant with many federal regulations. For many years, gravure printing was only used for long runs. Because of automation and scientific advances, runs can now be much shorter.

Review Questions

Please do not write in this book. Write your answers on a separate sheet of paper.

1. In what printing process are images manually etched or engraved onto a printing plate?
   A. Gravure.
   B. Rotogravure.
   C. Intaglio.
   D. Offset lithography.
2. Write the four basic steps in gravure printing.
3. List at least three advantages of gravure printing.
4. True or False? An engraved gravure cylinder damaged during shipping or production may have to be re-engraved.
5. Both line work and continuous tone images are reproduced with a(n) _____.
6. Continuous tone photographs and copy selected for reproduction should _____.
   A. not be reduced to less than 20% of their original size
   B. have average contrast
   C. have good tonal separation
   D. All of the above.
7. Why is the cylinder a popular image carrier configuration?
8. True or False? In electromechanical engraving, the scanner and engraver are not linked in any way.
9. What is the purpose of electrostatic assist?
10. True or False? The classification of gravure inks is only a guide, not a standard.
11. List the four common properties of gravure ink.

Suggested Activities

1. Select ten major magazines and determine if any of them are printed by the gravure process.
2. Identify five different products that have been printed by the gravure process.
3. Research and list technological changes that are taking place in gravure cylinder preparation.

Related Web Links

Castle Ink

www.castleink.com/_a-grav.html
Online store with a variety of articles regarding gravure printing.

Carbon Footprint

www.carbonfootprint.com
Resource for carbon dioxide information for personal and business needs.

BeGreenNow

www.begreennow.com
Resource for carbon offset information, including a carbon calculator.

CHAPTER 20

Screen Printing

Learning Objectives

After studying this chapter, you will be able to:

- Recall various applications of screen printing.
- Identify proper screen fabrics.
- Recall the qualities of a good screen frame.
- Explain how to attach fabric to a frame.
- Give examples of how to make knife-cut stencils.
- Categorize the different types of photographic stencils.

Important Terms

burned edges	retarders
cell distortion	sawtoothing
cell size	screen printing
durometer	squeegee
filament	tensiometer
mesh-bridging capability	thinners
mesh count	warp threads
percent open area	washup solvents
percent stretch	weft threads
pinholes	

Screen printing is the process of forcing ink through a porous fabric and the open areas of a stencil to produce an image. It has been known by several names: serigraphy, mitography, silk screen, stencil printing, and screen process. Only two terms are commonly used today: *serigraphy* in the field of fine arts and *screen printing* in the graphic communications industry.

Screen printing can be a very simple process, requiring only a few inexpensive tools and materials, or it can be extremely complex, requiring an array of sophisticated equipment and production techniques. The deciding factors are the complexity and level of quality required in the finished piece.

HISTORY OF SCREEN PRINTING

The origin of screen printing is difficult to determine, but the Chinese, Egyptians, and Japanese all are credited with first using a stencil process. The Japanese combined a screen with a stencil, cutting a stencil from two sheets of paper and sandwiching silk or hair between the sheets to form a screen. Printing with stencils spread to Europe in the fifteenth century and eventually to the American colonies.

In America, many people contributed to the improvement of the screen printing process through experimentation. In 1914, a multicolor screen printing process was perfected by John Pilsworth, a San Francisco commercial artist. In 1929, Louis F. D'Autremont, a screen printer in Ohio, developed the first material for knife-cut stencils. His stencil, called Pro-Film, was difficult to cut and adhere to the screen. Several years later, Joe Ulano, a New York screen printer, developed his own knife-cut stencil material, called Nu-Film. D'Autremont and Ulano became involved in a court battle over patent rights. The suit was eventually settled in favor of D'Autremont. However, Ulano's Nu-Film was a better, more easily used stencil, and it became the industry standard.

With a working stencil available, paint manufacturers saw a potential market for their products, and screen printing was established as an industrial process. The applications for screen printing were limited, however, by the availability of hand-cut stencils and inks. During World War II, screen printing began to have wider applications, in particular for identifying military vehicles and related equipment.

Modern screen printing developed in the 1940s and 1950s as new materials and production techniques were introduced. Today, rapid technological advances continue to improve the process and lead to expanded markets.

SCREEN PRINTING APPLICATIONS

The hallmark of screen printing is its diverse applications, **Figure 20-1.** It can be done on a wide variety of materials, including metal, glass, and wood. Images created using screen printing include posters, clothing, and printed circuit boards. Finished products are as diverse as a football jersey or a traffic sign. Screen printing is frequently the only

Figure 20-1. Screen printing is used on a variety of products. (John Walker)

screen printing: A printing process that uses a squeegee to force ink through a porous fabric covered by a stencil that blocks the nonimage areas. The ink pressed through the open image areas produces the image on a substrate.

process that can do the job. Like any process, it has advantages and disadvantages.

The advantages of screen printing include:

- Images can be printed on a wide variety of substrates.
- The production process is relatively easy.
- Costs are low compared to other printing processes.
- Images can be printed with glitter, flock, and other decorative finishes.
- The ink film is very resilient due to the thickness of the ink deposit because the film is up to 100 times as thick as in other printing processes.

Some disadvantages are:

- Rate of production is slow.
- Ink mileage is poor.
- Details and fine-line images may be difficult to print.

Images are created in much the same way as other printing processes. Handmade stencils are still used in the industry, but many are now created on the computer. Drawing and page composition programs are used to create the images. Existing digitized images may also be used. These images are commonly output on an imagesetter.

SCREEN PRINTING PROCESS

First, porous fabric is stretched across the frame. Next, a stencil is adhered to the fabric, blocking out portions of the fabric and leaving open the desired image areas. Ink is poured onto the fabric and forced through the image areas using a rubber or plastic blade called a *squeegee*. The ink is deposited on a substrate below, producing an image of the cut stencil, **Figure 20-2.** Additional prints are made by repeating the squeegee action on a new substrate.

Squeegees

A handheld squeegee has a smooth wooden or aluminum handle and a rubber or polyurethane blade. Squeegee blades are usually 3/16″ (4.7 mm) to 3/8″ (9.5 mm) thick and 2″ (5.1 cm) high.

Squeegee blades are rated by hardness, as determined by a *durometer*. A lower number indicates a softer blade: 60 durometers is soft, 80 durmoeters is hard. Most squeegee blades are rated between 50 and 90 durometers. A 70 durometer squeegee blade has a medium hardness and is recommended for general use.

Figure 20-2. Screen printing. A—Hold the squeegee at a 45° angle, press down, and pull it across the image. At the end of the stroke, use the squeegee to scoop up the ink and return it to the top of the frame. B—The image is transferred from the stencil to the substrate below the frame. (Bowling Green State University, Visual Communication Technology Program)

Blades are also distinguished by material used. Neoprene blades are the least durable and require frequent sharpening. Plastic blades are most frequently used and provide good durability and easy sharpening. Polyurethane blades provide maximum durability, but they are sometimes difficult to sharpen. Squeegee blades are sharpened either by cutting or by grinding. A knife-type sharpener uses a blade to cut the edge of a squeegee blade. A grinding sharpener uses either an abrasive belt or wheel to sharpen the edge of the blade, **Figure 20-3.**

Different substrates require different blade edges. Six squeegee blade shapes are shown in **Figure 20-4.** The squared-edge blade is used for flat surfaces and general-purpose printing. The squared-edge with rounded corners provides extra-heavy ink deposits on flat substrates and is used when a light color will be printed on a dark substrate. A rounded-edge blade is used primarily in textile printing where an extra-heavy ink film is required. Single-sided beveled edge blades are used for printing on glass. The double-sided beveled edge with flat point is used for printing on ceramics and the double-sided beveled edge is used for printing on cylindrical objects such as bottles and containers.

Machine squeegees are similar to hand squeegees. The machine squeegee handle is rectangular and has a thicker profile, **Figure 20-5.**

Squeegee blades lose their shape with use. Always keep squeegee edges sharp. Problems associated with dull squeegee blades include:

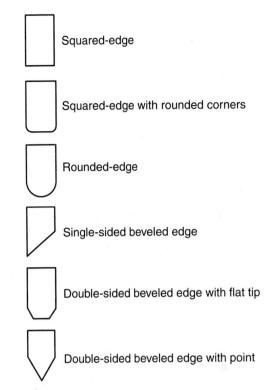

Squared-edge

Squared-edge with rounded corners

Rounded-edge

Single-sided beveled edge

Double-sided beveled edge with flat tip

Double-sided beveled edge with point

Figure 20-4. Squeegee blade shapes used for printing on various substrates.

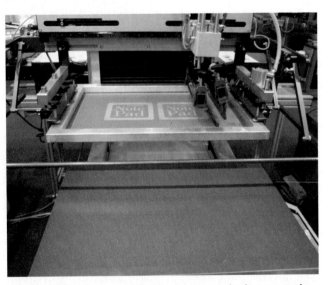

Figure 20-5. A squeegee on a screen printing press is automatically pulled across the image.

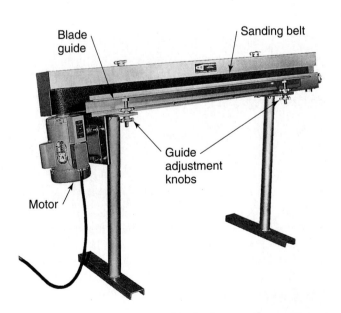

Blade guide

Sanding belt

Guide adjustment knobs

Motor

Figure 20-3. This squeegee blade sharpening machine uses a long sanding belt to grind new edges on used blades. (Advance Graphics Equipment)

squeegee: A rubber or plastic blade used to force ink through the open areas of a screen-printing stencil.

durometer: A measure of a rubber squeegee blade's hardness.

- Bubbles in the ink film.
- Poor edge definition in print.
- Excessive ink film thickness.
- Loss of detail.
- Spread images.
- Poor ink mileage.

Screen Inks

Selecting the proper ink is critical to the production of screen-printed images. The type of ink depends upon the type of stencil being used, the substrate, and the intended product. Should the ink be resistant to ultraviolet rays from the sun? Is moisture resistance important? These and other questions must be answered before the proper ink can be selected. Additional concerns include resistance to fading, chipping, and scratching; chemical resistance to acids and alkalis, and the ability to withstand the effects of vacuum packing.

Screen Solvents

Screen printing solvents are classified as thinners, retarders, and washup solvents. *Thinners* are solvents added to ink to change the viscosity (thickness) of the ink. Thinners do not affect drying time. The viscosity of thinned ink should resemble pancake syrup or 40-weight motor oil at room temperature. High ink viscosity can cause a mesh pattern to appear in the printed ink film.

Retarders are solvents added to ink to thin the viscosity and slow the drying time. Retarders are necessary with some fast-drying inks that may clog mesh openings in the screen fabric. This is an especially important factor in warm climates, where solvent evaporation and drying is accelerated.

Washup solvents are used to remove ink from the screen. They are inexpensive and their only function is to dissolve ink.

❶ ....
Prolonged exposure to solvent fumes can be harmful. Provide adequate ventilation and air exchange.
....

Drying Systems

At one time, large drying racks were used to air-dry substrates. Oven drying systems are used now that provide faster drying times and an efficient use of floor space. Three oven drying methods used often include conduction, convection, and radiation.

Conduction occurs when heat is generated within an object by contact with a heat source. Convection heating uses warm air to transfer heat to the object. Radiation heating occurs when heat is generated within an object through exposure to radiation. The popularity of radiation heating is growing as new inks are formulated that can be cured (dried) by infrared or ultraviolet radiation.

Most modern drying systems use a conveyor, **Figure 20-6.** The speed of the conveyor belt determines the length of time the ink is subjected to heat transfer. Faster drying inks use a faster conveyor belt speed, and vice versa.

SCREEN FRAMES

The screen frame serves several important functions. A frame:

- Provides a means of attaching fabric at the proper tension.
- Provides rigidity and dimensional stability.
- Resists mechanical stress and warpage.
- Resists chemical action and corrosion.
- Provides a means for register.

Frame Materials

Materials used to manufacture screen frames include wood, metal alloy, steel, and plastic. Wood and metal alloy are the most common, **Figure 20-7.**

Figure 20-6. A conveyor carries screen-printed items, such as these shirts, through the drying oven.

Figure 20-7. Wood and metal alloy are the most common materials used to manufacture screen printing frames. (Bowling Green State University, Visual Communication Technology Program)

Wood frames

Wood frames are still popular for general screen printing applications. A hardwood such as maple is ideal, but pine is most frequently used because of its low cost.

Wood frames may be constructed using screws, corrugated fasteners, dowels, splines, or nails. Whatever technique is used, remember that frames are continuously subjected to mechanical and chemical stress. Fasteners must be able to withstand the stress.

Frames and fasteners are under a constant deluge of water. Avoid metal fasteners when possible. Rust and corrosion will cause the frame joints to loosen and weaken. Wood frames should be glued using an adhesive that is waterproof. Apply a waterproof sealer before the frame makes contact with moisture.

As frame size increases, frame sidewall dimensions should also increase to withstand the mechanical strain of the fabric after tensioning. A larger frame also has less tendency to warp. As a rule of thumb, frame sizes up to 15″ × 15″ (38 cm × 38 cm) should be constructed of 1 1/8″ × 1 1/8″ (.3175 cm × .3175 cm) frame lumber. Sizes up to 24″ × 24″ (61 cm × 61 cm) should be constructed of 1 5/8″ × 1 5/8″ (4.1 cm × 4.1 cm) frame lumber. Beyond this size, frame lumber 2″ × 2″ (5.1 cm × 5.1 cm) or larger should be used.

Metal Alloy Frames

Metal alloy frames provide greater rigidity and dimensional stability than wood frames and are essential in commercial screen printing. While not susceptible to chemical attack from water, these frames have poor resistance to acids and soda solutions.

Metal alloy frames are available in a variety of styles and sidewall dimensions. Most have built-in mechanical clamps for attaching and stretching the screen fabric.

Metal alloy is rigid enough for frame sizes up to 36″ × 36″ (91.4 cm × 91.4 cm). For larger frames, steel is preferred. Some frames are constructed using a combination of metal and wood. The fabric may be glued to the wooden part of the frame.

Frame Profiles

If fabric tension causes the frame to bend inward, the fabric tension will be varied, causing the image to lose register or become distorted.

To compensate for the inward pull, some screen printers intentionally deflect frame sidewalls inward when attaching fabric, **Figure 20-8.** After the tensioned fabric is attached, the frame automatically relaxes, resulting in an outward pull of the frame sidewalls to balance the inward pull of the tensioned fabric.

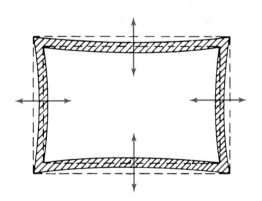

Figure 20-8. An inward deflection of the frame causes an outward pull on the fabric, which produces fabric tension. (Screen Printing Association International)

thinners: Solvents added to ink to change the viscosity of the ink. They do not affect drying time.

retarders: Solvents added to ink to thin the viscosity and slow the drying time.

washup solvents: Solvent used to dissolve ink from a screen.

Print Size

Maximum print size is determined by the inside dimensions of the screen frame. Generally, the nonimage area should be twice the size of the image area. An ideal frame size is four times the image area. Such dimensions are necessary for two reasons: proper flexibility of the fabric without excessive squeegee pressure and proper off-contact distance (distance from the screen to the substrate).

CLASSIFYING SCREEN FABRICS

Screen fabrics are classified according to filament, mesh count, strength, and weave pattern. A filament refers to the selected type of thread. The mesh is the number of threads per inch. The strength is designated by the diameter of the thread. The weave determines the pattern of the vertical and horizontal threads to make the screen.

Filament

A *filament* is a single thread. A fabric may be either multifilament or monofilament, **Figure 20-9.** Multifilament means there are several strands of material per filament. For example, sewing thread may have multiple strands. Monofilament means each filament is a single strand of material, or one thread. Fishing line is monofilament.

Multifilament fabrics usually print a slightly uneven ink film. The unevenness is due to the irregular size and shape of the cells caused by the differing cross sections of each thread. Multifilament fabrics lose some dimensional stability as a result of the stretching associated with their rope-like construction.

Monofilament fabrics provide better ink film thickness uniformity and dimensional stability than multifilaments. However, monofilaments cost more than multifilaments and are not as durable.

Mesh Count

Fabric *mesh count* is specified by the number of threads per linear inch. The higher the mesh count, the better the reproduction of fine details. A high mesh count also minimizes *sawtoothing*, a distortion in the design contours that causes a notched effect. As mesh count increases, fabric strength and durability decrease.

The mesh count in multifilament fabrics is specified by digits ranging from 5 to 25. Mesh count

Figure 20-9. Compare the magnified views of a multifilament fabric and a monofilament fabric. (Autotype USA)

per linear inch is estimated by multiplying the digit by 10. Thus, if the mesh number is 12, the mesh count per linear inch is 120 (12 × 10 = 120). This number is only approximate because little standardization exists between manufacturers. A 12-mesh fabric, for instance, could have 115 to 129 threads per linear inch.

Monofilament fabrics are specified by actual thread count. A 160-mesh fabric has exactly 160 threads per linear inch. The same is true for metal mesh.

Fabric Strength

Fabric strength is directly related to thread diameter. The strength of multifilament fabrics is specified by X, XX, or XXX. X has the smallest diameter, and XXX has the largest diameter and yields the strongest fabric. As mesh count increases, thread diameter must decrease or no porous areas (open cells) will exist, **Figure 20-10.**

Monofilament fabrics use a different system to specify strength. Either the actual thread diameter is given, expressed in thousandths of an inch, or a letter rating is given. S = small, T = medium, and HD = heavy-duty. In general, most screen printers select XX-multifilament and T-monofilament fabrics.

Figure 20-10. Magnified view of open cells in the image area on screen fabric.

Weave Patterns

Weave pattern determines how the vertical and horizontal threads are woven into the fabric. Threads that run horizontally are called *weft threads*. Threads that run vertically are called *warp threads*.

Three weave patterns used for screen fabrics are shown in **Figure 20-11.** The plain or taffeta weave is a general-purpose weave used in most situations requiring good strength and sharp detail.

The gauze weave is strong, so it is generally selected for extremely long runs. With this weave, the squeegee must move parallel to the double threads. Fine details cannot be printed due to the double threads.

The twill weave causes uneven ink film thickness and poor edge definition, resulting in a more

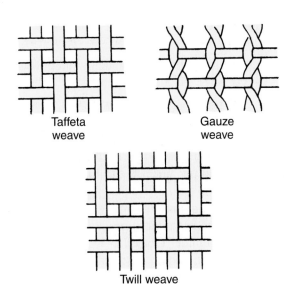

Figure 20-11. Three types of fabric weaves used for screen printing. (Screen Printing Association International)

pronounced sawtooth effect. Twill weave fabrics are not capable of producing fine details.

Ink film thickness and uniformity are related to weave pattern. *Percent open area* is the percentage of area per square inch through which ink can pass. The greater the percent open area, the thicker the ink film and the weaker the fabric.

Cell size is the distance across individual open areas between adjacent threads. It is specified in thousandths of an inch. As cell size increases, the percent open area increases, and fabric strength decreases.

TYPES OF SCREEN FABRIC

Three types of fabric are used as screens: natural, synthetic, and metal mesh. Natural fabrics are always multifilament. Synthetic fabrics may be either multifilament or monofilament. Metal mesh is always a monofilament. Natural fabrics are seldom used in industry today. Instead, most screen printers prefer synthetic and metal fabrics.

Silk

Silk is a natural fabric once used by most screen printers, giving rise to the term *silk screen*. Today, it is used largely by artists known as serigraphers. Silk has good durability and dimensional stability. It cannot be used with certain chemicals.

Polyester

Polyester is a synthetic fabric available as a multifilament or monofilament. The fabric has wide applications in almost all areas of screen printing and

filament: A single thread.

mesh count: The number of threads (or strands) per linear inch in a fabric.

sawtoothing: A distortion in a design contours that causes a notched effect.

weft threads: Threads that run horizontally, at a 90° angle to the warp threads.

warp threads: Threads that run vertically, at a 90° angle to the weft threads.

percent open area: Percentage of area per square inch in a fabric through which ink can pass.

cell size: The distance across individual open areas between adjacent threads.

can be used with any stencil. It is very durable in both multifilament and monofilament forms, but is slightly better as a multifilament. Monofilament polyester has better ink film uniformity and the best dimensional stability of any natural or synthetic fabric. Polyester, particularly monofilament, is very popular.

Nylon

Nylon is a synthetic fabric available only as a monofilament. Nylon has relatively good dimensional stability if used in a climate-controlled environment. It is the most durable of the natural or synthetic fabrics, and adapts well when printing on rough-textured or uneven substrates. Its flexibility makes it suitable for printing on concave or convex surfaces.

Metal Mesh

Metal mesh is a monofilament. Typically, it is stainless steel, but it can also be bronze, copper, or brass. It is used for printing with heated inks on plastic or when the excellent dimensional stability is required. Metal mesh is durable but fragile. Any kinks or deformities usually require replacement of the mesh.

Metalized Polyester

Metalized polyester is a hybrid monofilament fabric with a nickel-plated coating. The metallic surface is about 3 microns thick. The coating increases dimensional stability for printing critical tolerances, as with electronic circuit board printing. Each thread is "welded" in position. Metalized polyester is more durable than metal mesh and not as susceptible to kinks or deformities.

FABRIC ATTACHING AND TENSIONING

The practice of attaching and tensioning fabric to a frame is known as stretching. Despite the fact that it requires two actions, it is considered one operation. Fabric can be attached to the frame using one of four methods: stapling, cord and groove, mechanical clamping, or adhesive bonding.

Stapling

Staples are the least desirable means for attaching and tensioning fabric, **Figure 20-12,** because uniform fabric tension is difficult to achieve.

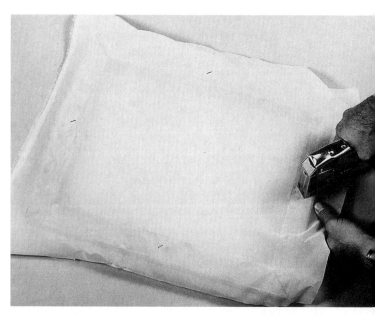

Figure 20-12. Staples can be used to attach and tension screens for low-quality printing.

Staples can also puncture and tear fabric. Tears weaken the weave and can lead to premature fabric failure. A continuous piece of staple tape is placed over the screen before stapling to help keep the screen from tears. However, staple tape does not solve the basic problems associated with stapling.

Staples are placed in the center of each side of the wood frame with the fabric. Stretch the fabric to a near corner and staple. Gradually pull and tension the fabric while installing the staples. Finish the side by placing the staples at an angle, about 1/8″ (.3175 cm) apart. Placing the staples at an angle allows the staple to cross several filaments and increase the strength. Then, pull the opposite side and staple. The remaining side is finished in the same way.

Cord and Groove

The cord and groove method is popular in small screen applications where printing requirements are not critical. A cotton or plastic cord is forced into a groove in the frame, **Figure 20-13.** As the cord moves down into the groove, the fabric is stretched across the frame.

Grooved-frame lumber and cord are available from a variety of manufacturers, or frames can be made by the printer. Cords of varying sizes are available. Correctly match cord diameter and groove width so a tight fit is created, without causing damage to the frame or fabric. A groove depth one and one-half times the cord diameter is recommended.

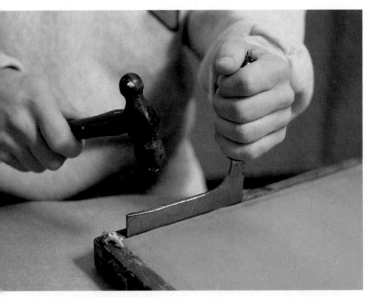

Figure 20-13. Fabric is being stretched using the cord and groove method. As the cord and fabric are forced into the groove, tension is placed on the fabric. (Bowling Green State University, Visual Communication Technology Program)

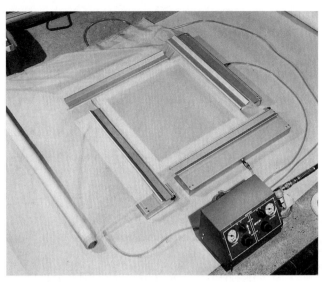

Figure 20-14. An automatic or pneumatic fabric stretching machine. Controlled air pressure is used to pull the fabric in all directions, resulting in an even stretch. (Autotype USA)

Mechanical Clamping

Mechanical clamps are available on many aluminum frames. The fabric is clamped in position on all four sides. Screws are then turned, forcing the movable clamps outward and resulting in fabric tension.

With mechanical clamping, the fabric may be tensioned to exact specifications. The screw threads should be lubricated periodically to prevent corrosion and wear.

Adhesive Bonding

To attach fabric to a frame with adhesive, a stretching machine is necessary. Stretching machines may be mechanical or pneumatic, **Figure 20-14.**

With a stretching machine, fabric may be tensioned to exact specifications without cell distortion. *Cell distortion* is the result of tensioning the fabric in one direction without stretching it equally in the other direction, **Figure 20-15.** Cell distortion is always present when using any method of stretching other than a stretching machine.

Stretching machines are generally used for high-volume printing, which compensates for the high initial cost of the machine. They are also used when fine detail and ink film uniformity are critical, such as printed circuit boards and four-color process printing.

Measuring Fabric Tension

Screen tension, or tightness, can be accurately measured using a tensiometer. Tension is expressed in *percent stretch*. Proper tension ensures the screen will create a quality image on the substrate.

When using a tensiometer, measurements are taken from all areas of the fabric. A *tensiometer* measures tension in Newtons per centimeter. The reading is compared to other areas of the fabric and to the manufacturer's specifications, **Figure 20-16.**

Fabric needs time to relax after tensioning before measurements are taken to obtain an accurate reading. Tensiometers are used in conjunction with mechanical or pneumatic stretching machines.

Fabric Treatment

For the stencil and fabric to adhere to each other, the fabric must be cleaned chemically, mechanically, or both. Proper cleaning removes surface grease, airborne contaminants, and residue.

Chemical treatment alters the adhesion characteristics of the fabric and allows for better

cell distortion: The result of stretching fabric openings unequally in two directions.

percent stretch: A technique for measuring screen tension that entails taking very accurate measurements before and during tensioning.

tensiometer: An instrument that measures screen fabric tension.

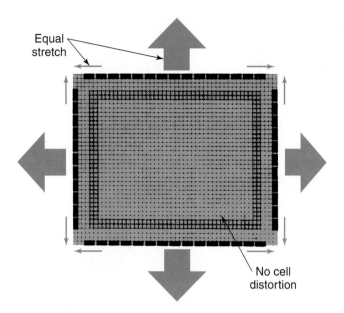

Figure 20-16. A tensiometer measures fabric tension. (Bowling Green State University, Visual Communication Technology Program)

! Always wear skin and eye protection when handling and using chemicals. Follow all safety precautions indicated on chemical containers.

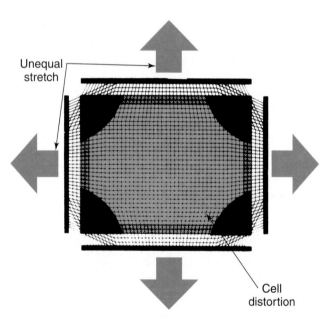

Figure 20-15. With equal tension applied, cells or openings in the fabric are not distorted. (Tetko, Inc.)

bonding between the stencil and fabric. Mechanical treatment changes the physical properties of the fabric to enhance the bond between stencil and fabric. Usually, chemical and mechanical treatments are done only once with new fabric. Repeated use of these treatments will degrade the fabric and cause premature fabric failure. Cleaning the fabric, or degreasing, should be done just before a new stencil is adhered to the fabric.

Different fabrics require different treatments. What is used on one fabric may be damaging to another fabric. Guidelines are given in **Figure 20-17.**

STENCILS

Proper selection and tensioning of fabric determines whether images will have quality edge definition, image resolution, ink film thickness, and ink uniformity. The stencil, however, determines whether the quality available in the selected fabric will be maintained. No matter how fine the fabric mesh or accurate the tension, an incorrect or improperly processed stencil will not produce the desired results.

Knife-Cut Stencils

The three types of knife-cut stencils are paper, water-soluble, and lacquer-soluble. Each has its own applications.

Paper Stencils

Paper stencils are cut from thin, durable types of paper, such as vellum. They are inexpensive and can produce excellent results. The amount of detail depends on the stencil cutter's talent. Generally, paper stencils are used for simple designs, especially if the production run is limited, **Figure 20-18.**

FABRIC	TREATMENT
Silk	No mechanical or chemical treatment. Degrease with a 2% solution of trisodium-phosphate (TSP) or other caustic soda.
Nylon	No mechanical treatment. Chemically treat once with a 5% solution of metacresol (cresylic acid). Remove chemical from the screen with cold water. Degrease with a 5% solution of TSP or other caustic soda.
Polyester	Monofilament polyester is mechanically treated with silicon carbide to roughen the threads. Do not use household cleaners, which damage threads and clog mesh. Treat only once if the fabric is new. It does not need to be degreased. Multifilament polyester does not require mechanical or chemical treatment. Degrease with a 5% solution of acetic acid and rinse with cold water.
Stainless steel mesh	No mechanical treatment. Flame-treating is optional; follow the manufacturer's directions. Degrease with a 5% solution of TSP or other caustic soda.

Figure 20-17. Review this chart to learn how to treat fabric before use.

Figure 20-18. A paper stencil on a screen press. (Bowling Green State University, Visual Communication Technology Program)

After the stencil is cut, it is placed beneath the screen frame. Ink is spread across the fabric. The tack of the ink causes the stencil to adhere to the underside of the fabric.

Water-Soluble Stencils

Water-soluble stencils consist of a plastic support sheet coated with a water-soluble gelatin. The gelatin is cut and removed from the image area to produce a stencil. Be careful not to cut into or remove the plastic support.

After stripping away the gelatin, position the stencil under the frame, with the gelatin side in contact with the underside of the fabric. Use a wet sponge to moisten the remaining gelatin portions of the stencil. Working in small sections, wet the stencil diagonally, from corner to corner. Allow to dry. Peel off the base support, leaving the adhered gelatin stencil. See **Figure 20-19.**

After printing and ink removal are completed, remove the stencil with a warm-water spray. If a spray unit is not available, soak the stencil in warm water until it can be flushed from the fabric. Water-soluble stencils cannot be used with water-based inks.

Lacquer-Soluble Stencils

Lacquer-soluble stencils are essentially the same as water-soluble stencils, except they are adhered to the screen using a lacquer-based solvent. They are composed of a lacquer-soluble material coated onto a plastic or paper support sheet.

Cut the stencil, taking care not to remove any of the support sheet. After stripping away all image area material, position the stencil beneath the frame. The lacquer side must be in contact with the underside of the fabric. Using a cloth wetted with a lacquer-adhering solvent, wet the stencil. Next, dab small sections of the stencil with a dry cloth, working diagonally, from corner to corner. After a suitable drying time, peel off the base support, leaving the adhered stencil.

After use, the stencil may be removed from the screen using lacquer thinner. Lacquer-soluble stencils produce excellent results but cannot be used with lacquer-based inks. They are ideal for use with water-based inks.

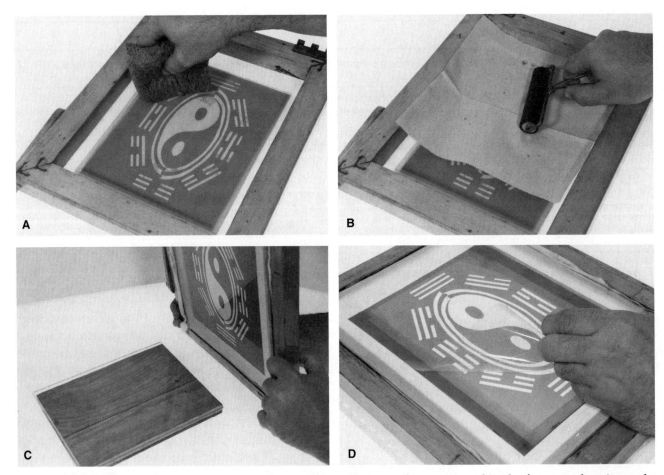

Figure 20-19. Steps in adhering a water-soluble stencil. A—The stencil is positioned in the frame and moistened with a damp sponge. B—Excess water is absorbed by a paper towel. C—The stencil is air-dried. D—The base support is peeled from the stencil.

Burned Edges

Both water-soluble and lacquer-soluble stencils can produce imperfect images if *burned edges* are present. Burned edges are the result of poor cutting or adhering techniques, **Figure 20-20.** If the backing sheet is cut, solvent will collect in the cut and burn the cut edge. Other causes of burned edges are:

- Cutting with a dull knife.
- Poor fabric and stencil contact during adhering.
- Using new fabric which has not been degreased.
- Using old fabric that is not clean.
- Using the wrong adhering liquid or adhering technique.
- Using rough, abrasive rags to apply adhering liquid.
- Failure to dry the screen immediately after adhering.
- Failure to keep the stencil clean while cutting.
- Kinks and creases in the stencil.

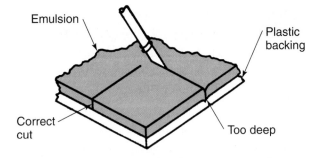

Figure 20-20. Cutting too deeply may groove the backing sheet. Solvent can collect in the groove and burn the stencil.

Photographic Stencils

Photographic stencils provide the detail, durability, and flexibility needed for many screen printing applications. They are light sensitive and are generally exposed using a positive film image. Newer computer-to-screen stencils produce a high-resolution screen stencil. The positive image is placed on an emulsion-coated screen. Photographic stencils are classified as indirect, direct, or direct-indirect.

Positives used to prepare photographic stencils must block light in the image areas and allow light to pass through the nonimage areas. Diffusion-transfer positives are suitable if the density is adequate to prevent exposure in the image areas.

Other types of positives include contact film positives made from film negatives, high-speed duplicating film positives exposed on a process camera, and rubylith masking film. Rubylith masking film acts as a barrier to light from an exposure frame light source.

For most applications, the film positive must be right-reading on the emulsion side. The exceptions are when printing a textile transfer or on a transparent substrate, such as glass. When printing on a transparent substrate, the image should be right-reading when viewed through the substrate from the unprinted side.

Indirect Stencils

Indirect stencils are exposed off the screen fabric. In other words, they are not in direct contact with the fabric. Indirect water-soluble stencils are used for relatively short production runs, and they reproduce fine detail well. Indirect stencils adhere particularly well to multifilament fabrics. Degreasing and mechanical treatment of monofilament polyester is essential if good adhesion is to be obtained. Indirect stencils have excellent *mesh-bridging capability*, the ability to bridge diagonally across a cell.

An indirect stencil has three layers: a light-sensitive gelatin, a plastic support, and an intermediate adhesive to keep the gelatin and base together until adhered to the fabric. The stencil is exposed in a contact frame (usually a lithographic platemaker) through the base, emulsion-side down, and in contact with the stencil base.

After exposure, the stencil is placed in a hardening solution for at least 1 1/2 minutes. After the stencil hardens, it is washed with a warm water spray. The softened stencil is placed base-side down on a flat buildup. The screen fabric is wetted, and the substrate side of the screen is brought into contact.

Unprinted newsprint or paper towels are used to remove excess water. After blotting five or six times with a cloth, the stencil is allowed to dry. Fans or blowers are ideal to speed drying.

A blockout solution may be applied to cover unwanted image areas on the stencil, **Figure 20-21.**

Figure 20-21. Blockout liquid is being used to cover the open area between the stencil and frame. (Bowling Green State University, Visual Communication Technology Program)

It is applied to the substrate side of the screen before or after the stencil has dried. Use caution to prevent the blockout liquid from filling the image area.

Direct Stencils

Direct stencils are exposed after a light-sensitive emulsion has been applied to the screen frame. Direct stencils, or photographic emulsions, are favored for their durability on long runs. By impregnating the fabric, direct emulsions can withstand abrasion and chemical action over time. When properly coated, they have nearly the mesh-bridging capability of indirect stencils.

Direct stencils are composed of a polyvinyl alcohol suspension and a sensitizer. Two common sensitizers are bichromate and diazo (ammonium or potassium bichromate).

If bichromated sensitizers are used, the direct emulsion must be sensitized, coated, dried, exposed, and washed within 24 hours. Coated screens using bichromated emulsions lose their sensitivity to light over time. Bichromated emulsions, if properly processed, have the shortest exposure time.

burned edges: An imperfection in a water- or lacquer-soluble stencil in which solvent collects in an improperly cut area of the stencil and melts (burns) the edge.

mesh-bridging capability: The ability of a stencil to bridge diagonally across an individual fabric cell.

❗ Bichromates are toxic. Adequately ventilate the area. Wear appropriate gloves and eye protection.

Diazo emulsions are nontoxic and biodegradable, two reasons for their popularity. They are also safer to handle than biochromates. Diazo-sensitized direct emulsions may be stored up to six weeks in a closed container, longer if refrigerated. Coated screens may be stored for three or four weeks before exposure.

Diazo emulsions are half as sensitive to light as bichromated emulsions; therefore, they require twice the exposure time. A variety of diazo direct emulsions are available for use with water-based or solvent-soluble inks.

A scoop coater is used to coat a screen with the photographic emulsion, **Figure 20-22.** Sensitized emulsion is poured into the scoop and applied to both sides of the screen fabric. Multiple coats are necessary to obtain a high-quality print.

Allow the emulsion to dry completely. The emulsion will shrink as it dries. If too much shrinkage occurs, thread profiles will appear on the substrate side of the emulsion, and the ink will seep out of the image area during printing. The results will be poor edge definition and a loss of resolution when printing fine-detailed images. It is important for the coating to be thicker than the fabric. The substrate side of the emulsion should be smooth.

A deep-bottom vacuum frame is used to expose a direct emulsion. The screen is positioned with the positive on the substrate side. The film emulsion should be in contact with the screen emulsion.

Exposure to light, **Figure 20-23,** causes a chemical reaction. Areas struck by light harden and become insoluble in water. The unexposed image area remains soluble and can be washed away using a warm water spray.

After the direct emulsion dries, a blockout solution can be applied to uncoated areas. *Pinholes* caused by dust or other airborne contaminants should also be retouched, **Figure 20-24.**

Reclaiming solutions are used to remove direct emulsions from the screen fabric. In the past, undiluted household bleach was used to remove direct emulsions. Because better reclaiming solutions are available today, bleach is no longer used.

Apply the reclaiming solution to a screen that is free of ink, and wait several minutes. The direct

Figure 20-22. A photographic emulsion is being coated directly on the screen using a scoop coater. (Bowling Green State University, Visual Communication Technology Program)

Figure 20-23. Exposing a direct stencil in a vacuum frame. (Bowling Green State University, Visual Communication Technology Program)

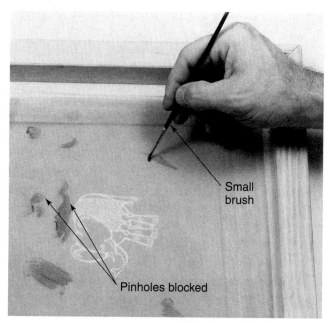

Figure 20-24. A small brush can be used to fill pinholes caused by dust or other contaminants.

emulsion will gradually change color. It can be removed using a warm or hot water spray. Special high-pressure screen washers are available to aid in the removal of the emulsion from the fabric mesh.

Direct-Indirect Stencils

Direct-indirect stencils are a combination of the two stencil techniques and materials. Direct-indirect stencils can be either emulsion-adhering or water-adhering. They are sometimes called direct-film stencils.

With emulsion-adhering stencils, a dry film or unsensitized gelatin on a polyester base is in contact with the substrate side of the fabric. A bichromate or diazo-sensitized direct emulsion is spread across the screen with a squeegee.

The direct emulsion is forced into the fabric mesh. As it softens the dry gelatin film, the indirect portion of the stencil is adhered and sensitized. After the direct emulsion dries, the polyester base support is stripped away, and the stencil is exposed in the same way as direct emulsion.

With water-adhering stencils, also known as capillary-system stencils, the dry gelatin is already light-sensitive. Water is spread across the screen to soften the stencil, allowing the gelatin to adhere to the screen fabric. After the direct emulsion dries, the polyester support is stripped away. The stencil is exposed in the same way as the direct emulsion.

A direct-indirect stencil is a compromise. Direct-indirect stencils last longer than indirect stencils. However, they cannot deliver the detail that indirect stencils provide. Direct-indirect stencils do not last as long as direct stencils. However, they can produce a finer image with more detail.

Photographic Stencil Exposure Calibration

All photographic stencils require a specific exposure. Calibration test images are used to determine the correct exposure, **Figure 20-25.** With any change in fabric, mesh count, stencil, or exposure device, a new exposure time needs to be determined.

Whenever a colored screen fabric is used to reduce light scatter within a direct or direct-indirect stencil, the exposure time must be increased by 1/3 to 1/2. **Figure 20-26** lists some common problems associated with improper stencil exposure.

Computer-to-Screen Stencils

This system produces a high-resolution screen stencil without film. First, the screen is coated with an emulsion. A positive image is then placed on the emulsion. This is accomplished by using wax rather than ink from an ink-jet setup. The imaged screen is exposed by using a standard exposure system.

Figure 20-25. A test image is used for the proper exposure calibration of photographic stencils.

pinholes: Imperfections on a photographic negative or stencil caused by dust and other airborne contaminants.

Indirect Stencil	
Underexposed	Overexposed
• Stencil becomes too thin after washout. • Excessive pinholes. • Early failure of stencil. • Images spread.	• Stencil fails to adhere to fabric. • Images choke. • Stencil is difficult to remove.

Direct Stencil	
Underexposed	Overexposed
• Stencil is soft in nonimage areas. • Stencil becomes too thin after washout. • Images spread. • Early failure of stencil. • Excessive sawtoothing at edges of image (poor mesh bridging).	• Stencil is difficult to wash out. • Loss of detail (such as serifs). • Images choke. • Stencil is difficult to remove.

Direct-Indirect Stencil	
Underexposed	Overexposed
• Stencil is soft in nonimage areas, or washes away completely. • Squeegee side of stencil becomes too thin. • Images spread. • Early failure of stencil. • Excessive sawtoothing at edges of image (poor mesh bridging).	• Stencil is difficult to wash out, or washes out completely due to high pressure required. • Loss of details (such as serifs). • Images choke. • Stencil is difficult to remove.

Figure 20-26. Common exposure problems for three types of stencils.

FABRIC AND STENCIL COMPATIBILITY

The fabric and stencil must be compatible to get the best image resolution and edge definition. Indirect stencils are best-suited to a multifilament polyester fabric, although they can be used successfully with any fabric. Direct stencils and direct-indirect stencils work well with any fabric, but are typically used with a dyed monofilament polyester when printing critical detail.

As light strikes each fabric thread, rays scatter to adjacent areas of the stencil. As a result, small, detailed images can be lost. Ruby, orange, or yellow fabrics reduce the chance of exposure in the image areas due to light refraction. The threads of dyed fabrics act as a safelight filter, refracting wavelengths of light to which the stencil is sensitive. Colored monofilament polyester should always be used when printing halftones or process color reproductions.

SCREEN IMAGES

Whenever a screened image is to be printed, the screen fabric tension, frame stability, and stencil processing become even more important in producing an acceptable product.

Using conventional process color angles, the fabric mesh count should be five to six times higher than the screen ruling of the halftone dots. This ratio should eliminate a moiré pattern between screen and fabric mesh. The angle between the screen ruling and the fabric mesh should be 22.5° for the least noticeable interference pattern between lines of halftone dots and fabric mesh.

SCREEN PRINTING PRESSES

Screen printing requires specialized equipment. The degree of equipment automation is determined by the type of substrate used. Semiautomatic presses require the operator to hand-feed the substrate into the printing position. After printing, the substrate may or may not be removed automatically. Once adjusted, the machine carries out all printing functions. Automatic presses infeed and outfeed automatically.

There are several types of presses used in screen printing. The most commonly used are the flatbed press, the cylinder press, and the rotary press.

- Types of flatbed screen printing presses include hand tables, semiautomatic, and automatic presses. **Figure 20-27** shows a large flatbed press set up to print colors. Replacing a printing frame on a large press requires additional personnel to handle the frame, **Figure 20-28.** The image carrier frames are clamped in place. Most production-type presses have vacuum tables or beds that hold the substrate in place during the printing process. A squeegee is pulled across the screen, forcing the ink through the open portion of the screen. On the return, the screen is coated with ink. This is called a flood coat.

- The cylinder press is used to print on substrates that are round, oval, or tapered. Bottles, pails, glasses, and toys are a few items using this type of printing press. The substrate is carried on the impression cylinder and the screen carrier supports the image. Both the cylinder and the carrier rotate while the squeegee remains stationary. Cylinder presses can be fully automated, semiautomated, or manually operated.

Figure 20-27. This flatbed screen press prints four colors.

Figure 20-28. The screens on this press are very large and heavy. Several workers are needed to change them.

- The rotary press has three main components: a fine-wire rotary screen, a squeegee, and an impression cylinder. The squeegee remains stationary while the rotary screen mesh revolves. The rotary screen is the image carrier. Ink is continually pumped into the cylinder and the squeegee forces the ink onto the substrate. Each cylinder unit carries an ink color or a clear coating. Items printed on rotary presses include gift wrap stock, textiles, and vinyl wall coverings.

Summary

A stencil attached to a screen is the simplest form of screen printing. The ink is forced through a mesh opening and it leaves an image on the selected stock. The process requires a frame, a squeegee, fabric, stencil, ink, and stock. The three types of presses commonly found in industrial settings include flatbed presses, cylinder presses, and rotary presses. A wide variety of products are produced by this printing method. Such examples include T-shirts, textiles, signs, pendants, and bottles.

Review Questions

Please do not write in this book. Write your answers on a separate sheet of paper.

1. What are some typical applications of screen printing?
2. Describe the basic printing process for screen printing.
3. _____ are solvents added to screen ink to alter viscosity and slow drying time.
4. Fabric mesh count is specified by the number of _____ per linear inch.
5. Distinguish between weft threads and warp threads.
6. What type of fabric is used for printing heated inks or when the ultimate of dimensional stability is needed?
   A. Organdy.
   B. Nylon.
   C. Polyester.
   D. Metal mesh.
7. What is the least desirable way of holding fabric on a wooden frame?
   A. Staples.
   B. Adhesive.
   C. Mechanical clamp.
   D. Cord and groove.
8. Chemical treatment alters the _____ characteristics of the fabric, and mechanical treatment changes the _____ of the fabric.
9. What is a burned edge?
10. What type of photographic stencil is used for long runs because of its durability?
    A. Indirect.
    B. Direct.
    C. Direct-indirect.
    D. None of the above.

Suggested Activities

1. Locate at least ten different products that were printed by the screen printing process. Explain how you determined screen printing was the process used.
2. Print an image on a T-shirt identifying your school or a student organization. Make the image at least two colors.

Related Web Link

Printing Process Descriptions

www.pneac.org/printprocesses/screen

Information about screen printing from the Printers' National Environmental Assistance Center.

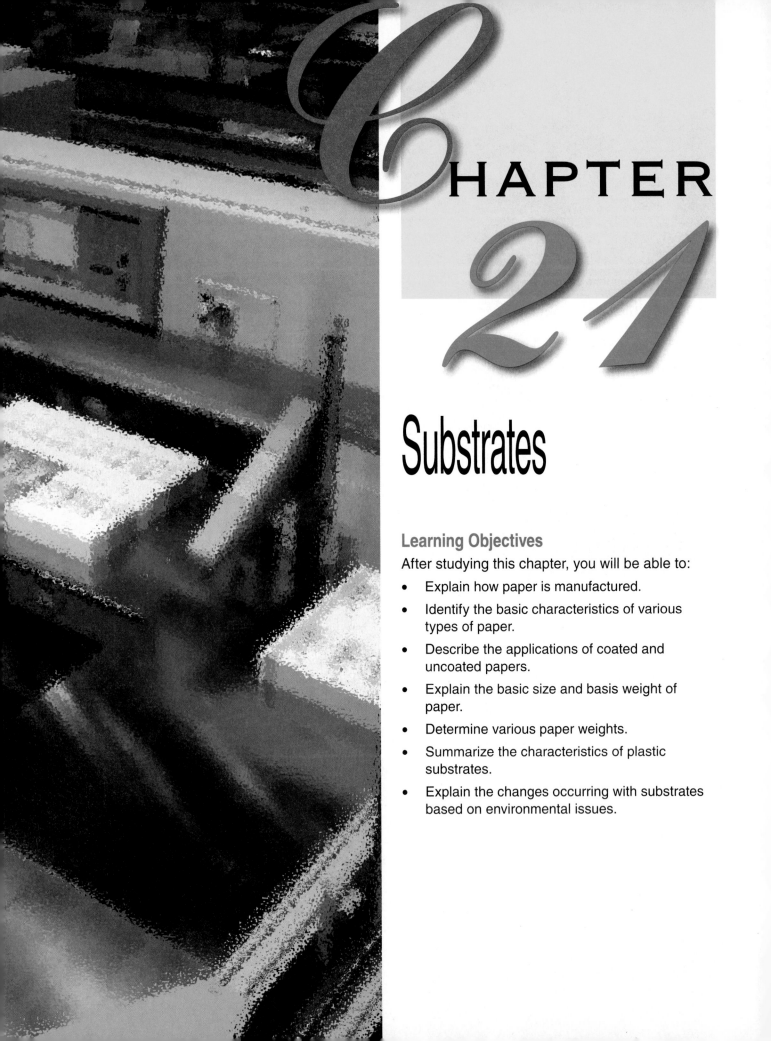

CHAPTER 21

Substrates

Learning Objectives

After studying this chapter, you will be able to:

- Explain how paper is manufactured.
- Identify the basic characteristics of various types of paper.
- Describe the applications of coated and uncoated papers.
- Explain the basic size and basis weight of paper.
- Determine various paper weights.
- Summarize the characteristics of plastic substrates.
- Explain the changes occurring with substrates based on environmental issues.

Important Terms

basic size
bleaching
calendering
cellulose
chain of custody
chipper
coated paper
de-inking
elemental chlorine
equivalent weight
fillers
fourdrinier machine
furnish
grades
grain
grain long
grain short
lignin
opacity
paper flatness
petrochemicals

postconsumer paper waste
preconsumer paper waste
print strength
printability
pulpers
ream
recycled paper
show-through
sizing
substance weight
substrate
supercalendering
tensile strength
thermoformed
totally chlorine free (TCF)
trim
uncoated paper
watermark

Substrates include any material with a surface that can be printed or coated. Although the most common printing substrate is paper, substances such as plastic, metal, and wood are also classified as substrates.

Matching the substrate to the job is critical. A high-quality layout, plate, ink, and printing technique will be wasted if a low-quality substrate is used. On the other hand, expensive stock should not be used to print low-quality products such as newspapers or sales flyers. Salespeople, designers, strippers, press operators, and finishing and binding personnel must have knowledge of the characteristics of paper and its applications. Its misuse can be very costly. More than one thousand different grades of paper are listed in paper merchant's catalogs.

PAPERMAKING HISTORY

Most paper is manufactured using machine technology, although some paper is still handmade. The use of handmade papers is usually limited to special applications, such as fine art reproductions, or limited editions of books printed and bound by craft workers using hand methods.

Some historical highlights of papermaking are:

- 105 A.D.—Ts'ai Lun, a Chinese official, mixed the bark of the mulberry tree with linen and hemp to make a crude form of paper.
- 500 A.D.—The Mayans produced paper using fig tree bark.
- 751 A.D.—Papermaking spread to Europe as a result of the Crusades and the Moorish conquest of northern Africa and Spain.
- 1400 A.D.—Papermaking by hand flourished.
- 1690 A.D.—The first paper mill in America was established near Philadelphia by William Rittenhouse and William Bradford.
- 1798 A.D.—Nicholas Louis Robert of France invented a machine with an endless wire screen to produce paper in rolls. The machine was financed by two English merchants, the Fourdrinier brothers, and was named the American fourdrinier machine.

Most of the paper manufactured in the United States today is made on the *fourdrinier machine*. It can produce continuous sheets of paper up to 33′ (10 m) wide at speeds faster than 3000′ (900 m) per minute. Some fourdrinier machines are more than 350′ (110 m) long. The mechanical principles of the original machine have remained nearly unchanged. Other inventions have occurred, but many are simply refinements.

Significant improvements in papermaking in recent years include thermomechanical pulping, synthetic wires and felts, twin-wire machines, and the use of computers to control pulping and papermaking operations. Paper manufacturers have also worked to improve pollution control and energy conservation in the industry.

MAKING PAPER

For centuries, the principle raw materials used in papermaking were cotton and linen fibers obtained from rags. Some cotton and linen fibers are still used for high-quality writing papers, business letterhead papers, art papers, and documents that will be kept for years. However, *cellulose* is the raw material used to make most paper today.

substrate: Any material with a surface that can be printed or coated.

fourdrinier machine: A paper machine that forms a continuous web of paper on a moving, endless wire belt.

cellulose: The raw material used to make paper.

Pine, fir, spruce, aspen, beech, birch, maple, and oak are typical species harvested for papermaking. The length of the tree fibers varies and determines, among other characteristics, the strength of the paper.

Papermaking is a complex manufacturing process. It uses both chemical and mechanical means to reduce wood fibers to pulp, which is the material used to ultimately produce paper in sheet form. See **Figure 21-1**.

Chipping

Harvested logs are cut to uniform length, debarked, **Figure 21-2,** and sent to a chipper or grinder. The

chipper cuts the logs into 3/8″ to 3/4″ chips. The chips are sized so the digester is able to separate the cellulose fibers. After the chips are screened for size, they are put in a huge cooking kettle called a digester.

Making Pulp

In the chemical pulpmaking process, chemicals in the sealed, pressurized digester break down the *lignin* present in the cellulose fibers. The cellulose fibers, which once resembled soda straws, become pulp, a mass of soft, spongy matter. The pulp is blown into a pit where the chemicals are washed away.

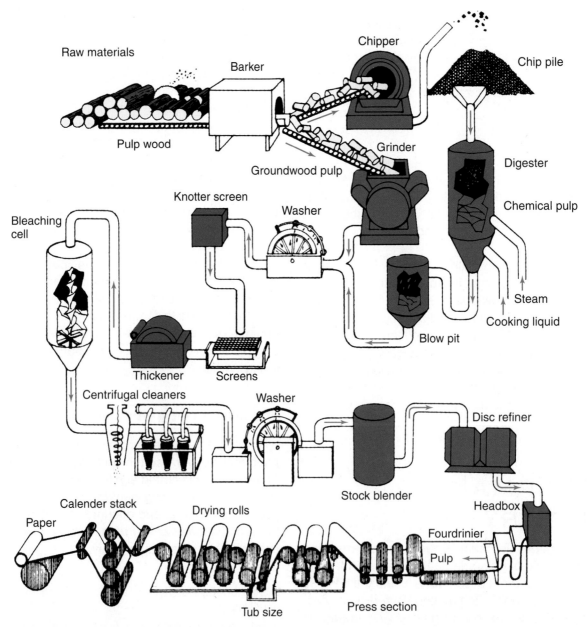

Figure 21-1. Major steps in the manufacture of paper. A modern papermaking operation requires a large investment in equipment and raw materials.

Figure 21-2. This huge machine rotates logs inside a toothed chamber to remove the bark. (Southern Forest Products Assn.)

The mechanical pulpmaking process (groundwood process) uses grinding wheels to reduce the logs to fiber. The by-product is pulp with high opacity but relatively low strength.

Sizing and Fillers

Sizing is added to the pulp slurry to make the paper more resistant to moisture. Rosin is a common sizing material. Alum is added as a binding agent. Binding is a part of the sizing process.

Fillers are needed to improve a paper's opacity, brightness, smoothness, and ink receptivity. Two common fillers are clay and titanium dioxide.

Dyes, Pigments, and Bleach

Dyes and pigments are added to produce colored substrates, while bleach makes the pulp white. Coloring or bleaching additives are mixed in vats called *pulpers*. The pulp goes through a final beating and refining stage before it is pumped to a stock chest.

Removing Water

A jordan machine is a beater or refiner of the fibers. A jordan machine refines the fiber slurry until it is about 99% water and 1% fiber and other solids. At this point, the paper is known as *furnish*. The solution is pumped into the headbox of the papermaking machine.

The pulp furnish is evenly dispersed on the fourdrinier wire, **Figure 21-3.** The wire screen vibrates as it travels along an endless belt, aligning the fibers in the direction of travel. A continuous web of paper is formed in the process. Gravity and suction remove about 35% of the water.

Figure 21-3. The fourdrinier wire section of the papermaking process. Wet paper fibers ride on an endless wire screen. This is known as the "wet end" of the machine. Water drains off as the fibers move toward the dryers. (Mead Publishing Paper Division)

Some papers are given a *watermark*, a translucent identifying design impressed in the paper while it is still wet. The symbols or images are created by rearranging the fibers with a tool known as a dandy roll. See **Figure 21-4.**

chipper: A machine that cuts logs into chips.

lignin: A glue-like substance that bonds wood fibers together.

sizing: Material, such as rosin, that is added to pulp slurry to make the paper stronger and more moisture-resistant.

fillers: Inorganic materials, such as clay or titanium dioxide, added to the papermaking furnish to improve opacity, brightness, smoothness, and ink receptivity.

pulpers: Vats in which coloring or bleaching additives are added to pulp.

furnish: The slurry of fillers, sizing, and colorants in a water suspension from which paper is made.

watermark: A translucent design impressed in paper.

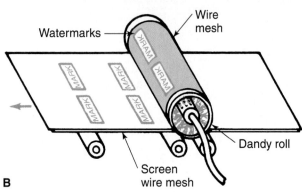

Figure 21-4. Creating a watermark. A—The watermark is simply a rearrangement of paper fibers. It identifies the grade of paper or the trademark of a company. B—A dandy roll is used to place the watermark on the paper.

Figure 21-5. Many of the papers used today for magazine and book publishing are coated for better reproduction of color and fine-screened halftones. Coating is applied on the papermaking machine. (Mead Publishing Paper Division)

Figure 21-6. Heated supercalender rolls are used to smooth and polish the paper surface to a high gloss. (Mead Publishing Paper Division)

Drying

When the furnish leaves the screen, it enters the press section, which removes more water. Then, the paper enters a dryer section consisting of large temperature-controlled rollers. More moisture is removed. Coatings are applied as the paper moves through the machine, **Figure 21-5.**

At some stage of the drying process, the paper must be calendered. *Calendering* is the process of flattening and smoothing the paper surface by passing it between a series of rollers. *Supercalendering* uses heated steel rollers and pressure to form a very smooth, high-gloss finish, **Figure 21-6.**

Rolling

The untrimmed paper is wound into rolls. Some rolls are rewound, slit, and cut into lengths to make flat packages of paper. Others remain as rolls for use in web-fed presses, **Figure 21-7.**

gloss might be used to convey a bright and exciting image. No. 1 paper produces very bright color through the use of transparent inks. Printed material, such as catalogs or posters, is typically printed on No. 2 or No. 3. Groundwood-processed sheets are of lower-grade stock, often No. 4 or No. 5.

Uncoated paper does not have a layer applied over the surface and tends to have a textured feel. Uncoated paper textures include laid, woven, and linen. These textures are suited to printed pieces that will be written on, such as stationery. Uncoated papers also enhance legibility, making them good choices for text-intensive printed material, such as textbooks or novels.

Adhesive-Coated Paper

Adhesive-coated stock is coated with an adhesive material that is permanently tacky or activated by water or heat. Labels are a common product that use this type of substrate. The heat-seal type of paper uses heat to melt the coating so it will stick to another surface. Stock with a coating that is permanently tacky is commonly called pressure-sensitive. These stocks require contact and pressure to make them adhere to another surface.

Safety Paper

Safety stock is typically used for printing checks. The specifications are very rigid because the stock must expose any attempted alteration of the document. If someone tries to alter it by erasure or by using chemicals, the paper automatically displays a change in the design or color. Some other documents using safety paper include bonds, deposit slips, coupons, tickets, certificates of title, warranties, and legal forms.

Bond Paper

Bond paper is a broad classification of quality paper used for business forms, letterheads, stationery, and many other products. Characteristics

Figure 21-7. On the machine in the background, rolls of paper are being rewound after being slit to different widths. Some of these rolls may later be cut into sheets and packaged; others will be used on web-fed presses. (Mead Publishing Paper Division)

PAPER TYPES

Adhesive-coated, safety, bond, carbonless, offset, duplicator, cover, ledger, index, newsprint, and recycled are some of the many types of paper. A general understanding of the characteristics and applications of various papers is important.

Coated and Uncoated Papers

Coated paper is a broad classification of paper that has layers of latex, pigments and adhesives applied to its surface. Coated papers typically have a smoother, stronger surface than uncoated papers. Finishes may be high-gloss, dull-coated, or matte-coated. They are more expensive than uncoated papers but yield better reproduction of images.

Coated papers are rated by brightness. A No. 1 rated paper is suitable for high-quality jobs, such as sales literature. Material intended to convey a prestigious image might use a matte finish, while high

calendering: Passing paper between rollers to increase the smoothness and gloss of the paper's surface.

supercalendering: Using heated steel rollers and pressure to form a very smooth, high-gloss finish on paper.

coated paper: Paper with a mineral substance applied to it for a smoother, stronger surface.

uncoated paper: Paper that does not have a mineral layer applied over the surface, so it has a slightly textured feel.

of bond paper include strength, good ink receptivity, and erasability.

Bond paper is used extensively for printers connected to desktop computers. Laser printers can provide acceptable quality using the same paper designed for photocopying machines. Paper for use in ink-jet printers has a coating formulated to accept the dye-like inks used by these printers.

Bond paper is made from cotton or rag fiber, or from chemical wood pulps. It has an even, hard finish on both sides. Rag bond is the most expensive type of paper and often has a watermark.

Duplicator Paper

Duplicator paper is an inexpensive bond paper designed for use in photocopying machines and laser printers. Duplicator paper should never be used as a stock for offset lithography or other forms of printing. Its surface strength and other qualities are not suitable for use on press.

Carbonless Paper

Carbonless paper is used to make multipart business forms that will be written on or used in some type of impact printer (a device, such as a typewriter, that makes a physical impression by striking the paper). Carbonless paper starts with a base stock similar to ordinary bond. The paper is coated with encapsulated colorless dyes and a receptor coating that reacts with the dye to produce an image. The capsules are broken when pressure is applied, releasing the dye onto the sheet below. The receptor coating develops the image.

Carbonless business forms have a variety of applications. Checks, vouchers, shipping labels in clear plastic envelopes, and continuous forms for impact-type printers are common uses.

Offset Paper

Offset paper is designed specifically for use on offset printing presses. It has good opacity, rapid ink absorption, and permanence. It can be coated or uncoated. Offset paper is used for a wide variety of products, such as books, form letters, magazines, manuals, and advertisements. See **Figure 21-8.**

Offset paper is sometimes called book paper because both have similar properties and construction methods. Offset papers are made from various materials, including chemical wood pulp, mechanical wood pulp, recycled papers, and even straw. Frequently, two or more of these raw materials are combined to make offset paper.

Impregnated offset paper receives a mineral film to smooth and strengthen the surface for better image reproduction. It is sometimes called pigmentized offset paper.

Text paper is an expensive grade of offset or book paper. Depending on its surface smoothness, it can be both attractive and functional. Smooth text paper is used for accurate reproduction of halftones. Rougher surfaces are used when halftone reproduction quality is not important.

Figure 21-8. Books and many other printed products are produced using offset paper, often on web-fed presses like this one. (Heidelberg Harris)

Cover Paper

Cover paper is a thick or heavy paper, typically used for the covers of books, catalogs, brochures, manuals, and similar publications. Sometimes, two layers of cover paper are bonded together to produce double thickness. When pasted together, it can be sold by caliper or thickness.

Ledger Paper

Ledger paper has a smooth, matte finish that resists erasing. It easily accepts pen and is both strong and durable. Ledger paper is used for accounting notepads, bookkeeping forms, business ledger sheets, and financial statement forms.

Index Paper

Index paper is a thick, stiff, smooth paper, frequently two-ply or greater. Index stock may be coated or uncoated. Its most common uses are index cards and postcards, so it must be sturdy enough to withstand frequent handling. Bristol paper is not as smooth as index paper, but the thickness and use is similar.

Newsprint Paper

Newsprint is one of the lowest grades of printing paper. It is made by the groundwood or mechanical method of papermaking. Newsprint has very short fibers which enable the paper to be folded easily in any direction. When new, it has a grayish-white color, but it turns yellow and becomes brittle with age. Since newsprint absorbs ink readily, a drying system on the press is not needed.

Zink Paper

Zink™ stands for Zero Ink. This product is a very unusual substrate. It is made of composite materials composed of different layers. Embedded between the top layer and the polymer base are dye crystals of cyan, yellow, and magenta. The paper is colorless and appears as a regular sheet of paper stock. The printer uses heat to activate the embedded crystals which in turn colorizes the stock.

Recycled Paper

Several environmental issues, such as depleting resources and landfill space, have contributed to the trend toward buying and using recycled paper.

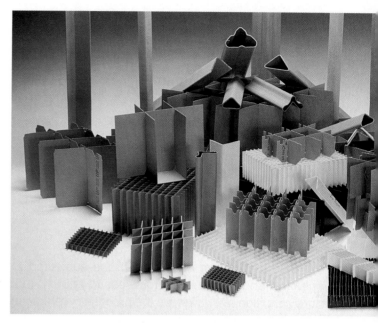

Figure 21-9. Corrugated packaging is a major user of fiber from recycled paper. (Sonoco Products Co.)

Recycled paper is made from old or used paper products, **Figure 21-9.** There are different grades of recycled paper. High grades can be made into quality printing paper. Low grades can be made into newsprint, cartons, and other products.

The recycled paper arena is dynamic. Guidelines relating to the manufacture of recycled paper are continually being reviewed by the United States Environmental Protection Agency (EPA). The federal government has established minimum-content standards for the paper it purchases.

Recycled papers may contain preconsumer waste, postconsumer waste, or both. Waste material created by manufacturing processes that would otherwise be disposed of is called *preconsumer paper waste*. Used materials that have served a purpose and may be recycled into new paper is called *postconsumer paper waste*.

Guidelines were issued by the Federal Trade Commission for the use of labeling products as recycled in a way that is clear and truthful for consumers. The label must consist of the percentage and type of recycled content, **Figure 21-10.**

recycled paper: Paper made from old or used paper products.

preconsumer paper waste: Scrap material generated by the papermaking process.

postconsumer paper waste: Used paper products that have served their intended purpose and are separated from solid waste for recycling into new paper.

10%
TOTAL RECOVERED FIBER
ALL POSTCONSUMER FIBER

Figure 21-10. A product must be labeled to indicate the percentage of recycled matter it contains. The recycled content of this product came entirely from postconsumer waste.

Before paper can be reused, it is subjected to chemical and mechanical processes to return it to a pure condition. *De-inking* is the process of removing inks, fillers, and coatings from waste paper. The mixture is reduced to cellulose fibers suspended in a water slurry.

After the waste paper is de-inked, the fibers are bleached. *Bleaching* is the use of chlorine bleach to give paper a bright white appearance.

Elemental chlorine was used to bleach paper. However, the waste given off from chlorine was linked to the creation of dioxin, which can cause health problems including cancer. Once this discovery was made, the EPA began to develop emission standards for the pulp and paper industry. Since then, alternatives to bleaching by chlorine have been used throughout the world.

Elementally chlorine-free (ECF) bleaching uses safer chemicals, such as chlorine dioxide or sodium hypochlorite, instead of chlorine gas. Using oxygen or other nonchlorine bleaching processes is another alternative to eliminate the formation of dioxins. Another alternative is to use unbleached (slightly brown) paper products known as *totally chlorine-free (TCF)*.

PAPER APPLICATIONS

Some papers are adaptable to different applications, while others are very limited in their use. The applications of paper to various printing processes will be discussed next.

Paper for Gravure

Newsprint produced for gravure printing typically contains mineral fillers and a calendered surface. Mail-order catalogs are a good example of this type of stock. When high-quality gravure printing is desired,

THINK GREEN
Paper Recycling

Recycling paper is one of the easiest ways to help protect the environment from the dangers caused by paper waste. There are multiple organizations dedicated to helping the graphic communications industry be less harmful to the environment. One example already discussed is the Forest Stewardship Council. Others include the Sustainable Forestry Initiative and the Green Press Initiative. These organizations ensure pulp for paper comes from recycled material or from approved forests. In order to be considered recycled, the paper must contain at least 30% recycled materials. Recycled paper comes in the forms of preconsumer waste or postconsumer waste. Preconsumer waste includes scraps or other types of leftover paper. Postconsumer waste is paper that has been printed on, used, and recycled. Recycled paper must be de-inked before it can be reused. In order to make recycled paper usable, it must be bleached. The most environmentally friendly process is elementally chlorine-free bleaching. Organizations like those mentioned offer assistance and certify the paper used by printers is environmentally safe. For more information, see www.sfiprogram.org.

the paper used contains mineral filler, but also a larger percentage of short-fiber chemical pulp.

Paper surfaces may be relatively soft, since gravure ink is not tacky. This eliminates the problem of ink picking fibers from the surface of the paper. Coated surfaces are widely used in gravure. Compressibility of paper is important because the gravure cells must make contact with the paper surface.

Because gravure is used in packaging, the stock must have dimensional stability, thickness must be controlled, and moisture content must be considered. The reaction of the stock to the process is critical in the high-production speeds required of gravure.

Paper for Offset Lithography

In offset lithography, fuzz, lint, and dust must be strictly limited. See **Figure 21-11.** A wide variety of papers can be printed by the lithographic process,

Figure 21-11. Papers used for offset lithography, whether printed on a small duplicator or a large web-fed press, must have a surface resistant to having fibers pulled loose by tacky ink. Loose fibers can cause specks and other defects in the printed product.

but any paper must have sufficient fiber-bonding strength to prevent the pulling of fibers from the stock by tacky ink. Because of the surface contact and tackiness of the ink, special coatings are applied to the paper.

Moisture is another consideration. The paper surface must not become weakened by moisture, or fibers will pick off with each successive impression.

Surface irregularity is not critical in offset lithography. The blanket is resilient and should return to its original shape, even if the paper has an irregular surface. Of course, limitations do exist. Halftones and solids do not print well on irregular stock.

Paper for Flexography

Flexography is ideal for printing packaging materials because the soft plates can transfer ink to almost any kind of substrate. Kraft linerboard and coated kraft are used in corrugated boxes. The ink is unable to be absorbed into kraft papers. Other paper and paperboard substrates include folding cartons, labels, gift wrap, and paperback books. Newsprint, corrugated linerboard, and paperboard are relatively rough and very absorbent. Calendered and coated papers are the smoothest and least absorbent. They also exhibit high ink holdout.

Paper for Laser Printing

In digital printing, errors in paper selection can cause such problems as misregistration and ink rub-off. The high speeds and temperatures of digital printing equipment require specially formulated papers, some of which are laser-compatible or laser-guaranteed, as well.

For medium- and high-speed black-and-white or color digital printers, smooth-finished laser papers have superior toner adhesion and excellent performance at high speeds and high temperatures. These printers typically print on papers ranging from 16-lb. bond to 60-lb. cover and 110-lb. index.

Dry-toner digital presses run well with smooth, bright papers from 24-lb. bond to 80-lb. cover stock, coated or uncoated.

Wet-toner digital presses require a special coating on substrates for optimal toner adhesion. A variety of substrates will work, from 50-lb. text to transparencies to labels, as long as they are coated.

PAPER CHARACTERISTICS

The directions of fibers in a sheet or web of paper must be a consideration in all printing processes. Another important factor is the stability of the sheet. Will it curl or have wavy edges? Paper also comes in a variety of weights and sizes.

Grain Direction

Paper made by the machine method has *grain*, which is determined by the direction in which the pulp fibers lie. Direction of grain becomes important when feeding the paper through the press and during some finishing procedures.

de-inking: The process of removing inks, fillers, and coatings from waste paper.

bleaching: A chemical treatment to whiten wood pulp.

elemental chlorine: Chlorine gas used to bleach paper pulp and to separate the pulp from lignin.

totally chlorine free (TCF): Refers to unbleached paper with a slightly brown appearance.

grain: The direction or structure of paper fibers.

The underlined dimension on a package of paper specifies the direction of the grain. Another way to find grain direction is to tear a sheet of paper in one direction and then the other. The straightest tear is parallel to the grain, **Figure 21-12.**

A third means of finding grain direction is to cut two strips of paper, each in a different direction. Lay the strips over a rod or straight surface. The sheet that curves the most is across or at right angles to the grain.

Grain may also be found by dampening one side of the sheet. The dampened paper will curl with the grain. Usually, a sheet of paper will fold easier and form a more even edge with the grain.

In most cases, sheets are fed through a press with the grain parallel to the cylinder of the offset press. The stock is referred to as *grain long*. During binding, the grain should be parallel to the binding edge so the fibers will not break. *Grain short* is a quality that indicates the grains run across the paper.

Paper Flatness

Paper flatness refers to how well the paper remains straight or unwarped. Flatness is a basic requirement if the stock is to feed through a sheet-fed press without problems.

Paper is naturally hygroscopic, meaning the cellulose fibers seek the moisture in the surrounding area. Most paper is shipped with 4% to 6% moisture content. In a facility with an air temperature of 70°F to 75°F (21°C to 24°C), that equates to 42% to 48% relative humidity.

Wavy paper edges indicate a greater amount of moisture in the edges than inside the sheet, **Figure 21-13.** Sometimes the opposite occurs, resulting in tight edges and a sheet that curls up or down.

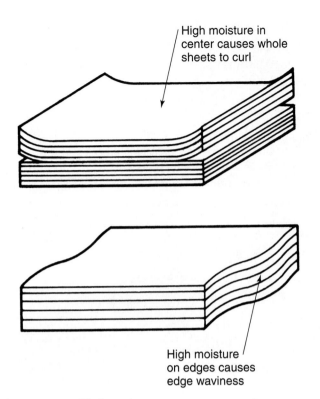

High moisture in center causes whole sheets to curl

High moisture on edges causes edge waviness

Figure 21-13. High moisture content can make paper warp or become wavy.

Paper handling must be closely supervised. Relative humidity and paper moisture are critical to smooth operation of the press. Packages of paper should be kept closed until needed to keep moisture out. Also, paper must be square and free of dust, lint, and dirt.

Paper Size and Weight

All paper has a grade, a basic size, and a basis weight. The types of paper are also known as *grades*. Each grade has certain characteristics and uses. The choice of paper grade depends on the intended use.

Basic size, specified by length and width, varies with grade, **Figure 21-14.** The basic size of bond paper is 17″ × 22″. One ream weighs 16 or 20 lbs.;

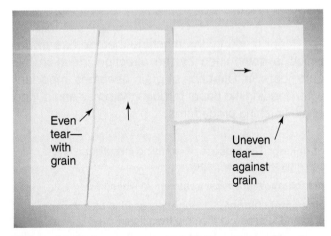

Figure 21-12 An easy way to tell paper grain direction is to tear two sheets in different directions. The straightest tear is parallel to the direction of grain.

Kind of Paper	Square Inches	Basic Size
Bond, ledger, writing	374	17″ × 22″
Cover	520	20″ × 26″
Newsprint	864	24″ × 36″
Book, offset, text	950	25″ × 38″
Index, bristols	778	25 1/2″ × 30 1/2″

Figure 21-14. Some common types of paper and their basic sizes.

16-lb. stock is thinner than 20-lb. stock. The basic size of book paper is 25″ × 38″. The substance weight of book paper is 2 1/2 times the weight of bond with 2 1/2 times the surface area.

Cover paper has a basic size of 20″ × 26″. It is a durable stock with many textures. It comes in 60-lb. to 80-lb. weights. The basic size of index stock is 25 1/2″ × 30 1/2″. It is a heavy stock and often identified by the number of plies. One-ply equals 90-lb. stock; two-ply equals 110-lb. stock; three-ply equals 140-lb. stock.

Basis weight is the weight in pounds of one ream of basic-sized stock. A *ream* has 500 sheets. Usually paper is referred to by its ream weight, as in 20-lb.

bond or 70-lb. book. A 20-lb. bond means that 500 sheets of 17″ × 22″ writing paper weigh 20 pounds.

If the letter M appears after the weight, it means per 1000 sheets. For example, 25 × 38 − 140M means 1000 sheets of 25″ × 38″ book paper weigh 140 pounds, **Figure 21-15.**

Substance weight is the actual weight of the ream. Papers have many basic sizes and basis weights. Therefore, the thickness of a ream of stock can vary based on its substance weight.

Equivalent weight is the weight of one ream of paper that is of a size larger or smaller than the basic size. Use the following formula to find the *equivalent weight* of paper, referring to Figure 21-15 for the basic size.

Type	Basic Size	Weights
Writing	17″ × 22″	26 32 40 48 56 64 etc.
Cover	20″ × 26″	100 120 130 160 180 etc.
Book	25″ × 38″	60 70 80 90 100 120 140 160 etc.
Index bristol	25 1/2″ × 30 1/2″	117 144 182 222 286 etc.

Figure 21-15. Some typical weights of paper for common sizes.

grain long: Important factor of paper that can affect folding and direction of feed for printing.

grain short: Indicates that the grain runs across the paper.

paper flatness: How well a sheet of paper remains straight or unwarped for feeding through a sheet-fed press.

grades: Categories or classes of paper.

basic size: The standard length and width, in inches, of a grade of paper.

ream: Five hundred sheets of paper.

substance weight: The actual weight of a ream of paper.

equivalent weight: The weight of one ream of paper of a size that is larger or smaller than the basic size.

$$\dfrac{\text{Length} \times \dfrac{\text{Width of}}{\text{sheets}} \times \dfrac{\text{Basis}}{\text{weight}}}{\text{Length} \times \text{Width of basic size}} = \text{Equivalent weight}$$

Example: What is the equivalent weight of a ream of 28″ × 34″ ledger paper, 32-lb. stock?

$$\dfrac{28 \times 34 \times 32}{17 \times 22} = 81.4 \text{ lbs.}$$

To find the *total weight* of a number of sheets, use the following formula:

$$\dfrac{\dfrac{\text{Weight of}}{\text{1000 sheets}} \times \dfrac{\text{Number of}}{\text{sheets}}}{1000} = \text{Total weight}$$

Example: What is the total weight of 1475 sheets of 17″ × 22″ − 56M, 28-lb. stock?

$$\dfrac{56 \times 1475}{1000} = 82.6 \text{ lbs.}$$

To find the *basis weight* (when the sheet size and ream weight are known) use the following formula:

$$\dfrac{\text{Basic size} \times \text{Ream weight}}{\text{Length} \times \text{Width of sheet}} = \text{Basis weight}$$

Example: What is the basis weight of a ream of book paper 23″ × 29″, with a ream weight of 56 pounds?

$$\dfrac{25 \times 38 \times 56}{23 \times 29} = \dfrac{53,200}{667} = 80 \text{ lbs.}$$

The length and weight of paper in rolls can be calculated by applying the factors shown in **Figure 21-16** to the appropriate formula.

To find the *length* of paper in a roll of known width and net weight (not including wrapper and core), use the following formula:

$$\dfrac{41.67 \times \text{Roll weight} \times \text{Factor}}{\text{Roll width} \times \text{Basis weight}} = \text{Length}$$

Example: How many feet of paper are in a 1000-lb. roll of 35″-wide offset book, 75-lb. stock?

$$\dfrac{41.67 \times 1000 \times 950}{35 \times 75} = 15,080'$$

Paper Computation Factors		
Type	**Basic size**	**Factor**
Business papers	17″ × 22″	374
Book papers	25″ × 38″	950
Cover papers	20″ × 26″	520
Printing bristols	22 1/2″ × 28 1/2″	641
Tag, news, conv.	24″ × 36″	864
Index bristols	25 1/2″ × 30 1/2″	778

Figure 21-16. A factor is derived by multiplying the dimensions of the basic size of a type of paper. For example, the basic size of business papers (bond) is 17″ × 22″, which equals 371. (Inter-City Paper Co.)

To find the *approximate weight* of rolls on a 3″ inner diameter core, use the following formula:

$$(\text{Roll diameter})^2 \times \text{Width} \times \dfrac{\text{Roll}}{\text{factor*}} = \text{Approximate weight}$$

*Roll factors:

Bond	0.021
Smooth Finish Offset	0.022
Vellum Finish Offset	0.018
C2S Web Offset	0.032

Example 1: What is the approximate weight of a 34 1/2″-wide, 40″-diameter roll of coated web paper?

$$(40 \times 40) \times 34.5 \times 0.032 = 1766 \text{ lbs.}$$

Example 2: What is the approximate weight of a 17 1/2″-wide, 40″-diameter roll of vellum offset?

$$(40 \times 40) \times 17.5 \times 0.018 = 504 \text{ lbs.}$$

Sometimes it is necessary to figure out how many pieces of paper can be cut out of a large sheet. A typical stock cutting sheet is shown in **Figure 21-17.**

To figure the number of pieces per sheet, the dimensions of the desired cut piece are written below the dimensions of the uncut sheet. First, each dimension of the cut size is divided into its corresponding full-sheet dimension. The resulting whole numbers (fractions are dropped) are multiplied to find the number of pieces that can be cut from the sheet. The computation is done two ways. In the vertical method, the dimensions are divided vertically; in the cross method, division is done diagonally.

An example of the two methods is shown in **Figure 21-18.** Stock size is 25″ × 38″, while the

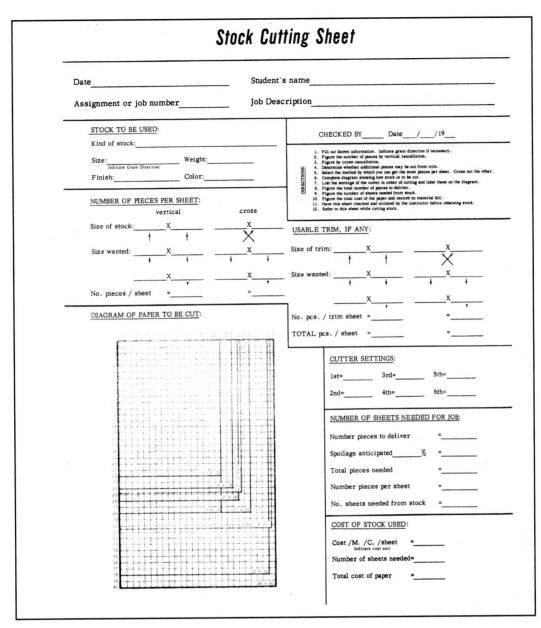

Figure 21-17. A stock cutting sheet form. (Central Missouri State University)

Number of pieces per sheet:

	Vertical	Cross
Size of stock:	25 × 38	25 × 38
Size wanted :	6 × 9	6 × 9
	4 × 4	6 × 2
No. pieces / sheet	= 16	= 12

Figure 21-18. How to determine the number of pieces per sheet.

desired cut size is 6″ × 9″. The result would be that 16 pieces can be obtained using the vertical method and 12 pieces using the cross method.

It is more economical to cut the short dimension of the piece out of the short dimension of the sheet, which is the number obtained using the vertical method. However, this is true only if it is satisfactory to have the grain run the long way on the piece.

If the grain had to run parallel to the short (6″) dimension of the piece, it would yield only 12 pieces (as determined using the cross method).

Sometimes, it is possible that the *trim* can be used for another job. To find out, utilize the same type of formula.

Metric Paper Sizes

In many countries, the SI Metric system is used for specifying paper size. The letters A and B each designate a different series. The sizes in each series are numbered 0 to 8 and represent the number of times a sheet can be folded to obtain a particular size. The sizes in a series are proportionate; any smaller size is always half the next larger size.

In the A series, A0 has an area of 1 m². The sheet is not a true square but has a proportion of 5:7, **Figure 21-19.** Using 1 m² as a starting point, the subsequently smaller sizes are determined by halving the larger size, **Figure 21-20.**

In the B series, the sizes fall between the A series measurements and are used for unusual situations. Standard metric sizes of paper are listed in **Figure 21-21.** The nearest metric equivalent to the 8 1/2″ × 11″

Designation	mm	Index
A0	841 × 1189	33.11 × 46.81
A1	594 × 841	23.39 × 33.11
A2	420 × 594	16.54 × 23.39
A3	297 × 420	11.69 × 16.54
A4	210 × 297	8.27 × 11.69
A5	148 × 210	5.83 × 8.27
A6	105 × 148	4.13 × 5.83
A7	74 × 105	2.91 × 4.13
A8	52 × 74	2.05 × 2.91
B0	1000 × 1414	39.37 × 55.67
B1	707 × 1000	27.83 × 39.37
B2	500 × 707	19.68 × 27.83
B3	353 × 500	13.90 × 19.68
B4	250 × 353	9.84 × 13.90
B5	176 × 250	6.93 × 9.84
B6	125 × 176	4.92 × 6.93
B7	88 × 125	3.46 × 4.92
B8	62 × 88	2.44 × 3.46

Figure 21-21. Alphanumeric designations, sizes, and indices for the metric-size paper sheets. An index is the decimal equivalent in inches.

standard sheet used in the United States is the A4 size. It is 210 mm × 297 mm (8.27″ × 11.69″).

QUALITIES OF PAPER

There are several physical qualities that can be used to make judgments about which paper is most well-suited for a particular printing job. These are color, smoothness, strength, brightness, and opacity.

Color

Paper color and ink color must be compatible. White paper is essential for full- or four-color printing. It reflects all the colors of the spectrum, while colored paper does not. Colored paper can create a process color value that is undesirable, producing a finished piece that may not be what the customer expected.

Smoothness

Smoothness and texture both greatly affect *printability*, or how well images show fine detail. Smoothness varies with paper type. A smooth sheet requires a very thin film of ink to produce sharp images. The opposite is true for rough papers.

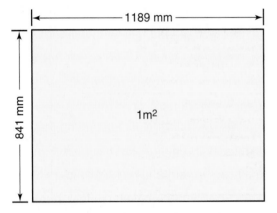

Figure 21-19. Size A0 is the basis for metric paper sizes. It is 1 m² in area, with a rectangular shape in a 5:7 proportion.

Figure 21-20. Metric paper sizes are simply halves of larger sizes.

Strength

The *tensile strength* of paper is determined by how well the inner fibers are bonded together. A roll of paper that cannot feed through a web-fed press without breaking easily has loosely bonded fibers and low strength.

Print strength is determined by how well the surface of the paper is bonded together. A low print strength could allow bits of fiber to be lifted off the paper surface by high-tack inks. Hickeys would appear on the printed image. Coated stock normally has higher print strength than uncoated stock.

Brightness

Brightness is determined by how well the paper surface reflects light. Paper brightness affects the contrast of the printed image. A bright paper makes colors, particularly black, stand out more.

Transparent ink on a bright paper also produces exceptional color rendition. More light reflects up through the ink layers to produce stronger colors.

Opacity

Opacity refers to the ability of light to pass through a sheet of paper. It is also the ability to see through the sheet. Poor opacity produces an undesirable result called *show-through*. The image on the back side of the sheet can be seen through the paper, and is a distraction to the reader. Examine stock carefully to make sure show-through will not occur. A heavyweight paper has high opacity, whereas a thin paper tends to have low opacity.

ENVELOPES

Envelopes come in many styles and sizes for a variety of applications. Envelopes used for postal purposes have a minimum size requirement of 3 1/2″ × 5″. Any size over 6 1/8″ × 11 1/2″, or thicker than 1/4″, is subject to additional postage fees. **Figure 21-22** illustrates common envelope styles.

- The commercial envelope is typically used to send correspondence. The No. 10 size (4 1/8″ × 9 1/2″) is the most widely used.

- The window envelope has an opening that allows the address to appear through the clear opening. This is a time-saving and convenient feature.

- The baronial envelope is used mostly for invitations, announcements, and greeting cards.

ACADEMIC LINK
Acid-Free Paper

The acid found in manufactured paper occurs naturally in wood pulp and may also be absorbed from the environment, printing processes, and human hands. This acid causes the paper to turn yellow in color and physically deteriorate. To ensure longevity, acid-free (or alkaline) paper has become the standard substrate used for archival and historical documents and projects.

During production, acid-free paper is treated with an alkaline compound, usually calcium carbonate, to neutralize the acid and bring the pH of the paper to 7 or slightly more. Acid-free paper also contains a reserve of the alkaline compound to neutralize any acids the paper may encounter once in use or that develop as the paper ages. The integrity of acid-free paper is expected to last hundreds of years. The life span of paper that has not been treated with an alkaline compound may only be a couple of decades.

What are some other common uses of calcium carbonate?

- The booklet envelope, with its opening on the side, is used to hold house publications and direct mail pieces.

- The clasp envelope is used to mail bulky materials. The manner of fastening will vary, but it is strong and can take abuse.

Figure 21-23 lists common envelope sizes. Envelope company catalogs provide more detailed information.

---

trim: The paper that is left over after cutting a sheet into smaller pieces.

printability: How well fine details are reproduced in a printed image.

tensile strength: The amount of stress that will break paper.

print strength: How well a paper surface resists lifting of its fiber by high-tack inks.

opacity: The quality of a paper that does not allow print from the opposite side to show through.

show-through: An undesirable result of poor opacity in which the image on one side of a sheet of paper is seen on the other side.

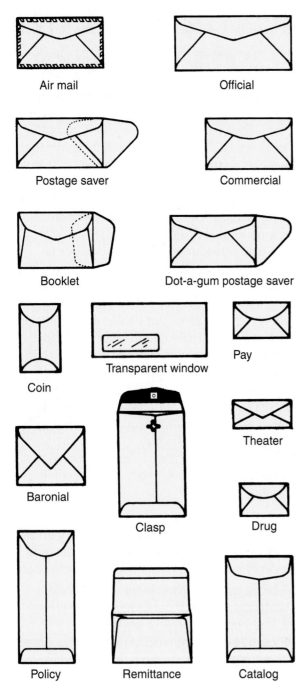

Air mail

Official

Postage saver

Commercial

Booklet

Dot-a-gum postage saver

Coin

Transparent window

Pay

Baronial

Clasp

Theater

Drug

Policy

Remittance

Catalog

Figure 21-22. Typical envelope styles. (Carpenter-Offutt Paper Co.)

Size	Dimensions (inches)		
Office and Commercial			
5	3 1/6	x	5 1/2
6 1/4	3 1/2	x	6
6 3/4	3 5/8	x	6 1/2
7	3 3/4	x	6 3/4
7 3/4	3 7/8	x	7 1/2
8 5/8	3 5/8	x	8 5/8
9	3 7/8	x	8 7/8
10	4 1/8	x	9 1/2
11	4 1/2	x	10 3/8
12	4 3/4	x	11
14	5	x	11 1/2
Baronial			
4	3 5/8	x	4 11/16
5	4 1/8	x	5 1/8
5 1/2	4 3/8	x	5 5/8
5 3/4	4 5/8	x	5 15/16
Booklet			
2 1/2	4 1/2	x	5 7/8
3	4 3/4	x	6 1/2
5	5 1/2	x	8 1/8
6	5 3/4	x	8 7/8
6 1/2	6	x	9
7	6 1/4	x	9 5/8
7 1/2	7 1/2	x	10 1/2
9	8 3/4	x	11 1/2
9 1/2	9	x	12
10	9 1/2	x	12 5/8
Clasp			
0	2 1/2	x	4 1/4
5	3 1/8	x	5 1/2
10	3 3/8	x	6
15	4	x	6 3/8
11	4 1/2	x	10 3/8
25	4 5/8	x	6 3/4
35	5	x	7 1/2
14	5	x	11 1/2
50	5 1/2	x	8 1/4
55	6	x	9
63	6 1/2	x	9 1/2
68	7	x	10
75	7 1/2	x	10 1/2
80	8	x	11
83	8 1/2	x	11 1/2
87	9 3/4	x	11 1/4
90	9	x	12
93	9 1/2	x	12 1/2
94	9 1/4	x	14 1/2
95	10	x	12
97	10	x	13
98	10	x	15
105	11 1/2	x	14 1/2
110	12	x	15 1/2

Figure 21-23. Common envelope sizes and dimensions.

PLASTIC SUBSTRATES

Plastic has many variations. Sometimes it is a thin film. Other times it is a sturdy yet flexible material. Another plastic might be stiff or even rigid. Plastic substrates are blended from various *petrochemicals* and other compounds. Most plastic substrates are available in both roll and sheet form.

Polyester

Polyester is one of the strongest plastic films used as a printing substrate. It has high clarity, toughness, durability, and good dimensional stability. It must be treated to prepare its surface for offset printing. Polyester substrates are used for decals, labels, and signs.

Copolyester

Copolyester is an extruded and dull-finished plastic substrate. It has a high degree of dimensional stability, clarity, and formability. It is available in matte finish or transparent colors. Copolyester is a comparatively inexpensive plastic substrate. Book report covers, overhead projector overlays, and flip charts are a few of its applications.

Polycarbonate Film

Polycarbonate film is a high-gloss substrate with good dimensional stability, good heat resistance, and excellent light transmittance. Low-haze polycarbonate film can be printed on offset presses without pretreatment. It is easily die cut and embossed. Polycarbonate film is used for decals, nameplates, membrane switch panels, overlays, and product identification.

Rigid Vinyl

A rigid vinyl substrate has good stability and is available in calendered gloss or matte finish. It comes in white translucent, white opaque, and standard opaque colors. Rigid vinyl is commonly used for identification cards or credit cards, but it is also used for shelf signs or labels, danglers, wall signs, and pocket calendars. Rigid vinyl is easily die-cut and *thermoformed* into shapes.

High-Impact Polystyrene

High-impact polystyrene is a versatile and economical plastic substrate. It is offset-printable and available in translucent and opaque colors. It is used for point-of-purchase display signs and toys.

Cellulose Acetate

Cellulose acetate is a plastic film. It provides outstanding clarity but poor dimensional stability and tear-resistance. Its soft surface is receptive to a wide variety of inks. Cellulose acetate is used for folders, book jackets, and overhead projector transparencies.

Clear-Oriented Polyester

Clear-oriented polyester is the cheapest plastic substrate available. It tears and scratches easily but provides good clarity. It is used for short-term display signs, labels, visual aids, and similar products.

Kimdura®

Kimdura® is a white opaque or translucent polypropylene film substrate. It serves as a "synthetic paper" that has been treated for offset printing. It is tough and durable, and can withstand repeated folding. Kimdura has good dimensional stability and a waterproof printing surface. It is used for posters, brochures, catalogs, children's books, outdoor maps, globes, menus, and instructional manuals.

Reemay®

Reemay® is a spunbonded polyester that is acrylic-coated on both sides. It is bright white. Reemay feels like fabric and can be sewn and grommeted. It is used for banners and similar applications and has excellent UV-resistance.

Tyvek®

Tyvek® is a strong spunbonded polyolefin plastic substrate. It has a smooth surface, good dimensional stability, resistance to ultraviolet light and moisture, and excellent opacity. Tyvek is treated with an antistatic agent to facilitate sheet handling. For printing purposes, it is commonly used for envelopes, tags, labels, maps, and book coverings.

ENVIRONMENTAL ISSUES

The paper industry is trying diligently to be good stewards of the earth's natural resources. Reforestation is taking place. Programs are ensuring that perpetual planting, growing, and harvesting of trees is taking place while protecting the environment. The driving force behind recycling advocacy is to keep

petrochemicals: Petroleum-based chemicals.

thermoformed: Formed by heat and pressure.

paper out of landfills. Another benefit of recycling is the saving of trees. It also takes less energy to make pulp out of a sheet of paper than a log.

Chain of Custody

The *chain of custody* is the process of tracking and recording the possession and transfer of wood and fiber from forests of origin, through the different stages of production, to the end user. This means that the responsibility now includes paper merchants, printers, agencies, and independent designers. The Sustainable Forestry Initiative (SFI) and the Forest Stewardship Council (FSC) are two programs that authenticate that the fiber source comes from responsibly managed forests.

Standards

Professionals and biologists are managing the forests to be in compliance with the standards of the SFI program. The FSC was established to create an honest and credible system for identifying well-managed forests. The Chlorine Free Products Association (CFPA) is a not-for-profit accreditation and standard-setting organization. The standards relate to the reduction of energy and water consumption, eliminating harmful toxins, provide a chain of custody for all fibers, and reviewing social, environmental and financial responsibility of their products and services.

Summary

The surface of many materials has the capability of being printed on to give a visible image. Although paper is the most commonly used substrate, plastics and metal have favorable surfaces. The papermaking process requires consistency so that the surface of the stock allows true repeatability of an image. Many types of paper are needed to produce a variety of products. It is essential to know the characteristics of paper when printing as all designed products may not be suitable for a selected stock. Knowledge of the quality of paper is also essential. Federal and state regulations have forced major changes within the manufacturing process as well as sustainable forestry and certification.

Review Questions

Please do not write in this book. Write your answers on a separate sheet of paper.

1. List three common materials used as printing substrates.
2. Most paper manufactured in the U.S. is made on what machine?
3. What is the raw material used to make paper?
4. _____ is added to the pulp to make paper moisture-resistant. _____ are added to improve opacity, brightness, smoothness, and ink receptivity.
5. The process that impresses a translucent design in paper is _____.
   A. watermarking
   B. calendering
   C. furnishing
   D. embossing
6. _____ paper is smoother, stronger, and yields a better image than _____ paper.
7. What are two alternatives to using chlorine gas to bleach paper?
8. What characteristic is contained by machine-made papers?
9. How many sheets are in a ream of paper?
10. What is the formula for determining basis weight?
11. How many sheets of 8″ × 10″ can be cut out of a 17″ × 22″ sheet?
12. What color of paper is essential for true process color reproduction?
13. Print _____ is an important factor affecting hickeys or specks on the printed image.
14. The _____ of paper affects whether the paper will exhibit an undesirable problem called _____.
15. Which plastic substrate is typically used to make identification cards and credit cards?
16. Explain the role of the chain of custody.

Suggested Activities

1. Explore the possibility of making handmade paper.
2. Using a rubber stamp, place the stamp image on seven different substrate surfaces. Analyze the effect of the stamp on each surface of the various substrates.

3. Visit a paper storage facility and list the paper classifications as well as the paper sizes associated with that classification.

4. As a group project, request the specifications for an actual job from a printing plant. Do all of the calculations necessary to determine how much paper is necessary for the job. Then visit the plant and find out if your calculations were correct.

Related Web Links

International Paper

www.ipaper.com
Site for the paper and packaging company with information on different types of forests and paper.

Forest Stewardship Council

www.fsc.org
Information and standards for responsible forest management.

ForestEthics

www.forestethics.org
An organization dedicated to the future health of endangered forests worldwide.

Green Seal

www.greenseal.org
Organization that offers studies, information, and standards about different environmental issues.

Green-e

www.green-e.org
Organization with standards for products made with renewable energy.

Chlorine Free Products Association

www.chlorinefreeproducts.org
Organization dedicated to creating products without the use of chlorine compounds.

Sustainable Forestry Initiative

www.sfiprogram.org
Organization with information and standards to help protect from deforestation.

chain of custody: The process of tracking and recording the possession and transfer of wood and fiber from forests of origin to the end user.

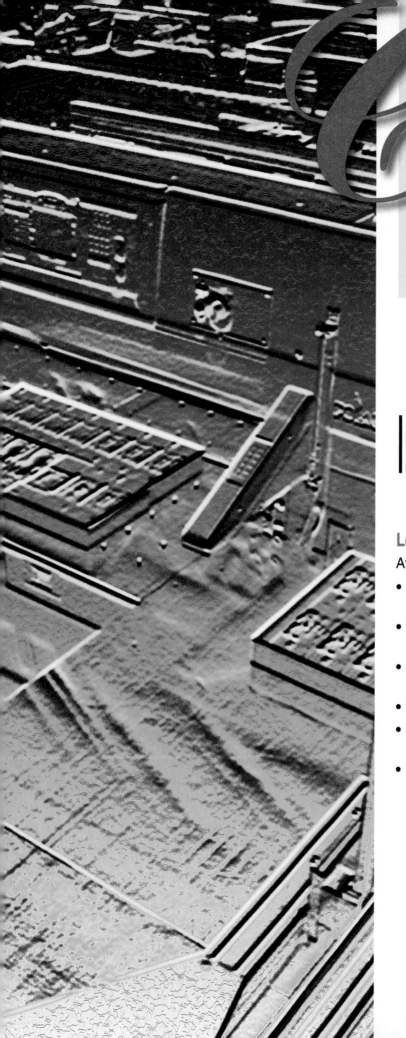

CHAPTER 22

Ink

Learning Objectives

After studying this chapter, you will be able to:

- Summarize the various ingredients and properties of ink.
- Identify the characteristics of ink formulations used for different printing processes.
- Summarize the characteristics of some specialized inks.
- Explain how to mix and match ink.
- Give examples of ways ink challenges affect the printed product.
- Identify methods used to analyze process inks.

Important Terms

additives	inkometer
brayer	livering
chalking	off color
color diagram	pigment
color strength	plate wear
drawdown test	reflection densitometer
dry	scumming
flooding	set
flush	setoff
ink	specking
ink body	spectrophotometer
ink fineness gauge	strike-through
ink formulation	thixotropy
ink length	tinting
ink mileage	vehicle
ink sticking	
ink tack	
ink thickness gauge	

Ink is the most common coating used to place a printed image on a substrate. Various inks are manufactured for use with the many printing processes and substrates available today. Inks have several properties that can affect printing quality. They must flow properly, have the correct stickiness, be permanent, dry properly, and have a workable consistency for the press rollers. This chapter will discuss the characteristics of printing inks and summarize how ink can affect a print job.

INK INGREDIENTS

The Egyptians and the Chinese first manufactured ink by binding soot with gums. They formed the mixture into rods and then it was dried. Moisture was added just before it was used. Many years later, the Chinese used the earth and plants as colors for pigments. Gums were still used as the binding agents. Around the time of Gutenberg, soot was mixed with varnish or linseed oil to make ink.

Ink formulation refers to the amount and type of ingredients used in a particular ink. Three ingredients are essential to the formulation of printing inks: vehicle, pigment, and additives.

The *vehicle* is a binding agent that holds the ink together. It also acts as a carrier for the pigment. A vehicle is often a solvent-resin or oil-resin combination, although soy-based paste inks are also widely used. Compounds, additives, oxidant agents, wetting agents, and antifoaming agents may be added, as well.

The *pigment* provides the color in an ink. A wide range of opaque and transparent pigments is available. Pigments are usually used dry and ground into a vehicle. They can also be used *flush*, as a paste dispersed in a vehicle. Dyes also may be used as coloring agents, particularly in flexographic inks.

Additives are ingredients added to ink to impart special characteristics. For example, certain additives reduce body tack, while others help make ink water-resistant. Driers, lubricants, waxes, and starches are common additives.

Driers accelerate drying, which permits the stacking of printed sheets without causing *setoff*, the transfer or smearing of ink. See **Figure 22-1.** Various devices or systems can assist with drying. Infrared (IR) radiation is used to accelerate oxidation. Ultraviolet (UV) radiation assists in curing. Spray powders are sometimes dispersed over the surface of the printed sheet to eliminate direct contact with the next printed sheet.

Ink is a chemical product and must be handled properly. Certain inks require special handling. Always follow the manufacturer's instructions.

INK PROPERTIES

Color strength, body, stability, length, tack, and drying are common properties of ink. These properties relate to the optical, structural, and drying characteristics of ink.

ink: A colored coating specially formulated to reproduce an image on a substrate.

ink formulation: The amount and type of ingredients used in a particular printing ink.

vehicle: The liquid component in ink that serves as a binding agent.

pigments: Colorants in the form of fine, solid particles that do not dissolve but spread through liquids or other substances.

flush: Term describing the dispersing of a pigment in an undried state (a paste) into a vehicle for ink.

additives: Ingredients such as driers, lubricants, waxes, and starches that are added to ink to impart special characteristics, improve desirable properties, or suppress undesirable properties.

setoff: A condition that results when wet ink on the press sheets transfers to the back of other sheets in a stack.

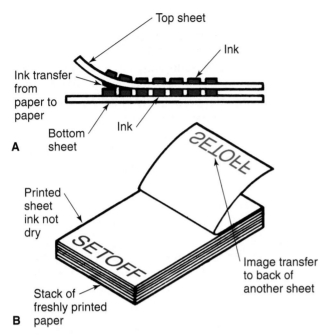

Figure 22-1. Setoff occurs when printed sheets output from a press are stacked on top of each other. Setoff is usually caused by improper drying of ink, but it can also be caused by excessively thick ink film, paper stacked too high, or an improper substrate and ink combination. A—How setoff occurs. B—The result of setoff.

Color Strength

Color strength is the ability of an ink to cover a substrate. Strong colorants produce vivid, sharp images and give good coverage. Weak colorants are generally not desirable. Pigments or dyes must be compatible with the ink base and carefully selected for the end use. Metallic, fluorescent, and pearl pigments are used to create special effects.

A transparent ink has weak color strength and is used when it is desirable for an image to show through the ink. Transparent inks are used in four-color printing where all colors of the spectrum are produced by overprinting the four process colors.

Ink Body

Ink body refers to an ink's consistency, thickness, or fluidity. Some inks are stiff and thick, while others are thin and fluid. The thickness of an ink can affect press operation considerably.

Inks used in relief or offset lithographic printing are very stiff, but flow more freely after being mixed by the press rollers. Gravure inks are formulated to be thin so they flow easily onto the substrate from the microscopic ink wells of the gravure cylinder.

With lithography, high ink body tends to thicken the deposit of ink on the substrate. A thinner ink does the opposite. High-speed presses use soft-bodied (more flowing) ink, while slower presses use heavy-bodied (less flowing) ink. Ink must be formulated for a specific printing process.

An *ink thickness gauge* is a device used to measure the thickness of the ink film on the press. Ink film is the thickness or depth of coating. The measurement is taken on the steel roller of the ink train of the press. The ink film gauge measurements are in mils (thousandths of an inch). An *ink fineness gauge* measures the pigment particle size in the ink with a very high degree of accuracy.

Ink Stability

Ink stability, or *thixotropy*, is the tendency of an ink to flow more freely after being worked. In relief printing, the press rollers work the ink by squeezing and depositing it on the press rollers before printing. Stirring ink tends to break down its internal cohesiveness. Ink that is agitated in the fountain flows more easily and distributes more evenly on the press rollers.

Many large presses have agitators to work the ink. The motion of the agitators helps keep the ink stable and fluid while it is in the fountain. Lack of motion causes the ink to become stiff and unable to transfer properly.

Ink Length

Ink length refers to the elasticity of an ink and its ability to form a filament or strand. The filament can be long or short, **Figure 22-2.**

If the ink forms a long filament, it will have a tendency to fly out on a high-speed press. Long inks,

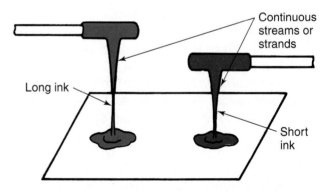

Figure 22-2. To form filaments, a rod is placed in ink, tapped on a surface, and then lifted. An ink that produces long filaments is called a "long" ink. "Short" inks produce shorter filaments.

such as those used on newsprint, flow more rapidly than short inks. Short inks flow poorly and have the consistency of butter.

Ink Tack

Ink tack refers to stickiness of the ink. It is a measurement of cohesion between the ink film and the substrate. The term is generally used when describing paste inks, such as those used in relief printing. When the ink is transferred from one roller to another, the ink must split. A portion stays on the first roller, but another portion must transfer to the next roller. If ink does not split, or has too much tack, it cannot be transferred from one roller to another, to the plate and blanket, or from the roller to a surface of the substrate.

An *inkometer* measures the tack of an ink to determine if it is too great for the surface strength of the paper. Too much tack can cause the paper to rupture, resulting in picking, splitting, or tearing. See **Figure 22-3.** Ink tack can be reduced. Liquid tack reducer cuts an ink's tack and body. It can be used to correct problems like picking and linting. Paste tack reducer cuts tack but does not affect ink body.

Ink Drying

An ink's ability to dry is important to the quality of the final product. Some common methods ink can use to dry are absorption, evaporation, oxidation, polymerization, and precipitation, **Figure 22-4.**

- Absorption-drying ink, also called penetrating ink, dries when the solvent is drawn into the paper. The ink does not dry hard but remains on the surface as a powder-like substance. Newspapers are a good example of inks that dry by absorption or penetration. If you rub your fingers over newsprint, a black powder will deposit on your skin.

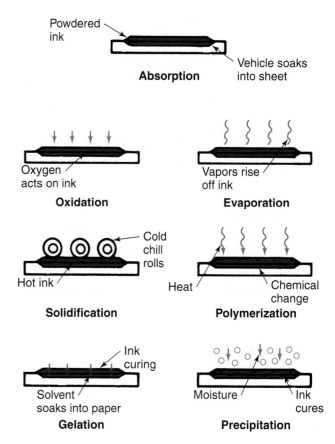

Figure 22-4. Inks dry in a number of ways.

- Evaporation-drying inks dry as the solvent is evaporated into the surrounding air, leaving a solid film of resin on the paper. Evaporation-drying inks are used in flexography, gravure, web-fed offset, and other processes where fast drying time is important. Solvent-evaporative inks consist of resins, solvents, and additives. Specific types include poster inks, lacquers, and textile dyes.

color strength: The amount of pigment in an ink that determines how well the ink will cover the substrate.

ink body: Term that describes the consistency of an ink.

ink thickness gauge: A device that measures the thickness of the ink film on the press rollers.

ink fineness gauge: A device that measures the pigment particle size in an ink.

thixotropy: The tendency of ink to flow more freely after being worked.

ink length: The elasticity of ink. It is referred to as long or short.

ink tack: The stickiness of the ink. A measurement of cohesion between the ink film and the substrate.

inkometer: An instrument that measures the tack of a printing ink.

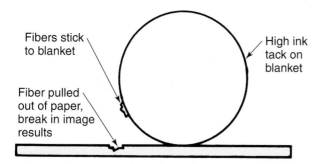

Figure 22-3. Picking can result when ink tack is not matched to stock. High tack can pull off fibers of paper.

- Oxidation-drying inks dry by absorbing oxygen from the surrounding air. Letterpress and offset printing commonly use oxidation-drying inks.
- Polymerization-drying inks dry by a chemical reaction that causes molecules in the ink to combine. Oxygen thickens the ink to a gel-like consistency, allowing the printed product to be handled without smearing before it is fully dried. Polymerization-drying inks can be used to print on metal.
- Chemical-reaction inks consist of resins, solvents, additives, and a drying-oil catalyst. These inks cure and dry by evaporation of the solvent and by oxidation. Specific types of ink include enamel, vinyl, epoxy, and polyester.
- Precipitation-drying inks, also called moisture-set inks, dry by reacting with water. Steam or water is sprayed on the ink after printing, causing the ink to set quickly. Glycol in the ink combines with the water and is absorbed into the paper.

Other Ink-Related Terms

Other important ink-related terms you should know include:

- Permanent or colorfast ink maintains its color with exposure to sunlight. It will not easily fade and is suitable for posters, signs, and other similar applications.
- Resistant ink is a very stable ink that can withstand exposure to forces that would fade other inks. It can tolerate sunlight, chemicals, heat, moisture, and gases without fading.
- Fugitive ink will fade and lose its color after prolonged exposure to sunlight. It is useful for temporary signs and posters.
- Viscosity refers to how easily an ink will flow. High-viscosity ink is thick and resists flow. Low-viscosity ink is fluid and flows more easily.
- Lake is an ink colorant formed when a soluble dye is converted to a pigment in a white base.
- Toner is a strong, concentrated ink colorant. Toner primarily consists of pure pigment ground and mixed into linseed oil.
- Job black refers to normal black ink used for a typical press run of average quality.
- Halftone black is a higher quality black ink designed for reproducing fine detail in halftone screen images.

- Watercolors are inks with a very flat or dull finish. They are water-based and do not contain varnish or oil.
- Metallic inks contain metal powders, such as aluminum or bronze, blended with an appropriate vehicle.
- Cleaning white is used to wash a press before changing from a dark to a light color.
- Liquid tack reducer cuts an ink's tack and body. It can be used to correct problems like picking and linting.
- Paste tack reducer cuts tack but does not affect ink body.
- Gloss/matte finishes are the visual effect of ink formulation. Gloss is achieved by the smoothness of the ink deposited on the substrate as well as the volume of dried ink the substrate retains. The surface of the substrate also contributes to gloss. Matte ink is achieved by the addition of flattening agents. The agents create microscopically irregular surfaces, which the eye sees as matte.
- Slow-dry additive can be used to lengthen ink drying time or skinning time in the fountain.
- Spray powder can be placed on ink after printing to prevent setoff. A special press attachment sprays the powder onto the printed images.
- Ink mill is a machine with steel rollers for crushing the ink ingredients into a fine substance.
- Nontoxic compounds must be used when dried ink has direct contact with food or edible materials.
- Fluorescent inks are special colored ink pigments that glow under black light.
- Opaque inks are capable of hiding the color of the stock on which an image is being printed.
- Vegetable oil–based inks are replacing those based on petrochemical (mineral) oils. Vegetable oils have replaced mineral oils for mostly environmental reasons. Petrochemical solvents and oils emit environmentally toxic volatile organic compounds (VOCs). In addition, ink wastes must be classified as "hazardous waste" and disposed of according to strict federal and state regulations.

INK TYPES

Special formulas are used to produce inks that are compatible with certain printing processes. The characteristics of ink formulation are determined by the plates, press units, and type of substrate. The types of ink used in producing images using the four basic printing processes are discussed next.

Relief Inks

Several types of inks are used to place an image on a substrate by raised surfaces, or relief. Letterpress inks for covering the face of electrotypes, foundry type, and similar printing surfaces are generally quite tacky and thick. An ink's viscosity refers to how easily an ink will flow. High-viscosity ink is thick and resists flow. Low-viscosity ink is fluid and flows more easily. See **Figure 22-5.** Letterpress inks usually dry by oxidation. However, the inks used to print on substrates, such as newsprint, dry by evaporation if heat is applied to the inked surface. Drying oils are used as vehicles to support the pigment. The pigment is often purchased in paste form.

Flexographic inks are fast-drying and used for printing on a variety of substrates, including paper, cloth, plastic, and metal. Alcohol-based flexographic inks dry by evaporation, while water-based flexographic inks dry by evaporation or absorption.

Typical kinds of relief printing ink include rotary, quick-set, precipitation-drying, water-washable, news,

and job. The inks are formulated for various types of presses and stocks for printing books, magazines, labels, packaging, or other commercial applications. Job ink is found in many commercial letterpress facilities, since it can be used on a wide variety of presses and papers. The quality of the ink varies with the types of images being printed. Linework ink does not need to be of as high quality as halftone ink.

Gravure Inks

Gravure inks are very fluid and dry rapidly, mainly by evaporation. The printing substrate must be capable of absorbing the ink from the recessed cells of a gravure plate or cylinder. Ink must be pulled from the cells and deposited on a substrate. Inking the cells is known as *flooding*. A doctor blade removes the ink from the surface of the nonimage areas of the cylinder or plate.

> **Many gravure inks are highly volatile and require certain precautions against fire. The area must be properly ventilated. Local, state, and federal requirements for pollution control, including solvent drainage, must be strictly followed. Solvent-recovery systems are commonly found in the industry.**

Screen Printing Inks

Screen printing inks are thicker than inks used for other processes. They are formulated to flow evenly when forced through the screen by the squeegee. Screen clogging can be a problem with screen printing inks; therefore, the solvent must not evaporate too quickly.

Conventional screen process inks contain pigments, binders, and solvents. The pigment is held together by the binder, which also assists in adhering the ink to the substrate. The solvents dissolve the resins and form a pliable material.

Screen ink formulas vary greatly, since substrates are numerous. Typical substrates include paper, cloth, plastics, metal, and glass. It is important to communicate clearly with ink suppliers and vendors to select the screen ink that best meets the product's requirements.

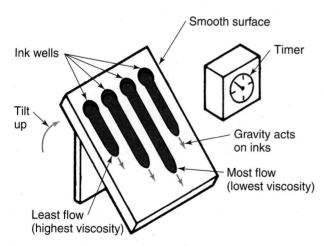

Figure 22-5. Viscosity is a measure of the thickness or fluidity of an ink. A basic method for comparing viscosity is to place the inks in small wells hollowed out of a flat surface. Tilt the surface upward so the inks flow out of the wells. The ink with the most (fastest) flow has the lowest viscosity; the ink with the least (slowest) flow has the highest viscosity. Flows can be timed to get accurate viscosity readings.

flooding: In gravure printing, the process of inking the cells of the plate or cylinder.

colorant: Chemical substance that gives color to such materials as ink, paint, crayons, and chalk.

Lithographic Inks

The image area of a lithographic plate is neither raised nor recessed. It is a flat surface with an image area that accepts ink. The nonimage areas are receptive to moisture.

Inks formulated for offset lithography must have high color strength. In lithography, the ink film placed on the substrate has less thickness than the ink film used in relief printing. A balance between ink and moisture is essential for complete and even ink transfer to the plate and substrate, **Figure 22-6.**

Lithographic inks dry by oxidation; therefore, it is essential that the ink set quickly. Moreover, the pigment must not bleed in water. Formulation of lithographic inks varies greatly since many types of substrates are used in sheet-fed and web-fed presses. Vehicles must be oxidative. Additives include soluble resins, drying and semidrying oils, and varnishes.

Inks that dry by ultraviolet radiation (UV-curable inks) are used in lithographic facilities. Thermal-curing inks are also used. The thermal technique uses low amounts of solvents and requires heat and a catalyst, such as drying oil or any other substance that assists in change.

The amount of moisture absorbed by the ink is critical. The vehicle for lithographic ink must be water-resistant, although the ink may accept 20% to 25% moisture before it emulsifies. Once emulsified, the surface will no longer distribute the ink throughout the inking system of the press. Too much moisture eliminates the tack needed for ink to transfer from one roller to another. The ink must split at the nip point of the press rollers, **Figure 22-7.**

A number of ink problems are associated with offset lithographic printing. Lithographic ink mixes with moisture to form an ink-in-water emulsion. This results in a problem known as *tinting*, in which a slight tint of ink is left on the nonimage area of the printed sheet.

Scumming is a problem that arises when the nonimage area of the plate accepts ink. There are two main causes of scumming: too much ink or too little fountain solution reaching the plate.

Most inks today contain a combination of vehicles that prevent the ink from scumming in the can or drying overnight if left on the press. Automated ink-dispensing systems also reduce costly ink waste by measuring the precise amount of ink into the fountain, **Figure 22-8.**

SPECIALIZED INKS

Lithography is the most widely used printing process and has spurred a demand for specialized lithographic inks. While the majority of inks used

Figure 22-6. A compressible inner layer on these offset ink rollers eliminates roller distortion throughout the nip and distributes ink more evenly. (American Roller Company)

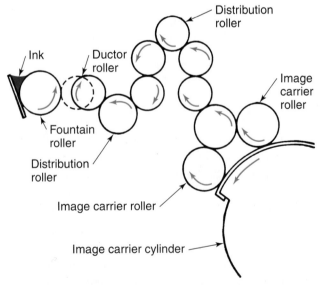

Figure 22-7. Ink formulation is critical to how well an ink splits and transfers from one press roller to the next.

Figure 22-8. Vacuum-sealed tubes in this ink-dispensing system prevent oxygen from contacting the ink and causing scumming. (Van Son Holland Ink)

Figure 22-9. Soy and other vegetable oil–based inks, which are free of environmentally harmful substances, are replacing solvent-based inks. (National Soy Ink Information Center)

are process colors in the basic ingredients in ink formulations, many specialized inks have been developed to satisfy specific needs.

Vegetable Oil–Based Inks

A substantial portion of color inks in use now are vegetable oil–based inks, **Figure 22-9.** Vegetable oils have replaced mineral oils for environmental reasons. Petrochemical solvents and mineral oils emit environmentally toxic volatile organic substances (VOCs). The level of VOCs must be controlled to meet local, state, and federal standards. The formula for determining the level of VOCs (by weight) is:

$$VOCs = \frac{\text{Total weight of formula} - \text{Water weight} - \text{Weight of nonvolatile compounds}}{\text{Total weight of formula}}$$

Apart from environmental benefits, vegetable oil–based inks have several technical benefits, such as cleaner and sharper printing and brighter colors. Transfer of ink in the system, rub resistance to surface damage, and the amount of ink needed has improved, as well. The price of vegetable oil–based color inks is comparable to the price of mineral oil color inks. Black ink, however, has fewer apparent technical benefits and a higher cost.

Vegetable oil–based inks do not dry as fast or as hard as conventional inks. As formulations for conventional inks become more environmentally safe, the popularity of vegetable oil–based inks may decline.

tinting: Problem that occurs when ink pigment particles bleed into the dampening solution, causing a slight tint of ink to appear on the nonimage area of the printed sheet.

scumming: A condition in lithography when the nonimage areas of the plate begin to accept ink.

Sheet-Fed Inks

Sheet-fed inks contain a high proportion of vegetable oil, most commonly linseed oil. They contain about 5% to 10% petroleum distillates to allow acceptable press speeds. Sheet-fed inks are suitable for use on eight-color perfecting machines, which require an ink that sets at exactly the correct speed.

Laser-Proof Inks

Electrostatic printing uses laser-proof inks for printing on laser printers and copiers. The image is fixed on the paper by heat up to 410°F (210°C) and pressure. The inks must be formulated to withstand intense heat without evaporating and to resist softening and transfer to the drum.

Hexachrome Inks

Conventional yellow, magenta, and cyan have been brightened by the addition of fluorescent colors to produce a specialized ink called Hexachrome™ by Pantone. It is suited for six- and seven-color process printing. Colors are brighter than are possible with standard four colors; however, press performance is compromised because of the presence of fluorescent pigments. Fluorescent pigments can have transfer problems because they are difficult to remove from ink rollers.

Proofing Inks

Despite the growth of digital proofing, ink proofs are still needed when accurate contract proofs are required. Proofing inks are formulated to compensate for the porosity that occurs on proofing press rollers, which are frequently washed with strong solvents. In addition to being stable, these inks are able to control dot gain.

Metallic Inks

Metallic inks contain metal powders, such as aluminum and bronze, blended with an appropriate vehicle. New gold and silver inks are free of heavy metals, a concern in food and toy packaging. Water-based metallic inks that deliver superior brilliance have been developed for use on multicolor presses.

UV-Curable Inks

Ultraviolet curable inks consist of resins, monomers, additives, and photoinitiators. These inks do not dry; instead they cure with no solvent evaporation. As ultraviolet light strikes the ink, a chemical reaction called polymerization occurs, which converts the ink from a liquid to a solid. Specific types of UV-curable inks are available for paper, plastic sheets, plastic bottles, and other substrates.

UV curing is comparable in cost to solvent- and water-based systems. The environmentally friendly aspect of UV technology may be the most important factor in the growth of UV inks. UV-curable inks contain less than 1% VOCs, and UV-printed papers can be repulped and recycled. An odor problem associated with curing has had a limiting effect on the use of UV inks with food packaging.

Waterless Inks

Waterless inks have attracted the attention of print shops because they allow for faster makeready and also dry quickly. Higher color density and good adhesion to nonabsorbent plastic substrates make them attractive, as well. Waterless inks have high viscosity and thickness. Raising the temperature during printing allows a waterless ink to flow more readily. See **Figure 22-10.**

Hybrid Inks

The development of hybrid inks came about because printers wanted a material with the qualities of UV ink at a lower cost. It is very expensive for a printer to dedicate one press to UV inks unless all a printer's business requires the use of UV ink. Hybrid inks can be used on a conventional press, which is then retrofitted with UV lighting stations. These energy-cured inks can perform as well or better than conventional inks. Most conventional inks don't dry quickly, but when hybrid inks are used, the image is dry when it arrives at the delivery end of the press.

Solid Inks

There are different ways of using ink to produce images on paper. So far, you've learned about such types as aqueous inks used in ink-jet printers, as well as ribbons containing pigments used in thermography. Technology using solid ink substitutes four sticks of process-colored ink for liquid ink. Ink from the sticks is melted to be put onto paper. Once the ink produces an image on the paper, it dries almost instantly. Because the sticks use vegetable oils, they are safe to handle and better for the environment than some liquid inks.

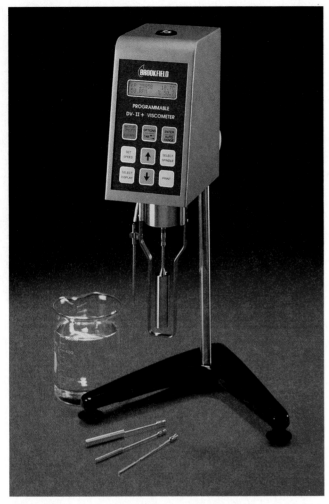

Figure 22-10. A viscometer is useful in determining the effect of temperature on the viscoelastic properties of ink used in waterless printing. (Brookfield Engineering Laboratories, Inc.)

MIXING, MATCHING, AND PROOFING

Mixing systems are available for all types of printing inks. These systems are used to blend basic inks. The inks are weighed to a prescribed amount based on information on a cataloged color selector.

The basic equipment for manual color mixing and matching consists of a hard, smooth surface; mixing knives or spatulas; scales; a color chart; and a record card. See **Figure 22-11.**

Color matching can be done by visually evaluating the color and substrate. The selection of pigments and dyes requires the eye of a talented and knowledgeable color specialist. Small adjustments are made to bring the color to exact specifications.

THINK GREEN
Volatlie Organic Compounds (VOCs)

As you have learned throughout this text, volatile organic compounds (VOCs) are toxic substances that evaporate into the atmosphere. They are most commonly found in blanket and roller washes, fountain solutions, plate cleaners, glaze removers, degreasers, and film cleaners. The evaporation of VOCs contributes to the development of such environmental hazards as smog. There are also health concerns associated with VOCs. VOCs are generally found in ink solvent. There are now several different types of ink available that contain little or no VOCs. UV-curable inks cure instead of dry, so there are no evaporating solvents. Vegetable oil–based inks, or soy inks, are an alternative to using inks with petrochemical solvents. Vegetable oil–based inks dry very slowly, but they are still commonly found in green printing facilities. For more information, visit www.soygrowers.com

Another color matching technique is to read the color values of a sample using a *spectrophotometer*, **Figure 22-12.** This computer-controlled instrument measures the relative intensity of radiation through the spectrum based on the sample.

Proofing of relief or lithographic ink is accomplished by a variety of instruments found in an ink manufacturing facility. Some are sophisticated, custom-built presses that simulate certain equipment and are able to determine the volume of ink used. Some are small hand-operated presses, while others are manual applicators.

Custom-built presses are available for flexographic proofing. Proofs can also be done manually using a *brayer*, a small, handheld roller used to spread ink with both a rubber plate–type roller and a metering steel roll. It simulates the "squeegee" application of ink on a full-size flexographic press. Gravure can be proofed very successfully on custom-built proofing presses and press-simulating instruments.

---

spectrophotometer: Instrument capable of measuring light of different colors or wavelengths.

Figure 22-11. Spatulas or mixing knives are used to mix ink by hand. (Van Son Holland Ink)

Figure 22-12. Accurate matches between digital color proofs and color samples can be made using a spectrophotometer. (Iris Graphics, Inc.)

Mixing and Matching Procedures

Color manuals or charts are available from ink manufacturers, **Figure 22-13.** The charts contain samples of ink on coated and uncoated stock.

Before mixing, make sure the work area is clean. Weigh out the designated amount of each ink on a scale, according to the manufacturer's specifications. Be sure to include the weight of the paper placed on the scale pan. Place the inks on a glass plate or smooth surface, and thoroughly mix them with an ink spatula until the color is uniform. Tap some of the ink onto the stock to be used, and compare the color with the sample. Continue selecting and weighing the ink according to the color system until the color matches the sample perfectly.

Figure 22-13. Color matching charts or manuals are used to match inks with sample colors. (Van Son Holland Ink)

Use only small amounts of ink to mix a trial batch. After the ink is thoroughly mixed, pull a proof. Compare the proof with the sample. When matching a tint, the color should be added to a white base in very small quantities until the desired tint is reached.

INK MILEAGE

How much ink is needed for a specific job? Finding the *ink mileage* is not easy, but it is crucial. Running out of ink can be disastrous. Tables can provide the approximate number of square inches that a given amount of ink will cover. For example, full-strength lithographic inks cover between 350,000 sq. in./lb. and 450,000 sq. in./lb. on coated, sheet-fed stock. On uncoated sheets, coverage is between 280,000 sq. in./lb. and 360,000 sq. in./lb. Absorption may result in a mileage loss of 20% or more.

When calculating the amount of ink needed, include the ink for makeready as well as the amount left in the ink fountain and on the rollers.

Several factors govern the amount of ink needed: specific gravity and color strength of the ink, stock surface, work to be printed, ink needed to prepare the press, type of press, and thickness of the ink film.

Ink can be purchased in tubes, cartridges, cans, pails, drums, and tanks, **Figure 22-14.** Ink containers should be stored in a cool, dry place and covered tightly to prevent contamination and drying. *Livering*, a chemical change that takes place during storage,

Figure 22-14. Today's inks are engineered to meet the high-speed requirements of technologically advanced printing presses. (Van Son Holland Ink)

is not reversible. Livering causes a hardened coating on the surface. When removed, the coating breaks up into flakes. Flakes of dried ink cause contamination and should be kept out of the ink fountain.

ORDERING INK

Consider the following questions when ordering ink:

- What colors will be used for the job?
- What printing process will be used: relief, gravure, offset, screen?
- What are the product requirements? For example, must the ink be long-lasting and weather-resistant?
- What substrate will be used: paper (smooth or rough, etc.), plastic, metal?
- Is ink cost a consideration?
- How many copies are to be printed for the job?

Asking these questions will help you and your ink sales representative select the appropriate ink for the job.

INK-RELATED CHALLENGES

Inks can cause a wide variety of printing problems. Sometimes ink *is* at fault; other times, the ink is blamed for what is, in fact, a press or a paper problem.

Setting and Drying

Set is the point at which an ink is dry enough to be lightly touched without smudging. *Dry* is the point at which the ink is free of volatile substances and has polymerized to a total solid state. Ink will dry relative to the substrate. On nonabsorbent substrates, ink must dry strictly by oxidation. This may take from 6 to 24 hours.

Chalking

Chalking is an ink-adherence problem that occurs when dried ink rubs off the substrate. Newspaper ink chalks by nature. Since a newspaper is only used once and then discarded, chalking does not pose a serious problem. Chalking would be unacceptable with a more permanent product, such as this textbook. Chalking can be prevented by applying a nonpenetrating varnish to the substrate surface to hold the pigment.

Adhesion in ink is relative to the printing process. Lithographic inks adhere best on porous substrates, while gravure and flexographic printing allow the use of solvents and resins that readily adhere to nonporous substrates, such as foils, vinyl, and polyester.

Strike-Through

Strike-through is an ink-penetration problem that occurs when the ink soaks into the paper too deeply and shows through the opposite side of the sheet. Usually, strike-through is caused by an excessively long ink-drying time. The long drying time allows the ink to soak into the paper. A highly absorbent paper can also cause strike-through.

brayer: A small, handheld roller used to distribute ink on a proof press.

ink mileage: The surface area that can be covered by a given quantity of ink.

livering: A chemical change in the body of an ink that occurs during storage.

set: The point at which an ink is dry enough to be lightly touched without smudging.

dry: The point at which the ink is free of volatile substances and has polymerized to a total solid state.

chalking: Condition that occurs when dried ink is easily rubbed off or lost from a printed sheet.

strike-through: An ink-penetration problem that occurs when the ink soaks into the paper too deeply and shows through the opposite side of the sheet.

Strike-through should not be confused with *show-through*. Strike-through is caused by excessive ink absorption. Show-through is a paper problem caused by thin or insufficiently opaque stock.

Setoff

As mentioned earlier, setoff occurs when wet ink transfers onto the back of a sheet that is stacked on top of the previously printed sheet. It is often incorrectly referred to as *offset*. Setoff can also be caused by an excessively thick ink deposit on the paper, improper ink, paper stacked too high, or a drying system problem.

Ink Sticking

Ink sticking can occur if two layers of ink film, on two different sheets, bond together. The problem is similar to setoff; both can be caused by improper drying.

Plate Wear

Plate wear can be caused by pigments that are not fully ground to a fine powder. The unground particles in the ink act as an abrasive, wearing away the surface of the plate. Excessive pigment can also cause plate wear. Always check the ink grind when plate wear is excessive. Excessive roller pressure or an abrasive substrate are two more reasons for plate wear.

Off-Color Problem

When the color of the printed job does not match the intended color, the job is said to be *off color*. Off-color problems have many causes. A dirty press can alter the colors of the ink. If the substrate is not a true white, its color can affect the printed color. Thickness, opacity, translucence, or other ink qualities can all affect the color of the printed product. Improper ink mixing can also result in an off-color problem.

A *drawdown test* can be used to check for proper ink mixing. A standard ink and the newly mixed ink are placed on the stock. Then, a thin blade is used to spread the inks down over the surface of the stock, **Figure 22-15.** After drying, the standard ink is compared to the newly mixed ink for proper color match, tone, and strength.

Specking

Specking is the appearance of tiny dots next to halftone dots or line art. Specking occurs when the ink is contaminated with paper fibers or other foreign

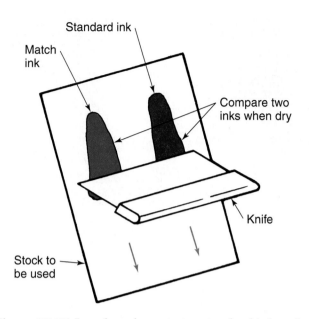

Figure 22-15. In a drawdown test, a standard ink and a mixed ink are placed on the chosen stock. A sharp blade is used to spread the inks onto the stock. After drying, ink qualities are compared.

material, or when it is not properly ground. Ink film that is too thick can also cause specking.

PROCESS INK ANALYSIS

Process inks (yellow, magenta, cyan, and black) differ from one ink manufacturer to another. Color bars printed under normal printing conditions may be used to evaluate a particular set of inks used in a printing facility. Most service bureaus or printers furnish test patterns, **Figure 22-16.**

A *reflection densitometer* is used for taking density readings from the printed control bars. This instrument measures the amount of light reflected from an object. Record the density readings on a process ink data sheet, **Figure 22-17.** The density readings can be used to determine the four principle working characteristics of a set of process inks: strength, hue, grayness, and efficiency.

Ink strength identifies the range and depth of colors that can be produced from a set of inks. Strength can be determined by visually comparing the density readings and selecting the highest reading for the yellow, magenta, and cyan inks.

Ink hue error identifies the percentage of reflection of colored light from a specific color of ink. A hue or color is determined by the eye in terms of cone stimulation to colors of light. The color or hue of magenta ink should

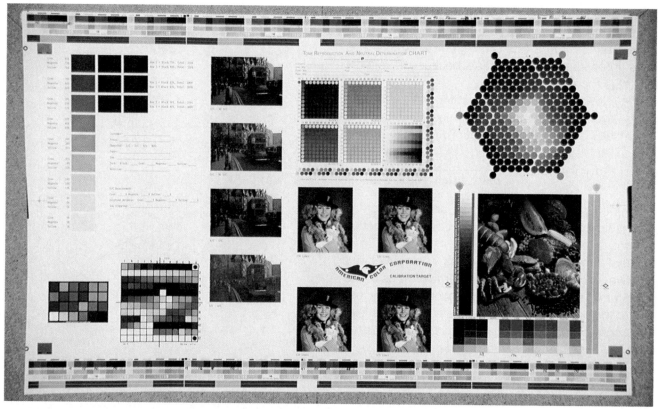

Figure 22-16. An ink analysis test pattern. (American Color Corp.)

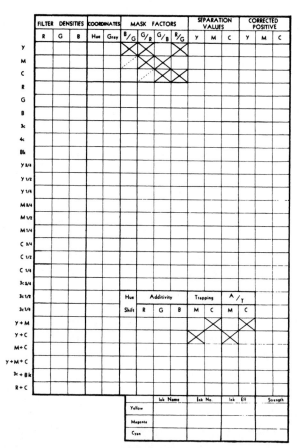

Figure 22-17. A process ink data sheet can be used to record information concerning methods used to produce separations.

absorb green light, preventing it from reflecting off the paper surface, while allowing all of the blue and red light to reflect. The ink impurities in the magenta ink pigmentation that distort this normal reflection ratio can be measured as a percentage of hue error.

To determine the hue error for one color of ink and its red, green, and blue filter readings, use the equation:

$$\frac{\text{Hue}}{\text{error}} = \frac{\text{Medium filter reading–Low filter reading}}{\text{High filter reading–Low filter reading}}$$

The purity of a process color is identified by a *grayness* factor. A color is considered gray when its

ink sticking: A press problem that occurs when two layers of ink film, on two different sheets, bond together.

plate wear: The wearing away of the surface of a plate by coarse particles in the ink.

off color: When the color of the printed job does not match the intended color.

drawdown test: A method of checking for proper ink mixing by placing a small amount of ink on paper, and then using a blade to spread it and produce a thin ink film.

specking: Tiny dots that appear near an image area, caused by paper fibers or other foreign material in the ink.

reflection densitometer: A device that reads reflected light to measure the density of an image.

predominant color reflects less light than the white sheet of paper it is printed on. For example, cyan should reflect 100% blue and green light, but it is considered gray in percentage because it reflects less blue than the white paper.

The lower the percentage factor, the higher the purity level. To determine the grayness factor for a given color of ink, use the equation:

$$\text{Grayness factor} = \frac{\text{Low filter reading}}{\text{High filter reading}}$$

Ink efficiency is similar to hue error, but instead of measuring the percentage of error in the reflection of light, a positive percentage is expressed. Each color of process ink filters out its complementary additive color and reflects the other two-thirds of the spectrum. This is the measurement of efficiency: the higher the percentage of an ink's efficiency, the less color correction will be required and the greater the gamut of possible colors that it can produce.

To determine a specific ink color efficiency percentage, use the equation:

$$\text{Ink efficiency} = 1 - \frac{\dfrac{\text{Low filter}}{\text{reading}} + \dfrac{\text{Medium}}{\text{filter reading}}}{2 \times \text{High filter reading}}$$

Color Diagrams for Ink Evaluation and Color Correction

When performing process ink analysis, it is beneficial to plot the information on a *color diagram* for the purpose of visual evaluation or comparison. Data such as hue error or grayness factor can be calculated and plotted on one of three types of diagrams: the hexagon, circle, or triangle. The ink data, represented by the plots, can then be visually compared to ideal colors on the diagram.

The color hexagon is one of the only diagrams that requires no major computations or formulas. It is one of the easiest and quickest diagrams used to plot color strength and hue differences. The hexagon is best suited for quality control or press control of primary printers and overprints, **Figure 22-18.**

The color circle is designed for visualizing the hue error and grayness factor of actual colors in relation to ideal colors. It is also valuable in determining the color correction system requirements for different inks and substrates. See **Figure 22-19.**

The subtractive color triangle is designed to illustrate the gamut of pure color that is possible with

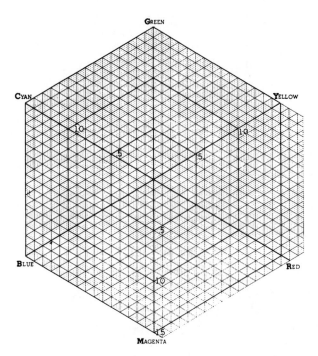

Figure 22-18. A color hexagon is used to plot color strength and hue differences to improve quality control. (Graphic Arts Technical Foundation)

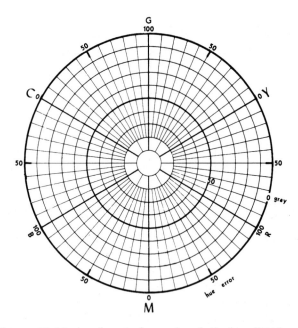

Figure 22-19. A color circle can be plotted so that hue error and grayness can be visualized and compared to ideal colors. (Graphic Arts Technical Foundation)

a set of process inks. The plots of ink data can also identify under- or over-trapping and predict overprints. Mask percentages are located along the sides of the triangle to identify masking requirements for color correction of the specific inks. See **Figure 22-20.**

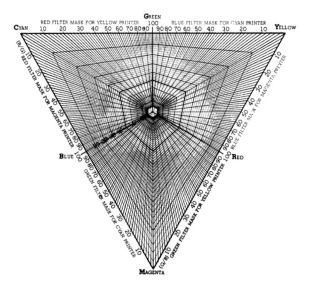

Figure 22-20. A color triangle indicates the gamut of color possibilities for a set of process inks. Mask percentages for color correction are located on the sides of the triangle. (Graphic Arts Technical Foundation)

The subtractive color triangle has two additional applications. It can be used to analyze new batches of process ink for hue and grayness by comparing the batches to successful proofs. The triangle can also be used to plot readings from the customer's reflective original art to immediately determine whether the important colors fall within the gamut of the process inks' capabilities.

Ink Impurities

The raw materials of a pigment used in making ink contain metals that appear naturally. Once they have been refined and qualify for printing pigments, they still contain impurities that cannot be removed. The processing operations are not capable of producing purity. Therefore, all inks have impurities.

The data derived from the analysis of a set of process inks will determine the exact masking or color correction requirements. When printing color, masking relates to the ink coverage and the density or reflection of ink film. Usually, the yellow pigment will be the purest. Magenta will typically contain a yellow impurity. Magenta ink can either be rubine or rhodamine in color. Rhodamine is a blue-magenta, which is more expensive and produces good fleshtones. Rubine magenta is more red.

Cyan ink contains the most impurities and will usually have a major impurity of magenta. If the cyan appears to have a magenta impurity, it will also contain a certain amount of yellow that is already in the magenta. Then the cyan ink is said to have a major impurity of magenta and a minor impurity of yellow.

During color correction, the cyan printer separation will receive the least amount of correction. Because the magenta impurity or yellow ink impurity in the cyan ink cannot be removed, less magenta and even less yellow must be printed. The yellow impurity is in both the cyan and magenta ink; therefore, it requires the most reduction, masking, and correction. Reduction is the process of bringing the image to a point where it looks as closely like the original as possible. It is accomplished by removing everything that conflicts with false appearance. The percentage of color correction is best determined by actual ink density readings and evaluation of the four basic ink characteristics.

Summary

Most of the printing processes require ink to create a visible image on a substrate. The essential ingredients to make ink have remained stable, but environmental issues have prompted changes to make the ingredients more friendly with the environment. Ink formulation must be compatible with the printing process. New technology is constantly changing the means of placing an image on a substrate. This advancement changes the ink or imaging materials formulation.

Review Questions

Please do not write in this book. Write your answers on a separate sheet of paper.

1. Explain the three main ingredients of ink.
2. _____ is the ink's ability to cover the substrate.
3. _____ refers to the ink's thickness or fluidity.
4. What type of press uses soft-bodied inks?
5. Define *thixotropy*.
6. Which ink quality would tend to make the ink fly out on a high-speed press?
   A. Short ink.
   B. Long ink.
   C. High tack.
   D. Low tack.

color diagram: A visual representation of color data, used for process ink analysis.

7. Low ink tack could cause which of the following problems?
   A. Paper tearing.
   B. Picking.
   C. Splitting.
   D. None of the above.

8. Describe the six ways ink can dry.

9. _____ viscosity ink is thick and resists flow, while _____ viscosity ink is fluid and flows more easily.

10. _____ can be found in many commercial letterpress facilities since it can be used on a wide variety of presses and papers.

11. Why are screen printing inks thicker than inks used for other processes?

12. Name two common problems associated with lithographic inks.

13. Give two advantages of using vegetable oil–based inks.

14. What is the most important factor in the growth of UV-curable ink use?

15. What is the function of a spectrophotometer?

16. What five factors should you consider when ordering ink?

17. True or False? Strike-through is an ink-penetration problem that is caused by thin stock.

18. What instrument is used to measure the amount of light reflected from an object?

19. What are the four principle working characteristics of a set of process inks?

20. What three types of color diagrams are used for process ink analysis?

Suggested Activities

1. Place a small amount of two kinds of ink on a sheet of glass. Tap the ink and check the length of each kind of ink by measuring the breaking point. What information is gained from this activity?

2. Mix ink to match a specified color requirement. What technique will you use to check the ink's color and strength?

Related Web Links

Print Ink History
www.cyberlipid.org/perox/oxid0012.htm
Information on the background of printing ink.

Ink World
www.inkworldmagazine.com
Online magazine with articles relating to new developments of ink.

National Soy Ink Information Center
www.soygrowers.com
Online resource providing information about vegetable oil–based inks.

You can research various inks and updates to ink technology online. Online magazines contain new and older articles related to developments.

CHAPTER 23

Finishing and Binding

Learning Objectives

After studying this chapter, you will be able to:

- Explain terms related to printing.
- Recall the types of folding processes.
- Explain different types of finishing operations.
- Summarize the processes needed for different binding techniques.
- Recall different types of packing used in the graphic communications industry.

Important Terms

banding machine
binding
blind embossing
collating
creasing
creep
cutting
debossing
die cutting
drilling
edition binding
embossing
finishing
gathering
laminating
lift
liquid lamination

mechanical binding
numbering
packaging
perfect binding
perforating
plastic comb binding
punching
scoring
shrink-wrap
slitting
spiral binding
stamping
stitching
taping machine
trimming
varnishing

Finishing is a general term that applies to many types of operations carried out during or following printing, include cutting, folding, slitting, perforating, creasing, scoring, die cutting, embossing, stamping, numbering, drilling, punching, varnishing, and laminating. Exact finishing methods will vary depending on the type of product and its specifications.

Binding is the process of fastening together the sheets of a product with methods including gluing, sewing, stapling, or other mechanical means. It can be considered a finishing operation, but is usually classified separately, since binding is often a operation subcontracted to a specialty house. Like finishing, binding is a general term that can be applied to slightly different tasks depending on the type of product and the process involved. **Figure 23-1** depicts the steps involved in a type of binding operation.

Finishing and binding are as important as the printing itself. If even one finishing process is poorly done, even a very well-printed job will have little or no value. The customer might reject the job, refusing to pay for it, or demand that it be done over without additional charge. In either case, the printing company will be faced with a financial loss on the job, instead of the expected profit. This makes it extremely

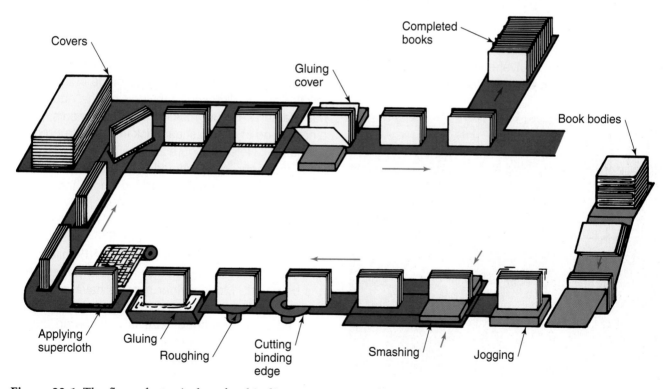

Figure 23-1. The flow of a typical perfect binding operation. Perfect binding is the process of attaching a paper cover to the book body with glue.

finishing: A general term that applies to the many operations carried out during or following printing.

binding: The process of joining together multiple pages of a printed product by various means including sewing, stapling, spiral wire, and adhesives.

important that all finishing and binding processes are performed correctly. Many printing facilities include packaging as part of the binding operation. Once the product is printed, it is distributed. A container is necessary to house the printed material. The purpose of packing is to contain, protect, preserve, and transport a product. Packaging is essential to the distribution process.

CUTTING

Making a large sheet of paper into several smaller sheets is termed *cutting*, which should not be confused with trimming. *Trimming* is the process of cutting off uneven edges of paper, as when trimming the three sides of a book. Types of cutting equipment include a guillotine cutter and a paper cutter.

Paper Cutter

The most common type of equipment used to cut paper stock is the guillotine cutter, **Figure 23-2**. The knife of a guillotine cutter is forced through the paper at a slight angle to produce an oblique shearing action, **Figure 23-3**.

The blade must be very sharp and free of nicks, since any roughness of the blade will appear as a jagged edge on the cut sheets. Keeping blades in excellent condition is essential for quality trimming or

Figure 23-2. This is a powerful computer-controlled guillotine cutter. Cuts can be preprogrammed into computer memory. To help in moving and positioning large stacks of paper, the cutting table is pierced with many tiny holes through which powerful jets of air are blown. The paper stack is slightly raised from the surface by the air, making it easy to move.

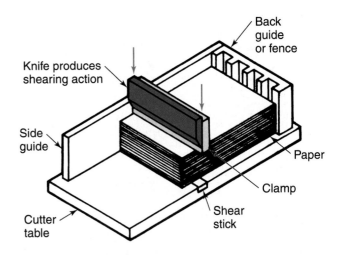

Figure 23-3. The guillotine cutter forces a blade through a stack of paper to produce shearing action.

cutting of stock. Most plants will send cutter blades out to be sharpened. Extreme care must be taken when removing or installing a cutter blade. Any blade that is out of the cutter should be placed in a sheath to eliminate the possibility of injury from the sharp edge.

> **Respect a cutter blade's sharpness. Handle a blade carefully, since it can cause severe cuts.**

Specific equipment instructions should be followed. To correctly position a sharpened blade in the cutter, follow specific directions provided by the equipment manufacturer. Before making any adjustments, place a new wood or plastic shear stick in the table's groove or channel. Refer to Figure 23-3.

The shear stick should be rotated or turned periodically to give a new surface under the cutting edge and produce a sharp, clean cut.

Today's paper cutters come in a wide variety of sizes from tabletop models to huge floor models. The simplest type is usually hand-operated while other models have power clamps to hold the paper while it is being cut. Modern floor models have automatic clamps and are computer-programmed to make planned cuts. The cutter size is designated by the length of cut. A 30″ paper cutter will take a sheet up to 30″ in width, **Figure 23-4**.

A dial gauge or digital readout indicates the distance of the back gauge to the cutting edge of the blade. A properly adjusted cutter will give very accurate cuts.

The amount of paper each cutter will cut depends on paper type, weight, and size. Six hundred sheets of narrow paper will cut much easier than 600 sheets that cover the full width of the cutter table.

Figure 23-4. The length of cut that can be made by a paper cutter is used to designate its size. Typical sizes are 30″ and 37″, although larger and smaller models are made.

Most large cutters have an air jet bed that allows for easy movement of heavy stacks of sheets. Air is pumped up through the table to form a cushion between the table and the paper. The air lifts the paper so it floats over the table for easy positioning, **Figure 23-5.**

Many of today's facilities have a vacuum system to remove all of the unwanted paper. The waste stock is sucked to a receiving area, where it is baled for recycling, **Figure 23-6.** Paper dust must be held to a minimum to comply with local, state, and federal regulations.

The cutting of paper is a very exacting task. A miscut can make a job a pile of waste, which is a very costly mistake. Accuracy is essential when paper is

Figure 23-6. Paper waste, such as trimmings from paper cutters, is usually baled for recycling.

cut down to the size for a given press run. Proper allowances must also be considered when bleeds and trims are specified.

Automatic paper cutters usually have safety features designed to prevent loss of fingers or hands. These include:

- **Nonrepeat device.** Cutter blade will only come down once until reset.
- **Two-handed operation.** Buttons on each side of the operator must be pressed simultaneously to make the cutter blade operate. See **Figure 23-7.**
- **Electric eye stop.** A detector that will automatically stop the descent of the cutter blade if a hand, arm, or other object is in its path.

Whatever the cutting device, safe operation is essential. If a cutter will slice through a pile of paper like butter, consider what it would do to a hand. Always follow manufacturer's directions and never bypass safety devices when operating a cutter.

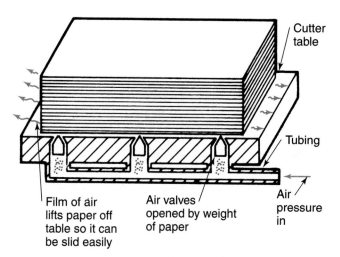

Figure 23-5. Most large cutters use an air jet bed on the table. Air flows up through holes in the table to lift paper for easy movement.

cutting: The process of making a large sheet of paper into several smaller sheets.

trimming: The process of cutting off uneven edges of a product after printing.

Figure 23-7. On most large paper cutters, the operator must use both hands to press buttons that make the cutter knife operate. This system keeps hands out of the area where the cut is performed.

FOLDING OPERATIONS

Once images have been printed on the substrate, they are often folded. Many jobs are printed on one side and backed up with a second printing, commonly called sheetwise imposition. The single sheet might be letter-size and small enough to be folded for insertion in an envelope, or large enough to have 8 or 16 book pages on each side.

The most common folding machine for smaller sheets is the buckle type, **Figure 23-8,** which uses roller action to buckle-fold the paper. The stock is placed in a friction- or suction-type feeder. The adjustment on the suction-type feeder is similar to a printing unit feeder, while the friction type requires a very exact setting.

As the sheet leaves the feeder, it travels on belts or rollers to two rollers that carry the sheet to the fold plate, **Figure 23-9.** As the sheet is forced against the fold plate, the sheet buckles and another combination of rollers folds the sheet and carries it to a delivery station or to another set of folding rollers. These rollers will place another fold if necessary. The fold will be either parallel with or right-angle to the first fold. **Figure 23-10** shows a parallel fold and a right-angle fold.

ACADEMIC LINK
Calculating Paper Requirements

Determining the amount of paper needed for a job must be an exact calculation. Ordering too much stock for a job is a waste of money and resources, while not ordering enough stock may delay completion of the job.

Several factors are included in calculating the paper requirements for a job, such as page size, stock size, order quantity, and waste percentage. A waste percentage is typically established when the order is received and should be added to the client's order quantity.

For example, a client orders 8000 copies of a 48-page, perfect bound booklet to be printed. The page size is 6″ × 9″, the allowable waste is 5%, and the full-size stock is 25″ × 38″. To determine the number of full-size sheets needed:

1. Determine how many 6″ × 9″ pages can be cut from a 25″ × 38″ sheet of stock.
2. Calculate the total number of 6″ × 9″ pages included in the order: 8000 × 48 = 384,000.
3. Divide the total number of finished pages by the number of 6″ × 9″ pages that can be cut from a 25″ × 38″ sheet of stock: 384,000 ÷ 16 = 24,000.
4. Calculate the allowable number of waste sheets: 24,000 × 5% = 1,200.
5. Add the number of sheets needed to print the job with the number of waste sheets allowed to determine the total number of full-size sheets of stock to order for the job.

How many 25″ × 38″ sheets are needed to complete this job?

Some folders use a folding knife to force the paper between rollers for folding. The operation of a knife-type folder is illustrated in **Figure 23-11.**

For larger folding jobs, floor-type folders in a variety of sizes are commonly found in graphic communications facilities. Some of these are used for smaller sheets, such as 11″ × 17″, others for very large sheets containing up to 32 book-size pages. Some newer folders, such as the one shown in **Figure 23-12,** have computerized controls to speed

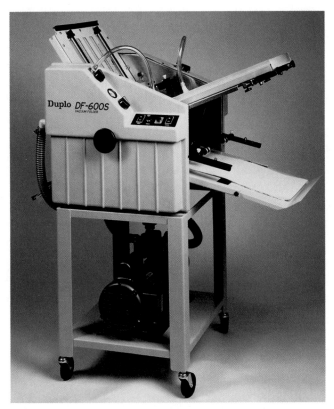

Figure 23-8. A small folder that uses a suction-type feeder. The suction is provided by a vacuum pump mounted below the folder. (Duplo USA)

up the process of setting up for different folds and different paper sizes.

The folding requirements of any project should be considered in the planning stage, since it can affect the choice of equipment and the overall production schedule. Most folds are a combination of parallel and right-angle folds, such as those shown in **Figure 23-13.**

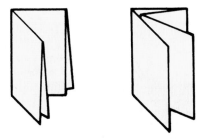

Figure 23-10. Examples of parallel and right-angle folds.

Special Types of Folds

Some printing jobs, especially those used for advertising and promotion purposes, have special folding requirements. A few of these are described below:

- **Self-cover stitched body.** The cover is the same stock as the sheets inside the book. Sheets are folded on the long side and stitched along the spine of the book.
- **Gate-fold book.** The front and back cover have panels that are folded in toward the spine of the book.
- **Folder.** A pocket or a flap that can be on one or both sides of the inside of the cover stock.
- **Fold-out book.** A fold-out in a book can fall anywhere in the book. Some books and magazines use the fold-out format.

This is not a complete list, but it conveys the idea that innovative types of folds require advance planning. Folding by hand should be avoided if possible, since it is a very costly operation.

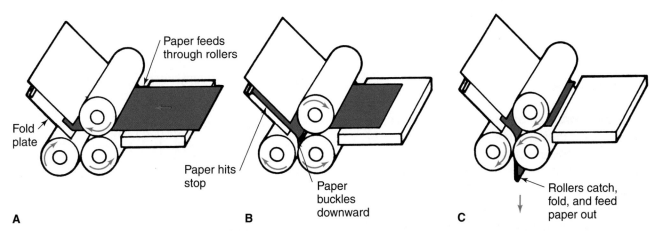

Figure 23-9. The basic operating principle of a buckle folder. A—Paper is fed into the machine by rollers. B—Paper hits the stop on the fold plate and buckles downward. C—Rollers catch the paper and feed it downward to make a fold.

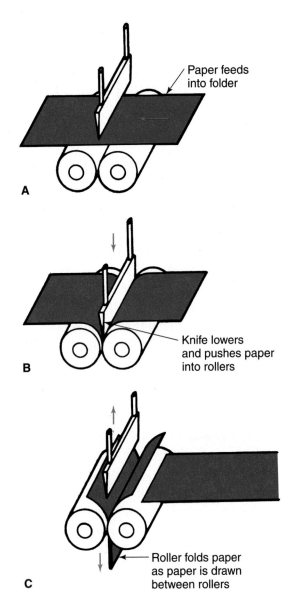

Figure 23-11. Operation of a knife type folder. A—Paper is fed into the folder by rollers. B—The folding knife comes down and pushes the paper between two rollers. C—The rollers fold and pull paper through machine.

Folding Area Safety

- Tie back long hair and secure any loose sleeves or similar clothing items. The rotating parts of folding machinery could grasp hair or loose clothing and pull it into the machine.

- Keep your fingers clear of pinch points, such as folding rollers.

- Handle paper carefully; the edges of sheets are very sharp and can cause painful cuts.

- Turn off any machine before making adjustments. Follow the manufacturer's

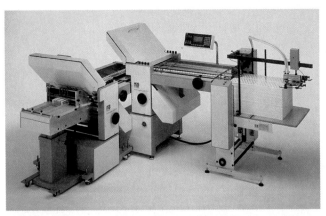

Figure 23-12. A computerized control panel on this floor model folder permits quick set-up for different paper sizes. Various attachments are available to permit use as a buckle-type folder or a combination buckle-type and knife-type folder. (Matthias Bauerle GmbH)

prescribed procedures for adjusting machine settings.

- Lock out electrical power when performing maintenance.

OTHER FINISHING OPERATIONS

In addition to cutting and folding, there are many other finishing operations that are used as required to produce the final product. Some of these are done "in-line" during the printing or folding processes; others are separate operations done on stand-alone equipment.

Perforating

Whenever it is necessary to remove a portion of the printed material, stock is perforated or "perfed." This makes it possible to readily tear off and remove a reply card on an advertising circular or a single page in a workbook. *Perforating* places a series of small cuts or slits in the substrate, using various types of blades or wheels, as shown in **Figure 23-14.**

Sometimes, the task can be completed while running the job on the press. This is a common practice with relief and planographic mechanical processes. The stock can also be perforated on the folder as an auxiliary process. The type of perforation and the number of teeth per inch to make the slits or holes will depend on the type of substrate used. **Figure 23-15** shows some examples of perforations.

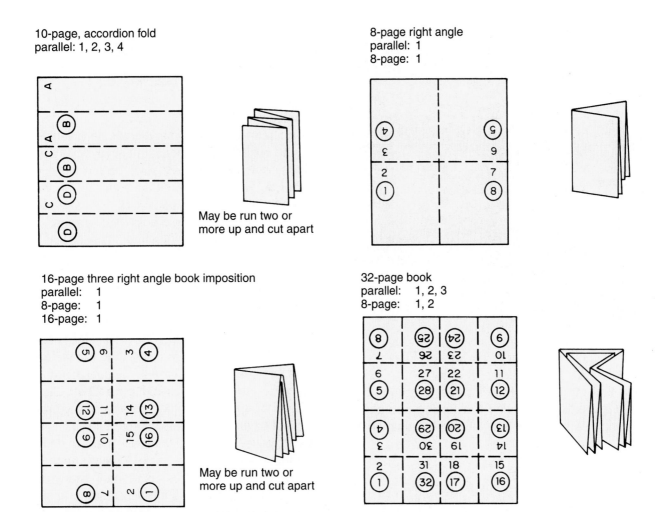

10-page, accordion fold
parallel: 1, 2, 3, 4

May be run two or
more up and cut apart

8-page right angle
parallel: 1
8-page: 1

16-page three right angle book imposition
parallel: 1
8-page: 1
16-page: 1

May be run two or
more up and cut apart

32-page book
parallel: 1, 2, 3
8-page: 1, 2

Figure 23-13. These are a few of the common folds used in the industry.

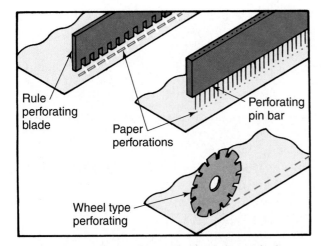

Rule
perforating
blade

Paper
perforations

Perforating
pin bar

Wheel type
perforating

Figure 23-14. Stock can be perforated through the use
of various devices on the press or the folder.

Pinhole	28T per inch
Slot	9T per inch
Slot	8T per inch
Slot	7T per inch
Slot	3 1/2T per inch
Knifecut	6 1/2T per inch
Knifecut	2 1//2T per inch
Knifecut	12T per inch

Figure 23-15. These are a few of the many different
perforations that are used. (Rollem)

perforating: Operation that places a series of small cuts
or slits in the substrate, using various types of blades or
wheels on the press or folder.

slitting: An operation similar to perforating that makes a
continuous cut, rather than a series of slits. It is usually
done by sharp-edged wheels that cut the stock as it passes
through the folder.

Slitting

Slitting is similar to perforating, but it involves
making a continuous cut rather than a series of
slits. It is usually done by one or more sharp-edged

Figure 23-16. Slitting is commonly done by a sharp wheel that cuts paper sheet as it exits the folder.

wheels that cut the stock as it passes through the folder, **Figure 23-16.** During the folding operation, for example, a leaflet or booklet can be trimmed to finished size by slitting wheels.

Creasing and Scoring

Creasing is the process of compressing the substrate so it will fold more easily. This is often accomplished with a rotary creaser attached to the folder, **Figure 23-17A.** Sometimes, creasing

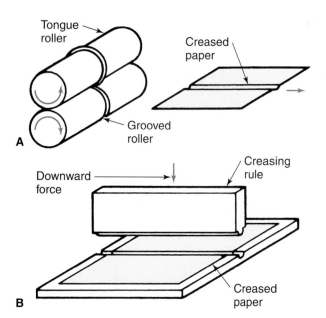

Figure 23-17. Creasing devices. A—The creasing roller method is used on a folder. B—Creasing rules are typically used on letterpress equipment.

is a separate operation using a creasing rule, **Figure 23-17B,** on letterpress equipment or specially designed finishing equipment. A creasing rule is made of a thin piece of metal that is pressed slightly into the stock. It is used to make folding easy. Rule thickness will vary with the stock.

The term *scoring* is used interchangeably with creasing in some operations, but *scoring* is actually a slight cut made in heavy stock before it is folded. The correct depth of the cut is important. Scoring is commonly done in the packaging industry, where scores are made at the fold points for cartons.

Die cutting

Whenever an irregular shape must be cut in a substrate, the method most often used to do the task is *die cutting.* In the die cutting process, pressure is used to force a sharp metal die through the stock, **Figure 23-18.**

The dies, which look somewhat like kitchen cookie cutters, are used to slice through the substrate to form tags, cards, labels, and boxes, **Figure 23-19.** Dies are also used to cut the irregular shapes after screen process printing of labels, decals, and stickers. Die cutting is not limited to paper but can be done with many materials.

Although relief printing is no longer done by most printers, a small relief press is found in many shops because of its usefulness for die cutting and similar tasks requiring pressure. The dies used in the process

Figure 23-18. Pressure applied to a die formed with sharp steel rules will cut irregular shapes, such as these arrows, out of a substrate. The pink material surrounding the rules is sponge rubber, which compresses and then springs back to push the cut shape out of the die.

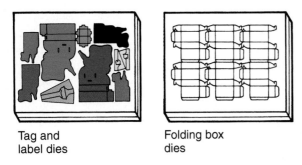

Tag and
label dies

Folding box
dies

Figure 23-19. Irregular shapes can be die cut. These are examples. (Accurate Steel Rule Die Mfg., Inc.)

consist of a base, or dieboard, with steel rules shaped and inserted in a saw kerf. The saw kerf is the open area left after sawing the material. Pieces of sponge rubber are glued to the dieboards on either side of the rules to release substrate material after cutting.

Embossing

Embossing is a process that creates a raised image on a substrate by pressing it between two dies, **Figure 23-20.** One die is in relief, while the other is recessed. When the two are brought together with the stock between them, the clamping force creates a raised image on the stock.

High-quality embossing requires expensive dies and must be done to close tolerances, but the results can be very impressive. See **Figure 23-21.** Sometimes, an image is printed, and the stock is then embossed. In other applications, the stock itself creates the image and ink is not used. This technique is called *blind embossing*. If an image is sunk into the substrate, rather than being raised, the process is called *debossing*.

Figure 23-21. Embossed surfaces create a very interesting pattern or design that has depth. This is an example of blind embossing, with no ink used on the raised image.

Stamping

The process of *stamping*, or foil stamping, is a method of transferring a thin layer of metallic tone or color to a substrate, using heat and pressure. Gold or simulated gold is commonly used as a stamping material, **Figure 23-22.** Silver and other metallics, as well as various color foils, are also available. Some other colors are also available as hot stamping materials.

Stamping is a form of relief printing process. The material to be stamped is set in raised metal type or produced as a cut (an engraving in metal which has a raised printing area), then clamped into a holding device. The type or other material is heated, then

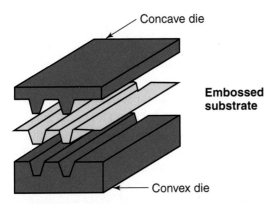

Concave die

Embossed
substrate

Convex die

Figure 23-20. A pair of dies is used for embossing an image on a substrate.

creasing: The process of compressing the substrate so that it will fold more easily; often done with a rotary creaser attached to the folder.

scoring: A slight cut made in heavy stock before it is folded.

die cutting: A process in which pressure is used to force a sharp metal die through the stock. It is used to make irregular shapes.

embossing: A process that creates a raised image on a substrate by pressing it between two dies.

blind embossing: An embossing process in which the stock itself creates the image and ink is not used.

debossing: The reverse of embossing, so that the image is sunk into the substrate, rather than being raised.

stamping: The process of transferring a thin layer of metallic tone or color to a substrate, using heat and pressure.

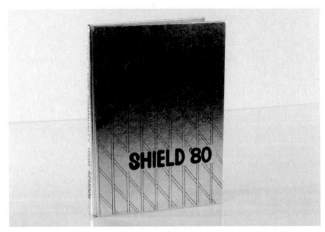

Figure 23-22. Foil stamping is used as an accenting or decorative device. It is frequently used on book covers.

Figure 23-23. Tickets are a printed product that commonly must be numbered as a finishing operation.

brought into contact with a coated foil laid over the substrate. The heat and pressure transfers the color or metallic film from the foil to the substrate. Proper image transfer depends on the amount of heat and pressure, and the length of time they are applied. In a production situation, the foil stamping unit is automated, but for small jobs, a hand-operated press is typically used.

Numbering

The process of imprinting tickets, certificates, checks, or other items with consecutive figures is called *numbering*. Using a device called a numbering machine, the figures are transferred from an inked relief image onto the stock. In operation, a plunger is automatically depressed by the press to ratchet the numbering head to a different figure or digit. This permits forward or backward numbering, **Figure 23-23.**

Often, the numbering machine is set to start on the maximum amount, so the last figure printed will be number 1. This prevents an overrun and places the tickets, forms, or other numbered materials in the correct numerical order.

Punching and Drilling

Both punching and drilling produce holes in a substrate, but use different means to do so. *Punching* is done by forcing a metal rod down through the paper to remove stock. The punch works in a shearing action with a die placed below the paper, **Figure 23-24.** Neither the punch nor the die rotate. Punching is used for such applications as producing the holes needed to do spiral binding.

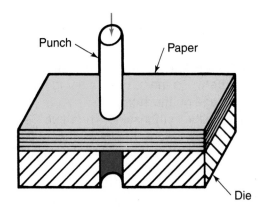

Figure 23-24. A punch forces a metal rod straight down through stock. It does not spin, as does a drill. The die located below the punch shears off stock to form a hole.

Drilling uses a revolving, hollow drill bit with very sharp edges, **Figure 23-25.** After placing stock on the drill table board, the revolving drill is forced through a *lift* of paper. The waste stock rises through the hollow center of the drill and is ejected out of the drill top. A guide at the back of the board regulates the distance the holes are drilled from the edge of the sheet, **Figure 23-26.** Most drills have stops to ensure the proper positioning for each lift to be drilled.

Drills are available in various diameters. Many drilling machines have auxiliary devices as attachments. These devices make it possible to slit, fillet, or notch a lift of paper. Also available are multiple spindle drilling machines that make it possible to drill ten or more holes at one time.

Figure 23-25. Paper drills have very sharp edges. Handle drills carefully when mounting or removing them.

Fence

Figure 23-26. A fence at the back of the drilling machine table can be set for proper positioning of the holes being drilled. This machine is operated with a foot switch, leaving the operator's hands free to position the material.

⚠ The drill spindle should be protected by a guard. The high-speed revolving action of the drill tends to draw hair toward it. This action is caused by static electricity. Hands and fingers must also be kept away from the revolving drill.

Varnishing

After an image has been printed on a substrate, *varnishing* is sometimes used to provide a clear protective surface. Usually, the coating makes the surface resistant to moisture and scuffing.

Glossy brochures, annual report covers, and similar products are typical examples of varnishing. The coating materials vary, but some of the latest coatings are epoxies that give excellent wear qualities. An epoxy is a resin that forms a very hard surface coating when combined with other chemicals.

Total area coverage can be accomplished by various processes but an offset press can be used if the dampeners are removed. Letterpress and screen processes can also be used for specific varnishing jobs.

Laminating

Laminating is the bonding of two or more materials together to become one common unit. A thin film of plastic with an adhesive coating is bonded to the substrate to provide protection against abrasion and moisture. The laminate material can be applied as an in-line operation on a web-fed press, **Figure 23-27,** or as individual sheets of various sizes. A common use of lamination is restaurant menus, which must be protected from moisture and constant handling.

The process often called *liquid lamination* is actually a coating method similar to varnishing. The plastic coating material is applied in liquid form and then cured into a tough protective layer by exposure to ultraviolet light. For this reason, it is sometimes referred to as a UV-cured coating.

numbering: The process of imprinting tickets, certificates, checks, or other items with consecutive figures, using a device that transfers the figures from an inked relief image.

punching: Piercing operation done by forcing a metal rod down through the paper to remove stock. The punch works in a shearing action with a *die* placed below the paper.

drilling: Piercing operation that uses a revolving, hollow drill bit with very sharp edges. The waste stock rises through the hollow center of the drill.

lift: Term describing a pile of paper, usually the amount cut or drilled in a single operation.

varnishing: A coating applied after printing to provide a clear protective surface.

laminating: Process in which thin film of plastic with an adhesive coating is bonded to a printed substrate to provide protection against abrasion and moisture.

liquid lamination: A coating method similar to varnishing. The plastic coating material is applied in liquid form and then cured into a tough protective layer by exposure to ultraviolet light.

Figure 23-27. Laminating material being applied at high speed on a web-fed press. The thin plastic layer protects the printed product.

BINDING

After printing and such finishing steps as folding, a product may be ready for shipment or it may require

binding to fasten the sheets or folded signatures together. Many printed press sheets are very large and must be folded, gathered and collated, stitched, and trimmed. See **Figure 23-28.**

Some general or basic types of binding include the following:

- **Adhesive binding.** Also called padding, this is a classification for methods that use glue or adhesive to hold the sheets together but allow them to be removed, as in the case of notepads.

- **Mechanical binding.** A broad category that includes many different devices used to hold sheets together. Spiral wire, metal posts, metal or plastic rings, plastic combs, and channels that rely on friction to hold are all mechanical methods. Since separate sheets are being fastened together, this is sometimes called loose-leaf binding.

- **Side stitching.** A form of stapling in which metal wire is forced through sides of sheets and formed to hold sheets together. Side sewing is similar, but uses threads rather than staples to bind sheets together.

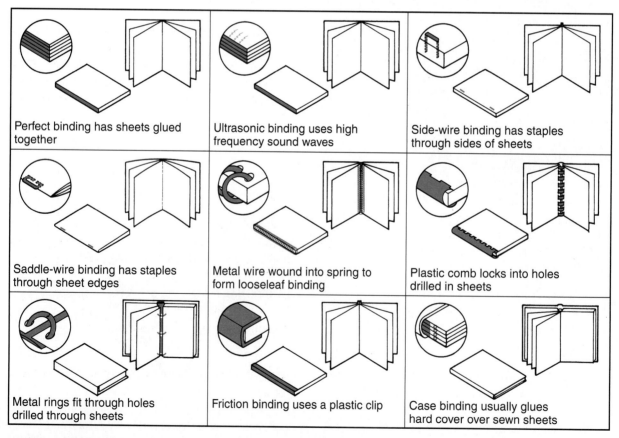

Perfect binding has sheets glued together

Ultrasonic binding uses high frequency sound waves

Side-wire binding has staples through sides of sheets

Saddle-wire binding has staples through sheet edges

Metal wire wound into spring to form looseleaf binding

Plastic comb locks into holes drilled in sheets

Metal rings fit through holes drilled through sheets

Friction binding uses a plastic clip

Case binding usually glues hard cover over sewn sheets

Figure 23-28. Various methods used to bind materials together after printing.

- **Saddle stitching.** A method in which metal wire is forced through the folded edge of a signature and formed into staples to hold the pages together. Saddle sewing is like saddle stitching, but is done with thread instead of wire.
- **Perfect binding.** Also called softcover binding, this method uses an adhesive to hold sheets or signatures together and to fasten the flexible cloth or paper cover onto the body.
- **Edition binding.** The most complex and permanent form of binding, in which a rigid cover is attached to a book body that is held together by sewing. Also called case binding or hard binding.
- **Self-cover binding.** A term used to describe using the same material for both the cover and body of the book. Self-cover books may be perfect bound, but are most often saddle stitched or side-stitched.

Some of the most widely used fastening techniques include pamphlet binding, edition binding, perfect binding, and mechanical binding.

Pamphlet Binding

Most of today's magazines, catalogs, and booklets fall into the pamphlet binding category. One of the simplest techniques is saddle wire stitching. Sheets are folded, gathered, and stitched through the center, or saddle, of the folded sheets.

Many booklets and magazines are fastened by this method. The folded sheets are placed one over the other and then placed on the saddle of the stitcher, **Figure 23-29.** The maximum number of pages is

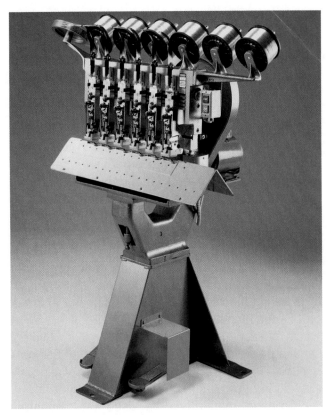

Figure 23-29. Stitching machine uses rolls of wire to produce staples that are inserted through the saddle of a signature. Signature is opened and positioned over the angled base for stitching. (Interlake Packaging Corp.)

regulated by the limit of the stitcher and/or the pamphlet thickness allowing the booklet or magazine to lie flat.

When larger publications are bound, the machine is capable of gathering the signatures and cover. They are then stitched and trimmed, **Figure 23-30.**

Figure 23-30. This saddle wire binding machine is used for high-volume production of magazines and booklets. (McCain Manufacturing Corp.)

gathering: The assembling of printed signatures.

collating: The gathering of sheets or signatures, usually after they are printed.

Gathering and Collating

Gathering is a general term associated with the assembling of signatures for a book or other multipage product. As discussed previously, a signature is a large sheet that has been folded to form a group of pages, **Figure 23-31.**

The term *collating* usually means the assembling of single sheets. However, the term can also mean the checking of signature placement after gathering.

The basic process of gathering is illustrated in **Figure 23-32.** It involves using a gathering machine to stack the signatures on top of each other in the correct order. Note that one type uses a rotating gripper bar and the other uses a gripper arm. Both place the signatures on a moving conveyor. Other variations are also available. **Figure 23-33** shows a gathering machine placing book signatures in the proper sequence.

A suction feed collator with in-line folding, stitching, and trimming for creating finished booklets is shown in **Figure 23-34.** It is shown collating six stacks of pages plus a cover.

Collating marks can be used on signatures to check the accuracy of the signature-gathering sequence. As illustrated in **Figure 23-35,** the collating marks should form a diagonal line when signatures are in the proper order. If the marks do not align, one or more signatures is out of sequence.

Stitching

Stitching is a common binding method that holds the sheets together with wire staples. It is typically used on products with fewer than 120 pages. Books with large numbers of pages are bound with other methods, such as sewing or mechanical devices.

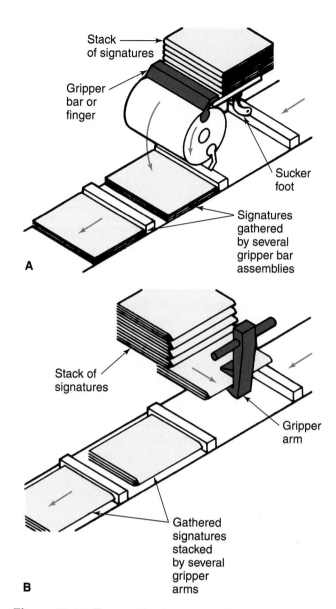

Figure 23-32. Two methods commonly used to gather signatures. A—Rotary gathering. B—Gripper arm gathering.

Figure 23-31. A signature is a larger sheet that is folded to produce a series of pages.

Figure 23-33. A gathering machine like this one places all signatures of a product in proper order for binding.

Figure 23-34. This is a suction feed collator with in-line fold, stitch, and trim units. It can be equipped with up to 18 bins and handle many different sheet sizes and paper weights. (Duplo USA)

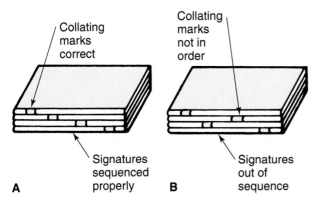

Figure 23-35. Collating marks placed on folded edges of signatures allow a visual check for proper gathering sequence. A—Marks align diagonally, showing correct signature order. As a further check, collating marks often are printed with letters or numbers in proper sequence. B—Marks not aligned diagonally. Signature order is incorrect.

Figure 23-36. Saddle-stitching involves stapling through the folded area, or saddle, of the product. It allows a booklet to lie relatively flat when opened.

Figure 23-37. Creep, or shingling, results when saddle-stitched products become thicker. The extended page edges will be trimmed off evenly.

Saddle stitching, **Figure 23-36,** is commonly used for booklets or magazines because they tend to lie more flat than side-stitched products when opened. When the thickness of a saddle-stitched product increases, the amount of *creep*, or shingling, becomes more evident. As shown in **Figure 23-37,** creep is a pushing out, or extension, of pages on the outer edge of the book, caused by the greater thickness at the spine. Although the finished pages will be trimmed evenly, an allowance for creep must be made in the prepress phase, when the pages are being laid out. If allowance is not made, page margins of the finished book will not be even. In extreme cases, type or illustrations along the outer edges could be cut off.

The side wire stitching technique is another method of fastening several signatures or many sheets, **Figure 23-38.** The cover could be of the same type of stock or a specially printed substrate. One of the drawbacks of this type of binding is that the booklet or magazine does not lie flat when opened.

Side stitch machines might be of the single-head type, like the one shown in Figure 23-38, or a multiple-head configuration that places several

stitching: A binding method that holds sheets together with staples. Typically used on books with fewer than 120 pages.

creep: A pushing out or extension of pages on the outer edge of a saddle-stitched book, caused by the greater thickness at the spine. An allowance for creep must be made in the prepress phase.

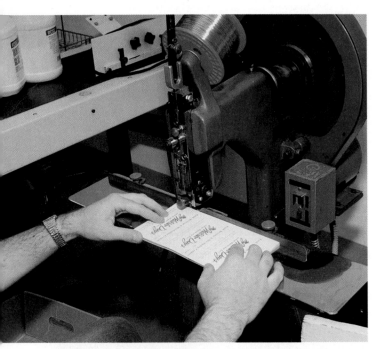

Figure 23-38. Side-wire stitching is used for some booklets and other products. A booklet bound by this method will not lie as flat when opened as will a saddle-stitched product.

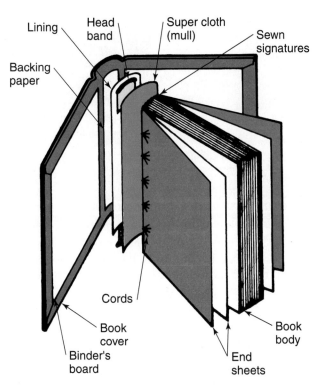

Figure 23-39. The basic parts of a case-bound book.

staples simultaneously. Multiple-head stitching increases binding speed or volume.

! Never place a finger or hand under a stitcher head. A staple could be driven through your finger or hand if the machine is activated.

Edition Binding

Edition binding, also called case binding, is considered the most durable and permanent method of binding books that will be used extensively over a period of time, such as textbooks and reference volumes. The parts of an edition-bound book are identified in **Figure 23-39.**

The binding process involves gathering and sewing the signatures together, then compressing the signatures, and trimming the edges with a three-knife trimmer, **Figure 23-40.** The book body is then glued, the spine rounded, and lining applied. The book cover is manufactured separately by wrapping and gluing a printed cover on binder's board. It is then attached to the body with an adhesive in a process called casing in. The bound book is then clamped in a fixture until the adhesive dries. The steps in the binding process are shown in order in **Figure 23-41.**

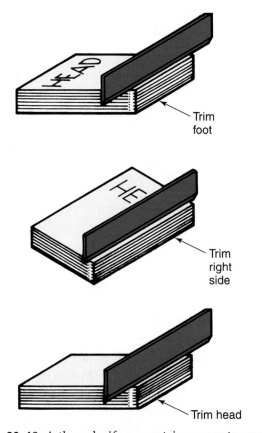

Figure 23-40. A three-knife paper trimmer cuts excess material off the foot, right side, and head of the book body after signatures are sewn together. Although the three trimming steps are shown separately here, they are completed in a single operation.

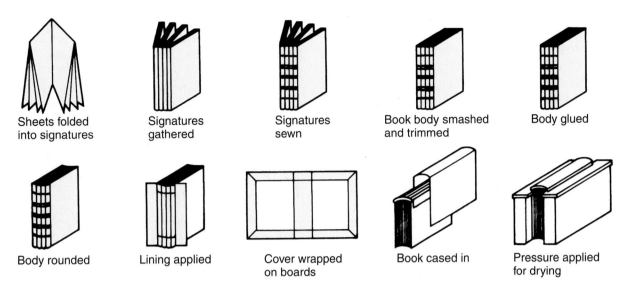

Sheets folded into signatures   Signatures gathered   Signatures sewn   Book body smashed and trimmed   Body glued

Body rounded   Lining applied   Cover wrapped on boards   Book cased in   Pressure applied for drying

Figure 23-41. These are the major steps that occur during the edition binding of a book.

Although the vast majority of case-bound books produced today are manufactured with machine binding methods, hand-binding is still done for special volumes and other uses. Knowing how to do hand-binding is a useful skill and an aid to understanding the binding process.

Perfect Binding

The *perfect binding* process, used for producing books that are usually described as softcover or paperback, is a fast and relatively low-cost method. Since it eliminates the need for sewing and constructing a hard cover, it is more economical than edition binding. Perfect binding is not as long-lasting or rugged as edition binding. For this reason, it is often selected for products that will have a limited lifespan, such as telephone directories, magazines, and some books for children. Its low cost has made it popular for mass-market novels and other books where price is a competitive factor. See **Figure 23-42.**

In this process, either signatures or single sheets can be gathered or collated to form the book body. The binding equipment then grinds or saws the binding edge of the book body to roughen the surface, and a flexible glue is applied. The cover is placed on the body and clamped until the glue sets. The book is then trimmed, usually with a three-knife trimmer. Refer to Figure 23-1.

Perfect-bound books intended for greater permanence, such as some textbooks and reference volumes, often are bound with a system called burst binding. This method involves notching the spine of the book body and applying a high-strength adhesive

Figure 23-42. Perfect binding is a very popular method for use with products as diverse in size as magazines, books, and telephone directories.

under pressure. Another method that provides greater permanence is sewing the signatures together (like an edition-bound book) before the gluing and covering operations are performed. These methods virtually eliminate pages coming loose and falling out, which has been a problem with some softcover books in the past.

edition binding: The most complex and permanent form of binding, in which a rigid cover is attached to a book body that is held together by sewing.

perfect binding: Method that uses an adhesive to hold sheets or signatures together and to fasten the flexible cloth or paper cover onto the body.

Mechanical Binding

The broad category called *mechanical binding* consists of a number of methods that employ a mechanical device (metal spring, plastic fastener, etc.) to hold sheets together in loose-leaf form. Two of the methods usually used are plastic comb binding and spiral binding.

Plastic comb binding is commonly used for booklets that might have to be altered by adding or removing pages. Books bound with this method permit the pages to lay perfectly flat when open.

The binding method involves using a special machine, **Figure 23-43,** to punch rectangular holes along one edge of the printed material. After the sheets are punched, they are positioned over the spread or expanded plastic teeth of the fastener. When released, the plastic teeth extend through the punched holes to bind the publication. The same machine can be used to open the comb teeth so pages can be removed or added. Combs are available in various diameters to suit the number of pages being fastened.

Spiral binding is similar to the plastic comb method, but does not allow opening the binding for the addition or removal of pages. In this method, smaller round holes are punched, then the wire is spiral fed through the booklet using automatic equipment. The method is used for many types of products from small pocket notebooks to calendars, to books an inch or more in thickness, **Figure 23-44.** Several variations of the spiral method are used, but all follow the same principle. The diameter of each type of binding wire varies with the need.

Like most mechanical bindings, the spiral wire method allows a book to be opened flat and remain that way. The spiral allows for the tearing out of a page but not the insertion of sheets.

PACKAGING

In graphic communications, *packaging* basically involves wrapping, strapping, or boxing the printed pieces together for delivery to the customer. While printed products were once typically wrapped in paper and then packed in boxes, the more common method today is the use of plastic *shrink-wrap*. In this method, a stack of printed pieces is placed on the conveyor of a shrink-wrapping machine, **Figure 23-45,** and enclosed with a thin plastic in sheet form. The wrapped stack then passes through a heated tunnel where the plastic shrinks to form a tight, sealed package.

The shrink-wrapped products may then be packed in boxes of corrugated board to protect them during shipment. Other printed products, such as books, may be packed in boxes without being wrapped beforehand. Several boxes can be stacked on a pallet and then strapped in place for shipping.

An alternative to shrink-wrapping is to use a *banding machine*, also called a loop press, to wrap and bond a plastic or metal band around a bundle of booklets, books, boxes, or other products. This holds the products together for shipping.

Figure 23-43. A special machine is used to punch the product and insert a plastic binding comb. The finished plastic bound book can be taken apart to easily add or remove pages. (General Binding Corp.)

Figure 23-44. Spiral fastening uses metal or plastic wire wound through holes to bind together loose sheets.

Bindery Operator

A bindery operator is responsible for completing all binding and finishing services required for each job, which includes operating and maintaining all bindery equipment and applying hand-finishing techniques when required. Typical bindery operations include cutting, folding, drilling, stapling, packing, hot stamping, laminating, collating, inserting, padding, wrapping, gathering, and numbering.

Bindery operators typically work very closely with other team members, as many bindery operations are completed in an assembly line of repetitive tasks. Some plants still have equipment that requires manual operation, while many facilities use highly-automated and computerized machines.

Bindery operators are expected to operate and maintain all bindery equipment, enforce all applicable OSHA safety regulations, dispose of all waste material in compliance with EPA regulations, and pay close attention to specifications and details while performing all bindery tasks to ensure quality on every job. Manual dexterity and mechanical abilities are also important qualities. A high school diploma or an associate's degree is needed for entry level bindery positions, and on-the-job training is often provided by employers. Certification programs are available and may be a requirement for advancement opportunities.

"The more we know, the more we are able to cope in an ever-changing, highly technological society. Various communication systems will be the major link for this rapid dissemination of information."

Jack Simich
Former GATF Educational Director

Figure 23-45. A shrink-wrapping machine wraps bundles of product in plastic, then passes the bundles through a heated tunnel (at left end of the machine) to shrink the plastic tightly around the product. (Doboy Packaging Machinery)

Larger forms of the banding machine may be used to strap stacks of boxes onto pallets to keep them securely in place during shipping. Plastic wrapping material, similar to shrink-wrap, is often used to bind a stack of boxes on a pallet into a single unit.

A *taping machine* is used in shipping departments to automatically apply tape to seal the tops of boxes. As the boxes are fed through the machine, a series of rollers and brushes applies the tape to the top of each box. A cutter also slices off the tape to the correct length. Two belts move the boxes through the taping machine. This helps automate the shipping department of a facility.

mechanical binding: A broad category that includes many different devices used to hold sheets together.

plastic comb binding: A mechanical binding method commonly used for booklets that might have to be altered by adding or removing pages.

spiral binding: A mechanical binding method in which small round holes are punched through the pages and metal or plastic wire is spiral fed through them.

packaging: The process of wrapping, strapping, or boxing the printed pieces together for delivery to the customer.

shrink-wrap: A packaging method in which a stack of printed pieces is enclosed with a thin plastic in sheet form.

banding machine: Device that is used to wrap and bond a plastic or metal band around a bundle of booklets, books, boxes, or other products. This holds the products together for shipping.

taping machine: Device used in shipping departments to automatically apply tape to seal the tops of boxes.

Summary

Often after printing, the product needs further operations to be finished. The two most common types of classifications are finishing and binding. Those operations associated with finishing include cutting, folding, creasing, die cutting, embossing, numbering, drilling, varnishing, and laminating. These finishing operations will be written up in the specifications. Binding operations include those processes that fasten the product together. The product can be greatly enhanced by proper binding and finishing. This makes it extremely important that all finishing and binding processes are performed correctly.

Review Questions

Please do not write in this text. Write your answers on a separate sheet of paper.

1. What does the term *finishing* mean to a printer?

2. Which term refers to making three sides of a book even and square?
   A. Cutting.
   B. Scoring.
   C. Sheathing.
   D. Trimming.

3. What is a *shear stick*?

4. Explain why a folding machine operator should tie back long hair and secure loose clothing.

5. A(n) _____ lifts heavy stacks of paper off the cutter table for easy movement.

6. How does a buckle folder work?

7. _____ is similar to cutting but it can be done by a set of wheels as the sheet passes through the folder.

8. Describe the processes and uses of pamphlet binding, edition binding, perfect binding, and mechanical binding.

9. _____ is a general term associated with the assembling of signatures.

10. Why are collating marks used?

Suggested Activities

1. Complete an edition binding project. Visit a writing class in your school and suggest to the teacher that each student write a poem and that your class would print the poems and bind them into a book.

2. Diagram the workflow of a perfect-bound book.

3. Visit a printing plant and identify the binding and finishing tasks that were used to finish three different jobs.

Related Web Links

Print Net Inc.

www.printnetinc.com

Green printer with resources on how the binding process can be made green.

Handbound Book

www.instructables.com/id/Handbound-Book

Instructions for binding books by hand.

About Bookbinding

www.aboutbookbinding.com

Information on the history of binding books.

High-speed web offset presses, such as this one at a metropolitan newspaper, are often custom-designed to meet a specific publication's needs. Web offset is extensively used for magazine and book printing, as well.

CHAPTER 24

The Business of Printing

Learning Objectives

After studying this chapter, you will be able to:

- Summarize practices for planning and growing a successful business.

- Explain the basic fundamentals of business, such as costs, estimates, and productivity.

- Summarize the use and application of various industry standards and specifications.

- Explain how copyright laws apply to printing companies.

Important Terms

business plan
copyright
corporation
fair use
fixed cost
infringement
labor cost

materials cost
partnership
printing estimate
productivity
profit
single proprietorship
trade customs

Printing and publishing is a big business that is comprised of many small businesses. It is a big business in terms of the dollar value of products (approaching $200 billion), the number of establishments (more than 40,000), and the number of employees (approximately 1.1 million). More than 70% of commercial printing businesses, however, employ 20 or fewer people, with nearly 35% of all shops having less than five employees. Only about 6% of all commercial printers employ more than 100 workers.

PLANNING FOR GROWTH AND SUCCESS

The growth and success of a graphic communications operation is dependent on every employee, every process, every supplier, and every piece of equipment. The location of various departments, placement of equipment, geographic location of the facility, and many other factors affect the success of a business. Careful business planning is tremendously important. If a planner or manager makes mistakes, it can cost the firm time, money, and personnel.

The success of a graphics firm is measured by the cost and quality of finished products. The employees, raw materials, and equipment dictate the cost and quality of a printed product. Every phase of production must be well thought out and reviewed periodically. As the old saying goes, "A chain is only as strong as its weakest link." If one phase of production is a weak link in the chain, it can affect the final product and the future of the company.

To help achieve growth and success, effective managers rely on proven business and personnel practices, which include:

- Use efficient, cost-effective equipment to produce better products at a lower cost.
- Develop a "team effort" attitude, where all employees work and communicate as a cohesive unit to outperform competing companies.

- Use worker feedback to analyze and improve production steps. The person performing a task usually has the best idea of how it can be done better.
- Determine pay increases, in part, on company profits. This can generate incentive to improve job performance.
- Make it known that promotions and salary increases are based on job performance. Use qualities like dependability, work quality, efficiency, cooperation, initiative, and innovation.
- Provide workers with the capability of advancement within the company as a performance incentive and means of building employee morale.
- Carefully analyze and select outside sources of supplies and services, weighing cost versus quality factors.
- Apply modern quality control and production control methods to all appropriate operations within the company.
- Develop and implement a continuous training program to help employees keep up-to-date with advances in technology.

Developing a Business Plan

A *business plan* is a document that states the goals of a business and presents a framework for achieving those goals. In any business, planning is essential to success. Once a business plan has been developed, it must be used. The plan is a tool to measure success.

Some of the basic reasons to have a business plan are that it helps the executive officer focus on the factors relating to success and growth; it is a management tool; it defines many aspects of the business; it is a communication tool; and it helps keep the financial picture in focus. See **Figure 24-1** for basic factors in business plan development.

Establishing the Organization

Three of the most common organization types for businesses are single proprietorship, partnership, and corporation. Each type has unique characteristics and advantages.

A *single proprietorship* is a business owned by one person; also known as a sole proprietorship. The business and the owner are a single entity, and the owner has full control of the business operations. The owner's income is the business' profits. The

Factors in Business Plan Development	
Vision statement	Production Staffing Equipment Facilities Projected growth Funding
Product	Range of products Competitive pricing
Market and Strategy	Target audience Niche Need for the product Growth potential Advertising Sales Promotion package
Customers	List clients Gain and loss factors
Competitive advantage	Reason for success Why is product better Customer service Distribution Prompt and courteous service
Management team	Qualification of personnel Duties and responsibilities Available resources Accounting system Salaries Benefits
Personnel	Current workforce Future workforce Job descriptions Benefits Salaries

Figure 24-1. Basic factors in developing a business plan.

owner of a single proprietorship also carries 100% of the liability of running a business. For example, if the business incurs bad debt or is sued, the owner is personally liable even if the business closes.

A *partnership* is a business owned by two or more persons. The owners and the business are considered a single entity and pay income tax on the profits of the business. In this type of business, the ownership responsibilities and legal liability is split between or among all the partners. Unlike a single proprietorship, a partnership shares both the profits and liabilities of a business.

A business that is a *corporation* is a separate legal entity from the people who own or manage it. This type of business pays taxes on its own tax return and is liable for its own debt and other legal responsibilities. Typically, a corporation has shareholders who invest in the company and share in the profits of the company.

With a large number of small companies in the printing industry, most businesses are single proprietorships or partnerships. The larger companies (and some smaller ones) are typically corporations. Single owners and most partners are actively involved in operating their businesses, while many of the stockholders in a corporation are not involved in the day-to-day operations of the business.

BUSINESS BASICS

The success of any type of business involves certain operations tasks that must be performed in order to stay in business.

- **Sales.** Obtaining orders for the company's products or services.

- **Business.** Handling all the financial operations of the company.

Many business plans in the graphic communications industry now include a sustainability plan. A sustainability plan contains the guidelines and procedures used in order to help organizations use, develop, and protect resources in a way that meets needs without harming the environment. As the demands on our natural resources increase, companies must implement sustainable practices to safeguard the environmental health, economic growth, and quality of life. The creation of a company's sustainability plan may rely on individual employee input, but the goals are simple. The sustainable practices a company implements must focus on reducing the use of materials, energy, and water; reducing the pollution put out by the company; reducing the amount of waste produced by the company; and using more nontoxic, recycled, and remanufactured materials. Communication and education within the company are necessary to meet these goals. For more information on sustainability plans, see www.kab.org.

- **Production.** All the activities necessary to produce goods or services.
- **Administration.** Coordinating and overseeing all aspects of the company.

In a large business, there may be dozens of people fulfilling each of these responsibilities. In a small company or single proprietorship, however, very few people may fill all the roles, **Figure 24-2.** In a small company, for example, the owner handles both the sales and administrative responsibilities, the office manager sends out invoices, pays bills from suppliers, and keeps business records, and the production manager operates press equipment and oversees the prepress worker and press helper.

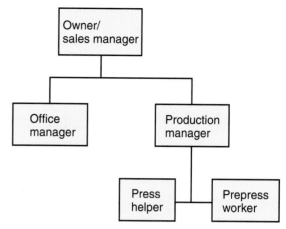

Figure 24-2. In the organization of a typical small, single-proprietor printing business, the owner also serves as sales manager. Such enterprises are often family businesses, with all or most of the employees related to the owner.

As company size increases, the responsibility for carrying out business operations is divided among a greater number of people, **Figure 24-3.** For example, a company that is a two-person partnership may designate one partner as the company president (administrator) and the other as controller (business manager). A variation on this organization might be the addition of a production manager, to whom the prepress manager and the plant manager report. The production manager is responsible to the president, as are the controller and sales manager. When a company becomes large enough to be incorporated, a Board of Directors is elected by the company's stockholders to oversee the business, **Figure 24-4.** Day-to-day operation is conducted by the president or chief executive officer (CEO). Larger organizations are more complex, with a number of different levels of supervision and responsibility.

business plan: A document that states the goals of a business and presents a framework for achieving those goals.

single proprietorship: A type of business owned by one person in which the business and the owner are a single entity; the owner's income is the business' profits.

partnership: A type of business that is owned by two or more persons. The owners and the business are considered a single entity and pay income tax on the profits of the business.

corporation: A type of business that is a separate legal entity from the people who own or manage it. A business that is a corporation pays taxes on its own tax return and is liable for its own debt and other legal responsibilities.

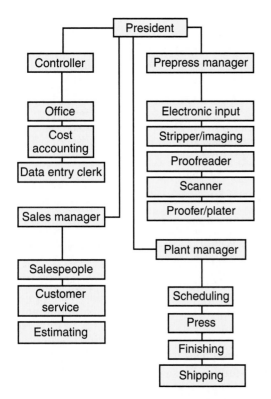

Figure 24-3. A company with approximately 50 employees is capable of spreading business responsibilities across a larger number of people. In this example, the president and the controller are joint owners/partners.

Business Costs

To remain in business, a company must make a *profit*. This means that it must receive more income from the sale of products or services than it spends for raw materials, employee salaries, building rent, utility bills, and other costs of doing business. The difference between income and expenses is the profit of a business.

The key to success is identifying and controlling business costs, and setting prices that cover the costs and provide a desired percentage of profit. A company that does not accurately determine its costs or sets prices too low to make a profit, will soon be out of business.

Business costs can be grouped into three categories: materials costs, labor costs, and fixed costs. Accountants have various formulas to assign a portion of the fixed costs to each job that is printed. Materials costs and labor costs are specific to each job: a particular number of worker hours to produce it, along with measurable quantities of paper, ink, and other materials.

- *Materials costs* are the prices paid for items that are consumed as a job is printed, primarily paper and ink. Other items, such as packaging for the finished product, are also included in materials costs.

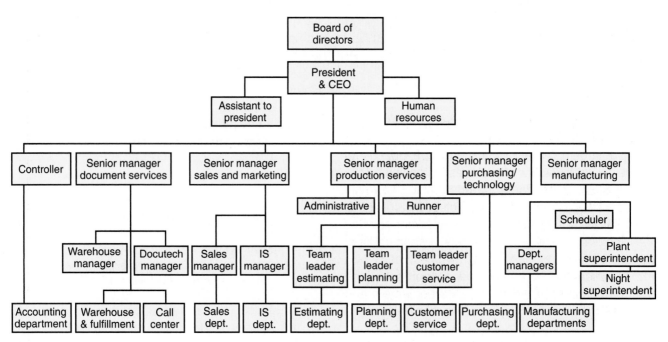

Figure 24-4. The organization of large companies is more complex than smaller firms and includes several levels of management.

- *Labor costs* are the "people costs" involved in operating a business. These include the hourly wages or salaries for workers, the cost of health insurance, paid holidays and vacations, and other employee benefits. Services purchased from outside suppliers, such as illustrators, are also considered labor costs.

- *Fixed costs* (also known as overhead) are expenses that remain the same, regardless of the volume of business. For example, rent or mortgage payments for the shop premises are the same whether the printing presses are running round-the-clock, or the business is closed for the weekend. Fixed costs also include electricity, gas, telephone, the equipment needed to run the business, office supplies (ranging from copier toner to floor wax), and even the cost of an advertisement in the telephone directory.

The computer has become a major tool in almost every aspect of graphic communications, from the creative and prepress areas through all phases of production and business operations. In addition to software for estimating, accounting, billing, and purchasing, programs have been developed to simplify personnel and equipment scheduling and more efficient equipment operation, **Figure 24-5.** Some systems use computer terminals at various workstations to gather information that can be used for more accurate cost calculations. Precise information on costs allows more closely calculated estimates, which may provide a competitive advantage for a printer. Better cost control can also improve a company's profitability.

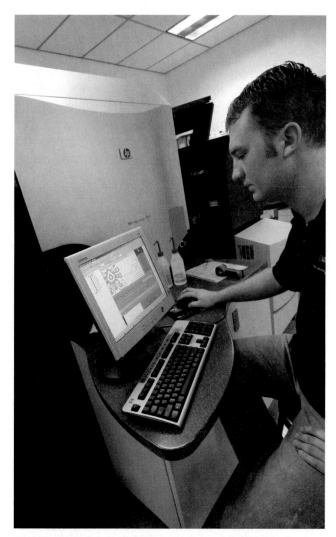

Figure 24-5. The computer station on this digital printing system functions as a print server with available image enhancement packages. (GIT, Arizona State University)

Job Estimates

After a job is completed, it is a fairly simple matter to accurately calculate the costs involved in producing it. It then would be easy to determine a price for the job that covers costs and provides a fair profit. However, customers want to know in advance what they are going to pay for their order. This is where a printing estimate comes in. A *printing estimate* is an offer to print a particular job for a specified price. If the customer accepts the estimate, it becomes a contract that is binding for both the printer and customer.

Developing an estimate can be very simple or extremely complicated, depending on the circumstances. At the simple end are jobs performed day-in and day-out by small shops and quick printers. These jobs are usually handled with a fixed price schedule rather than an actual estimate and are typically priced in units, such as 100 or 500 sheets. A base price for printing is established and additional charges are applied for variables, such as

profit: The difference between sales income and business expenses.

materials cost: The prices paid for items that are consumed as a job is printed, such as paper, ink, and packaging materials.

labor cost: The "people costs" involved in operating a business, including hourly wages, salaries, and benefits for employees.

fixed cost: Business expenses that remain consistent, regardless of the volume of work in the shop.

printing estimate: An offer to print a particular job for a specified price. If the customer accepts the estimate, it becomes a contract that is binding for both the printer and customer.

a different paper stock or color ink. Finishing steps, such as folding or tabbing, are also listed on a price schedule.

More complicated jobs require custom-developed estimates that meet specifications provided by the customer. A custom estimate requires careful calculation of every aspect of the project, from paper cost and availability to operating cost of each piece of equipment, percent of spoilage, and final packaging and delivery.

Preparing an accurate estimate requires a precise knowledge of costs. Many successful firms have developed detailed breakdowns of their operations, which created a data base of information for use in developing estimates. Using these breakdowns, a company can determine exactly how much per hour it costs to operate a specific piece of equipment, **Figure 24-6,** or how many worker hours must be allotted to carry out a particular operation. The hourly cost rates developed using this method include a portion of the company's overhead (fixed cost), as well as labor costs. Cost of materials is determined separately because it varies from one job to another. An estimate is developed using hourly cost rates and the specific materials cost for the job.

Many printing firms, especially smaller companies or those performing various types of printing operations, relied on pricing guides that provided average costs for virtually every type of prepress, printing, and finishing operation. Following instructions provided in guides such as the *Franklin Offset Catalog*, an estimate could be developed fairly quickly. Although pricing guides are still in use, they have been replaced in many plants by specialized estimating software used with computers, **Figure 24-7.** There are a number of different estimating programs on the market, but most operate in a similar manner. An estimator enters the specifics of a job, such as size, quantity, paper to be used, and equipment required. The software then calculates an estimate based on cost data and presents it for review.

Some estimating software is designed for use on standalone desktop computers, while other programs are intended for larger operations where a number of different sites are linked by telephone lines or even satellite systems. Some estimating programs allow outside sales personnel with laptop computers to prepare an estimate right at the customer's office or plant. Information is exchanged with the printing company's computer through a wired modem or wireless connection, allowing confirmation of prices, scheduling, and material availability.

Figure 24-6. Accurate printing estimates depend upon precise costing information. The hourly cost of operating equipment is a combination of labor costs and overhead. (GIT, Arizona State University)

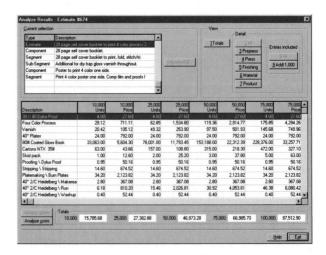

Figure 24-7. Estimating software can simplify the process of preparing a printing estimate. This summary screen provides the estimator with pricing for various quantities of a job. With software such as this, information can be viewed many different ways before preparing and printing an estimate. (Hagen Systems, Inc.)

Organizing Work

Productivity is the amount of quality work completed in a given time span, and is a key word in a printing plant. Efficiency (maximum output with minimum effort) and utilization (maximum use of people and equipment) are two factors that contribute to productivity. To achieve high productivity, good communication is essential.

To track printing jobs as they move through the plant and provide job-specific information to all departments, some type of job ticket is typically used, **Figure 24-8.** Job tickets are generally designed to meet the specific needs of a company or area within a company. Job tickets often take the form of a jacket or pouch that hold loose papers, such as purchase orders or other forms relating to the job.

The information that appears on a job ticket is necessary job specifications for various workers and departments. For example, the stock and ink required for the job is important information for

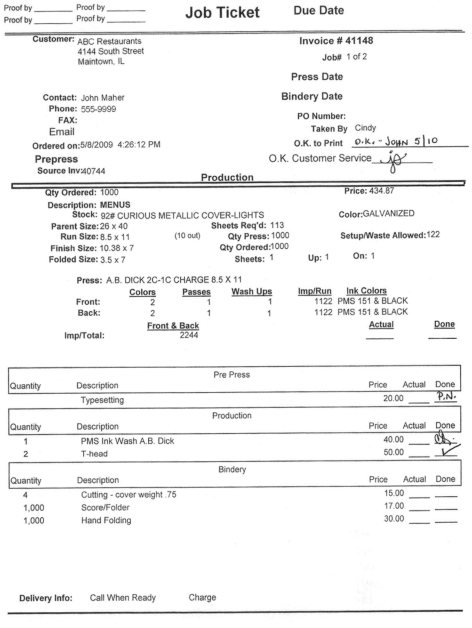

Figure 24-8. A job ticket holds specifications and details about printing jobs that are useful to all departments involved in completing the order.

productivity: The amount of quality work that is completed in a given time span.

both the purchasing department and press room, and the finishing information applies to the bindery department. In addition to job specs, a job ticket records the customer contact and billing information, proof or approval details, and job delivery information. With computer programs, it is possible to trace a job throughout the plant or off-site location any time a client requests job status information.

Matching the Job to the Equipment

To ensure efficient and profitable printing operations, each job should be matched with the most appropriate equipment available. Using a piece of equipment that is not particularly suited for a job can cause delays, increase waste, and cut profit margins. One common choice printers face today is whether to print a job using conventional means or electronic (digital) methods. There is frequently no clear indication of when it is better to use conventional printing or digital printing. Speed, quality, and economics are some determining factors. Run length, page count, and bindery processes are also considerations in determining the optimum equipment.

Run length and page count are primary factors in choosing between conventional printing and digital printing. The per-page cost typically remains constant as volume increases with digital printing. Using conventional printing, however, per-page cost decreases with higher page counts and longer run lengths, **Figure 24-9.** For each printing process, a point of optimum return can be determined. With experience, users learn to optimize job requirements and printing method.

Most digital systems have integrated sorting with limited in-line binding. If the desired result is complete units, then the run length and page count become critical aspects in determining the reprographic method. Conventional printing allows more variability and customization in the manufacturing process. Digital systems, on the other hand, can produce short-run, fully completed products, if product specifications conform to the options available. Additionally, a digital system operator can simultaneously run more than one printer, which increases the production volume. Conventional printing typically requires at least one dedicated operator for each press. In some shops, however, it is not uncommon for one person to operate two small offset presses at the same time.

First-copy time favors the digital printer because makeready costs do not apply. However,

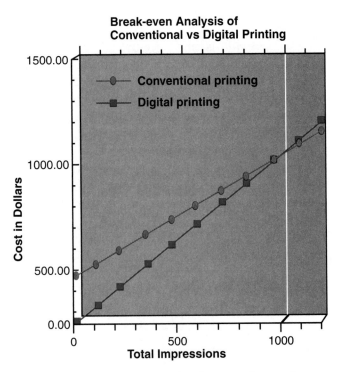

Figure 24-9. Digital color technology can be used cost effectively for short runs, although conventional printing clearly has advantages for longer runs.

the makeready costs with conventional printing are changing favorably due to technological advancements. High-volume electronic printers have an interrupt feature that requires minimum time and effort to produce another job, even if a different paper is involved. In the same situation, conventional printing presses require considerable downtime to allow the operator to put the job plate back on the press, change inks, get the ink levels correct, register the image, and anywhere from three to several hundred sheets of paper before the first good copy is achieved.

Plates are an element of traditional printing that introduces variable costs for material, labor, and time. Because digital printers do not require a platemaking step to produce copies, they have a decisive cost advantage. Once running, though, printing ink and chemistry will cost much less than the fuser and toner used in the digital press. Printing presses cost considerably more to get the first copy, but each additional copy has a much lower unit cost than the copier.

Digital printers have no makeready cost: the first copy produced is the same as the second and the last copies. Thus, the break-even point is when the cost of total copies made on the digital press equals the makeready cost on the printing press plus the lower cost per copy volume.

Career Link

Customer Service Representative

A customer service representative (CSR) in the printing industry is the first, and often only, line of contact customers have with the company. To provide the best customer service possible and build professional relationships with clients, CSRs must have thorough knowledge of the printing plant operations, the computer system for order entry and tracking, and the specifications and needs of each job.

CSRs act as a liaison between the customer and other shop personnel by accurately communicating the customer's requirements, tracking the progress of jobs through the shop, and making the best use of the shop's resources and schedules. In handling orders and customer requests, a CSR may need to calculate figures, such as proportions, discounts, percentages, area and volume, analyze and interpret technical procedures, and create written and oral reports. In smaller operations, the CSR may also have responsibilities related to sales activities.

The minimum educational requirement for a CSR position is an associate's degree from a two year college or technical school, however, many CSR positions require a bachelor's degree from a college or university. Depending on the position available, a combination of education and experience may also be given consideration.

"Print has an unequalled history of strength and believability. It has the power to shape ideas and influences action. It is important to note in today's world of sound bites of fleeting impressions, print lasts."

Michael Makin
Printing Industries of America

Multiple-page documents require added consideration to be given to the type of binding necessary and the corresponding equipment. Usually, bindery operations for conventionally printed sheets are done off-line. Some electronic printers can saddle stitch work on-line; others require an off-line operation. The key considerations are run length and page count.

TRADE CUSTOMS

It would be time-consuming and inefficient to write a contract that covers all aspects of each new print job. In the printing industry, trade customs are used rather than formal, individual contracts. *Trade customs* are understood rules or implied laws used in the printing industry that have been validated by courts as binding agreements. At times, specific contracts are issued when additional or special terms are desired, however.

The National Association of Printers and Leadership (NAPL) issued guidelines for the use of trade customs. These state that the printer should:

- Print trade customs on the back of estimates and other order acknowledgments.

- State that all work is subject to trade customs on the order acknowledgment.
- Make sure that customized terms and conditions are enforced in the same manner as trade customs.
- Ensure that salespersons are knowledgeable about trade customs and how they protect the printer.

For years, the industry followed a document that was called Trade Customs of the Printing Industries of North America, **Figure 24-10**. It was considered the guide to transactions such as Terms and Conditions of Sale. The technology has changed dramatically, making the document obsolete in many areas and not informative in others. The new publication, the Best Business Practices for the Printing Industry, is intended to fill that void.

trade customs: Understood rules or implied laws used in the printing industry that have been validated by courts as binding agreements.

Terms and Conditions of Sale

1. **Quotation.** A quotation not accepted within 30 days may be changed.

2. **Orders.** Acceptance of orders is subject to credit approval and contingencies such as fire, water, strikes, theft, vandalism, acts of God, and other causes beyond the provider's control. Canceled orders require compensation for incurred costs and related obligations.

3. **Experimental Work.** Experimental or preliminary work performed at customer's request will be charged to the customer at the provider's current rates. This work cannot be used without the provider's written consent.

4. **Creative Work.** Sketches, copy, dummies and all other creative work developed or furnished by the provider are the provider's exclusive property. The provider must give written approval for all use of this work and for any derivation of ideas from it.

5. **Accuracy of Specifications.** Quotations are based on the accuracy of the specifications provided. The provider can re-quote a job at time of submission if copy, film, tapes, disks, or other input materials don't conform to the information on which the original quotation was based.

6. **Preparatory Materials.** Art work, type, plates, negatives, positives, tapes, disks, and all other items supplied by the provider remain the provider's exclusive property.

7. **Electronic Manuscript or Image.** It is the customer's responsibility to maintain a copy of the original file. The provider is not responsible for accidental damage to media supplied by the customer or for the accuracy of furnished input or final output. Until digital input can be evaluated by the provider, no claims or promises are made about the provider's ability to work with jobs submitted in digital format, and no liability is assumed for problems that may arise. Any additional translating, editing, or programming needed to utilize customer-supplied files will be charged at prevailing rates.

8. **Alterations/Corrections.** Customer alterations include all work performed in addition to the original specifications. All such work will be charged at the provider's current rates.

9. **Prepress Proofs.** The provider will submit prepress proofs for the customer's review and approval. Approval form will be returned to the provider marked "O.K.," "O.K. with corrections," or "Revised proof required" and signed by the customer. Until approval is received, no additional work will be performed. The provider will not be responsible for undetected production errors if:
- proofs are not required by the customer.
- the work is printed per the customer's O.K.
- requests for changes are communicated orally.

10. **Press Proofs.** A press sheet may be submitted for the customer's approval. Any press time lost or alterations/corrections made because of the customer's delay or change of mind will be charged at the provider's current rates.

11. **Color Proofing.** Because of differences in equipment, paper, inks, and other conditions between color proofing and production press-room operations, a reasonable variation in color between color proofs and the completed job is to be expected. When variation of this kind occurs, it will be considered acceptable performance.

12. **Over-runs or Under-runs.** Over-runs or under-runs will not exceed 10% of the quantity ordered. The provider will bill for actual quantity delivered within this tolerance. If the customer requires a guaranteed quantity, the percentage of tolerance must be stated at the time of quotation.

13. **Customer's Property.** The provider will only maintain fire and extended coverage on property belonging to the customer while the property is in the provider's possession. The provider's liability for this property will not exceed the amount recoverable from the insurance. Additional insurance coverage may be obtained if it is requested in writing, and if the premium is paid to the provider.

14. **Delivery.** Unless otherwise specified, the price quoted is for a single shipment, without storage, F.O.B. provider's platform. Proposals are based on continuous and uninterrupted delivery of the complete order. If the specifications state otherwise, the provider will charge accordingly at current rates. Charges for delivery of materials and supplies from the customer to the provider, or from the customer's supplier to the provider, are not included in quotations unless specified. Title for finished work passes to the customer upon delivery to the carrier at shipping point; or upon mailing of invoices for the finished work of its segments, whichever occurs first.

15. **Production Schedules.** Production schedules will be established and followed by both the customer and the provider. In the event that production schedules are not adhered to by the customer, delivery dates will be subject to renegotiation. There will be no liability or penalty for delays due to state of war, riot, civil disorder, fire, strikes, accidents, action of government or civil authority, acts of God, or other causes beyond the control of the provider. In such cases, schedules will be extended by an amount of time equal to delay incurred.

16. **Customer-Furnished Materials.** Materials furnished by customers or their suppliers are verified by delivery tickets. The provider bears no responsibility for discrepancies between delivery tickets and actual counts. Customer-supplied paper must be delivered according to specifications furnished by the provider. These specifications will include correct weight, thickness, pick resistance, and other technical requirements. Artwork, film, color separations, special dies, tapes, disks, or other materials furnished by the customer must be usable by the provider without alteration or repair. Items not meeting this requirement will be repaired by the customer, or by the provider at the provider's current rates.

17. **Outside Purchases.** Unless otherwise agreed in writing, all outside purchases as requested or authorized by the customer, are chargeable.

Figure 24-10. The Terms and Conditions of Sale section of the Best Business Practices for the Printing Industry address common printing trade business customs. (Printing Industries of America)

STANDARDS AND SPECIFICATIONS

Under certain circumstances, such as producing work for government agencies, printers may be required to conform to certain standards set by organizations such as ISO or ANSI. In other situations, customers may require the printer to meet specifications set by the company or by specialized organizations. Such specifications as SWOP®, GRACoL®, G7, and DISC are set by IDEAlliance.

International Organization for Standardization (ISO)

The International Organization for Standardization (ISO) is a nongovernmental, worldwide organization of national standards bodies. It covers all fields except electrical and electronic engineering standards, which are covered by another organization. ISO coordinates the exchange of information on international and national standards and publishes its technical work in the form of international standards. The ISO technical committee for graphic technology is TC 130.

American National Standards Institute (ANSI)

The American National Standards Institute is an impartial organization that validates work conducted by organizations accredited as standards development groups. Standards are considered to be voluntary, not mandated. Each standard is identified with the letters ANSI and a number.

Committee for Graphic Arts Technologies Standards (CGATS)

The Committee for Graphic Arts Technologies Standards (CGATS) is accredited by ANSI. The goal of CGATS is to have the entire scope of printing and publishing recognized as the national standards group, and intends to coordinate the efforts of other bodies.

NAICS Code

The North American Industry Classification System (NAICS) provides codes to classify businesses in order to collect and report statistical data, **Figure 24-11.** This information is used to compare data within each industry and among participating regions: United States, Canada, and Mexico. The

NAICS Printing Industry Codes	
NAICS Code	**Printing Operation Type**
323	Printing and Related Activities
3231	Printing and Related Activities
32311	Printing
323110	Commercial Lithographic Printing
323111	Commercial Gravure Printing
323112	Commercial Flexographic Printing
323113	Commercial Screen Printing
323114	Quick Printing
323115	Digital Printing
323116	Manifold Business Forms
323117	Book Printing
323118	Blankbooks, Loose-leaf Binder, and Device Manufacturing
323119	Other Commercial Printing
32312	Support Activities for Printing
323121	Trade Binding and Related Work
323122	Prepress Services

Figure 24-11. NAICS codes and printing industry-related categories.

first two digits in the NAICS code designate industry sectors, the third digit represents the subsector, the fourth represents the industry group level, the fifth digit identifies the international industry level, and the sixth digit designates the national detail.

COPYRIGHT LAWS

A *copyright* provides legal protection against unauthorized reproduction of literary works (books and other printed materials), musical compositions and recordings, artworks, photographs, film and video works, and dramatic works. Copyright gives authors, artists, and other copyright owners the opportunity to exclusively profit from their creations for a stated period. It protects against financial loss resulting from the sale of their work by someone who has not paid a fee to them. In the U.S., a copyright lasts for the life of the author or creator, plus 70 years after his or her death.

In graphic communications or printing, copyrights primarily address printed materials. A textbook like this one, for example, usually has copyright information on the page immediately following the title page. Smaller printed pieces, such as booklets, might have a copyright notice on the first page or inside the front cover. Single page items, such as posters, usually have a copyright notice on the front side. There are a number of forms that the copyright notice can take, but it should include the word "copyright," the abbreviation "copr.," or the symbol ©. A copyright notice should also include the name of the copyright owner and the year first published, **Figure 24-12.**

© **Jones Publishing 1999**

Copyright Jones Publishing 1999

Copr. Jones Publishing

© **JP**

Copr. JP 1999

Figure 24-12. There are a number of ways that a copyright notice can be presented.

When a customer brings in materials and asks the printer or copy service to reproduce it, there is a risk of violating copyright law. If the item bears a copyright notice, the customer must produce written evidence of permission from the copyright holder to reproduce the material. It might be wise to have customers sign a release form that protects the printer from liability for *infringement*. Being convicted of copyright infringement can cost thousands of dollars in fines and damages payable to the copyright holder.

Factors commonly used by the courts to determine and remedy copyright infringement include:

- How the material was used.
- The type of work copied.
- The amount of the material copied.
- The impact on the monetary and market value of the original copyrighted material.

There are exceptions to the law that allow some duplication of copyrighted materials without infringement. These exceptions are known as the *fair use* provisions of the law. The most common example of fair use is in education. Materials may be copied and used in the classroom for direct teacher-to-student educational purposes only. This means that an instructor may copy a reasonable portion of a copyrighted work (such as a magazine article or book chapter) for classroom use by students. Additionally, students may copy material and use it in a classroom presentation or discussion. If the copyrighted material is to be used outside of the classroom, however, the appropriate permissions *must* be secured.

Summary

The graphic communications industry has a tremendous impact on our society. A printing business relies on its operation, as well as the government, education, and everyday life. Society would not be the same without the printing business. Understanding the basic components of running a business helps employees know why certain operations and actions are essential to be successful.

Review Questions

Please do not write in this text. Write your answers on a separate sheet of paper.

1. Identify five business and personnel practices that are effective in growing a successful business.
2. Explain the purpose of a business plan.
3. Describe the characteristics of a corporation

business type.

4. What are some examples of expenses that are categorized as *materials costs*?

5. Which business expenses are included when calculating hourly cost rates?

6. _____ is the amount of quality work completed in a given time span.

7. How are job tickets used within a printing company?

8. The two primary factors in deciding if a job should be produced using conventional printing or digital printing are _____ and _____.

9. What is the ISO technical committee for graphic technology?

10. Explain the purpose of NAICS codes.

11. How long is a copyright in effect in the U.S.?

12. Describe the *fair use* provisions of the copyright laws.

Suggested Activities

1. Since digital printing has made great strides within the printing industry, identify the products that are commonly printed by the digital process. Before digital printing, what printing process was used to produce these products?

2. What are the benefits of incorporating national specifications in printing operations?

3. Visit the NAICS section of the U.S. Bureau of Labor Statistics Web site. Research the number of printing establishments in your state and note the number of employees in each category.

Related Web Links

U.S. Census Bureau–North American Industry Classification System (NAICS)

www.census.gov/eos/www/naics
NAICS section of the U.S. Census Bureau's Web site. Contains the most current NAICS reference information.

United States Copyright Office

www.copyright.gov
Web site of the U.S. Copyright Office. Contains copyright information, laws, application forms, a searchable database, and many other tools and resources.

Keep America Beautiful

www.kap.org
Organization offering resources for learning about sustainability with information on individual contribution.

copyright: A legal protection against unauthorized copying of original, creative works.

infringement: The unauthorized use of copyrighted material.

fair use: Certain exceptions to U.S. Copyright Laws that allow duplication and use of copyrighted materials without infringement.

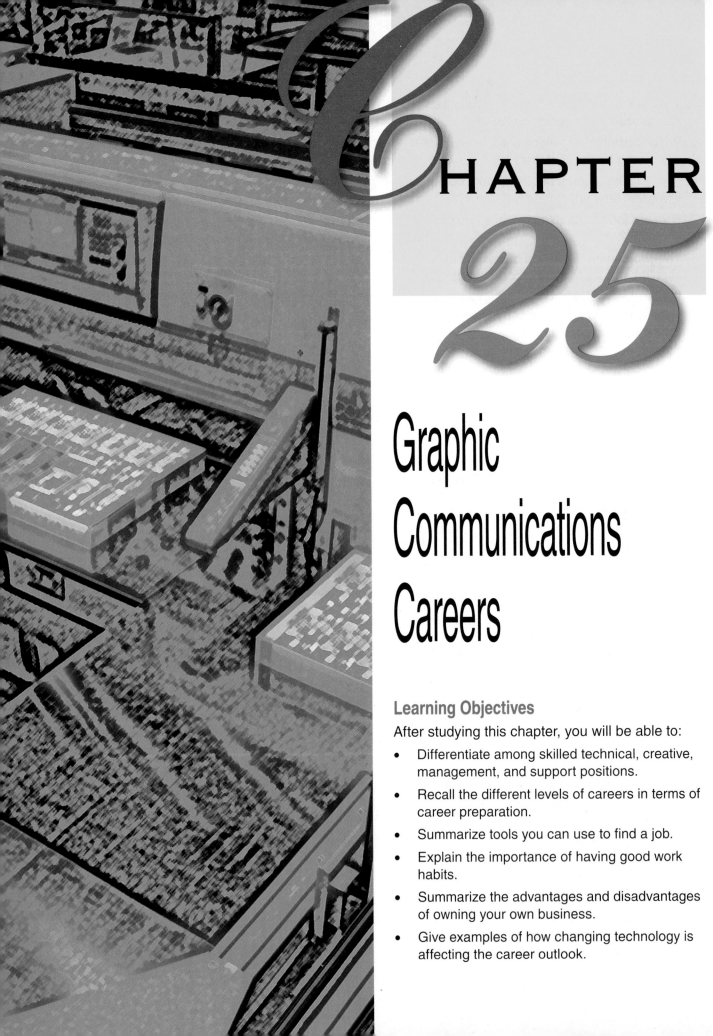

CHAPTER 25

Graphic Communications Careers

Learning Objectives

After studying this chapter, you will be able to:

- Differentiate among skilled technical, creative, management, and support positions.

- Recall the different levels of careers in terms of career preparation.

- Summarize tools you can use to find a job.

- Explain the importance of having good work habits.

- Summarize the advantages and disadvantages of owning your own business.

- Give examples of how changing technology is affecting the career outlook.

Important Terms

apprenticeship
career
craft-centered jobs
electronic information
    transfer
entrepreneur

lifelong learning
manager
outsourcing
robotics
turnaround
work ethic

The graphic communications industry encompasses a multitude of challenging *careers* for skilled technical, creative, management, and support personnel. Educators, engineers, and scientists can also find positions in the graphic communications industry. Entrepreneurship is yet another avenue open to someone who wants to own and operate a company. This chapter will summarize and help you more fully understand these positions.

CAREERS IN THE GRAPHIC COMMUNICATIONS INDUSTRY

The graphic communications industry needs people with many different interests, talents, and abilities. The workforce can be organized into six general categories:

- Skilled technical positions include those who can operate sophisticated machinery and carry out tasks that directly involve machines, materials, and products.
- Creative positions include those who have skills in writing, art, and design.
- Management positions include those who like to work with people and can supervise the work of others.
- Support positions include people who are the link between products and customers.
- Engineers and scientists are people whose jobs focus on research.
- Educators are people who teach students to prepare them for careers in the graphic communications industry.
- Service operation positions are available to those who want to work for a company that provides a specific service to other printing companies.

Skilled Technical Positions

Skilled technical workers are involved in the prepress and press stages of production. Changes in technology have brought about changes in these career positions. Many formerly *craft-centered jobs* that were traditionally performed by artisans or others with manual skills, now require specialized technical skills.

Prepress Imaging Specialist

Technological changes have and continue to change in the prepress area. Most of the prepress work is accomplished by using electronic devices and software. Preflighting of customer materials is one of the first activities commonly preformed in the prepress area. Image manipulation is accomplished to produce the desired results. Some of the tasks performed by personnel in the department include scanning images into digital format, creating digital artwork, and checking and fitting files. Working closely with customers is also imperative.

Pressroom Personnel

No matter what printing process is involved, pressroom workers are responsible for the quality of the final printed product, **Figure 25-1.** The efforts of

Figure 25-1. Press operators are checking a run of a printed product. (USA Today)

career: A position you train for and seek employment for your life's work.

craft-centered jobs: Refers to work performed by artisans or others with manual skills.

many individuals are needed to transfer the image from an image carrier to a substrate. The number of people involved depends on the type and size of the press. Some presses are small and simple to operate, but many are complex and require extensive technical knowledge.

Controlling ink, solutions, and paper are basic activities of pressroom workers. Quality control is imperative. Knowledge of paper, ink, and press operations is essential. Mechanical aptitude is a desirable quality.

Activities performed by lithographic press operators include positioning plates, filling the ink fountain, loading stock; controlling ink flow, fountain solution, and press speed; and inspecting finished sheets, **Figure 25-2.**

The web lithographic press operator must set up a press using huge rolls of paper, rather than sheets of stock, **Figure 25-3.** Press size and complexity varies. Newspaper and other large presses print on both sides of the stock, fold, and deliver a finished product with great speed. Press assistants working under experienced press operators are common on many of the large presses.

The letterpress operator runs a smaller press. Common job-shop printing includes letterheads, forms, cards, and envelopes. Today, these presses are used primarily for finishing operations, such as die cutting and numbering.

The gravure press operator runs a press at very high speeds and usually has a crew assigned to specific responsibilities. See **Figure 25-4.**

Screen presses have a configuration uncommon to the other processes. The screen press operator must set up the press to print on a variety of materials. Knowledge of inks, screens, and image carriers is essential.

Figure 25-3. The operator of this web offset book printing press is responsible for maintaining quality on very long runs. (Strachan Henshaw Machinery, Inc.)

Figure 25-4. This technician is operating a gravure cylinder engraving machine. The finished cylinders will be transported to the pressroom. (Linotype-Hell)

Figure 25-2. Press operators must set up, run, and maintain complex printing presses. Mechanical aptitude and knowledge of ink, paper, and solutions are important.

Bindery and Finishing Personnel

Accuracy and mechanical aptitude are required of bindery and finishing personnel. Physical strength is sometimes necessary. Workers use sophisticated equipment to cut stock to size for the press or once it has been printed, **Figure 25-5.** Machine operators must have knowledge of slitting, perforating, and folding techniques. Gathering and collating operations require machine operators and setup personnel who can do accurate work. Skills in die cutting, embossing, foil stamping, and printing are also utilized.

Creative Positions

Creative people are needed in many roles within the graphic communications industry. Talented designers, editors, illustrators, writers, and photographers conceptualize and create products that go to print.

Writer

As the name implies, the writer generates any copy to be printed. Creative writing talent and thorough knowledge of the language is imperative. A willingness to write on a wide variety of topics is usually needed. Many times the writer is not employed by the printer, but by an agency or other business firm.

Graphic Designers

Graphic designers are artists who are responsible for planning printed pieces. Creative talent is imperative. Expressing an idea visually is the primary role of a graphic designer. An appreciation for beauty and an eye for composition and color are essential traits. These traits may be natural in an individual or developed through training and experience, **Figure 25-6.**

The computer has nearly replaced the traditional cut-and-paste method of production. Desktop systems are utilized at nearly every workstation. Familiarity with design programs is a standard job requirement, with small variations in software proficiency. Working knowledge of several of the common drawing, image editing, and page layout programs is expected. See **Figure 25-7.**

Despite the advances in computer technology, traditional artistic composition and design skills remain important. Some graphic designers design exclusively on the computer, while others may use both the computer and hand drawing or painting. The future trend in hiring will focus on creative talent.

Figure 25-5. Bindery and finishing personnel must operate and maintain various types of complex equipment.

Figure 25-6. Artists must understand color theory and be able to visualize a concept.

Figure 25-7. Graphic artists use computers to design and lay out text and images for print.

Figure 25-8. Managers are part of a team. They must be able to plan, organize, and direct activities.

Editor

The editor prepares the written material and illustrations for publication by revising and rewriting copy and checking it for accuracy. Copy editing entails sequencing content, marking the copy for style, and ensuring consistency throughout the manuscript. A command of the language is essential. Sometimes technical expertise is also needed.

Publishers of books, magazines, and newspapers employ editors. Freelance editorial work is also possible for those who prefer self-employment.

Photographer

A photographer may be called on to take high-quality photographic illustrations for a publication. The photographer must create the image based on the customer's stated objective and parameters. A working knowledge of traditional and digital camera equipment and photographic techniques is expected.

Many photographers work independently, while others are employed by newspaper and magazine publishers. Advertising and public relations agencies also employ photographers.

Management Positions

Managers direct a team of workers who affect the entire organization. Part of being a good manager is being able to get work done through other people. It also requires excellent organizational abilities. See **Figure 25-8.**

Management must work in a team with other employees to accomplish the objectives of the company. Communication, cooperation, and understanding between departments are the ingredients for a productive, innovative workforce. Managers are responsible for ensuring a job gets done right and on time.

Management-level employees in a graphic communications facility typically include executive officers, plant managers, plant superintendents, managing editors, production managers and schedulers, controllers, sales managers, supervisors, estimators, and planners.

Characteristics important to being an effective member of the management team include being able to:

- Make logical decisions.
- Get work done through others.
- Communicate well with others.
- Motivate personnel.
- Apply factual information and not opinions.
- Act maturely and fairly.

The management team must be concerned with the following aspects of the business:

- Increased specialization of production equipment.
- High investment requirements for new equipment.
- Rising costs of materials and energy.
- Shortages or lead times for critical materials.
- Rapid introduction of new technology.
- High interest rates for capital equipment purchases and short-term borrowing.
- Excess production capacity.
- Slow real growth in market areas.
- Threat of increased international competition.
- Government regulations affecting manpower, fiscal and manufacturing operations, and environmental compliance.

Typically, management personnel have several responsibilities in different areas. At times, the executive officer can be the chief financial officer and also have responsibilities for sales. Such a mix of duties is common to the graphic communications industry.

Chief Executive Officer

The president or chief executive officer (CEO) of a company is the top administrator. He or she is the policymaker and overseer of the total operation. The president is interested in employing skilled and reliable personnel to contribute to the effective and efficient operation of the company.

Controller

The controller is responsible for the financial operation of a company. He or she ensures the company operates by sound methods and practices. Contact with financial institutions, as well as preparing budgets, forecasts, analyses, reports, and statements are functions of this position. An aptitude for mathematics and a thorough knowledge of accounting practices are essential. See **Figure 25-9.**

Figure 25-9. Controllers are responsible for all financial aspects of a company. They must have an aptitude for mathematics and a knowledge of accounting practices.

EDP Supervisor

The EDP supervisor is in charge of all the electronic data processing (EDP) functions in the plant. Knowledge of computer programming and applications is essential.

Estimator

The estimator calculates the costs used to bid or price a job. Understanding all plant operations is essential. Accurate calculations are required, since the figures will reflect the technical capabilities of the various operations as well as the cost of materials. Business and technical experience is needed.

Plant Manager

The plant manager is responsible for the plant's manufacturing operations. Products must be produced on time, at the lowest possible cost, at a level of quality acceptable to the customer. Another critical concern to the plant manager is the safety and health of all employees. The ability to analyze results and understand people is important.

Plant Superintendent

The plant superintendent directs all manufacturing operations of the company as well as first-line supervisors. The plant superintendent makes sure all equipment is working efficiently and kept in good condition. The position is high-pressure and requires patience and direct control.

Production Manager

The production manager is a liaison between sales and production personnel. The production manager is in charge of cost estimates, job entry, job planning, and scheduling. Keeping accurate records and getting along with others is essential.

Production Scheduler

The production scheduler sets up timetables for all jobs in an efficient and effective manner. After the job is in production, each phase must be recorded so the product can be traced at any phase of production. Being able to plan and understand the capabilities of equipment and personnel is important. The application of computer technology to production scheduling must be understood.

manager: A leadership position whose responsibility it is to manage a company, business, or part of a business.

Quality Control Supervisor

The quality control supervisor sets standards for production and finished products, **Figure 25-10.** The job requires constant sampling to ensure consistent quality and to reduce waste or spoilage. Knowledge of control devices as a means to measure quality is basic to the position.

Sales Manager

The sales manager is responsible for establishing a profitable sales staff. Among the manager's responsibilities are supervising sales activities, customer relations, and budgeting; setting sales quotas and profit margins; and overseeing sales service. The sales manager must have a good aptitude for business and leave a favorable impression on people.

Support Personnel

Support personnel reinforce the work of the technical, creative, and managerial departments through two main channels: customer service and sales and marketing. These employees are the important link between products and customers.

Customer Service Representative

A customer service representative is the liaison between customers, management, and the sales force. Knowledge of job schedules and job progress is essential. Understanding the operation of the firm is also imperative. Good interpersonal skills, particularly on the telephone, are necessary to the position.

Sales Representative

A sales representative position requires basic sales techniques, but it also requires a knowledge of printing processes. In a way, a sales representative is a trusted advisor to the customer. The representative must be able to provide the greatest product or service for the customer's investment. Meeting and being accepted by people is a prime requisite for the position. Being ambitious, highly organized, and able to project a professional image are contributors to success. See **Figure 25-11.**

Marketing Coordinator

The fundamental objective of any company is to market its products or services profitably. Personnel with positions in marketing, advertising, and public relations are responsible for promotional activities, including identifying potential customers. In a small firm, a single marketing coordinator may handle all these activities. The marketing and sales departments often work together closely. Both managerial- and support-level positions are available in marketing.

Figure 25-11. Sales representatives must understand processes and be able to work with customers. (Heidelberg, Inc.)

Figure 25-10. The quality control supervisor ensures that every aspect of production is within specifications.

THINK GREEN
Environmental Consultant

As a result of the growing concerns over environmental issues, the printing industry has become dedicated to becoming more green. Before becoming more environmentally compliant, a company must first be educated about the issues, as well as discovering how that specific company impacts the environment. Following this, a plan must be established to address how to reduce the company's impact. Frequently, an outside individual or company is hired to help start the process. It is the job of an environmental consultant to instruct and help companies plan on how to reduce their environmental impact. It is then up to the companies to implement the plan and work toward helping the environment. For a printer, an environmental consultant would take into account the energy expended to run a printer, the amount and type of paper used, and even the energy used to light the space. For more information, see www.beagreenirene.com.

Preflight Technician

The preflight technician is a person who works with computers and software applications. This person is a troubleshooter. When a computer file arrives, the preflight technician goes over the file and identifies problems within the file that could prevent the job from printing successfully.

Color Specialist

The color specialist works closely with the printer and the customer. If the customer indicates that "the green is not green enough," the color specialist checks the copy and informs the printer what changes need to be made to produce a job acceptable to the customer. A thorough knowledge of color theory as it relates to printing processes is essential.

Engineers and Scientists

Engineers and scientists are able to find positions in research and development in the graphic communications industry. Engineers are needed to improve industrial

processes, **Figure 25-12.** Positions are often product-oriented and exist to provide quality control.

Scientists, particularly those with a strong background in chemistry, are also hired as researchers. They may experiment with and test equipment, inks, and printing paper. The paper and pulp industry, in particular, conducts much of its own research.

With the ever-increasing focus on environmental issues, environmental engineers and scientists are being hired by industry to ensure compliance standards are met, **Figure 25-13.**

Positions for engineering and science technicians are also available. Often, four or five technicians are hired to support the activities of a single scientist or engineer.

Educator

Educators have the responsibility of preparing capable people for careers in the graphic communications industry. An effective educator must have an in-depth knowledge of the industry, have a strong desire to work with young people, and be a strong communicator.

Positions with Service Operations

Printing is a cooperative enterprise. One component depends on another. Since most firms do not have an integrated facility, *outsourcing* to

Figure 25-12. Engineers in industrial settings work to improve processes and products. (Martin Marietta Corp.)

outsourcing: Sending a product to a service company for specified work needed to complete a product.

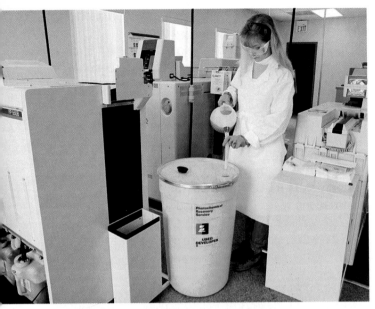

Figure 25-13. Stringent federal, state, and local waste-reclamation standards have created a need for waste management professionals with a background in science. (Safety-Kleen)

service companies is essential for the completion of a product. Positions supporting the printing process are available in all service operations.

Agency or Studio

An agency or studio is a type of service operation. It helps a larger company with advertising, packaging, and producing printed or media-oriented materials. Many graphic communications positions are available in agencies.

Bindery and Finishing Services

Specialized bindery and finishing operations are often beyond the capability of a printing facility. The operations are subcontracted to a company that has equipment capable of rapidly folding, trimming, and packaging printed products.

Typographic Service

Typographic service facilities design, lay out, compose, assemble, and output on a variety of materials using electronic means. Computer oriented imaging operations have become very sophisticated as a result of the technological advances in the industry.

Vendors

The graphic communications industry depends on many types of machines and materials. Suppliers provide opportunities for the plant owner to buy

equipment, but from time to time the equipment needs to be serviced. Someone must also supply inks, solutions, and paper.

Jobs exist for people to sell and service products used by the graphic communications industry, **Figure 25-14.** Ink manufacturers, for example, supply a great service to the industry. Chemists have the important job of formulating ink so it is compatible with the press, substrate, and various other requirements of the process.

Quick Printing and Copy Services

The role of quick printing and copy services is to provide printing services quickly, with different levels of quality. The level of technical knowledge and skills needed depends on the job. Some operators have more manual skills, while others are highly skilled technicians operating sophisticated systems.

Positions in quick printing require employees to be versatile. They may be responsible for managing others, selling services, estimating job costs, or operating equipment. Job requirements vary with the owner or franchise, and should be made clear to prospective employees. See **Figure 25-15.**

Screen Process Service

Screen printing drives the need for specialty-type printing facilities and workers with a wide variety of skills. Typical screen applications include sign printing, fabric imaging, printing on vinyl, and the manufacture of printed electronic circuit boards and components. See **Figure 25-16.**

Figure 25-14. Manufacturing provides the materials and machinery that equip graphic communications plants. (basysPrint Corporation)

Figure 25-15. Service companies include advertising agencies, quick printing shops, specialty printers, and composing services. These smaller companies do work for larger companies or individuals. (National Association of Quick Printers, Inc.)

Figure 25-16. Screen process services fill a niche for such specialty products as T-shirts with images.

Specialty Printing Service

Specialty printing shops do not have a wide market but provide a service for specialized products. These shops do engraving, label-making, and similar types of printing. Engraving, for example, is needed for producing high-quality business cards, stationery, and invitations.

PREPARING FOR A CAREER IN THE GRAPHIC COMMUNICATIONS INDUSTRY

Choosing a career is one of the most important decisions you will ever make. It can affect many aspects of your life, including level of education, income potential, working conditions, and types of coworkers. A career choice can also affect your family. It determines your geographic location, the number of hours spent on the job, possibilities for advancement, and many other considerations. Above all, your career choice can affect your satisfaction with life in general.

Job satisfaction is important. You need to feel good about your work and your future. Choosing the right career requires you to look ahead. What kind of work do you expect to be doing five years from now? ten years from now? Which occupation will offer advancement and bring satisfaction? What areas are in demand?

Begin your search for a career by listing your aptitudes and goals. Then, try to match those to a career. The Interest Survey given on the States' Career Clusters Web site may help you better define your interests. You will then need to learn the requirements of different jobs in a particular field.

What are the entry-level jobs within the graphic communications industry? Most of the skill areas require at least a high school education, general equivalency diploma (GED), or vocational/technical training. See **Figure 25-17.** Students who apply for part-time work during high school can get a head start toward full-time employment after graduation.

The *apprenticeship* educational plan is another entry method. In union shops, it is the only means of becoming a journeyman, or experienced worker. Under this plan, the employee is a registered apprentice for a designated period of time (usually four to six years). An agreement is signed that the apprentice will receive classroom and on-the-job training in specific skill areas.

apprenticeship: A method of job training in which an employee in a union shop receives classroom training and on-the-job experience as a means of becoming an experienced journeyman.

Figure 25-17. These young people are in training for positions as skilled technicians. (GIT, Arizona State University)

Formal training is available in private or public post-secondary institutions. These schools provide technical education, where specific skills are being developed for jobs within an industry. Because many jobs now require higher level skills, community colleges are offering technical skills training programs. A four-year program in graphic communications is another career path, **Figure 25-18.**

Teaching or educational administration opportunities in the field of graphic communications require a college degree from an accredited institution. Positions including technologists, scientists, researchers, and engineers also require a degree.

The employment outlook in the graphic communications industry is very good. Constantly changing technology will make necessary ongoing

Figure 25-18. Many students prepare for careers in graphics and printing at a four-year educational institution.

retraining and upgrading of skills and knowledge, a trend in education and business known as *lifelong learning*.

Try to obtain a broad knowledge of products and processes. Courses in basic electronics and computer science should be taken during high school and college. Typesetting, quality assurance, cost analysis, inventory, color separating, production scheduling, and robot control are just a few of the careers that require the use of electronic equipment. Computer literacy is a necessity.

FINDING A JOB

Several resources are available to help you search for a job. One such tool is the *Occupational Outlook Handbook* published by the United States Department of Labor and Bureau of Statistics. Another is the States' Career Clusters Initiative, which provides detailed pathways for different careers.

Once you have chosen a job you want, you must apply and interview for it. You will likely have to fill out a job application, and you must submit your résumé. Contact a company's human resources department for more information on how to apply. Your résumé should include your personal information, objective, educational background, previous work experience, any special skills, organizations and activities, and personal references. See **Figure 25-19.**

After filling out the application and creating your résumé, you must prepare for a job interview. Before the interview, research the company. Prepare to ask questions about the position and company if necessary. Be prompt when arriving at the interview. During the interview, be sure to answer all the employer's questions concisely and honestly.

WORK HABITS

Good work habits are important for both finding and keeping a job. Having a good *work ethic* means being dependable. You must be honest, cooperative, and respectful with your coworkers. It is also important to develop your communication skills. These traits will translate into skills for becoming a good team member. They will also help you progress into a position of leadership.

Solving problems often requires you to work with other people as a member of a team. A team usually consists of team members and one or more team leaders. Teamwork can help get a job done more quickly than doing it alone, and it allows for

Patricia White

Address	3131 Glenwood Avenue Frankfort, IL 60423 815/599-4212
Objective	To obtain a position as a graphic designer in a medium-sized printing or publishing firm.
Education	Eastern Illinois University, Charleston, IL Bachelor of Arts in Graphic Design, May 2008
Work Experience	8/06 to present Pepco Print, Charleston, IL Type of business: Small quick printer serving mostly walk-in trade. Produces bound/collated copies, letterheads, reports, brochures, cards, tickets, and invitations. Job duties: Electronic and manual layout and design; document center equipment operation; customer service at front counter.
Special Skills	Experienced in the following design applications: QuarkXpress, Adobe Illustrator, Adobe Photoshop, Director, Fractal Design Detailer.
Organizations and Activities	*Member*, Graphic Design Association, Eastern Illinois University, *Committee Member*, University Board Graphics, Eastern Illinois University. *Conference Attendee*, American Center for Design Conference, Chicago, 2008.
	References available upon request.

Annotations: Let employers know how well your needs match theirs. — Provide most recent employment information, including starting and ending dates. — Briefly describe your areas of responsibility. — List skills most appropriate to the job you are seeking. — Get permission from references before giving out their names and addresses.

Figure 25-19. Example of a résumé, highlighting the main points that should be included.

more possible solutions to be considered. Problems are successfully solved using teamwork when all the members provide their ideas and abilities. See **Figure 25-20.** Working in teams takes organization and cooperation among the team members, and the exercise of leadership skills by the team's leaders.

The team's leaders are in command of the rest of the team. The quality of their leadership determines whether the team will be a success or a failure. Important characteristics of leadership include:

- Good leaders have a vision of what must be done and look for ways to reach the team's goals.
- Good leaders are skilled communicators who are able to encourage the team members to assist each other and cooperate. They work to ensure all the team members contribute to the team's success.
- Good leaders are willing to work as long as it takes to achieve success. They can organize and direct the team's activities.
- Good leaders are fair and honest. They take responsibility for their own actions and give credit to others when it is due.
- Good leaders know how to delegate authority. They may even assign leadership roles to other team members to get the job done as efficiently as possible.

lifelong learning: Upgrading and updating one's job skills and knowledge to keep pace with technological changes in a field.

work ethic: Standard to which on-the-job conduct and performance is based.

Figure 25-20. Teamwork is an important aspect of a career. Working in teams helps get jobs done more quickly and can produce different perspectives on solutions.

Figure 25-21. An owner of a facility has responsibilities similar to an executive officer or president of a company. Overseeing operations and accomplishing work through others is vital.

ENTREPRENEURSHIP

An *entrepreneur* is someone who starts his or her own business. In the graphic communications field, it might be a small print shop, silk screen facility, color specialist house, or similar endeavor.

Thousands of new businesses are started every year. Small businesses provide over 50% of all jobs in the United States.

A good entrepreneur must be a self-starter, in good health, and self-confident. He or she should be able to differentiate a calculated risk from a foolish chance. An entrepreneur must be responsible, dependable, hardworking, and able to motivate the workers and utilize their talents. He or she will set specific goals and work until these goals are achieved. See **Figure 25-21.**

Advantages and Disadvantages of Entrepreneurship

Before deciding to start your own business, consider the advantages and disadvantages of entrepreneurship. Some advantages are:

- More control over income if the business is successful and grows.
- More control over job responsibilities.
- Meaningful professional relationships with talented people.
- Recognition as a leader.

Some disadvantages are:

- Working long hours to keep the business profitable.
- Work worries go home with you.
- Success or failure is on your shoulders.
- Loss of money, even life savings, if the business fails.
- Repaying business loans for many years.
- Inconsistent or unpredictable income.
- Large amount of paperwork for recordkeeping.
- Need to discipline workers for unsatisfactory performance.

Starting the Business

You can either buy an existing business or start a new one. When buying an existing business, you have the advantage of being able to check financial records to determine if it has been profitable in the past. Also, you will already have customers that know about and patronize the business. Equipment costs, facility planning, and other concerns are taken care of.

If you decide to start a new business, much more work is involved. You must find a suitable location, rent or build a facility, order equipment and supplies, and more. Until customers start patronizing the facility, it can be difficult to meet financial obligations. Financial backing can also be more difficult to obtain with a new business because of the high risk of failure.

To obtain information on buying or starting a business, you can contact the Small Business Administration or small business assistance centers at community colleges.

Do not expect instant fame and fortune when starting a business. Instead, look realistically at the inherent advantages and disadvantages. It is easy to get excited about starting a business and overlook how much work and money is involved. You may not realize the consequences of failure. Keep in mind that there may be less stress and more money working for someone else.

Technological Growth

Changes in technology have brought about changes in traditional careers in printing. For example, the manual aspects of prepress are being replaced by a fast-paced, all-digital workflow.

The computerized workplace has made for faster work patterns, with clients expecting projects to be completed in short periods of time. In addition to fast *turnaround*, the ability to function through electronically linked sites, modems, and faxes has changed how work gets done, **Figure 25-22.**

Telecommunications and *electronic information transfer* over telephone lines or by satellite permits almost instant transmission of digitized (computer-coded) images and proofs around the globe. Subsequently, information management positions are being created to handle job ticketing, tracking, processing, and billing.

Beyond prepress considerations are the capabilities for multimedia. Printing customers want to tap into the mass-marketing capability of the Internet, creating positions for web designers, computer graphics designers, and people in sales and marketing. Web-to-print is a factor of the future the industry cannot overlook.

Robotics, the use of machines to do repetitive tasks, is utilized in various manufacturing venues. Robots are ideal in the bindery area of a printing plant where highly repetitive tasks are done. While many traditionally labor-intensive activities are being eliminated by robots, positions requiring higher technical skills are opening in other areas.

Our technological age has revolutionized the way we communicate and work. The field of graphic communications is in the forefront of this revolution. Diverse employment opportunities will continue to emerge in such a dynamic, global industry.

Figure 25-22. The computer terminals in this office are electronically linked to each other. Faxes, modems, and Internet services link terminals around the world.

Summary

Many positions are available in the graphic communications industry. The skills range from very creative to very technical. Leadership and science-oriented positions are also found in the industrial environment. The level of educational requirements varies. It is imperative that you match your interests, aptitudes, and goals in life.

Review Questions

Please do not write in this book. Write your answers on a separate sheet of paper.

1. What are the six general employment categories in graphic communications?
2. How have changes in technology brought about changes in careers in prepress and press work?
3. Who is responsible for the quality of the final printed product?
4. List six characteristics important to the management team.
5. Name three methods for entering a career in graphic communications.

entrepreneur: Someone who starts his or her own business.

turnaround: The completion time for a product from its inception.

electronic information transfer: Sending digital information instantly via telephone lines and satellites.

robotics: The use of machines to do repetitive tasks, particularly in manufacturing.

6. What is *lifelong learning*?

7. Why should someone preparing for a career in graphic communications take courses in basic electronics and computer science?

8. List at least three types of information to be included on your résumé.

9. What is a *work ethic*?

10. Name three advantages and three disadvantages of entrepreneurship.

11. Why should an entrepreneur avoid expecting fortune and fame when starting a business?

12. In what area of a printing plant is the use of robots ideal?

Suggested Activities

1. What types of jobs are found in the printing plants in your area?

2. Write the job description for a specific job that has the greatest interest to you.

3. Contact one of your local printing organizations and find out what opportunities are available in the local area of the country.

4. Explain the qualifications and duties of a position within the prepress area of the plant.

Related Web Links

Occupational Outlook Handbook

www.bls.gov/oco

Government site providing information on various occupations.

States' Career Clusters

www.careerclusters.org

Organization that provides detailed information on different career pathways.

Graphic Comm Central

teched.vt.edu/GCC

Comprehensive site for students that contains information relating to careers in the graphic communications industry.

Be A Green Irene

www.beagreenirene.com

Online resource containing information on environmental consultants.

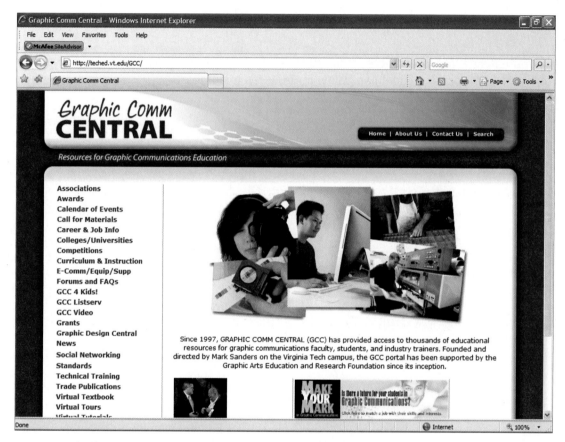

Web sites may provide the resources you need to research a specific career in the graphic communications industry. This Web site contains information on what types of classes to take as well as what types of jobs are available.

APPENDIX

Several typefaces are presented here, grouped by each of the five classifications. As you study these type designs, refer to the components identified below for features to compare.

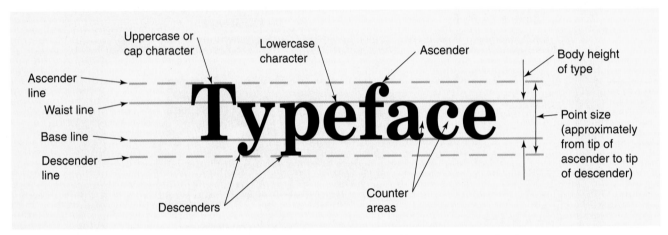

When discussing typefaces, using the correct terminology ensures effective communication.

Serif

Palatino
abcdefghijklmnopqrstuvwxyzABCDEFG

Times
abcdefghijklmnopqrstuvwxyzABCDEFGHIJ

Century Old Style Standard
abcdefghijklmnopqrstuvwxyzABCDEFG

Bauer Bodoni
abcdefghijklmnopqrstuvwxyzABCDEFGHIJKL

Cheltenham
abcdefghijklmnopqrstuvwxyzABCDEFGHIJK

ITC New Baskerville
abcdefghijklmnopqrstuvwxyz

Minion Pro
abcdefghijklmnopqrstuvwxyzABCDEFGHI

Italian Garamond
abcdefghijklmnopqrstuvwxyzABCDEFGHI

Caslon 540
abcdefghijklmnopqrstuvwxyzABCDEFGHI

ITC Garamond
abcdefghijklmnopqrstuvwxyzABCDEFGH

Casablanca
abcdefghijklmnopqrstuvwxyzABCDE

Square Serif

Geometric Slabserif 703
abcdefghijklmnopqrstuvwxyzABCDEF

Courier
abcdefghijklmnopqrstuvwxyzABCD

Playbill
abcdefghijklmnopqrstuvwxyzABCDEFGHIJKLMNOPQRSTUVWXYZ12

Sans Serif

Helvetica
abcdefghijklmnopqrstuvwxyzABCDEFG

Futura
abcdefghijklmnopqrstuvwxyzABCDEFGHIJ

Formata
abcdefghijklmnopqrstuvwxyzABCDEF

Ottawa
abcdefghijklmnopqrstuvwxyzABCDEFGHI

Gothic 812
abcdefghijklmnopqrstuvwxyzABCDEFGHIJKLMNOPQR

KabanaBook
abcdefghijklmnopqrstuvwxyzABCD

News Gothic Standard
abcdefghijklmnopqrstuvwxyzABCDEFGHIJK

Myriad
abcdefghijklmnopqrstuvwxyzABCDEFGHIJ

Swiss 721
abcdefghijklmnopqrstuvwxyzABCDEFGHI

Vogue
abcdefghijklmnopqrstuvwxyzABCDEFGHIJK

Cursive and Script

Ex Ponto
abcdefghijklmnopqrstuvwxyzABCDEFGHIJKL

Amazone
abcdefghijklmnopqrstuvwxyzABCDEFGH

Commercial Script
abcdefghijklmnopqrstuvwxyzABCDEFGHIJ

Freehand 591
abcdefghijklmnopqrstuvwxyzABCDEFGHIJKLM

Berthold Script
abcdefghijklmnopqrstuvwxyzABCDEFGHI

Tekton
abcdefghijklmnopqrstuvwxyzABCDEFGHIJKL

Novelty, Decorative, and Miscellaneous

IRONWOOD
ABCDEFGHIJKLMNOPQRSTUVWXYZABCDEFGHIJKLMNOPQRSTUVWXYZ1

Hollow
abcdefghijklmnopqrstuvwxyzABCDEFG

Lincoln
abcdefghijklmnopqrstuvwxyzABCDEFGHIJ

LIBERTY
ABCDEFGHIJKLMNOPQRSTUVWXYZABCDE

**Madrone
abcdefghijklmn**

Merlin
abcdefghijklmnopqrstuvwxyzABCDE

Kids
abcdefghijklmnopqrstuvwxyzABC

GEOMETRIC SLABSERIF 703
ABCDEFGHIJKLMNOPQRSTUVWXYZABCD

Caslon Openface
abcdefghijklmnopqrstuvwxyzABCDEFGHIJ

Southern
abcdefghijklmnopqrstuvwxyzABCDEFGH

Orbit-B
abcdefghijklmnopqrstuvwxyzABCDEFGH

PALETTE
ABCDEFGHIJKLMNOPQRSTUVWXYZABCDEFG

Penguin
abcdefghijklmnopqrstuvwxyzABCDEFGHIJKLMN

ROSEWOOD STANDARD
ABCDEFGHIJKLMNOPQRSTUVWXYZABCD

STENCIL
ABCDEFGHIJKLMNOPQRSTUVWXYZ

UMBRA
ABCDEFGHIJKLMNOPQRSTUVWXYZABCD

APPENDIX

Useful Information

Prefix	Symbol	Multiplication Factor	
exa	E	$10^{18} =$	1,000,000,000,000,000,000
peta	P	$10^{15} =$	1,000,000,000,000,000
tera	T	$10^{12} =$	1,000,000,000,000
giga	G	$10^{9} =$	1,000,000,000
mega	M	$10^{6} =$	1,000,000
kilo	k	$10^{3} =$	1,000
hecto	h	$10^{2} =$	100
deca	da	$10^{1} =$	10
(unit)		$10^{0} =$	1
deci	d	$10^{-1} =$	0.1
centi	c	$10^{-2} =$	0.01
milli	m	$10^{-3} =$	0.001
micro	u	$10^{-6} =$	0.000001
nano	n	$10^{-9} =$	0.000000001
pico	p	$10^{-12} =$	0.000000000001
femto	f	$10^{-15} =$	0.000000000000001
atto	a	$10^{-18} =$	0.000000000000000001

Figure B-1. U.S. Customary and metric conversion factors and prefixes.

When you know	Multiply by: Very accurate	Multiply by: Approximate	To find

Length

inches	*25.4		millimeters
inches	*2.54		centimeters
feet	*0.3048		meters
feet	*30.48		centimeters
yards	*0.9144	0.9	meters
miles	*1.609344	1.6	kilometers

Weight

grains	15.43236	15.4	grams
ounces	*28.349523125	28.0	grams
ounces	*0.028349523125	0.028	kilograms
pounds	*0.45359237	0.45	kilograms
short ton	*0.90718474	0.9	tonnes

Volume

teaspoons	*4.97512	5.0	milliliters
tablespoons	*14.92537	15.0	milliliters
fluid ounces	29.57353	30.0	milliliters
cups	*0.236588240	0.24	liters
pints	*0.473176473	0.47	liters
quarts	*0.946352946	0.95	liters
gallons	*3.785411784	3.8	liters
cubic inches	*0.016387064	0.02	liters
cubic feet	*0.028316846592	0.03	cubic meters
cubic yards	*0.764554857984	0.76	cubic meters

Area

square inches	*6.4516	6.5	square centimeters
square feet	*0.09290304	0.09	square meters
square yards	*0.83612736	0.8	square meters
square miles	*2.589989	2.6	square kilometers
acres	*0.40468564224	0.4	hectares

Temperature

| Fahrenheit | | * 5/9 (after subtracting 32) | Celsius |

* = Exact

Figure B-2. Conversion table—U.S. Customary to SI metric.

When you know	Very accurate	Approximate	To find
		Length	
millimeters	*0.03933701	0.04	inches
centimeters	*0.3937008	0.4	inches
meters	*3.280840	3.3	feet
meters	*1.093613	1.1	yards
kilometers	*0.621371	0.6	miles
		Weight	
grams	*0.03527396	0.035	ounces
kilograms	*2.204623	2.2	pounds
tonnes	*1.1023113	1.1	short tons
		Volume	
milliliters	*0.20001	0.2	teaspoons
milliliters	*0.06667	0.067	tablespoons
milliliters	*0.03381402	0.03	fluid ounces
liters	*61.02374	61.024	cubic inches
liters	*2.113376	2.1	pints
liters	*1.056688	1.06	quarts
liters	*0.26417205	0.26	gallons
liters	*0.03531467	0.035	cubic feet
cubic meters	*61023.74	61023.7	cubic inches
cubic meters	*35.31467	35.0	cubic feet
cubic meters	*1.3079506	1.3	cubic yards
cubic meters	*264.17205	264.0	gallons
		Area	
square centimeters	*0.1550003	0.16	square inches
square centimeters	*0.001077639	0.001	square feet
square meters	*10.76391	10.8	square feet
square meters	*1.195990	1.2	square yards
square kilometers	*0.3861019	0.4	square miles
hectares	*2.471054	2.5	acres
		Temperature	
Celsius		* 9/5 (then add 32)	Fahrenheit

* = Exact

Figure B-3. Conversion table—SI metric to U.S. Customary.

Measures of Length		Measures of Weight		Measures of Liquid Volume	
10 millimeters	= 1 centimeter (cm)	10 milligrams	= 1 centigram (cg)	10 milliliters	= 1 centiliter (cl)
10 centimeters	= 1 decimeter (dm)	10 centigrams	= 1 decigram (dg)	10 centiliters	= 1 deciliter (dl)
10 decimeters	= 1 meter (m)	10 decigrams	= 1 hectogram (hg)	10 deciliters	= 1 liter (l)
10 meters	= 1 decameter (dam)	10 hectograms	= 1 kilogram (kg)	10 liters	= 1 decaliter (dal)
10 decameters	= 1 hectometer (hm)	10 kilograms	= 1 myriagram (myg)	10 decaliters	= 1 hectoliter (hl)
10 hectometers	= 1 kilometer (km)	10 myriagrams	= 1 quintal (q)	10 hectoliters	= 1 kiloliter (kl)
10 kilometers	= 1 myriameter (mym)	10 quintals	= 1 millier or metric ton (MT or t)		

Figure B-4. Metric units.

FRACTION	INCHES	M/M	FRACTION	INCHES	M/M
1/64	.01563	.397	33/64	.51563	13.097
1/32	.03125	.794	17/32	.53125	13.494
3/64	.04688	1.191	35/64	.54688	13.891
1/16	.6250	1.588	9/16	.56250	14.288
5/64	.07813	1.984	37/64	.57813	14.684
3/32	.09375	2.381	19/32	.59375	15.081
7/64	.10938	2.778	39/64	.60938	15.478
1/8	.12500	3.175	5/8	.62500	15.875
9/64	.14063	3.572	41/64	.64063	16.272
5/32	.15625	3.969	21/32	.65625	16.669
11/64	.17188	4.366	43/64	.67188	17.066
3/16	.18750	4.763	11/16	.68750	17.463
13/64	.20313	5.159	45/64	.70313	17.859
7/32	.21875	5.556	23/32	.71875	18.256
15/64	.23438	5.953	47/64	.73438	18.653
1/4	.25000	6.350	3/4	.75000	19.050
17/64	.26563	6.747	49/64	.76563	19.447
9/32	.28125	7.144	25/32	.78125	19.844
19/64	.29688	7.541	51/64	.79688	20.241
5/16	.31250	7.938	13/16	.81250	20.638
21/64	.32813	8.334	53/64	.82813	21.034
11/32	.34375	8.731	27/32	.84375	21.431
23/64	.35938	9.128	55/64	.85938	21.828
3/8	.37500	9.525	7/8	.87500	22.225
25/64	.39063	9.922	57/64	.89063	22.622
13/32	.40625	10.319	29/32	.90625	23.019
27/64	.42188	10.716	59/64	.92188	23.416
7/16	.43750	11.113	15/16	.93750	23.813
29/64	.45313	11.509	61/64	.95313	24.209
15/32	.46875	11.906	31/32	.96875	24.606
31/64	.48438	12.303	63/64	.98438	25.003
1/2	.50000	12.700	1	1.00000	25.400

Figure B-5. A decimal conversion chart.

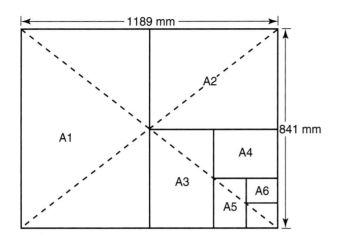

Figure B-6. ISO A-series paper.

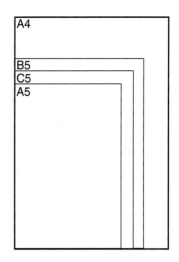

Figure B-7. The relationships among ISO A-, B-, and C-series papers.

ISO Sizes	Millimeters	Inches
2A	1189 x 1682	46.81 x 66.22
A0	841 x 1189	33.11 x 46.81
A1	594 x 841	23.39 x 33.11
A2	420 x 594	16.54 x 23.39
A3	297 x 420	11.69 x 16.54
A4	210 x 297	8.27 x 11.69
A5	148 x 210	5.83 x 8.27
A6	105 x 148	4.13 x 5.83
A7	74 x 105	2.91 x 4.13
A8	52 x 74	2.05 x 2.91
A9	37 x 52	1.46 x 2.05
A10	26 x 37	1.02 x 1.46

Figure B-8. ISO A-series paper sizes (metric and U.S. Customary measurements).

ISO Sizes	Millimeters	Inches
B0	1000 x 1414	39.37 x 55.67
B1	707 x 1000	27.83 x 39.37
B2	500 x 707	19.68 x 27.83
B3	353 x 500	13.90 x 19.68
B4	250 x 353	9.84 x 13.90
B5	175 x 250	6.93 x 9.84
B6	125 x 176	4.92 x 6.93
B7	88 x 125	3.46 x 4.92
B8	62 x 88	2.44 x 3.46
B9	44 x 62	1.73 x 2.44
B10	31 x 44	1.22 x 1.73

Figure B-9. ISO B-series paper sizes (metric and U.S. Customary measurements).

R Series	Bond 17" x 22" (432 mm x 559 mm) (g/m²)	Cover 20" x 26" (508 mm x 660 mm) (lb/ream)	Index 25 1/2" x 30 1/2" (648 mm x 775 mm) (lb/ream)	Newsprint 24" x 36" (610 mm x 914 mm) (lb/ream)	Book 25" x 38" (635 mm x 965 mm) (lb/ream)
20.0	5.32	7.39	11.00	12.29	13.51
22.4	5.95	8.28	12.39	13.77	15.13
25.0	6.65	9.24	13.83	15.36	16.89
28.0	7.44	10.35	15.49	17.21	18.92
31.5	8.37	11.65	17.43	19.36	21.28
45.0	11.97	16.64	24.89	27.66	30.40
50.0	13.30	18.49	27.66	30.73	33.78
56.0	14.89	20.71	30.98	34.42	37.84
63.0	16.75	23.30	34.85	38.72	42.57
71.0	18.88	26.26	39.28	43.63	47.97
85.0	22.61	31.45	46.90	52.27	57.46
100.0	26.60	36.98	55.32	61.46	67.57
112.0	29.79	41.42	61.96	68.83	75.68
140.0	37.24	51.78	77.45	86.04	94.60
180.0	47.88	66.57	99.58	110.62	121.63
200.0	53.20	73.97	110.64	122.91	135.14
250.0	66.50	92.46	138.30	153.64	168.93
400.0	106.41	147.95	221.29	245.83	270.29

Figure B-10. The R20 series of paper weights and equivalent weights.

Trimmed Page Size (Inches)	Number of Printed Pages	Number from Sheet	Standard Paper Size
4 x 9	4	12	25 × 30
	8	12	38 × 50
	12	4	25 × 38
	16	6	38 × 50
	24	2	25 × 38
4 1/4 x 5 3/8	4	32	35 × 45
	8	16	35 × 45
	16	8	35 × 45
	32	4	35 × 45
4 1/2 x 6	4	16	25 × 38
	8	8	25 × 35
	16	4	25 × 38
	32	2	25 × 38
5 1/2 x 8 1/2	4	16	35 × 45
	8	8	35 × 45
	16	4	35 × 45
	32	2	35 × 45
6 x 9	4	8	25 × 38
	8	4	25 × 38
	16	2	25 × 38
	32	2	38 × 50
8 1/2 x 11	4	4	25 × 35
	8	2	25 × 35
	16	2	25 × 45
9 x 12	4	4	25 × 38
	8	2	25 × 38
	16	2	25 × 50

Figure B-11. Cutting charts. Using standard paper sizes can prevent waste, while using odd-size pages can create excess waste and also increase costs, if the correct quantity has not been ordered or there is not enough time to order special-size paper. This chart shows the number of pages to several standard paper sizes. The paper size includes trim top, bottom, and sides. This size does not include bleed.

Grade of Paper	Book 25 x 38	Bond 17 x 22	Cover 20 x 26	Bristol 22 1/2 x 28 1/2	Index 25 1/2 x 30 1/2	Tag 24 x 36	g/m²
Book	**30**	12	16	20	25	27	44
	40	16	22	27	33	36	59
	45	18	25	30	37	41	67
	50	20	27	34	41	45	74
	60	24	33	40	49	55	89
	70	28	38	47	57	64	104
	80	31	44	54	65	73	118
	90	35	49	60	74	82	133
	100	39	55	67	82	91	148
	120	47	66	80	98	109	178
Bond	33	**13**	18	22	27	30	49
	41	**16**	22	27	33	37	61
	51	**20**	28	34	42	46	75
	61	**24**	33	41	50	56	90
	71	**28**	39	48	58	64	105
	81	**32**	45	55	67	74	120
	91	**36**	50	62	75	83	135
	102	**40**	56	69	83	93	158
Cover	91	36	**50**	62	75	82	135
	110	43	**60**	74	90	100	163
	119	47	**65**	80	97	108	176
	146	58	**80**	99	120	134	216
	164	65	**90**	111	135	149	243
	183	72	**100**	124	150	166	271
Bristol	100	39	54	**67**	81	91	148
	120	47	65	**80**	98	109	178
	148	58	81	**100**	121	135	219
	176	70	97	**120**	146	162	261
	207	82	114	**140**	170	189	306
	237	93	130	**160**	194	216	351
Index	110	43	60	74	**90**	100	163
	135	53	74	91	**110**	122	203
	170	67	93	115	**140**	156	252
	208	82	114	140	**170**	189	328
Tag	110	43	60	74	90	**100**	163
	137	54	75	93	113	**125**	203
	165	65	90	111	135	**150**	244
	192	76	105	130	158	**175**	284
	220	87	120	148	180	**200**	326
	275	109	151	186	225	**250**	407

Figure B-12. Equivalent weights, in reams of 500 sheets. Basis weights are in bold type.

Book (25 x 38)	This grade encompasses the widest range of printing papers. As the name implies, book grade is widely used for books. Other uses include magazines, folders, pamphlets, posters, and other commercial printing. The different grades of book paper are coated (enamel), uncoated, offset, text, and label.
Cover (20 x 26)	Many grades of coated, text, and book papers are made in matching cover weights. There are also many special cover papers with a variety of surface textures, coatings, and finishes.
Bond (17 x 22)	Primarily used for stationery and business forms, this category also includes ledger and writing grades. Available in a wide range of colors and weights. Surfaces accept typewriter and writing inks and erase easily. There are two types: sulphite and cotton fiber (rag content). More costly bonds are made with 25% to 100% cotton fiber.
Index Bristol (25 1/2 x 30 1/2)	Characterized by stiffness and receptivity to printing inks, index is used wherever a stiff, inexpensive paper is required.
Printing (Mill) Bristol (22 1/2 x 28 1/2)	Generally stiffer than index, printing bristols are widely used for menus, greeting cards, covers, and tickets.
Newsprint (24 x 36)	This inexpensive grade is limited primarily to cost-critical uses.

Figure B-13. Printing papers. All papers have certain properties and characteristics affecting printability and quality. Printability and quality are not always related. The finest quality of paper might not always print well. Weight, bulk, caliper, grain direction, color, opacity, surface texture, coatings, and strength are some of the factors to consider before selecting paper. Papers are generally classified and defined in terms of use, as suggested by the grade names listed in this chart. Basic sizes are shown in parentheses.

Basis 25 x 38	30	35	40	45	50	60	70	80	90	100	120	150
17½ x 22½	25	29	33	37	41	50	58	66	75	83	99	124
19 x 25	30	35	40	45	50	60	70	80	90	100	120	150
20 x 26	33	38	44	49	55	66	77	88	99	109	131	164
22½ x 29	41	48	55	62	69	82	96	110	124	137	165	206
22½ x 35	50	58	66	75	83	99	116	133	149	166	199	249
23 x 29	42	49	56	63	70	84	98	112	126	140	169	211
23 x 35	51	59	68	76	85	102	119	136	153	169	203	254
24 x 36	55	64	73	82	91	109	127	146	164	182	218	273
25 x 38	60	70	80	90	100	120	140	160	180	200	240	300
26 x 40	66	77	88	99	109	131	153	175	197	219	263	328
28 x 42	74	87	99	111	124	149	173	198	223	248	297	371
28 x 44	78	91	104	117	130	156	182	207	233	259	311	389
30½ x 41	79	92	105	118	132	158	184	211	237	263	316	395
32 x 44	89	104	119	133	148	178	207	237	267	296	356	445
33 x 44	92	107	122	138	153	183	214	245	275	306	367	459
35 x 45	99	116	133	149	166	199	232	265	298	332	398	497
35 x 46	102	119	136	153	169	203	237	271	305	339	407	508
36 x 48	109	127	146	164	182	218	255	291	327	364	437	546
38 x 50	120	140	160	180	200	240	280	320	360	400	480	600
38 x 52	125	146	166	187	208	250	291	333	374	416	499	624
41 x 54	140	163	186	210	233	280	326	373	419	466	559	699
41 x 61	158	184	211	237	263	316	369	421	474	527	632	790
42 x 58	154	179	205	231	256	308	359	410	462	513	615	769
44 x 64	178	207	237	267	296	356	415	474	534	593	711	889
44 x 66	183	214	245	275	306	367	428	489	550	611	734	917
46 x 69	200	234	267	301	334	401	468	535	601	668	802	1000
46½ x 67½	198	231	264	297	330	396	463	529	593	661	793	991
52 x 76	250	291	333	374	416	499	582	666	749	832	998	1248

Book, Offset, Label (Coated and Uncoated), and Text

Basis Size 17 x 12	13	16	20	24	28	32	36	40
8½ x 11	6.5	8.0	10	12	14	16	18	20
8½ x 14	8.3	10.2	12.7	15.3	17.8	20.4	22.9	25.5
11 x 17	13	16	20	24	28	32	36	40
16 x 21	23	29	36	43	50	57	65	72
16 x 42	47	58	72	86	101	115	130	144
17 x 22	26	32	40	48	56	64	72	80
17 x 26	31	38	47	57	66	76	85	95
17½ x 22½	27	34	42	51	59	67	76	84
17 x 28	33	41	51	61	71	81	92	102
18 x 23	29	36	44	53	62	71	80	89
18 x 46	58	71	89	106	124	142	160	117
19 x 24	32	39	49	59	68	78	88	98
19 x 28	37	46	57	68	80	91	102	114
19 x 48	63	78	98	117	137	156	176	195
20 x 28	39	48	60	72	84	96	108	120
21 x 32	47	58	72	86	101	115	130	144
22 x 25½	39	48	60	72	84	96	108	120
22 x 34	52	64	80	96	112	128	144	160
22½ x 22½	35	43	54	65	76	87	97	108
22½ x 28½	45	55	69	82	96	110	123	137
22½ x 34½	54	66	83	100	116	133	149	166
22½ x 35	55	67	84	101	118	135	152	168
23 x 36	58	71	89	106	124	142	159	177
24 x 38	63	78	98	117	137	156	176	195
24½ x 24½	42	51	64	77	90	103	116	128
24½ x 28½	49	60	75	90	105	120	135	150
24½ x 29	50	61	76	91	106	122	137	152
24½ x 38½	66	81	101	121	141	161	182	202
24½ x 39	66	82	102	122	143	164	184	204
25½ x 44	78	96	120	144	168	192	216	240
26 x 35	61	76	94	113	132	151	170	189
28 x 34	66	82	102	122	143	163	184	204
28 x 38	74	91	114	136	159	182	205	228
34 x 44	104	128	160	192	224	256	288	320
35 x 45	109	135	168	202	236	270	303	337

Bond, Business, Writing, and Ledger

Figure B-14. Standard paper sizes and weights. It has been traditional practice to price papers based on a ream (500 sheets). 1M pricing is replacing this. These tables give the weight per 1M sheets for common sizes and weights of different paper grades.

Basis Weights in Boldface

	Bond 17 x 22	Book 25 x 38	Cover 20 x 26	Index 25½ x 30½	Bristol 22½ x 28½
Bond	**13**	33	18	27	22
	16	41	22	34	28
	20	51	28	42	34
	24	61	33	50	42
	28	71	39	58	48
	32	81	45	66	55
	36	91	50	75	62
	40	102	56	83	68
Book	12	**30**	16	25	20
	16	**40**	22	33	27
	18	**45**	25	37	30
	20	**50**	27	41	33
	22	**55**	30	45	37
	24	**60**	33	49	41
	26	**65**	36	53	44
	28	**70**	38	57	47
	30	**75**	41	61	50
	31	**80**	44	65	54
	35	**90**	49	74	61
	39	**100**	55	82	68
	47	**120**	66	98	81
Cover	18	46	**25**	38	31
	25	64	**35**	52	42
	29	73	**40**	60	50
	36	91	**50**	75	62
	40	100	**55**	82	68
	43	110	**60**	90	74
	47	119	**65**	97	80
	58	146	**80**	120	99
	65	164	**90**	135	111
	72	183	**100**	150	123
Index	43	110	60	**90**	74
	53	135	74	**110**	91
	67	171	93	**140**	116
	82	208	114	**170**	140
Bristol	52	133	73	109	**90**
	58	148	81	121	**100**
	70	178	97	146	**120**
	82	207	114	170	**140**
	93	237	130	194	**160**
	105	267	146	218	**180**

**Equivalent Weights in Reams
of 500 Sheets**

Figure B-14. *(Continued)*

Weight per 1000 Sheets

Basis Size 22½ x 28½	67	80	90	94	100	110	120	140	160
22½ x 28½	134	160	180	188	200	220	240	280	320
22½ x 35	165	196	221	231	246	270	295	344	393
23 x 35	168	201	226	236	251	276	301	352	402
26 x 40	217	259	292	305	324	357	389	454	519
28½ x 45	268	320	360	376	400	440	480	560	640

Printing Bristol

Weight per 1000 Sheets

Basis 20 x 26	50	60	65	80	90	100	130
20 x 26	100	120	130	160	180	200	260
22½ x 28½	123	148	160	197	222	247	321
23 x 29	128	154	167	205	231	257	333
23 x 5	155	186	201	248	279	310	403
26 x 40	200	240	260	320	360	400	520
35 x 46	310	372	403	495	557	619	805

Cover

Weight per 1000 Sheets

Basis Size 25½ x 30½	90	120	140	170	220
20½ x 24¾	117	157	183	222	287
22½ x 28½	148	198	231	280	263
22½ x 35	182	243	284	344	446
25½ x 30½	180	240	280	340	440
28½ x 45	297	356	462	561	726

Index Bristol

Formula:	Weight of 1000 sheets x the number of sheets ÷1000 = total weight
Example:	Determine the weight of 1765 sheets of 25 x 38 x 80 (160M) lb. stock.
Solution:	160 x 1765 = 282,400 ÷ 1000 = 282.4 lbs.

Figure B-15. Finding the weight of a number of sheets.

Basis Weight	Paper Finish			
	Coated	Smooth	Vellum	Antique
Book				
40		.0025	.0031	.0034
45	.0021	.0028	.0035	.0037
50	.0023	.0031	.0038	.0041
60	.0028	.0038	.0046	.0050
70	.0034	.0044	.0054	.0058
80	.0040	.0050	.0059	.0065
90	.0046	.0057	.0065	.0074
100	.0052	.0063	.0071	.0082
120	.0060	.0076	.0082	.0100
150	.0072	.0095	.0106	.0123
Cover				
50		.0058	.0070	.0075
60	.0056			
65		.0075	.0092	.0097
80	.0072	.0093	.0113	.0120
90		.0106	.0130	.0135
100	.0092	.0116	.0140	.0150
130		.0150	.0184	.0190
Bond				
13		.0021	.0025	.0027
16		.0026	.0031	.0033
20		.0032	.0039	.0042
24		.0038	.0047	.0050
Index				
90		.0080	.0084	
110		.0096	.0104	
140		.0132	.0140	
170		.0144	.0160	
Bristol				
90	.0055	.0069	.0084	.0090
100	.0061	.0076	.0093	.0100
120	.0073	.0092	.0111	.0120
140	.0085	.0107	.0130	.0140
160	.0097	.0122	.0148	.0160
180	.0110	.0137	.0167	.0180
200	.0122	.0153	.0185	.0200
220	.0134	.0167	.0204	.0220

Figure B-17. Caliper equivalents. The numbers provided are averages. Variations occur in mill runs.

Problem: Determine the weight of a roll of coated (2 sides) book paper that is 30" in diameter and 38" wide.

1. Square the diameter: 30 x 30 = 900

2. Multiply the result by the roll width: 900 x 38 = 34,200

3. Multiply by given factor (.034): 34,200 x .034 = 1162.8

Answer: 1163 lbs.

Factors:	(These average factors apply for all weights)
Newsprint	0.016
Antique finish	0.018
Machine finish, English finish, Offset, Bond	0.027
Supercalendered (coated 1 side)	0.030
Coated 2 sides	0.034

Figure B-16. How to find the weight of a roll of paper.

Diameter (Inches)	All Bond	Regular Ledger	Posting Ledger	Regular Offset	Regular Tagboard
10	1.86	2.34	1.98	2.10	2.55
12	2.83	3.37	2.94	3.12	3.74
14	3.92	4.58	4.07	4.32	5.07
16	5.13	5.99	5.38	5.71	6.86
18	6.60	7.58	6.86	7.27	8.01
20	8.23	9.35	8.51	9.04	10.21
22	10.00	11.16	10.28	10.90	12.47
24	11.90	13.34	12.30	13.05	14.56
25	13.10	14.62	13.42	14.22	15.96
26	14.10	15.80	14.53	15.41	17.24
27	15.30	17.05	15.68	16.63	18.60
28	16.40	18.33	16.88	17.90	20.00
29	17.70	19.66	18.12	19.22	21.46
30	18.90	21.05	19.40	20.58	22.96
31	20.02	22.45	20.73	21.99	24.62
32	21.60	23.93	22.10	23.45	26.10
33	22.90	26.52	23.52	24.95	27.78
34	24.20	27.89	24.98	26.49	29.49
35	25.70	29.86	26.48	28.06	31.25
36	27.00	31.60	28.03	29.73	33.06
37	28.70	33.39	29.61	31.41	34.93
38	30.20	35.23	31.25	33.15	36.83
39	31.90	37.13	32.93	34.92	38.81
40	33.70	39.06	34.65	36.75	40.82

Figure B-18. Approximate roll weights per inch of width. (International Paper Co.)

No. Out of Sheet	Quantity of Pressrun									
	500	1000	1500	2000	2500	3000	3500	4000	4500	5000
1	500	1000	1500	2000	2500	3000	3500	4000	4500	5000
2	250	500	750	1000	1250	1500	1750	2000	2250	2500
3	167	334	500	667	834	1000	1167	1334	1500	1667
4	125	250	375	500	625	750	875	1000	1125	1250
5	100	200	300	400	500	600	700	800	900	1000
6	84	167	250	334	417	500	584	667	750	834
7	72	143	215	286	358	429	500	572	643	715
8	63	125	188	250	313	375	438	500	563	625
9	56	112	167	223	278	334	389	445	500	556
10	50	100	150	200	250	300	350	400	450	500
11	46	91	137	182	228	273	319	364	410	455
12	42	84	126	168	209	250	292	334	375	417
13	39	77	116	154	193	231	270	308	347	385
14	36	72	108	144	179	215	250	286	322	358
15	34	67	100	134	167	200	234	267	300	334
16	32	63	94	125	157	188	219	250	282	313
17	30	59	89	118	148	177	206	236	265	295
18	28	56	84	112	139	167	195	223	250	279
19	27	53	79	106	132	158	185	211	237	264
20	25	50	75	100	125	150	175	200	225	250
21	24	48	72	96	120	143	167	191	215	239
22	23	46	69	91	114	137	160	182	205	228
23	22	44	66	87	109	131	153	174	196	218
24	21	42	63	84	105	125	146	167	188	209
25	20	40	60	80	100	120	140	160	180	200
26	20	39	58	77	97	116	135	154	174	193
27	19	38	56	75	93	112	130	149	167	186
28	18	36	54	72	90	108	125	143	161	179
29	18	36	54	72	87	103	121	138	156	173
30	17	34	51	67	84	100	117	134	150	167
31	17	33	49	65	81	97	113	130	146	162
32	16	32	47	63	79	94	110	125	141	157
33	16	31	46	61	76	91	107	122	137	152
34	15	30	45	59	74	89	103	118	133	148
35	15	29	43	58	72	86	100	115	129	143
36	14	28	42	56	70	84	98	112	125	139
37	14	28	41	55	68	82	95	109	122	136
38	14	27	40	53	66	79	93	106	119	132
39	13	26	39	52	65	77	90	103	116	131
40	13	25	38	50	63	75	88	100	113	125

Figure B-19. Paper-stock estimator. Use this chart to determine how many sheets are needed for a particular job. For example, a job calls for 4000 pieces that cut 16 out of 1 sheet. Follow the first column to 16, and then read across that line to the 4000 column. The result is 250 sheets. (No spoilage is included.)

To determine the approximate number of linear feet in a roll of paper, use the formula and factors shown below.

Formula: $$\frac{\text{Net Weight x 12 x (Factor)}}{\text{Basis Weight x Width}} = \text{Linear Feet}$$

Paper	Factors
Bond	1300
Cover	1805
Book or Offset	3300
Vellum Bristol (22 1/2″ x 28 1/2″)	2230
Index (25 1/2″ x 30 1/2″)	2700
Printing Bristol (22 1/2″ x 35″)	2739
Wrapping, Tissue, Newsprint, Waxing (24″ x 36″)	3070
Tag	3000

Example: Find the number of linear feet in a roll of form bond (20″ width, sub. 16 lbs., net weight 750 lbs.)

$$\frac{750 \times 12 \times 1300}{16 \times 20} = 36,562.5 = 36,563 \text{ Linear Feet}$$

To obtain a more exact approximation of linear feet, use the formula below:

$$\frac{[(\text{Roll Radius})^2 \times (3.1416)] - [(\text{Core Radius})^2 \times 3.1416)]}{\text{Paper Thickness}} = \text{Linear Inches}$$

$$\frac{\text{Linear Inches}}{12} = \text{Linear Feet}$$

Figure B-20. The approximate number of linear feet in rolls. (Zellerbach Paper Co.)

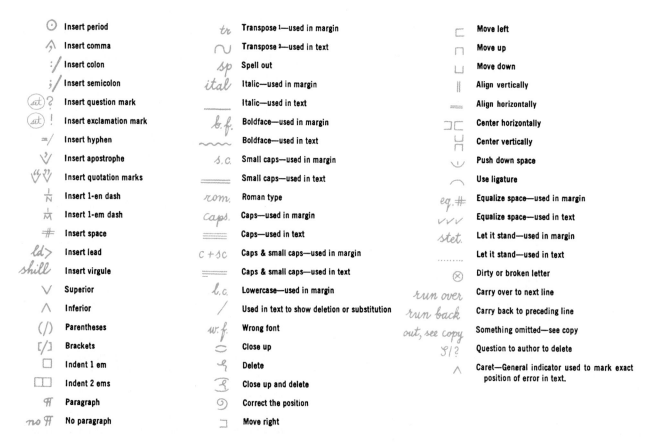

Figure B-21. Proofreader's marks.

GLOSSARY

A/D converter: A device used to convert an analog charge into digital form. The result of this conversion is stored as pixel data. (8)

achromatic vision: Blindness to all colors; ability to see only in shades of white, gray, and black. (9)

adaptation: Adjustment that eyes make in different lighting conditions. (9)

additive: Ingredients such as driers, lubricants, waxes, and starches that are added to ink to impart special characteristics, improve desirable properties, or suppress undesirable properties. (22)

additive color: Theory based on mixing red, green, and blue light in various combinations to create a color reproduction or image. (7)

additive color formation: Theory based on mixing red, green, and blue light in various combinations to create a color reproduction or image. (9, 10)

adjacency: A property of the eye that changes the perception of a color based on the adjacent or surrounding color. A color will appear brighter if surrounded by dark colors, or darker when surrounded by light colors. (9)

afterimage: An image that viewer continues to see after the actual object is no longer in sight. The image is created by the eye's attempt to restore equilibrium. (9)

aliasing: The process in which smooth curves and other lines become jagged because an image is enlarged or the resolution of the graphics device or file is reduced. (7)

analog charge: A series of electrical impulses created with the light received by the CCD. (8)

analog format: The principal feature of something in analog format is that it is continuous. An image in analog format has smooth, continuous gradations of tone from light to dark. (8)

anilox roll: A metal or ceramic roll engraved with cells that carry ink to the plate cylinder. (18)

antialiasing: Software technique for diminishing the jagged edges of an image that should be smooth. It reduces the prominence of jaggies by surrounding them with intermediate shades of gray or color. (7)

antihalation backing: A biodegradable dye coating on the back of most films that absorbs light so it will not reflect back to the emulsion and produce a shadow or double image. (11)

apprenticeship: A method of job training in which an employee in a union shop receives classroom training and on-the-job experience as a means of becoming an experienced journeyman. (25)

aqueous inks: Inks that are based on a mixture of water, glycol, and dyes or pigments. (13)

artwork: The graphic elements (line art and photographs) used in producing printed products. (1)

ascender: The part of a letter that extends above the body height. (4)

automatic film processing: A process that uses a mechanical device used to develop the latent image on photographic material. (11)

automatic trap: Trap set by building art with common colors. See also *trapping*. (10)

autotracing: A feature of some graphics programs; allows bitmapped images to be converted into object-oriented format. (7)

banding machine: Device that is used to wrap and bond a plastic or metal band around a bundle of booklets, books, boxes, or other products. This holds the products together for shipping. (23)

bank: A compositor's workstation; used to hold a job case when hand-setting foundry type. (6)

barrier guards: Machine guards that can be hinged or moved. (2)

base material: The layer of film that supports the emulsion. It is commonly made from plastic or a special grade of paper. Most of today's graphic films use a polyester base. (11)

basic size: The standard length and width, in inches, of a grade of paper. (3, 21)

basis weight: The weight, in pounds, of a ream of paper cut to its basic size. (3)

Bezier curve: A vector graphic defined mathematically by two endpoints and two or more other points that control its shape. Named after French mathematician Pierre Bezier. (7)

binding: The process of joining together multiple pages of a printed product by various means including sewing, stapling, spiral wire, and adhesives. (1, 23)

bit: Binary digit. The basic unit of digital information. (7)

bit depth: The number of bits of color or grayscale information that can be recorded per pixel. The greater the bit depth, the more colors or grayscales can be represented. Also referred to as tonal resolution. (8)

bitmapped images: Graphics files that contain a map of pixels (tiny rectangular picture elements), each of which is assigned characteristics such as color and brightness, to make up the image. Artwork created by a paint program is a bitmapped image, and so is a continuous tone image (photograph) that has been digitized by use of a scanner. (7)

black letter: A classification of type consisting of faces that resemble the hand-drawn lettering of German monks in the Middle Ages. (4)

blanket: A resilient material that is attached to a cylinder and used as an image transfer material from the plate cylinder to the substrate. (14)

blanket cylinder: A printing system component that holds the image-receptive blanket on the press and receives the image from the plate cylinder. (15)

bleaching: A chemical treatment to whiten wood pulp. (21)

blind embossing: An embossing process in which the stock itself creates the image and ink is not used. (23)

blueline proof: Proof produced from imageset film. A photographic procedure is used in which light-sensitive compounds are applied to paper, plastic, or metal sheets. The substrate is then exposed to intense blue and/or ultraviolet light and developed with ammonia vapors or an alkaline solution to form an image. The images and text on the proofs are usually blue in color. Also referred to as diazo proof. (10)

body type: Type sizes that range from 4-point through 12-point that are used for setting straight matter. (4, 5)

book printing: Graphic communications industry segment that produces trade books (general interest nonfiction and fiction) sold in bookstores and other retail locations, and textbooks providing instruction on a great variety of subjects. (1)

brake mechanism: A tension control device designed to produce a slight amount of drag on the web as it travels through a web-fed press. (15)

brayer: A small, handheld roller used to distribute ink on a proof press. (22)

brightness: For paper classification, the percent reflectance of blue light only, centering on the wavelength of 457 nm. (4) Often referred to as lightness or luminosity, brightness can be defined as a value indicating how light or dark a color is. For paper classification, the percent reflectance of blue light only, centering on the wavelength of 457 nm. (9, 10)

brownline proofs: Single-color printing proofs that are used to evaluate the placement of page elements. (10)

brush system: A continuous dampening system that uses a brush roller to transfer fountain solution from the fountain roller to the rest of the system. (15)

burned edges: An imperfection in a water- or lacquer-soluble stencil in which solvent collects in an improperly cut area of the stencil and melts (burns) the edge. (20)

burnish: To rub down a dry transfer image onto a substrate with a smooth wood, plastic, or metal tool. (6)

business plan: A document that states the goals of a business and presents a framework for achieving those goals. (24)

byte: A binary word, or group of eight individual 1s and 0s (called bits) or binary digits. (7)

calendering: Passing paper between rollers to increase the smoothness and gloss of the paper's surface. (21)

calibration: A process by which a scanner, monitor, or output device is adjusted to provide a more accurate display and reproduction of images. (10)

calligraphy: The art of hand-drawing letters, also known as manuscript writing. (4)

camera bed: The main support for the other camera parts. It determines the sturdiness of the camera. (11)

career: Positions you train for and seek employment for your life's work. (25)

cell distortion: The result of stretching fabric openings unequally in two directions. (20)

cell size: The distance across individual open areas between adjacent threads. (20)

cellulose: The raw material used to make paper. (21)

chain of custody: The process of tracking and recording the possession and transfer of wood and fiber from forests of origin to the end user. (21)

chalking: Condition that occurs when dried ink is easily rubbed off or lost from a printed sheet. (22)

character compensation: A method of tight-setting copy by electronically reducing the width of each character and space very slightly, which reduces the white space between characters. (4)

characterization: Describes the color limitations or color profile of a particular device. (10)

characters: The individual visual symbols, such as letters, numerals, and punctuation marks, in a particular typeface. (4)

charge-coupled device (CCD): A solid-state, light-sensitive chip receptor that converts light into an analog charge; commonly built into image capturing devices (scanners and digital cameras). (8)

chase: A metal frame that supports the type set into the galley for printing on a relief printing press. (6)

chipper: A machine that cuts logs into chips. (21)

choke trap: Trap performed by spreading the background under the foreground object. See also *trapping*. (10)

chroma: A term used in the Munsell system to indicate the extent to which the color is diluted by white light. The chroma value represents how much a given hue deviates from a neutral gray of the same value. (9)

chromatic adaptation: The adjustment our eyes make to color conditions. For example, if you were reading next to a lamp that emits light with a yellow cast, your eyes would quickly adapt so the yellow color would not be noticeable. (9)

chromatic induction: A change in perception where the eye causes a color to look different when surrounded by or adjacent to other colors. A color appears brighter when surrounded by dark colors, and the same color appears darker when surrounded by light colors. Also called simultaneous contrast. (9)

chromaticity: The color quality of an image. (3) A quality of color that includes hue and saturation (chroma), but not brightness (lightness). (9)

chromaticity coordinates: The *x* and *y* values of the CIE Yxy color space; they represent the hue and saturation of a color. (9)

CMOS APS: Complementary metal oxide semiconductor active pixel sensor. An active light sensor chip commonly used in low-end digital cameras. (8)

coated paper: Paper with a mineral substance applied to it for a smoother, stronger surface. (21)

collating: The gathering of sheets or signatures, usually after they are printed. (23)

color: A visual sensation produced in the brain when the eye views various wavelengths of light. Color viewing is a highly subjective experience that varies from individual to individual. In the graphic arts industry, lighting standards and color charts help ensure the accuracy of color reproduction. (5)

colorant: Chemical substance that gives color to such materials as ink, paint, crayons, and chalk. The colorants that dissolve in liquids are called dyes. Colorants that do not dissolve but spread through liquids or other substances as tiny solid particles are called pigments. (9)

color constancy: The tendency to perceive the color of an object to be constant, even when specific conditions (such as lighting) are changed. (9)

color correction: Adjusting images to optimize values for highlight and shadow, neutral tones, skin tones, and sharpness, used to compensate for impurities in the printing ink and color separation. (10, 19)

color diagram: A visual representation of color data, used for process ink analysis. (22)

color formation: Additive and subtractive systems that create different colors from primary colors. (5)

color gamut: Common expression for the entire (greatest possible) range of color that can be shown on a computer display or reproduced by another output device. See also *palette*. (9, 10)

colorimeter: A color measurement device that measures and compares the hue, purity, and brightness of colors in a manner that simulates how people perceive color. (9)

Color Key™ proofs: A color proofing system that generates a set of process-color transparent film positives from separation negatives so registration and screen-tint combinations can be checked before actual press proofs are produced. (10)

Color management module (CMM): Color transformation engine that translates data from one device's color space to another. (10)

Color management system (CMS): An electronic prepress tool that provides a way to correlate the color-rendering capabilities of input devices (scanners, digital cameras), color monitors, and output devices (digital proofers, imagesetters, and color printers) to produce predictable, consistent color. (7, 10)

color sensitivity: A measure of how receptive a material is to the colors of light. (11)

color separation: Process of dividing the colors of a multicolored original into the printing primaries (CMY) and black (K). The CMYK color separations are made into film and used to prepare printing plates. (3, 9, 11)

color space: A three-dimensional area where three color attributes, such as hue, value, and chroma, can be depicted, calculated, and charted. (9)

color strength: The amount of pigment in an ink that determines how well the ink will cover the substrate. (22)

color temperature: The degree to which a black body must be heated to produce a certain color radiation; it is the method of rating the quality of a light source. (11)

color wheel: A visual tool that illustrates the basics of color. (5)

combination densitometer: A color measurement device that computes both the reflection and transmission densities of an image or surface material. (9)

commercial printing: A segment of the graphic communications industry that produces various products for customers, including forms, newspaper inserts, and catalogs. (1)

common impression cylinder: A web-fed press design in which one cylinder is surrounded by a group of printing units. Each printing unit prints a separate color on the web. (15)

comparison proofing: A proofreading method done primarily by one person to find such major problems as copy deletion, incorrect sequence, or copy duplication. It is best suited for jobs containing a small amount of copy. Also called one-person proofing. (7)

complementary colors: Any two colors that lie directly opposite each other on the color wheel. (9)

composing stick: A device used to hold foundry type when performing hand composition. The stick has a movable knee that can be set to the determined line length. (6)

composition: The process of organizing, setting, and production of type, line art, and photographs for printed communication. (5, 6)

composition depth: The space measuring from the beginning of a composition until the end of the composition. (4)

compositor: A person who sets type; also referred to as a typesetter. (6)

comprehensive layout: A detailed layout showing how the printed piece will look when finished. (5)

computer-to-plate (CTP): Technology that uses imaging systems that take fully-paginated digital materials and expose this information to plates in platesetters or imagesetters without creating film intermediates. (1, 14)

condensed typefaces: Those intended to get more words in less space by narrowing the width (but not height) of the characters. They are used rather than going to a smaller typeface. (4)

cones: Light-sensitive nerve cells of the retina that help us perceive light and color (red, green, and blue). Cones detect both intensity and wavelength (color). (9)

constructive interference: When two light waves cross a single point at the same time and combine to create brighter light than one wave can emit alone. (9)

contact printing: Process that produces a photographic print by exposing a light-sensitive material (film, photographic paper, or plate) held against a negative or positive in a contact printing frame. The resulting copy is the same size as the original. (11)

context-sensitive menu: The characteristic of a selection menu in page composition software in which the options that display are dependent on the type of material being worked on. (7)

continuous ink-jet printer: Printer in which a continuously circulating flow of ink through the printhead is maintained while the power is on. (13)

continuous spectrum: Spectrum of colors that is created when sunlight passes through a prism. The spectrum blends smoothly from one color to the next. (9)

continuous tone: An image with an infinite number of tone gradations between the lightest highlights and the darkest shadows. (9, 11)

continuous tone copy: An image with an infinite number of tone gradations between the lightest highlights and the darkest shadows. (1)

contrast: The variation of elements in a printed product. (5, 10)

control lines: Markings on originals and along the margins of negative film flats to aid in color registration and correct alignment. (12)

control strips: Continuous wedges of film with graduated densities that are pre-exposed under exacting conditions. They are used to test the development solution in automatic processors. (11)

conversion: Step of color management systems that performs color correction between imaging devices. (10)

copy: The text elements (words) used in producing printed products. (1)

copyboard: A glass-covered frame at one end of a process camera that holds the original image while it is being shot. (11)

copyboard controls: Controls used for positioning the copyboard in relation to other parts of the process camera. (11)

copyfitting: The process of fitting together copy and illustrations in a specific amount of space. (5)

copyright: A legal protection against unauthorized copying of original, creative works, including literary works, musical compositions and recordings, artwork, photographs, film and video works, and dramatic works. (24)

cornea: A transparent window at the front of the eye that refracts light to the retina. (9)

corporation: A type of business that is a separate legal entity from the people who own or manage it. A business that is a corporation pays taxes on its own tax return and is liable for its own debt and other legal responsibilities. (24)

craft-centered jobs: Refers to work performed by artisans or others with manual skills. (25)

creasing: The process of compressing the substrate so it will fold more easily; often done with a rotary creaser attached to the folder. (23)

creep: A pushing out or extension of pages on the outer edge of a saddle-stitched book, caused by the greater thickness at the spine. An allowance for creep must be made in the prepress phase. Also called shingling. (12, 23)

Cromalin™ proofs: A type of single-sheet color proof. (10)

cross-platform: Describes applications, formats, or devices that work on multiple computer operating system platforms. (7)

cursive: A typeface designed to simulate handwriting, in which the letters are not joined. (4)

cutting: The process of making a large sheet of paper into several smaller sheets. (23)

D log E chart: A graphic representation of the relationship between exposure and density. It indicates how a given film reacts to light and development. Also called characteristic curve. (11)

dampening system: A group of rollers designed to apply moisture to the nonimage area of the printing plate. (15)

debossing: The reverse of embossing, so the image is sunk into the substrate, rather than being raised. (23)

decibels (dBA): A unit for expressing the intensity of sound. (2)

definition: The sharpness or distinction of the printed image. (4)

de-inking: The process of removing inks, fillers, and coatings from waste paper. (21)

delivery pile: A uniform stack of paper that accepts sheets from the delivery system of a sheet-fed press. (15)

delivery system: A press system that removes the printed substrate from the printing system and prepares it for finishing operations. (15)

densitometer: An electronic instrument that uses a photocell to accurately measure the amount of light reflected from or through different values. (3, 9, 11)

density: The light-stopping ability of a material. The ability to hold back or block light. (11)

density capacity: The theoretical maximum density allowed by a given film. (11)

descender: The part of a letter that extends below the body or baseline. (4)

design: The application of proper methods to produce a product that is both artistic and functional. (5)

design axes: Variable typeface attribute (weight, width, style, optical size). The base design determines the range of variations available. (7)

desktop publishing system: A computerized system commonly used in the graphic communications industry to produce type and images. (3)

destructive interference: When two light waves cross at a single point at the same time and intersect to cause a dimmer light or a dark spot. This occurs when the crest of one wave intersects the trough of another wave, reducing the height of the crest. (9)

detail printer: The black printer in a set of color separations. Also called the skeleton printer. (9)

dialog box: A page composition software feature that permits the operator to input information, such as specifying an action, inputting a measurement, or selecting a color. (7)

dichromatic vision: A form of color blindness where only yellows and blues are visible. (9)

didot point system: The standard system of print measurement used in Europe. The didot point is equal to 0.0148″. Twelve didot points equal one Cicero (0.1776″). (3)

die cutting: A process in which pressure is used to force a sharp metal die (steel rule) through the stock. It is used to make irregular shapes. (23)

diffraction grating: An optical device used to study the colors in light. The grating uses thousands of thin slits to diffract light and separate it into its component parts. (9)

digital asset management (DAM): The protocol and resources established to handle all digital files and data. (13)

digital blueline proofs: Two-sided digital position proof for eight-page impositions (sixteen-page signatures). (10)

digital format: Data stored with measured values and distinct points or positions. A digital image is stored with distinct points of varying brightness and color, which are recorded as pixels. (8)

digital prepress system: A computer-centered process that consists of preparing content (text and graphics), then composing pages (design/layout), and outputting the finished file to an imagesetter, directly to a platemaker, or directly to a digital press. (7)

digital printing technology: Any reproduction technology that receives electronic files and uses dots for replication. (13)

digital proofs: Proofs generated by outputting files on a high-resolution, high-quality printer. (10)

direct imaging (DI): The process of sending a digital file directly to a press without the use of traditional offset or computer-to-plate processes or chemistry. (13)

direct screen photographic color separation: A method in which a process camera, contact printing frame, or enlarger is used to make color separation exposures through a photographic mask and a halftone screen onto high-contrast panchromatic film. Color-corrected halftone separation negatives are produced in one step, eliminating the need to screen tone values separately. (9)

display type: Type sizes above 12-point, used to emphasize the importance of a message and capture the reader's attention. (4)

distributed printing: A system of digital printing in which the electronic files for a job can be sent anywhere in the world, through a wide area network (WAN), for output. Commonly used for localized editions of newspapers and magazines. (13)

doctor blade: A thin metal blade that clears excess ink from the noncell areas of the anilox roll. (18)

dot etching: Manual alteration of the dot structure to correct color. Also a contacting technique used to spread or choke the dot structure. (10)

dot gain: Optical increase in the size of a halftone dot during prepress operations or the mechanical increase in halftone dot size that occurs as the image is transferred from plate-to-blanket-to-paper in lithography. (10)

dot pitch: A measurement of the vertical distance between rows of pixels on a monitor, stated in decimal fractions of a millimeter. The image quality becomes crisper as the fraction becomes smaller. A common dot pitch measurement on monitors for general computer use is 0.28. (7, 10)

dots per inch (dpi): Measuring units for image resolution; the number of dots a printing device can generate in one linear inch. It is also used to describe pixels per inch in a bitmapped image. (3)

double-sheet detector: A control device that prevents more than one sheet of paper from entering the press. (15)

drawdown: The amount of time required to remove all air from a vacuum frame to allow the original and the film to achieve uniform contact before exposure. (11)

drawdown test: A method of checking for proper ink mixing by placing a small amount of ink on paper, and then using a blade to spread it and produce a thin ink film. (22)

drawsheet: A sheet of tympan paper that provides the holding surface for paper to be printed on a platen press. (17)

drilling: Piercing operation that uses a revolving, hollow drill bit with very sharp edges. The waste stock rises through the hollow center of the drill. (23)

drop-down menus: A selection list within software programs that extends downward from the menu bar on the computer display screen. The list contains choices that can be used to create or modify documents. (7)

drum scanner: A type of scanner that scans images mounted on a rotating drum. The drum spins quickly in front of a stationary reading head. As the drum rotates, the original material is illuminated by a light source that pans slowly across the front of the drum. Also referred to as a rotary scanner. (8)

dry: The point at which the ink is free of volatile substances and has polymerized to a total solid state. (22)

dummy: A representative layout of a printed piece showing the folds, page numbers, and positions of text and illustrations. (12)

duotone: A two-color halftone reproduction from a black-and-white photograph. (11)

duplicate plate: In relief printing, a secondary plate or copy of the original type form of composed characters. (17)

duplicator: A small sheet-fed press typically used for short printing runs. (16)

durometer: A measure of a rubber squeegee blade's hardness. (20)

dye: A type of colorant that dissolves in liquid. (9)

dye sublimation: A type of thermography that uses heat and pressure to change solid dye particles on a ribbon into a gas to produce an image on a substrate. (13)

dynamic range: The gradations from light to dark that a digital imaging device can read or produce. (8)

E

editing: The final preparation of the author's or writer's manuscript for publication. It involves checking the text, line art, and photographs. Content editing involves checking the material to make sure it is up-to-date, technically accurate, organized in a logical sequence, and covers all important ideas. Copy editing is done to correct spelling and punctuation, to mark for style, and to assure proper grammar. (1)

edition binding: The most complex and permanent form of binding, in which a rigid cover is attached to a book body that is held together by sewing. (23)

E gauge: A device used to measure point sizes and leading of printed type. (3)

electromagnetic spectrum: The entire range of wavelengths of electromagnetic radiation, extending from gamma rays (very short) to radio waves (very long). The wavelengths are usually measured in nanometers (nm). (9, 11)

electronic color separation: The process of separating process colors and black (CMYK) with an electronic (computer-assisted) imaging system. (9)

electronic information transfer: Sending digital information instantly via telephone lines and satellites. (25)

electrophotography: Printing process that uses a drum coated with chargeable photoconductors, dry or liquid toners, and a corona assembly to produce an image on a substrate. (13)

electroplating: An electrical-chemical process of applying copper plating to a gravure cylinder. (19)

electrostatic assist: A process in which a power source feeds electrical charges between the impression roller (negative) and the printing cylinder (positive), creating a force that achieves a nearly complete release of ink from the etched cells. (19)

electrostatic plates: Light-sensitive plates that are imaged by a charge of electrostatic energy. (14)

electrostatic printing: A printing method that uses the forces of electric current and static electricity. It is commonly found in office copying machines. Machines capable of producing copies in multiple colors have become common in recent years. (1, 13)

electrotype: A duplicate relief plate that is produced from a mold through an electrochemical process. (17)

elemental chlorine: Chlorine gas used to bleach paper pulp and to separate the pulp from lignin. (21)

elements of design: The fundamental elements used by the graphic designer. Elements of design include lines, shapes, mass, texture, and color. (5)

elements of layout: The fundamental elements used by the layout artist to make a composition. The elements of layout include body type, display type, illustrations, and white space. (5)

embossing: A process that creates a raised image on a substrate by pressing it between two dies. (23)

em quad: In foundry type, a nonprinting type block that is a square of the type size, typically used to indent the beginning of the paragraph. (4)

emulsion: Chemical compounds that form a light-sensitive coating on the base material. It is usually made up of silver halides suspended in a gelatin. (11)

emulsion sensitivity: A measure of how light-sensitive material reacts to light exposure. It is rated by an arbitrary numerical system known as ISO. The higher the ISO rating assigned to a film emulsion, the faster the film will react to a light exposure. (11)

en quad: In foundry type, a spacing element half an em quad in width, typically used to separate words. (4)

entrepreneur: Someone who starts his or her own business. (25)

equivalent weight: The weight of one ream of paper of a size that is larger or smaller than the basic size. (21)

ergonomics: The science of fitting the job to the worker. (2)

error-diffusion screening: Screening method that places dots randomly. (10)

expanded faces: Those intended to fill more space without going to a larger point size. Also called extended faces, they consist of letters that have been made wider without increasing their height. (4)

eye span: The width of body type a person can see with one fixation (sweep or adjustment) of the eye muscles. The normal eye span is about one and one-half alphabets. (4)

fair use: Certain exceptions to U.S. Copyright Laws that allow duplication and use of copyrighted materials without infringement. (24)

feeding system: A press system that transfers individual sheets of paper to the press and places them in register. (15)

filament: A single thread. (20)

fillers: Inorganic materials, such as clay or titanium dioxide, added to the papermaking furnish to improve opacity, brightness, smoothness, and ink receptivity. (21)

film: A material that is chemically altered after it is exposed to light. It is made up of a protective overcoating, an emulsion, a base material, and an antihalation backing. (11)

film back: The hinged assembly on the process camera used to hold a sheet of film flat in the focal plane. (11)

film scanner: A specially designed CCD scanner that captures images from various types of film. (8)

filter: A feature of image manipulation programs used to apply special effects to images, such as textures and patterns. (8)

financial printing: A segment of the graphic communications industry consisting of plants that primarily print materials such as checks, currency, and legal documents. (1)

finishing: A general term that applies to the many operations carried out during or following printing, such as cutting, folding, slitting, perforating, creasing and scoring, die cutting, embossing, stamping, numbering, drilling and punching, varnishing, and laminating. (1, 23)

FIRST: Flexographic Image Reproduction Specification and Tolerances. A set of guidelines and data to be used as communication and production tools in the flexographic reproduction process. (18)

fixed cost: Business expenses that remain consistent, regardless of the volume of work in the shop. Also known as overhead. (24)

flat: A large support sheet to which images (films) have been attached (stripped) for exposure onto a printing plate. (12, 14)

flatbed scanner: A type of scanner that scans images placed on a glass bed, or scan area. (8)

flexography: A relief printing process that uses flexible (usually plastic) printing plates. Flexography is extensively used in packaging, and is achieving growing use in printing newspapers and other long-run jobs. (1, 6, 17, 18)

flooding: In gravure printing, the process of inking the cells of the plate or cylinder. (22)

floor horizontal camera: A horizontal process camera with a large bed that mounts on the floor of the facility. (11)

flush: Term describing the dispersing of a pigment in an undried state (a paste) into a vehicle for ink. (22)

flying splicer: A splicer unit that bonds a new web to the existing web without stopping any operations on a web-fed press. (15)

focal plane: The plane on a camera where the images transmitted by the lens are brought to sharpest focus. (11)

font: In computer-based or phototypesetting composition methods, a font consists of all the characters that make up a specific typeface. (4) A font in foundry type, where each character is on a separate piece of metal, consists of different quantities of each character in one size and style of type. (6)

font set: The font list for a document. Font sets can be created for individual jobs and activate only the set needed. (7)

form: A set of foundry type consisting of different quantities of each character in one size and style. (6) A guide for determining how images on a signature will be laid out to meet folding, trimming, and bindery requirements. (12)

formal balance: A design principle that is achieved when the elements of a design are of equal weight and are positioned symmetrically. (5)

former board: A curved or triangular plane that serves as the folding surface on a web-fed press. (15)

forms printing: Companies that design and print special paper forms used in many businesses. (1)

foundry type: Individually metal-cast type (letters, numbers, characters) that can be arranged to form words and sentences for printing on paper. (4, 6)

fourdrinier machine: A paper machine that forms a continuous web of paper on a moving, endless wire belt. (21)

fovea: The most sensitive part of the eye's retina and the area of sharpest vision. It is located at the center of the macula and is packed with cone cells. (9)

front-end platforms: The combination of desktop computer hardware, peripherals, and software that allow users to create, manipulate, and store documents prior to printing. (12)

furnish: The slurry of fillers, sizing, and colorants in a water suspension from which paper is made. (21)

furniture: Wood or metal spacers arranged around a block of type in a chase to position the type for printing. (6)

galley: A three-sided metal tray used to store type forms or slugs before they are assembled into page form. (6)

gamma: A measure of film contrast resulting from length of development. (11)

gamma levels: Degrees of contrast of a screen image of a monitor. (10)

gamut: Common expression for the entire (greatest possible) range of color that can be shown on a computer display or reproduced by another output device. (21)

gamut alarm: Warning used by many imaging or page composition programs to indicate the presence of colors that are out of the printing range. (10)

gamut compression: Technique used to compress colors to fit into a smaller color gamut. The compression gives the illusion that all color chroma, saturation, and value are present. (10)

gathering: Assembling printed signatures. (23)

gigabyte: One billion bytes, abbreviated GB. (7)

grade: Category or class of paper. (3, 21)

grain: The direction or structure of paper fibers. (21)

grain long: Important factor of paper that can affect folding and direction of feed for printing. (21)

grain short: Indicates that the grain runs across the paper. (21)

gram: The standard unit of mass in the metric system. (3)

graphical user interface (GUI): A method of representing computer operations and programs on the screen with small pictures (icons) that can be selected with a mouse to perform activities. The GUI is considered far easier and more rapid to use than the command method, which involved typing directions from the keyboard. (7)

graphic communications: A general term for the exchange of information in a visual form, such as words, drawings, photographs, or a combination of these. More specifically, a term describing printing and related industries. (1)

gravure: A method of printing from cells or depressions that are engraved below the nonimage area of the printing cylinder. (19)

gray component replacement (GCR): The removal of equal amounts of cyan, magenta, and yellow areas of a four-color halftone and replacement of these colors with a higher proportion of black. This produces a clearer, less muddy effect. (10)

grayscale: A continuous tone strip used to visually gauge exposure of an image. (3, 10)

grayscaling: The process of converting a continuous-tone image to an image in shades of gray. (10)

gripper allowance: The unprinted space allowed at the edge of a printing sheet. (12)

gripper edge: The side of the flat that enters the press and is held by the mechanical fingers of the press gripper. (12)

ground glass: A piece of grained, matte, or frosted glass mounted onto the back of the process camera with hinges or on rails. It is used to view and focus on the original copy before it is exposed as a latent image on film. (11)

halftone grade film: Film used to create halftones. It is considered to be more sensitive and dimensionally stable than line film. (11)

halftone gravure: A gravure method that uses halftone separations rather than continuous-tone separations for image reproduction. (19)

halftone screen process: The procedure of converting a continuous-tone original into a dot structure. (11)

handheld scanner: A small scanner is moved across a page or image by hand. Also referred to as half-page scanners. (8)

hardware: A computer and its associated devices. (7)

heavy elements: The darker strokes of a type character that give it identity. (4)

high-key photograph: Photo that contains the most important details in the highlights, or lighter tones. (11)

highlight: Tones with the lightest value. In halftone, the area with the smallest dots. (11)

hinting: Application that optimizes how type prints at small point sizes on printers with a resolution of 600 dpi or lower. (10)

histogram: A graphic display of highlight, midtone, and shadow values that correspond to the number of pixels affected in each part of the tonal scale. (8)

horizontal camera: A process camera that has a horizontal optical axis. (11)

hue: The color of an object perceived by the eye, and determined by the dominant light wavelengths reflected or transmitted. (9)

ICC color profiles: Profiles based on the CIELAB color space and used as standards for describing the color characterizations of different devices. ICC color profiles contain information on the device's color space and the compensation required to bring the device to its ideal level of performance. (10)

illumination: The brightness of light in an image. (3)

illustrations: The elements of layout that include the ornamentation, photographs, and artwork, such as line art. (5)

image assembly: The process of electronically assembling line and halftone negatives or positives into pages. See *stripping*. (1)

image carrier: A device on a printing press, such as a press plate, used to transfer inked images onto another intermediate carrier or directly onto a substrate, such as paper. (1, 6)

impactless printing: Term for several types of printing (such as ink-jet or electrostatic) that do not require direct contact between an image carrier and the substrate. (1)

imposition: The layout of copy on a page in preparation for the photographic process. (12)

impression cylinder: A printing system component that brings the paper to be printed in contact with the blanket cylinder. (15)

incident beam: The beam of light coming toward a surface. (9)

indirect screen photographic color separation: A two-step process in which continuous-tone separations are produced from full-color originals, and halftone negatives or positives are made from the continuous-tone separations. (9)

informal balance: A design principle that is achieved by changing the value, size, or location of elements in a design. (5)

infringement: The unauthorized use of copyrighted material. (24)

ink: A colored coating specially formulated to reproduce an image on a substrate. (22)

ink agitator: A revolving device that is used to maintain a consistent flow of ink from the ink fountain. (16)

ink body: Term that describes the consistency of an ink. (22)

ink darkness: A factor that affects the contrast of printed materials. Darkness depends on the ink's covering power. Complete coverage hides the surface of the paper. (4)

ink fineness gauge: A device that measures the pigment particle size in an ink. (22)

ink formulation: The amount and type of ingredients used in a particular printing ink. (22)

inking and dampening system: A combined system of rollers that applies both ink and fountain solution to the plate during operation of the press. (15)

inking system: A group of rollers designed to carry ink to the image area of the printing plate. (15)

ink-jet printing: A direct-to-paper technology that uses digital data to control streams of very fine droplets of ink or dye to produce images directly on paper or other substrates. (13)

ink-jet proofs: A type of job proof that provides four-color proofs generated directly from the digital files. The color simulates what will be produced on a press. (7)

ink keys: Adjustable devices used to control the flow of ink from the ink fountain to the printing plate. (16)

ink length: The elasticity of ink. It is referred to as long or short. (22)

ink mileage: The surface area that can be covered by a given quantity of ink. (22)

inkometer: An instrument that measures the tack of a printing ink. (22)

ink sticking: A press problem that occurs when two layers of ink film, on two different sheets, bond together. (22)

ink tack: The stickiness of the ink. A measurement of cohesion between the ink film and the substrate. (16, 22)

ink thickness gauge: A device that measures the thickness of the ink film on the press rollers. (22)

inline: Done as a continuous process on a single piece of equipment. (18)

in-plant printing: Term for printing facilities operated by companies whose business is not the production of printed materials. (1)

intaglio: A printing process in which words, pictures, or designs are engraved into a printing plate or cylinder. (19)

International Color Consortium (ICC): Organization established in 1993 by leading manufacturers to create a cross-platform standard for color management. (10)

interpolation: A mathematical technique used to increase the apparent resolution of an image. Image resolution is increased by adding data in intermediate shades of gray or color to surrounding areas. (8)

interpreter: A computer program used with output devices that receive PDL page descriptions. After receiving a page description, the interpreter constructs a representation of the page to suit the output device. (7)

ionography: Printing process that uses an electron cartridge, a nonconductive surface, and a magnetic toner to produce an image on a substrate. (13)

iris: An opaque diaphragm that contracts and expands to control the amount of light that enters the eye. The iris is the colored portion of the eye. (9)

ISO series: The series of standard paper and envelope sizes established by the International Organizations for Standardization (ISO). (3)

IT8 reflective target: Standard color reference tool used to calibrate input and output devices. (10)

italic type: A slashed type, modeled on a form of handwriting. It was developed and first used by Aldus Manutius, a printer in Italy. Most Roman and sans serif faces have a companion italic of the same design. (4)

J

job case: A storage drawer with individual compartments for the letters and spacing material used in hand-setting foundry type. (6)

Job Definition Format (JDF): A file format based on Extensible Markup Language (XML), which provides a standard format that is compatible with any JDF-enabled equipment. JDF files can contain information on the document designer, fonts used, images contained, stock type and size, ink colors, bindery instructions, and instructions for JDF-enabled devices used in the production process, including ink fountain settings on a press and the configuration of bindery equipment. (7)

job ticket: A work order that gives the imposition for a particular job and provides a checklist of general information for use by the stripper or others in the prepress department. (12)

justify: To adjust letter-spacing and word-spacing so lines of type in a block are all equal in length, resulting in even left and right margins. (4)

K

kerning: A typesetting technique in which space between certain pairs of characters is tightened to improve appearance and readability. (4)

knockout: Clean break between design elements. (10)

L

labor cost: The "people costs" involved in operating a business, including hourly wages, salaries, and benefits for employees. (24)

laminating: Process in which thin film of plastic with an adhesive coating is bonded to a printed substrate to provide protection against abrasion and moisture. (23)

laser plates: Carriers that are imaged digitally by a laser platemaking system. (14)

layers: A feature of image editing programs that creates multiple, editable levels of a single piece of artwork. (8)

layout: The sketch or plan for the finished page when assembling a mechanical. (5)

leading: The vertical distance separating each line of typeset copy, measured in points from one line to the next. Pronounced "ledding." (3)

legibility: A measure of how difficult or easy it is to read printed matter. (4)

lensboard: The support that holds the lens in alignment with the optical axis of the camera. (11)

lensboard controls: Controls used for positioning the lensboard and making other adjustments to the lens on process cameras. (11)

letterspacing: Changing the spacing between typeset letters, for better appearance or to fit copy in a given space. (4)

lifelong learning: Upgrading and updating one's job skills and knowledge to keep pace with technological changes in a field. (25)

lift: Term describing a pile of paper, usually the amount cut or drilled in a single operation. (23)

ligatures: Joined letter combinations, such as *fi, ff, fl, ffi,* or *ffl,* found in some typefaces. (4)

light elements: The hairlines or other less-dark strokes that tie together the heavy elements of a type character. (4)

lignin: A glue-like substance that bonds wood fibers together. (21)

line art: A drawing with no grays or middletones. Traditionally, black lines on white paper. In computer publishing, an object-oriented graphic. While scanned-in line art is bitmapped, line art created (mathematically) in the computer is a vector, or object-oriented graphic. (1)

line gauge: A device used to measure type sizes and line lengths in picas or inches. (3)

line length: The distance from the left to right sides of a line or body of copy, usually measured in picas. Also called line width. (4)

lines: Design elements that form the shapes of an image. (5)

Linotype: The most common type of mechanical linecasting machine. It permitted the compositor to use a keyboard to quickly assemble brass letter molds, then cast an entire line of type. (6)

liquid lamination: A coating method similar to varnishing. The plastic coating material is applied in liquid form and then cured into a tough protective layer by exposure to ultraviolet light. Also called UV-cured coating. (23)

liter: The standard unit of capacity in the metric system. (3)

lithography: A method of printing directly from a flat surface or plate containing an image formed in ink. (14)

livering: A chemical change in the body of an ink that occurs during storage. (22)

lockout devices: A key or combination-type lock used to hold an energy isolating device in the safe position to prevent the machine from energizing. (2)

lookup tables: Chart stored in computer memory that lists the dot sizes needed to produce given colors. (10)

loose set: Term describing wider than normal letterspacing. (4)

lossless compression algorithms: A mathematical formula for image compression that assumes that the likely value of a pixel can be inferred from the values of surrounding pixels. Because lossless compression algorithms do not discard any of the data, the decompressed image is identical to the original. (7)

lossy compression algorithms: A mathematical formula for image compression in which data in an image that is least perceptible to the eye is removed. This improves the speed of data transfer, but causes a slight degradation in the decompressed image. (7)

low-key photograph: Contains primarily shadows, or darker tones. (11)

Ludlow: A type of linecasting machine that was used primarily to set larger point sizes, which was typically used as display type. (6)

luminance: The amount of light in an image. (3)

M

machine guards: Metal or plastic enclosures that cover moving machine parts and protect the operator from being cut, squashed, or hit by flying fragments. Guards also protect the equipment from foreign objects. (2)

macula: A small hollow in the middle of the eye's retina where the cones are concentrated. (9)

magnetography: Printing process that uses a drum, magnetic toner, and high pressure to produce an image on a substrate. (13)

makeready: The process of preparing a press for printing a job. (13)

manager: A leadership position whose responsibility it is to manage a company, business, or part of a business. (25)

manuscript: A style of hand lettering used by the scribes of Germany, France, Holland, and other countries in the Middle Ages. (4)

mask: A feature of image editing programs that protects a specified area of an image from changes, filters, and other effects applied to the rest of the image. (8)

mass: A measure of volume that adds definition to shapes in a visual presentation. (5)

Matchprint proofs: Industry-standard contract proof produced from the actual film that will create the printing pages. This enables accurate evaluation of the film for trapping, moiré, and other conventional printing problems. (10)

Material Safety Data Sheets (MSDS): A document, produced by a chemical manufacturer, that summarizes the physical properties of a particular chemical and the health and safety hazards associated with its use. (2)

materials cost: The prices paid for items that are consumed as a job is printed, such as paper, ink, and packaging materials. (24)

matrix: A mold used with molten metal to produce individual pieces of foundry type. In molded-rubber platemaking, a phenolic resin mold that captures the details of the original plate. (6, 18)

maximum resolution: Maximum number of pixels that a computer screen can represent in both horizontal and vertical dimensions. (10)

mechanical binding: A broad category that includes many different devices used to hold sheets together. An example is loose-leaf binding. (23)

megabyte: One million bytes; usually abbreviated MB. (7)

mercury vapor lamps: Light source that produces radiation by passing an electrical current through gaseous mercury. At one time, these lamps were the primary means of exposing sensitive printing plates. (11)

mesh-bridging capability: The ability of a stencil to bridge diagonally across an individual fabric cell. (20)

mesh count: The number of threads (or strands) per linear inch in a fabric. (20)

metal halide lamps: Mercury lamp that has metal halide additives. (11)

meter: The standard unit of length in the metric system. (3)

metric conversion chart: A table of equivalencies used to convert US Conventional and metric values from one system to another. (3)

metric prefix: Word prefix that indicates multiples or divisions of measuring units in the metric system. (3)

midtones: Tones with gray values. (11)

modem: A device used with computers to send and receive digital information through telephone lines. (7)

Modern Roman typefaces: Typefaces that have increased contrast between very thin, light elements and heavy elements. (4)

moiré pattern: A visually undesirable dot-exaggerating effect that occurs when two different screen patterns are randomly positioned or superimposed. (3, 11)

molleton cover: A cloth tube that fits over the body of a dampening roller and helps it retain fountain solution. (15)

monochromatic colorimeter: A color measurement device that measures the intensity of a particular color and does not depend on the eye's perception of color. (9)

Monotype: A composing machine with a keyboard and a separate metal caster that produced individual cast letters. (6)

mottling: The blotchy or cloudy appearance of an image, instead of a smooth, continuous tone. (8)

movable type: Individual type characters, usually cast in metal, that can be assembled into words, disassembled, and later reassembled into different words. (6)

near-complementary color: A color that harmonizes with colors that lie next to its complement on the color wheel. For example, near-complementary colors to red are blue-green and yellow-green. Also called split-complementary color. (9)

negative leading: The practice of reducing spacing below the type size, resulting in lines that are set very close together vertically. (4)

newspaper printing: A segment of the graphic communications industry that involves publishing and printing daily or weekly newspapers. (1)

Newton's rings: An undesirable color pattern that results from interference between the exposure light and its reflected beam from the closest adjacent surface. Commonly referred to as "Newton rings." (8)

nip points: The point of contact where two cylinders, gears, or rollers meet or come close to one another. (2)

nonpareil: Measuring unit on a line gauge that is equal to one-half pica. A pica is equal to 0.166″; a nonpareil is 0.083″. (3)

Novelty typeface: A typeface designed primarily to command special attention, express a mood, or provide a specific appearance for a theme or an occasion. Also called "decorative" or "occasional" typefaces. (4)

numbering: The process of imprinting tickets, certificates, checks, or other items with consecutive figures (numbers), using a device that transfers the figures from an inked relief image. (23)

oblique: In electronic composition, the term used to describe a simulated italic character produced by slanting an upright Roman typeface. (4)

off color: When the color of the printed job does not match the intended color. (22)

offset printing: A printing method in which inked images are offset or transferred from one surface to another. (14)

oil mounting: A method of mounting transparent original material onto a drum scanner. The originals are coated with a small amount of mounting oil or gel to reduce scratches and imperfections before being mounted on the drum. (8)

Old English: A text typeface often used for such applications as diplomas, certificates, and religious materials. (4)

Oldstyle Roman typefaces: A group of typefaces that have a rugged appearance, with relatively little contrast between heavy and light elements. They reflect the earliest Roman designs. (4)

opacity: The quality of a paper that does not allow print from the opposite side to show through. See *show-through.* (4, 21)

open press interface (OPI) system: A computer configuration and software that allows the designer to use low-resolution images when creating document layouts in page composition programs, and high-resolution images automatically replace the low-res images when the file is sent to an output device. (7)

optical character recognition (OCR): A system used to translate the bitmap image of scanned text into ASCII characters. (8)

output device: A piece of equipment used to display, produce, or transfer information processed by a computer, such as monitors and printers. (7)

outsourcing: Sending a product to a service company for specified work needed to complete a product. (25)

overhead horizontal camera: A horizontal process camera that has the camera bed and copyboard attached to the overhead framework. (11)

overprinting: When image elements are specified to be printed over or on top of other colors. (10)

package printing: Industry that uses images printed on many different types of materials, such as plastic, paper, cardboard, corrugated board, and foil. (1)

packaging: The process of wrapping, strapping, or boxing the printed pieces together for delivery to the customer. (23)

page composition: Prepress process of setting type and image layout for a page. (1)

page description language (PDL): A file format that describes a page's layout, contents, and position within the larger document in a manner the output device can understand. Adobe® PostScript®, Adobe® PDF, and Hewlett Packard PCL are examples of common PDLs. (7)

page grid: A nonprinted set of guidelines on each composition page that includes guidelines for margins, columns, gutters, and other basic page elements. Also called baseline grid or frame. (7)

paint effects: A feature of image manipulation programs that contains several tools that allow the user to create and color images. Some tools fill in and erase colors and assign and adjust color values and gradations. (8)

palette: A modified form of a program menu that can be resized and positioned on the screen to suit the operator's preferences. When displayed, it always remains visible, overlaying any other images on the screen. (7)

paper caliper: A device used to measure paper thickness. (3)

paper flatness: How well a sheet of paper remains straight or unwarped for feeding through a sheet-fed press. (21)

paper size: Measurements that describe the length and width dimensions of paper. Sizes are expressed in inches or metric units. (3)

partnership: A type of business that is owned by two or more persons. The owners and the business are considered a single entity and pay income tax on the profits of the business. In this type of business, the ownership responsibilities and legal liability is split between or among all the partners. (24)

pasteboard: An on-screen work area in page composition programs; used for temporary storage of layout elements (such as a piece of art or a section of typeset material) before moving them onto the page. (7)

percent open area: Percentage of area per square inch in a fabric through which ink can pass. (20)

percent stretch: A measurement of screen tension. (20)

perfect binding: Method that uses an adhesive to hold sheets or signatures together and to fasten the flexible cloth or paper cover onto the body. Also called softcover binding. (23)

perfecting press: Printing system that prints both sides of the substrate at once. (15)

perforating: Operation that places a series of small cuts or slits in the substrate, using various types of blades or wheels on the press or folder. (23)

periodical printing: That segment of the graphic communications industry consisting of plants that are designed primarily to print magazines. (1)

personal protective devices: Clothing or equipment worn for protection from potential bodily injury associated with chemical use or machine operation. Devices worn in graphic communication plants include safety glasses, face shields, plastic or rubber gloves, earplugs, dust masks, respirators, and safety shoes. (2)

petrochemicals: Petroleum-based chemicals. (21)

photoconversion: The general term for processes that use light to place the original image onto a light-sensitive material. It includes the use of process cameras to make negatives and screened (halftone) images, digital cameras and scanners used for image capture, and exposure units for platemaking. (1)

photo-density range: The density difference between the highlight value and shadow value. Also referred to as copy-density range. (11)

photo direct plates: Image carriers that are imaged directly from camera-ready copy or a paste-up. (14)

photoengraving: A platemaking method that produces relief images by exposing a light-sensitive plate coating through a negative. (17)

photographic masking: Method of color manipulation that is accomplished by creating film images from an original using filters. (10)

photomultiplier tube (PMT): A light-sensing device composed of highly sensitive photocells that transform variations in light into electric currents. The photocells create input signals for the computing circuits in electronic scanners. (8)

photopigments: Light-sensitive chemicals in the cones of the human eye. Photopigments respond to red, green, or blue light. (9)

photopolymer plates: Plastic relief plates commonly used in flexographic printing that contain a light-sensitive polymer coating that hardens after exposure. (14, 17, 18)

pH scale: A measuring scale used to determine the acidity or alkalinity of a solution. The pH scale is numbered from 0–14, with 7 designated as neutral. A pH value below 7 indicates an acidic solution; a value above 7 indicates an alkaline solution. (15)

pH value: A measurement that indicates the acidity or alkalinity of a solution, as measured on the pH scale. (15)

pica: One of the principal units of measure used in the graphic communications industry. A pica is equal to 0.166″. Six picas almost equals one inch (0.966″). (3)

pi characters: In fonts for computer of phototypesetting, such symbols as stars, asterisks, arrows, percent signs, or check marks. In foundry type, such special characters are called sorts or dingbats. (4)

piezoelectric ink-jet printer: Printer in which a piezocrystal is charged to cause pressure, which forces droplets of ink from the nozzle. (13)

pigments: Colorants in the form of fine, solid particles that do not dissolve but spread through liquids or other substances. They have varying degrees of resistance to water, alcohol, and other chemicals and are generally insoluble in the ink vehicle. (9, 22)

pinholes: Imperfections on a photographic negative or stencil caused by dust and other airborne contaminants. (20)

pixel: Abbreviation for *picture element*, the tiniest image component in a digital imaging or display system. On a computer monitor screen, pixels are arranged in rows and columns that glow to display the image. (3)

plastic comb binding: A mechanical binding method commonly used for booklets that might have to be altered by adding or removing pages. Books bound with this method permit the pages to lay perfectly flat when open. (23)

plate: An image carrier used for printing multiple copies on a press. (14)

plate bend allowance: A portion of the leading edge of the plate that is inserted into a plate-holding device. (12)

plate coatings: Layers of light-sensitive material on the surface of plates that form or harden when exposed to light. (14)

plate coverings: Layers of material bonded to the plate base material, used to help hold the image area in place. (14)

plate cylinder: A printing system component that holds the plate on the press. (15)

plate elongation: The physical stretching of an image carrier when mounted on the plate cylinder, which may distort images and text. (18)

plate grain: The surface texture of a plate base. (14)

platen press: A relief press that prints by pressing a type form or plate against a platen, the surface that holds the paper to be printed. (17)

plate wear: The wearing away of the surface of a plate by coarse particles in the ink. (22)

platform: The computer system, or hardware, that is used to operate the software. The platform defines the standard around which a system can be developed. Popular platforms are PC and the Apple Macintosh. (7)

point: One of the principal units of measure used in the graphic communications industry. A point is equal to 0.0138″. Twelve points equal one pica. (3)

point size: A vertical measurement used to identify or specify the size of a typeface. Measurement is from the top of the ascender space to the bottom of the descender space. (4)

point system: The system of print measurement used throughout the graphic communications industry in the United States. The standard units in the point system are the point and pica. (3)

portable document format (PDF): A file format developed by Adobe Systems for representing documents in a manner that is independent of the original application software, hardware, and operating system used to create those documents. A PDF file can describe documents containing any combination of text, graphics, and images independently of output device or resolution. It is ideal for delivering entire documents over electronic mail, the World Wide Web, CD-ROM, or other media. (12)

postconsumer paper waste: Used paper products that have served their intended purpose and are separated from solid waste for recycling into new paper. (21)

posterization: The technique of changing a black-and-white, continuous-tone picture into a multicolor or multitone reproduction. (11)

PostScript: A programming language, commonly referred to as page description language, developed by Adobe Systems, Inc. PostScript language is specially designed for describing text and graphics on a printed page. (7)

PostScript printer typeface file: One of two component files that make up a PostScript type family. The PostScript printer typeface file is used for printing PostScript Type 1 fonts. (7)

PostScript Type 1 font: Consists of all the variations of one style of type; includes the suitcase file and PostScript printer typeface file. (7)

preconsumer paper waste: Scrap material generated by the papermaking process. (21)

preflighting: The process of checking documents for completeness to avoid unnecessary or unsuccessful processing. Missing fonts, missing graphics and images, and PostScript errors are detected early in production to avoid wasted resources and time. (7)

prepress: The production steps that are carried out prior to printing. (12)

press proofs: Proof generated with a proof press. One of the best verification proofs; also very slow and expensive. (10)

primary colors: Colors that can be used to generate secondary colors. In the additive system, these colors are red, green, and blue (RGB). In the subtractive system, these colors are cyan, magenta, and yellow (CMY). On the color wheel, the colors are red, green, and yellow. (5)

principles of design: The basic guidelines used by a design artist. The principles of design are balance, contrast, unity, rhythm, and proportion. (5)

printability: How well fine details are reproduced in a printed image. (21)

print engine: A small computer component inside a laser printer that translates the output of the computer into a bitmapped image for printing. (7)

printing: A process involving the use of a specialized machine (a printing press) to transfer an image from an image carrier to a substrate, usually paper. Most often, printing involves making duplicates of the printed product in large quantities. (1)

printing estimate: An offer to print a particular job for a specified price. If the customer accepts the estimate, it becomes a contract that is binding for both the printer and customer. (24)

printing press: A specialized machine used to transfer an image from an image carrier to a substrate, usually paper. (1)

printing system: A group of cylinders used to transfer images from the printing plate to the substrate. In a lithographic press, the printing system consists of a plate cylinder, a blanket cylinder, and an impression cylinder. (15)

print strength: How well a paper surface resists lifting of its fiber by high-tack inks. (21)

process camera: Device used to make enlargements, reductions, and same-size reproductions of originals for use in page composition or stripping work. The camera may be used to produce a film negative (opposite original), a film positive (film like original), or a print (photo like original). (1, 11)

process color printing: The method of printing full-color materials using the transparent cyan, magenta, yellow, and black (CMYK) inks. (9)

process colors: The printed reproduction of full-color photographs using the transparent inks of cyan, magenta, yellow, and black (CMYK). (1)

productivity: The amount of quality work that is completed in a given time span. (24)

profit: The difference between sales income and business expenses. (24)

proof: Any copy or art that is checked before going into print. Also, a prototype of the printed job made photomechanically from plates (a press proof), photochemically from film and dyes, or digitally from electronic data (prepress proofs). (7)

proofreader's marks: Widely used symbols that single out and explain when something in typeset copy is to be taken out, added, or changed. (7)

proofreading: The process of checking for typesetting errors and marking them for correction. (7)

proportion: The relationship between elements in an image. (5)

proportional scale: A measuring device used to determine the correct reproduction percentage for the enlargement or reduction of images. (3)

protective overcoating: A material that helps keep a film emulsion from being scratched and marred while being handled. (11)

pulpers: Vats in which coloring or bleaching additives are added to pulp. (21)

pulsed xenon lamps: The primary light source found in graphic communication facilities. These lamps are an excellent light source with spectral output close to daylight. (11)

punching: Piercing operation done by forcing a metal rod (a punch) down through the paper to remove stock. The punch works in a shearing action with a die placed below the paper. (23)

quantizing: A filtering process that determines the amount and selection of data to eliminate, which makes it possible to encode data with fewer bits. (8)

quartz-iodine lamps: An incandescent lamp with a tungsten filament surrounded by iodine and inert gases, all enclosed in a quartz bulb. (11)

quick printing: A subdivision of commercial printing, consisting of shops specializing in rapidly completing short-run printing and photocopying work for business customers. (1)

quoins: Expanding metal locking devices used to wedge a type form and furniture in place in a chase. (6)

RAID: Redundant Array of Independent Disks. A hard drive configuration that connects a number of high-capacity hard disk drives together. The connected drives act like a single, huge hard drive. (7)

random-access memory (RAM): Type of short-term computer memory that stores information in process. It is the most common type of memory found in computers and other devices, such as printers. Storage capacity is measured in kilobytes (1024 bytes), megabytes (1024 kilobytes), and gigabytes (1024 megabytes). (7)

raster image processor (RIP): A device that interprets all of the page layout information for the marking engine of the output device. PostScript or another page description language serves as an interface between the page layout workstation and the RIP. (7)

rasterized: To convert image data into a pattern of dots (pixels) for the production of film. (12)

ream: Five hundred sheets of paper. (3, 21)

recycled paper: Paper made from old or used paper products. (21)

refined layout: Layout in which the positioning of the images represents the exact location of all images without having the composed material in place. (5)

reflected beam: A beam of light that has bounced off a surface. (9)

reflection copy: An original that will reflect different amounts of light from the different tone values of the original. Examples are photographs, oil paintings, chalk or charcoal renderings, and watercolor work. (11, 19)

reflection densitometer: Instrument used to accurately determine different tone values, such as the highlights and shadows of an original. See *densitometer*. (3, 9, 11, 22)

reflection density guide: Measuring instrument used to visually compare the example density to the image density. It has precalibrated density steps that are assigned a numerical value, which represent the photo-density range. See *photo-density range*. (11)

refresh rate: The speed with which the screen is redrawn. The refresh rate controls the amount of detectable screen *flicker*. (10)

register unit: A feeding system mechanism that places paper in register for printing on a press. (15)

relief printing: The process of printing from a raised surface. Ink is applied to the raised image and transferred to the paper or other substrate. Letterpress and flexography are both relief printing processes. (6, 17)

repeat length: Distance equal to one revolution of a press cylinder. (18)

resolution: An image's sharpness or clarity; the number of pixels per unit of linear measurement on a video display or the number of dots per inch (dpi) in printed form. (3, 8)

retarders: Solvents added to ink to thin the viscosity and slow the drying time. (20)

retina: A layer of light-sensitive cells at the back of the eye. When light reaches the eye, it is focused onto the retina. (9)

retouching tools: Tools used in image manipulation programs to modify images in ways similar to methods used in darkroom photography. They can "dodge" areas that are too dark and lack detail, or "burn" areas to increase exposure to areas that are too light. Retouching tools also include features for adjusting color, contrast, hue, and saturation. (8)

reverse type: White characters on a solid black or color background. (4)

rhythm: The use of elements in an image to create visual movement and direction. (5)

ribbons: Rows of pages engraved on a cylinder. (19)

rider: Company-specific stipulations or slight alterations to the traditional trade customs. (24)

robotics: The use of machines to do repetitive tasks, particularly in manufacturing. (25)

rods: Light-sensitive nerve cells of the retina that help us perceive light and intensity. There are about twelve million rods in the human eye. The rods detect light intensity and are most sensitive to black, white, and shades of gray. (9)

Roman typeface: A type style based on the capital letters cut into stone monuments by the ancient Romans. Nicolas Jenson developed Roman lowercase letters that would merge readily into word forms. Jenson's designs were the models used by type designers for hundreds of years. (4)

rough layout: A redrawn version of a thumbnail sketch, closely resembling the final layout. (5)

rubber plates: Flexible relief plates commonly used in flexographic printing. (17)

sans serif: The classification for typefaces without serifs (stroke endings). This typeface classification is second only to Roman in popularity. Sans serif typefaces usually have heavy and light elements that are approximately the same thickness. (4)

saturation: An attribute of color that defines its degree of strength or difference from white. It can also be defined as the extent to which one or two of the three RGB primaries is predominant in a color. (9)

sawtoothing: A distortion in design contours that causes a notched effect. (20)

scan area: The section of a scanning device on which images are placed for scanning. (8)

scanner: An electronic imaging device that measures color densities of an original, stores those measurements as digital information, manipulates or alters the data, and uses the manipulated data to create four color separations. Scanners use either a CCD array or PMTs to capture the image as a raster or bitmapped graphic. (8, 9)

scoring: A slight cut made in heavy stock before it is folded. (23)

screen: Used to change continuous-tone photographs into dotted halftones for printing. (3)

screen angles: Angular relationships of line screens used in making color separations for four-color printing. (3)

screen flicker: Rapid changes in light intensity produced by a monitor screen. (10)

screen printing: A printing process that uses a squeegee to force ink through a porous fabric covered by a stencil that blocks the nonimage areas. The ink pressed through the open image areas produces the image on a substrate. (20)

screen ruling: The number of ruled grid lines per inch (lpi) on a halftone screen. (8)

screen tint: Reproduction screen used to provide a tint percentage of a solid color. (3)

scriber: A tool for following a template; an attached pen deposits ink onto a sheet of paper. (6)

script typeface: A typeface designed to simulate handwriting, in which the letters are joined. (4)

scumming: A condition in lithography when the nonimage areas of the plate begin to accept ink. (22)

selective compression: A compression option that allows the user to specify compression levels for different elements within a single file. (7)

sensitometry: The study and measurement of the sensitivity of photographic materials, in relationship to exposure and development. (11)

separation plates: Special outputs for each color on a page created by page composition software; similar in purpose to the physical overlays used in paste-up to prepare material for color printing. (7)

serif: The thickened tips or short finishing-off strokes at the top and bottom of a Roman typeface character. (4)

set: The point at which an ink is dry enough to be lightly touched without smudging. (22)

setoff: A condition that results when wet ink on the press sheets transfers to the back of other sheets in a stack. (16, 22)

set size: The width of a typeset character. Electronic composition makes it possible to change the set size of characters. (4)

shade: A color gradation created by adding black to a color. For example, if black is added to red, the color maroon is created. Maroon is a shade of red. In ink manufacture, shade is a common synonym for hue. (9)

shadow: Darkest parts of an image or photograph, represented as the largest dots in a halftone. (11)

shapes: Elementary forms that define specific areas of space. (5)

sheet-fed press: A lithographic press that prints paper one sheet at a time as it is fed through the system. (15)

sheet separators: Air-producing devices that separate the top sheet from the rest of the pile in a feeding system. (15)

sheetwise imposition: A printing layout that uses separate flats and plates to print the front and back of a single press sheet. Different pages appear on each side of the sheet. (12)

show-through: An undesirable result of poor opacity in which the image on one side of a sheet of paper is seen on the other side. (21)

shrink-wrap: A packaging method in which a stack of printed pieces is enclosed with a thin plastic in sheet form. The wrapped stack is heated, causing the plastic to shrink and form a tight, sealed package. (23)

signatures: Folded sheets that form multiple-page sections of a book. Each signature contains 4, 8, 16, or 32 pages. (12)

SI Metric system: The modern version of the metric system, based on seven internationally recognized units of measure. (3)

single proprietorship: A type of business owned by one person in which the business and the owner are a single entity; the owner's income is the business' profits. The owner has full control of the business operations and also carries 100% of the liability of running a business. Also known as a sole proprietorship. (24)

sizing: Material, such as rosin, that is added to pulp slurry to make the paper stronger and more moisture-resistant. (21)

slitting: An operation similar to perforating that makes a continuous cut, rather than a series of slits. It is usually done by sharp-edged wheels that cut the stock as it passes through the folder. (23)

slugs: An entire line of type produced by a hot metal typesetting machine. (6)

small caps: Capital letters smaller than the normal caps of the font. (4)

smoothing: A technique used by some printers to reduce jaggies. Most printers that support smoothing implement it by reducing the size and alignment of the dots that make up a curved line. (7)

smoothness: Freedom from surface irregularities. As a quality of paper, smoothness affects the visibility of printed images. (4)

soft image: A loss of image that occurs when the outside edges of an image contain less density or tone quality than that of the inside portion of the image. (14)

soft proof: Press-ready, electronic files that represent what the final printed page will look like. Soft proofs are most often PDF files that can be viewed on a computer monitor. (7)

soft proofing: Proofreading of an image or page layout on a computer monitor. (10)

software: Computer programs that initiate and accomplish various computer-based tasks. (7)

software-as-a-service (SaaS): A type of data management system in which the data is managed and maintained externally. Clients access the data on demand using system-specific software and an Internet connection. (13)

solvent inks: Inks that have a main ingredient of a solvent that evaporates and produces VOCs. (13)

spaceband: Wedge-shaped devices used to justify a line of matrices in a hot-metal linecasting machine. (6)

spatial resolution: The ability of a digital imaging device to address data in two dimensions—horizontal and vertical. (8)

specifications: The overall layout guidelines relating to such information as type style, type size, line width, color use, and page organization. (5)

specking: Tiny dots that appear near an image area, caused by paper fibers or other foreign material in the ink. (22)

spectrodensitometer: A color measuring instrument that serves all the functions of a spectrophotometer, densitometer, and colorimeter in one device. In addition to measuring color value and optical density, many of these instruments can also measure paper attributes and special colors. (9)

spectrophotometer: Instrument capable of measuring light of different colors or wavelengths. When used for measurement in the graphic communications industry, a spectrophotometer converts this data to CIE color specifications. Spectrophotometers are the most accurate type of color measurement device. A spectrophotometer uses a prism or diffraction grating to spread the light and slits to isolate narrow bands of light between 1 nm and 10 nm. (3, 9, 22)

spectrum locus: A horseshoe-shaped curve that results when the chromaticity coordinates of visible light are plotted on the CIE chromaticity diagram. Since all visible colors are mixtures of these wavelengths, all visible colors must occur within the boundary formed by this curve. (9)

spiral binding: A mechanical binding method in which small round holes are punched through the pages and metal or plastic wire is spiral fed through them. (23)

spontaneous combustion: Ignition by rapid oxidation without an external heat source. (2)

spot screening: Screening method in which dots are laid in a grid pattern based on the color tone. The spacing between the dot centers is held constant, but the dot size (amplitude) is varied to produce different shades or tones. Also known as amplitude modulation. (10)

spread trap: Trap created by spreading the foreground over the background color. Typically used when a lighter object is knocked out of a darker background. (10)

squeegee: A rubber or plastic blade used to force ink through the open areas of a screen-printing stencil. (20)

stamping: The process of transferring a thin layer of metallic tone or color to a substrate, using heat and pressure. Also called foil stamping. (23)

star target: A quality control device used to detect slurring of ink. (12)

stereotype: A duplicate relief plate that is cast by pouring molten metal into a mold or mat made from the original type form of composed characters. (17)

stitching: A binding method that holds sheets together with staples. Typically used on books with fewer than 120 pages. (23)

stochastic screening: Halftone method that creates the illusion of tones by varying the number (frequency) of micro-sized dots (spots) in a small area. Unlike conventional halftone, the spots are not positioned in gridlike pattern. Instead, the placement of each spot is determined as a result of a complex algorithm that statistically evaluates and distributes spots under a fixed set of parameters. With first-order stochastic screening, both the number and size of dots vary. Also referred to as FM dots or FM screening. (10)

strike-through: An ink-penetration problem that occurs when the ink soaks into the paper too deeply and shows through the opposite side of the sheet. (22)

stripping: The physical assembly of film negatives and positives on a flat for platemaking. Also called image assembly. (12)

stroke: The thickness of a line forming a character element. (10)

style sheet: A formatting tool, often used in page composition programs, that combines a number of attributes, such as type size, alignment, and other characteristics. (7)

stylus: A diamond cutting tool used to form the tiny ink wells on the metal surface of a gravure cylinder. (19)

Subiaco face: An early version of the Roman typeface, used for several books and named for the town where the printing was done. (4)

substance weight: The actual weight of a ream of paper. (21)

substrate: Any material with a surface that can be printed or coated. (1, 21)

subtractive color formation: The combining of inks in the colors cyan, magenta, yellow, and black to produce the printed image. Usually referred to as the CMYK system. (7, 9, 10)

successive contrast: A color-vision effect that causes the viewer to see afterimages. (9)

sucker feet: Devices that provide a vacuum to remove sheets from a stack and position them for access to the press. (15)

suitcase file: One of two component files that make up a PostScript type family. The suitcase file is used for the screen display of fonts. (7)

supercalendering: Using heated steel rollers and pressure to form a very smooth, high-gloss finish on paper. (21)

surface plates: Presensitized plates coated with light-sensitive material. (14)

sweet spot: A 3″ or 4″ area in the center of a flatbed scanner at which the scanner scans material at full resolution. (8)

tagout device: A prominent warning device, such as a tag, securely fastened to an energy isolating device, to indicate that electrical power is off and must remain off until the tag is removed. (2)

taping machine: Device used in shipping departments to automatically apply tape to seal the tops of boxes. (23)

template: A pierced or cut guide, usually plastic, used to create lettering and symbols, or to draw shapes by hand. (6) In a page composition program, a reusable form that can be set up to include the page geometry, typography, and other elements of a page that recur in a document. (7)

tensile strength: The amount of stress that will break paper. (21)

tensiometer: An instrument that measures screen fabric tension. (20)

text: Words, sentences, or paragraphs. (4)

text filter: A page composition program feature that allows the original text formatting applied to be retained when the text is imported into the page composition program. (7)

texture: A projection of emphasized structure or weight. (5)

thermal ink-jet printer: Printer in which the ink is superheated to form a bubble, which expands through the firing chamber, forcing ink out of the nozzle. (13)

thermal plates: Image carriers that can be exposed optically or digitally through the use of heat. (14)

thermal transfer: A type of thermography that uses heat and pressure to change solid dye particles on multiple ribbons into a gas to produce an image on a substrate. (13)

thermoformed: Formed by heat and pressure. (21)

thinners: Solvents added to ink to change the viscosity of the ink. They do not affect drying time. (20)

thixotropy: The tendency of ink to flow more freely after being worked. (22)

thumbnail sketches: Simple, rapidly drawn designs of a layout. (5)

tick mark: A V-shaped notch in the lead edge of the flat that identifies the gripper edge. (12)

tight set: Term describing narrower than normal letterspacing. (4)

tint: A color gradation created by adding white to a color. For example, adding white to red creates pink. Pink is a tint of red. (9)

tinting: Problem that occurs when ink pigment particles bleed into the dampening solution, causing a slight tint of ink to appear on the nonimage area of the printed sheet. (22)

tone: The degree of lightness or darkness of a color. The tone of a color may be lowered or heightened by adding some of its complementary color. (9)

tone curve adjustment: The use of curves to make tonal adjustments to an image. (10)

tone-line process: The process used to convert continuous-tone originals into line reproductions that resemble pen-and-ink sketches or other fine-line drawings. It is used to create a detailed outline reproduction of a continuous tone original. (11)

toner: Positively charged powder used in laser printers and photocopiers that is attracted to negatively charged image dots to make up the printed image on a page. Heated rollers fuse the powder onto paper to produce a permanent image. (7)

totally chlorine free (TCF): Refers to unbleached paper with a slightly brown appearance. (21)

toxic substance: A poisonous substance. (2)

tracking: A feature of computer typesetting programs that allows control of letterspacing and wordspacing together. (4)

trade customs: Understood rules or implied laws used in industry that have been validated by courts as binding agreements. (24)

Transitional Roman typefaces: Typefaces that are a remodeling of Oldstyle faces. There is greater contrast between the heavy and light elements, and the characters are wider than the equivalent Oldstyle characters. Baskerville, a Transitional Roman, was the first typeface designed to print on smooth paper. (4)

transmission copy: An original that allows light to pass through. (11)

transmission densitometer: Color measurement device that measures the fraction of incident light conveyed through a negative or positive transparency without being absorbed or scattered. See *densitometer*. (3, 9, 11)

trapping: Method used to create a small area of overlap (trap) between colors to compensate for potential gaps; how well one color overlaps another without leaving a white space between the two or generating a third color. (10)

trichromatic colorimeter: A color measurement device that relies on the perception of the eye to match a patch of light by combination of the three primary colors. (9)

trim: The paper that is left over after cutting a sheet into smaller pieces. (21)

trimming: The process of cutting off uneven edges of a product after printing. (23)

tristimulus: A densitometer reading through all three color separation filters. (11)

tristimulus values (X, Y, Z): Three values that designate the amount of red, green, and blue light in an image. (9)

tungsten-filament lamps: An incandescent lamp with a filament of tungsten metal surrounded by gases, all enclosed in a glass bulb. (11)

turnaround: The completion time for a product from its inception. (25)

two-cylinder system: A press system that combines the printing operations of the plate cylinder and impression cylinder into one. (15)

two-person proofing: A proofreading method that requires the reader to work with an assistant, called the copyholder. The reader follows the printed design proof, checking for errors, while the copyholder follows the original manuscript. (7)

typeface: Distinctive designs of visual symbols used to compose a printed page. (4)

typeface family: A grouping consisting of all the variations of one style of type. (4)

typeface series: The range of sizes of each typeface in a family. The common type sizes used in printing are 6, 8, 10, 12, 14, 18, 24, 36, 48, 60, and 72 point. (4)

type metal: A low-melting-point alloy of lead, tin, and antimony used to cast foundry type. (4)

type size: Measurements that describe the size of printed type, commonly expressed in points. (3)

typographer: A print designer who determines how a manuscript should be expressed in type as well as other details of reproduction. (4)

typography: The art of expressing ideas in printed form through the selection of appropriate typefaces. (4)

U

uncoated paper: Paper that does not have a mineral layer applied over the surface, so it has a slightly textured feel. (21)

undercolor addition (UCA): The inverse function of undercolor removal. Undercolor addition is used with gray component replacement to produce better shadow quality. (10)

undercolor removal (UCR): Technique used to reduce the yellow, magenta, and cyan dot percentages in neutral tones by replacing them with increased amounts of black ink. See also *gray component replacement* and *undercolor addition*. (10)

undercut: The vertical distance between the surface of the cylinder bearers and the cylinder body. The undercut allows for the thickness of the plate or blanket and packing. (15)

unity: The proper balance of all elements in an image so a pleasing whole results and the image is viewed as one piece. (5)

unsharp masking (USM): A function of some scanners that increases tonal contrast where light and dark tones come together at the edges of the images. (8)

US Conventional system: The standard system of weights and measures used in the United States. (3)

UV-curable inks: Inks that are forced onto the substrate, then subjected to UV light to be polymerized. (13)

vacuum frame: A glass frame used to hold the film and plate in tight contact for exposure on a platemaker. (14)

value: Describe the lightness or darkness of a color; used in Munsell's color system. The darkest value is at the bottom and the lightest value is at the top. The value of pure black is designated as 0/, pure white as 10/, and middle gray as 5/. (9)

variable data printing: A digital printing process that enables quick and easy content changes at several points within a print run. The "on the fly" imaging resident allows customized and personalized printed materials to be produced. (13)

varnishing: A coating applied after printing to provide a clear protective surface. (23)

vector fonts: Fonts represented with object-oriented graphics, also known as scalable fonts or outline fonts. An example of a vector font system is PostScript. (7)

vector images: Images that are defined in terms of mathematical parameters (Bezier curves), which gives the artist or designer control over shape, placement, line width, and pattern. Because the objects are defined geometrically, the visual quality of the shapes does not degrade when enlarged or reduced. In computer graphics, a *vector* is a line that is defined by its start point and endpoint. (7)

vehicle: The liquid component in ink that serves as a binding agent. (22)

vertical camera: A process camera that has a vertical optical axis. The copyboard and filmholder are perpendicular to the optical axis. (11)

video card: Board that plugs into a computer to give it display capabilities. Also referred to as a video adaptor. (10)

viewing booth: A booth or defined area illuminated with color-balanced lighting (5000 K). Images are viewed at a 90° angle to reduce glare. (9)

vignette: Pictorial material (photograph) in which the background color gradually decreases in strength toward the edge until it appears as the stock. (14)

viscosity: The internal resistance of an ink to flow. It is the opposite of fluidity. (18)

visibility: A legibility factor that results from the contrast of a dark typeface against the light reflected by the paper. (4)

visible spectrum: The electromagnetic wavelengths visible to the human eye. (11)

volatile organic compounds (VOCs): Toxic substances contained in blanket and roller washes, fountain solutions, plate cleaners, glaze removers, degreasers, and film cleaners. VOCs evaporate into the atmosphere, contributing to the development of such environmental hazards as ground-level ozone (smog) and other health concerns. (2, 18)

warp threads: Threads that run vertically, at a 90° angle to the weft threads. (20)

washup solvents: Solvent used to dissolve ink from a screen. (20)

waste stream: The solid, liquid, or contained gaseous material that is produced and disposed of, incinerated, or recycled by a facility. (2)

waterless plates: Presensitized plates that use an ink-repellent substance other than water to separate the nonimage area from the image area. (14)

waterless press: An offset lithographic press system that eliminates the use of a dampening system during the printing process. (15)

watermark: A translucent design impressed in paper. (21)

web-break detector: A device that automatically shuts down the press if the web snaps or tears. (15)

web-fed press: A lithographic press that prints with one long, continuous web of paper that is fed from a roll. (15)

web splicer: A device used to bond a new roll to the end of an existing web on a web-fed press. (15)

weft threads: Threads that run horizontally, at a 90° angle to the warp threads. (20)

weight: The degree of boldness of the printing surface of a letter. The readable image might have a light, medium, bold, or extra-bold printing surface. (4)

well sites: Hundreds or thousands of photosensitive elements on a CCD. Also referred to as photosites. (8)

white point: A movable reference point that defines the lightest area in an image displayed on a cathode ray tube (CRT) causing all other areas to be adjusted accordingly. (10)

white space: The areas of the layout that are void of printed images. (5)

widow: A very short word, or part of a word, forming the final line of a paragraph. (4)

wordspacing: Changing the spacing between typeset words, for better appearance or to fit copy in a given space. (4)

work-and-tumble imposition: A printing method in which one flat is prepared, but the sheet is tumbled (or flopped) so the gripper edge changes when the second side is printed. Only one plate and press makeready are needed. (12)

work-and-turn imposition: A printing method in which one plate surface is used for printing both sides of a sheet without changing the gripper edge. (12)

work ethic: Standard to which on-the-job conduct and performance is based. (25)

WYSIWYG: What You See Is What You Get. A monitor display method used by word processing and page layout programs, in which the monitor displays a RGB representation of the printed output. (7)

WYSIWYP: What You See Is What You Print. A monitor display method used by word processing and page layout programs that uses color management software to produce a CMYK representation of the printed output, which is closer to the final printed product. (7)

x-height: The height of the lowercase "x." Also called body height. (4)

XY scanning technology: Scanning technology that optimally positions the scanning head along an XY axis. The scanner head slides both up and down and side-to-side beneath the bed. (8)

Z

Zahn cup: A gravitational flow device used to measure the viscosity of ink. (18)

zero-speed splicer: A splicer unit on a web-fed system that uses a set of festoon rollers to draw out slack from the web and feed the press while a splice is being made. (15)

INDEX

A

achromatic vision, 202–203
adaptation, 201–202
A/D converter, 160–161
additive color formation, 132–133, 193–194, 214–215
additives, 403
adhesive bonding, 373
adhesive-coated paper, 387
adjacency, 202–203
afterimages, 201
aging, 203
aliasing, 136–137
American National Standards Institute (ANSI), 453
analog charge, 160–161
analog format, 159
analog images, 159
anilox roll, 340–341, 348
antialiasing, 136–137
antihalation backing, 234–235
apprenticeship, 465
aqueous inks, 267
art preparation requirements, 25–26, 355
artwork, 25
ascenders, 83
assembly procedures, 256–258
    quality control devices, 258
automatic film processing, 248–249
automatic proofreading systems, 227–228
automatic trap, 220–221
autotracing, 137

B

balance, 104
banding machine, 438–439
bank, 121
barrier guards, 43
base material, 234–235
basic size, 68–69, 392–393
basis weight, 70–71, 393
batteries, 165
Bezier curve, 137
binding, 32–33, 421, 432–438
    edition, 436–437
    mechanical, 438
    pamphlet, 433–436
    perfect, 437
bit depth, 159
bitmapped images, 136–137
bits, 127
black letter, 81, 85
black printer, 245–246

blanket, 278–279
blanket cylinder, 301–302, 318–319
bleach, 385
bleaching, 390–391
blind embossing, 429
blueline proofs, 226–227
body type, 90–91, 108–109
bond paper, 387–388
book printing, 35–36
brake mechanism, 298–299
brayer, 411, 413
brightness, 93, 190, 213, 397
brownlines, 226–227
brush system, 305
burned edges, 376–377
burnished, 124–125
business, 443–454
    basics, 444–451
    copyright laws, 454
    costs, 446–447
    job estimates, 447–448
    matching jobs to equipment, 450–451
    organizing work, 449–450
    planning, 443–444
    standards and specifications, 453–454
    trade customs, 451–452
business plan, 443–445
    developing, 443
    establishing organization, 443–444
bytes, 127

C

calendering, 386–387
calibration, 213
calibration schedules, 216–217
calligraphy, 85
camera bed, 238–239
carbonless paper, 388
careers, 456–469
    creative positions, 459–460
    educators, 463
    engineers and scientists, 463
    entrepreneurship, 468–469
    finding jobs, 466
    management positions, 460–462
    preparing for, 465–466
    service operations, 463–464
    skilled technical positions, 457–459
    support personnel, 462–463
    technological growth, 469
    work habits, 466–467

D

E

X

Y

Z